The Global Trading System

Kym Anderson is Professor of Economics and Executive Director of the Centre for International Economic Studies at the University of Adelaide, Australia. He was a WTO Dispute Settlement Panelist during 1996–2000.

Bernard Hoekman leads the International Trade Group at the World Bank in Washington, DC.

The editors worked together in the Economic Research and Analysis Division of the GATT Secretariat in Geneva during the latter years of the Uruguay Round. Both have authored and edited several books on trade policy and the global trading system.

Tauris Guides to Global Economic Issues

International Debt
S.E. Corbridge
ISBN 1 86064 274 8

The Global Trading System
K. Anderson and B. Hoekman
ISBN 1 86064 058 3

Global Transport Issues
R. Tolley and B. Turton
ISBN 1 86064 564 X

The Global Trading System

Edited by

Kym Anderson

Professor of Economics and Director, Centre for International Economic Studies, University of Adelaide

and

Bernard Hoekman

Senior Economist, International Trade Group, World Bank

Volume 1: Genesis of the GATT

I.B.Tauris *Publishers*
LONDON • NEW YORK

Published in 2002 by I.B.Tauris & Co. Ltd
6 Salem Road, London W2 4BU
175 Fifth Avenue, New York NY 10010

In the United States of America and in Canada distributed by
St Martin's Press, 175 Fifth Avenue, New York NY 10010

A full CIP record for this book is available from the British Library
A full CIP record for this book is available from the Library of Congress

ISBN 1 86064 058 3

Library of Congress catalog card number: available

Typeset by I.T.S., Edinburgh
Printed and bound in Great Britain by MPG Books Ltd, Bodmin, Cornwall

Contents

Introduction to Volume 1: Genesis of the GATT

Kym Anderson and Bernard Hoekman

Trading has been going on ever since humankind began seeking to improve well-being. It involves exchanging either endowments or the goods and services produced with them, including through specialization in production: between individuals within households or tribes, between households or tribes located within walking distance of each other, between rural and urban areas within nation states, between nation states and, for more than half a millennium, between continents. The Silk Road provided the first major inter-continental trade link, between Europe and Asia, but it was not until the expeditions of European mariners to the Americas, the Far East and Australasia from the middle of the past millennium that truly global trade began.

Anyone familiar with the history of international trade prior to the mid-twentieth century is acutely aware of its unruliness. Indeed it often took a war between nations before leaders would get together to develop a trade agreement. Even then it would typically be a limited bilateral agreement which, if it hurt other economies, could exacerbate tensions elsewhere. The recent popular history of the spice trade from 1553 to 1667 by Milton (1999) is a reminder of the brutal lawlessness with which international trade was conducted in centuries past. Certainly trade relations were relatively tranquil in the five decades to World War I, but they became unruly again in the interwar period.

When viewed from this historical perspective, the development of the modern global trading system since World War II has been both extremely rapid and far more successful than its planners dared hope for. The modern, legally binding, rules-based global trading system originated with the 1947 General Agreement on Tariffs and Trade (GATT). This was encapsulated in the World Trade Organization (WTO) that came into being in 1995 following the successful completion of the Uruguay Round of multilateral trade negotiations. Over that half-century international trade rose rapidly: more than one-fifth of global output is now exported, double the proportion of the 1950s. The GATT was a major contributor to that growth, as it proved to be a powerful vehicle through which nations were able to overcome domestic resistance to trade liberalization. GATT rules outlawing quantitative restrictions on trade, and successive GATT rounds of negotiations that resulted in cuts in bound tariffs on imports of manufactures by industrial countries led to tariffs coming down to 'nuisance' levels for many products. Manufacturing tariffs of OECD countries now average less than 4 per cent, compared with more than 40 per cent when the GATT was first signed in

1947 by the original 23 contracting parties (who at that time accounted for four-fifths of world trade). That membership, incidentally, has since grown to more than 140, with another 30 in the process of joining. Once the largest traders in that latter group accede, which include China and Taiwan (whose accession is imminent), as well as Russia, the WTO membership will account for more than 95 per cent of global international trade.

Appreciating the differences between the trading environment pre-GATT and today's system is an essential precursor to evaluating the latter. The GATT and now the WTO provide not only a set of multilateral rules and disciplines but also a forum to negotiate tariff reductions and rules changes, plus a legal mechanism to settle trade disputes that is recognized as an integral part of the world's body of international law. The WTO has added three other contributions to those of the earlier GATT: to monitor and report on trade and trade-related policy developments on a regular basis, thereby adding to policy transparency; to facilitate the fuller integration of developing and transition economies into the global trading system; and to improve cohesion between the WTO and other international economic agencies such as the World Bank and International Monetary Fund.

Superior though it is, the current system nonetheless still has plenty of room for improvement. Indeed much attention has been directed in recent years at its shortcomings. Among the issues that have focused attention are globalization, regional integration, noisy trade disputes across the North Atlantic and elsewhere, a perception by some that the system is unfair to developing countries, linkages between trade and other policy areas such as foreign investment or competition policy, and concerns about possible adverse impacts of trade on such things as inequality, poverty, the environment, labour standards, and food safety and security. These concerns were voiced loudly at the third WTO trade ministerial meeting in Seattle in late 1999, contributing to the postponing of the first comprehensive round of multilateral trade negotiations under WTO auspices.

There is thus a need for more-accessible information, knowledge and understanding of what the global trading system is about, how it evolved, how it works, why the world needs it, and what more it can, should, or should not try to do to make the world a more peaceful and prosperous place. These needs were accentuated at Seattle (and subsequently at other economic meetings of world leaders) where it was clear that many of the protesting groups knew little about the WTO and the workings of the rules-based global trading system, nor about what the world might be like without that institution and its rules and procedures.

There are a number of books on the GATT/WTO rules-based global trading system that are readily available.[1] The present set of readings is designed to complement those books with less-readily available journal articles and chapters from edited volumes. They come from the core trade disciplines of economics, law, and political science, but with an emphasis on the editors' profession of economics.[2] Our objective was to collect papers that have been cited often, provide a pertinent historical perspective, and/or address current and future issues that confront the trading system. Because of space constraints, quantitative ex ante and ex post assessments of the economic effects of trade reforms are explicitly excluded.[3] The selection is based on responses to a survey of around one hundred of our colleagues, whom we sincerely thank (with apologies for not being able to include more of their papers!). We also thank the original publishers of the included papers for permission to reproduce them in this collection. A list of the full set of papers in the four volumes, together with their original source, is provided in the Acknowledgements.

The present four-volume set has been prepared around the following topics: the genesis of the GATT; the rules and procedures embodied in the GATT (and, since its inception in 1995, the General Agreement on Trade in Services, or GATS); the exceptions to those rules; and the 'new' issues that confront the WTO membership in the twenty-first century as internationalization progresses further (the lowering of the transactions costs of doing business across national borders). Within each of the four volumes the readings appear in alphabetical order, since that makes them easier to find than if they were ordered chronologically or by sub-topics.

The rest of this chapter provides an introduction to the readings in the current volume. This first volume deals with both history and theory: the events leading up to the establishment of the rules-based multilateral trading system as embodied in the GATT, and the politico-economic ideas behind it.

HISTORICAL BACKGROUND TO THE GATT'S CREATION

A very succinct history of the evolution of trade agreements over the 150 years up to the establishment of the WTO in 1995 is provided by Irwin in reading 10. The period neatly divides into three quite different sub-periods: up to World War I, the interwar years, and post-World War II. As Irwin's Figures 1 to 3 depict, the first and third sub-periods are characterized by steady growth in output and exports with trade growing nearly twice as fast as production. During the years from 1860 to 1913 the world enjoyed relative serenity in terms of international trade and monetary relations. Even though economic growth then was proceeding at less than half the post-World War II pace, it was very rapid by previous standards. The interwar years, by contrast, were disastrous.

Reading 9, also by Irwin, provides a more detailed history. The seventeenth, eighteenth, and early nineteenth centuries are characterized as an era in which trade negotiations were 'ever pending, never ending'. Frustration with that state of affairs set the stage for unilateral tariff cuts by the major economic power of the time, namely Britain, with the repeal of its Corn Laws in 1846. British policy-makers were left to hope that their trading partners would see the benefits of unilateral liberalization and follow their example.

That was not immediately forthcoming. However, by 1860, with war clouds gathering over Austria's involvement in Italy, Britain and France felt a commercial treaty was needed to diffuse tensions and improve diplomatic relations. The resulting Cobden-Chevalier Treaty of 1860 contained a most-favoured-nation (MFN) clause. This required that the agreed cut in the tariff on each item in their bilateral trade was to be applied also to their imports from other countries. It also meant that every European country that subsequently signed a trade treaty with either Britain or France (and most had done so by 1867) signed onto MFN. Especially important was the Treaty of Frankfurt concluded by Bismarck with France in 1871: its Article XI provided for permanent, unconditional MFN and was thereby a key stabilizer of European commercial policy. The systemic effect of the 1860 Anglo-French accord was thus of much greater significance than its importance to either country alone, as it led to a network of treaties that lowered hugely both the average level of tariff protection and the extent of trade discrimination in Europe.

Reading 16, a report by the United States Tariff Commission, covers the same period of history but from a US perspective. In contrast to Europe, the USA during this period sought mainly exclusive reciprocity agreements or, at best, conditional MFN treaties. While those agreements freed up some trade, they explicitly retained a degree of discrimination. Evidently the US perceived the cost to themselves of that discrimination to be more than outweighed by the incentive it provided to trading partners to join in. Yet as Viner put it in 1924 (see reading 17), the conditional MFN clause in American commercial treaties in the preceding century probably caused "more diplomatic controversy, more variations in construction, more international ill-feeling, more conflict between international obligations and municipal law and between judicial interpretation and executive practice, more confusion and uncertainty of operation, than have developed under all the unconditional most-favored-nation pledges of all other countries combined."

While the trade policy actions taken during this period allowed world output and trade to boom for several decades, there was no binding of tariffs in these trade agreements. Thus when countries began to face economic difficulties, some of them began to raise tariffs again. This was especially the case when agricultural incomes fell, particularly if falling import prices were the cause – as indeed they were from the 1870s because of falling rail and shipping costs in eastern Europe and the New World. It was not every grain-importing country that became more protectionist though. In reading 12, Kindleberger points out that Italy allowed huge numbers of peasants to migrate to America; Britain allowed them to migrate to its urban areas for industrial or service sector jobs; and Belgium, Denmark and the Netherlands left farmers to take advantage of low grain prices by specializing in livestock production. It was mainly France and Germany who reacted by raising tariffs on agricultural imports so as to appease farm lobby groups.

Later that century, when many of the European trade treaties were reaching their expiry date (nearly fifty of them were to expire in the first half of the 1890s), economic difficulties were making their renegotiation more contentious than earlier. Tariff wars ensued, so that the threat of retaliation – which had served as a deterrent to raising tariffs – was no longer a constraint on reform reversal. Even so, MFN was retained, and there was no recourse to anti-dumping or countervailing duties or to export subsidies, despite the appearance of a 'fair trade' movement in Europe in the 1890s.

In short, the great trade policy achievement of the period from 1860 to 1913 as compared with earlier periods was the establishment of non-discrimination in Europe via the widespread use of the unconditional MFN clause. However, the absence of bindings on tariffs (to prevent backsliding), of an outlawing of nontariff trade-distorting measures, and of a legal means of resolving trade disputes, not to mention the unwillingness of America or others to adopt the unconditional MFN principle, meant the sustainability of the achievements of that period was far from certain. Indeed, the bilateral treaty regime ended abruptly with the outbreak of World War I in 1914.

Following that war, efforts to restore liberal trade centred on international conferences. However, despite the rhetoric in support of open markets, they did not lead to renewed trade treaties with binding commitments to openness based on MFN. With no country willing or able to replace Britain as the hegemon, there was (as Kindleberger puts it in reading 13) trade policy anarchy. When recession and low agricultural prices hit in the late 1920s, and the USA introduced the Smoot-Hawley tariff hikes of June 1930, governments elsewhere responded with beggar-thy-neighbour protectionist trade policies that together drove the world economy into depression. The volume of world trade shrunk by one-quarter between 1929 and 1932, and its value fell by 40 per cent.

The trade policy instruments used in the 1930s included quantitative restrictions and prohibitions on trade, exchange controls, and clearing agreements. State bureaucracies were established to monitor financial and merchandise transactions, state planning overshadowed the market, and regulatory control of trade in Europe and elsewhere proliferated. Moreover, the first attempts to reverse that protection growth were discriminatory, as with the Ottawa Conference of 1932 that led to preferential tariffs on trade among members of the British Commonwealth. Nor did the politics of the situation in France at the time allow for cross-issue trades and linkages that might have seen Britain stabilize sterling and the USA forgive debt in return for France lowering its tariffs on agricultural imports in 1933 (see reading 5 by Eichengreen and Uzan). Hence by the end of the 1930s protectionism was far more entrenched than in the previous century when only non-discriminatory tariffs had to be grappled with. Indeed non-tariff trade barriers were so rife as to make tariffs redundant and hence a return to MFN irrelevant unless and until 'tariffication' of those barriers occurred.

Out of the inter-war experience came the conviction that a return to the beneficent noncooperative equilibrium of the nineteenth century was highly unlikely. Instead, Britain and the USA were convinced that liberal world trade required a set of multilaterally agreed rules and binding commitments based on non-discriminatory principles. A proposal for such an agreement was put to the British War Cabinet in 1942 by Meade (reading 14), and was developed further at the Bretton Woods conference in 1944 out of which grew also the IMF and World Bank. In the Anglo-American view, the post-war international economic system was to be constructed in such a way as to remove the economic causes of friction that were believed to have been at the origin of the Second World War. An important element in this vision was the establishment of a stable world economy that would provide all trading nations with non-discriminatory access to markets, supplies and investment opportunities. There was a strong perception that there was a positive correlation between trade and peace, and, as important, between non-discrimination and good foreign relations.

As it happened, the efforts in the latter 1940s to create an International Trade Organization (ITO) to complement the IMF and World Bank were unsuccessful.

The negotiations on the charter of such an organization, although concluded successfully in Havana in 1948, did not lead to the establishment of the ITO because the proposed organization was perceived by the US Congress as taking away too much national sovereignty (see reading 4 by Diebold). As a result, the ITO Charter was never submitted to Congress for ratification by the American government. Nonetheless, many of the key elements of the ITO proposal were encapsulated in a General Agreement on Tariffs and Trade that was signed by 23 trading countries—12 developed and 11 developing—in 1947 (before the ITO negotiations were concluded). These countries were anxious to pursue liberalization, and did not want to wait for the conclusion of the ITO talks. They created the GATT as an interim agreement that embodied many of the draft ITO disciplines. As the ITO never came into being, the GATT was the only concrete result of post-war efforts to create an international trade body.

The GATT provided not only a set of multilateral rules and disciplines but also a forum to negotiate tariff reductions and rules changes, plus a mechanism to help settle trade disputes. Eight so-called rounds of negotiations took place in the subsequent 46 years, the last one (the Uruguay Round) culminating in the so-called Interim Commission of the International Trade Organization (ICITO, better known as the GATT Secretariat) being converted into the World Trade Organization in January 1995. Probably none of those involved in the negotiations of the 1940s that led to the establishment of the GATT dared to hope that it would contribute to the extraordinarily long period of rapid output and trade growth depicted in Irwin's Figure 3 (reading 10).

THEORETICAL FOUNDATIONS OF THE GATT

Do the key objectives of the GATT – the setting and enforcing of rules, and the pursuit of trade liberalization through multilateral negotiation of tariff cuts — have an economic logic? On the first of those objectives, Corden suggests in reading 2 that it does if it is less costly to national economies to work within rules over the long term than to have to cope with their trading partners (and themselves) continually changing policies to satisfy domestic vested interests. A basic role of the GATT/WTO is to provide an 'anchor' for trade policy—the institution provides a mechanism for governments to 'lock-in' policy commitments by imposing costs on themselves if they later renege. Political economy and trade policy are indissolubly linked because every trade intervention potentially creates conflict between winners and losers – producers vs. consumers, agriculture vs. industry, skilled vs. unskilled labor. All political systems find it difficult to deal with redistribution explicitly and so trade policy presents both problems and opportunities. Supporting a trade liberalization with explicit redistribution to prevent anyone from losing is a big political challenge, whereas using trade intervention as a form of covert redistribution may be a politically attractive way of rewarding specific interests. Empirical work by Staiger and Tabellini in reading 15 supports the view that governments are more able to resist domestic political pressures for protectionist measures in an environment of rules than one allowing discretion.

Politics and political economy also played a major role in the shaping of GATT rules. Goldstein (reading 7) notes that the sanctioning of agricultural protectionism in the GATT was driven by the agricultural lobby in the USA. This helped 'sell' the GATT domestically, but later came back to haunt US farmers as they came to confront the effects of active intervention by the EU in agriculture, which led to recurrent disputes and decades of cross-Atlantic tensions. A major challenge during the 1980s and 1990s was to find other issues that could be linked to agriculture and alter the domestic political economy balance in the EU (and other protectionist nations).

As to the second key purpose of GATT, the question is whether a multilateral negotiating forum is needed to cut tariffs. Many economists would say no. Their reasoning is that the optimal unilateral policy for a national-welfare maximizing government is free trade. Why then, they ask, would a government be willing to help its economy by cutting an import tariff only if its trading partners made a 'concession' of a similar magnitude? An early attempt to approach that question is provided by Johnson in reading 11. He begins by assuming a country wishes to protect a sector for some 'non-economic' reason such as boosting the industrial sector. In a two-country world there would then be the possibility that through an exchange of tariff reductions both countries could end up better off. However, when he extends his analysis to a many-country world, there are limits to the extent of the reciprocal preferential tariff cuts that can be negotiated on an MFN basis; and tariff cuts that discriminate among foreign countries will be more attractive than non-discriminatory ones.

The basic rationale for reciprocity can be found in the political economy literature. Costs of liberalization generally are concentrated in specific industries, which often will be well organized and oppose reductions in protection. Benefits, in the aggregate usually greater than costs, accrue to a much larger set of agents, who thus do not have a great individual incentive to organize themselves politically. In such a setting, being able to point to reciprocal, sector-specific export gains may help to sell the liberalization politically. By obtaining a reduction in foreign import barriers as a quid pro quo for a reduction in domestic trade restrictions, specific export-oriented domestic interests that will gain from liberalization have an incentive to support it in domestic political markets.

For reciprocity to work it is important that lobbies favoring open markets do not have other means of getting what they want. Finger (reading 6) points out that large countries increasingly negotiate increased market access for their exporting firms bilaterally. Such bilateral alternatives weaken the power of reciprocity in the multilateral context, as they reduce the incentives for export interests to support liberalization in the context of WTO negotiations.

Bagwell and Staiger (reading 1) construct a rigorous comprehensive economic theory of the GATT, formalizing many of the insights and intuitions of practitioners, and demonstrating that the practice of reciprocity has a strong economic foundation. They note that reciprocity in trade negotiations can help to offset the externalities that are imposed by countries on each other as they implement trade policies. In effect, by insisting on reciprocity countries can ensure that their terms of trade are not affected detrimentally.

Agreements have little value if they cannot be enforced. Enforcement requires access to information on the trade regimes that are maintained by members. Deardorff (reading 3) notes that the provision of information is one of the main roles of the WTO, which has numerous mechanisms to facilitate communication and the exchange of information. This helps defuse potential conflicts in an efficient manner. Transparency is also vital in terms of ensuring 'ownership' of the WTO as an institution—if citizens do not know what the organization does, its legitimacy will be eroded. However, pressures will invariably arise that induce governments to violate agreements. A unique feature of the WTO is that there is a binding dispute settlement process. Given the absence of supra-national powers, such enforcement must ultimately rely on the threat of retaliation and on the costs of a breakdown of future cooperation. As argued by Hungerford (reading 8) the objective of the GATT/WTO dispute settlement process is to induce cooperation in a regime that is by definition one in which countries interact in a non-cooperative manner (in a game-theoretic sense). In practice, the system has been remarkably successful—retaliation was quite rare indeed in the GATT years, and most countries abided by the recommendations of dispute settlement panels. The reason for this was that the short-term gains that could be had by defecting (not implementing dispute settlement findings) were outweighed by the cost of a breakdown of cooperation that would arise if all countries pursued such short-term self-interest.

Writing in 1951, Diebold openly expressed doubt that, with the ITO being stillborn, the GATT would survive (end of reading 4). Certainly when one contemplates his list of the difficulties to be surmounted, including the discriminatory trading by the Sterling bloc and the Organization for European Economic Cooperation (OEEC), it is remarkable that the ICITO achieved so much and eventually became a permanent organization in the form of the WTO. True, it left some gaping holes (see Volume 3 of this collection) and many new issues confront the WTO (see Volume 4). But its basic rules and procedures (see Volume 2) have served the world well, and they provide a strong foundation on which the WTO has begun and will continue to build.

NOTES

1. See, for example, Diebold (1952), Curzon (1965), Jackson (1969, 1997), Dam (1970), Hudec (1975, 1987, 1993), Tumlir (1985), Winham (1992), Davey, Jackson and Sykes (1995), Hoekman and Kostecki (2001), and Trebilcock and Howse (1999). A new one by economic theorists is due shortly (Bagwell and Staiger, 2002). The legal texts of the GATT/WTO rules are collected in WTO (1995a), while GATT legal case history is summarized in WTO (1995b). Detailed negotiating histories of the Uruguay Round can be found in Stewart (1993, 1999) and Croome (1998).
2. A lawyer's collection is available in Howse (1997).
3. See, for example, Deardorff and Stern (1981) on the Tokyo Round and Martin and Winters (1996) on the Uruguay Round of GATT negotiations.

REFERENCES

Bagwell, Kyle and Robert W. Staiger (2002), *The Economics of the World Trading System*, Cambridge, MA: MIT Press (forthcoming).

Croome, John (1998), *Reshaping the World Trading System: A History of the Uruguay Round* (revised edition), Geneva: World Trade Organization.

Curzon, Gerard (1965), *Multilateral Commercial Diplomacy*, London: Michael Joseph.

Dam, Kenneth W. (1970), *The GATT: Law and International Economic Relations*, Chicago: University of Chicago Press.

Davey, William, John H. Jackson and Alan Sykes (1995), *Legal Problems of International Economic Relations*, St. Paul: West Publishing Co.

Deardorff, Allan V. and Robert Stern (1981), 'A Disaggregated Model of World Production and Trade: An Estimate of the Impact of the Tokyo Round', *Journal of Policy Modeling* 3(2): 127–52.

Hoekman, Bernard and Michel Kostecki (2001), *The Political Economy of the World Trading System: The WTO and Beyond*, London and New York: Oxford University Press.

Howse, Robert (ed.) (1997), *The World Trading System* (4 vols of readings), London: Routledge.

Hudec, Robert E. (1975), *The GATT Legal System and World Trade Diplomacy (2nd edition)*, Salem, New Hampshire: Butterworth.

Hudec, Robert E. (1987), *GATT and the Developing Countries*, Aldershot: Gower for the Trade Policy Research Centre.

Hudec, Robert E. (1993), *Enforcing International Trade Law: The Evolution of the Modern GATT Legal System*, Salem, New Hampshire: Butterworth.

Jackson, John H. (1969), *World Trade and the Law of GATT*, Indianapolis, Indiana: Bobbs-Merrill.

Jackson, John H. (1997), *The World Trading System: Law and Policy of International Economic Relations (2nd edition)*, Cambridge, Massachussetts: MIT Press.

Martin, Will and L. Alan Winters (eds.) (1996), *The Uruguay Round and the Developing Countries*, Cambridge and New York: Cambridge University Press.

Milton, Giles (1999), *Nathaniel's Nutmeg*, London: Sceptre (Hodder and Stoughton).

Stewart, Terence (1993), *The GATT Uruguay Round, A Negotiating History (1986–1992)*, Volumes I to III.

Stewart, Terence (1999), *The GATT Uruguay Round, A Negotiating History (1986–1992)*, Volume IV.

Trebilcock, Michael J. and Robert Howse (1999), *The Regulation of International Trade (2nd edition)*, London and New York: Routledge.

Tumlir, Jan (1985), *Protectionism: Trade Policy in Democratic Societies*, Washington D.C.: American Enterprise Institute.

Winham, Gilbert R. (1992), *The Evolution of International Trade Agreements*, Toronto: University of Toronto Press.

WTO (1995a), *The Results of the Uruguay Round of Multilateral Trade Negotiations: The Legal Texts*, Geneva: World Trade Organization.

WTO (1995b), *Analytical Index: Guide to GATT Law and Practice*, Vols. I and II, Geneva: World Trade Organization.

ACKNOWLEDGEMENTS

The publishers and editors are grateful for permission to use copyright material.

VOLUME 1: GENESIS OF THE GATT

1. BAGWELL, KYLE AND ROBERT W. STAIGER (1999), 'An Economic Theory of GATT', *American Economic Review* 89(1): 215–48, March. Nashville, Tennessee: American Economic Association
2. CORDEN, W. MAX (1987), 'On Making Rules for the International Trading System', Ch. 10 in Robert Stern (ed.), *U.S. Trade Policies in a Changing World Economy*, pp. 413–26. Cambridge, Massachusetts: MIT Press.
3. DEARDORFF, ALAN V. (1996), 'An Economist's Overview of the World Trade Organization', in Gordon Flake and Florence Myeong-Hwa Lowe-Lee (eds), *The Emerging WTO System and Perspectives From East Asia*, Washington, D.C.: Korea Economic Institute of America.
4. DIEBOLD, WILLIAM, JR. (1952), *The End of the ITO*, Essays in International Finance No. 16, pp.1–37. Princeton, New Jersey: International Finance Section, Department of Economics and Social Institutions, Princeton University Press.
5. EICHENGREEN, BARRY AND MARC UZAN (1993), 'The 1933 World Economic Conference as an Instance of Failed International Cooperation', Ch. 6 in Peter Evans, Harold Jacobson and Robert Putnam (eds), *Double-Edged Diplomacy: International Bargaining and Domestic Politics,* pp. 171–206. Berkeley: University of California Press.
6. FINGER, J. MICHAEL (1991), 'The GATT as an International Discipline Over Trade Restrictions: A Public Choice Approach', Ch. 7 in Roland Vaubel and Thomas Willett (eds), *The Political Economy of International Organizations: A Public Choice Approach*, pp. 125–41. Boulder, Colorado: Westview Press.
7. GOLDSTEIN, JUDITH (1993), 'Creating the GATT Rules: Politics, Institutions and American Policy', Ch. 6 in J. Ruggie (ed.), *Multilateralism Matters: The Theory and Praxis of an Institutional Form*, pp.201–32. New York: Columbia University Press.
8. HUNGERFORD, THOMAS L. (1991), 'GATT: A Cooperative Equilibrium in a Noncooperative Trading Regime?' *Journal of International Economics* 31: 357–69. Elsevier Science Publishers.

9. Irwin, Douglas A. (1993), 'Multilateral and Bilateral Trade Policies in the World Trading System: An Historical Perspective', Ch. 4 in Jaime De Melo and Arvind Panagariya (eds), *New Dimensions in Regional Integration*, pp.90–119. Cambridge and New York: Cambridge University Press.
10. Irwin, Douglas A. (1995), 'The GATT in Historical Perspective', *American Economic Review* 85(2): 323–8, May. Nashville, Tennessee: American Economic Association.
11. Johnson, Harry G. (1965), 'An Economic Theory of Protectionism, Tariff Bargaining and the Formation of Customs Unions', *Journal of Political Economy* 73(3): 256–83, June. Chicago: University of Chicago Press.
12. Kindleberger, Charles P. (1951), 'Group Behaviour and International Trade', *Journal of Political Economy* 59(1): 30–46, February. Chicago: University of Chicago Press.
13. Kindleberger, Charles P. (1989), 'Commercial Policy Between the Wars', Ch. 2 in Peter Mathias and Sidney Pollard (eds), *The Cambridge Economic History of Europe, Vol. 8*, pp. 161–96. Cambridge: Cambridge University Press.
14. Meade, James (1942), 'A Proposal for an International Commercial Union', British War Cabinet paper reproduced in *The World Economy* 10: 399–407, 1987, and in Susan Meade (ed.), *The Collected Papers of James Meade, Volume III: International Economics*, London: Unwin Hyman, 1988.
15. Staiger, Robert and Guido Tabellini (1999), 'Do GATT Rules Help Governments Make Domestic Commitments?' *Economics and Politics* 11(2): 109–44, July. Oxford: Blackwell.
16. United States Tariff Commission (1919), *Reciprocity and Commercial Treaties*, pp.17–48 & 9–14. Washington, D.C.: Government Printing Office.
17. Viner, Jacob (1924), "The Most-Favored-Nation Clause in American Commercial Treaties', *Journal of Political Economy* 32(1), February, pp.17–39. University of Chicago Press. (Reprinted as Ch. 1 in his *International Economics: Studies by Jacob Viner*, Glencoe, Illinois: The Free Press.)

VOLUME 2: CORE RULES AND PROCEDURES

1. Baldwin, Robert (1986), 'Toward More Efficient Procedures for Multilateral Trade Negotiations', *Aussenwirtschaft* 41: 379–94. *The Swiss Review of International Economic Relations.* Swiss Institute for Research in International Economics, University of St Gallen, Switzerland.
2. Baldwin, Robert E. and Richard N. Clarke (1988), 'Game-Modeling Multilateral Trade Negotiations', *Journal of Policy Modeling* 9: 257–84. Elsevier.© Society for Policy Modeling 1987.
3. Caplin, A. and Karla Krishna (1988), 'Tariffs and the Most-Favored-Nation Clause: A Game Theoretic Approach', *Seoul Journal of Economics* 1(3): 267–89.
4. Conybeare, H.A.C. (1988), 'Managing International Trade Conflicts: Explanations and Prescription', *Journal of International Affairs* 42(1): 75–91.© Trustees of Columbia University in the City of New York.

5. Finger, J. Michael (1974), 'GATT Tariff Concessions and the Exports of Developing Countries – United States Concessions at the Dillon Round', *Economic Journal* 84(335): 566–75, September. Oxford: Blackwell.
6. Hillman, Arye and Peter Moser (1995), 'Trade Liberalization as Politically Optimal Exchange of Market Access', in M. Canzoneri, Wilfred Ethier and Vittorio Grilli (eds), *The New Transatlantic Economy*, Cambridge and New York: Cambridge University Press.
7. Jackson, John H. (1998), 'Designing and Implementing Effective Dispute Settlement Procedures: WTO Dispute Settlement, Appraisal and Prospects', Ch. 5 in Anne O. Krueger (ed.), *The WTO as an International Organization*, pp.161–80. Chicago: University of Chicago Press.
8. Kovenock, Dan and Marie Thursby (1992), 'GATT, Dispute Settlement and Cooperation', *Economics and Politics* 4(2): 151–70, July. Oxford: Blackwell.
9. Laird, Sam (1999), 'The WTO's Trade Policy Review Mechanism – From Through the Looking Glass', *The World Economy* 22(6): 741–64, August. Oxford: Blackwell.
10. Ludema, Rodney D. (1991), 'International Trade Bargaining and the Most-Favored-Nation Clause', *Economics and Politics* 3(1): 1–20, March. Oxford: Blackwell.
11. McMillan, John (1989), 'A Game-Theoretic View of International Trade Negotiations: Implications for the Developing Countries', Ch. 2 in John Whalley (ed.), *Rules, Power and Credibility*, pp. 26–44. London: University of Western Ontario.
12. Rhodes, Carolyn (1989), 'Reciprocity in Trade: The Utility of a Bargaining Strategy', *International Organization* 43(2): 273–99. ©1989 World Peace Foundation and the Massachusetts Institute of Technology.
13. Schwartz, Warren F. and Alan O. Sykes (1996), 'Toward a Positive Theory of the Most-Favored-Nation Obligation and Its Exceptions in the WTO/GATT System', *International Review of Law and Economics* 16(1): 27–51, March. Elsevier Science.
14. Stern, Robert M. (1976), 'Evaluating Alternative Formulae for Reducing Industrial Tariffs', *Journal of World Trade Law* 10(1): 50–64.
15. Viner, Jacob (1931), 'The Most-Favored-Nation Clause', *Index 6*, pp.94–108. Stockholm: Svenska Handelsbanken, January. (Reprinted as Ch. 5 in his *International Economics: Studies by Jacob Viner*, Glencoe IL: The Free Press.)
16. Winters, L. Alan (1987), 'Negotiating the Abolition of Non-Tariff Barriers', *Oxford Economic Papers* 39: 465–80. Oxford: Oxford University Press.
17. Winters, L. Alan (1987), 'Reciprocity', Ch. 7 in J. Michael Finger, and Andrzej Olechowski (eds), *The Uruguay Round: A Handbook on the Multilateral Trade Negotiations*, pp. 45–51. Washington, D.C.: The World Bank.
18. Wolf, Martin (1984), 'Two-Edged Sword: Demands of Developing Countries and the Trading System', Ch. 9 in Jagdish Bhagwati and John Gerard Ruggie (eds), *Power, Passions, and Purpose: Prospects for North-South Negotiations*, pp. 201–29. Cambridge, Massachussetts: MIT Press.

VOLUME 3: EXCEPTIONS TO THE CORE RULES

1. ANDERSON, KYM (2001), 'Bringing Discipline to Agricultural Policy via WTO', Ch. 3 in Bernard Hoekman and Will Martin (eds), *Developing Countries and the WTO: A Pro-active Agenda*, Oxford: Blackwell.
2. FINGER, J. MICHAEL (1991), 'Development Economics and the General Agreement on Tariffs and Trade', Ch. 13 in Jaime De Melo and Andre Sapir (eds), *Trade Theory and Economic Reform: North, South, and East: Essays in Honor of Bela Balassa*, pp. 203–23. Oxford: Blackwell.
3. FINGER, J. MICHAEL, H. KEITH HALL AND DOUGLAS R. NELSON (1982), 'The Political Economy of Administered Protection', *American Economic Review* 72(3): 452–66, June. Nashville, Tennessee: American Economic Association.
4. FINGER, J. MICHAEL AND L. ALAN WINTERS (1998), 'What Can the WTO Do for Developing Countries?' Ch. 14 in Anne O. Krueger (ed.), *The WTO as an International Organization*, pp. 365–93. Chicago: University of Chicago Press.
5. HIGGOTT, RICHARD A. AND ANDREW F. COOPER (1990), 'Middle Power Leadership and Coalition Building: Australia, the Cairns Group and the Uruguay Round of Trade Negotiations', *International Organization* 44(4): 589–632, Autumn. ©1990 World Peace Foundation and the Massachusetts Institute of Technology.
6. HOEKMAN, BERNARD (1996), 'Assessing the General Agreement on Trade in Services', Ch. 4 in Will Martin and L. Alan Winters (eds), *The Uruguay Round and the Developing Countries*, pp. 88–123. Cambridge and New York: Cambridge University Press.
7. INGCO, MERLINDA D. (1996), 'Tariffication in the Uruguay Round: How Much Liberalisation?' *The World Economy* 19(4): 425–46, July. Oxford: Blackwell.
8. KAHLER, MILES AND JOHN ODELL (1988), 'Developing Country Coalition-Building and International Trade Negotiations', Ch. 8 in John Whalley (ed.), *Rules, Power and Credibility*, pp.149–67. London: University of Western Ontario.
9. MESSERLIN, PATRICK A. (1989), 'The EC Antidumping Regulations: A First Economic Appraisal, 1980–85', *Weltwirtschaftliches Archiv*, 125(3): 563–87.
10. MICHALOPOULOS, CONSTANTINE (1999), 'The Developing Countries' Participation in the WTO', *The World Economy*, 22(1): 117–43, January. Oxford: Blackwell.
11. SAMPSON, GARY AND RICHARD H. SNAPE (1985), 'Identifying the Issues in Trade in Services', *The World Economy*, 8: 171–81. Oxford: Blackwell.
12. SNAPE, RICHARD H. (1991), 'International Regulation of Subsidies', *The World Economy,* 14: 139–64. Oxford: Blackwell.
13. SNAPE, RICHARD H. (1992), 'History and Economics of GATT's Article XXIV', Ch. 12 in Kym Anderson and Richard Blackhurst (eds), *Regional Integration and the Global Trading System*, pp.273–91. London: Harvester Wheatsheaf and New York: St Martin's Press.
14. WINTERS, L. ALAN (1998), 'Regionalism versus Multilateralism', in Richard Baldwin, David Cole, Andre Sapir and Anthony Venables (eds), *Regional*

Integration, pp. 1–39. Cambridge and New York: Cambridge University Press.

15. WOLF, MARTIN (1990), 'How to Cut the Textile Knot: Alternative Paths to Liberalization of the MFA', Ch. 9 in Carl Hamilton (ed.), *Textiles Trade and the Developing Countries: Elimination of the MFA in the 1990s*, pp. 215–37. Washington, D.C.: World Bank.

VOLUME 4: 'NEW' ISSUES FOR THE WTO

1. ANDERSON, KYM (1998), 'Environmental and Labor Standards: What Role for the WTO?' Ch. 8 in Anne O. Krueger (ed.), *The WTO as an International Organization*, pp. 231–55. Chicago: University of Chicago Press.
2. BHAGWATI, JAGDISH N. (1994), 'Fair Trade, Reciprocity and Harmonization: The New Challenge to the Theory and Policy of Free Trade', Ch. 13 in Alan V. Deardorff and Robert M. Stern (eds), *Analytical and Negotiating Issues in the Global Trading System*, pp.547–61. Ann Arbor: University of Michigan Press.
3. BHAGWATI, JAGDISH N. AND T.N. SRINIVASAN (1996), 'Trade and the Environment: Does Environmental Diversity Detract from the Case for Free Trade?' Ch. 4 in Jagdish N. Bhagwati and Robert E. Hudec (eds), *Fair Trade and Harmonization: Prerequisites for Free Trade? Vol. 1: Economic Analysis*, pp. 159–99. Cambridge, Massachusetts: MIT Press.
4. BROWN, DRUSILLA K., ALAN V. DEARDORFF AND ROBERT M. STERN (1996), 'International Labor Standards and Trade: A Theoretical Analysis', Ch. 5 in Jagdish N. Bhagwati and Robert E. Hudec (eds), *Fair Trade and Harmonization: Prerequisites for Free Trade? Vol. 1: Economic Analysis*, pp. 227–80. Cambridge, Massachusetts: MIT Press.
5. DAVIDOW, JOEL (1981), 'The Seeking of a World Competition Code: Quixotic Quest?' pp. 361–403 in Oscar Schachter and Robert Hellawell (eds), *Competition in International Business*, New York: Columbia University Press.
6. DEARDORFF, ALAN V. (1992), 'Welfare Effects of Global Patent Protection', *Economica* 59: 35–51, February. Oxford: Blackwell.
7. HAMILTON, BOB AND JOHN WHALLEY (1984), 'Efficiency and Distributional Implications of Global Restrictions on Labour Mobility', *Journal of Development Economics* 14: 61–75. Elsevier Science Publishers.
8. HOEKMAN, BERNARD (1997), 'Competition Policy and the Global Trading System', *The World Economy* 20(4): 383–406, July. Oxford: Blackwell.
9. MCCULLOCH, RACHEL AND ROBERT OWEN (1983), 'Linking Negotiations on Trade and Foreign Direct Investment', Ch. 14 in Charles Kindleberger and David Audretsch (eds), *The Multinational Corporation in the 1980s*, pp. 334–58. Cambridge, Massachusetts: MIT Press.
10. NOGUES, JULIO (1990), 'Patents and Pharmaceutical Drugs: Understanding the Pressures on Developing Countries', *Journal of World Trade* 24(6): 81–104.
11. PALMETER, DAVID (1999), 'National Sovereignty and the World Trade Organization', *Journal of World Intellectual Property* 2(1): 77–91. Geneva, Switzerland: Werner Publishing Company.

12. SYKES, ALAN O. (1999), 'Regulatory Protectionism and the Law of International Trade', *University of Chicago Law Review* 66(1): 1–46, Winter. ©1999 University of Chicago.
13. TUSSIE, DIANA (1994), 'The Policy Harmonization Debate: What Can Developing Countries Gain From Multilateral Negotiations?' *UNCTAD Review* 5: 1–8. Geneva and New York: United Nations.
14. VOGEL, DAVID (1997), 'Trouble for Us and Trouble for Them: Social Regulations as Trade Barriers', Ch. 3 in Pietro Nivola (ed.), *Comparative Disadvantages: Social Regulations and the Global Economy*, pp. 98–145. Washington, D.C.: Brookings Institution.
15. WILLIAMSON, JEFFREY G. (1998), 'Globalization, Labor Markets and Policy Backlash', *Journal of Economic Perspectives* 12(4): 51–72, Fall. Nashville, Tennessee: American Economic Association.

1. An Economic Theory of GATT

K. Bagwell and R. W. Staiger

The central role played by the General Agreement on Tariffs and Trade (GATT) in shaping postwar trade policy is widely accepted. Through the eight rounds of trade negotiations that have followed since the inception of GATT in 1947, average ad valorem tariffs on industrial goods have fallen significantly from over 40 percent to less than 4 percent. Over the same period of time, membership in GATT [and now its successor organization, the World Trade Organization (WTO)] has risen from 23 countries to well above 100. Despite the important role played by GATT in the world economy, however, economists have not yet developed a unified theoretical framework that interprets and evaluates the principles that form the foundation of GATT. Our purpose here is to propose such a framework.

We begin with a first and most basic question: What can governments gain from a trade agreement? We adopt the view that a trade agreement is appealing to governments if it offers them greater welfare than they would receive in the absence of the agreement. If in the absence of an agreement, governments set trade policies in a unilateral fashion, then a trade agreement is appealing provided that an inefficiency (relative to governments' preferences) exists under unilateral tariff setting. Viewed from this perspective, the role of a trade agreement is then to remove the inefficiency, so that member governments can enjoy higher welfare. The principles embodied in the trade agreement can then be interpreted and evaluated in this light.

What, then, is the inefficiency that trade agreements are designed to remedy? Working with models in which governments maximize national income, previous authors have established that the classic terms-of-trade externality creates an inefficiency in unilateral trade policies.[1] Intuitively, when a government imposes an import tariff, some of the cost of this policy is shifted to foreign exporters, whose products sell at a lower world price (i.e., at less favourable terms of trade). This temptation to shift costs naturally leads governments to set unilateral tariffs that are higher than would be efficient. A trade agreement can then promote a more efficient outcome for its member governments if it serves as a means to eliminate the terms-of-trade-driven restrictions in trade that arise when policies are set unilaterally. The assumption that governments maximize national income, however, stands in contrast to the manifest political constraints under which real governments operate. It is thus important to consider further the rationale for a trade agreement, within a richer model in which governments may have political concerns.

To this end, we construct a general model that allows for a wide class of government preferences. The economic environment is captured with a standard two-good general equilibrium model of trade between two countries, and we represent each government's welfare as a general function of the local and world prices that the tariff selections imply. This formulation allows us to associate a government's motivation to manipulate the terms of trade with the welfare gain that the government receives when its tariff choice changes the world price (holding fixed the local price). The government's preferences as to the local price are unconstrained and may reflect general economic and political (i.e., distributional) considerations. Our representation of government preferences thus includes the traditional case in which governments maximize national income as well as the possibility emphasized in leading political-economy models that governments are concerned with the distributional implications of their tariff choices.

Working with this general framework, we observe that political motivations influence the determination of the tariff policies to which governments aspire. For example, when governments have political motivations, free trade may not rest on the efficiency frontier. But it is the terms-of-trade externality – and this externality alone – that creates an inefficiency when governments set their trade policies unilaterally. For the class of government preferences that we entertain, we thus offer as our first broad conclusion that trade agreements are appealing to governments solely as a means to remedy the inefficient terms-of-trade-driven restrictions in trade that arise when trade policies are set unilaterally. To establish this conclusion, we demonstrate that unilateral trade policies would be efficient in a hypothetical world in which governments pursued political goals but were not motivated by the terms-of-trade implications of their trade policies. In other words, if governments were not motivated by the terms-of-trade implications of their trade-policy selections, then there would be no reason for the creation of GATT.[2] This hypothetical experiment yields a set of *politically optical* tariffs, which are efficient precisely because the motivation for such tariffs is separate from any cost-shifting incentive.[3]

Armed with this basic conclusion as to the purpose of trade agreements, we next interpret and evaluate the key principles on which GATT is founded. Following the legal literature on GATT (see, e.g., John H. Jackson, 1989 pp. 85–89), we interpret GATT as a "rules-based" institution whereby, prior to negotiating over trade policy, member governments agree to a set of rules or principles which describe the limits of acceptable behavior and thereby govern the "bargaining chips" that can be brought to the actual trade-policy negotiations that follow.[4] While GATT has a large number of specific articles, it is widely accepted that the two "pillars" of the GATT approach are the principles of reciprocity and nondiscrimination. The principle of reciprocity is a GATT norm under which one country agrees to reduce its level of protection in return for a reciprocal "concession" from its trading partner. At the broadest level, this principle refers to the "ideal" of mutual changes in trade policy which bring about equal changes in import volumes across trading partners. The principle of nondiscrimination is a separate norm, under which a member government agrees that any tariff on a given product applied to the imports of one trading partner applies equally to all other trading partners. This discussion motivates our second question: Do the principles of reciprocity and nondiscrimination serve governments as simple rules of negotiation that promote efficiency, by "undoing" the terms-of-trade-driven inefficiency that arises in the absence of an agreement?

We begin with the principle of reciprocity. Our discussion here builds upon a key observation: mutual changes in trade policy that conform to the principle of reciprocity leave world prices unchanged. Recalling that trade-policy decisions are inefficient if and only if governments are motivated by their abilities to *change* the world price, we propose at a general level that the principle of reciprocity can be efficiency enhancing, since it neutralizes the terms-of-trade externality that underlies inefficient behavior. To develop this general proposal in a more concrete fashion, we then identify and consider the two specific applications of reciprocity that arise in GATT practice.

A first application arises when governments seek negotiated tariff reductions. While there is no formal requirement in GATT articles that governments exchange reciprocal tariff reductions in these negotiations, it has been observed that governments in fact seek a *balance of concessions* (i.e., tariff cuts). This emphasis on reciprocal tariff reductions contrasts sharply with the standard economic argument that unilateral free trade is the best policy for a (small) country, independent of the tariff selected by its trading partner, and this contrast has led many to conclude that governments approach trade negotiations from a mercantilist perspective that is driven by political forces and divorced from sound economic reasoning. We show instead that the principle of reciprocity as it arises in this application can be given a rather direct economic interpretation: whatever their underlying political motivations, governments are driven to choose overly protective trade policies because of the cost-shifting effects of the world-price movements associated with their unilateral tariff choices, and they would therefore seek lower tariffs if the world-price implications of their liberalization could be neutralized – a feat that reciprocity achieves.

A second application of reciprocity in GATT practice occurs when a government decides to increase a previously "bound" (i.e., negotiated) tariff and invokes GATT's procedures for renegotiation. Here, GATT's reciprocity rules explicitly require moderation on the part of trading partners, who are permitted to withdraw *substantially equivalent concessions* of their own. In this case, the principle of reciprocity governs the manner in which tariffs may be *increased* as part of a renegotiation. In light of this possibility for renegotiation, an important issue is whether *any* efficient set of tariffs that might be agreed to in an original negotiation is in fact "renegotiation proof" under the rules of GATT. We show that GATT's insistence on reciprocity in renegotiations is indeed compatible with an efficient set of tariffs, and we further find that the only efficient tariffs that are impervious to renegotiation of this nature are the politically optimal tariffs. If governments seek an efficient outcome that will not be renegotiated as allowed under the principle of reciprocity, they therefore will negotiate to the politically optimal tariffs.

We then turn to the principle of nondiscrimination. Extending our framework to a multi-country setting, we begin by establishing an "affinity" between politically optimal tariffs and the principle of nondiscrimination: while there will in general be many points on the efficiency frontier that entail discriminatory tariffs, we show that politically optimal tariffs are efficient if and only if they conform to the principle of nondiscrimination. We next explore the implications of reciprocity in our multicountry setting, finding that an efficient multilateral trade agreement is impervious to renegotiation as allowed under the principle of reciprocity if and only if it is characterized by politically optimal tariffs that satisfy the principle of nondiscrimination. Thus, if a trade agreement permits renegotiation that conforms to the principle of reciprocity, then governments can achieve an efficient outcome only if the agreement also imposes the principle of nondiscrimination.[5]

The complementary relationship between the principles of reciprocity and nondiscrimination in generating efficient outcomes rests upon a simple intuition. As we have discussed above, the principle of reciprocity has the effect of neutralizing the world-price effects of a government's decision to raise tariffs, and so it can eliminate the externality that causes governments to make inefficient trade-policy choices provided that trade-policy externalities travel only through world prices. While externalities indeed travel only through world prices in the basic two-country model, when the modeling framework is extended to include multiple countries, there arises as well the possibility of a local-price externality. In particular, if a country discriminates when setting its trade policy, then, all else equal, it would prefer that a greater fraction of a given import volume be provided by the export source on whom it places the highest tariff. But the export volumes from trading partners are in turn determined in part by the local prices in these countries, and so a local-price externality is created. If the importing country adopts a policy of nondiscrimination, however, the preference for one export source over another is removed, and the only remaining externality is again the world-price externality, which the principle of reciprocity is well designed to neutralize.

Drawing on these findings, we offer as our second broad conclusion that the principles of reciprocity and nondiscrimination may be interpreted as simple negotiation rules that work hand in hand to assist governments as they attempt to undo the terms-of-trade-driven trade policies. In fact, we offer the more specific finding that these principles direct negotiation outcomes toward the tariffs that are both politically optimal and nondiscriminatory, and hence toward the tariffs that governments would have chosen had they not been motivated by cost-shifting incentives in the first place. We interpret these results as establishing an efficiency-enhancing role for the two principles that form the pillars of the GATT architecture.

Finally, we consider the implications of a major exception to the principle of nondiscrimination that must be granted whenever GATT's member governments negotiate *preferential agreements*. This exception, embodied in Article XXIV of GATT, was controversial in its inception and has met with renewed controversy recently as many GATT members have increasingly exercised their rights under this article to negotiate preferential agreements. Against this backdrop, we use our modeling framework to address a third question: Will preferential agreements interfere with the efficiency properties of a multilateral trading system that is otherwise built upon the pillars of reciprocity and nondiscrimination?

In accord with Article XXIV, we consider two forms of preferential agreements: *free-trade areas*, in which member countries eliminate internal barriers to trade, and *customs unions*, in which members also adopt a common external tariff. Preferential agreements are inherently discriminatory, and so they revive the local-price externality described above. As a consequence, the principle of reciprocity typically does not deliver an efficient outcome when preferential agreements are in place. The only exception arises in the special case in which the preferential agreement takes the form of a customs union formed by members with sufficiently similar preferences. In this case, the customs union can be regarded as a "single" country with no internal tariff, and our previous results then imply that the principles of reciprocity and nondiscrimination can serve to deliver an efficient outcome. More generally, we offer as our third broad conclusion that preferential agreements pose a threat to the efficiency properties of the existing multilateral system.

This paper builds on the approach from Bagwell and Staiger (1996), in which we study the purpose of reciprocal trade agreements but do not interpret and evaluate the principles of reciprocity and nondiscrimination as embodied in GATT practice. A more closely related paper is Bagwell and Staiger (1997a), where we adopt a partial equilibrium framework, impose a particular representation of political economy, and explore similar themes.

The remainder of the paper proceeds as follows. Section 1 presents our basic framework in a two-country setting and examines the purpose of reciprocal trade agreements. Section II then turns to an interpretation and evaluation of the principle of reciprocity. A multicountry extension of the modeling framework is developed in Section III, and the principle of nondiscrimination is analyzed. Preferential agreements are examined in Section IV. Next, in Section V we consider why governments might choose to design an institutional arrangement such as GATT that adopts a rules-based approach to trade negotiations. We argue that this approach can encourage participation of weaker countries in GATT, and we show that stronger countries might support the creation of such an institution for this reason. Finally, in Section VI, we conclude the paper with a discussion of evidence relating to our implicit hypothesis that governments have the ability and the desire to manipulate the terms of trade in a quantitatively significant fashion.

I. THE PURPOSE OF RECIPROCAL TRADE AGREEMENTS

In this section, we develop a model of the economic environment for the case in which two countries trade two goods. Allowing for a wide range of government preferences, we then show that trade agreements are appealing to governments if and only if they serve as a means to remedy the inefficient terms-of-trade-driven restrictions in trade that arise under unilateral trade policies.

A. The Economic Environment

We begin with a description of the economic environment in which trade takes place. We work within a standard two-sector, two-country perfectly competitive general equilibrium trade model. Two countries, home (no*) and foreign (*), trade two goods, x and y, taken to be normal goods in consumption and produced under conditions of increasing opportunity costs. Production takes place under perfect competition, facing tariffs on imports by each country. Let $x(y)$ be the natural import good of the home (foreign) country, and define $p \equiv p_x/p_y$ ($p^* \equiv p_x^*/p_y^*$) to be the local relative price facing home (foreign) producers and consumers. With $t(t^*)$ representing the home (foreign) ad valorem import tariff which we take to be nonprohibitive, and with $\tau \equiv (1 + t)$ and $\tau^* \equiv (1 + t^*)$, we have $p = \tau p^w \equiv p\,(\tau, p^w)$ and $p^* = p^w/\tau^* \equiv p^*(\tau^*, p^w)$, where $p^w \equiv p_x^*/p_y$ is the "world" (i.e., untaxed) relative price. The foreign (domestic) terms of trade are then measured by p^w $(1/p^w)$. We interpret $\tau > 1$ $(\tau < 1)$ to be an import tax (import subsidy) and similarly for τ^*.[6]

Production in each country is determined by selecting the point on its production possibilities frontier at which the marginal rate of transformation between x and y is equal to the local relative price: $Q_i = Q_i(p)$ and $Q_i^* = Q_i^*\ (p^*)$ for $i \in \{x, y\}$. Consumption is a function of the local relative price – which defines the trade-off faced by consumers and determines the level and distribution of factor income in the economy – and of tariff revenue $R(R^*)$, which is distributed lump sum to domestic (foreign) consumers and which we measure in units of the local export good at local prices. We represent domestic and foreign consumption, respectively, as $D_i = D_i\,(p, R)$ and $D_i^* = D_i^*\ (p^*, R^*)$ for $i \in \{x, y\}$. Tariff revenue is defined implicitly by $R = [D_x\,(p, R) - Q_x(p)][p - p^w]$ or $R = R(p, p^w)$ for the domestic country, and similarly by $R^* = [D_y^*\ (p^*, R^*) - Q_y^*\ (p^*)][1/p^* - 1/p^w]$ or $R^* = R^*(p^*, p^w)$ for the foreign country, with each country's tariff revenue an increasing function of its terms of trade under the assumption that goods are normal. National consumption in each country can thus be written as $C_i\,(p, p^w) \equiv D_i(p, R(p, p^w))$ and $C_i^*\,(p^*, p^w) \equiv D_i^*\,(p^*, R^*(p^*, p^w))$.

We next introduce notation for imports and exports, so that the trade balance and equilibrium conditions may be expressed. For the home country, imports of x are denoted as $M_x(p, p^w) \equiv C_x(p, p^w) - Q_x(p)$ and exports of y are represented as $E_y(p, p^w) \equiv Q_y(p) - C_y(p, p^w)$. Foreign country imports of y, M_y^*, and exports of x, E_x^*, are similarly defined. Home and foreign budget constraints imply that, for any world price, we have balanced trade:

(1)
$$\begin{aligned} &p^w M_x(p(\tau, p^w), p^w) \\ &\quad = E_y(p(\tau, p^w), p^w); \\ &M_y^*\,(p^*(\tau^*, p^w), p^w) \\ &\quad = p^w E_x^*(p^*(\tau^*, p^w), p^w), \end{aligned}$$

where we now represent explicitly the functional forms of the local prices. Finally, the equilibrium world price $(\tilde{p}^w(\tau, \tau^*)$ is determined by the y-market-clearing condition

(2)
$$\begin{aligned} &E_y(p(\tau, \tilde{p}^w), \tilde{p}^w) \\ &\quad = M_y^*\,(p^*(\tau^*, \tilde{p}^w), \tilde{p}^w) \end{aligned}$$

with market clearing for good x then implied by (1) and (2).

In summary, given an initial pair of tariffs, the equilibrium world price is implied by (2), and the equilibrium world price and the given tariffs then together determine the local prices. In this way, the initial tariffs imply local and world prices and thereby the levels for production, consumption, imports, exports, and tariff revenue. Finally, we add the standard restriction that $dp/d\tau > 0 > dp^*/d\tau^*$ and $\partial\tilde{p}^w/\partial\tau < 0 < \partial\tilde{p}^w/\partial\tau^*$, which ensures that the prices so determined do not succumb to the Lerner and Metzler paradoxes.

B. Government Objectives

We next offer a general representation of government preferences. While it is customary to represent a government's payoff (i.e., welfare) in terms of the underlying choice variables (i.e., tariffs), we choose instead to represent each government's welfare as a function of the local and world prices that the tariffs imply, as this approach enables us to isolate the terms-of-trade externality that tariff selections generate. We thus represent the objectives of the home and foreign governments by the general functions $W(p(\tau, \tilde{p}^w), \tilde{p}^w)$ and $W^*(p^*(\tau^*, \tilde{p}^w), \tilde{p}^w)$, respectively.

The essential structure we place on W and W^* is that, holding its local price fixed, each government achieves higher welfare when its terms of trade improve:

$$(3)\qquad \partial W(p, \tilde{p}^w)/\partial\tilde{p}^w < 0 \text{ and } \partial W^*(p^*, \tilde{p}^w)/\partial\tilde{p}^w > 0.$$

Figure 1 illustrates. An initial tariff pair $A \equiv (\tau, \tau^*)$ and is associated with a domestic iso-local-price locus, $p(A) \rightarrow p(A)$, and an iso-world-price locus, $p^w(A) \rightarrow p^w(A)$.[7] Also depicted is a second iso-world-price locus, $p^w(C) \rightarrow p^w(C)$, along which the world price is lower than at point A, indicating an improved terms of trade for the domestic country. A reduction in the world price that maintains the domestic local price is thus achieved with the movement from point A to B, corresponding to a higher (lower) domestic (foreign) import tariff. We assume only that the implied income transfer from the foreign to the domestic country is valued by the domestic government.

This representation of government preferences is quite general, as it includes both the traditional possibility that governments maximize national income as well as the possibility that governments are also motivated by distributional concerns. With respect to the latter possibility, as Richard E. Baldwin (1987) observes, the political economy models of trade policy proposed by Mancur Olson (1965), Richard E. Caves (1976), William A. Brock and Stephen P. Magee (1978), Robert C. Feenstra and Jagdish Bhagwati (1982), and Ayre L. Hillman (1982) can all be represented in this way. Similarly, the median-voter model of Wolfgang Mayer (1984), the lobbying models of Gene M. Grossman and Elhanan Helpman (1994, 1995) and Dixit et al. (1997), and the political-constraint model of Robert E. Baldwin (1985) fit within this framework.[8]

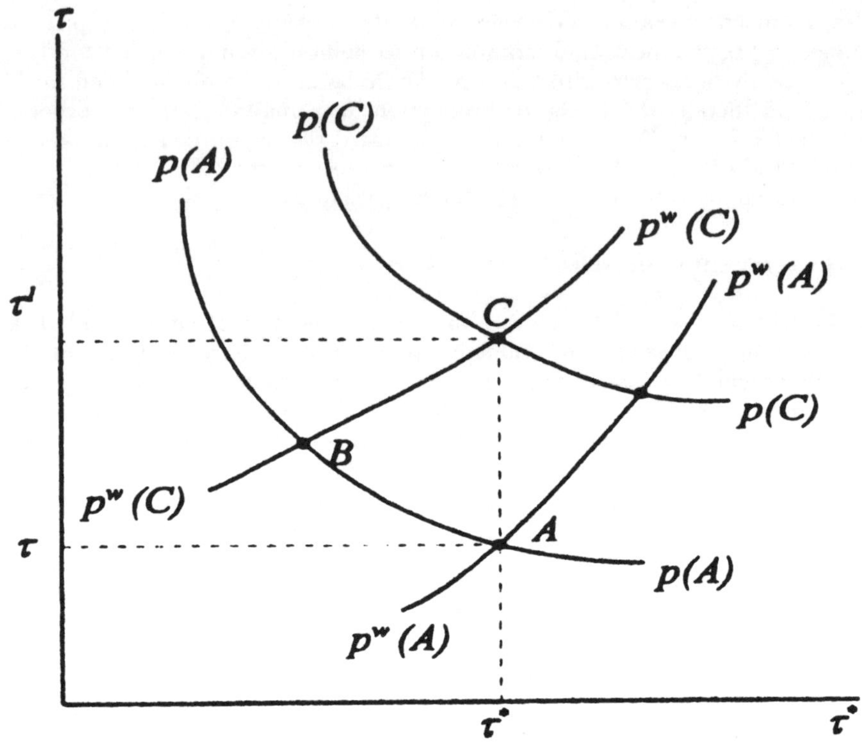

FIGURE 1 The World- and Local-Price Effects of a Tariff Change

C. The Purpose of Reciprocal Trade Agreements

We assume that governments seek *reciprocal trade agreements* to achieve mutually beneficial changes in trade policy; that is, through a reciprocal trade agreement governments seek tariff changes that result in Pareto improvements for member countries (as measured by W and W^*) over what could be achieved by unilateral tariff setting. *Reciprocal trade liberalization* then refers to mutual reductions in tariffs implemented through a reciprocal trade agreement. Finally, if the tariffs negotiated under a reciprocal trade agreement reach the efficiency locus, defined by

(4) $$[d\tau/d\tau^*]\,|_{dw=0} = [d\tau/d\tau^*]\,|_{dW^*=0},$$

then the governments have formed an *efficient reciprocal trade agreement*.

We begin our exploration of reciprocal trade agreements by considering the trade-policy inefficiencies that arise in their absence. To this end, we first suppose that each government sets its trade policy unilaterally, selecting a tariff to maximize its objective function taking the tariff choice of its trading partner as given. The resulting reaction functions are defined implicitly by

(5a) Home: $W_p[dp/d\tau] + W_{p^w}[\partial\tilde{p}^w/\partial\tau] = 0,$

(5b) Foreign: $W^*_{p^*}[dp^*/d\tau^*] + W^*_{p^w}[\partial\tilde{p}^w/\partial\tau^*] = 0,$

where subscripts denote partial derivatives.[9] Thus, with $\lambda \equiv [\partial\tilde{p}^w/\partial\tau]/[dp/d\tau] < 0$ and $\lambda^* \equiv [\partial\tilde{p}^w/\partial\tau^*]/[dp^*/d\tau^*] < 0$, (5a) and (5b) can be rewritten as

(6a) Home: $W_p + \lambda W_{p^w} = 0,$

(6b) Foreign: $W^*_{p^*} + \lambda^* W^*_{p^w} = 0.$

Each government's best-response tariff is therefore determined by the combined impact that the induced local- and world-price movements have on welfare.

The forces that determine best-response tariffs are illustrated in Figure 1. Consider an initial tariff pair represented by the point $A \equiv (\tau, \tau^*)$. Holding fixed τ^*, if the domestic government were to unilaterally increase its tariff from τ to τ^1, a new tariff pair corresponding to the point $C \equiv (\tau^1, \tau^*)$ would be induced. This tariff pair lies on a new iso-local-price locus, given as $p(C) \rightarrow p(C)$, and also on a new iso-world-price locus, represented as $p^w(C) \rightarrow p^w(C)$. By increasing its tariff, the domestic government thus induces a local price that is higher and a world price that is lower. As Figure 1 illustrates and (6a) suggests, the overall movement from A to C can be disentangled into separate movements in the local and world prices, respectively. The movement from A to B isolates the world-price change. The welfare gain for the domestic government that is associated with this change is captured in (6a) with the term λW_{p^w}, which is strictly positive by (3). The movement from B to C then reflects the induced increase in the local price, and the effect of this change on the domestic government's welfare is represented in (6a) by the term W_p.

We now define *Nash equilibrium tariffs* as a pair of domestic and foreign tariffs (τ^N, τ^{*N}) which simultaneously satisfy (6a) and (6b).[10] Our first pair of results establish that a Pareto improvement from the Nash equilibrium can be achieved through a reciprocal trade agreement, but only if the agreement is characterized by reciprocal trade liberalization.

PROPOSITION 1: *Nash equilibrium tariffs are inefficient.*

PROPOSITION 2: *A reciprocal trade agreement must entail reciprocal trade liberalization.*

Proofs of these propositions are found in the Appendix.

These results reflect a familiar intuition. When a government imposes an import tariff, its terms of trade improve, and part of the cost of this policy is borne by its trading partners, whose products sell at a lower world price. This terms-of-trade externality implies that the government faces less than the full costs of protecting its import-competing sectors. As a consequence, governments oversupply policies directed toward import protection relative to the efficient intervention levels given their preferences, and a reciprocal trade agreement can therefore benefit all governments if it serves as a mechanism through which the protection levels of each country can be reduced. An implication of our analysis is that the benefits of reciprocal trade liberalization are quite robust, as they arise for a very general class of government preferences.

More strikingly, for the class of government preferences entertained here, we find that the terms-of-trade externality is the *only* inefficiency that a reciprocal trade agreement can remedy. To establish this conclusion, we consider a hypothetical world in which governments are assumed not to value the terms-of-trade effects that their unilateral tariff choices imply.[11] if under this hypothesis unilateral tariff choices are efficient, then we may conclude that the terms-of-trade externality is the only rationale for a trade agreement. With this experiment in mind, we define *politically optimal tariffs* as any tariff pair (τ^{PO}, τ^{*PO}) that simultaneously satisfies:

(7a) Home: $W_p = 0$,

(7b) Foreign: $W^*_{p^*} = 0$.

In the special case where the domestic and foreign governments seek to maximize national income, politically optimal tariffs correspond to reciprocal free trade.[12]

We now find that the terms-of-trade externality is indeed the only inefficiency that a trade agreement can remedy.

PROPOSITION 3: *Politically optimal tariffs are efficient.*

This proposition is proved in the Appendix, but the intuition follows from Figure 1. When choosing its tariff, the domestic government considers the domestic costs and benefit that a tariff increase has through the corresponding increase in the domestic local price (the movement from *B* to *C*), and it also considers the extent to which the costs associated with a higher local price are shifted onto its trading partner through the corresponding reduction in the world price (the movement from *A* to *B*). In the hypothetical case in which the domestic government does not value the world-price change that a tariff increase implies, however, it is motivated only by the former consideration. When both governments behave in this fashion, the resulting politically optimal tariffs are thus efficient.

Of course, the politically optimal tariffs are not the only efficient tariffs. To see this, we use (4) to recast the efficiency locus in the form

(8) $(1 - AW_p)(1 - A^*W^*_{p^*}) = 1$,

where $A \equiv (1 - \tau\lambda)/(W_p + \lambda W_{pw})$ and $A^* \equiv (1 - \lambda^*/\tau^*)/(W^*_{p^*} + \lambda^* W^*_{pw})$, with $A \neq 0$ and $A^* \neq 0$ under the further assumption that the partial derivatives of the welfare functions are always finite. Observe that (8) is satisfied when $W_p = 0 = W^*_{p^*}$, confirming that politically optimal tariffs are efficient; however, (8) can also be satisfied if $W_p \neq 0$ and $W^*_{p^*} \neq 0$, and politically optimal tariffs thus define only a particular point on the efficiency locus. Starting from the political optimum, other points on the efficiency locus can be reached by altering tariffs so as to generate local prices that are efficient given the new distribution of world income implied by the associated world-price movements.[13]

We now add some additional structure to the model and assume that: (i) a unique Nash equilibrium exists; (ii) a unique political optimum exists; and (iii) the political optimum lies on the contract curve (i.e., it corresponds to a point on the efficiency locus that yields mutual gains for each government relative to its Nash welfare).[14] These assumptions are imposed in Figure 2, which illustrates the three propositions of the section. As Proposition 1 indicates, the Nash tariffs (point *N*) lie off of the efficiency locus as defined by (8) (the curve $E \rightarrow E$). The figure also depicts the Nash iso-welfare curves for the domestic and foreign governments, and these curves illustrate the message of Proposition 2: relative to the Nash equilibrium, a trade agreement can increase the welfare of both governments only if the agreement calls for a reduction in both tariffs. Finally, as Proposition 3 requires, the politically optimal tariffs (point *PO*) lie on the efficiency locus. Notice that the iso-welfare curves are tangent at every point along this locus. A novel feature of the politically optimal point is that the iso-welfare curves are also tangent to the iso-world-price locus. The bold portion of the efficiency locus corresponds to the contract curve.

More broadly, Figure 2 illustrates the general purpose of a reciprocal trade agreement. When governments interact unilaterally, the associated Nash tariffs are inefficient as a consequence of the terms-of-trade externality. A reciprocal trade agreement is then attractive to governments if it enables them to cooperate and replace the high Nash tariffs with lower tariffs that rest on the contract curve. While the rationale for a reciprocal trade agreement may be understood in these general terms, there remains an important practical issue: How is the trade agreement to be designed?

There are two basic approaches. In a "rules-based" approach, governments agree to certain principles under which subsequent negotiations will be undertaken. Alternatively, governments might adopt a "power-based" approach in which they bargain in a direct fashion that is not constrained by agreed-upon principles of negotiation. With the creation of GATT, governments chose to adopt a rules-based approach, and two foundational rules of GATT are reciprocity and nondiscrimination. We focus in the next two sections on the efficiency properties of these simple rules.

II. RECIPROCITY

In this section, we define and interpret GATT's principle of reciprocity. We then show that reciprocity can enhance efficiency, as it can guide governments toward the politically optimal tariffs.

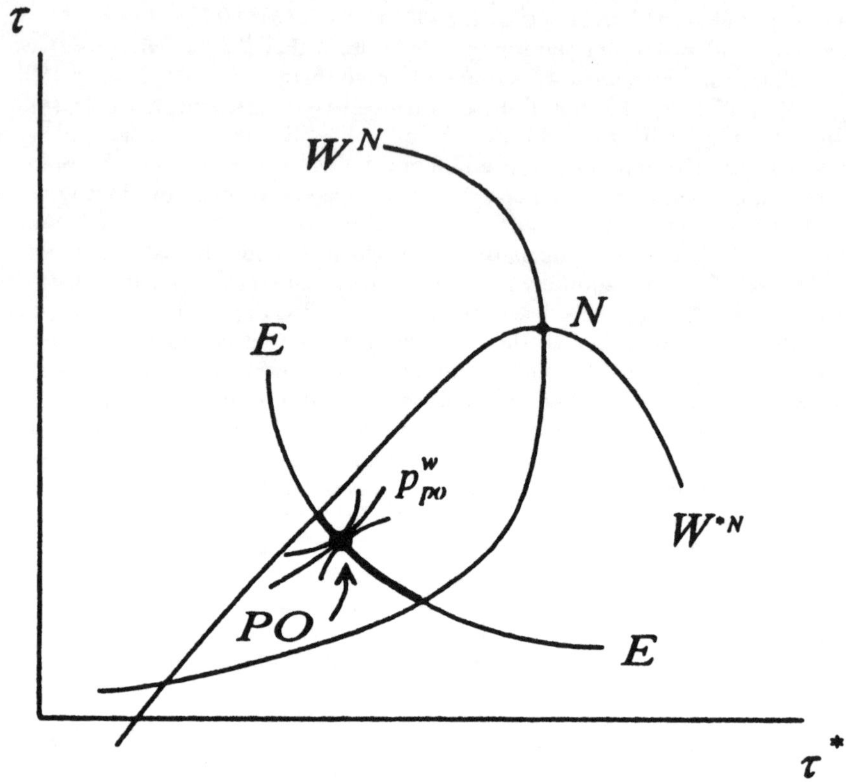

FIGURE 2 The Purpose of a Reciprocal Trade Agreement

A. The Principle of Reciprocity

We begin with a definition of reciprocity. At the broadest level, reciprocity refers to the "ideal" of mutual changes in trade policy that bring about equal changes in import volumes across trading partners.[15] We thus propose the following definition: a set of tariff changes $\Delta\tau \equiv (\tau^1 - \tau^0)$ and $\Delta\tau^* \equiv (\tau^{*1} - \tau^{*0})$ conforms to *the principle of reciprocity* provided that

$$\tilde{p}^{w0}[M_x(p(\tau^1, \tilde{p}^{w1}), \tilde{p}^{w1}) - M_x(p(\tau^0, \tilde{p}^{w0}), \tilde{p}^{w0})] = [M_y^*(p^*(\tau^{*1}, \tilde{p}^{w1}), \tilde{p}^{w1}) - M_y^*(p^*(\tau^{*0}, \tilde{p}^{w0}), \tilde{p}^{w0})],$$

where $\tilde{p}^{w0} \equiv \tilde{p}^w(\tau^0, \tau^{*0})$, $\tilde{p}^{w1} \equiv \tilde{p}^w(\tau^1, \tau^{*1})$ and changes in import volumes are measured at existing world prices. Using the trade-balance condition (1) and the equilibrium condition (2), it is now direct to show that this expression reduces to

$$[\tilde{p}^{w1} - \tilde{p}^{w0}]M_x(p(\tau^1, \tilde{p}^{w1}), \tilde{p}^{w1}) = 0$$

Hence, *mutual changes in trade policy that conform to reciprocity leave world prices unchanged.*

With this observation in hand, we may anticipate the general manner in which reciprocity can be efficiency enhancing. Intuitively, as we argued above, unilateral tariff choices are inefficient if and only if governments are motivated by their abilities to *change* the world price. When governments negotiate tariffs under the rule of reciprocity, however, this terms-of-trade externality is neutralized, as the mutual tariff changes that occur under reciprocity leave the world price *fixed.* This feature of reciprocity, which can be seen transparently in our two-country, two-good model but which also extends beyond the 2 × 2 case, will play a central role in our analysis.[16]

To explore this general proposal more fully, we identify the two specific applications of reciprocity that occur within GATT practice. First, the principle of reciprocity is often associated with the informal idea that governments seek a "balance of concessions" (i.e., reciprocal tariff cuts) when they enter into trade negotiations. The emphasis that governments place upon reciprocity in this sense has attracted the interest of many economists, and we therefore pause and offer an economic interpretation of this application in the next subsection. A second application of reciprocity can be found within the formal rules of GATT itself. We give this application primary emphasis, and it concerns the rules by which GATT members must abide when they renegotiate agreements. In the final subsection, we interpret and evaluate the agreements that governments can implement when they recognize that the principle of reciprocity governs any renegotiation process.

B. Reciprocity and the Balance of Concessions

When governments negotiate tariff reductions in a GATT round, they do so under GATT Article XXVIII bis. As the language therein makes clear, participation in negotiations is voluntary and suggests a desire to arrange "reciprocal and mutually advantageous" reductions in tariffs. At the same time, there is no formal requirement in GATT that negotiated tariff reductions conform to the principle of reciprocity as defined above. Rather, governments have developed an informal reliance upon this principle, as they typically seek a *balance of concessions* through a negotiated agreement.[17]

This informal principle of reciprocity appears to defy standard economic logic, which holds that unilateral free trade is the optimal policy for a country. Why should a government require a "concession" from its trading partner in order to do what is in any event best for its country? Indeed, the observation that governments seek reciprocity in negotiated agreements is sometimes interpreted as evidence that government negotiators adopt a mercantilist perspective that is inconsistent with economic reasoning and derives from political forces. For example, Paul R. Krugman (1991 p. 25) observes the following.

> To make sense of international trade negotiations, one needs to remember three simple rules about the objectives of the negotiating countries:
>
> (1) *Exports are good.*
> (2) *Imports are bad.*
> (3) *Other things equal, an equal increase in imports and exports is good.*
>
> In other words, GATT-think is enlightened mercantilism.

By contrast, we argue next that the informal principle of reciprocity that characterizes actual trade negotiations admits a direct and simple economic interpretation.[18]

To develop this argument, we assume for the moment that governments begin at the Nash equilibrium point, and we show formally in the Appendix that reciprocal trade liberalization that satisfies the principle of reciprocity raises the welfare of each government in a monotonic fashion, at least if the liberalization effort does not proceed too far.

PROPOSITION 4: *Beginning at a Nash equilibrium, reciprocal trade liberalization that conforms to reciprocity will increase each government's welfare monotonically until this liberalization has proceeded to the point where* min $[-W_p, W^*_{p^*}]$. *If countries are symmetric, this liberalization path leads to the politically optimal outcome.*

Intuitively, at a Nash equilibrium, each government would prefer more trade, if only it could achieve this increase without experiencing a decline in its terms of trade. For example, it is direct from (3) and (6a) that $W_p < 0$ at a Nash equilibrium, which indicates that the domestic local price is higher than the domestic government prefers, taking as given the Nash world price. The domestic government would thus prefer to reduce its tariff, lower the local price, and experience a corresponding increase in trade volume, if it could do so without reducing its terms of trade. While a unilateral liberalization effort is unappealing at the Nash equilibrium as a consequence of the associated deterioration in the terms of trade, a negotiated *mutual* reduction in tariffs that conforms to the principle of reciprocity results in a higher trade volume without a terms-of-trade loss for either government. Both governments thus benefit from reciprocal tariff reductions of this form, provided that the reciprocal liberalization effort does not proceed past the point at which min $[-W_p, W^*_{p^*}]$, where one government obtains its preferred local price given the initial Nash world price.

Figure 3A and 3B illustrate the liberalization paths described in Proposition 4. In Figure 3A, the countries are symmetric, and so the iso-world-price locus that runs through the Nash point *N* also intersects the politically optimal point *PO*. In this case, as governments liberalize according to the principle of reciprocity, each government benefits until both simultaneously achieve their preferred

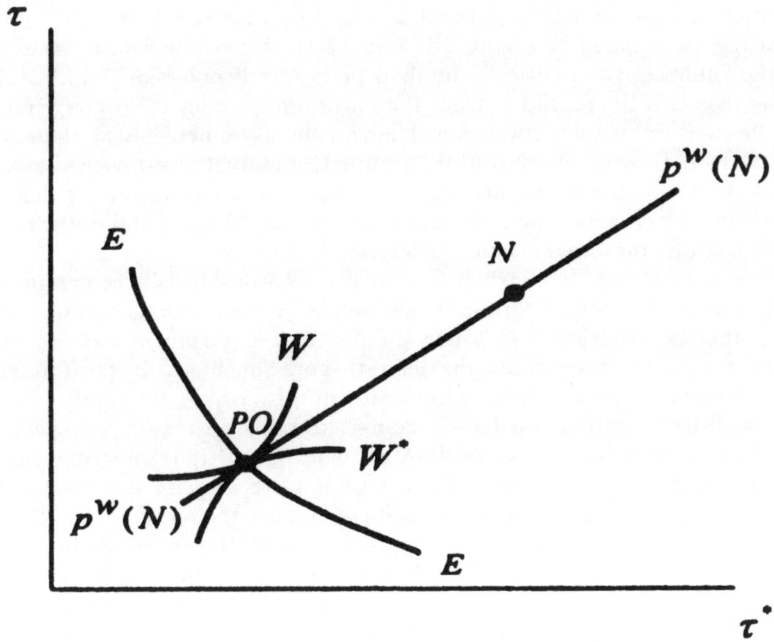

FIGURE 3A Liberalization According to Reciprocity – The Symmetric Case

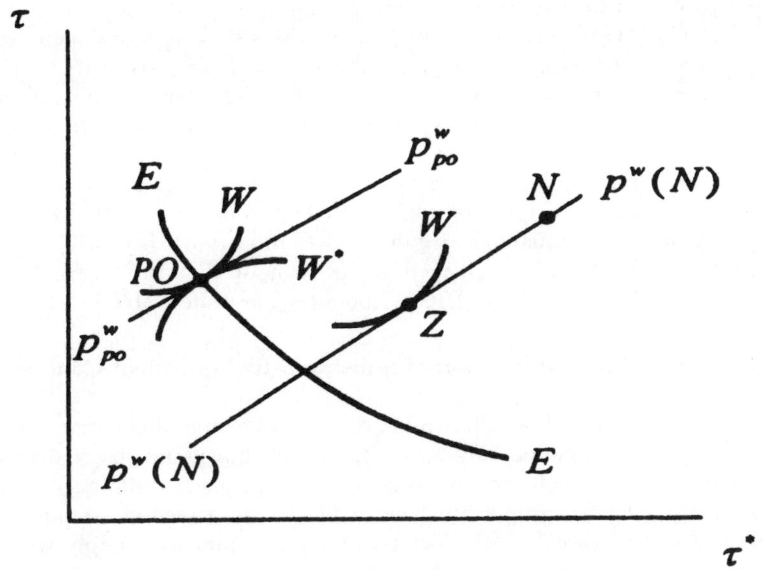

FIGURE 3B Liberalization According to Reciprocity – The Asymmetric Case

local prices at the politically optimal tariffs. The case in which countries are asymmetric is depicted in Figure 3B, and the Nash iso-world-price locus now need not intersect the politically optimal point. As Proposition 4 indicates, it remains true that liberalization from the Nash point under reciprocity initially raises the welfare of each government; but in the asymmetric case, the mutual benefits from further liberalization terminate before the efficiency locus is reached. For instance, in Figure 3B, it is the domestic government that first achieves its preferred local price at the given Nash world price, and so the mutual benefits from further liberalization terminate at point Z.

It is convenient now to consider further the relationship between reciprocity and the politically optimal tariffs. As discussed in the previous section, under the hypothetical experiment in which the domestic government does not value movements in the terms of trade, the domestic government sets its tariff to satisfy $W_p = 0$. When both governments select tariffs in this fashion, the resulting tariffs are the politically optimal tariffs. Of course, there is no reason to expect that actual governments would be indifferent to terms-of-trade movements. The experiment is instructive, though. We may think of reciprocity as corresponding to a related experiment, in which governments ignore the terms-of-trade implications of their tariff selections, not because such a movement would be without value, but rather because the mutual adjustments in tariffs implied by reciprocity guarantee that the world price is, in fact, fixed. The domestic government's preferred tariff thus again satisfies $W_p = 0$, which is to say that reciprocity induces governments to act as *if* they did not value the terms-of-trade movements associated with their unilateral tariff selections.[19]

Finally, we return to Krugman's (1991) three rules of "enlightened mercantilism" that characterize actual negotiations, and we note that Propositions 1 through 4 provide a formal economic interpretation of these rules. Specifically, we find that: (1) governments enter into negotiations seeking more open export markets ("exports are good"), because a reduction in the import tariff levied by the trading partner serves to improve the terms of trade; (2) import liberalization is viewed by governments as a concession ("imports are bad"), because it implies reducing the import tariff below the best-response value and suffering a terms-of-trade decline; and (3) each government benefits from a concession at home that is balanced under reciprocity against an "equivalent" concession abroad ("other things equal, an equal increase in imports and exports is good"), because the balance of concessions so achieved serves to neutralize the terms-of-trade decline that would have made unilateral liberalization undesirable.[20]

C. Reciprocity and the Withdrawal of Substantially Equivalent Concessions

There is nothing in GATT which *requires* that the outcome of negotiations produce a balance of concessions; rather, reciprocity in this circumstance describes the broad manner in which governments seem to approach trade negotiations. Reciprocity also plays an important role in GATT in a second circumstance, however, and in this case GATT does require that countries comply with the rule of reciprocity. This second application of reciprocity concerns the manner in which countries may lawfully renegotiate a previous agreement. Under GATT

Article XXVIII (Dam, 1970 pp. 79–99; Jackson, 1989 p. 119; Alice Enders, 1999), a country may propose to modify or withdraw a tariff concession to which it had previously committed in a round of tariff negotiation. In the circumstance in which the country fails to reach agreement with its trading partners over a renegotiated tariff schedule, the country is free to carry out the proposed changes anyway, and the notion of reciprocity is used to moderate the responses of its trading partners, who are permitted to withdraw *substantially equivalent concessions* of their own.[21]

By requiring moderation on the part of trading partners, this second application of reciprocity ensures that the proposing country's unilateral decision to increase a previously bound tariff results in an offsetting tariff adjustment from its trading partner which preserves the original world price. Consequently, under GATT's rules, any agreement that leaves some government wanting less trade at the prevailing world price will be renegotiated. For the remainder of the paper, we will focus on reciprocity as it applies in this second circumstance, and we will consider the trade agreements that can be implemented when governments negotiate an initial set of tariff "bindings", where subsequently either government is free to increase its previously bound tariff with the understanding that the outcome of any renegotiation that follows will preserve the world price implied by the previous agreement. We wish to characterize the set of trade agreements that can be implemented as the end result of this process, i.e., once no further renegotiation is desired by either government.

Formally, we consider a negotiation process that entails three stages. In the initial negotiation stage (corresponding to Article XXVII bis), governments agree to bind their tariffs at specified levels.[22] The second stage is a renegotiation stage (corresponding to Article XXVIII), where any renegotiation satisfies the restriction of reciprocity as outlined above, and thus results in mutual changes in tariffs that preserve the world price from the first stage. Finally, to ensure that the renegotiation process achieves eventual resolution (and in line with Article XXVII), we introduce a third stage that arises if governments fail to agree on a renegotiated set of tariffs. In this final stage, the tariffs that are implemented are those that achieve the greatest trade volume consistent with the restriction of reciprocity and the requirement that no country is asked to import a volume greater than is implied by its government's proposal in the renegotiation stage.

We begin our analysis with some definitions. Given a world price $\tilde{p}^w$ that is determined in the first stage of negotiations, we will say that a renegotiated tariff pair (τ, τ^*) satisfies the *restriction of reciprocity* if the tariff pair preserves the original world price: $\tilde{p}^w(\tau, \tau^*) = \tilde{p}^w$. If in the renegotiation stage the domestic government proposes a domestic tariff $\hat{\tau}$ and the foreign government proposes a foreign tariff $\hat{\tau}^*$, then under the restriction of reciprocity the tariff proposed by one government will "imply" a world-price-preserving tariff for its trading partner. We thus define the domestic government's implied foreign tariff, $\tau^* = \tau^*(\hat{\tau}, \tilde{p}^w)$, and the foreign government's implied domestic tariff, $\tau = \tau(\hat{\tau}^*, \tilde{p}^w)$, by the requirements that $(\hat{\tau}, \tau^*(\hat{\tau}, \tilde{p}^w))$ and $(\tau(\hat{\tau}^*, \tilde{p}^w), \hat{\tau}^*)$ satisfy the restriction of reciprocity. We may then say that the proposed tariffs, $\hat{\tau}$ and $\hat{\tau}^*$, *agree* if they imply the same tariff pair along the iso-world-price locus: $(\hat{\tau}, \tau^*(\hat{\tau}, \tilde{p}^w)) = (\tau(\hat{\tau}^*, \tilde{p}^w), \hat{\tau}^*)$. When the proposed tariffs do not agree, the tariff pair (τ, τ^*) that is implemented in the final stage satisfies the *restriction of proposed import limits* if the domestic import volume under (τ, τ^*) is no greater than the implied import volume $M_x(p(\hat{\tau}, \bar{p}^w), \bar{p}^w)$ and the foreign import volume under (τ, τ^*) is likewise no greater than the implied import volume $M_y^*(p^*(\hat{\tau}^*, \bar{p}^w), \bar{p}^w)$. This final restriction formalizes the idea that neither government can be forced to import a volume greater than implied by its own proposal in the renegotiation stage.

We are prepared now to formally define the *Bilateral Negotiation Game*:

Stage 1: Governments bargain over tariffs and a world price, $\bar{p}^w$, is determined.

Stage 2: The domestic government propose a domestic tariff, $\hat{\tau}$, at the same time that the foreign government proposes a foreign tariff, $\hat{\tau}^*$. If the tariff proposals agree, then they are implemented as the outcome of the negotiation.

Stage 3: If the tariff proposals to not agree, then the tariffs that are implemented are those which achieve the greatest trade volume while satisfying the restrictions of reciprocity and proposed import limits.

Our approach is to first determine the tariffs that can be achieved under the representation of reciprocity given in stages 2 and 3, and then later provide a description of the stage-1 bargaining process that encompasses a range of possibilities.

While there are a variety of simple rules under which governments might negotiate, we will argue that an appealing feature of reciprocity is that this rule is compatible with an efficient outcome. In fact, negotiations under reciprocity results in an efficient outcome if and only if tariffs are ultimately set at their politically optimal levels. The key intuition is again that the rule of reciprocity eliminates the ability of any government to shift costs onto its trading partner through a change in the world price. This rule therefore induces each government to behave as if it did not value world-price movements, a behavior which leads naturally toward the selection of politically optimal tariffs.

The main ideas can be developed more concretely with reference to Figure 4. There, we identify three pairs of efficient tariffs, labeled A, B, and PO. We represent as well the iso-world-price loci that run through each of the three tariff pairs. Finally, we also illustrate the loci that represent tariffs for which $W_p = 0$ and $W^*_{p^*} = 0$, respectively. For illustrative purposes only, these loci are assumed downward sloping. According to (8), each locus intersects the efficiency frontier at the politically optimal point PO and nowhere else.[23]

Suppose now that the governments' initial agreement corresponds to point A. In this case, the foreign government would prefer to move up the associated iso-world-price locus to point A', where it achieves its preferred local price. The foreign government thus has incentive to propose the tariff $\tau^*(A')$, with the corresponding implied domestic tariff $\tau(A')$; in fact, for the bilateral negotiation game represented above, this proposal is a dominant strategy for the foreign government.[24] The efficient tariff pair at A is thus not "renegotiation proof" under GATT rules, since the foreign government would request a renegotiation to raise its tariff to $\tau^*(A')$, knowing that the domestic government would then

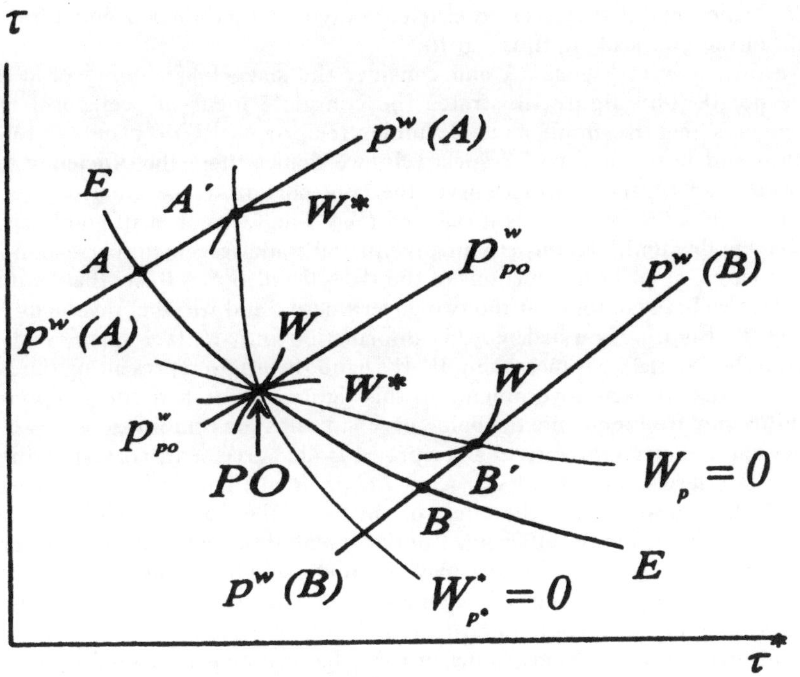

FIGURE 4 Renegotiation Under Reciprocity

withdraw a substantially equivalent concession that preserves the world price and delivered the point A'. Using a similar argument, it is apparent that the point B also fails the renegotiation test, although in this case it is the domestic government that withdraws its original concession in order to induce the point B'. It is now direct to see that there is exactly one efficient tariff pair which, if agreed to initially, would be impervious to the renegotiation process. This tariff pair is the politically optimal tariff pair, since this is the only point on the efficiency locus at which each government achieves its preferred local price for the given world price.[25]

We now say that a tariff pair (τ, τ^*) can be *implemented under reciprocity* if there exists a world price $\tilde{p}^w$ such that the outcome of stages 2 and 3 of the Bilateral Negotiation Game is uniquely (τ, τ^*), when governments make dominant proposals. Arguing in this general fashion described above, we show formally in the Appendix that the following proposition obtains.

PROPOSITION 5: *An efficient trade agreement can be implemented under reciprocity if and only if it is characterized by tariffs which are set at their politically optimal levels.*

Thus, if governments recognize the potential for renegotiation as allowed by

GATT rules, and if they seek an efficient outcome, then their negotiations will result in the politically optimal tariffs.

We turn now to Figure 5A and consider the stage-1 bargaining process in more detail. This figure illustrates the complete locus of reciprocal trade agreements that are implementable under reciprocity. With τ and τ^* on the vertical and horizontal axis, respectively, we depict there the efficiency locus (labeled $E \rightarrow E$), the contract curve (the bold portion of the efficiency locus), and the politically optimal point (labeled *PO*). The locus of tariff combinations implementable under reciprocity in a reciprocal trade agreement corresponds to the upper envelope of the portions of the $W_p = 0$ and $W^*_{p^*} = 0$ loci that lie inside the Nash welfare contours of the two governments, and we label this locus $R \rightarrow PO \rightarrow R$. Figure 5B translates this information into welfare space, with the vertical (horizontal) axis measuring $W(W^*)$ and the origin representing the Nash welfare levels of each government. In this figure, the dashed curve represents the efficiency frontier, while the bold curve indicates the combinations of welfare achievable under reciprocity in a reciprocal trade agreement, corresponding to the welfare levels along the locus $R \rightarrow PO \rightarrow R$ in Figure 5A. As depicted in Figure 5B, reciprocity has the effect of shrinking the feasible set of bargaining outcomes to lie within the efficiency frontier at all but the politically optimal point.

With reference to Figure 5B, we may now understand the constraint of reciprocity more broadly as a rule of negotiation that has the effect of steering the stage–1 bargaining outcome toward the political optimum. To make this point, we consider any stage–1 bargaining process that can be represented in terms of the maximization of a general function, the iso-quantity contours of which are downward sloping and convex in the space of welfare. The objective function specified in the Nash bargaining solution is one example. The maximization is taken over a set of feasible tariff/welfare outcomes, and the feasible set is determined in turn by the bargaining format.

We compare two bargaining formats.[26] Suppose first that governments bargain directly in stage 1 over final tariff/welfare outcomes, without the possibility of subsequent renegotiation. The feasible set of welfare outcomes then corresponds in Figure 5B to those welfare levels that lie on or within the efficiency frontier. Assuming that the efficiency frontier is concave, the bargaining outcome is uniquely determined as a tangency between an iso-quantity contour and the efficiency frontier. We represent this solution as point *A*. The second format corresponds to the Bilateral Negotiation Game. In this case, the feasible set of welfare outcomes is represented in Figure 5B as those welfare levels that lie on or within the bold curve. If this curve is concave, the bargaining solution is uniquely determined as a tangency between the iso-quantity contour and the bold curve. The solution under this second format is depicted at point *B*, where the stage-1 bargaining outcome is now closer to the political optimum.[27]

This discussion indicates that the restriction of reciprocity directs the bargaining outcome toward the political optimum. Intuitively, this restriction limits the extent to which one government can gain when the other government's welfare is diminished (relative to the political optimum), and this "efficiency penalty" ensures that governments will not venture too far from the political optimum in their stage–1 negotiations. Finally, we also observe that, as Proposition

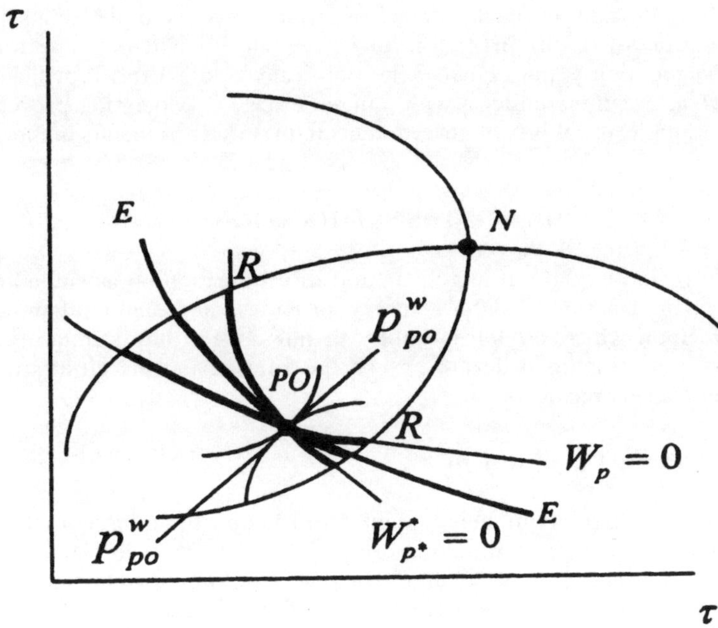

FIGURE 5A The Locus of Tariffs Implementable Under Reciprocity

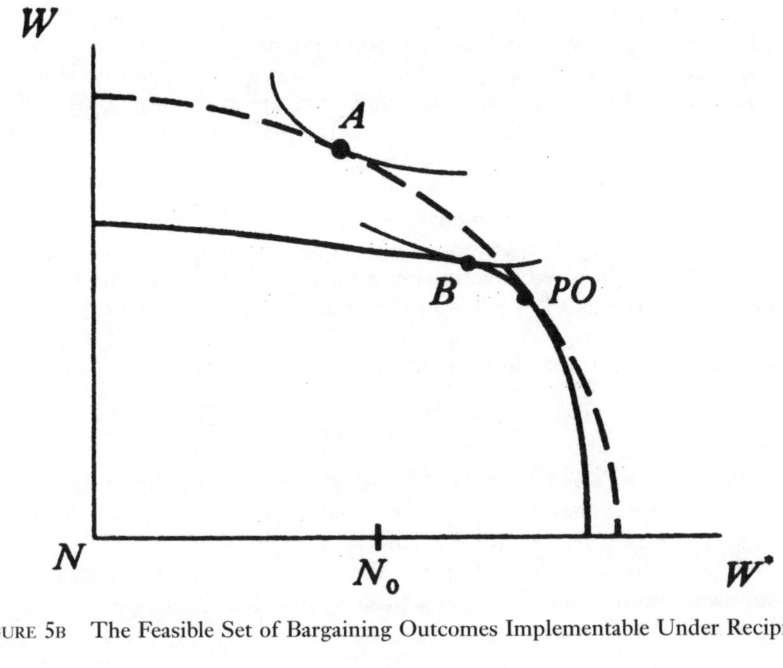

FIGURE 5B The Feasible Set of Bargaining Outcomes Implementable Under Reciprocity

5 states, the politically optimal outcome is itself necessary under any stage–1 bargaining process, if this process is to deliver an efficient outcome for the Bilateral Negotiation Game. Hence, the politically optimal tariffs will be the outcome of negotiations under a wide range of stage–1 bargaining procedures when, for example, the ability of governments to make side payments is allowed.[28]

III. NONDISCRIMINATION

Along with reciprocity, the principle of non-discrimination — as embodied in the most-favored-nation (MFN) clause – provides the second pillar of the foundation upon which GATT is built. We now extend our framework to a multicountry setting in order to assess the role of nondiscrimination in multilateral trade agreements.

A. The Economic Environment

WE assume that there is one home country (no *) and three foreign countries (*).[29] The home country is a natural importer of x, and the three foreign countries are natural importers of y. We assume that the three foreign countries have no basis for trade among themselves in the absence of discriminatory tariffs. Furthermore, if tariffs are discriminatory, we assume that the "natural" flow of trade is not altered: discriminatory tariffs do not induce trade among the foreign countries, and they also do not reverse the pattern of trade between the home country and any of its foreign trading partners.[30] As such, each foreign country trades only with the home country, and the home country is thus the only country that has the opportunity to set discriminatory tariffs.

We now introduce some notation. The set of foreign countries is denoted by $\aleph^* \in \{1, 2, 3\}$, and we use $j \in \aleph^*$ as an index for foreign country j. We continue to define $p \equiv p_x/p_y$, as the home local relative price, and we now denote the local relative price in foreign country j as $p^{*j} \equiv p_x^{*j}/p_y^{*j}$. The ad valorem tariff levied by the home country on imports from foreign country j as denoted as t^j, and similarly t^{*j} is the ad valorem tariff imposed by foreign country j on imports from the home country. We assume these tariffs are nonprohibitive. Next, we define the "world" (untaxed) relative price for trade between the home country and foreign country j as $p^{wj} \equiv p_x^{*j}/p_y$. Defining $\tau^j \equiv (1 + t^j)$ and $\tau^{*j} \equiv (1 + t^{*j})$, we then have that $p = \tau^j p^{wj} \equiv p(\tau^j, p^{wj})$ and $p^{*j} = p^{wj}/\tau^{*j} \equiv p^{*j}(\tau^{*j}, p^{wj})$. Finally, we note that bilateral trades link world prices according to:

$$p^{wj} = [\tau^k/\tau^j]\cdot p^{wk}, \textit{ for } j, k \in \aleph^*. \tag{9}$$

Thus, a home-country policy of MFN (i.e., $\tau^1 = \tau^2 = \tau^3$) implies a single world price: $p^{wj} \equiv p^w$. By contrast, tariff discrimination across imports from foreign countries j and k(i.e., $\tau^j \neq \tau^k$) implies different world prices: $p^{wj} \neq p^{wk}$.

Foreign production and consumption decisions can be characterized exactly as in our two-country model, since each foreign country j has only one trading partner, and so its terms of trade are given simply by p^{wj}. Thus, production, consumption, exports and imports for foreign country $j \in \aleph^*$ are denoted respectively by $Q_i^{*j} = Q_i^{*j}(p^{*j})$ for $i \in \{x, y\}$, $C_i^{*j}(p^{*j}, p^{wj})$ for $i \in \{x, y\}$, $E_x^{*j}(p^{*j}(\tau^{*j}, p^{wj}), p^{wj})$, and $M_y^{*j}(p^{*j}(\tau^{*j}, p^{wj}), p^{wj})$. The presence of multiple trading partners for the domestic country potentially complicates the expression of domestic quantities, as the home country may face different terms of trade with each of its trading partners. This complication does not affect the determination of domestic production, which is still represented as a function of local relative prices: $Q_i = Q_i(p)$ for $i \in \{x, y\}$. Likewise, domestic consumption of good i is still determined as a function of the local relative price and domestic tariff revenue: $D_i(p, R)$ for $i \in \{x, y\}$. But, in light of the possibility of discriminatory tariffs, domestic tariff revenue now depends both on the total volume of x imported by the domestic country and the composition of this given volume across the foreign trading partners.

To construct an expression for domestic tariff revenue, we let $\{p^{*j}\}$ and $\{p^{wj}\}$ denote the set of foreign local and world prices, respectively, and we define bilateral trade shares by

$$s_x^{*j}(\{p^{*j}\}, \{p^{wj}\}) \equiv E_x^{*j}(p^{*j}, p^{wj}) \Big/ \Big[\sum_{i \in \aleph^*} E_x^{*i}(p^{*i}, p^{wi})\Big].$$

We then define the domestic country's *multilateral* terms of trade by the trade-weighted average of the set of bilateral world prices:

$$T(\{p^{*j}\}, \{p^{wj}\}) \equiv \sum_{i \in \aleph^*} s_x^{*i}(\{p^{*i}\}, \{p^{wi}\}) \cdot p^{wi}.$$

With this definition in place, domestic tariff revenue is given implicitly by

$$\begin{aligned} R &= [D_x(p, R) - Q_x(p)] \times \sum_{i \in \aleph^*} s_x^{*i}(\{p^{*i}\}, \{p^{wi}\}) \cdot [p - p^{wi}] \\ &= [D_x(p, R) - Q_x(p)] \cdot [p - T], \end{aligned}$$

or $R = R(p, T)$.

We may now represent the domestic country's consumption as $C_i(p, T) \equiv D_i(p, R(p, T))$. It follows that home-country imports of x may be denoted as $M_x(p, T) \equiv C_x(p, T) - Q_x(p)$, while home-country exports of y may be represented as $E_y(p, T) \equiv Q_y(p) - C_y(p, T)$. Henceforth, we will refer to T simply as the home country's terms of trade, and it will play a role analogous to p^w in the two-country model of the previous sections. In fact, as (9) indicates, if the home country adopts a MFN tariff policy, then $T = p^{wj} \equiv p^w$. However, a discriminatory tariff policy implies $T \neq p^{wj}$ for $j \in \aleph^*$.

We turn finally to the trade-balance and market-clearing conditions. Home and foreign budget constraints imply that, for any world prices, we have

$$(10) \qquad \begin{aligned} & T(\{p^{*j}\}, \{p^{wj}\}) \\ & \times M_x(p, T(\{p^{*j}\}, \{p^{wj}\})) \\ & = E_y(p, T(\{p^{*j}\}, \{p^{wj}\})); \\ & M_y^{*j}(p^{*j}, p^{wj}) \\ & = p^{wj} \cdot E_x^{*j}(p^{*j}, p^{wj}), \text{ for } j \in \aleph^*. \end{aligned}$$

With $\{\tau^j\}$ and $\{\tau^{*j}\}$ representing the set of domestic and foreign tariffs, respectively, we denote the equilibrium world price for trade between the home and foreign country j by $\tilde{p}^{wj}(\{\tau^j\}, \{\tau^{*j}\})$. Equilibrium world prices are then determined by (9) and the market-clearing condition for good x:

$$(11) \qquad \begin{aligned} & M_x(p, T(\{p^{*j}\}, \{\tilde{p}^{wj}\})) \\ & = \sum_{i \in \aleph^*} E_x^{*i}(p^{*i}, \tilde{p}^{wi}). \end{aligned}$$

The equilibrium in the y-market is then assured by (10).

B. Government Objectives

We again represent the objectives of each government as a general function of its local price and terms of trade. Thus, the home government maximizes $W(p, T)$ while foreign government j maximizes $W^{*j}(p^{*j}, \tilde{p}^{wj})$. We assume only that, with local prices held fixed, each government strictly prefers an improvement in its terms of trade: $W_T(p, T) < 0$ and $W^{*j}_{p^{wj}}(p^{*j}, \tilde{p}^{wj}) > 0$.

The home government welfare function embodies a novel pattern of externalities. As in the two-country model, the tariff level selected by a foreign government alters world prices, and this in turn affects the home country's terms of trade T and imparts a home-government externality through the consequent change in tariff revenue. In the multicountry model, however, the tariff level selected by the foreign government may also exert a home-government externality through the effect that the tariff has on the foreign local price and thereby the home country's terms of trade and tariff revenue. Intuitively, for any given total import volume for the home country, if the home country set tariffs in a discriminatory fashion, then the home government receives greater tariff revenue when a larger fraction of imports emanates from the foreign country on whom it places the highest import tariff. The foreign export volumes, however, are determined in part by foreign local prices, and therefore foreign local prices impart a home-government externality when home tariffs are discriminatory. Importantly, this "local-price externality" disappears when the home governments tariffs satisfy MFN, since in that event the home country's terms of trade is independent of foreign local prices and is given simply by the (common) world price.

C. Tariff Policies

As in our analysis of the two-country model, we compare the Nash, politically optimal, and efficient tariffs. We begin with the Nash tariffs. Let the domestic government select a tariff policy, (τ^1, τ^2, τ^3), to maximize its welfare. W, at the same time that each foreign government j chooses its tariff policy, τ^{*j}, to maximize its welfare, W^{*j}. The resulting best-response conditions are

(12a) $$\text{Home:} = W_p + \tilde{\lambda}^j W_\tau = 0, \text{ for } j \in \aleph^*,$$

(12b) $$\text{Foreign: } W^{*j}_{p^{*j}} + \tilde{\lambda}^{*j} W^{*j}_{p^{wj}} = 0, \text{ for } j \in \aleph^*,$$

with $\tilde{\lambda}^j \equiv [dT/d\tau^j]/[dp/d\tau^j]$ and $\tilde{\lambda}^{*j} \equiv [\partial\tilde{p}^{wj}/\partial\tau^{*j}]/[dp^{*j}/d\tau^{*j}]$. A set of tariffs $(\{\tau^j\}, \{\tau^{*j}\})$ for $j \in \aleph^*$ forms a *Nash equilibrium* if each government's tariff policy satisfies its best-response condition(s).

We next extend to our multicountry setting the definition of politically optimal tariffs. In analogy with our two-country model, we define *politically optimal tariffs* as a set of tariffs $(\{\tau^{jPO}\}, \{\tau^{*jPO}\})$ for $j \in \aleph^*$ that satisfies

(13a) $$\text{Home: } W_p = 0,$$

(13b) $$\text{Foreign: } W^{*j}_{p^{*j}} = 0, \text{ for } j \in \aleph^*.$$

Notice that (13a) and (13b) comprise a set of four equations that must be met by a set of six tariffs (three domestic, three foreign). As such, in the multicountry setting, there are in general many combinations of tariffs that are politically optimal. however, if the additional restriction of MFN is imposed, the number of tariffs drops to four (one domestic, three foreign), and so it may be expected that there is a unique set of politically optimal tariffs that conform to MFN.

We consider next the set of *efficient tariffs*. To characterize this set, we may fix the welfare levels of each foreign government and determine the set of tariffs that maximizes the welfare of the domestic government. this defines a point on the efficiency locus. By varying foreign welfare levels over all feasible values, the entire efficiency locus can be described. We carry out this analysis in the Appendix, where we confirm that the Nash equilibrium tariffs are again inefficient. We establish as well the following proposition.

PROPOSITION 6: *Politically optimal tariffs are efficient if and only if they conform to MFN.*

This proposition thus reports an "affinity" between politically optimal tariffs and the principle of nondiscrimination. Intuitively, politically optimal tariffs are efficient provided that the externalities countries impose on one another in their tariff choices travel only through world prices. In a multicountry world, trade policy externalities indeed travel in this way if and only if tariffs conform to MFN. Tariff discrimination complicates the transmission of externalities across trading partners by allowing bilateral trade volumes, and hence local prices, to transmit externalities as well. Finally, we note that nondiscrimination is not a general property of points on the efficiency frontier, but is rather a special property required by political optimality.

D. Reciprocity and Nondiscrimination

We now interpret and evaluate the role of nondiscrimination in the presence of reciprocity. To this end, we first adapt our earlier definition of reciprocity to a multicountry setting. Maintaining our interpretation of reciprocity as calling for equal changes in exports and imports across trading partners, we say that a set of tariff changes $\Delta\tau^j \equiv (\tau^{j1} - \tau^{j0})$ and $\Delta\tau^{*j} \equiv (\tau^{*j1} - \tau^{*j0})$ conforms to reciprocity provided that, for $j \in \aleph^*$,

$$\begin{aligned}
&\tilde{p}^{wj0} \cdot [E_x^{*j}(p^{*j}(\tau^{*j1}, \tilde{p}^{wj1}), \tilde{p}^{wj1}) \\
&\quad - E_x^{*j}(p^{*j}(\tau^{*j0}, \tilde{p}^{wj0}), \tilde{p}^{wj0})] \\
&\quad = M_y^{*j}(p^{*j}(\tau^{*j1}, \tilde{p}^{wj1}), \tilde{p}^{wj1}) \\
&\quad - M_y^{*j}(p^{*j}(\tau^{*j0}, \tilde{p}^{wj0}), \tilde{p}^{wj0}),
\end{aligned}$$

where we now make explicit the dependence of local prices on tariffs and the market-clearing world prices. Trade balance [condition (10)] implies that this expression can be reduced to

$$\begin{aligned}
&[\tilde{p}^{wj1} - \tilde{p}^{wj0}] \cdot E_x^{*j}(p^{*j}(\tau^{*j1}, \tilde{p}^{wj1}), \tilde{p}^{wj1}) \\
&\qquad\qquad = 0 \text{ for } j \in \aleph^*.
\end{aligned}$$

Hence, as before, mutual tariff changes that conform to reciprocity leave world prices unchanged.

Our next task is to develop the appropriate extension of the Bilateral Negotiation Game for the multicountry model. As before, we posit a three-stage negotiation process that begins with an initial stage in which tariffs are bound at specified levels, determining a set of bilateral world prices. In the second stage, governments make renegotiation proposals, where under the restriction of reciprocity the bilateral world prices must be preserved. If governments fail to reach an agreement in this renegotiation stage, a third stage is entered in which tariffs are implemented that achieve the greatest multilateral trade volume consistent with the constraints that the tariffs satisfy the restriction of reciprocity and require no government to import a bilateral volume in excess of that implied by its proposal in the renegotiation stage.

We now develop a formal representation of the trade negotiation process. Letting $\{\tilde{p}^{wj}\}$ denote the set of bilateral world prices determined in the first stage, we say that a renegotiated set of tariffs $(\{\tau^j\}, \{\tau^{*j}\})$ satisfies the *restriction of reciprocity* if the tariff set preserves the bilateral world prices: $\tilde{p}^{wj}(\{\tau^j\}, \{\tau^{*j}\}) = \bar{p}^{wj}$ for each $j \in \aleph^*$. We now consider the foreign tariffs and bilateral trade volumes that are "implied" by the domestic government's proposal in the renegotiation stage, where the domestic proposal is a set $\{\hat{\tau}^j\}$ of domestic tariffs that satisfy (9) given $\{\bar{p}^{wj}\}$. In contrast to the two-country model, the proposed tariff set when combined with the fixed set of bilateral world prices $\{\bar{p}^{wj}\}$ does not uniquely imply domestic import volumes nor foreign tariffs.[31] We therefore assume that the domestic government also proposes the shares $\{\hat{s}_x^{*j}\}$ of its total import volume that are to come from each foreign trading partner, where these proposed shares are nonnegative and sum to one. When the domestic government proposes $\{\hat{\tau}^j\}$ and $\{\hat{s}_x^{*j}\}$ the implied foreign tariffs, $\tau^{*j} = \tau^{*j}(\{\hat{\tau}^j\},\{\hat{s}_x^{*j}\},\{\bar{p}^{wj}\})$, are defined by the requirements that the tariffs $(\{\hat{\tau}^j\},\{\tau^{*j}\})$ satisfy the restriction of reciprocity and generate the proposed set of trade volume shares:

$$E_x^{*j}(p^{*j}(\tau^{*j}(\cdot), \bar{p}^{wj}), \bar{p}^{wj}) = \hat{s}_x^{*j} \cdot \sum_{j \in \aleph^*} E_x^{*i}(p^{*i}(\tau^{*i}(\cdot), \bar{p}^{wi}), \bar{p}^{wi})$$

for $j \in \aleph^*$,

where $\tau^{*j}(\cdot)$ denotes the value $\tau^{*j}(\{\hat{\tau}^j\},\{\hat{s}_x^{*j}\},\{\bar{p}^{wj}\})$.[32]

We consider next the foreign trade volumes and domestic import tariffs that are implied by the proposals of the foreign governments in the renegotiation stage. We assume that, in this stage, each foreign government j proposes its tariff, $\hat{\tau}^{*j}$. Given the bilateral world price $\bar{p}^{wj}$, this proposal directly implies an import volume for foreign country j, which is given as $M_y^{*j}(p^{*j}(\hat{\tau}^{*j}, \bar{p}^{wj}), \bar{p}^{wj})$. In addition, the three foreign tariff proposals together imply a set of domestic tariffs, when the bilateral world prices are fixed.[33] Thus, if in the renegotiation stage each foreign government j proposes tariff $\hat{\tau}^{*j}$, then the set $\{\hat{\tau}^{*j}\}$ defines an implied set of domestic tariffs, with member $\tau^j = \tau^j(\{\hat{\tau}^{*j}\}, \{\bar{p}^{wj}\})$, by the requirement that the tariffs $(\{\tau^j\},\{\hat{\tau}^{*j}\})$ satisfy the restriction of reciprocity.

We are now prepared to state two final definitions. First, we say that the proposals $(\{\hat{\tau}^j\},\{\hat{s}_x^{*j}\})$ and $\{\hat{\tau}^{*j}\}$ *agree* if $(\{\hat{\tau}^j\}, \{\tau^{*j}(\cdot)\}) = (\{\tau^j(\cdot)\}, \{\hat{\tau}^{*j}\})$, where as above $\tau^{*j}(\cdot)$ denotes the implied value $\tau^{*j}(\{\hat{\tau}^j\}, \{\hat{s}_x^{*j}\}, \{\bar{p}^{wj}\})$ and where $\tau^j(\cdot)$ denotes the implied value $\tau^j(\{\hat{\tau}^{*j}\}, \{\bar{p}^{wj}\})$. Second, when the proposals do not agree, the tariff set $(\{\tau^j\}, \{\tau^{*j}\})$ that is implemented in the final stage is said to satisfy the *restriction of proposed import limits* if the domestic import volume from any foreign trading partner j under $(\{\tau^j\}, \{\tau^{*j}\})$ is no greater than the implied import volume from this partner $E_x^{*j}(p^{*j}(\tau^{*j}(\cdot), \bar{p}^{wj}), \bar{p}^{wj})$ and the import volume for any foreign country j under $(\{\tau^j\}, \{\tau^{*j}\})$ is no greater than the implied import volume $M_y^{*j}(p^{*j}(\hat{\tau}^{*j}, \bar{p}^{wj}), \bar{p}^{wj})$, for every $j \in \aleph^*$.

We now define the *Multilateral Negotiation Game*.

Stage 1: Governments bargain over tariffs and a set of bilateral world prices, $\{\bar{p}^{wj}\}$, *is determined.*

Stage 2: The domestic government proposes a set of domestic tariffs, $\{\hat{\tau}^j\}$, and trade-volume shares, $\{\hat{s}_x^{*j}\}$, at the same time that each foreign government j proposes a foreign traffic, $\hat{\tau}^{*j}$. If the proposals agree, then the tariffs are implemented as the outcome of the negotiation.

Stage 3: If the proposals do not agree, then the tariffs that are implemented are those which achieve the greatest multilateral trade volume while satisfying the restrictions of reciprocity and proposed import limits.

As before, we concentrate on stages 2 and 3, in order to determine the tariffs that can be implemented when reciprocity is represented in this way.

We say that a tariff set $(\{\tau^j\}, \{\tau^{*j}\})$ can be *implemented under reciprocity* if there exists a set of bilateral world prices $\{\bar{p}^{wj}\}$ such that the outcome of stages 2 and 3 of the Multilateral Negotiation Game is uniquely $(\{\tau^j\}, \{\tau^{*j}\})$, when foreign governments choose dominant proposals and the proposal of the domestic government is a best response to the foreign proposals.[34] We can now state our next proposition.

PROPOSITION 7: *An efficient multilateral trade agreement can be implemented under reciprocity if and only if it is characterized by tariffs which conform to the principle of MFN and are set at their politically optimal levels.*

A proof of this proposition is provided in the Appendix.

Intuitively, nondiscrimination ensures that all international externalities are channeled through world-price movements, and the principle of reciprocity serves effectively to neutralize externalities of exactly this nature. Alternatively, if stage-1 bargaining results in discriminatory tariffs, then the tariff choices of each foreign country will impart externalities on the home country through both world price and foreign local-price effects, and reciprocity is ill suited to handle the latter. Reciprocity and nondiscrimination are thus simple rules that, when used together, can deliver an efficient outcome. Furthermore, these rules direct attention toward a particular set of tariffs – the politically optimal MFN tariffs – along the efficiency frontier.[35]

IV. PREFERENTIAL AGREEMENTS

While the principles of reciprocity and non-discrimination form the pillars of GATT, a major exception to the latter principle, is allowed for the purpose of creating preferential agreements. As mentioned in the introduction, this exception, embodied in GATT Article XXIV, was controversial in its inception and has met with renewed controversy recently. In this section, we use our modeling framework to address a central question in this controversy: Will preferential agreements interfere with a multilateral trading system that is built upon the pillars of reciprocity and nondiscrimination?

In accord with Article XXIV, we consider two forms of preferential agreements. First, the domestic country forms a *free-trade area* with foreign i if $\tau^i = 0 = \tau^{*i}$

and $\tau^j > 0$ for some $j \neq i$. As free-trade areas are inherently discriminatory, the next result is a direct implication of Proposition 7.

PROPOSITION 8: *An efficient multilateral trade agreement can not be implemented under reciprocity in the presence of a free-trade agreement.*

Free-trade agreements are thus fundamentally at odds with a multilateral trading system that is built on the pillars of reciprocity and non-discrimination. This is because, to deliver efficiency, reciprocity requires a world in which the transmission of externalities is contained within world-price movements, but externalities travel through local prices as well when tariffs are discriminatory.

A second preferential agreement is a *customs union*, in which members eliminate all internal trade barriers and adopt a common external tariff as well. Proposition 7 no longer directly applies to this case, since the creation of a customs union reduces the number of external tariff authorities from four to three. But Proposition 7 is instructive, in that it suggests that reciprocity might continue to deliver efficiency, provided that the union can be viewed as a single country in the previous analysis that sets its external tariffs at the politically optimal MFN levels.

To explore this possibility, we must define the objectives of the tariff authorities in the customs union. If the domestic country forms a customs union with foreign country i, we assume that the customs union sets external tariffs to maximize a function $U(W, W^{*i})$, where U is increasing in each argument. The elimination of internal barriers implies that $p = p^{*i} = \tilde{p}^{wi} = p^{cu}$ and that the two countries experience a common external terms of trade, $T \equiv T^{cu}$. The objectives of the customs union may thus be represented further as $U(W, W^{*i}) = U(W(p^{cu}, T^{cu}), W^{*i}(p^{cu}, T^{cu}) \equiv W^{cu}(p^{cu}, T^{cu})$, with $W^{cu}_{T^{cu}} < 0$. With $W^{*j}(p^{*j}, \tilde{p}^{wj})$ still representing the objectives of each foreign government $j \neq i$, it follows from Proposition 7 that an efficient multilateral trade agreement between the customs union and the remaining foreign countries can be achieved under reciprocity if and only if the external tariffs of the customs union and the tariffs of all other countries conform to the principle of MFN and are set at their politically optimal levels.

This conclusion is appropriate if we define efficiency in terms of the welfare of the customs union itself and the remaining foreign countries. When we define efficiency in terms of the welfare of individual countries, however, we must determine as well whether it is internally efficient (i.e., with respect of W and W^{*i}) for members of the customs union to share a common local-market price. If the tariff revenue collected by the customs union can be divided among members in a way that achieves internal efficiency at this common price, we will call the two countries *natural integration partners*. This possibility is ensured if the political preferences and income levels of the two countries are sufficiently similar. We can now state the following proposition.

PROPOSITION 9: *An efficient multilateral trade agreement can be implemented under reciprocity in the presence of a customs union if and only if the members of the customs union are natural integration partners and the external affairs of the customs union and the tariffs of all other countries conform to the principle of MFN and are set at their politically optimal levels.*

Together, Propositions 8 and 9 identify a rather limited set of circumstances under which preferential agreements can exist without compromising the effectiveness of the principles of reciprocity and nondiscrimination in delivering an efficient multilateral trading agreement.

V. PARTICIPATION

GATT is a "rules-based" approach to trade negotiations. While there are all manner of rules that might be contemplated when designing a rules-based institution, an important feature of the GATT rules of reciprocity and nondiscrimination is that they steer negotiations toward a particular point on the efficiency frontier: the political optimum. As mentioned in Section I, an alternative negotiation approach is "power-based." Under this approach, governments negotiate directly over tariffs, without reference to any previously agreed-upon rules, and the outcome of the negotiations is thus especially sensitive to the "bargaining power" that the governments respectively possess. Natural formalizations of the power-based approach, such as the Nash bargaining solution, indicate that power-based negotiations may result in an agreement that rests on the efficiency frontier. Yet these negotiations, by favoring the more powerful country, would typically not deliver the political optimum. This raises a central question: How might governments choose between alternative institutional designs (e.g., rules-based versus power-based approaches)?

This is a fundamental question within the field of international relations, and we do not presume to provide a complete answer here. Some of the broader considerations involved are described below by Jackson (1989 pp. 85–86), who concludes that the history of international relations has witnessed a gradual evolution from a power-based to a rules-based approach:

> In broad perspective one can roughly divide the various techniques for the peaceful settlement of international disputes into two types: settlement by negotiation and agreement with reference (explicitly or implicitly) to relative power status of the parties; or settlement by negotiation or decision with reference to norms or rules to which both parties have previously agreed.
>
> For example, countries *A* and *B* have a trade dispute regarding *B*'s treatment of imports from *A* to *B* of widgets. The first technique mentioned would involve a negotiation between *A* and *B* by which the most powerful of the two would have the advantage. Foreign aid, military maneuvers, or import restrictions on other key goods by way of retaliation would figure in the negotiation. A small country would hesitate to challenge a large one on whom its trade depends . . .
>
> On the other hand, the second suggested technique – reference to agreed rules – would see the negotiators arguing about the application of the rule . . . During the process of negotiating a settlement it would be necessary for the parties to understand that an unsettled dispute would ultimately be resolved by impartial third-party judgements based on rules so that the negotiators would be negotiating with reference to their respective predictions as to the outcome of those judgments and not with reference to potential retaliation or actions exercising power of one or more of the parties of the dispute.

> In both techniques negotiation and private settlement of disputes is the dominant mechanism for resolving differences; but the key is the perception of the participants as to what are the "bargaining chips." . . .
>
> All diplomacy, and indeed all government, involves a mixture of these techniques. To a large degree, the history of civilization may be described as a gradual evolution from a power-oriented approach, in the state of nature, toward a rule-oriented approach. . . .[36]

While our simple modeling framework can not capture the breadth of themes to which Jackson alludes, it can be used to explore a pair of important issues that are associated with the choice between rules-based and power-based approaches to trade-policy negotiations.

The first issue concerns the scene in which GATT is a rules-based institution. Up to this point, we have regarded any negotiating approach as "rules-based," if the approach involves agreed-upon rules under which subsequent negotiations are undertaken. Certainly, GATT satisfies this standard. As Jackson's discussion above suggests, however, there is also a second standard that might be put forth: a rules-based agreement is designed so that the outcome of negotiations is insulated from the power positions of the parties involved. While it is inevitable that real-world negotiations are influenced to some degree by the power positions of the participants, we argue that GATT also satisfies this second standard, since it is designed in a manner that reduces the effect of bargaining power on negotiation outcomes. In particular, the rule of reciprocity neutralizes power asymetries and guides governments toward the political optimum, an outcome that is defined without reference to countries' relative power status. In this sense, our results confirm the widely held view that reciprocity is one "pillar" of GATT's architecture, with nondiscrimination then required as a second pillar that preserves the effectiveness of reciprocity in a multicountry world.

This discussion leads naturally to a second issue: Why would powerful countries agree to participate in GATT under the rule of reciprocity? In the remainder of the section, we offer one possible answer: by serving to moderate the lawful response of powerful countries in case of disagreement, GATT's rule of reciprocity may encourage weaker countries to participate in GATT negotiations without the fear of exploitation by their stronger trading partners.

To develop this point, we return to the Bilateral Negotiation Game described in Section II and consider the addition of a stage 0 in which each government decides whether or not to participate in negotiations in light of the bargaining format which follows. As with reference to Figure 5B, we may consider the possibility of two bargaining formats: a "power-based" format, in which governments bargain directly in stage 1 over final tariff/welfare outcomes without the possibility of subsequent renegotiation, and a "rules-based" format corresponding to the Bilateral Negotiation Game. As described in Section II, the power-based format gives rise to a negotiation outcome corresponding to the point labeled *A* in Figure 5B, while the rules-based format gives rise to the negotiation outcome labeled *B* in Figure 5B.

The question we now pose is whether the stage-0 participation decision might be influenced by the bargaining format. More specifically, we ask whether, in directing the bargaining outcome toward the political optimum, GATT's rule of reciprocity might encourage weaker countries to participate in GATT negotiations without the fear of exploitation by their stronger trading partners. Essentially, the answer to this question is "yes," provided that there exists a distinction between stage-0 and stage-1 government preferences which leads to a difference between the Nash (disagreement) welfare levels as viewed from stage-1 negotiations (labeled N in Figure 5B) and the Nash welfare levels as viewed from the stage-0 participation decision (which we depict for illustrative purposes by the point labeled N_0 in Figure 5B). Here we briefly consider one way in which such a difference could arise: from sunk costs associated with the actions of private agents.[37]

If production requires irreversible investments, then private-sector decisions made in anticipation of negotiations to liberalize markets may alter the payoffs to governments should negotiations break down. John McLaren (1997 p. 404) has argued that this observation may be particularly relevant in describing the plight of a small country negotiating to gain access to the markets of a large trading partner, where "the rational investments undertaken by small-country citizens . . . in anticipation of future bargaining can rob the small country of its flexibility . . ." and make it worse off under the resulting bargain than if the opportunity to negotiate had never arisen. This point may be illustrated in the present context with the use of Figure 5B, if we think of the foreign government as representing the smaller country, and we think of the irreversible small-country investments in serving the large-country market as being determined between stages 0 and 1.

Consider first the possibility of a power-based bargaining format. The curves represented in Figure 5B will correspond to the situation as viewed in stage 1 (i.e., after the decision to negotiate has been made and the investment decisions of the small country have been sunk), with the welfare levels at point N depicting the respective payoffs for the two governments in the event that stage-1 negotiations break down, and the point A reflecting the bargaining outcome under a power-based format. The point labeled N_0 depicts the respective payoffs for the two governments if either government decides in stage 0 not to participate in negotiations, and the payoff to the foreign government is larger at N_0 than at N as a result of the sunk investments associated with the latter. If, as depicted in Figure 5B, N_0 lies to the right of the outcome under the power-based bargain A, then the foreign country would do better to pass up the opportunity to negotiate a trade agreement with its large trading partner, much as McLaren's (1997) remarks suggest. As a result, negotiations do not occur, and governments receive the Nash payoffs associated with N_0 in this case.

Now consider the possibility of a rules-based bargaining format. In particular, suppose that the stage-0 participation decision is made with reference to the Bilateral Negotiation Game, whose outcome is depicted in Figure 5B by the point B. It is here that, by guiding countries toward the political optimum in their tariff negotiations, the introduction of a rule such as reciprocity can diminish power asymmetries, thereby relaxing the participation constraint for the weaker country and facilitating its entry into tariff negotiations. In terms of Figure 5B, the foreign government will agree to participate in negotiations under the rule of reciprocity provided that, as depicted, the point N_0 lies to the left of the rules-based negotiating outcome depicted at B. It is now apparent that, as long as B lies to the northeast of N_0, it will also be in the interest of the more powerful country to agree to a rule of reciprocity, so as to encourage the widest participation of its trading partners.

VI. CONCLUSION

Working within a general equilibrium model and adopting a representation of government trade-policy objectives that accommodates the major formulations of political economy motives, we have shown that governments can shift the cost of their intervention onto trading partners by altering world prices with their unilateral tariff choices, and that this is the source of the inefficiency which a reciprocal trade agreement must address. From this perspective, we have offered an interpretation of GATT's principles of reciprocity and non-discrimination as rules that work in concert to guide governments toward efficient multilateral trade agreements. While we establish circumstances under which customs unions are compatible with an efficient multilateral trading system built on these principles, we have shown that these circumstances are quite narrow, and that in addition free-trade agreements are fundamentally incompatible with such a system. As such, we offer support for the view that preferential agreements pose a threat to the multilateral trading system.

Our basic argument is developed in four main steps. First, we establish that governments' unilateral tariffs are higher than is efficient, because of the temptation to shift costs onto trading partners via the world-price externality. Second, utilizing the requirement of balanced trade, we find that the principle of reciprocity as practised in GATT serves to neutralize the world-price implications of tariff negotiations. Reciprocity can thus assist governments in achieving efficient trade-policy outcomes. Third, we construct a multicountry model and observe that externalities then may travel to the home government both through world and foreign local prices. When the home government sets MFN tariffs, however, externalities travel only through the world price, and so the principle of reciprocity is again well suited to address the inefficiencies with which a trade agreement must contend. Finally, we observe that exceptions to MFN for the purpose of creating preferential agreements revive the local-price externality, thus frustrating the ability of a multilateral system governed by the principle of reciprocity to deliver an efficient outcome.

The empirical relevance of our theory requires that governments are able to shift the costs of their intervention onto trading partners and that the implications of such cost-shifting activities are quantitatively significant. The first requirement is met if governments are able to improve their terms of trade with their trade-policy choices, which is the case when foreign exporters incur some of the incidence of an import tariff (i.e., when the full tariff is not passed through to domestic consumers). Equivalently, the hypothesis that governments can improve their terms of trade with their tariff choices is supported if a reduction in the domestic import tariff is not fully passed through as a reduced price for domestic consumers. It is therefore relevant to refer to the study of GATT negotiations by Mordechai E. Kreinin (1961 p. 314), who suggests that "less than a third . . . of the tariff concessions granted by the United States were passed on to the U.S. consumer in the form of reduced import prices, while more than two-thirds . . . accrued to the foreign suppliers and improved the terms of trade of the exporting nations."[38] It is also relevant to note that a large empirical literature exists that documents imperfect pass-through of exchange-rate shocks. Presumably, if the cost increase to foreign exporters takes the form of a tariff increase as opposed to an exchange-rate shock, imperfect pass-through would once again occur, confirming that some of the incidence of the import tariff is borne by foreign exporters. Empirical support for this presumption is offered by Feenstra (1995).[39]

Evidence also exists that supports the requirement that the terms-of-trade effects of trade-policy choices influence the national cost of intervention in quantitively important ways. In particular, this requirement is strongly supported in the empirical studies by Stephen T. Berry et al. (1995) and Pinelopi K. Goldberg (1995). In both studies, it is found that the terms-of-trade implications of the U.S. decision in the 1980s to restrict automobile imports from Japan with voluntary export restraints (VERs) (rather than tariffs) increased substantially the cost to the United States of achieving the reduced import volumes. Berry et al. report a particularly striking experiment. They compare the actual VER policy with a hypothetical equivalent-tariff policy and calculate that the equivalent-tariff policy would have yielded revenue sufficient to turn what was a losing trade policy in terms of U.S. national income into a policy that would have generated a net gain to U.S. national income of $12.5 billion. The study is relevant for our arguments, since the only difference between the two policies is that they generate distinct world prices. It is precisely this role of world prices to affect the incidence of the cost of intervention across trading partners that is the starting point of our theory.[40]

Finally, we note that relevance of cost-shifting motives for the purpose and design of trade agreements had been suggested as well by GATT legal scholars. For example, in discussing rationales for departing from a goal of free trade, Jackson (1989 p. 19) observes:

> More subtle is the possibility that a national consensus could explicitly opt for a choice of policies that would not maximize wealth (in the traditionally measurable sense, at least), but would give preference to other non-economic goals . . . It can be argued that when a nation makes an "uneconomic" choice, it should be prepared to pay the whole cost, and not pursue policies which have the effect of unloading some of the burdens of that choice on to other nations. In an interdependent world, paying the whole cost is not often easy to accomplish.

We conclude by mentioning two caveats that apply to our analysis. First, we have interpreted reciprocity and nondiscrimination as principles that can help guide governments from inefficient unilateral outcomes to the efficiency frontier. In practice, however, enforcement difficulties at the international level (see, e.g., Dam, 1970) may preclude governments from eliminating fully the terms-of-trade driven restrictions in trade volume and arriving at the efficiency frontier. When this is the case, the efficiency properties of reciprocity and nondiscrimination may be weakened. For example, it then becomes possible that the formation of preferential agreements may enhance the efficiency of the multilateral trading system, by providing additional enforcement ability that results in multilateral tariffs that are closer to the efficiency frontier.[41]

Second, while the government welfare function that we have employed in our analysis is quite general, it does not capture all of the reasons that governments might pursue trade agreements in practice. For example, regional integration initiatives may reflect broader objectives, such as military security and political stability, which are not captured by local and world prices. This suggests that GATT's willingness to allow Article XXIV exceptions to MFN might be understood in terms of the broader benefits that regional integration may confer. Our framework also excludes the possibility that governments seek trade agreements as a commitment device in a game with domestic agents. These and other possibilities are important topics for future research.

APPENDIX

PROPOSITION 1: *Nash equilibrium tariffs are inefficient.*

PROOF:

We begin by noting that

$$\text{(A1)}\quad \left.\frac{d\tau}{d\tau^*}\right|_{dW=0} = -\frac{\partial\tilde{p}^w/\partial\tau^*}{dp/d\tau}\left[\frac{\tau W_p + W_{p^w}}{W_p + \lambda W_{p^w}}\right];$$

$$\left.\frac{d\tau}{d\tau^*}\right|_{dW^*=0} = -\frac{dp^*/d\tau^*}{\partial\tilde{p}^w/\partial\tau} \times \left[\frac{W^*_{p^*} + \lambda^* W^*_{p^w}}{W^*_{p^*}/\tau^* + W^*_{p^w}}\right].$$

At a pair of Nash equilibrium tariffs (τ^N, τ^{*N}), $[d\tau/d\tau^*]|_{dW=0} = \infty > 0 = [d\tau/d\tau^*]|_{dW^*=0}$ by (6a), (6b), and (A1). Thus, by (4), the tariff pair (τ^N, τ^{*N}) is inefficient.

PROPOSITION 2: *A reciprocal trade agreement must entail reciprocal trade liberalization.*

PROOF:

We establish that a necessary condition for a tariff pair (τ^0, τ^{*0}) to yield welfare improvements for both the domestic and foreign government relative to the Nash tariffs (τ^N, τ^{*N}) is that $\tau^0 < \tau^N$ and $\tau^{*0} < \tau^{*N}$. To establish this we suppose that $\tau^0 > \tau^N$ and show that the foreign government must lose. The other case in which $\tau^{*0} > \tau^{*N}$ can be handled in an analogous way. First consider the impact of each country's tariff change on the welfare of its trading partner, given by $dW/d\tau^* = [\tau W_p + W_{p^w}][\partial\tilde{p}^w/\partial\tau^*]$ and $dW^*/d\tau = [W^*_{p^*}/\tau^* + W^*_{p^w}][\partial\tilde{p}^w/\partial\tau]$, respectively. Recalling that (6a) and (6b) define, respectively, the domestic and foreign reaction functions $\tau^R(\tau^*)$ and $\tau^{*R}(\tau)$, we note that when the domestic or foreign government, respectively, is on its reaction function, the impact on its welfare of a rise in its trading partner's tariff is

$$dW/d\tau^* = [1 - \tau^R(\tau^*)\lambda]W_{p^w}][\partial\tilde{p}^w/\partial\tau^*] < 0;$$

$$dW^*/d\tau = [1 - \lambda^*/\tau^{*R}(\tau)]W^*_{p^w}[\partial\tilde{p}^w/\partial\tau] < 0.$$

These inequalities imply that, along each government's reaction function, its welfare is strictly declining in the tariff of its trading partner. With this we now have that $\tau^0 > \tau^N$ implies

$$\begin{aligned} &W^*(p^*(\tau^{*0}, \tilde{p}^w(\tau^0, \tau^{*0})), \tilde{p}^w(\tau^0, \tau^{*0})) \\ &\leq W^*(p^*(\tau^{*R}(\tau^0), \tilde{p}^w(\tau^0, \tau^{*R}(\tau^0))), \\ &\tilde{p}^w(\tau^0, \tau^{*R}(\tau^0))) < W^*(p^*(\tau^{*R}(\tau^N), \\ &\tilde{p}^w(\tau^N, \tau^{*R}(\tau^N))), \tilde{p}^w(\tau^N, \tau^{*R}(\tau^N))) \\ &= W^*(p^*(\tau^{*N}, \tilde{p}^w(\tau^N, \tau^{*N})), \\ &\tilde{p}^w(\tau^N, \tau^{*N})). \end{aligned}$$

Thus, the foreign government must be hurt by any change in tariffs that involves increasing the domestic tariff from its Nash level.

PROPOSITION 3: *Politically optimal tariffs are efficient.*

PROOF:

Using (A1), we have $[d\tau/d\tau^*]|_{dW=0} = -[\partial\tilde{p}^w/\partial\tau^*]/[\partial\tilde{p}^w/\partial\tau] = [d\tau/d\tau^*]|_{dW^*=0}$ at politically optimal tariffs defined by (7a) and (7b), which therefore by (4) are efficient.

PROPOSITION 4: *Beginning at a Nash tariff equilibrium, reciprocal trade liberalization that conforms to reciprocity will increase each government's welfare monotonically until this liberalization has proceeded to the point where* $\min[-W_p, W^*_{p^*}] = 0$. *If countries are symmetric, this liberalization path leads to the politically optimal outcome.*

PROOF:

Consider reciprocal reductions in τ and τ^* beginning from the Nash equilibrium and moving along the positively sloped iso-world-price locus that passes through (τ^N, τ^{*N}). With $dp^w = 0$, the impact of a small amount of reciprocal liberalization along this path on domestic government welfare W is just $-W_p(\partial p/\partial\tau)d\tau$ while the impact on foreign government welfare W^* is $-W^*_{p^*}(\partial p^*/\partial\tau^*)d\tau^*$. Both are strictly positive around the Nash equilibrium, and both continue to be strictly positive until liberalization has proceeded down this path to the point where $\min[-W_p, W^*_{p^*}]$. If countries are symmetric, then both W_p and $W^*_{p^*}$ will reach zero at the same point on the iso-world-price locus through (τ^N, τ^{*N}), defining a pair of politically optimal tariffs by (7a) and (7b).

PROPOSITION 5: *An efficient trade agreement can be implemented under reciprocity if and only if it is characterized by tariffs which are set at their politically optimal levels.*

PROOF:

A tariff pair (τ, τ^*) can be implemented under reciprocity if there exists a world price $\bar{p}^w$ such that the outcome of stages 2 and 3 of the Bilateral Negotiation Game is uniquely (τ, τ^*), when governments make dominant proposals. Therefore, to prove the proposition, we must establish that politically optimal tariffs are the only tariffs on the efficiency frontier that can be implemented under reciprocity. Expression (8) characterizes the efficiency frontier, and along this frontier it is necessary that $W_p = 0 = W^*_{p^*}$ or $W_p \neq 0 \neq W^*_{p^*}$. Observe as well that the restriction of proposed import limits will bind in stage 3 at the highest proposed tariff from stage 2, and therefore that the mapping from tariff proposals to the tariffs $(\tilde{\tau}(\bar{p}^w), \tilde{\tau}^*(\bar{p}^w))$ that are actually implemented as the outcome of the Bilateral Negotiation Game is given by $\tilde{\tau}(\bar{p}^w) = \max\{\hat{\tau}, \tau(\hat{\tau}^*, \bar{p}^w)\}$ and $\tilde{\tau}^*(\bar{p}^w) = \tau^*(\tilde{\tau}(\bar{p}^w), \bar{p}^w)$. The proposition now follows once it is observed that, for any world price $\bar{p}^w$ determined in stage 1 of the Bilateral Negotiation Game, it is a dominant strategy in the subgame corresponding to stages 2 and 3 for the domestic government to propose $\hat{\tau} = \tau^0(\bar{p}^w)$ and for the foreign government to propose $\hat{\tau}^* = \tau^{*0}(\bar{p}^w)$ where $\hat{\tau} = \tau^0(\bar{p}^w)$ satisfies $W_p(p(\tau, \bar{p}^w), \bar{p}^w) = 0$ and $\hat{\tau}^* = \tau^{*0}(\bar{p}^w)$ satisfies $W^*_{p^*}(p^*(\tau^*, \bar{p}^w), \bar{p}^w) = 0$.

PROPOSITION 6: *Politically optimal tariffs are efficient if and only if they conform to MFN.*

PROOF:

We first characterize the efficiency locus. Define $\tilde{p}^{wj}(\tau^{*j}, \bar{W}^{*j})$ as the equilibrium world price for trade between the domestic country and foreign country j that would provide the government of country j with the welfare level $\bar{W}^{*j}$ when its tariff is set at τ^{*j}. This magnitude is defined implicitly by $W^{*j}(p^{*j}(\tau^{*j}, \tilde{p}^{wj}), \tilde{p}^{wj}) = \bar{W}^{*j}$. For simplicity we treat $\tilde{p}^{wj}(\tau^{*j}, \bar{W}^{*j})$ as a well-defined function of τ^{*j}, which it must be provided that W^{*j} is sufficiently close to a representation of national income. Cases where $\tilde{p}^{wj}$ is not uniquely defined can be handled with appropriate modifications without changing our results. For future reference we note that

(A2) $$\partial\tilde{p}^{wj}(\tau^{*j}, \bar{W}^{*j})/\partial\tau^{*j} = [p^{*j} \cdot W^{*j}_{p^{*j}}]/[W^{*j}_{p^{*j}} + \tau^{*j}W^{*j}_{p^{wj}}] \text{ for } j \in ℵ^{*}.$$

Since the three foreign tariff and welfare levels, $\{\tau^{*j}\}$ and $\{\bar{W}^{*j}\}$, determine a complete set of both world and foreign local prices, they also imply a value for the domestic terms of trade:

$$\bar{T}(\{\tau^{*j}\}, \{\bar{W}^{*j}\}) \equiv T(\{p^{*j}(\tau^{*j}, \tilde{p}^{wj}(\tau^{*j}, \bar{W}^{*j}))\}, \{\tilde{p}^{wj}(\tau^{*j}, \bar{W}^{*j})\}).$$

Finally, by equilibrium condition (11), a value for the domestic local price is implied as well, and we denote it by $\bar{p}(\{\tau^{*j}\}, \{\bar{W}^{*j}\})$. Domestic welfare can now be written as a function of the three foreign tariffs and foreign welfare levels, or $W(\bar{p}(\{\tau^{*j}\}, \{\bar{W}^{*j}\}), \bar{T}(\{\tau^{*j}\}, \{\bar{W}^{*j}\}))$. Fixing foreign welfare levels and choosing foreign tariffs to maximize the domestic welfare level then defines a point on the efficiency frontier. The first-order conditions are

(A3) $$W_p + \bar{\lambda}^{*j}W_T = 0 \text{ for } j \in ℵ^{*},$$

where $\bar{\lambda}^{*j} \equiv [\partial\bar{T}/\partial\tau^{*j}]/[\partial\bar{p}/\partial\tau^{*j}]$and where $\partial\bar{p}/\partial\tau^{*j}$ is nonzero and finite. An implication of (A3) is that Nash tariffs are inefficient. This can be seen by fixing foreign welfare levels at their Nash values and observing that efficient tariffs satisfy (A3), while Nash tariffs satisfy (12a).

Now suppose that a set of tariffs are politically optimal. Then by (A3) and (13a), they will be efficient if and only if $\partial\bar{T}/\partial\tau^{*j} = 0$ for $j \in ℵ^{*}$. From the definition of $\bar{T}$, we have

(A4) $$\frac{\partial\bar{T}}{\partial\tau^{*j}} = \frac{1}{M_x} \cdot \left[\frac{\partial E_x^{*j}}{\partial p^{*j}} \frac{dp^{*j}}{d\tau^{*j}} + \frac{\partial E_x^{*j}}{\partial p^{wj}} \frac{\partial\tilde{p}^{wj}(\tau^{*j}, \bar{W}^{*j})}{\partial\tau^{*j}} \right) \cdot (\tilde{p}^{wj}$$

$$- \bar{T}) + E_x^{*j} \cdot \frac{\partial \tilde{p}^{wj}(\tau^{*j}, \bar{W}^{*j})}{\partial \tau^{*j}} \Bigg] .$$

But political optimally implies, by (A2) and (13b), that $\partial \tilde{p}^{wj}(\tau^{*j}, \bar{W}^{*j})/\partial \tilde{p}^{wj} = 0$, and hence

$$\text{(A5)} \quad \frac{\partial \bar{T}}{\partial \tau^{*j}} = \frac{1}{M_x} . \left[\frac{\partial E_x^{*j}}{\partial p^{*j}} \quad \frac{dp^{*j}}{d\tau^{*j}} \right] . (\tilde{p}^{wj} - \bar{T}),$$

which will be zero if and only if tariffs also conform to MFN.

PROPOSITION 7: *An efficient multilateral trade agreement can be implemented under reciprocity if and only if it is characterized by tariffs which conform to the principle of MFN and are set at their politically optimal levels.*

PROOF:

To prove this result we add an additional regularity condition that $\partial E_x^{*j}/\partial p^{*j} > 0$ for $j \in \aleph^*$, which will be met as long as substitution effects dominate income effects. We must establish that the only set of world prices for which the outcome of stages 2 and 3 of the Multilateral Negotiation Game rests on the efficiency frontier, when foreign governments make dominant proposals and the proposal of the domestic government is a best response to the foreign proposals, is the politically optimal MFN world price (i.e., the world price associated with politically optimal MFN tariffs). We outline the general argument here; a more detailed argument is found in our discussion paper (Bagwell and Staiger, 1997c).

We begin with the possibility of MFN tariffs. Arguments analogous to the proof of Proposition 5 establish that politically optimal MFN tariffs can be implemented under reciprocity given the politically optimal MFN world price, and by Proposition 6 these tariffs are efficient. Moreover, arguments analogous to those in Proposition 5 establish that efficient tariffs cannot be implemented under reciprocity given any other MFN world price.

We next consider the possibility of discriminatory tariffs. We establish that efficient tariffs cannot be implemented under reciprocity given any set of discriminatory world prices that such tariffs might imply. Again, as each foreign country faces a single world price, arguments analogous to those in the proof of Proposition 5 establish that for any world price $\bar{p}^{wj}$ determined in stage 1 of the Multilateral Negotiation Game, it is a dominant strategy in the subgame corresponding to stages 2 and 3 for foreign government j to propose $\hat{\tau}^{*j} = \tau^{*j0}(\bar{p}^{wj})$ where $\hat{\tau}^{*j} = \tau^{*j0}(\bar{p}^{wj})$ satisfies $W_{p^{*j}}^{*j}(p^{*j}(\tau^{*j}, \bar{p}^{wj}), \bar{p}^{wj}) = 0$. The best response of the domestic government to these foreign proposals is to propose tariffs and bilateral trade shares such that either: (i) its proposal is nonpivotal with each foreign trading partner, in which case it (weakly) desires more multilateral trade volume (at the fixed terms of trade defined by the given set of world prices and the bilateral trade volumes implied by the proposals of its trading partners) than its trading partners are willing at those world prices to accommodate, so that $\{W_p \leq 0, W^{*j}_{p^{*j}} = 0 \text{ for } j \in \aleph^*\}$, or (ii) its proposal is pivotal with at least one foreign trading partner, in which case the foreign trading partner H with which it shares the least-favorable (highest) world price among all foreign countries with which it trades will obtain (weakly) less trade than it desires at the given bilateral world price, while the domestic government achieves its desired multilateral trade volume (at the fixed terms of trade defined by the given set of world prices and the bilateral trade volumes implied by the pivotal foreign proposals and its proposed bilateral trade volume with H), so that $\{W_p = 0, W^{*j}_{p^{*j}} \geq 0 \text{ for } j \in \aleph^*\}$. If the conditions in (i) or (ii) hold with strict equality, then the implemented tariffs will be discriminatory politically optimal tariffs, which by Proposition 6 are inefficient. Hence, there are two cases left to consider (we now maintain the assumption that all bilateral trade flows are strictly positive, though this is inessential for the proof):

(i) $\{W_p < 0, W^{*j}_{p^{*j}} = 0 \text{ for } j \in \aleph^*\}$: In this case, (A2) implies that $\partial\tilde{p}^{wj}(\tau^{*j}, \bar{W}^{*j})/\partial\tau^{*j} = 0$ for $j \in \aleph^*$, and thus that $\partial\bar{T}/\partial\tau^{*j}$ is given by (A5) for $j \in \aleph^*$. Then by (A3) and (A5), tariffs must be discriminatory if they are to be efficient, and noting that $\partial\tilde{p}^{wj}(\tau^{*j}, \bar{W}^{*j})/\partial\tau^{*j} = 0$ also implies $\partial\bar{p}/\partial\tau^{*j} > 0$ for $j \in \aleph^*$, it follows from (A3) that $\partial\bar{T}/\partial\tau^{*j}$ must then be strictly negative for each j if efficiency is to be achieved. But then let k solve $\min_j \{\bar{p}^{wj}\}$ and observe that $\partial\bar{T}/\partial\tau^{*k} > 0$ by (A5).

(ii) $\{W_p = 0, W^{*j}_{p^{*j}} \geq 0 \text{ for } j \in \aleph^*$, with a strict inequality for at least one $j\}$: In this case, (A3) implies that we have efficiency if and only if $\partial\bar{T}/\partial\tau^{*j} = 0$ for $j \in \aleph^*$. By (A2), we must have $\partial\tilde{p}^{wj}(\tau^{*j}, \bar{W}^{*j})/\partial\tau^{*j} > 0$ and thus, by (A4), efficiency requires discriminatory tariffs. But noting that $dp^{*j}/d\tau^{*j} < 0$ for $j \in \aleph^*$, we may then let k solve $\min_j \{\bar{p}^{wj}\}$ and observe that $\partial\bar{T}/\partial\tau^{*k} > 0$, provided that $\partial E^{*j}_x/\partial p^{*j} > 0$ and $\partial E^{*j}_x/\partial p^{wj} < 0$. The latter condition is ensured by our assumption that all goods are normal in consumption, while the former condition is posited above and will be met as long as substitution effects dominate income effects.

NOTES

Bagwell: Department of Economics, International Affairs Building, Columbia University, 420 West 118th Street, New York, NY 10027, and National Bureau of Economic Research; Staiger: Department of Economics, Social Science Building, university of Wisconsin, 1180 Observatory Drive, Maidson, WI 53706, and National Bureau of Economic Research. We think Jim Anderson, Jagdish Bhagwati, Alan Deardorff, Ronald Findlay, Ronald McKinnon, T. N. Srinivasan, three anonymous referees, and seminar participants at Boston University, Columbia University, the University of Michigan, Harvard University, the University of Toulouse, Stanford University, the University of Wisconsin, the World Trade Organization, and the 1997 NBER Summer Institute for helpful comments. This paper was written while Staiger was a Fellow at the Center for Advanced Study in the Behavioral Sciences. Staiger is also grateful for financial support provided by the National Science Foundation Grant No. SBR-9022192.

1 For an early formal analysis of the terms-of-trade externality, see Harry G. Johnson (1953–1954). More recent discussions include John McMillan (1986, 1989), Avinash Dixit (1987), and Bagwell and Staiger (1990).

2 A political motivation for trade agreements might arise if governments seek such agreements to gain commitment relative to their private sectors. This possibility, which is not included in our modeling framework, is explored by Staiger and Guido Tabellini (1987), Staiger (1995), and Giovanni Maggi and Andres Rodriguez-Clare (1998). However, whether this commitment theory of trade agreements offers an interpretation of the basic principles of GATT is still an open question.

3 The politically optimal tariffs correspond to reciprocal free trade when governments maximize national income.

4 A separate question is how these rules are to be enforced. We abstract from the issue of enforcement in the body of the paper, but return to it in the concluding section.

5 The principle of nondiscrimination is trivially satisfied in the basic two-country model described earlier.

6 The Lerner symmetry theorem ensures that trade taxes or subsidies can be equivalently depicted as applying to exports or to imports in this two-sector general equilibrium setting.

7 Given the assumptions that Metzler and Lerner paradoxes are absent, the iso-local-price locus exhibits negative slope and the iso-world-price locus is positively sloped.

8 Baldwin (1985) proposes that a government has autonomous *ideological* concerns (e.g., it may be a "free trader") but faces a *political-support constraint* (e.g., export-sector support for proposed liberalization efforts must counterbalance import-competing-sector opposition) when pursuing these goals. To see that this case is included, let G be the objective of the domestic government and let the political-support constraint be given by the inequality restrictions $S(p(\tau, \tilde{p}^w), \tilde{p}^w) \geq \bar{S}$. Then W is the Lagrangian $W(p(\tau, \tilde{p}^w), \tilde{p}^w) = G(p(\tau, \tilde{p}^w), \tilde{p}^w) + \bar{p}[S(p(\tau, \tilde{p}^w), \tilde{p}^w) - \bar{S}]$, where the multiplier p depends also on $p(\tau, \tilde{p}^w)$ and $\tilde{p}^w$.

9 We also assume throughout that second-order conditions are globally satisfied.

10 We postpone for now discussion regarding the existence and uniqueness of Nash equilibria, choosing instead to focus on statements that are true for any Nash equilibrium with positive trade that is not Pareto dominated by other Nash equilibria. An implication of this focus is that we ignore here and throughout the paper the possible gains from a reciprocal trade agreement that could come from coordinating across Pareto-ranked Nash equilibria. The emphasis placed on enforcement issues in actual trade agreements suggests that the achievement of coordination gains is not the primary purpose of such agreements. Similarly, we ignore for now issues associated with the existence and uniqueness of politically optimal affairs, as defined in the text.

11 The assumption here is not that governments fail to understand that their tariff choices affect the terms of trade; rather, the hypothetical situation we consider is that governments are not motivated by the world-price implications of their tariff choices. In terms of (6a), governments recognize that $\lambda < 0$, but we now consider the tariffs that they would select were their welfare functions such that $W_{p^w} \equiv 0$. Our thought experiment identifies these hypothetical preferences and evaluates the efficiency properties of these tariffs with respect to actual government preferences.

12 When the domestic government maximizes the utility of a representative agent, its objective can be represented as $W(p, p^w) \equiv V(p, I(p, p^w))$, with V denoting the indirect utility of the representative domestic agent and with I denoting the domestic national income measured in units of y at local prices. With a similar expression for the foreign government, a direct application of Roy's identity indicates that $W_p = 0 = W^*_{p^*}$ implies $\tau = 1 = \tau^*$.

13 In the special case of national-income-maximizing governments, as Mayer (1981) shows, the efficiency locus is described by the set of tariffs that satisfy $\tau = 1/\tau^*$. In this case,

along the efficiency locus, tariffs are adjusted so as to maintain equality in relative local prices across countries, with different efficient tariff pairs resulting in different world prices and thus different distributions of income across countries. In the more general formulation considered here, it remains true that the efficiency locus determines a relationship between domestic and foreign tariffs, but it need not be the case that this relationship equates relative local prices across trading partners.

14 The political optimum lies on the contract curve if the countries are not too asymetric. As Johnson (1953–1954), Mayer (1981), and John Kennan and Raymond G. Riezman (1988) show for the case in which governments maximize national income, when governments are sufficiently asymmetric, the political optimum (which is then free trade) need not offer Pareto gains relative to the Nash equilibrium for all governments.

15 See, for example, Kenneth W. Dam (1970, pp. 58–61; 87–91) on the concept of reciprocity in GATT and the various ways in which reciprocity is measured in practice.

16 To see that this property of reciprocity holds more generally, consider a two-country, N-good world economy. Let $(p^{w0'}, p^{o'}, E^0)$ denote an initial triple consisting of a $(1 \times N)$ vector of equilibrium world prices, a $(1 \times N)$ vector of equilibrium local home country prices, and an $(1 \times N)$ vector of equilibrium trades with the jth element of E positive (negative) if good j is imported by the foreign (home) country. Similarly, let $(p^{w1'}, p^{1'}, E^1)$ denote a second set of equilibrium prices and quantities that arise under an alternative set of trade policies. In analogy with our approach above, the view that reciprocity reflects mutual changes in trade policy which bring about equal changes in import volumes across trading partners can be represented with the restriction that tariff changes conforming to reciprocity lead to changes in trade volumes which satisfy $p^{w0'}[E^1 - E^2] = 0$. Utilizing the balanced trade conditions $p^{w0'}E^0 = 0$ and $p^{w1'}E^1 = 0$ and proceeding as above, the restriction of reciprocity can be rewritten as $(p^{w1'} - p^{w0'})\, E^1 = 0$. Thus, mutual changes in trade policy continue to satisfy the restriction of reciprocity if world prices are unchanged. In the many-good case, however, it is also possible that reciprocity can be satisfied even when world prices change. To evaluate this possibility, we note that the restriction of reciprocity can be further rewritten as $(p^{w1'} - p^{1'})E^1 = (p^{w0'} - p^{1'})E^1$. This indicates that any trade-policy adjustment giving rise to the price vectors p^{w1} and p^1 results in the same aggregate tariff revenue as would an alternative tariff-policy adjustment that gave rise to the price vectors p^{w0} and p^1, when each adjustment is consistent with the restriction of reciprocity. Since world prices affect welfare only through tariff revenue, we may therefore restrict attention to tariff-policy adjustments that preserve the world prices. These properties of reciprocity also extend naturally to a many-country setting.

17 For a discussion of the informal application of reciprocity, see, e.g., Dam (1970 p. 59) and Bhagwati (1991).

18 Krugman (1997) develops more fully the view that GATT negotiations are incompatible with economic reasoning and reflect mercantilist logic. Some of the advantages of reciprocity described by McMillan (1986, 1989) and Bhagwati (1990 p. 15) are more in line with the results we discuss here.

19 This discussion may be made more concrete with reference to (6a). As this equation makes clear, the domestic government's preferred tariff satisfies $W_p = 0$ when the term λW_{p^w} is zero. This would in fact be the case, either if the government were hypothesized not to value a change in the terms of trade (i.e., if $W_{p^w} \equiv 0$) or if it were to expect a reciprocal tariff adjustment from its trading partner that would remit in no change in the terms of trade (i.e., if $\lambda = 0$).

20 It is interesting to note that, according to a popular political argument, the appeal of reciprocity is that it mobilizes export-sector support for liberalization. In fact, however, this political argument can be captured by our model. The key point is that the proposed export-sector support for reciprocity is ultimately tied to the anticipated

economic benefits of a lower foreign import tariff, and these benefits travel through the world price. See also footnote 8.

21 In fact, it is in the context of Article XXVII renegotiations that perhaps the clearest statement of the measurement of reciprocity in GATT practice has been given. In describing the "fairly well-established criteria" that were considered in determining what would constitute the withdrawal of substantially equivalent concessions, the Legal Adviser to GATT's Director-General observed (WTO, 1995 p. 949): 'The first criterion was the development of the imports during, normally, the three years before the renegotiations started. What was taken into account was not just a statistical average, but also the trend in the development of trade during that period. Furthermore, account was taken of the size of the tariff increase being negotiated. Moreover, an estimate was made of the price elasticity of the product concerned.'

22 Our purpose here is to examine the tariffs that *can* be implemented in the presence of renegotiation as formally allowed by GATT rules. Consistent with this objective and the formal content of GATT rules, we thus allow that governments are unconstrained with respect to the tariff bindings to which they initially agree. In particular, we depart from the focus of the previous subsection, in which negotiated tariffs are constrained (at least informally) to lie on the Nash iso-world-price locus. This focus served well to illustrate the point that the informal pursuit of reciprocity in trade negotiations has a direct economic interpretation, but it is an unduly restrictive focus in light of our present objectives.

23 Using (8), efficiency is possible if and only if both $W_p = 0$ and $W^*_{p^*} = 0$ (corresponding to the politically optimal point) or both $W_p \neq 0$ and $W^*_{p^*} \neq 0$.

24 The restriction of proposed import limits ensures that, if the proposals do not agree, the tariff pair that is implemented is the proposed tariff pari that is the "highest" (i.e., most restrictive) pair. Thus, if the domestic government proposes a tariff pair that is lower than A', then the foreign government's proposal is pivotal, and the foreign government achieves its preferred point on the given iso-world-price locus. On the other hand, if the domestic government proposes a tariff pair that is higher than A', then the foreign proposal is nonpivotal, and the foreign government's proposal would matter only if it were higher yet, which would result in an even worse (i.e., further above A') outcome for the foreign government.

25 In the special case in which governments maximize national income, the political optimum corresponds to reciprocal free trade and the locus at which $W_p = 0$ ($W^*_{p^*} = 0$) is horizontal (vertical) out of this point. The efficiency locus passes through the reciprocal-free-trade point as well, but it otherwise lies below the loci at which $W_p = 0$ and $W^*_{p^*} = 0$. If governments maximize national income, therefore, the point of reciprocal free trade is the only point on the efficiency frontier that is impervious to renegotiation as allowed by GATT rules.

26 We explore the differences between these two formats at greater length in Section V, where we refer to the first (second) format as a power- (rules-) based approach.

27 The details depicting the positions of points A and B in Figure 5B will depend on the specific stage–1 bargaining process adopted, but the general point illustrated by the figure – that each government's payoff lies closer to its politically optimal payoff under the second bargaining format – will hold in a variety of settings. For example, this will always be the case if countries are not too asymmetric, or with sufficient concavity of the reciprocity-constrained efficiency frontier relative to the unconstrained frontier. It will also hold if stage–1 bargaining is characterized by the generalized Nash bargaining solution with sufficiently large bargaining-power asymetries, under the added regularity condition that the reciprocity-constrained frontier is globally more concave than the unconstrained frontier.

28 Government-to-government side payments are often considered in theoretical analyses

of trade agreements (e.g., Grossman and Helpman, 1995; Eric W. Bond and Constantinos Syropoulos, 1996). The general relevance of such side payments in practice is less clear, though important cases are discussed in Carsten Kowalczyk and Tomas J. Sjostrom (1994) and John Whalley (1998).

29 There is the minimal number of foreign countries that will allow us to consider the role of nondiscrimination in a multilateral agreement when the domestic country is also a member of a preferential agreement. The topic is the subject of Section IV.

30 These assumptions will be met if, for example, transportation costs between foreign countries are large as compared to the extent of discriminatory home tariffs. Their only role in our analysis is to ensure that it is possible for the home country to select discriminatory tariffs without prohibiting trade between it and its less-favored trading partners.

31 For a fixed set of domestic tariffs $\{\hat{\tau}^j\}$ and bilateral world prices $\{\bar{p}^{wj}\}$, the local domestic price $p(\tau^j, \bar{p}^{wj})$ is implied. In the multicountry model, however, this price alone is insufficient to determine domestic import volume, as T is affected by the set of foreign tariffs, $\{\hat{\tau}^{*j}\}$, when domestic tariffs are discriminatory. See equilibrium condition (11).

32 Given $\{\bar{p}^{wj}\}$, $\{\hat{\tau}^j\}$, and $\{\hat{s}_x^{*j}\}$, foreign tariffs and bilateral trade volumes are implied as follows. First, p is determined as $p = p(\hat{\tau}^j, \bar{p}^{wj})$ while T is determined as $T = \sum_{i \in \aleph^*} \hat{s}_x^{*j} \cdot \bar{p}^{wj}$. Total import volume is then determined as $M_x = M_x(p, T)$, where under (11) we have $M_x = \sum_{i \in \aleph^*} E_x^{*j}$ as well. E_x^{*j} is then implied as $E_x^{*j} = \hat{s}_x^{*j} \cdot \sum_{i \in \aleph^*} E_x^{*j}$, and this in turn implies p^{*j} as $p^{*j} = p^{*j}(\tau^{*j}, \bar{p}^{wj})$, and hence a value for τ^{*j}, for each $j \in \aleph^*$.

33 Given $\{\bar{p}^{wj}\}$ and $\{\hat{\tau}^{*j}\}$, we have that $\{p^{*j}\}$ is determined, and so the right-hand side of (11) is also determined. Furthermore, with $\{p^{*j}\}$ determined, we see that T is determined as well. Thus, satisfaction of (11) determines p. But this means that (τ^j) is implied as $\tau^j = \bar{p}^{wj}/p$.

34 In the multicountry model, we no longer require that the domestic-government proposal is dominant. Intuitively, the domestic government will wish to choose its share proposal so as to trade as much as possible with the partners with whom it has the most favorable terms of trade. The optimal domestic share proposals are thus sensitive to the anticipated foreign proposals, as the latter bound the import volumes that the respective foreign partners will accept.

35 At this point it is useful to comment on the relation between the Bilateral and Multilateral Negotiation Games. In our analysis of the latter we have allowed for the possibility of discriminatory tariffs and have shown that MFN is required for efficiency. This possibility introduces some complications, as we then must consider share announcements and best-response choices by the domestic government. If we had instead imposed MFN from the outset, then the analysis would again be exactly analogous to the Bilateral Negotiation Game.

36 As Jackson's discussion goes on to suggest, a separate issue is how agreements are to be enforced. Whether the agreement is over tariff levels directly or rather over rules within which governments agree to operate when determining their tariff policies, enforcement of the agreement is an issue which should not be ignored. We return to this important issue in our concluding section.

37 An alternative way to generate a difference between *ex ante* (prior to initiating negotiations) and *ex post* government preferences would be to focus on changing political constraints associated with the resolution of uncertainty over the effects of liberalization, along the lines of Raquel Fernandez and Dani Rodrik (1991). See also footnote 8.

38 A recent study which finds large terms-of-trade effects from regional liberalization is L. Alan Winters and Won Chang (1999).

39 In this context, it is instructive also to mention the theoretical analysis of Daniel

Gros (1987). He finds that even apparently small countries have some power over the terms of trade, provided that the industry is monopolitically competitive. We also stress that our theory does not require that all countries are able to alter the terms of trade. Our theory suggests that truly "small" countries should be extended MFN treatment under GATT without a requirement that they offer reciprocal liberalization of their own. (This is because the unilateral tariff policies of small countries impart no externality; see Bagwell and Staiger, 1996.) To some extent, this treatment is represented in GATT through MFN combined with the "principle supplier" rule (see Dam, 1970 p. 61) as it applies to reciprocal tariff negotiations.

40 At the same time, the decision of the United States to "give away" such an amount might be taken as evidence that governments in fact do not care about the terms of trade, even when the associated implications for income are large. This inference, however, does not follow from the U.S. VER experience. The relevant policy alternative for the United States was not a set of unilateral tariff increases (corresponding to the equivalent-tariff policy above), which surely would have incited a retaliatory "trade war" with Japan, but rather a set of tariff changes from the United States and Japan that were consistent with GATT rules.

41 As we show in other work (Bagwell and Staiger, 1999), however, the enforcement implications of preferential agreements for multilateral tariff cooperation are complex, and there is as yet no basis from which to conclude that such agreements are necessarily efficiency enhancing. See also Bond and Syropoulos (1996), Bond et al. (1996), and Bagwell and Staiger (1997b, d). Maggi (1999) offers a broader perspective as to the role of enforcement in the multilateral trading system.

REFERENCES

Bagwell, Kyle and Staiger, Robert W. "A Theory of Managed Trade." *American Economic Review*, September 1990, *80*(4), pp. 779–95.

____, "Reciprocal Trade Liberalization." National Bureau of Economic Research (Cambridge, MA) Working Paper No. 5488, March 1996.

——, "Reciprocity, Non-discrimination, and Preferential Agreements in the Multilateral Trading System." National Bureau of Economic Research (Cambridge, MA) Working Paper No. 5932, February 1997a.

——, "Multilateral Tariff Corporation during the Formation of Customs Unions." *Journal of International Economics*, February 1997b, *42*(1–2), pp. 91–123.

——, "An Economic Theory of GATT." National Bureau of Economic Research (Cambridge, MA) Working Paper No. 6049, May 1997c.

——, "Multilateral Tariff Cooperation during the Formation of Free Trade Areas." *International Economic Review*, May 1997d, *38*(2), pp. 291–319.

——, "Regionalism and Multilateral Tariff Cooperation," in John Piggott and Alan Woodland, eds., *International trade policy and the Pacific Rim*. London: Macmillan, 1999, pp. 157–85.

Baldwin, Richard E. "Politically REalistic Objective Functions and Trade Police." *Economics Letters*, August 1987, *24*(1), pp. 287–90.

Baldwin, Robert E. *The political economy of U.S. import policy*. Cambridge, MA: MIT Press, 1985.

Berry, Stephen T.; Levinsohn, James A. and Pakes, Ariel. "Voluntary Export Restraints on Automobiles: Evaluating a Strategic Trade Policy." National Bureau of Economic Research (Cambridge, MA) Working Paper No. 5235, August 1995.

Bhagwati, Jagdish, "Aggressive Unilateralism: An Overview," in Jagdish Bhagwati and

Hugh T. Patrick, eds., *Aggressive unilateralism: America's 301 trade policy and the world trading system*. Ann Arbor, MI: University of Michigan Press, 1990, pp. 1–45.
——. *The world trading system at risk*. Princeton, NJ: Princeton University Press, 1991.
Bond, Eric W. and Syropoulos, Constantinos. "Trading Blocs and the Sustainability of Interregional Cooperation," in Matthew B. Canzoneri, Wilfred J. Ethier, and Vittorio Grilli, eds., *The new transatlantic economy*. Cambridge: Cambridge University Press, 1996, pp. 118–41.
Bond, Eric W.; Syropoulos, Constatinos and Winters, L. Alan. "Deepening of Regional Integration and External Trade Relations." Center for Economic Policy Research Discussion Paper No. 1317, 1996.
Brock, William A. and Magee, Stephen P. "The Economics of Special Interest Politics." *American Economic Review*, May 1978 (*Papers and Proceedings*), *68*(2), pp. 246–50.
Caves, Richard E. "Economic Models of Political Choice: Canada's Tariff Structure." *Canadian Journal of Economics*, May 1976, *9*(2), pp. 278–300.
Dam, Kenneth W. *The GATT: Law and international economic organization*. Chicago: University of Chicago Press, 1970.
Dixit, Avinash. "Strategic Aspects of Trade Policy," in Truman F. Bewley, ed., *Advances in economic theory: Fifth World Congress*. Cambridge: Cambridge University Press, 1987, pp. 329–62.
Dixit, Avinash; Grossman, Gene M. and Helpman, Elhanan. "Common Agency and Coordination: General Theory and Application to Government Policy Making." *Journal of Political Economy*, August 1997, *105*(4), pp. 752–69.
Enders, Alice. "Reciprocity in GATT: 1942– 1967,– in Jagdish Bhagwati, ed., *Going alone: Historical country and sectoral experience*. Cambridge, MA: MIT Press, 1999 (forthcoming).
Feenstra, Robert C. "Estimating the Effects of Trade Policy," in Gene M. Grossman and Kenneth Rogoff, eds., *Handbook of international economics*, Vol. 3. Amsterdam: North-Holland, 1995, pp. 1553–95.
Feenstra, Robert C. and Bhagwati, Jagdish, "Tariff Seeking and the Efficient Tariff," in Jagdish Bhagwati, ed., *Import competition and response*. Chicago: University of Chicago Press, 1982, pp. 245–58.
Fernandez, Raquel and Rodrik, Dani, "Resistance to Reform: Status Quo Bias in the Presence of Individual-Specific Uncertainty." *American Economic Review*, December 1991, *81*(5), pp. 1146–55.
Findlay, Ronald and Wellisz, Stanislaw. "Endogenous Tariffs, the Political Economy of Trade Restrictions and Welfare," in Jagdish Bhagwait, ed., *Import competition and response*. Chicago: University of Chicago Press, 1982, pp. 223–43.
Goldberg, Pinelopi K. "Product Differentiation and Oligopoly in International Markets: The Case of the U.S. Automobile Industry." *Econometrica*, July 1995, *63*(4), pp. 891–951.
Gros, Daniel, "A Note on the Optimal Tariff, Retaliation and the Welfare Loss from Tariff Wars in a Framework with Intra-industry Trade." *Journal of International Economics*, November 1987, *23*(3/4), pp. 357–67.
Grossman, Gene M. and Helpman, Elhanan. "Protection for Sale." *American Economic Review*, September 1994, *84*(4), pp. 833–50.
——, "Trade Wars and Trade Talks." *Journal of Political Economy*,. August 1995, *103*(4), pp. 675–708.
Hillman, Arye, L. "Declining Industries and Political-Support Protectionist Motives." *American Economic Review*, December 1982, 72(5), pp. 1180–87.
Jackson, John H. *The world trading system*. Cambridge, MA: MIT Press, 1989.
Johnson, Harry G. "Optimum Tariffs and Retaliation." *Review of Economic Studies*, 1953–1954, *21*(2), pp. 142–53.

Kennan, John and Riezman, Raymond G. "Do Big Countries Win Tariff Wars?" *International Economic Review*, February 1988, *29*(1), pp. 81–85.

Kowalczyk, Carsten and Sjostrom, Tomas J. "Bringing GATT into the Core." *Economica*, August 1994, *61*(243), pp. 301–17.

Kreinin, Mordechal E. "Effect of Tariff Changes on the Prices and Volume of Imports." *American Economic Review*, June 1961, *51*(3), pp. 310–24.

Krugman, Paul R. "The Move Toward Free Trade Zones," in *Policy implications of trade and currency zones: A symposium sponsored by the Federal Reserve Bank of Kansas City*. Jackson Hole, WY: Federal Reserve Bank of Kansas, August 22–24, 1991, pp. 7–41.

——, "What Should Trade Negotiators Negotiate About?" *Journal of Economic Literature*, March 1997, *35*(1), pp. 113–20.

Maggi, Giovanni. "The Role of Multilateral Institutions in International Trade Cooperation." *American Economic Review*, March 1999, *89*(1), pp. 190–214.

Maggi, Giovanni and Rodriguez-Clare, Andres. "The Value of Trade Agreements in the Presence of Political Pressures." *Journal of Political Economy*, June 1998, *106*(3), pp. 574–601.

Mayer, Wolfgang. "Theoretical Considerations on Negotiated Tariff Adjustments." *Oxford Economic Papers*, March 1981, *33*(1), pp. 135–53.

——, "Endogenous Tariff Formation." *American Economic Review*, December 1984, *74*(5), pp. 970–85.

McLaren, John. "Size, Sunk Costs, and Judge Bowker's Objection to Free Trade." *American Economic Review*, June 1997, *87*(3), pp. 400–20.

McMillan, John. *Game theory in international economics*. New York: Harwood, 1986.

——, "A Game-Theoretic View of International Trade Negotiations: Implications for the Developing Countries," in John Whalley, ed., *Developing countries and the global trading system: Volume 1*. Ann Arbot, MI: University of Michigan Press, 1989, pp. 26–44.

Olson, Mancur. *The logic of collective action*. Cambridge, MA: Harvard University Press, 1965.

Staiger, Robert W. "International Rules and Institutions for Trade Policy," in Gene M. Grossman and Kenneth Rogoff, eds., *Handbook of international economics*, Vol. 3. Amsterdam: North-Holland, 1995, pp. 1495–551.

Staiger, Robert W. and Guido Tabellini. "Discretionary Trade Policy and Excessive Protection." *American Economic Review*, December 1987, *77*(5), pp. 823–37.

Whalley, John. "Why Do Countries Seek Regional Trade Agreements?" in Jeffrey A. Frankel, eds., *The regionalization of the world economy*. Chicago: University of Chicago Press, 1998, pp. 63–87.

Winters, L. Alan and Chang, Won. "Regional Integration and the Prices of Imports: An Empirical Investigation." *Journal of International Economics*, 1999 (forthcoming).

World Trade Organization. *Analytical index: Guide to GATT law and practice, volume 2*. Geneva: World Trade Organization, 1995.

2. On Making Rules for the International Trading System

W. M. Corden

10.1 INTRODUCTION

WHAT ISSUES ARE INVOLVED in making rules for the international trading system? The issues are immediate. First, the existing set of rules seems to be breaking down, with countries bypassing GATT in numerous ways, and there is a general sense that this cannot continue. Second, the view of the Japanese and U.S. governments suggest that new multilateral negotiations may be initiated soon.

My approach will be somewhat taxonomic. I wish to sort out and highlight issues. While concluding with some particular recommendations, I aim to contribute to clarification rather than urge a particular point of view.

One might be concerned with the probable, the possible, or the desirable. Economists, who claim to be realists but are often idealists, devote much of their writing to the last in the hope that by doing so, it will become the first. Like most other economists, I have never been very good at long-term forecasts, so I shall be concerned with the second and especially the third.

10.2 ON THE MAKING OF RULES

Should there be formal international trade rules, whether simple or complex, and, if so, how should they be made? The alternative to rules is a system of continuous negotiations and power play. Rules themselves have to be constructed through negotiations and power play, but the establishment of a rules-based system economizes on the amount of the latter required. In addition rules provide the benefit of certainty. On the other hand there is a loss of flexibility. These are trade-offs in choosing between a rules-based and a negotiations-based system. I need hardly add that since the early 1970s, the international trading system has been slowly moving from a rules-based system toward a negotiation-based one, but also that, for trade to continue at all, there must be some rules, even if implicit.

Let me begin by turning to the second question: how the rules should be made. They will, of course be made by negotiations, but what are the principles that negotiators should have in mind? Here I will focus on one issue highlighted in the theory of the social contract and of justice. One could argue that participants should establish a just system that each will find satisfactory in whatever relative situation they eventually find themselves. With hindsight, particular participants might have benefited from different rules, but rules are made at a time when participants cannot be sure about their eventual situations, so any participant should bear in mind the possibility of being at some stage in a relatively weak situation.

In practical terms negotiators should take a long-term view. They should not just try to forecast the actual situation their particular country will be in and then try to negotiate rules that will be favorable for that situation. They should bear in mind that their country may later be in quite a different situation, one they are not able to forecast. One can hardly take this to the theoretical (I think, Rawlsian) extreme and suggest that negotiators should imagine that they know nothing at all about the prospective situations of their countries – that the United States and New Zealand know nothing about their likely relative size or bargaining power in the future. But a country should not assume that because it is in a current account deficit now, it will always be so, or because it is a net exporter of primary products now, it will always be one.

This is not a minor point. Great and powerful nations, such as Britain, have become less powerful and more dependent on rules. The United States initiated the exemption of agriculture from the GATT rules and now finds its interests have changed. Some developing countries have become major exporters of manufactures, and others will no doubt move in that direction. There are certainly many other examples. The issue comes down to one that lies behind so much economic policy debate: the short-term versus the long-term view, economists usually favoring the latter.

The central issue is rules versus continuously negotiated or discretionary equilibria (or disequilibria). The key point is that there is a trade-off between the costs of continuous negotiations and continuous power play, with threats, possibly culminating in trade warfare and political crises, and the costs resulting from loss of flexibility. The more stable the underlying environment is believed to be – that is, the more the parties feel that they can forecast the future – the more they would be likely to choose rules. On the other hand, great uncertainty might also lead to a bias for rules, which might succeed in reducing the uncertainty.

One might argue that countries that expect to be weak (that is, small countries, including most or all developing countries) would favor rules. It is generally assumed that any rules that are now made for the international trading system (such as the existing GATT system, if it were enforced) will protect the weak. This may be one reason why the EC, which feels itself to be in a strong bargaining position, is not enthusiastic about a stricter rules-based system. This is also the reason why many people argue that the developing countries would benefit from a system where GATT was strengthened and properly enforced.

Yet one might note a qualification to this view. It seems to be assumed that the rules would actually protect the weak in the way in which a Rawlsian social contract would. But if countries likely to be weak in the future are also weak at the time the negotiations to frame the rules are made, there may be no net gain to them. The position of the United States is interesting. Presumably the United States can confidently expect to be very powerful for many years to come.

Therefore it would not seem to have a strong incentive to support a rules-based system that protects the weak. The only incentive would be to move to such a system in order to economize on later negotiation (and related) costs. For the United States, and to a lesser extent other countries, it is a matter of weighing the short run versus the long run. Negotiating for rules is a form of investment: costly negotiations now are the investment, and fewer negotiations later are the returns. To repeat, the cost of negotiations includes the cost of breakdowns, power play, and so on, including the spillover of conflicts into areas outside trade.

In explaining U.S. attitudes, there is another consideration. Many ideas for tightening up and constructing rules, and indeed for constructing complex legalistic systems, seem to have come from the United States because, for various historical reasons, this is a legalistic country and, above all, a country that always thinks in terms of constitutions and rules because it is held together by a constitution. This is well known. But some other countries, notably Japan and Britain, are very different. Whatever system is constructed will have to be a compromise between different attitudes to rules versus discretion and negotiation. The interesting point is that insofar as rules protect the weak, other countries should welcome the U.S. bias toward rules.

10.3 CRITERIA FOR JUDGING POLICIES AND SYSTEMS

Let us take as given that a system with rules will be constructed or that the existing system will be amended in various ways. Before discussing various detailed issue, there are some further general principles that need to be explored. I am concerned not with the probable or the possible but the desirable. In other words, I am concerned with welfare economics.

10.3.1 Efficiency and Long-term Mutual Gain

Economists' recommendations are usually based on the efficiency criterion, defined as Pareto efficiency. A policy is efficient if the gainers could compensate the losers and still have something left over. Actual compensation does not have to take place, but it must be possible. This is the basis of the argument for free trade, subject to the numerous qualifications (often second best or worse) that have been explored in the literature of international trade theory. In discussing the rules-versus-discretion trade-off, I referred to costs of both types of systems, and these were meant to be Pareto-efficiency costs.

The problem about this efficiency criterion that economists use so much – and politicians and others are often so reluctant to accept – is that efficiency is not optimality. How can one say that a policy represents an improvement if some people are made better off and some worse off and full compensation does not take place? This issue is important even within countries where there is often some element of compensation through the fiscal system (gainers pay more taxes, and losers may be the beneficiaries of more support from government) but where compensation is rarely if ever complete. But it must be a major concern in the international arena since there is no intercountry system of compensation, and no system of rules is likely to create it (other than possibly in a partial way). This problem led at one stage in the development of welfare economics to a nonsolution: the nihilistic answer of the new welfare economics that economists can (in effect) make no prescriptions about anything. This was the orthodoxy in economic theory for a brief period, but it was an uncomfortable position for a profession to get itself into.

A way out, much used in cost-benefit analysis, implicit in a great deal of policy analysis, and formalized earlier by Samuelson, Meade, and others, is to attach welfare weights to different incomes and so combine the efficiency and the income distribution criteria. The welfare-weights approach encourages explicitness in policy recommendations, which economists normally regard as a virtue, but gives no criteria for agreement. A social welfare function is required to provide the welfare weights, and every person – or every government – can have his or her own. To get some generally agreed prescriptions, one must then look for some generally acceptable social welfare functions, or – put less formally – generally acceptable approaches to income distribution effects of policy changes.

Two kinds of social welfare functions must play some role. One is the egalitarian social welfare function, which gives more weight to the poor than the rich. It certainly influences my own thinking and policy proposals. In the present context it means that relatively more weight should be given to the interests of the developing countries, especially the least developed among them. This is, of course, an arbitrary judgment. The second is the conservative social welfare function, a concept that describes or rationalizes an approach that can be found to underlie policy advocacy in many countries. Severe adverse effects on incomes of any sections (though they may already be relatively well off) should be avoided, and, to prevent such effects, policy interventions are justified. Clearly this criterion underpins the numerous safeguard arrangements in trade policy (whether within or outside the famous GATT escape clause article XIX) and justifies, at least to politicians and the general public, so much protection. Economists cannot ignore this criterion, though they may realize that regular application of it will reduce national income. There is a moral hazard problem in systematically rescuing industries or people in trouble. The traditional position of economists is to argue against policies that reflect a conservative social welfare function in favor of the efficiency criterion.

We are still left with the problem of justifying our traditional efficiency approach when compensation does not take place. Must we always take distribution effects, including intercountry distribution, into account when considering any policy? And does this not completely destroy the market-based noninterventionist rules that many of us favor? The answer must be in probability terms. It might be called the long-term mutual gain argument. I shall put it here in world rather than national terms, though it applies at both levels. It has to be conceded that any policy or set of rules that raises world national income (that is, that is favorable on the efficiency criterion) is likely in the short run to make some countries better off and some worse off. But if such policies are consistently follows over a longer period, it is probable that eventually everyone will be better off. This seems to provide some defense for advocacy of systematic efficiency and growth-oriented policies.

10.3.2 Restraining Governments for the Good of Their Countries

Should international rules restrain governments not for the sake of protecting other governments or countries as part of an international social contract but rather for the sake of protecting the peoples of individual countries from their own governments and protecting the governments from the continuous pressures that act upon them? Some advocacy of rules in international trade – or advocacy that international organizations or committees that themselves have discretion should have some authority in particular fields over governments – runs along these lines. To some extent the role of the IMF is seen in these terms. The idea is that we need international rules and international organizations to allow governments to resist pressure groups. But it is worth remembering that this implies that when the rules are made and the organizations are staffed, the governments are able to resist these pressures. Perhaps the idea is that it is possible to resist these pressures once (when the rules are made) but not continuously.

There is also the idea that politicians do not generally understand economists' efficiency-based arguments against protection, so somehow we should get some rules imposed that will enforce the desirable policies, possibly not just through enforcement procedures in the international system that is created but also through the policy inertia that convenient, simple rules allow.

One might then ask, if we cannot persuade politicians of our views, how can we get the rules established? I can think of an answer only in terms of economies of scale and efficiency. We have something to teach (the gains from trade and the efficiency arguments against protection) that is basically correct and of which we can convince people if only there is time and effort enough available. We can succeed once every twenty years or so, when a system of rules is established or revised, but we cannot succeed continuously other than at excessive cost. Thus one might use an efficiency argument for the establishment of proefficiency rules.

There are arguments against the view that international rules should be established that restrain governments from pursuing policies that (in the belief of economists or of other governments) are against their own countries' interests. One argument is that the presumption should be that each government knows best what is good for its citizens. People who believe in the need for a government to plan the economy, and believe their government would do so beneficially, are naturally opposed to international constraints. This was an element in the opposition by the left wing of the British Labour party to Britain's joining the EC. More generally it seems that one cannot just assume that international rules will impose better arrangements than would any particular government. For example, international trading rules imposed by majority vote in the United Nations might well be inferior to those imposed unilaterally by the United States.

My view is that there is still some presumption that governments are better judges of the possible trade-offs and appropriate equilibria in their countries than are centralized bureaucracies, intergovernmental committees, or other governments. This does not deny that governments may be unwise or ill intentioned, but there is a case for decentralized decision making between countries just as there is within countries.

Inevitably international rules will be made primarily by the powerful countries. The fact that they are big and powerful economically is some indication of the economic success of their policies. Thus the rules they make, influenced by the ideologies that have helped to make them successful, may also be good for other countries. Nevertheless other countries should be encouraged more by example than by international rules to follow in their footsteps.

10.3.3 Harmonious International System

One criterion should have a high place in setting up or reforming an international trading system, or indeed any other international system: one should aim to have a harmonious international system where political tensions generally are minimized and economic policy warfare is avoided. Countries should not feel aggrieved about each others' policies and not inclined to retaliate. This idea represents the idea of the conservative social welfare function interpreted across borders. Countries should not affect each other adversely in a marked way. The efficiency criterion (long-term mutual gain argument) should in general be the guiding star for setting the rules for an international system, but it should be qualified by this consideration. The advocacy of this approach rests on the eventual cost – not just economic but also political – resulting from lack of the required harmony. Rules should be devised that make for harmony, that minimize costly negotiations and conflicts, but also that do not place unnecessary restraints on governments.

10.4 SPECIAL ROLE OF THE UNITED STATES

The United States will have the dominant role in any reconstruction of the rules for the international trading system. Nothing can happen without it, and a great deal can happen if both the administration and Congress want it to happen. The United States has inevitably inherited the leadership mantle from Great Britain. Japan has supported a new initiative but for good reasons is generally reluctant to take on a position of leadership. The EC lacks the ability to lead because of the decentralized nature of its decision making. The division of powers in the EC is much greater than in the United States. Furthermore if Europe did lead, it might well be in the wrong direction – wrong from the point of view of the economist's efficiency criterion, that is. The EC is racked by the central economic problem of excessive real wage levels and social security arrangements relative to productivity, which had led to unemployment beyond the power of orthodox macroeconomic policy to reduce, and this generates inflexibility, feelings of insecurity, and protectionist pressures. In addition, a key role, indeed a veto role, is played in its decision-making process by France, a country where the belief in free or freer trade is somewhat less than in other major Western countries.

The major role of the United States must be as the successful market economy, which by its visible success sets an example to other countries and spreads the belief in some simple principles that should also guide the international trading system. Of course, the United States has been and is an offender against these principles. The examples are well known. But its militant proclamation of belief in the basic market principles should foster a more widespread commitment to efficiency-oriented and market-based policies. At the same time the United States must bear in mind the legitimacy of other ideologies – more interventionist and often with more emphasis on sectoral income conservation – prevalent in other countries.

10.5 DISCRIMINATION AND NONDISCRIMINATION

There are many specific issues relating to the making of international trading rules that one can and should discuss. Here I select two: the question of nondiscrimination and that of subsidies.

One of the central issues that will arise in any new negotiations is whether a new safeguards code, involving a revision of article XIX of GATT, should be negotiated and whether countries that subscribe to the new system should be compelled to use this article and not bypass it, as they do now, with VERs and other devices. The article insists on nondiscrimination, but the devices that are being used outside the GATT framework are always severely discriminatory, usually directed against particular developing countries or Japan. The notorious Multi-Fiber Arrangement is grossly discriminatory against developing countries and outside GATT rules.

The nature of the current problem is the following. Let us assume for the moment that discrimination is undesirable from the point of view of the international system but is seen as being in the national interest of particular major countries. Article XIX might be revised through negotiation of a new safeguards code that allows for discrimination, possibly subject to some limitations, subject to transparency, and so on. In that case countries might cease to bypass GATT. That would be desirable for the system. On the other hand, the force of antidiscrimination arguments within each country would be weakened if discrimination were made legal within the GATT system. It is the old issue of whether use of an undesirable but popular drug should be legalized. The EC has blocked negotiation of any new safeguards code that does not permit discrimination. Perhaps one must then explore the possibilities of permitting very limited and temporary discrimination within a new code or article XIX while trying to convert the Europeans to the virtues of nondiscrimination.

Nondiscrimination and the MFN clause have been at the center of the GATT system that emerged postwar, mostly as a reaction against the mutually destructive discriminatory and discredited policies of the 1930s, as well as the hostility of the United States to imperial preference. But in the last twenty-five years or so, nondiscrimination has broken down in three ways.

First, there has been the establishment of the European Common Market and its preferential arrangements for the associated territories. This has clearly had a trade diversion element in it, but it has been widely thought acceptable because it was, after all, associated with trade creation, and the usual presumption (with some empirical support) is that trade creation far outweighed trade diversion. In fact outsiders may have been net gainers as a result of the higher real incomes that resulted from the net beneficial effect within the EEC. Second, there has been the GSP in favor of LDCs. This has been seen as acceptable because it is discriminated in favor of the poorer countries. But more important the effects have been so small, and the exceptions so large, that it has been no threat to the system. On the other hand, it has diverted the developing countries from pushing hard for universal nondiscrimination, which would be much more in their interests. Third, there has been the discrimination through the Multi-Fiber Arrangement and, more recently, through the widespread use of VERs in many other product areas. These developments are far more of a threat because they are so widespread and because they are wholly associated with protection; they do not represent a partial movement to free trade. They represent a combination of trade destruction (negative trade creation) and trade diversion. It is this development that requires the current international trading system or nonsystem to be reviewed.

Let me now come to the more basic question. What really is wrong with discrimination? Who gains and who loses? The orthodox world efficiency approach, basing itself on Viner, gives the well-known answer: every act of discriminatory reduction trade barriers has a favorable trade creation and an unfavorable trade diversion effect, and nondiscriminatory reduction of trade barriers would always be better. Going beyond this type of analysis, there seem to me three considerations.

One argument weighs in favor of permitting discrimination. Discrimination may be necessary as part of a process of moving to world free trade. For example, a group of countries might successfully negotiate a free trade area or customs union arrangement, but they might be unable to persuade some outside countries to join. For a variety of reasons they may not be willing to offer free trade unilaterally to these other countries. This unwillingness may be desirable, in any case, because it puts some incentive on the other countries to join the free trade area, hence removing their own barriers as well. A customs union or free trade area that is genuinely wide open to new members seems to me a highly desirable development, though it involves discrimination against outsiders and hence some (possibly short-term) trade diversion cost. If such a union begins, say, with the United States, the EC, and Japan, it may be the best way in which a movement toward the world freeing of trade can be revived. If fact proposals of this kind have frequently been made.[1]

Two other considerations count against discrimination. First, the opportunity for discrimination produces continuous opportunities for bargaining, which is costly. Partly as a result, it is conducive to international ill will, as the experience of the 1930s testifies. It does not contribute to a harmonious international system. Second, it is inevitable that it would damage those in a weak bargaining position, notably the developing countries. The fact that it tends to be particularly directed against developing countries, as evidenced by numerous VERs and the Multi-Fiber Arrangement, and that is antiharmony leads me to favor strongly the nondiscriminatory approach other than that which is involved in the free trade area process.

10.6 ON SUBSIDIES

Optimal intervention theory tells us that well-chosen subsidies are almost always preferable to tariffs, and even more, to quotas. This does not mean that all subsidies are desirable but that particular objectives – such as fostering an infant industry or offsetting a distortion in the labor market that raises the cost of labor to an industry or throughout the economy - can be more efficiently achieved by subsidies than by trade intervention. Before this theory was developed, many economists preferred subsidies to tariffs because the former are more transparent. The cost is more visible, going through the annual budget, and there is therefore a built-in restraint on pressures for protection.

The general decline of tariffs and the willingness in OECD countries to allow government expenditures in relation to GNP to rise to unprecedently high levels has made subsidies relatively more important as instruments of intervention. Forms of subsidization are numerous and sometimes quite indirect. Some built-in restraint must still be there, but it is now frequently argued that subsidies, because they take so many forms and are not always measured on an equivalent basis to tariffs, are less transparent. Surprisingly there is a hankering for tariffs, and sometimes it even seems to be suggested that the replacement of subsidies by tariffs would be desirable. I suspect that this is mainly explained not by any change in the nature of either device but by the fact that tariffs have been reduced over the years.

A subsidies code has emerged out of the Tokyo Round of multilateral trade negotiations, and it is widely proposed that all subsidies that might affect trade should be brought within the GATT framework. The principal feature of present arrangements is that GATT allows countries to impose countervailing duties on imports in cases where the suppliers of imports have benefited from export subsidies, while the subsidies code (to which not all members of GATT have subscribed) prohibits export subsidies completely, other than in agriculture and when imposed by developing countries. The code is somewhat vague on other kinds of subsidies, but there is pressure, particularly in the United States, to restrict them further and to allow countervailing action.

The GATT opposition to export subsidies has often been queried. Export subsidies may well benefit the importing country (by having a favorable national effect in terms of the efficiency criterion) because of improved terms of trade. The adverse effect will be sectoral. From a world efficiency point of view, if the export subsidies offset tariffs and quotas, the net effect may, on second-best grounds, also be efficient. If country A subsidizes exports on a long-term basis, from the point of view of country B the effect may, on second-best grounds, also be efficient. If country A subsidizes exports on a long-term basis, from the point of view of country B the effect is no different than when there has been a sectoral productivity improvement in country A that cheapens particular exports and so changes the conditions of comparative advantage. Thus the concern with export subsidies cannot be based either on the efficiency (long-term mutual gain) argument or on the conservative social welfare argument. It rests on the fairness argument, whereby any unfavorable comparative advantage change brought about by policy is considered to be unfair to the adversely affected parties. Only if the adverse effect is sudden and severe would some temporary protection be justified on conservative-social-welfare-function grounds.

Subsidies in general cannot be prohibited by international rules or be used as a justification for permitting other countries to impose trade restrictions. Subsidies can fulfil many social purposes, including the provision of adjustment assistance, encouraging the training of labor, and regional development. And what is a subsidy? Is the United States subsidizing technological development through its military budget, for example? Surely the United States would not agree that this be placed within the ambit of international trade negotiations. This is just one example, but numerous other items of public expenditure can be described as subsidies to someone or something. Proposals to maintain or strengthen the rule of law in international trade will be bound to fail if it is attempted to extend the scope of the law so widely that it digs deep into the sovereignty of governments.

It would seem to me much wiser to allow full subsidy freedom, including export subsidies. If country A wants to protect its own industry against the consequences of country B's subsidies on exports or production of a competing product, let country A countervail with a subsidy of its own. In both cases there is the built-in constraint of the cost to the budget. Both governments will have some incentive to negotiate to reduce their subsidies if they find that they are getting too expensive. Perhaps each country should be required to produce an annual subsidies report and to supply statistics on subsidies to GATT.

10.7 CONCLUSION

So many considerations have been introduced here that one can hardly claim that a clear-cut policy recommendation inevitably emerges. Nevertheless starting from some simple presumptions, it seems that one can arrive at a set of recommendations for a new system that may not be probable but is just possible and would certainly be desirable.

The presumptions are that the major negotiating nations, in particular the big three, broadly accept the long-term mutual gain argument for free trade, that they accept the relevance of the concern with sectoral income maintenance, that they wish to have as far as possible a harmonious international system, and that they see some virtues in policy openness and in decentralization of decision making.

This leads me to the following package, at least as a long-term target at which the negotiating nations should aim.

1. Complete free trade (no tariffs or quantitative import restrictions among the countries that agree to participate). This should include both agriculture and textiles. With all trade restrictions completely ruled out, there should be no incentive for exporting countries to accept VERs.

2. This may be qualified by a safeguards code that allows for temporary, nondiscriminatory tariffs, the rules being similar to those of article XIX. This qualification is meant to take some account of the sudden injury problem (that

is, the concern with the temporary conservation of sectoral incomes or, at least, avoiding sudden declines).

3. Developed countries that do not participate do not get the benefits of free trade or the safeguards code, so discrimination against them is permitted. But they should be free to enter the system without any negotiations.

4. There shall be subsidy freedom.

5. With regard to protection imposed under safeguards and protection imposed against those outside the agreement, there shall be complete transparency, including regular international examinations along OECD lines.

6. There will be no restrictions on imports from developing countries other than those imposed under the same safeguards code, but developing countries will not be required to join the scheme until they have reached particular levels of income per head or exports per head. These should not be set too low, roughly drawing the line where it is now drawn in United Nations and World Bank categorizations. When they reach these levels ("graduate"), they will be invited to join the scheme, with transitional arrangements lasting some years to allow for infant industry protection and gradual dismantling of trade barriers. They will retain their subsidy freedom, as the others do. If they do not join the scheme when they graduate, they will gradually lose the privilege of free entry into the free trade area.[2]

It seems to me that all this is desirable, little of it is probable, but some of it is at least possible.

NOTES

1 The *Annual Report of the Council of Economic Advisers* (1985, pp. 125, 26) suggests the free trade area approach as a secondary strategy for trade liberalization if fully multilateral negotiations do not succeed. The correct point is made that free trade area negotiations "tend to reverse the usual incentives in international trade negotiations by making countries more eager to be among the first to agree to liberalise trade rather than among the last" and "as the number of countries joining an FTA grows, the incentives for outsiders to join increase."

2 At the conference the recommendation to allow free entry for imports from developing countries, even when they themselves still have trade restrictions, was queried. The issue is not whether the markets of the developed countries should be wide open to imports from developing countries, for given trade restrictions in the developing countries, whether positive or zero, this is clearly desirable from an efficiency point of view and if one agrees that developed countries' trade policies should generally help, rather than discriminate against developing countries. The issue is whether pressure should be put on developing countries to reduce their own restrictions, possibly moving to complete free trade, in their own interests. Is it asking too much from their policymakers, or is the carrot of open markets in the developed countries what is needed?

One consideration to bear in mind is that there are some conceivably valid arguments for tariffs at modest levels, at least on second-best grounds, in developing countries, primarily on infant industry grounds or for the raising of revenue (such a view must be stated with careful qualifications). Probably more important, given that protection levels are high in many developing countries, the adjustment problems involved in moving rapidly to free trade in order to gain the benefits of open markets in the developed countries may be perceived as too great. On balance many of the developing countries may then decline to join, possibly because they incorrectly perceive the adjustment problems to be too great or because their decision makers are not intellectually convinced of the case for free trade.

3. An Economist's Overview of the World Trade Organization

A. V. Deardorff

I. INTRODUCTION

THE ARENA OF INTERNATIONAL trade has provided ample evidence over the years of the destructive chaos that can ensue when nations are left completely on their own in conducting trade policies. At the beginning of the Great Depression of the 1930s, the United States led the world in raising its trade barriers in order to stimulate its domestic economy at the expense of economies abroad. Since World War II, fortunately, the United States has also led in bringing down these and other barriers to trade. But powerful economic and political forces continue to exist through the world that push for whatever protection might be available in particular sectors, again at the expense of those sectors elsewhere. International trade theory tells us that increased barriers to trade reduce world welfare, and that the outcome of these "beggar-thy-neighbor" policies is likely to be that all countries are worse off. Still, each country individually may perceive correctly that it stands to gain in some way from its own protection, whether or not protection is used abroad. This means that the world is in something like the classic "prisoners' dilemma" situation of game theory, where each player individually has incentive to act in ways that make the players collectively worse off.[1] As Dixit (1996, p. 124) has remarked, "The key political conflict in international trade is a Prisoners' Dilemma for the group [of] countries seeking to agree to a more liberal trading regime." In such a prisoners' dilemma, players who are left alone in their actions cannot be expected to behave in the general interest, and it follows that some mechanism of international cooperation may be needed to prevent such mutually destructive policy competition. The World Trade Organization (WTO) provides this mechanism in a variety of ways that will be reviewed in this paper.[2]

The WTO and its predecessor, the General Agreement on Tariffs and Trade (GATT) have an interesting and somewhat peculiar history that I will review initially, in Section II below. This history contributed to the institutional structure of the WTO, as containing three components: the revised GATT, the General Agreement on Trade in Services (GATS), and the Agreement on trade-related intellectual property issues (TRIPs). It is customary, therefore, to organize a discussion of the WTO in this same way, dealing first with the GATT, then the GATS, then TRIPs. However, from a functional point of view these distinctions are not very helpful, and I will instead organize my discussion of the WTO around the following four functions that, to a greater or lesser extent, all three of these components collectively provide:

1. **Communication**: Constitutes a forum for exchange of information, consultation, and negotiation.
2. **Constraint**: Constraints on the trade-policy actions of member governments.
3. **Exception**: Permits exceptions from these constraints for prescribed reasons and with prescribed means.
4. **Dispute Settlement**: Offers a mechanism for settlement of disputes among members.

These four functions are broken down into their various components in Table 1, which also provides an outline of the discussion in this paper. Those who are already familiar with the GATT and the WTO may find this organizational structure unfamiliar, because of its grouping by function. In particular, many of the familiar provisions of the GATT and WTO – such as tariff bindings, quantitative restrictions, anti-dumping, and safeguards – are split between the section on constraints and the section on exceptions, reflecting my view that there is an important difference between what countries are *required* to do and not do, the constraints, and what countries are merely *permitted* optionally to do, the exceptions. Similarly, the single issue of subsidies/countervailing duties is itself split here between the constraints on the use of subsidies, on the one hand, and the exceptions that permit, but do not require, countervailing duties on the other. Finally, the issues that prior to the WTO were handled outside the GATT in the Tokyo Round codes – such as customs valuation and product regulations (standards) – are here listed on an equal footing with both the more venerable GATT provisions and the new agreements on services and intellectual property. The purpose of this organizing framework, then, is to convey a picture of the WTO as it now is, not as it evolved in the past.

The four main functions listed above in Table 1 can be easily understood in terms of the prisoners'-dilemma nature of the problems that the WTO seeks to resolve.[3] First, the prisoners' dilemma arises most clearly from the assumed inability of the prisoners to communicate with each other, and thus to agree to remain silent. Therefore the first and most important role for an international mechanism to escape the prisoners' dilemma in trade policy is to get the players into the same room to facilitate communication. The WTO is that room. I will discuss the various means that the WTO provides for communication in Section III.

The strategies available to trade policy makers are of course far more complicated than the simple prisoners' choices of whether or not to confess. Therefore it is necessary to define what will constitute cooperation, that is, what constraints should be placed on behavior in order for it to be viewed as cooperative. This is important, first because such cooperation should lead in fact to a desirable outcome, and it is not always obvious whether particular policies affecting trade are good or bad. But it is also important because observed departures from such

TABLE 1: *Functional Outline of the World Trade Organization*

Communication	Ministerials	
	Negotiating Rounds	
	Working Groups	
	Trade Policy Review Mechanism	
	Councils and Committees	
Constraints	Tariff Bindings	
	Customs Valuation	
	Product Regulations	
	Quantitative Restrictions	
	Subsidies	
	Foreign Direct Investment (TRIMs)	
	Service (GATS)	
	Intellectual Property (TRIPs)	
Exceptions	Anti-Dumping	
	Countervailing Duties	
	Safeguards	
	Balance of Payments Protection	
	Preferential Trade Agreements	
Dispute Settlement	Consultation	
	Panel Recommendation	
	Appellate Body	
	Remedy	Implementation
		Compensation
		Retaliation

agreed behavior will be taken by the players to indicate that cooperation has broken down, and the constraints should not be so onerous or ambiguous that cooperation is not sustainable. The constraints that the WTO places on trade policy will be discussed in Section IV.

These constraints define what countries *must do* and *must not do*. However, any set of constraints is likely to be too strict, either because special circumstances may arise in which the constraints are inappropriate, or because events may make adhering to the constraints too difficult. There is therefore also a need to permit exceptions to these rules, defining what countries *may do*. That is, the exceptions permit, but do not require, certain forms of behavior that would otherwise have been viewed as non-cooperative. These exceptions will be the topic of Section V.

Finally, there needs to be some mechanism for enforcing any agreement. This requires a way of determining whether a country has departed from it, as well as some form of penalty that will be imposed if it does. This is the dispute settlement mechanism that will be the subject of Section VI. Section VII concludes with a brief evaluation of how well the WTO structure succeeds in the objective of fostering international cooperation in trade policy.

Underlying the entire WTO and its GATT predecessor is the single principle of nondiscrimination: that economic welfare is greatest if policies do not discriminate among suppliers and among demanders of economic goods and services. This principle may have been motivated originally by some notion of fairness, but the basis for it may today be found among the theorems of welfare economics. These argue that consumer welfare will be maximized if both consumers and producers bear the full marginal costs and marginal benefits of their own actions. In particular, consumers should face prices from alternative suppliers that reflect their true marginal costs, undistorted relative to one another by policy. In the WTO, the principle of nondiscrimination takes two forms: Most Favored Nation (MFN) treatment and National Treatment (NT). MFN assures that there is nondiscrimination among foreign suppliers, while NT assures that there is nondiscrimination between foreign suppliers and domestic suppliers. Most of the constraints of the WTO can be understood as attempts to maintain or move towards MFN and NT.

II. A VERY BRIEF HISTORY OF THE WTO[4]

The WTO came into existence on January 1, 1995, as one result of the agreement reached in the seven-year-long Uruguay Round of multilateral trade negotiations that was completed the previous year. Its history, however, extends much further back, at least to the proposed International Trade Organization (ITO) that was designed in the mid-1940s alongside the other Bretton Woods institutions, the IMF and the World Bank. The ITO was never approved, and part of its intended purpose was served instead by the GATT, which had been agreed upon originally as only a temporary measure pending approval of the ITO. Although it was formally only a treaty and therefore not an organization *per se*, the GATT served much the same functions that were listed above for the WTO. The scope of the GATT, however, was limited to trade in goods.

As a vehicle for communication, the GATT sponsored a series of "rounds" of trade negotiations, the Uruguay Round being the most recent. Early rounds were primarily intended to reduce tariffs, the most successful of these being the Kennedy Round that was completed in 1967. It was followed by the Tokyo Round, begun in 1974 and completed in 1979. In addition to negotiating further tariff reductions, the Tokyo Round also succeeded in extending the negotiations to several nontariff barriers (NTBs), which were covered in several "codes" that countries who were signatories of the GATT had the option of signing and that bound only the signatories of the respective code.

The original GATT included many of the same constraints and exceptions that remain part of the WTO and that will be discussed below. Successive rounds of negotiation expanded the lists of both, while the Tokyo Round codes extended some of these optionally to certain NTBs.

All of these rules were minimally enforced by means of several distinct dispute settlement mechanisms, one for the GATT itself and additional ones for separate codes. These mechanisms were also similar to the single mechanism that will be described below for the WTO. However, the earlier dispute mechanisms provided only minimal discipline, because of a feature that each country could in effect veto any decision that went against it. This, as we shall see, has been changed fundamentally in the WTO.

III. COMMUNICATION IN THE WTO

As the example of the prisoners' dilemma suggests, effective communication is a fundamental prerequisite for cooperation. In the sphere of trade policy, countries need ways to know what others are doing as well as what commitments others are making. The WTO provides several of these.

At the highest level, the trade ministers or their equivalents from the member countries meet every two years to discuss trade policies. These "Ministerials" also occurred under the GATT, although not always with such regularity. They are preceded by a great deal of communication among lower level trade diplomats, who seek to lay the foundation for agreement among the ministers. Frequently in past ministerials, agreement has been reached to initiate another in the series of rounds of trade negotiations, which constitute another critical mechanism of communication among countries. At this time, however, it is not clear whether future ministerials under the new WTO will again initiate such rounds of negotiation, since the WTO includes more mechanisms for the gradual evolution of the trade institutions than were part of the GATT, and such major initiatives as the recent trade rounds may therefore be unnecessary in the future. The next ministerial is scheduled for this December 1996, in Singapore. As the first ministerial under the new WTO, it may lay out the parameters that future ministerials will follow. If a new round of negotiations is not initiated, as seems likely, then the purpose of the Singapore Ministerial will be more one of plotting the course for future smaller negotiations within the WTO framework.

Trade rounds, when they have occurred in the past under the GATT and if they occur in the future under the WTO, do serve a purpose for cooperation among the diverse players in the world trading system that cannot be understood within the simple framework of the prisoners' dilemma. This is the fostering of trade-offs. While there are many issues in international trade policy in which, like the prisoners, all countries can be made better off if they can only agree, there are also many other issues for which agreement necessarily implies both winner and losers. Thus, for example, negotiations in the Uruguay Round dealing with the Multi-Fiber Arrangement (MFA) were well understood to be leading, if they were successful, toward losses for firms within the developed world and toward gains for potential producers of textiles and apparel in the developing world that were being denied access to developed country markets by the MFA.[5] At the same time, negotiations on intellectual property were widely regarded as likely to benefit developed countries and harm developing countries. Had negotiations on either of these issues been attempted independently, it is therefore unlikely that agreement could have been reached, since in each case the losing group of countries would have nothing to gain. However, by combining a variety of such issues within the framework of a negotiating round, the GATT has successfully permitted countries to trade off losses on some issues in exchange for gains on others. It is not clear that anything but such a round, therefore, will permit the WTO to make progress on many of the issues that remain before it.[6]

Currently, the way that members of the WTO are communicating on many of these issues is through "working groups."[7] In addition to direct changes in the international trade policy environment that have been negotiated in recent rounds, the Uruguay Round also included agreement to form several of these working groups. This has been a typical response to issues where the discussions are not yet far enough along for agreement to be foreseeable, and instead those who advocate consideration of such issues have had to content themselves with more formal discussion. By forming a working group on an issue, the WTO gives it a legitimacy that may lead in the longer run to formal negotiation and agreement. In addition, it alerts those parties who might oppose an initiative to voice their objections. Working groups are currently in place on several issues, including one on trade and the environment and another on trade and competition policy. That these working groups do have some substantive significance is indicated by those issues where even the formation of a working group has been opposed, in spite of a strong constituency in favor. The United States pushed in the Uruguay Round for the formation of a working group on labor standards, but the developing countries successfully prevented that.

Ministerials, rounds of negotiation, and working groups are all designed as means of communication over primarily large issues. The WTO also includes several facilities for communication on a more regular basis. One is the Trade Policy Review Mechanism (TPRM). First established in 1988, the TPRM has been made a formal part of the WTO, which includes a Trade Policy Review Body (TPRB) to oversee it. Under the TPRM, countries are required to undergo periodic reviews of their trade policies, based on information that both they themselves and the TPRB assemble. Done as frequently as every two years for the largest WTO members, these reviews are intended to identify all of the policies affecting the international trade of the focus countries, including both goods and services. Therefore, to the extent that membership in the WTO has committed any country to policies that it would be in its unilateral interest to abandon, these regular reviews should facilitate cooperation. However, the scope of the TPRM is limited to trade. It does not currently deal with investment regulations, and it is now being debated whether to expand its scope to other "new" issues, such as environment and labor standards.

Channels for even more frequent communication on a day-to-day basis also exist in the form of the Councils and Committees of the WTO. The former are three Councils for Trade and Goods, Trade in Services, and Trade-Related Aspects of Intellectual Property. The first of these oversees the many agreements covering trade in goods, while the other two are responsible for the respective agreements on services and intellectual property. There are also three special purpose Committees – on Trade and Development, on Balance of Payments, and on Budget – that deal with the areas indicated. All of these Councils and Committees report to the General Council, composed of all WTO member countries, which conducts the day-to-day work of the WTO.

In addition, membership in the WTO obligates countries to notify the WTO whenever they engage in policies in a variety of areas that might be trade restricting. Technical regulations, for example, must be notified to the WTO Secretariat with sufficient lead time for exporters to adapt to the new rules. Similar notification requirements apply, for example, to sanitary and phytosanitary measures and state-trading enterprises.

Ultimately, however, for many trade policy actions, the most effective means of communication will be formal filing of a WTO case against a country by another country that perceives itself to be aggrieved by that action. Thus the most important and effective means of communication is probably the WTO dispute settlement process, to be discussed below. In some cases, the mere filing of such a case (or even the threat of filing) may be enough to persuade the offending party to change its behavior, especially in situations where its violation of WTO cooperation was inadvertent.

The drawback of the dispute settlement process, however, is that it gives voice to objections to a country's policies only if they are explicitly constrained under one or more WTO rules, and even then only if the aggrieved country or countries want the practices to stop. In some cases, these conditions are not satisfied. Voluntary export restraints (VERs) for example were not mentioned in the old GATT, and therefore could not generate GATT disputes. And even in the WTO, where the rules do prohibit VERs as we shall see, there is the question of whether the countries whose exports have been constrained by the VERs will complain about them. In such cases, it may well be in the political interests of producers in both exporting and importing countries to maintain the VERs because of the rents that they generate, even though consumer welfare in at least the importing country is being reduced. Therefore it is to be hoped that the TPRM and other means of communication under the WTO will be sufficient to alert the world to policies that undermine the broader public interest.

IV. CONSTRAINTS IMPOSED BY THE WTO

Had the players in the prisoners' dilemma been able to talk to each other, their agreement could have been very simple: don't confess. Trading nations have a much more complicated form of cooperation to achieve. The general principle, that their trade policies should be nondiscriminatory, conforming to the principles of MFN and NT, is far too imprecise to be operational, although for some categories of trade, such as state trading, the WTO includes explicit requirements that such trade be MFN. Therefore the WTO spells out in some detail a long list of constraints on member country behavior – things that they either must do or must not do in order to be viewed as cooperating. Many of these constraints appeared as provisions of the original GATT agreement of 1947, which took the form of a treaty and consisted of XXXV Articles of Agreement.[8] These articles have been reviewed, extended, and supplemented with additional agreements in the rounds of negotiation that have occurred since then.[9] The major provisions constraining member behaviour are listed in Table 1 and discussed below. Note again that other important provisions such as those dealing with anti-dumping and safeguards are left to the next section of the paper dealing with exceptions.

Some of the more noteworthy constraints, then, are as follows.

Tariff Bindings

Basic to the GATT and the WTO is the commitment of the member countries to constrain their use of tariffs on imports. Tariffs were, of course, the most obvious and common form of trade policy that existed when the GATT was first negotiated, and their adverse effects are well understood. However, the GATT did not, and the WTO still does not, prohibit the use of tariffs completely. On the contrary, it only requires countries to commit not to raise tariffs above certain levels that they negotiate on entry or in multilateral negotiating rounds. These levels are called the tariff "bindings," and it is on these that the early rounds of negotiation focused. Even after many such rounds, however, it remained true before the Uruguay Round that not all traded goods were covered by tariff bindings, especially in developing countries. One achievement of the Uruguay Round, therefore, was the commitment of most member countries to bind almost all of their tariffs. These tariff bindings, however, are often well above the actual tariffs that developing countries especially are currently levying, so that there remains a substantial risk that such countries may raise their actual tariffs and still be in accord with their WTO commitments.

Notice too that by permitting members to continue to levy positive tariffs in all sectors where they have not explicitly bound themselves voluntarily at zero, the WTO is necessarily departing from its own NT principle for a large portion of trade in goods. That is, imports are not being accorded NT whenever they are subject to a tariff, since domestically produced goods clearly are not subject to the tariff. NT in goods remains, therefore, only a long-run goal towards which the international trading system attempts to move over time, rather than an immediate requirement. As will be discussed below, this is in marked contrast to what has been attempted with regard to services. Because services do not physically cross borders, they are not subject to tariffs, and the use of tariff buildings in services would therefore be meaningless. Negotiations have therefore centered on achieving NT immediately in these sectors, wherever countries can be persuaded to do so.

Customs Valuation

Because of the prisoners'-dilemma nature of trade policy cooperation, there will always be an incentive to cheat on any agreement. Therefore, having bound their tariffs, countries will sometimes seek ways to increase the restrictiveness of these tariffs without violating the tariff bindings. There are many ways of administering tariffs that can have this effect, and the WTO seeks to prevent such behavior.

For example, *ad vaolrem* tariffs are levied on the value of the imported goods, and unless the method of valuation is precisely circumscribed, customs officers may seek to exaggerate the value of a good in order to increase the tariff collected on it. Of course, the importers have an even stronger incentive to understate the value of an imported good, so that one cannot simply rely on an importer's declaration of value as definitive. These declarations are especially problematic when trade is between subsidiaries of a single multinational firm, and the transfer prices that they report have no counterpart on the open market. The WTO therefore includes explicit rules on customs valuation that are intended to reduce the discretion that countries and their customs officers, as well as the traders themselves, have in valuing goods at the border.

Note that these constraints on customs valuation serve another important purpose, in addition to making it harder for governments to undermine their WTO agreements. By reducing uncertainty over the amount of tariff that an exporter will pay at the border, potential traders become more confident of the profits they will make from trade, and they may therefore be expected to trade more. That is, uncertainty over customs valuation itself acts as a barrier to trade, and by committing themselves to predictable and transparent valuation procedures, countries reduce this barrier.

Product Regulations

Governments engage in a wide variety of regulatory actions, many of which are not targeted at international trade but which nonetheless may affect the costs or feasibility of trade. Most obvious are the many regulations, standards, and other measures that restrict the form that a good may take or the manner in which it may be produced for sale in the domestic market. Such rules may be intended to protect the public safety or health, or they may only seek to insure compatibility of products that must be used in combination. But in either case it is possible for such a rule to be biased against imported products, perhaps in the form that a product must take, or perhaps in the procedures that are laid out for certifying that a rule has been obeyed. The WTO therefore includes its own constraints on how such rules should be established and enforced so as not to be biased against imports. Two sets of constraints appear, one on Technical Regulations and Standards and another on Sanitary and Phytosanitary Measures,[10] but both have essentially the same purpose. They do not prescribe what such regulations should be, only that they should be designed and enforced in ways that do not discriminate against imports. Like the agreement on customs valuation, these too provide the additional benefit of reducing uncertainty in international trade.

Quantitative Restrictions

Quantitative restrictions (QRs) are usually regarded as more onerous than tariffs because of the more limited flexibility that they permit in trade and because they place greater limits on the extent to which foreign and domestic sellers can compete. In addition, it is very difficult to measure the restrictiveness of a QR,[11] and this makes it hard to negotiate only their partial liberalization. It is therefore only recently that QRs have come under the effective discipline of the GATT.[12] The WTO, with some exceptions, largely simply prohibits their use. This includes both explicit quotas that are imposed on particular products, and also import licensing schemes that allocate scarce foreign exchange in a manner that is discriminatory across goods or countries. VERs, which typically have taken quantitative form, are also prohibited as part of the safeguards rules discussed in the next section. QRs are still permitted for a few specific purposes to be discussed below, but for the most part they are forbidden. Since until the Uruguay Round QRs were quite commonly used in some sensitive sectors – especially agriculture and textiles/apparel – implementation of this prohibition has required some major changes in policy. In agriculture, existing QRs have been replaced by "tariff equivalents" — additional tariffs that are intended to restrict imports to the level of the QR. These tariff equivalents will then be subject to future liberalization through the same process of negotiated tariff bindings that has long been used for other goods. In the case of textiles and apparel, on the other hand, the complex web of quotas that has spread over recent decades under the MFA is allowed to continue to exist temporarily, with WTO members committed to a schedule of removing them over the next ten years.[13]

Subsidies

Subsidies that are provided by governments directly for exports have always been prohibited in the GATT, although until the Uruguay Round and the formation of the WTO there have been very large exceptions to this prohibition. Now, all export subsidies are forbidden. Subsidies to production, on the other hand, are a much thicker problem. On the one hand it is clear that some production subsidies can adversely affect producers in other countries. On the other hand, there exist a multitude of solid economic reasons why some production subsidies are at least second-best, and sometimes even first-best, means of achieving various legitimate objectives.[14] This ambiguity has been dealt with in the WTO by first identifying three classes of subsidy, classes that are sometimes conveniently identified by the colors of a traffic light. "Red light subsidies" are those for which no redeeming value can be identified, and these are simply prohibited. They include export subsidies, as already mentioned, plus subsidies that are contingent upon the use of domestic over imported goods, as well as an illustrative list of very explicit subsidies that fall into this category. "Yellow light subsidies," on the other hand, are not prohibited at all, but their possible adverse effects on other countries' producers are nonetheless recognized by permitting importers to levy countervailing duties against them in specified circumstances. They are there called "actionable subsidies", and we will discuss them further in the next section. Finally, "green light subsidies" are "non-actionable" and include both subsidies that are not specific to particular firms or industries, plus certain subsidies for research and development, regional development, and adaptation to environmental regulations.

Foreign Direct Investments

So much international commerce is today conducted by multinational corporations, with substantial investments in many countries, that there has long been call for international constraints not only on trade policies, but also on policies affecting foreign direct investment. As a result, the Uruguay Round included negotiations on Trade Related Investment Measures (TRIMs), and the WTO too includes a TRIMs agreement. In fact, however, the TRIMs agreement only prohibits investment measures that directly affect trade flows in a manner that violates NT or that violates the prohibition of QRs. Prohibited most clearly are local content and trade balancing requirements, both of which would restrict the trade of an international direct investor.

Services

Services were not included under the GATT, largely because they were not viewed as being tradable when the GATT was created. Most services require the simultaneous presence of both the producer and consumer, so that if a service provider from one country wishes to sell to a buyer from another, either the seller must establish a presence in the buyer's country, which typically requires foreign direct investment and/or movement of labor, or the buyer must travel to the seller's country, as in the case of tourism.[15] However, the increasing volume of international transactions in services industries, such as finance, transportation, and telecommunications, led to powerful political forces in the developed world, pushing to provide for services industries the same sorts of protections against capricious government policies that were provided for goods producers under the GATT. The result is the General Agreement on Trade in Services, GATS, which is a part of the WTO.

The aim of the GATS is to require that services providers from all countries, when they compete in other countries, be subject to the same principles of MFN and NT that are the objectives of the GATT. In fact, because traded services do not themselves cross national borders and are therefore not subject to the same kinds of tariffs and other border measures as are goods, the approach followed in the GATT of gradually bringing down those barriers through negotiation is not available for services. Instead, members of the WTO have committed themselves to go all the way to national treatment in those service industries in which they have promised to do anything at all. In the Uruguay Round negotiations leading to the WTO, countries negotiated not on service barriers, but rather on lists of service sectors, identifying those sectors that they were willing to make subject to liberalization. Unfortunately, the number of such sectors turned out to be quite small, and the extent of actual liberalization of trade in services that was achieved by the Uruguay Round was essentially zero.[16] Continued negotiation of liberalization for the excluded service sectors has been underway in the WTO since it began, although with limited success.

Intellectual Property

Much as developed-country service providers sought to benefit from a GATT-like structure, owners of many forms of intellectual property (IP) – copyrights, patents, trademarks, etc. – in the developed countries also began seeking during the 1980s to include intellectual property issues in GATT negotiations. In order to justify their inclusion in a trade negotiation, discussion was nominally restricted to Trade Related Intellectual Property Rights, or TRIPs, although in fact the negotiations covered almost all aspects of IP protection. The major issue, for all forms of IP protection, was that many countries, especially in the developing world, either did not have IP laws that were comparable to those in the developed world, or they had such laws but were lax in enforcing them. As a result, owners of copyrights, patents, and trademarks were finding their products copied and counterfeited in the developing world with impunity.

The result of these negotiations was that the WTO now includes, alongside the GATT and GATS agreements, a TRIPs agreement on intellectual property. This agreement goes considerably beyond the MFN and NT principles of the two trade agreements, however, in that it seeks to harmonize the actual policies of the member countries. In particular, all but the very poorest WTO members are now required to adhere to certain minimum standards regarding intellectual property, and these standards are comparable to those prevailing in the developed countries (who also agree to remove various differences among their own IP laws).

V. MISSING CONSTRAINTS ON UNILATERAL ACTION

Noticeably absent from the list of constraints just considered is any constraint on the sorts of unilateral action that the United States and other large trading blocs have used in the past to pressure other countries in their trade policies and even in their domestic policies. Indeed, movement toward some of the objectives of the WTO, especially the TRIPs agreement, already occurred before the Uruguay Round was completed, as the United States negotiated bilaterally with countries where it felt that its intellectual property rights were being abused. In addition, the United States has made frequent use of Section 301 of its trade law, which triggers unilateral retaliation against countries with perceived barriers to market access, and it has a long history of negotiating bilaterally with Japan, especially, seeking quantitative targets on Japanese market penetration by foreign firms.

Nowhere in the constraints discussed above are countries prevented from further use of such unilateral action. Nor, however, do the exceptions discussed below explicitly permit such action either. Use of Section 301 and similar bilateral initiatives are therefore left in an ambiguous state in the WTO, and there is disagreement among trade policy authorities as to whether particular ones of these initiative do or do not violate the GATT. The one such initiative on which the WTO does take a position is VERs, which are explicitly prohibited as mentioned above. Otherwise there seems to be no reason within the legal framework of the WTO that countries will not be able to continue acting unilaterally and bilaterally for their own purposes. On the other hand, the more that countries find themselves able to deal with perceived trade conflicts within the context of the WTO, the less they may feel the need to go outside it. There is some reason for hope on this score, since countries do seem to be taking their disputes increasingly to the WTO.

VI. EXCEPTIONS PERMITTED BY THE WTO

Simple agreements, like that between our prisoners not to confess, can be essentially absolute ("I will not confess.") because the actions being agreed to and the circumstances of the agreement are both well understood.[17] But complex agreements amount national governments must permit a fair amount of flexibility. Any rules that are adopted will inevitably be subject to interpretation, and the effects of these rules on the economy can never be known with certainty. Therefore, international trade agreements typically include some sort of "escape clause" that allows the parties to back partially out of the agreement in the event that it proves to be more injurious than expected. Furthermore, governments always have well-established policies that they are reluctant to relinquish as well as powerful constituents who benefit from those policies. The latter may interfere with adoption of any agreement, and therefore may need to be bought off by permitting some form of these policies to continue, hopefully in weakened form. The WTO, like the GATT before it, includes a number of such policy options that either protect members partially from adverse outcomes or, more commonly, that are needed to make membership in the organization acceptable to powerful domestic political interests.

I discuss these exceptions in this section, separate from the restrictions on member country behavior considered above, in part because these exceptions are all optional. That is, while countries are required to keep their tariffs at or below their bound levels under normal circumstances, they are only permitted, not required, to make exceptions to this binding in the case of, say, dumped imports. There is nothing in the WTO that says a country must have and use an anti-dumping law. Indeed, most of the exceptions to be discussed below are, in their nature, rather antithetical to the larger objectives of the WTO.

Anti-Dumping

The WTO follows long established practice in permitting the use of anti-dumping (AD) duties under certain circumstances. Dumping is defined as the export of a good for an unfairly low price, defined either as below the price on the exporter's home market or as below some definition of cost. In spite of this designation of unfairness, however, nothing in the WTO prohibits dumping itself, or asks member governments to try to restrain their firms from doing it. Rather, the WTO only addresses how importing countries may respond to dumping. When dumping is shown to cause injury, WTO rules permit importing countries to levy AD import duties equal to the "dumping margin" – the difference between the actual and the fair market price. And note, of course, that the WTO does not *require* the use of AD duties, it only permits them and says how they may be used.

There are numerous details of the AD rules in the WTO, which are far too complex to cover here. Some would say that the AD rules that preceded the WTO were so lax that an affirmative finding of dumping in the United States and Europe was almost assured, as long as a company seeking such protection asked for it enough times.[18] These rules were tightened in some respects in the Uruguay Round, but they were loosened in other respects. The result is that AD continues to be a tool of protection that is readily available to those who want to use it. For all its accomplishments, therefore, the WTO leaves open the question of whether AD will be used to undermine the liberalization efforts in goods and services.

Countervailing Duties

Countervailing duties (CVDs) were already mentioned above as being permitted in response to "actionable" subsidies. When an importer establishes that domestic producers have been injured by imports that have benefited from a government subsidy abroad, and when the nature of that subsidy satisfies certain requirements – most importantly, perhaps, being that it not be generally available to other industries – then the importing country is permitted to levy a CVD equal in size to the subsidy. The purpose is to offset the harm that the subsidized imports do to domestic industry, not to punish the foreign exporters. For again the WTO does not take a position on whether such subsidies are good or bad. It says only that other countries should be permitted to protect their competing domestic producers from any adverse effects that the foreign subsidies may cause them. Of course, the WTO also identifies another group of "prohibited" subsidies – primarily export subsidies and their equivalents – that are also subject to CVDs and that are designated as undesirable.

Once again, the use of CVDs is only permitted, not required, and this is interesting from an economist's perspective for two reasons. First, it can be argued that the use of some subsidies – those that are not responding to some other distortion in the economy – does lower world welfare, and therefore that they should be prohibited. That is in fact what the designation of red light subsidies seeks to do, although there are undoubtedly also many yellow light subsidies that are unjustified and should be prohibited as well. However, merely prohibiting a subsidy may not have much effect, and it is here that CVDs could be useful.

To see how, consider the use of competitive export subsidies, such as have emerged in agriculture in recent years. These, once again, put countries in the position of a prisoners' dilemma, since each country's subsidy undermines the gains that others' subsidies were seeking, and makes all worse off. An effective deterrent to the use of such subsidies would be CVDs, but only if they were expected with certainty by governments that were contemplating use of subsidies. Thus one could argue that the use of CVDs should not just be permitted, but rather should be required, even in (or especially in) countries that have no domestic competing producer interests to ask for them. Of course, this presupposes that one can adequately make the necessary distinction between economically justified and unjustified subsidies, and while the traffic light approach of the WTO does attempt this, few would argue that it gets it exactly right.

Safeguards

The Safeguards Clause of the WTO serves the purpose identified above of permitting members to partially and temporarily back out of their agreements if they prove too costly. Thus, if the concessions made in joining the WTO are causing serious injury[19] to domestic producers, then countries are permitted to protect those producers temporarily with a trade barrier. Such a facility has been available throughout the history of the GATT, but it was used less and less over time. The reasons for this were several, including the requirement that users of safeguards compensate the foreign countries who were adversely affected by them, the prohibition under the old rules against discriminatory safeguards tariffs, and the greater difficulty of getting safeguards protection, in comparison to an AD duty, due to the more stringent injury requirement. Instead, industries routinely sought AD protection rather than safeguard protection, even when the reason for their petition had more to do with injury than with the low foreign price. Alternatively, for major industries, governments negotiated VERs with the relevant foreign exporters, thus achieving both discrimination and compensation without needing to formally contravene the GATT.[20] Under the new rules of the WTO, VERs are formally prohibited, as mentioned above. Rules for safeguards have been modified to permit some discrimination, and the requirement of compensation has been weakened. The hope is that the new safeguards rules will attract greater use, diverting governments from excessive use of AD duties and other measures for safeguards purposes. It remains to be seen whether this will in fact happen.

Balance of Payments Protection

From the beginning, the GATT has permitted exceptional use of protection for balance of payments purposes, and this continues to be the case in the WTO. That is, if a country is experiencing severe excess demand for foreign exchange that is making it difficult to retain foreign reserves, it is permitted to use quotas to restrict trade, even on a discriminatory basis. From an economist's perspective this is an odd exception, since trade restrictions, especially at the sectoral level, make little sense as means to solve the macroeconomic problem that a balance of payments deficit represents. Furthermore, since almost by definition something like half of all countries are likely to be indeficit positions, this exception opens a huge hole in the WTO restrictions against trade barriers. The surprise to me is that the balance of payments exception has not been more used.

Preferential Trade Agreements (PTAs)

Despite its underlying principle of nondiscrimination embodied in the MFN requirement, the WTO permits preferential trade agreements so long as they reduce to zero essentially all of the tariffs among the participates. Thus it is permitted to form free trade areas, where this is done without changing each country's tariffs against nonmembers, as well as customs unions that also include a common external tariff. In the latter case the WTO requires that the external tariff not increase the average protection against nonmember exports. That restriction does not, unfortunately, assure that PTAs are beneficial from the perspective of world welfare, since they still inevitably cause welfare reducing trade diversion as well as trade creation.[21] Since the proliferation of PTAs that began in the 1980s and 90s with the expansion of the European Union, the North American Free Trade Agreement, and arrangements such as ASEAN, APEC, and Mercósur, there has been controversy among economists as to their desirability. However, they are certainly a reality, and it was inevitable that the WTO, like the GATT, would permit them. Unfortunately the WTO has done little to increase the likelihood that the movement toward PTAs will be beneficial, as it could have done, for example, if it had done more to insist that PTAs stand ready to admit new members on the same terms as existing members.

VII. DISPUTE SETTLEMENT IN THE WTO

Agreements are worthless without enforcement. If the prisoners in the prisoners' dilemma were allowed to communicate, but were then separated again, they would surely agree to cooperate by not confessing. But if that is all they agree to, then once they are separated, they still have an incentive to break their agreement by confessing, regardless of whether each believes that the other will confess or not. On the other hand, if their agreement includes not only a commitment not to confess, but also a threat by each that if the other confesses they will manage, even though incarcerated, to do them harm, then cooperation may be sustained. What matters then is the seriousness of the threat and its credibility.

Similarly, the WTO involves a long list of commitments by the member countries, as we have seen above. But without some mechanism to enforce these agreements, countries will depart from them whenever they perceive it in their interest to do so, which it often will be. The first line of defense against violation of the WTO agreements is provided by the regular WTO bodies – the Councils and Committees mentioned above – where many disagreements can be resolved. As a last resort, however, the WTO includes a formal dispute settlement mechanism provides more explicit procedures for enforcing the agreements.

To be effective, an enforcement mechanism would ideally provide some sort of punishment to a defector from an agreement if and only if they do defect, and this punishment should be viewed as worse than any advantage they might otherwise get from defecting. It is critical that the punishment be highly correlated with defection, since the possibilities of defecting without being punished, and of being punished without defecting, both make defections more likely. In the complex world of trade policy, the hardest part of this may be the determination of whether or not a country has violated the agreement, and this is the main purpose of the WTO dispute settlement mechanism.

Once the mechanism has identified a violation of the WTO agreement, then the punishment that is supposed to follow, if the violation is not corrected, is the withdrawal of certain concessions that the offended country had previously made to the offending party. In practice this means that selected trade barriers will be raised against (and only against) the offending country.

The dispute settlement mechanism of the WTO works as follows. First, when one country believes that another is violating any aspect of the agreement (including GATS and TRIPs, as well as GATT), the complaining country first requests consultation with the offending country, and the two seek to resolve the dispute on their own. If consultation fails, then the complaining country requests establishment of a panel, consisting of three persons with appropriate expertise from countries not party to the dispute. This panel assesses the evidence in the context of its interpretation of the WTO rules and issues a report. This report is automatically accepted unless all WTO members, acting through their Dispute Settlement Body (DSB), decide by consensus against its adoption, or if one of the parties to the dispute voices its intention to appeal. Therefore, the process requires unanimity among WTO members *not* to accept a panel report, in marked contrast to the procedures of the old GATT, where a panel report could be blocked by any one country, including the country that was complained against.

To hear appeals, the WTO has established an Appellate Body, composed of seven members, of which three will serve on any given case. This Appellate Body is to consider only issues of law and legal interpretations by the panel, and it too issues a report which must be accepted except by a unanimous decision of the DSB.

Once this process is completed, countries are expected to implement any recommendations of the panel report. If they do not, then complaining countries are entitled to compensation from them, or to use suspension of concessions (usually increased trade barriers) against them. If suspension of concessions occurs, it is to be done preferably in the same sector as the dispute, or failing that under the terms of the same agreement (GATT, GATS, or TRIPs). But if this too is impractical, suspension can come under another agreement. Thus, in particular, violations of the TRIPs agreement can lead to increased barriers to trade in goods, if the violations are not corrected in accordance with the recommendations of a panel report. This ability to extend dispute settlement across agreements is one of the strengths of the WTO, and no doubt is one of the things that motivated advocates of extended intellectual property protection to incorporate it into the Uruguay Round negotiations.

One might think that this mechanism, with its ultimate reliance on suspension of concessions, would be defeating the purpose of the WTO. After all, the presumption is that the "concessions" made by WTO members have been for the general good, so that to respond to one violation by creating a second violation is just making matters worse. Two wrongs, we were taught as children, do not make a right.

But of course the hope is that suspension of concessions will rarely be needed – that countries will sometimes reach an understanding in the initial consultations, and that when they do not, the cases will be settled either by implementing the panel's recommendation or by compensation. Suspension of concessions is always the last resort. But it is the possibility of suspension that makes the rest of the process work. It is critical to achieving cooperation.

One might also think that this whole procedure should be unnecessary. Why not just threaten every member with expulsion from the WTO if they violate its rules? Surely the gains from membership are large enough that no member would risk expulsion from it. The difficulty here is that this threat is not credible.

Membership in the WTO is indeed valuable, so valuable in fact that the other members will be reluctant to set a precedent by expelling another, lest the same thing later happen to them.

Indeed, I would argue that the WTO dispute settlement mechanism comes reasonably close to the "tit for tat" strategy that Axelford (1983) has shown to be most successful in achieving cooperation in prisoner-dilemma games. It also comes as close as is probably possible to incorporating the four characteristics that Axelford argues are needed to foster cooperation: (1) clarity; (2) niceness; (3) provocability; and (4) forgiveness. The WTO rules are as clear as it has been possible to make them, and the panel and appellate body decisions as they begin to appear should make them clearer. Niceness is implicit in WTO membership, which presumes that countries initially do not set out to break the rules. But it is both quite possible to act in such a way that will lead to an adverse panel report (provocability), while at the same time a country can avoid retribution by ceasing its behavior (forgiveness).

VIII. CONCLUSION

The WTO has brought a remarkable degree of order to the world economy. While its precise structure to some extent still reflects the odd circumstances of its history, the institution as it is designed makes very good sense. Viewed as a facility for fostering cooperation in trade policy, set it in a world where underlying incentives are to use trade policies in beggar-thy-neighbor ways, the WTO appears to succeed admirably in providing the necessary tools for cooperation. It constructs a variety of channels through which countries can communicate. It lays out a detailed set of rules defining cooperative behavior, rules that are well-grounded in either economic theory or history so as to be acceptable to the member countries. It permits an assortment of exceptions to these rules, some of which are regrettable but all of which were probably necessary to make it possible for many countries to participate. And finally it creates a streamlined dispute settlement mechanism that seems well-tailored to encouraging cooperation and adaptation by the participating countries.

It is too early to know for sure how successful all of this will be. But the biggest danger for any international agreement is not that it will fail to be achieved (witness the success, in a sense, of the still-born International Trade Organization), but that it will be ignored. There are signs already that countries are turning increasingly to the WTO to settle disputes that earlier they would have handled bilaterally. And the list of countries seeking membership in the WTO continues to grow.[22] The world of international trade policy will probably never be truly peaceful, but the WTO offers our best hope that future competition in international trade will be productive, not destructive.

NOTES

The author has benefitted from frequent discussions of trade policy and the WTO with

John H. Jackson and Robert M. Stern. I am indebted as well to Joseph Francois and Bernard Hoekman for their insights into the WTO and their pointers to the literature dealing with it. I would also thank my discussants, Ernie Preeg and Chul-Su Kim, as well as other participates at the KEI conference, for corrections and suggestions that have improved the revised version of the paper.

1 In the classic prisoners' dilemma, two prisoners are suspected of jointly committing a crime, but neither has yet confessed. They are placed in separate rooms and told: (1) that if neither confesses both will go free; (2) that if both confess they will both be imprisoned; and (3) that if only one confesses, turning state's evidence against the other, that one will be positively rewarded, while the other will serve a longer prison term. Since each prisoner is better off confessing, given the action of the other (the reward is better than just going free, and the short prison term is better than the long one), the normal outcome in the absence of cooperation between the prisoners (called a Nash equilibrium) is for both to confess. Both could be better off than that equilibrium however, if they could somehow agree to cooperate and neither confess. However, such cooperation is bound to be difficult, since both have an incentive to break any agreement by confessing.

2 This paper will not attempt to cover every detail of the WTO agreements. For other somewhat more detailed summaries, see GATT (1993) and Martin and Winters (1995). Also, a very detailed presentation of the many components of the WTO is provided by both Hoekman (1995b) and Hoekman and Kostecki (1995). I have drawn heavily upon all three of these sources in preparing this paper.

3 I am using game theory here, and the prisoners' dilemma gave in particular, in only an informal and very loose way. As colleagues have pointed out, the strict framework of the simple prisoners' dilemma game does *not* imply the usefulness of at least some of the functions provided by the WTO. For example, if the prisoners' dilemma is a one-shot game, then getting the players together to discuss their actions will not help, since any agreement they make will be broken when they are separated. On the other hand, if the game is repeated indefinitely, then cooperation can arise after all spontaneously without anything like the WTO, out of fear of the consequences if a player defects. I am, however, less interested in the formal solutions to such abstract games than in using the game as a motivator for my exposition. Those who wish to relate the discussion to formal results in game theory should interpret my prisoners' dilemma game as one that occurs in real time, with multiple and continuous variables under the players' control, with uncertainty, and with whatever other realistic complications will suffice to make the game too difficult for my learned colleagues to solve.

4 For a more detailed history of the international trading system prior to the Uruguay Round, see Jackson (1989), which also includes detailed explanation of the structure of the GATT system. For a history of the Uruguay Round itself see Preeg (1995).

5 Other firms and developing countries that had quotas, however, might well lose from textile liberalization, as these quotas would lose their value.

6 The importance of such tradeoffs has been stressed by Hoekman (1989).

7 Communication also takes place outside the WTO, most importantly through the OECD. For example, it will be noted that the WTO says very little about foreign direct investment (FDI). The OECD is currently in the process of trying to design a multilateral code for FDI, which then might become a model for future agreement within the WTO. On this and other issues, the OECD Trade Committee plays an important role of helping to define the future negotiating agenda of the WTO.

8 GATT articles are numbered with Roman numerals.

9 The number of articles was increased to XXXVIII in the Kennedy Round that went into force in 1966, while additional agreements were negotiated as separate codes during the Tokyo Round.

10 Phytosanitary measures refer to the health of plants, while sanitary measures evidently refer to health of animals and people.
11 See Deardorff and Stern (1985, 1996).
12 QRs were banned under the GATT, but the ban was not effective especially in sensitive sectors.
13 The schedule for eliminating these quotas leaves the bulk of the trade to be liberalized only at the end of this ten-year period, and it leaves to the discretion of importing countries which product lines they liberalize before that. How successful this effort at liberalization will turn out to be therefore remains to be seen.
14 The simplest example in economic terms is the use of a subsidy to the production of a good that yields an external economic benefit for other parts of the economy. A more common and familiar example, however, is the use of a subsidy to promote growth of an infant industry.
15 Modern technologies have created other modes of delivery of some services, but it remains true that it is often difficult to observe traded services moving across national borders. See Hoekman and Stern (1991).
16 See Hoekman (1995a).
17 Although even here I suppose there could be some ambiguity. Does "not confess" mean not talk at all? Or does it permit talking, and if so, about what? Can the prisoner admit to being on the scene? And so forth. A skilful interrogator can no doubt exploit both ambiguities in any agreement, getting one to say more than intended while still not confessing, or using silence on some issues as itself incriminating.
18 See Finger (1993).
19 The injury test for safeguards is stronger than those for AD duties and CVDs.
20 See Deardorff (1987) for more discussion of the need for both discrimination and compensation in safeguards policies.
21 Trade creation occurs when members of a PTA import from each other what they previously produced themselves, presumably at higher cost. Trade diversion occurs when members import from each other what they previously imported from nonmembers, presumably a lower cost.
22 As of November 5, 1996, there were 125 members of the WTO, according to WTO (1996). An additional 31 have requested to join, and their applications are being considered. The latter include several cases that are bound to be difficult, such as the People's Republic of China, Chinese Taipei, and the Russian Federation. One of the challenges for the future of the WTO is how to deal with such major political and economic decisions as the admission of these countries.

REFERENCES

Axelrod, Robert 1983 *The Evolution of Cooperation*, New York: Basic Books.

Deardorff, Alan V. 1987 "Safeguards Policy and the Conservative Social Welfare Function," in H. Kierzkowski, ed., *Protection and Competition in International Trade*, Blackwell.

Deardorff, Alan V. and Robert M. Stern 1985 *Methods of Measurement of Non-Tariff Barriers*, United Nations Conference on Trade and Development. UNCTAD/ST/MD/28 (January).

Deardorff, Alan V. and Robert M. Stern. 1996. *Measurement of Nontariff Barriers*, report prepared for the Organization of Economic Cooperation and Development.

Dixit, Avinash K. 1996 *The Making of Economic Policy: A Transaction-Cost Politics Perspective*, Cambridge, MA: M.I.T. Press.

Finger, J. Michael, ed. 1993 *Antidumping: How It Works and Who Gets Hurt*, Ann Arbor: University of Michigan Press.

General Agreement on Tariffs and Trade (GATT) 1993 "The Final Act of the Uruguay Round," in *News of the Uruguay Round of Multilateral Trade Negotiations* 93–2180, (December 14), pp. 1–32.

Hoekman, Bernard 1989 "Determining the Need for Issue Linkages in Multilateral Trade Negotiations," *International Organization* 43, (Autumn), pp. 693–714.

Hoekman, Bernard 1995a "Assessing the General Agreement on Trade in Services," in Will Martin and L. Alan Winters, *The Uruguay Round and the Developing Economies*, World Bank Discussion Paper No. 307, pp. 327–364.

Hoekman, Bernard 1995b "Trade Laws and Institutions: Good Practices and the World Trade Organization," World Bank Discussion Paper No. 282, (April).

Hoekman, Bernard and Michel Kostecki 1995 *The Political Economy of the World Trading System*, Oxford, U.K.: Oxford University Press.

Hoekman, Bernard and Robert M. Stern 1991 "Evolving Patterns of Trade and Investment in Services," in Peter Hooper and J. David Richardson (eds.), *International Economic Transactions: Issues in Measurement and Empirical Research*, Chicago: University of Chicago Press for the NBER.

Jackson, John H. 1989 *The World Trading System*, Cambridge, MA: MIT Press.

Martin, Will and L. Alan Winters 1995 *The Uruguay Round: Widening and Deepening the World Trading System*, Washington, D.C.: The World Bank.

Preeg, Ernest H. 1995 *Traders in a Brave New World: The Uruguay Round and the Future of the International Trading System*, Chicago: University of Chicago Press.

WTP 1996 *The World Trade Organization (WTO)*, home page on the World Wide Web, http://www.unicc.org/wto/Welcome.html.

4. The End of the ITO

W. Diebold, Jr.

Trouble, violence and discontent marked the close of 1950. New fears swept the United States and its allies as MacArthur's troops retreated before the Chinese forces pouring across the Yalu. A remark by President Truman was misconstrued to mean he was planning to use the atomic bomb in Korea. Prime Minister Attlee flew to Washington to discover American intentions and, if necessary, to counsel caution. Asiatic countries asked the Chinese not to cross the 38th parallel; the American Chief of Staff flew to Tokyo to see General MacArthur who had just publicly questioned the orders that prevented him from bombing the enemy's "privileged sanctuary" in Manchuria. The House of Representatives voted new taxes. The President asked for still larger military appropriations. A price controller and a civil defense administrator were appointed during the first week of December.

Naturally, in such times, few paid much attention to a State Department press release about the international trade conference under way at Torquay, England. Yet there, almost lost in the long mimeographed sheet, a subordinate clause announced a major change in American trade policy. On the recommendation of the interested federal agencies, said the announcement, the President had agreed that "the proposed Charter for an International Trade Organization should not be resubmitted to the Congress. . . ."[1] In form the decision seemed one of administration tactics; with a crowded Congressional agenda, passage of a bill for customs simplification and the forthcoming renewal of the Trade Agreements Act were more urgent than a long debate on a trade convention that had been pending for several years. The decision meant that the United States was dropping the ITO Charter. Since no other governments wanted to create the trade organization without the United States, the most ambitious attempt ever made to reach agreement on a comprehensive code of rules for international trade quietly ended in failure.

More than nine years had passed since the Atlantic Charter registered the desire of the countries fighting fascism "to bring about the fullest collaboration between all nations in the economic field." The further formulation of that aim in pledges, commitments and institutions can be traced through the lend-lease agreements, wartime discussions, the Bretton Woods conference, the creation of the Food and Agriculture Organization and UNRRA, the Charter of the United Nations and the British loan agreement. All these acts pointed toward an eventual comprehensive agreement removing barriers to world trade. The Bretton Woods agreements, for instance, and the American act adhering to them, were premised on the forthcoming creation of effective arrangements for cooperation in international trade. Capstone, keystone, cornerstone were the words repeatedly used, but whatever the metaphor, an agreement on trade principles was to be an essential part of the structure of international economic cooperation.

That agreement was the Charter for an International Trade Organization. *Quellenforschung* aside, the Charter's history covers nearly five years of preparation in wartime, over two years of lengthy, laborious, full-dress negotiations that eventually involved over fifty governments, and then nearly three years more of waiting and arguing, ending with what an Italian journal has called a "second-class funeral" in the dying days of 1950.[2] There followed a coda as other governments chimed in and announced that in view of the American decision they would not act on the ITO Charter.

From the first, the ITO was primarily an American idea. Only constant drive from the United States turned sketchy projects into concrete proposals and brought the long negotiations to completion. As late as January 1950, in his State of the Union message, President Truman called for Congressional action on the proposed Charter. He echoed the language with which he had submitted it to Congress in April 1949: "This Charter is an integral part of the larger program of international economic reconstruction and development. . . An essential forward step in our foreign policy. . . ." Then, at the end of 1950, this favored American project was quietly dropped, and the American public, like the rest of the world, scarcely noticed its fall.

What had happened? How did it come about that this "necessary part" of the "solid foundation of continuous cooperation in economic affairs," as the President had called it, should now disappear "not with a bang, but a whimper"? The explanations seem to me to fall broadly into three categories: changes in the world setting between 1945 and 1950, the political situation in the United States, and the defects of the Charter from the point of view of American business. The pages that follow set out some of these explanations. They do not give a documented, play-by-play account of events. Many of the details are still locked away in archives or, in this telephone age, perhaps only in men's memories. Those that are published are available elsewhere. This is an essay in interpretation, not an historical narrative.

I. THE WORLD SETTING

The ITO appeared on the world stage in preliminary form in December 1945 when the American loan to Britain was negotiated.[3] The war was not long over. The postwar world which had excited so much hope and such thoughtful attempts to foresee its difficulties realistically was at hand. The United Nations was getting under way. The organs and arrangements for postwar international cooperation prepared so carefully while the battles still raged were now to come into their own. Soon, many hoped, they would dominate the scene. Plans for economic reconstruction usually envisaged a "transitional period" in which war damage would have to be repaired and dislocation set right. The United States was prepared to help. The time would be used, too, to create the most favorable possible conditions for the kind of international economic relations prescribed in the Bretton Woods agreements, the *Proposals* and other postwar plans. The economic aims of the recovery plans were well-phrased in Article VII of the lend-lease agreements. There was to be "expansion, by appropriate international and domestic measures, of production, employment and the exchange and consumption of goods, which are the material foundations of the liberty and welfare of all peoples." The victors would move toward "the elimination of all forms of discriminatory treatment in international commerce; to the reduction of tariffs and other trade barriers. . . ."

It would not be any easy task to create this kind of a world, but with good will, care, effort and some luck it could be done; that was the prevalent mood. There were danger signals. Lend-lease had been cut off abruptly, before arrangements had been made to ease our European allies, and particularly the United Kingdom, into a position where they could pay for essential imports. The strains and suspicions of the wartime alliance with Soviet Russia were growing; Potsdam had not been a pleasant conference. The ITO itself was very late; negotiations should have been much farther advanced before peace set in. Yet it was an essential part of the structure. Clair Wilcox, chairman of the United States delegation, put the dominant view clearly at the outset of the first ITO negotiations in London in October 1946:

> Of the many tasks of economic reconstruction that remain, ours is by all odds the most important. Unless we bring this work to completion, the hopes of those builders who preceded us can never be fulfilled. If the peoples who now depend upon relief are soon to become self-supporting, if those who now must borrow are eventually to repay, if currencies are permanently to be stabilized, if workers on farms and in factories are to enjoy the highest possible levels of real income, if standards of nutrition and health are to be raised, if cultural interchange is to bear fruit in daily life, the world must be freed, in large measure, of the barriers that now obstruct the flow of goods and services. If political and economic order is to be rebuilt, we must provide, in our world trade charter, the solid foundation upon which the superstructure of international cooperation is to stand.

Few questioned the need for some kind of trade organization. The great differences of opinion were about the powers the international body should have, the practices that were to be outlawed, the extent to which existing trade barriers were to be lowered, and how soon the rules were to come into play for countries whose economic position had been seriously damaged by the war. This last issue became familiar in the ITO negotiations as the question of what exceptions to the general rules should be provided for countries in balance-of-payments difficulties. For Western Europe a large part of the answer – perhaps most of it, according to the thinking of 1945 and 1946 – depended on how much financial aid the United States was prepared to give. Unless the help were adequate, the European governments saw no chance of reducing trade barriers and ending discrimination; with substantial aid, and the further protection of escape clauses if their difficulties recurred, they could look forward, with varying degrees of hope and skepticism, to a successful transition period after which an agreement liberalizing international trade could come fully into play. It was no accident that the ITO *Proposals* were launched at the time the British loan was negotiated. Britain and the United States were the key countries, without whose concerted action a world trade agreement would be sadly restricted, if it were workable at all. The loan agreement was a kind of capsule of the prevalent thinking about the postwar world economy. The joint statement on commercial policy, which supported the ITO *Proposals*,[4] stood for the economic world that was to be; the loan was a substantial fraction of the American aid that was to make that world possible.

By March 1948, when the *Draft Charter for an International Trade Organization* was signed at Havana, the postwar world had shown itself to be quite different from that envisaged in 1945. European reconstruction had proved to be a harder task than was expected. Prewar levels of production had been reached in many fields but were proving inadequate to satisfy the postwar expectations of Europeans plus the need for increased exports. The transition period was obviously going to be longer than that contemplated in 1945. What it was a transition to was becoming doubtful. Relations between the United States and the USSR had changed from uneasy alliance to cold war. Communists seized control of the government of Czechoslovakia just a month before the Charter was signed. When the negotiators came home from Havana, Congress was debating the Marshall Plan which registered two major changes in postwar plans: more American aid for Western Europe and a stronger political motive for providing it.

The hopes embodied in the ITO were not dead, but they were dimmed. The Marshall Plan showed that the period during which governments would be in financial troubles requiring the continued use of trade controls was likely to last for a while yet. The ITO negotiations themselves showed how important the exceptions to the rules favoring liberal trade had become. The political alignment of the cold war was not a serious barrier to putting the Charter into effect. Few had expected that Russia would join the organization.[5] Czechoslovakia, which had participated throughout the negotiations, signed the Charter; Poland came to Havana but did not sign. In any case, the Iron Curtain countries accounted for a very small part of world trade; the ITO could work without them. On the other hand, the ITO had little to contribute to the cold war. It could be argued that in the long run international trade on the ITO pattern would strengthen the free world and make it a better place to live in, but that was a distant prospect. For the immediate future the attraction lay in measures, like the Marshall Plan, that promised quick political and economic gains. Any immediate benefits from removing trade barriers could be obtained through the General Agreement on Tariffs and Trade (GATT), negotiated in 1947 as an interim arrangement pending adoption of the ITO.

In the circumstances, the ITO lacked urgency. No one could argue that its main principles would quickly take effect and change the face of the free world's economy. The opposition to Soviet policy that had helped pass economically enlightened measures like the British loan and the Marshall Plan did not generate support for the ITO. The Administration had its hands full getting other measures through Congress and could see no gain in loading one more controversial item onto a crowded schedule. As a result, the Charter was held over until the new

Congress met in 1949. In April of that year President Truman sent the Charter to the Hill and asked for a joint resolution authorizing American participation. But by then Congress was busy with the North Atlantic Treaty, the Military Defense Assistance Program, and legislation for the second year of ECA. The Administration apparently agreed with Congressional leaders that it was better not to press for quick action on the ITO since these other foreign affairs measures took precedence. The slight recession of mid-1949 brought on a series of complaints about unemployment allegedly traceable to imports, thus helping to create a poor atmosphere for the ITO. Not until April and May 1950 did the House Committee on Foreign Affairs hold hearings on the joint resolution. The Committee did not report, and the matter never came to the floor of the House.

By the end of 1950, when the ITO was dropped, all these factors had intensified. Americans, and their United Nations allies, were fighting in Korea. General Eisenhower was getting ready to take command of a new allied headquarters in Europe. The United States was feeling its way toward some kind of mobilization economy. The aspirations of 1945 seemed more remote than ever. The Charter was adrift in a world for which it was never made.

II. AMERICAN POLITICS AND THE ITO

Depression is traditionally a poor time to get acceptance of trade barrier education. Yet the Reciprocal Trade Agreement Act, the most effective step the United States has taken to reduce its tariffs in at least half a century, was put up to Congress in 1933 and passed in 1934, both depression years. Part of the explanation is that the Act was presented largely as a means of fostering exports, and so helping recovery, by breaking down foreign trade barriers. It was presented as a contrast to the Hawley-Smoot Tariff, the retaliations which followed it and the increased use of quotas and exchange controls by foreign countries to close markets to American goods. While Cordell Hull always emphasized that trade was "a two-way street" and stressed the element of reciprocity in the program, it was the prospect of larger exports, not larger imports, that won votes for the bill.

Even more important was the Democratic landslide of 1932 and the composition of the new Administration. In power for the first time since Woodrow Wilson, the victors naturally felt that Democratic policies should be substituted for Republican ones in as many fields as possible. The tariff was an issue on which the tradition of party difference was strong. This may have been something of a myth, at least in the twentieth century, but in some circumstances it could be an effective myth. The traditional Democratic attitude toward the tariff, together with newer ideas for making the policy effective by keeping the tariff out of Congress, were embodied in Cordell Hull, the Secretary of State. Hull's position was particularly strong as an alumnus of Congress and a leading figure in what became the conservative wing of the Democratic party, a key element in the coalition by which Roosevelt kept power. Hull won a sharp fight within the Administration on the kind of trade policy to be advocated and thereafter the field was his. The Trade Agreements Program was not part of the mainstream of economic and social reform of the New Deal. It had a different logic from the NRA, the AAA, and the monetary policy that upset the London Economic Conference, and it clashed concretely with those measures at certain points. Still, its rationale was politically effective, and it is an aspect of the New Deal's pluralism and eclecticism that the break from existing trade policy should have taken this form.

Once enacted, the Trade Agreements Program gained the advantages of inertia that belong to "established policy." The President's power to cut tariffs was used very cautiously. It was concentrated on "excessive protection," the tariff margin that American producers did not need to compete successfully against lower-cost imports. The selective cutting of rates provided a degree of flexibility that could also be used, when necessary, to temper the program to the requirement of votes for renewal every three years. Mr Hull continued to regard the Trade Agreements Program as a major feature of his foreign policy. Mr Roosevelt continued to back Hull. The American electorate continued to give Roosevelt large majorities. The Democratic members of the House and Senate continued to follow the leadership of the White House. After war broke out in 1939, the impact of tariff reductions was reduced. Then the Trade Agreements Program became linked to war aims and probably gained a certain amount of support – or at least avoided some overt opposition – on this count. It costs little to vote for an inoperative ideal.

The general pattern of the legislative history of the Trade Agreements Act and its renewals in Hull's and Roosevelt's time was about as follows. The initiative and main drive for the program came from the State Department. Renewal of the Act was regularly a "must" on the President's list of requests to Congress. A minority of the Democrats in Congress opposed the program, for the most part because of protectionist sentiment in their constituencies. The majority that supported the program included men who favored its principles or whose constituencies included an active export or trading interest, and also a number of "doubtful" Senators and Representatives who might well have voted against the Act on one ground or another, or at least remained indifferent to it, had it not been for the arsenal that a strong Administration has at its command when "must" legislation is at issue. To determine how great the otherwise "doubtful" vote was would require careful analysis of the votes at each renewal[6] but there is little doubt that it was sizable and that in some years, at least, the Administration's ability to sway it was decisive in continuing the Trade Agreements Program.

Though there was always some Republican support for the Trade Agreements Program, most of that party's representatives in Congress usually voted against renewal. When the Trade Agreements Act came before a Republican Congress for the first time, in 1948, the President's power was circumscribed by the introduction of "peril points" below which he could not reduce duties without explaining his action to Congress. This provision was eliminated in 1950 but made its reappearance – along with other limitations – in the 1951 renewal, when there was a Democratic majority no longer so strongly under the influence of the White House as in Roosevelt's presidency and when the Secretary of State's status on the Hill was not what Mr Hull's had been.[7]

This rough sketch of the political pattern on which the Trade Agreements Act depended helps us to understand some of the ITO's difficulties. The issues were not identical, of course. The Charter covered a broader field and entailed new obligations. One might, therefore, support the Trade Agreements Program while opposing the Charter.[8] Important segments of the business community did just this and thereby played a significant part in bringing about the demise of the ITO.

What these businessmen did not like about the ITO is the subject of the next section. The fact that the merchant and export groups who regularly supported the Trade Agreements Act were split over the ITO removed an important prop on which the Administration's case with Congress would otherwise have rested. It is impossible to say that business opposition meant so-or-so many votes in Congress and thus made passage of the ITO resolution impossible. Only the Administration officials and Congressmen who engaged in the actual head-counting that must have preceded the decision to drop the matter could estimate that. Perhaps we shall someday learn how close the count stood, what the pattern of support and opposition was, who might have been brought around if the Truman Administration had possessed the persuasive forces the Roosevelt Administration used to have. Lacking that, we do not even know for a certainty that the crucial votes may not have been those of a few men whose unwillingness to support the Administration in this matter may have rested on considerations irrelevant to the Charter. Certainly the Republican gains in the elections of November 1950 added to the Administration's difficulties in mustering support for the ITO.

In any case the opposition of certain business groups was undoubtedly a major factor in the defeat of the ITO. The loss of business support worked in two ways. Congressmen close to the business groups and likely to be much influenced by their views became opponents instead of supporters of the ITO. It was not only their votes that were lost but also their help in the intra-Congressional discussion and log-rolling which are so important in putting through a measure of this sort on which there is a sizable doubtful vote. Secondly, the more or less neutral Representatives and Senators, whose convictions and whose constituents' direct interests were not already heavily committed, would be much harder to rally in support of the ITO if they saw that major groups directly affected by the measure were opposed or uninterested. Of course, certain business groups had regularly opposed the Trade Agreements Program but it was kept alive despite them. Not their opposition, but the opposition of merchants and manufacturers who had supported the Trade Agreements Program, marked the difference in the position of the ITO Charter before Congress.

Apart from this shift in business support, the line-up for and against the Charter was similar to that called forth by the Trade Agreements Program in recent years. Except for America's Wage Earners' Protective Conference – the protectionist wing of the AF of L – and certain unions in protected industries, labor generally supported the Charter, but acceptance of the ITO was not a major concern of either the CIO or the AF of L. The American Farm Bureau Federation and the National Farmers Union supported the Charter while the Grange hedged. The farmers' main foreign trade bogey was laid by provisions, introduced into the Charter on American initiative, permitting the use of import quotas in connection with farm programs. Farmers had an interest in the removal of foreign trade barriers on their exports, but the ITO did not promise enough immediate action to stimulate much enthusiasm. Many civic organizations and women's groups endorsed the ITO, and some committees were organized especially to urge American adherence to it, but the Charter's length and complexity, among other things, prevented it from becoming an object of great public interest.

Professional economists and academic people concerned with foreign affairs for the most part favored the ITO, but usually with explicit recognition of its limitations and often with a feeling that it was desirable principally because the other possible alternatives were so unattractive. This somewhat reserved attitude, stemming from the Charter's mixture of high principle with detailed compromises that were distasteful, even if necessary, checked the growth of enthusiastic activity among independent liberals. Even those who had a firm conviction that acceptance of the imperfect Charter was in the American interest admitted that the ITO might not work out as they hoped. Beneath these doubts and reservations was the realization that the Charter was an attempt – a necessary and proper attempt, but one whose chances of success were inevitably uncertain – to bridge a gap between a doctrine of the sound ordering of international trade and a situation in which many of the premises of that doctrine were no longer valid. This was an understanding, and in my opinion correct, view of the matter, but it was not one to generate the kind of political steam needed to pass the Charter.

Two other factors probably played a part in reducing the ITO's chances of success. Great export crops like cotton and tobacco were no longer quite so important as they had been in the South, traditional home of Democratic free trade attitudes. Foreign aid programs were helping to provide current export markets. Peanuts, meat and dairy products were providing a growing share of the South's farm output industry, especially the manufacture of textiles, was expanding. Some of these new activities, instead of increasing the South's interest in exports, were protected from foreign competition by tariffs and other import controls. So the South could no longer be counted on for solid support on measures aimed at reducing trade barriers. The other factor was that the ITO lacked a backer of the political power of Cordell Hull who could have mobilized more active support for the ITO within the Administration. Nor did any postwar Secretary of State have as great a personal interest in trade barrier reduction as had Hull.

While it is hard to judge how important each of these many factors was, there can be little doubt that business opposition and the Administration's lack of influence with Congress, compared to Roosevelt's day go far to explain why the Charter was dropped. It remains to explain the business attitudes.

III. BUSINESS CRITICISM OF THE ITO

The men who propounded the ITO were trying to be very realistic. They wanted to avoid the errors which had led to the failure of many efforts to remove the world trade barriers in the 'twenties and 'thirties. They were also anxious to produce an agreement that would be acceptable to a large number of countries. These praiseworthy efforts contained the seeds of the ITO's failure.

Thought about the postwar world began early in the Second World War. Those who planned and who thought about plans tried to find guidance in the peace settlement after the First World War and in its unsatisfactory aftermath. They were especially bent on avoiding "the errors of last time." Perhaps they were too much influenced by what they thought of the past and failed to show enough ingenuity and imagination in anticipating some of the less attractive possibilities of the postwar world. However that may be, two conclusions from the inter-war experience with international trade policy had great influence it shaping the ITO.

One was that many of the interwar efforts to remove trade barriers had failed because international conferences had limited themselves too much to recommending the endorsement of broad principles, leaving it to each government to act according to the exigencies of its position. As a result, little came of the pledges to reduce trade barriers. This lesson the drafters of the ITO Charter tried to apply by making their document detailed, and including in it specific commitments to avoid particular trade practices except under certain extenuating circumstances, which they also tried to specify.

The second conclusion was that "commercial policy cannot be considered by itself. . . . It must be considered as a part of the more general constructive policies agreed among governments for the prevention (or mitigation) of economic depressions and assurance of social stability."[9] Moreover, in the past the emphasis on tariffs, quotas, taxes, subsidies, etc., slighted the special problems of raw materials that gave rise to private or public commodity agreements and left out of account cartels, monopolies, and private restrictive practices in international trade. Wartime developments stressed and gave immediacy to this view of the weaknesses of the older approach. One or another governments were committing themselves to "full employment" as the primary and overriding aim of national economic policy. Plans abounded for bringing "stability" to the world's raw material markets. Economic warfare and the seizure of alien property were producing reams of material on cartel connections and practices, many of them linked to German aggression.

Therefore, the drafters of the ITO gave their creation a much broader scope than any previous international trade agreement. There were to be detailed rules not only for tariffs, quotas, exchange controls and state trading, but also for international commodity agreements and inter-governmental measures to check restrictive trade practices. Provisions concerning the maintenance of full employment in each country and the avoidance of policies that would create unemployment abroad were left rather general because no one could devise detailed provisions likely to be acceptable to fifty governments.

The desirability of including such a wide range of subjects in the Charter was emphasized by widely-held views in other countries. There, as the American drafters knew, employment policy and raw materials problems were considered much more important than the removal of trade barriers. To make substantial progress in the removal of trade barriers it seemed necessary to show that the United States was not proposing merely to get rid of quotas and reduce tariffs without regard to other conditions affecting international trade. The League report noted above had spoken of "the absolute necessity of adapting commercial policies to the circumstances influencing national balances of payments." Wartime conversations with the British had made it clear that there was no hope of any comprehensive trade agreement's being adopted unless there were escape clauses for countries in balance-of-payments difficulties. The Chapultepec Conference of 1945 had emphasized that economically underdeveloped countries were unwilling to talk about removing trade barriers unless it were very clear that their infant industries were exempted. The United States itself was not prepared to accept the logic of a liberal foreign trade policy in all fields, notably agriculture and shipping. How far it would go in the reduction of tariffs remained to be seen.

Casting a shadow on all calculation and discussion was the fear that when the insatiable war demand ended, the United States would plunge into depression. Apart from the special problem of reconversion, it was also widely held that the American economy was inherently unstable and might at any time in the future set off another world depression. Foreign countries naturally wanted to protect themselves, though the means of doing this were far from clear and the chances of success none too good. But the apprehension colored the attitude of many governments, leading them to look for possible safeguards against too close a link with the United States and in any case to demand a free hand to try to protect themselves against an American depression by the use of trade and exchange controls.

Recognizing all this, the drafters of the ITO tried from the first to make their proposals "realistic," by recognizing the limits on governments' willingness to carry out liberal trading principles, and by trying to reach agreement on terms and procedures for applying exceptions to the basic rules laid down in the Charter. This, they felt, was better than proposing a rigid body of principles which would not be carried out by the signatories. Moreover, they wanted to show from the first that the United States understood the difficulties of less favored countries and was prepared to try to accommodate them in the proposed trade organization.

These endeavors – to be specific, to be comprehensive, and to recognize the problems of other countries – explain much of the character of the ITO. The Charter's length, its complexity, and the mixture of general principles with extensive lists of exceptions to them, all stem from these efforts. The American policy that led to these results was understandable, consciously arrived at with a recognition of the risks involved, and seemed to most informed observers at the same time to be the only course feasible if the aim was to get a charter acceptable to enough governments to cover a substantial portion of world trade. But this essay does not aim at re-arguing the case or suggesting whether another course of action would have produced better results (or of judging what "better" results would be).[10] Here the significant point is that the effort to be realistic produced a document that proved to be unacceptable to that reputed arch-realist, the American businessman.

Business opposition to commercial policies that are alleged to go too far in removing trade barriers is an old story. The new element in this case was the opposition the Charter met from businessmen who felt it did not go far enough in removing trade barriers. The people who took this view were not primarily concerned about the effect of the Charter on American trade barriers. Their objection was that the Charter would do little to remove the trade barriers set up by foreign countries and might even strengthen some of them. The essence of this view was that the exceptions to the Charter's general rules, and the escape clauses applicable to special circumstances, were so numerous that most foreign countries could comply with the Charter without actually freeing trade from existing restrictions. Moreover, the businessmen who took this view usually also believed that the Charter went too far in subordinating the international commitments of signatory countries to the requirements – real or imagined - of national economic plans and policies. They believed, too, that the Charter was too heavily laden with the ideological and practical paraphernalia of government regulation and control, so that it would not help, and very likely would hinder, the development of private enterprise. In short, the businessmen who took these views held that the Charter was not "liberal" enough and not "internationalist" enough. Because of their emphasis on these imperfections in the Charter, and their desire for an instrument that approached nearer to their ideals of economic policy, it will be convenient, and not too unfair, to call this group the "perfectionists," in contrast to the "protectionists" who opposed the Charter for quite different reasons, and about whom I shall say a word later in this essay.

There have always been people who felt that the Trade Agreements Program was too modest to make a major contribution to the improvement of world trade. But they supported it for what help it could be, and because the alternative seemed a less liberal policy. That perfectionist sentiment should be important enough to constitute a major influence on the shaping of American commercial policy, and that it should work *against* a measure designed to remove trade barriers, are something new in American politics.

Protectionists aside, not all business groups took the perfectionist view. The National Council of American Importers supported adherence to the Charter because "the United States and the world have more to gain than to lose by its acceptance. . . ." The Committee for Economic Development recommended that the Charter be adopted if the provisions concerning international investment were eliminated. Other businessmen, acting as individuals or as members of such organizations as the National Planning Association and the Committee for the International Trade Organization, also supported American adherence. But the United States Chamber of Commerce, the National Association of Manufacturers, the National Foreign Trade Council and the United States Council of the International Chamber of Commerce all opposed the Charter. The NAM and the U.S. Chamber of Commerce are the largest of the business organizations; their position on international economic matters is not easily predictable since their membership includes firms benefiting from tariff protection as well as those favoring freer foreign trade. The U.S. Council of the ICC is traditionally internationally-minded. The National Foreign Trade Council, made up exclusively of firms concerned with foreign trade and investment, is generally regarded as the principal spokesman for the foreign trade community as a whole. The Council has been a consistent supporter of the Trade Agreements Program and still maintains that position. The difficulty the Council had in reaching a conclusion about what stand to take on the ITO may be guessed from the remarkable fact that the *Final Declaration* of the Thirty-fifth National Foreign Trade Convention held by the Council in November 1948 said not a word about the ITO, though it contained recommendations on twenty-one subjects, including many suggestions for executive or legislative action and a thirteen-page essay on the conference's theme: Private Enterprise is the World's Best Hope. A few weeks later the Council came out against the Charter. Additional evidence of divided counsels is the presence of some businessmen on the committees or boards of several organizations, some of which endorsed the Charter while others opposed it.

The attitude of the business groups opposing the Charter on non-protectionist grounds varied somewhat in the emphasis given to one argument of another, and in the interpretation of certain parts of the Charter. Nevertheless the common ground was wide enough so that a survey of its main features can stand as a sketch of the perfectionist position without great violence to the views of any one group.[11]

The perfectionists did not seriously object to the principles of trade policy laid down in the Charter. Their complaint was that the principles were not carried out. The exceptions and escape clauses seemed so numerous and extensive that the Charter held little promise of leading to the removal of trade barriers. Objections were particularly strong to the complicated rules sanctioning the use of import quotas – sometimes discriminatory ones – by countries in balance-of-payments difficulties. True, many governments were already engaging in such practices but in the Bretton Woods Agreements and elsewhere most nations had professed their desire to eliminate controls as soon as they could safely do so. The Charter, according to the view of these business groups, made no progress along this road; it was more likely to perpetuate the undesirable practices and so seemed a step toward the restriction of trade, not its liberation.

Two special considerations gave a particular edge to this argument. One was the prevalent view among businessmen that economic difficulties could not be cured by exchange controls and quotas. Convertibility, freer trade and freer play for the profit and price system seemed to them essential for the adjustments that national economies had to undergo; at some point each country would have to take the medicine of such a course; perpetuation of the controls only delayed the day and made the dose harder to swallow. The second consideration arose out of Article 21, paragraph 4(b) of the Charter which appeared to mean that no country could be required to alter policies directed toward the maintenance of full employment or the promotion of economic development even if these created balance-of-payments difficulties. This looked like a perfect loophole for the indefinite retention of controls, especially since most of the businessmen believed that government-sponsored full employment polices were bound, if they worked, to be inflationary and so to exercise pressure on foreign exchange reserves. Moreover, the way to engineer balance-of-payments difficulties seemed not only paved but marked.

In the matter of full employment, the business groups objected to the principles they saw in the Charter. The articles on employment were rather general and somewhat vague because, it will be recalled, the negotiators had felt the need to recognize the link between trade and employment but had not found any precise rules acceptable to all governments. When Administration spokesmen pointed out that the language of the ITO Charter's provisions conformed to American legislation and that obligations were carefully qualified to allow each country to find its own way of maintaining a high level of economic activity, the businessmen answered that if the employment provisions meant nothing they had better be left out of the Charter. Otherwise, governments that put faith in them were bound to be disappointed. Furthermore, the provisions might be read as relieving countries of all their obligations concerning trade policy in times of recession, and particularly if the recession occurred in the United States. The businessmen were really concerned about more than the ITO Charter. Their criticisms reflected general uneasiness about the implications of statements that governments were responsible for the level of employment. In part, their attitude was a carryover from the domestic debate at the time of the passage of the Employment Act of 1946 when the proposition that the United States Government should commit itself to maintaining "full employment" had become a symbol of government intervention, the New Deal, the welfare state and all the other large issues that had disturbed American political economy since the depression. To some extent, indeed, the presence of the employment provisions may have stood for the businessmen as an indication that the Charter was not a trade-liberalizing document of the traditional sort, but an instrument linked to planning and government control.

Concern over governmental controls also led the perfectionists to oppose the Charter's chapter on international commodity agreements. The aim of the chapter was to limit the use of such agreements to certain circumstances, to specify what might be done under a commodity agreement, and to establish rules that would insure fair treatment, for instance by requiring equal representation for consumers as well as producers. Prewar commodity agreements had not come up to these standards. Nevertheless, the business groups were inclined to oppose the whole chapter on the ground that it went too far in sanctioning governmental restriction of production and regulation of trade. "Private cartels are bad, . . . government cartels are worse," read a statement by the National Association of Manufacturers.

As to the sections of the Charter dealing with private cartels and restrictive practices, the attitude of the business groups was a little less clear cut. They all abjured restriction and took a stand in favor of competition. But they were dubious of the Charter provisions. On the one hand there seems to have been some feeling that the scope of the provisions was uncertain, so that governments or international agencies might interpret them to ban useful business arrangements as well as undesirable ones. On the other hand, the fact that the Charter's provisions left each government with a good bit of discretion in the enforcement of the ban on restrictive practices suggested to the business critics that the rules would turn out to mean different things in different countries. What one government held to be legal another might ban. The result would be not only confusion and legal uncertainty, but an advantage for one businessman over his foreign competitor. Underlying this concern was the suspicion that an active Anti-Trust Division in the United States would be diligent in the prosecution of cases, while in Western Europe and elsewhere general tolerance of cartels and industrial agreements would result in the acceptance of quite a different standard of business behavior.

One of the greatest stumbling blocks for the business groups was the Charter's treatment of investment. The Committee for Economic Development, which accepted the rest of the Charter, objected to the articles on this subject. The basic complaint was that the Charter did not provide private foreign investments with any firm protection against confiscation or discrimination by governments. The crucial passages were full of adjectives like "just," "reasonable," and "appropriate." Nothing was done to check the freedom of action of countries receiving foreign investment to decide what investment to permit and on what terms. So far as equal treatment was concerned, governments merely undertook "to give due regard to the desirability of avoiding discrimination as between foreign investments."

Such provisions, said the businessmen, were worse than nothing at all. "This article not only affords no protection for foreign investments of the United States but it would leave them with less protection than they now enjoy."[12] By committing itself to the Charter, ran this argument, the United States would give up its right to take independent action to protect American investors. Acceptance of the Charter would weaken the efforts being made publicly and privately to create a proper "climate" for private investment. This would discourage private capital and postpone the day when the governments of underdeveloped countries would come to realize that in their own interests they would have to provide more freedom and security for potential investors.

There was a good bit of irony in this situation. The offensive passages would not have been in the Charter at all if it had not been for the efforts of American business. The first drafts of the Charter had said nothing about investment. American business groups complained to the State Department about this omission. Foreign investment, they pointed out, was an important factor in international trade; moreover, as the main potential source of capital the United States had an interest in seeing to it that a sound legal framework should be constructed that would encourage investment. State Department officials, resisting these suggestions, undoubtedly pointed out that the chances were poor of getting the kind of investment provisions the businessmen wanted. The United States was already having to bargain hard on the trade provisions. Safeguards for investment worked out by a sizable group of nations, many of them underdeveloped, were likely to be much weaker than those that might be arrived at in bilateral negotiations with countries anxious to have American capital for their development. The elaboration of a comprehensive investment code might prove at least as complicated as the working out of the trade charter, which had already taken several years.

However, the business groups stuck to their position, the State Department finally yielded, and the American representatives at the Geneva conference proposed an article on investment. Its final version, reached only after difficult negotiations, "instead of promising to stimulate the flow of private capital, threatened to check it," according to Clair Wilcox, head of the American delegation.[13] So the subject was reopened at the final conference in Havana and, after another round of hard bargaining, new articles were substituted. No one claimed the new provisions went very far toward providing what American business wanted but the representative of the National Association of Manufacturers at Havana called them "the most important gains made by the United States delegation" and said that they "offer foreign investors greater protection than they ever had previously against unjust, arbitrary acts by governments." On further reflection, the National Association of Manufacturers and other business groups rejected this view and made the investment provisions one of their main targets in attacking the Charter.

It is not the purpose of this essay to discuss the validity of the businessmen's criticisms of the Charter, some of which are open to serious objection. Supporters of the Charter maintained that the compromises to which the perfectionists objected were essential to any comprehensive trade agreement. They claimed that within the framework of the ITO the United States could work for improvement of the unsatisfactory provisions and could check the abuse of escape clauses. The business groups disagreed. They saw the whole history of Charter negotiations as a retreat from what the United States wanted (or ought to want) and held that if the ITO were set up the process would continue. Since each government would have only one vote under the Charter, they thought it certain that the United States would consistently be on the losing end of the arguments, with debtor countries, or control-minded governments, or underdeveloped countries, or countries in balance-of-payments difficulties, combining to defeat it on major issues.

The businessmen thought the Charter too one-sided to be of any great commercial value to them. Tariff reductions made by the United Stated would be effective, and this country would be bound by the general provisions of the Charter. But most other countries, being in balance-of-payments difficulties, or underdeveloped, or in need of special measures for economic reconstruction, would be able to take advantage of the exceptions. They would maintain barriers on the importation of American goods and would be allowed to discriminate against exports from this country. Their tariff concessions would mean little because their trade would be held down by quotas and exchange controls. Supporters of the Charter pointed out that the countries in question were doing these things anyhow. Failure to adopt the ITO would not improve matters, while the Charter's exceptions at least laid down rules to govern the application of trade restrictions, provided means of policing them, and gave some hope of eventually getting rid of the restrictions as world economic conditions improved. But the perfectionists would not accept this reasoning. They took the view that by ratifying the Charter the United States would be sanctioning these undesirable trade practices. It would not only have agreed that they were right in principle but would have given up the freedom to use its own economic strength to press for the removal of the foreign controls.

The whole perfectionist case was clearly summarized in one paragraph by the Executive Committee of the United States Council of the International Chamber of Commerce in its *Statement of Position* on the Charter:

> It is a dangerous document because it accepts practically all of the policies of economic nationalism; because it jeopardizes the free enterprise system by giving priority to centralized national governmental planning of foreign trade; because it leaves a wide scope to discrimination, accepts the principle of economic insulation and in effect commits all members of the ITO to state planning for full employment. From the point of view of the United States, it has the further very grave defect

> of placing this country in a position where it must accept discrimination against itself while extending the Most-Favored-Nation treatment to all members of the Organization. It places the United States in a permanent minority position owing to its one-vote-one-country voting procedure. Because of that, membership in the ITO based on this Charter would make it impossible for the United States to engage in an independent course of policy in favor of multilateral trade.

This is strong language. It is worth bearing in mind that by the time this and similar statements were written the business groups were actively working against the Charter. Blunt, categorical and rather extreme statements may have seemed more effective than more balanced analyses. Provisions that in other circumstances might have been regarded as dubious but tolerable because they were necessary parts of an acceptable compromise could be denounced as violations of fundamental principles once it had been decided to oppose the Charter. But we cannot be sure that tactical considerations of this sort provide the principal explanation of the all-out condemnation of the Charter by the perfectionists. Many American businessmen – especially when they come together in a group – seem to feel that their constant combat against "government control," "socialism," and the like requires the propagation of basic principles in very clear, simple and absolute terms. Naturally, these statements depict a world in which blacks and whites appear to be more sharply defined than they are in fact. Sore subjects excite extremism; many postwar statements about free enterprise have been heavily freighted with ideology. It is not always easy to tell when these statements are setting out utopian ideals and when they are describing a state of affairs the business groups think is really attainable. Because the drafters and negotiators of the ITO Charter were trying to bridge gaps between different kinds of economic systems and different philosophies of economic organization, their document inevitably diverged considerably from the pure principles subscribed to by many American businessmen. Tactics apart, this taint undoubtedly played its part in stimulating the perfectionist reaction.

Statements made in 1950 were also colored by the hopeful signs the businessmen saw in the improvement in Western Europe's payments position (even before Korea), the defeat of socialist governments in several countries (including Australia and New Zealand), and a wide-spread relaxation of governmental controls. The devaluations of September 1949 were regarded as a big step toward equilibrium in international trade. The difficulties of low production and dollar shortage that lay behind many of the ITO's exceptions and escape clauses were held to be largely overcome. Therefore, some perfectionists felt, the Charter was "now obsolete." The same evidence could have been used to demonstrate that the Charter as it stood would be less obnoxious than the perfectionists claimed because, as their payments positions improved, governments would lose the right to invoke many of the escape clauses.

The Administration took the view that the Charter would have to be accepted as it stood; reservations would invite similar action by other governments, pulling apart the agreement already reached; renegotiation was impossible. "For better or worse," wrote Clair Wilcox, the Havana Charter "is the only charter that can be considered or adopted by the nations of the world."[14] The perfectionists did not disagree. They felt they had shot their bolt on modifications of the Charter in proposals made during the course of negotiations. Their suggestions as to what the United States should do instead of ratifying the agreement came almost as an afterthought, produced under questioning by their critics. The National Foreign Trade Council simply urged action under the Trade Agreements Act, the negotiation of more commercial treaties, and pushing ahead with Point Four. The other business groups also supported the idea of making more bilateral agreements on trade with countries willing to accept principles the United States could endorse. The National Association of Manufacturers and the U.S. Council of the International Chamber of Commerce suggested that a commercial policy commission under the United Nations Economic and Social Council might provide a means of advancing the interests of multilateral trade on sound principles. The U.S. Chamber of Commerce proposed an agreement limited to strictly trade matters, centering on a simple statement of basic principles, containing a declaration in favor of free enterprise, including no restrictions on domestic freedom of action of member countries, and operating with a system of weighted voting. Such an agreement, they thought, might be negotiated by representative business delegations under the aegis of the International Chamber of Commerce, thus smoothing the way to governmental action.

Opinions about these alternative courses played no appreciable part in the demise of the ITO. The perfectionists opposed the Charter because it was not good enough, not because they were sure they had something better to offer. This is not the place to criticize the alternative proposals or to rehearse the debate about the businessmen's objections to the Charter. Nor need I speculate on the interesting possibility that in this case the businessmen were the "hopeless idealists" while the bureaucrats and college professors who supported the Charter, without being enamored of it, were the "realists." For present purposes, the exposition of the perfectionist point of view is sufficient; it helps explain why the ITO lacked the support needed for American ratification.

Of course, not all the opposition to the Charter came from perfectionists. Protectionists were against it, too. Statements opposing the Charter were submitted to the House Foreign Affairs Committee from a familiar array of protected industries: chemicals, dairy products, livestock and allied industries, nut growers, makers of glassware and glass containers, woolen manufacturers, independent petroleum producers, rayon manufacturers, the paper and pulp industry, the makers of woven wire cloth, and the National Labor-Management Council on Foreign Trade Policy in which a number of protected industries are represented. The American Tariff League was in its accustomed place. The line-up was similar to that on renewals of the Trade Agreements Act, but there were some striking differences in what was said. The protectionist groups presented their familiar arguments warning against the effect on the American economy of permitting freer entry of low-cost foreign goods. But in most of the protectionist statements the emphasis was on the more broadly conceived disadvantages of the ITO – its one-sidedness, its alleged support for governmental control and planning, the freedom of most countries to use escape clauses. In short, the protectionists found it convenient to present much of their position in terms of perfectionist arguments. Observing this, Representative Fulton ironically remarked, ". . . the American Tariff League is the most liberal organization that I have heard before this committee for a long time because they throw the pebble clear out in the pond and say, 'Here is this high level that we want to reach that is even above what the New Dealers ask. And if the charter is not that progressive and so highly moral in principle, we are not going into the charter with its present practical exceptions because it is based on conditions as they now exist.'"[15]

Many of the protectionist groups used other arguments as well, frequently of an "anti-internationalist" sort. They pictured the ITO as a superstate capable of directing American trade policy. Some spoke as if the ITO were going to set tariff levels. There was a certain amount of concern about changes in American laws that would be required by adherence to the Charter and an even greater emphasis – supported by the American Bar Association – on the alleged unconstitutionality of delegating certain powers to an international body.

Whether the protectionists' use of perfectionist arguments was merely "the homage vice pays to virtue" or whether it has some deeper significance as a sign of the times does not concern us here. The fact that groups traditionally in favor of the removal of trade barriers were against the ITO enabled those who opposed the removal of import barriers to take the same stand without sharply delineating their real position. The result was to make business opposition to the Charter seem more of a piece than it really was.[16] More important than the appearance was the political reality. In a manner new to the history of American commercial policy, the ITO was whipsawed between the protectionists and the perfectionists.

IV. IS IT THE END?

Normally, all the President did in December 1950 was to withdraw the Charter from Congress. There was no Congressional action. No one repudiated the American signature. The Charter retained its legal status of an international agreement awaiting ratification.[17] But in 1951, Secretary Acheson testified before a Congressional committee that it was his firm policy that the Charter would never be resubmitted to Congress. Subsequent official remarks on foreign trade policy have referred to the Charter only occasionally, in quick-passing historical reminiscence. United States Government opinion appears to favor putting GATT on a more nearly permanent basis, with the implication that the ITO is dead. No one has suggested that the Charter might be modified to be more acceptable or to fit changed world conditions. Among government officials there is an understandable revulsion from the idea of trying to renegotiate this complex instrument which has had such little political magnetism. Nor can the objective observer who would be spared the grueling grind of negotiation make much of a case for the view that renegotiation would be desirable.

Many suggestions have been made as to how the Charter's chances of passage might have been improved. If businessmen had been on the American delegation from the first, would they have had a better understanding of Washington's point of view? Would the State Department have made more headway if it had offered less defense of the weaker parts of the Charter and instead had singled them out as unsatisfactory but unavoidable features that the American representatives would try to change, or at least prevent the misuse of, once the ITO was set up? Could a system of weighted voting have been devised that would have reduced opposition at home and still been acceptable abroad because it reflected the actual bargaining power the United States would have in any trade organization regardless of voting arrangements? Would the Charter have been more acceptable if it had been in two parts: a code of principles toward which the signatories were to work, and an interim "code of exceptions" that would apply in an initial transitional period and in later times of abnormal difficulties? Ought the State Department to have suggested that Congress agree to American adherence to the Charter but at the same time pass a resolution expressing dissatisfaction with some parts of it, directing American delegates to work for its improvement, and stating the principles to which the United States would commit itself?

Any of these questions is good for an argument. But there is little present profit in hypothetical history. None of the devices suggested by these questions holds any serious promise of regaining acceptability for the Charter. The circumstances of world conditions and United States politics that contributed to the rejection of the Charter have not changed in ways favorable to it. There have been no indications of a change of heart among the perfectionists. The protectionists, or at least many of them, appear to be growing more active in the course of 1952. In the election campaign no party has taken a stand on the Charter, and its prospects of revival by the new Administration, of whatever party, seem absolute zero. Nor does there appear to be any force outside the United States pushing for acceptance of the Charter. Early in 1951 several governments withdrew the Charter from their parliaments, explaining that there was no point in going ahead with the project so long as the United States had dropped it. Without American leadership there can be no revival of the ITO or of any reasonable facsimile. The direction of American foreign trade policy is in doubt, but the least likely direction for it to take is the revival or renegotiation of the ITO Charter.

So the ITO is dead. But some of its parts are still alive. Certain of its provisions have acquired a sort of shadow existence by incorporation in other agreements. For instance, the OEEC's Code of the Liberalization of Trade says that state trading should be conducted "in accordance with the general principles laid down" in the Havana Charter. The Code incorporated by reference the Charter's definition of dumping. The Schuman Plan treaty empowers the High Authority to recommend action against countries that do not belong to the coal and steel community if they or their nationals "are engaging in dumping operations or other practices condemned by the Havana Charter." The Charter's definition of an acceptable customs union as one in which the external trade barriers are about midway between those previously applied by member nations turns up frequently.[18] There are several other instances of Charter provisions achieving some kind of legal status even though the Charter itself is dead.

The Charter's provisions concerning intergovernmental commodity agreements have also had a kind of independent existence. In a resolution of March 1947, reaffirmed in September 1951 after the ITO was plainly dead, the United Nations Economic and Social Council recommended that member countries "accept the principles" of the commodity chapter of the Charter "as a general guide in intergovernmental consultation or action with respect to commodity problems."[19]

Under the 1947 resolution an Interim Co-Ordinating Committee for International Commodity Arrangements was set up with a chairman representing the Preparatory Committee that was working on the Charter. Later the nominating function passed to the Interim Commission for the ITO and then, in 1951, it was given to the Contracting Parties to GATT. Each year the Co-Ordinating Committee publishes a *Review of International Commodity Problems* that gives particular attention to international consultation on commodity problems, the work of various commodity study groups, and the terms of commodity agreements proposed or adopted. While dropping hints and leaving implications,[20] the *Reviews* have not formally passed judgment as to whether the Charter's principles are in fact being fully applied.

In a somewhat different way, the Economic and Social Council has acted on the Charter's provisions regarding restrictive business practices. On the initiative of the American representative, the Council in September 1951 recommended that member governments take measures "based on the principles set forth in Chapter V of the Havana Charter . . ." to prevent harmful restrictive practices. A committee was set up to propose international measures that would achieve these purposes and provide for continuing consideration of the problem. At several key points the resolution borrows language from the Charter and in reciting the rationale of the recommendation it states that restrictive practices "may have harmful effects on the . . . aims and objectives listed in Chapter I of the Havana Charter."[21] In the discussion of the resolution there was some objection to inclusion of the ITO principles on the ground that "attempts to resuscitate parts of a dead body" were a "deplorable procedure."[22] Although Isador Lubin, the American representative, had cited examples of how restrictive practices inhibited economic development, spokesmen for a number of underdeveloped countries showed their old suspicion that the United States was trying to impose free competition on the world. However, the Uruguayan delegate explained that he had proposed that the Charter's cartel chapter be taken as a guide just because it did not condemn all restrictive practices, but only those having harmful effects. He interpreted the Charter as sanctioning various government monopolies regarded as essential to Uruguay's development. There was no real challenge to the substance of the Charter's chapter (except from the Iron Curtain representatives, who regarded the whole thing as a fraud), and the Belgian and Canadian delegates maintained that the Charter was the logical starting place because it embodied a satisfactory compromise between those who wanted to check restrictive practices as such and those who condemned them only when they had clearly harmful effects.

Thus, two important chapters of the Charter have attained a limited sort of existence despite the failure of the ITO. There have also been fairly extensive international discussions and proposals in the fields of economic development and international action to check depressions but with much less reference to the Charter. However, the principal survival of the Charter is in the field of commercial policy – GATT, the General Agreement on Tariffs and Trade.

Conceived as an interim measure, GATT was a kind of advance instalment of the Charter. It put into effect temporarily most of the provisions of the Charter's chapter on commercial policy and provided for multilateral negotiations to reduce tariffs, which were carried out at Geneva in 1947, Annecy in 1949, and Torquay in 1950–51. GATT also obliges its signatories "to observe to the fullest extent of their executive authority the general principles" of most parts of the Charter "pending their acceptance of it in accordance with their constitutional procedures." The limitation, "to the fullest extent of their executive authority," applies also to many of the commercial policy provisions since the protocols under which the signatory countries apply GATT exempt them from the need to change existing legislation in many important matters. Indeed, the only articles not included in this exemption are those covering general most-favored-nation treatment, the granting of tariff concessions, the territorial application of the agreement, frontier traffic, customs unions and free trade areas, the joint action of the contracting parties, and a number of provisions essential to carrying out the agreement.

GATT, to which 33 countries now adhere, was originally concluded for three years. During this time, in addition to negotiating tariff reductions, the signatories settled some trade disputes among members and passed on various issues concerning the application of the Agreement's provisions to particular cases. As the failure of the Charter to gain acceptance became evident, considerable energy had to be put into extending GATT, and in particular into preventing extensive cancellation of tariff concessions previously negotiated. These things were done at Torquay, when the agreement was renewed for three years. GATT also lacks a continuing organization and for a secretariat has been relying on the Interim Commission for the ITO, another orphan.

GATT, then, differs from the ITO in covering a narrower sphere of policy, requiring little if any legislative action by signatories, lacking a permanent organization, and committing signatories less firmly (they may withdraw on 60 days' notice). These differences are sources of both weakness and strength.

Because the commitments are less binding, GATT has been more easily accepted than the ITO was. But the counterpart of this advantage is an element of uncertainty, a threat that governments may not stick to GATT if the going gets rough. At the opening of the sixth session of the contracting parties Sir Hartley Shawcross stressed the fact that Britain had only committed itself to GATT provisionally. Since then the wisdom of continued adherence to the agreement has been repeatedly challenged in Parliament and government spokesmen have answered that they were still considering the matter. And in the United States, Congress made it plain that it was not endorsing GATT when it extended the Trade Agreements Act in 1951.

The fact that GATT is largely limited to traditional commercial policy subjects protects it from the disputes that arose over other parts of the ITO Charter. But by the same token this limited coverage makes GATT somewhat unsatisfactory to those who are particularly concerned that tariffs and quotas shall not be considered separately from the problems of raw materials, economic development, restrictive practices, and measures to check depressions. The Norwegians have proposed the inclusion in GATT of the Charter's main provisions on the maintenance of full employment. While this proposal, opposed by the United States, has been withdrawn, there is no evidence that it is dead. When the Economic and Social Council was discussing the American cartel resolution in September

1951, the British representative said that his delegation "felt strongly that restrictive business practices could be satisfactorily dealt with only in a body which was equally concerned with tariffs, quantitative restrictions and similar measures affecting trade. . . . His Government believed that in those circumstances the only appropriate body to deal with restrictive practices was represented by the Contracting Parties to the General Agreement on Tariffs and Trade."

There is nothing surprising in these views. They have the same rationale as that followed by the drafters of the Charter. Therefore, they inevitably point to the same result. As one observer expressed it, "If these claims are met in part or fully, a kind of new Charter might be the result which, in turn, would come up against the same strong opposition that has brought the full Havana Charter to its fall. Clearly, if the GATT is to be successful within its narrower sphere it must remain a relatively narrow agreement, retaining, in particular, its present legal characteristics as a multi-nation trade agreement that can be kept in force without ratification by the United States Congress. . . ."[23]

Similarly, there is a widespread opinion that GATT should be given a firmer, clearer juridical status, and there is a general feeling that it requires its own secretariat and some separate organizational existence. But on this matter, too, Sir Hartley Shawcross registered British doubts in the statement already referred to. There is also danger that attempts to strengthen the form of GATT and the national commitment to it will be regarded in the United States as an attempt to slip across the essence of the ITO without benefit of Congress. O. R. Strackbein, a protectionist spokesman, has already transferred to GATT virtually the same attack that was made on the ITO as a super-state. While acknowledging that the Contracting Parties did release the United States from its most-favored-nation commitment to Czechoslovakia under the Agreement, and sanctioned this country's use of the escape clause to withdraw a tariff concession on women's fur felt hats and hat-bodies, he demanded to know, "how it has come about that action of the United States Congress and action of the President in carrying out powers delegated to him by Congress are now subject to review by an international body . . . when such authority of review was never conferred upon it by Congress."[24]

* * * * * *

Thus GATT is the ITO *manqué*. There is a constant striving to fulfil the original pattern. If this striving should be satisfied, GATT would risk going over the same precipice as the Charter. So long as the striving is frustrated, GATT's strength is in doubt and it becomes the vortex of many strong and conflicting pressures. These pressures would exist without GATT; GATT may be able to survive them and to help control them, but the issue is in doubt.

V. WHAT NOW?

Much might be said about the ways and means of improving or strengthening GATT. The canvassing of these possibilities is an important part of the reconsideration of American foreign trade policy. But, in order to sketch the problems that face us, let us instead look briefly at the kind of pressures to which GATT and some other multilateral trading arrangements are subjected.

American participation in GATT is by executive action under the Trade Agreements Act. When Congress renewed the Act in 1951 it stipulated that the Tariff Commission must investigate all complaints that American producers were being damaged by imports resulting from tariff concessions made under the Act. If it finds the complaints to be justified, the Commission is to recommend remedial action to the President who must explain himself to Congress if he does not order the tariff increased. This virtual invitation to try to counter tariff reductions – what can the producer lose? – has been responded to with a wave of applications for the withdrawal of concessions. At the time of writing, a few have been turned down and a few have been acted on. Some concessions made under GATT have been withdrawn, with the result – as the Agreement provides – that countries affected have withdrawn some matching concessions on American exports. To check imports of products on which there are no concessions, producers have appealed directly to Congress to raise the tariff, as in the case of tuna fish. By a rider to the Defense Production Act, imports of cheese have been restricted by quotas, in isolation of GATT. Other amendments were proposed, but defeated, that would have treated feed grains the same way and curtailed imports of goods made from scarce materials.

There is, then, a new wave of protectionism in the United States. Its material results are not yet clear. Its causes are probably numerous. A contributing factor is undoubtedly the weakening of the Administration's foreign trade policy, accelerated by the events with which this essay has been concerned. Accompanying the drive for higher import barriers is a tendency for Congress to reassert its authority over foreign trade matters, a familiar phenomenon in many fields during the dying months of an Administration.

Along with the attempt to raise new trade barriers has come a resistance to attempts to remove existing ones. The Administration's efforts to get Congress to simplify customs administration have been fruitless, in part because the bill would be reduced what Percy Bidwell named "the invisible tariff." Despite the Secretary of Defense's finding of several years ago that it would be against the national interest to apply Buy American clauses to all military procurement, there is still a marked preference for the domestic produce, even at a higher price. Even the provisioning of American troops abroad shows some of the marks of such a policy. As a *New York Times* reporter commented, "An Army that is still hauling canned beer 4,000 miles to be drunk by people living in Heidelberg and Munich presents a formidable psychological problem. . . ."

Of course, the United States was never prepared to accept the pure principles of the ITO in all its own commercial behavior. Loopholes of American design were built into the Charter to permit the use of import quotas in connection with domestic farm programs and the withdrawal of tariff concessions if imports damaged domestic producers. Shipping was excluded from the Charter largely because the United States was not prepared to alter its subsidy policy. But the recent protectionist drive raises the specter of a sharper reversal in trade policy. Events seem to be bearing out a fear expressed by Jacob Viner in 1947. Writing about the ITO he said, "The old schoolmen distinguished between the grace which inspires good resolutions and that other grace which provides the will to fulfil them. There is great danger that the American supply of the latter will fall far short of the State Department's supply of the former."[25]

GATT, and the general approach to trade problems it embodies, have been challenged from other quarters as well. At the tariff-bargaining session at Torquay in 1950–51 the United States was unable to conclude any new tariff agreements with the United Kingdom or with several major members of the Commonwealth because these countries were unwilling to make further substantial reductions in the margins of preference they granted to one another under the Ottawa agreements of 1932. Some American officials interpreted this to mean that Britain was unwilling to go any farther in the making of global multilateral trade agreements and was withdrawing to the shelter of imperial preference-sterling area trading. The return to power of the Conservative Party plus the renewed payments crisis have stimulated a demand in Britain for getting free of the limitations GATT puts on the extension of imperial preference. This attitude, coupled with the building up of a case against recent trends in American trade policy – which to some extent has exaggerated the material effects of the new protectionist drive – may presage proposals for loosening GATT. If the United States remains in violation of GATT as a result of such measures as the cheese import quotas, or if it has to resort more frequently to the escape clause, this country will be in a poor position to defend the agreement against British pressure for change. The outcome might well be steps sanctioning the American actions in return for adjustments to meet the desires of other countries, such as the granting of greater freedom of action for the British on imperial preference. The result would be to leave GATT considerably weaker.

GATT is not the only multilateral arrangement dealing with the conditions of international trade, and the others are also subject to disturbing pressures. The trade liberalization program of the Organization of European Economic Cooperation, and the related provisions of the European Payments Union, led to the removal of quotas on a portion of trade among the European Marshall Plan countries and to the introduction of a considerable degree of non-discrimination among them. Progress in these matters, which began late in 1949, was hampered first by a German balance-of-payments crisis which curtailed the area of liberalized trade and then, more seriously, at the end of 1951 and early in 1952 by British and French measures restoring import restrictions to check drains on their foreign exchange reserves. The French and British actions were in large part a response to economic disturbances caused by the impact of the Korean War, rearmament and the expectation of rearmament.

A third multilateral trade and payments arrangement is the sterling area. Within the group, current payments are free from exchange control and trading privileges are exchanged which are not extended to outsiders. But here, too, there have been disturbances, leading to new trade restrictions within the sterling area and added strains in its relations with the rest of the world. It has apparently come as something of a shock to many Britons to discover that the process of putting each sterling area country's foreign accounts in balance may involve cuts in imports from the United Kingdom as well as from the United States. The recurrence of dollar difficulties raises the specter of a breaking-up of the sterling area, or at least the partial withdrawal from it of members who feel they could make out better in their dollar affairs, and perhaps their external trade and payments generally, if they operated independently of the sterling area dollar pool.

These three arrangements for the removal of barriers to multilateral trade — GATT, the OEEC program, and the sterling area – do not dovetail neatly. GATT, which includes substantially all of the countries in the other two groups as well as the United States and Canada, is based on the most-favored-nation principle. The OEEC quota reductions are for the most part limited to trade among member countries (but a country is not forbidden to extend these concessions to outsiders). So long as the pound is inconvertible the sterling area entails discrimination against payments in hard currencies. The preferential tariff arrangements in the British Commonwealth, largely overlapping the sterling area but not identical with it, introduce still further complications. The absence of a link between quota reductions in the OEEC and tariff reductions in GATT creates trouble for low-tariff countries in Western Europe. The Schuman Plan will create a customs union for iron, coal and steel among the member countries, requiring further derogation of the most-favored-nation rights of outside countries. The discrepancies among these trading arrangements cause some current difficulties and, looking at the long run, both the sterling area and the OEEC trading program raise a basic problem in relation to GATT: How much "regionalism" – a misleading word with its geographic connotations – is compatible with the "globalism" of GATT (and of the ITO principles)? Can trade barriers be removed by both approaches until they merge, or is the inherent exclusiveness of regionalism bound to hamper cooperation in the larger area?[26]

The forces that curtail the area of liberalized trade within each of these trading arrangements may also increase the discrepancies between GATT and the two "regional" groups. The OEEC's trading system and the sterling area are both based on discrimination against American goods and if the troubles that manifest themselves as "the dollar shortage" grow, the severity of the discrimination may grow. But the disruptive forces work within each group as well. It seems illogical that nations should raise trade barriers instead of lowering them at a time when a more effective international division of labor would enable them to carry the burden of rearmament more easily. But unless there is a strong binding force – and even that of the sterling area, the most cohesive of the groups, may not be sufficient – each government is likely to try to deal with its own particular set of problems by the most effective *national* action open to it. To safeguard the balance of payments, import barriers are likely to be the easiest method at hand.

Rearmament not only disrupts trade and checks efforts to remove trade barriers. It substitutes a whole set of different criteria for the principles embodied in multilateral trade agreements such as GATT. The flow of strategic materials must be controlled, not set free. Prices may have to be manipulated, not left to the market. Cost must sometimes be disregarded. In a time of cold war, non-discrimination becomes strategically unwise and insistence on it would be stultifying. When last renewing the Trade Agreements Act, Congress excluded the countries of the Soviet orbit from its benefits by directing that American tariff concessions to them be withdrawn and that they be denied most-favored-nation treatment. In trade terms the consequences were not great or the resulting sanctions very strong. The gesture was largely emotional. But the denial of the principle of non-discrimination goes much further, especially in the matter of export controls. ". . . For if there is anything that strategic considerations demand," says Professor Viner, "it is discrimination in the treatment of different countries, according as they are friends, or foes, or would-be neutrals."[27]

Serious as it is, rearmament is not the main challenge to international trade policy. If it were, the debate would be whether the best course was to put the liberal ideals on ice for the time being or to try to find a way of applying multilateral trading principles within NATO, or some other free-world grouping, while applying the principles of economic warfare to the rest of the world. This is one of the problems we face. Another is how to check protectionist tendencies that conflict with the purposes of programs for strengthening the free world and that increase the need for foreign aid by making it harder for countries to support themselves by exports. But there is another basic problem of continuing importance that exists independently of the present crisis in world politics. If there were no rearmament and no cold war, we should still be confronted by the question: Can the principles on which GATT and the ITO are based be successfully applied in the contemporary world?

Although political tension has increased the economic difficulties of many countries and has made some postwar adjustments more difficult than they would have been in a less threatening world, cold war cannot be considered the primary cause of some major difficulties that plagued the drafters and negotiators of the Charter and that would have continued to plague the ITO if it had been established. Mere enumeration is sufficient to indicate the kind of difficulties I have in mind: the troubles that express themselves in the chronic dollar shortage; extensive government controls over both domestic and foreign transactions; price-fixing and subsidies, whether aimed at keeping prices high or low; widespread inflationary pressures coupled with professed fears of the onset of recession; the contrary pulls of the desire for domestic stability at all costs and the desire for international stability.

Out of each of these circumstances comes a horde of troubles for any attempt to fit the traditional methods of a liberal trade policy to current circumstances. Only a few of these difficulties can any longer honestly be set aside as phenomena of the "transition period" – even if that term retains any meaning. Some of the difficulties arise from practices not covered by the old rules, such as state trading, for which new rules have to be invented, without great success so far. In other cases, the adaptation of old rules produces peculiar results; it has long been plain that allocating shares in import quotas according to the pattern of trade in a base period is a very different kind of "equal treatment" from the avoidance of tariff discrimination among competing suppliers. In still other cases, formal application of old principles in new circumstances produces results contrary to intentions. This is the case, for instance, when "you accept prices as the regulator or allocator of production and the regulator of where commodities should go, even though these prices may reflect nothing more than the arbitrary whim of a dictator or the snap judgment of a petty bureaucrat."[28]

One way of summarizing these difficulties is to say that the trade theory underlying GATT and ITO is largely a nineteenth-century product that does not fit twentieth-century facts. Another is to say that the world can have a flourishing multilateral trade based on national specialization only if free enterprise or the price system are allowed greater roles, internationally and within each country, than they have had for some time. These and other ways of stating the issue all contain part of the truth, but whatever the formulation, the basic fact is that there is a gap between major features of the present world economy and the known means of securing the most economical pattern of international trade. The ITO was an attempt to bridge that gap. How it might have worked we shall never know. Everyone concerned had reservations about the prospects and, as we have seen, the Charter proved unacceptable partly because of lack of confidence in what it could do. It is conceivable that the problem will be largely eliminated by the freeing of markets and the dropping of policies that conflict with liberal trading principles. But the evidence that this will happen is not very persuasive; the political forces in most countries seem to set more strongly in the other direction. At best only part of the problem is likely to be solved in this way. In any case, we are left with the question of what is to be done if events work out differently.

"The time is out of joint." But we cannot simply suspend trade policy until the world is again orderly and then hope to resume a course based on the old principles. The main end of the principles is certainly valid: an international division of labor that permits maximum production. But, more obviously than ever before, we lack the means of achieving this end. It is not just political support for a wise course that is lacking. We also lack an intellectual reconciliation between multilateral international trade based on a high degree of specialization and the concept of managed and stable national economies. Perhaps there is no reconciliation. Insoluble problems exist. At some points we seem to have come to an intellectual impasse, but there is still much work to be done in clarifying issues before we can say that these problems really defy solution. Meanwhile, men must conduct their affairs and governments their foreign trade policies as best they can, improvising where known methods prove inadequate. And it would not be unprecedented if the intellectual solution followed instead of preceded the evolution of practice.

The ITO was an attempt to find a practicable compromise between the old aims and methods and the new ones. It contained some inventions that may seem worth resuscitating. But the way of the ITO is closed and we face the problem of starting again. In which direction should the United States try to go? We may attempt to keep GATT in as good repair as possible and build on it an adaptation of the multilateral approach. We may seek a liberal trading world by bilateral or even unilateral measures. We may revert to a greater degree of economic nationalism. We may put principles on the shelf and improvise to keep our footing in an unsettled world where the aims of foreign trade policy seem to change frequently. Or we may devise some wholly new line of approach. The new Administration, whatever its party, will have to face these issues, not only because the Trade Agreements Act expires in June 1953 but because a convergence of forces has pushed the underlying trade problems to the surface. Whether or not a consciously elaborated policy is adopted, action will be taken or not taken which will be a policy in fact.

The core of the postwar trade policy of the United States was the ITO, which was in many ways the fusion and highest development of the main elements in the policies that had gone before, since 1934. The ITO failed in part because the world was not the kind of world on which the Charter was premised. The world has not changed back. The ITO failed in part because of shifts in American politics. Those shifts, and others, are still going on. The ITO failed, finally, because not enough people had confidence in the way it tried to bridge gaps between different concepts of the nature of the economic process, between the supposed interests of the United States and most of the rest of the world, and between faith and practice. The gaps are still there; they may narrow or widen; but a multilateral trading arrangement, covering most of the free world, cannot be successful unless it can bridge them.

The failure of the ITO leaves the United States with only the remnants of a foreign trade policy. It is doubtful that they can survive the buffeting, internal and external, political and economic, that they are now undergoing. The postwar planners were right when they said that an international understanding on trade policy was essential to the success of most other measures of international economic policy, so the whole structure of the free world is affected.

The need for a new foreign trade policy is clear and urgent. But the shape that policy ought to have is obscure. How much can we adapt from past policies? Can we invent new means of attaining old aims? How can we devise a policy that is not only promising but politically acceptable? The dynamics of the world of the 1950's are different from those of the world for which the ITO and its companion international agreements were made. We do not seem to know the commercial policy corollaries of the new propositions; indeed we are not even sure of the new propositions themselves. Our need is for a restatement of what we are after and a fresh analysis of how to get it. The end of the ITO has forced us to face these problems but it has provided no clear guides to their solutions.

NOTES

1 Department of State, *Bulletin*, December 18, 1950, p. 977. The only public harbinger of this action that I have seen is a dispatch from Torquay, England to *The New York Times*, November 10, 1950. The reporter, presumably Michael Hoffman who was covering the tariff conference then in progress, said that after noting the Republican gains in the Congressional elections that had just taken place, "both Americans and non-Americans here have written off any possibility of United States ratification in the next two years. . . . A delay of two years more is likely to mean that the Havana Charter never will be pushed forward again in its present form. . . ."

2 *Italian Economic Survey* (Rome) January-February 1951, p. 1. The end was so quiet and unceremonious that on April 26, 1951 *The New York Times* was still discussing the effect of the Torquay conference on the Administration's case for the Charter before Congress.

3 It was presented in *Proposals for Expansion of World Trade and Employment*, prepared by United States officials after consultation with the British. In September 1946 a

more elaborate draft appeared, called *Suggested Charter for an International Trade Organisation of the United Nations*, which the United States presented to the Preparatory Committee created by the Economic and Social Commission, which had its first meeting in London in October.

4 The *Proposals* were American; the *Joint Statement* said that the British government was "in full agreement on all important points" and would "use its best endeavors to bring [international] discussions to a successful conclusion, in the light of the views expressed by other countries." There were, of course, some misgivings, especially among the British. And some Americans put more store in the long run political consequences of strengthening Britain than in facilitating a liberal system of world trade. But for most these aims appeared to merge.

5 However, early drafts of the Charter contained a provision in the state trading section intended to provide a Soviet *quid pro quo* for tariff reductions on Russian exports.

6 In some years it is hard to say which was the critical vote since the passage of the bill often got the support of men who had shortly before voted for modifications or delaying motions which, if carried, might well have drastically altered the shape of the program.

7 The Administration's insistence that it never reduced tariffs if that would harm American producers weakened its case against the peril points which, it could be argued, were merely legislative assurance of the same practice. This is a fallacious argument, but I am not here discussing the case for or against the Trade Agreements Program. The point illustrates the difficulty of building up political support for a fairly complex, and to some extent procedural, case, especially when the alternative has the attraction of ambiguity.

8 On the other hand, supporters of the Charter would have to support some kind of Trade Agreements Act so that the United States could carry out its obligation to negotiate in good faith with other members of the ITO for the reduction of tariffs. It could have been argued, however, that a modified form of the Act would be consistent with this obligation. Without reference to the ITO, Senator Vandenberg apparently regarded his co-sponsorship (with Senator Millikin) of the original peril-point procedure as a measure of bipartisan foreign policy consistent with preservation of the spirit of the Trade Agreements Act.

9 League of Nations, Economic, Financial and Transit Department, *Commercial Policy in the Interwar Period: International Proposals and National Policies* (Geneva, 1942) p. 157. This report authoritatively sets out a number of views, widely held among economists and officials, which influenced the making of the ITO.

10 The American literature for and against the Charter is extensive. The authoritative defense of the ITO, by one of its principal authors, is Clair Wilcox, *A Charter for World Trade* (New York: Macmillan, 1949). See also, W. A. Brown, *The United States and the Restoration of World Trade* (Washington: The Brookings Institution, 1950). A shorter statement favorable to the Charter is Percy W. Bidwell and William Diebold Jr., "The United States and the International Trade Organization," *International Conciliation*, March 1949. An endorsement that emphasizes the difficulties and risks is given by Jacob Viner in "Conflicts of Principle in Drafting a Trade Charter," *Foreign Affairs*, July 1947, 612–628.

The fullest statement of the business case against the Charter appears in the statements and documents presented in the Congressional *Hearings* cited below. See also the writings of Michael Hellperin, especially "How the U.S. Lost the ITO Conferences," *Fortune*, September 1949, 80–82, which argues that a different negotiating technique would have produced a better charter. For an extreme case against the ITO, see Philip Cortney, *The Economic Munich* (New York: Philosophical Library, 1949).

11 The survey that follows is based principally on a number of reports issued at various times during the ITO negotiations by committees of the business organizations

mentioned. The final positions of all but the United States Council of the International Chamber of Commerce are presented in *Membership and Participation by the United States in the International Trade Organisation, Hearings* before the Committee on Foreign Affairs, House of Representatives, 81st Congress, 2d Session (G.P.O., 1950). The U.S. Council's Executive Committee issued a mimeographed *Statement of Position* on May 9, 1950.

12 Statement by the National Foreign Trade Council, *Hearings*, cited, p. 200. Moreover, another article pledged all ITO members to cooperate in helping the economic development of others. The businessmen regarded this as a surrender of American bargaining power and undue emphasis on the role of government capital. Government spokesmen challenged this interpretation.

13 Wilcox, cited, p. 146. Some language about investment had been introduced into the Charter at the first ITO conference in London where the underdeveloped countries pressed for inclusion of an article saying that members would not put "unreasonable impediments" in the way of others' getting the facilities they needed for development. This was matched by a provision that the receiving countries would "take no unreasonable action injurious to" the suppliers of capital. The business groups objected to the inadequacy of the latter provision, but they did not argue that it was positively harmful.

14 Wilcox, cited, p. 199.

15 *Hearings*, cited, p. 406.

16 The agreement on the end to be achieved, regardless of a difference about the reasons, probably also helped organizations that included both protected industries and those concerned with increased foreign trade to take clear-cut positions on the Charter. It is interesting to note that the U.S. Chamber of Commerce – which opposed the Charter on perfectionist grounds – was represented at the Havana conference by Elvin Kilheffer who appeared before the House Foreign Affairs Committee on behalf of several protectionist groups in the chemical industry.

17 Only Liberia ratified the Charter unconditionally. Australia and Sweden ratified it, but made their adherence conditional on similar action by the United States and, in the former's case, also Britain.

18 This definition is in any case binding on a number of countries because it is incorporated in GATT. For comments on the imprecision and possible meaninglessness of the criterion, see Jacob Viner, *The Customs Union Issue* (New York, 1950) pp. 66–68.

19 The language quoted is from the 1951 resolution. The earlier version was that governments should "adopt as a general guide" the principles of the commodity chapter. The words "pending the establishment of the International Trade Organization" which had appeared earlier were dropped in 1951. The Economic Commission for Latin America passed a similar resolution (pertaining only to countries that had signed the Charter) at its first meeting in 1948.

20 For instance, the 1949 *Review* says of the tea agreement of that year, "It will be seen from the text . . . that the present arrangement, although controlling exports, nevertheless does not provide for equal representation of producing and consuming countries." Such equal representation was one of the principal requirements of the Charter; it is applied in the wheat agreement, the most important intergovernmental commodity agreement of the postwar period. In the same *Review* the Committee suggested that somewhat more publicity might be given to discussion in various commodity study groups; this, too, is in line with Charter principles.

21 The text of the resolution, as passed, appears in U.N., Economic and Social Council, *Official Records*, Thirteenth Session, 549th Meeting, 13 September 1951, (E/SR549), pp. 645–646. The discussion took place at that meeting and the three previous ones.

The original American resolution made no specific reference to the Charter, though it incorporated its gist and some of its language. The paragraph establishing Chapter V as a guide was introduced in a Uruguayan amendment, and the reference to Chapter I by Chile.

22 Statement by the Chilean representative, 548th meeting, p. 634. The Indian representative took much the same view and the Chinese spokesman doubted the propriety of mentioning the Charter since it had not been widely accepted.

23 Heinz Heymann, "The G.A.T.T. at Crossroads," Skandinaviska Banken, *Quarterly Review* (Stockholm) July 1951, pp. 58–64 at 63.

24 Radio address reprinted in the *Congressional Record*, January 14, 1952, pp. A124–A125.

25 Jacob Viner, "Conflicts of Principle in Drafting a Trade Charter," *Foreign Affairs*, July 1947, pp. 612–628 at 614.

26 For a fuller discussion of these issues see Howard S. Ellis, *The Economics of Freedom* (New York), 1950, pp. 431–443, 493–507, and my *Trade and Payments in Western Europe* (New York), 1952, pp. 405–417.

27 Jacob Viner, *Rearmament and International Commercial Policies*, Department of State, Foreign Service Institute (Washington, 1951, multigraphed) p. 9.

28 Same, p. 23.

5. The 1933 World Economic Conference as an Instance of Failed International Cooperation

B. Eichengreen and M. Uzan

The 1933 World Economic Conference is a classic example of failure to achieve international agreement. In June of that year representatives of the nations of the world assembled in London to negotiate a coordinated response to the economic crisis of the 1930s. They achieved nothing. The issues that led them to convene the conference included exchange-rate instability, deflation, tariffs, and external debts. They made no significant progress on any of these fronts. Following the conference, the already fragmented international monetary system splintered into yet additional currency blocs. Deflationary pressure on the gold-standard countries intensified accordingly. International trade was stagnant. The problem of intergovernmental debts remained a bone of contention among the Allies, while the overhang of defaulted commercial debts impeded the recovery of international capital markets. The economic crisis lingered, doing nothing to nurture political moderation at home or to encourage collaboration in the diplomatic sphere.

No existing explanation for the failure of the conference is entirely satisfactory. One thesis is that U.S. insistence that certain issues (war debts, tariff rates) be declared off limits doomed the conference to failure. Unfortunately, it is not clear why this should have made agreement on issues such as exchange rates and monetary reflation more difficult. A second popular thesis is that Roosevelt's decision to take the dollar off gold torpedoed the conference. Again, it is not clear why, if it was possible to envisage an agreement prior to dollar devaluation, Roosevelt's action should have so dramatically transformed matters. Nor is there in the literature an adequate explanation for Roosevelt's decision.[1]

In this chapter we reassess the failure of the 1933 World Economic Conference, adding what are, relative to the existing literature, two novel elements. The first is domestic politics. In 1933, we argue, domestic politics severely restricted the scope for agreement. Those who, prior to the conference, thought that they envisaged the outlines of an agreement neglected this critical influence.

The second element is the conceptual framework that negotiators brought to the table. Policy-makers were unable to agree on a concerted response to the economic crisis because they perceived it in very different ways. Lacking a shared diagnosis of the problem, they were unable to prescribe a cooperative response. Actions that are commonly portrayed as perverse appear logical once the absence of a common conceptual framework is recognized.

Both elements are necessary to understand the failure of the conference. Had negotiators possessed compatible conceptual frameworks, it might have been possible to strike a purely monetary deal. France, Britain, and the United States could have agreed to simultaneous changes in domestic monetary cum exchange-rate policies, none of which were desirable in isolation but, when undertaken simultaneously, would have left all three nations better off. That national delegations conceived the role of monetary policy in very different ways prevented them from negotiating a mutually acceptable monetary response.

Even with a purely monetary agreement ruled out, conceptual differences did not in principle preclude a cross-issue deal involving monetary concessions by Britain, tariff concessions by France, and war-debt concessions by the United States. But such cross-issue agreement foundered on domestic politics (primarily the opposition of French agriculture to trade liberalization). Domestic political obstacles proved insurmountable because the structure of domestic political institutions, particularly in France, vested special-interest groups with considerable leverage.

Our analysis has implications for several separate literatures in economics and political science. It illustrates some of the uses of the literature on issue linkage[2] and of that relating domestic and international policies.[3] Its emphasis on the importance of negotiators' conceptual frameworks bears on the role of ideas in policy-making.[4] It provides an application of the literature in economics concerned with the scope for cooperation when national policy-makers subscribe to different models.[5] But it transcends that literature by endogenizing policy-makers' choice of model.

The first section of this chapter sketches the background to the period and provides a narrative of events. In light of this account, the next section indicates the limitations of existing explanations for the failure of the conference. The third section introduces the role of competing conceptual frameworks, and the next adds domestic politics. The conclusion attempts to relate these strands to the recent literature on diplomacy and domestic politics.

THE 1933 WORLD ECONOMIC CONFERENCE

This section provides an account of the 1933 World Economic Conference to familiarize the reader with the principal events that we seek to explain.[6] It documents the ways in which those events have been analyzed by previous scholars and allows us to identify some limitations of the interpretations that dominate the literature.

Background

The year 1932 marked the trough of the business-cycle downturn that began in 1929. By 1932 the volume of global manufacturing production had fallen to less than 60 percent of 1929 levels. Primary production fell less dramatically, but it too reached its trough in 1932.[7]

The collapse of foreign trade and finance encouraged the belief that the crux of the problem lay in the international sphere. By 1932 the value of trade had fallen to less than half of its 1929 value. Following the imposition of the U.S.

Smoot-Hawley Tariff in 1930, trade barriers around the world reached new heights. International lending, which had peaked in 1928, evaporated with the outbreak of sovereign default in Latin America in 1931 and its spread to Central and Eastern Europe in 1932. Debtor countries such as Argentina, Australia, Brazil, New Zealand, and Venezuela had been forced off the gold standard soon after the Great Depression struck. With Britain's devaluation in September 1931, international monetary instability spread to the core of the gold-standard system. By the end of 1931, more than two dozen countries were off the gold standard. What had once been a unified international monetary system was, like Gaul, divided into three parts: countries with devalued currencies, those under exchange control, and a residual bloc still on the gold standard.

These problems pointed to the issues that would form the agenda for a prospective conference: deflation, trade barriers, external debts, and exchange-rate instability. Discussion of deflation emphasized not only the collapse of price levels; the decline in output and the rise in unemployment also fell under this heading. There was a tendency to impute a causal connection to the simultaneous collapse of prices and production. Action to stabilize prices, and ultimately to raise them, was viewed in some circles as necessary and sufficient to bring the Depression to an end.

The problem of trade barriers encompassed both tariffs and quotas. The United States had imposed the Smoot-Hawley Tariff in the summer of 1930. Within months of sterling's devaluation, Britain had imposed a general tariff and negotiated tariff preferences with the members of its Commonwealth. France, Belgium, and the Netherlands responded with increasingly comprehensive import quotas. Particularly troubling to contemporaries was the growing prevalence of clearing arrangements. Starting in 1932, Germany negotiated clearing arrangements designed to maximize its market power internationally and balance its trade bilaterally. Central and Eastern European nations in Germany's orbit followed suit.

Under the heading "external debts" fell a potpourri of financial obligations. The most controversial item remained German reparations and Allied war debts to the United States. Germany's obligation, established originally at another London conference in 1921, had been scaled back under the Dawes Plan in 1924, under the Young Plan in 1930, and at the Lausanne Conference in 1932. Controversy arose from the fact that war debts had not been reduced commensurately. To gain access to the U.S. capital market, the European Allies had negotiated and war-debt settlements with the United States, generally between 1923 and 1926. These agreements remained in place until in June 1931 the Hoover Moratorium suspended war-debt and reparations payments for a year. At Lausanne in the spring of 1932, Germany's obligation was extinguished in return for its promise to deliver 3 billion reichsmarks of bonds. But the French and British publics objected to an agreement eliminating German reparations without also writing down Allied war debts to the United States. The representatives of the European Allies therefore signed a gentleman's agreement not to ratify the Lausanne Convention until a settlement had been reached with the U.S.

The exchange-rate problem was the most contentious of all. Sterling fell from U.S. $4.86 on September 19, 1931, to $3.25 by the beginning of December. It fluctuated between $3.15 and $3.70 over the course of 1932. In the absence of significant inflation in Britain, this was a dramatic shift in relative prices to be accommodated by the remaining gold-standard countries. In addition to the Commonwealth, most of Britain's foreign trading partners depreciated their currencies along with sterling.

The 1933 World Economic Conference was not the first international meeting at which such problems were discussed. Previous economic conferences at Brussels in 1920 and Genoa in 1922 had been less than totally successful, however. Neither led to reconstruction of the international economic system along the lines envisaged in the delegates' resolutions. It was some years, therefore, before another such meeting was convened. Finally in 1930, Germany, dissatisfied that the Young Plan negotiations had been limited to a subset of economic issues, proposed a world economic conference. The possibility was raised again in 1931 during the Franco-American dispute over the Hoover Moratorium and in 1932 during Anglo-American discussions. The Lausanne Conference set the stage. The delegates at Lausanne, in addition to annulling Germany's reparations schedule, called upon the League of Nations to convoke an "International Monetary and Economic Conference" to address economic problems on a global scale.

Objectives of the Participants

The central participants at the London Conference were the United States, the United Kingdom, and France. Dozens of other nations attended, and some, such as Germany, were prominent in the proceedings. But the United States, Britain, and France were the central players. Any cooperative response to the economic crisis hinged upon their agreement.[8]

France attached priority to the restoration of international monetary stability, by which was meant a return to the gold standard by Britain and its trading partners and the removal of exchange control by Germany and other Central European countries.[9] Monetary stabilization along orthodox lines was, in the French view, the only means of reviving investor confidence and laying the basis for sustainable growth. The French regarded tampering with the gold standard as inconsistent with this end. Here they opposed schemes to redistribute the Bank of France's excess gold reserves to other countries, to reduce gold cover ratios, to encourage central banks to hold foreign-exchange reserves, and to moderate the independence of central banks. The Bank of France and its governor, Clement Moret, were even more hostile to these expedients than was the French Treasury under Georges Bonnet. The French also wished to preserve their freedom to use instruments such as tariffs and quotas which insulated them from financial and economic disturbances abroad.

Britain's priority was reflation, which meant freedom from external constraints on the policy of cheap money.[10] By 1932 the British Treasury, which took the lead in international negotiations, had been converted to the advantages of low interest rates and rising prices. Unless Britain received a guarantee that other countries would adopt a similar posture, it was unwilling to return to gold. To insure that the stabilization of sterling would not prevent Britain from pursuing reflationary policies, the British asked for four specific concessions: a war-debt settlement, which would stem the drain of gold to the United States; a commitment by foreign central banks to initiate expansionary open-market operations, which required changes in the statutes preventing the Bank of France from engaging in such actions; a redistribution of existing gold to countries with insufficient reserves, enabling them to relax their exchange controls and stabilize their currencies; and finally, commercial policy concessions by the United States and France, which would prevent their trade balances from moving into strong surplus and keep them from draining gold from other countries pursuing reflationary policies.

Both Britain and France hoped that a war-debt settlement might be negotiated in London. Though war debts were formally outside the terms of reference of the conference, they nonetheless figured in the calculations of British and French negotiators. For their part, some U.S. officials recommended offering war-debt concessions if the Europeans acceded to other American demands.[11]

U.S. demands were difficult to anticipate. The Hoover Administration was thought to support the French campaign for a generalized return to gold. Hoover's 1931–32 moratorium had demonstrated a new flexibility on the issue of intergovernmental debts. The position of the incoming Roosevelt Administration was less clear. Roosevelt had avoided addressing the merits of the gold standard and devaluation during the election campaign. But by delegating such discussion to hard-money Democrats, he left the impression that he too was sympathetic to the French position. Unlike the Republicans, the traditional party of protection, a Democratic administration was seen as more likely to press for tariff reductions.

No international conference could succeed without U.S. participation. American isolationists having thwarted efforts to include the United States in previous international economic conferences, by 1932 the U.S. had acquired a reputation for boycotting such assemblies. Knowing this, the U.S. could demand a price for its participation. With the dollar still on gold, it was likely to be asked for concessions on war debts and import tariffs. It therefore demanded that war debts be excluded from the agenda and that there be no discussion of specific tariff rates. Neither sanction was binding, however. Tariffs and war debts featured in the informal discussions of treasury and central-bank officials and were alluded to in conference proceedings, starting with British Chancellor Neville Chamberlain's opening address.

Preliminary Discussions

At Lausanne it had been agreed to appoint a Committee of Experts to set the agenda for the London Conference. The British and French experts were clearly affiliated with their countries' respective treasuries. On the British side, they were Sir Frederick Leith-Ross, long-time high Treasury official, and Sir Frederick Phillips, head of domestic financial affairs at the Treasury. On the French side they were Charles Rist, long-time government adviser, and Jean Parmentier, honorary director of the Treasury. The American experts were less intimately associated with the U.S. State and Treasury departments: they were John H.

Williams, professor of economics a Harvard University, and Edmund E. Day, a former Harvard professor currently director for social sciences at the Rockefeller Foundation.

The Committee of Experts convened in Geneva at the end of October 1932. Deep divisions immediately surfaced between countries on and off gold. The French and American experts demanded that Britain restore gold convertibility as a precondition for further talks. Leith-Ross and Phillips countered with a demand for international action to raise the level of prices in gold-standard countries as a precondition for currency stabilization. The French dismissed reflationary initiatives, especially when undertaken by countries off the gold standard, as not merely ineffectual but counterproductive. Only currency stabilization on a gold basis, they argued, would succeed in restoring confidence and encouraging investment.

At this stage, the U.S. position had more in common with France's than with Britain's, although the experts' statements remained vague pending the outcome of the November presidential election. That outcome was known when the experts reconvened in the second and third weeks of January, but not the intentions of the president-elect. With the United States and France preoccupied by domestic affairs (the interregnum between administrations in the U.S., a budgetary crisis in France), the British experts assumed responsibility for drafting the annotated agenda. Their document, when it emerged, recommended establishing a common international monetary standard, increasing the level of prices, abolishing exchange controls, and removing trade restrictions. Jockeying took place over the order of the list, but the final version of the agenda made clear that these four objectives were linked.

To achieve them, governments were encouraged to take a mixture of steps, some reflecting French gold-standard orthodoxy, others British insistence on cheap money. The former included balancing budgets, removing exchange controls, and enhancing central-bank independence. The latter included liberal money and credit policies and steps such as debt settlement to encourage international lending. The question was whether what were in effect two distinct strategies could be successfully reconciled.

The Conference and Its Breakdown

Roosevelt's decision on April 19 to accept the Thomas Amendment and take the United States off gold threw a wrench into conference preparations. It seemed likely that the dollar would fall significantly against gold and that, to keep pace, the Bank of England would depreciate sterling. Exchange-rate fluctuations might be considerable. It seemed doubtful that countries would be able to agree to a general currency stabilization or to negotiate a package of bilateral parities and tariff reductions with currencies fluctuating violently against one another.

Hence, the Washington Conversations, of late April and early June, in which Roosevelt and his advisors met with representatives of 11 nations, came to be seen as a critical opportunity to negotiate a tariff truce and an exchange stabilization agreement. The truce was successfully concluded: the United States, the United Kingdom, France, Germany, Italy, Japan, Belgium, and Norway agreed not to increase tariffs or tighten quotas for the duration of the conference. Exchange-rate stabilization proved a more difficult nut to crack. Starting on April 25, Leith-Ross, now the British government's Chief Economic Adviser, met with James Warburg, Roosevelt's confidant on monetary matters, to discuss stabilization. The views Warburg conveyed to Leith-Ross were personal; they had not yet been endorsed by the President.[12] Warburg suggested that the franc and the dollar be stabilized at par and that sterling be stabilized in the neighborhood of $3.50. This $3.50 was acceptable to the British, who also found congenial Warburg's proposal that countries reduce gold cover ratios to 25 or 30 percent, remove exchange controls, and readjust war debts.[13]

Unfortunately, neither Roosevelt nor the financial markets were of the same mind as Warburg. Within a fortnight of the Warburg-Leith-Ross conversations, the dollar had fallen to $4 against the pound. Warburg modified his plan to incorporate a 15 percent discount of the dollar against gold.[14] The French, invited to contribute their opinion, rejected anything less than dollar stabilization at the old gold parity. By mid-May, however, they were forced to acknowledge the unrealism of this demand. They then pressed for stabilization at current levels. Warburg offered a plan under which the three governments would each contribute 500 million dollars to a joint stabilization fund, without saying anything about the level at which exchange rates would be stabilized. The British refused to peg sterling to the dollar without further information about the new U.S. administration's monetary intentions. The French fears that if Roosevelt utilized the inflationary powers granted him under the Thomas Amendment, France's 500 million dollar contribution would be expended immediately in support of the dollar and the President's reckless monetary experiment. And Roosevelt was not yet prepared to commit himself. Each government held its breath, hoping that the others would give in first.

As May turned to June, still no agreement to stabilize exchange rates had been reached. Responding to French requests, the three countries convened exchange-rate stabilization talks at the British Treasury on June 10, two days before the conference was scheduled to open. Representatives of the three treasuries met in one room, and Clement Moret of the Bank of France, Montagu Norman of the Bank of England, and George Harrison of the Federal Reserve Bank of New York met in another.

The French opened with a demand for immediate stabilization of sterling and the dollar within 1 percent bands, offering no quid pro quo. Stabilization would be feasible, argued the Bank of France's representatives, only if each government issued a detailed statement of intentions. The French Treasury representatives, Jacques Rueff (financial attaché to the French Embassy in London) and Jacques Bizot, more cognizant of British and American resistance, accepted a counterproposal that the three nations jointly issue only a general statement of their desire for exchange-rate stability. The British and Americans agreed on the desirability of 5 percent bands, but disagreed on the appropriate level for the sterling-dollar rate, the Americans preferring more than $4, the British preferring less.

Within five days negotiators agreed to compromise. The British and American governments would limit currency fluctuations for the duration of the conference. The pound would be held at $4 plus or minus 3 percent. Only in the event of "exceptional and unforeseen circumstances" would currencies be allowed to deviate from this band.

Rumors surfaced that there existed an agreement, but without confirmation of the rate. On June 16 the dollar gained 4 percent against gold, and U.S. stock and commodity prices tumbled, anticipating that the Federal Reserve would be forced to adopt a more restrictive stance. If Roosevelt retained doubts about the connection between currency depreciation and commodity prices, they were vanquished by these events. On June 17 he instructed his representatives to disown the agreement, rejecting stabilization of the sterling-dollar rate at current levels but leaving open the possibility of future action at a more favorable level. The impression gained by their foreign counterparts was that prospects were bleak for dollar stabilization at any level.

France's fall-back position was a currency stabilization agreement which excluded the United States. The British agreed to consider yet another joint declaration if the French would draft it and secure the support of the other gold countries. The document resembled nothing so much as the general statement of principles that had been suggested by British and U.S. treasury representatives at the outset of talks. Specific exchange rates and techniques for achieving them were conspicuous by their absence.

French hopes that Britain would accept even a weak stabilization agreement without U.S. concurrence proved mistaken. The British forwarded the document to the Americans, making clear that their participation was contingent upon that of the United States. Roosevelt's closest adviser, Raymond Moley, recently arrived in London, was favorably inclined. In New York, Treasury Secretary Woodin and Bernard Baruch concurred. Once again, however, Roosevelt ignored his advisors' recommendations. On July 1, he informed London of his decision. The next day his famous "bombshell" message to the conference, in which he denounced the argument in favor of stable exchange rates as a "specious fallacy" and derided "old fetishes of so-called international bankers," put an end to tripartite talks.[15]

In despair, the French suggested immediate adjournment. The British were inclined to agree. To save face, it was decided to soldier on. The subcommission on financial reconstruction issued a vague statement that debtors should pay their debts, but that creditors should be understanding if they did not. The subcommission on monetary problems affirmed the superiority of the gold standard over alternative monetary arrangements, but offered no useful suggestions of how it might be re-established. The conference adjourned at the end of July with negligible accomplishments to its credit.

LIMITATIONS OF EXISTING EXPLANATIONS

The two leading explanations for the failure of the conference both blame the United States. One emphasizes U.S. insistence that war debts and specific tariff rates be excluded from the agenda, the other Roosevelt's bombshell rejecting stabilization. Neither is wholly satisfactory.

The first explanation has two limitations. First, it is not obvious why the exclusion of war debts and tariff rates rendered agreement on exchange rate and monetary questions impossible. Excluding war debts and tariff rates from the agenda did not prevent the three countries from agreeing to stabilize their currencies, reduce their gold cover ratios, and expand their money supplies. France would have obtained the exchange-rate stability it desired, the United States and Britain the reflationary initiatives to which they attached priority. The U.S. would not have granted war-debt concessions, nor would it have been forced to reduce tariffs. Thus one can plausibly argue that the U.S. could have emerged from the conference as well off as in the hypothetical situation in which both war debt and tariff revision had been negotiated. Other countries would have obtained neither debt relief nor improved access to the U.S. export market. Hence their enthusiasm for a prospective agreement surely was dimmed by the U.S. strategy. But it was the U.S., not other countries, that refused to stabilize. The problem was not that the U.S. had too little to offer; rather, it was that Roosevelt regarded France and Britain's counteroffer as inadequate.

The second limitation of this explanation is that, in the case of war debts at least, it is not clear that the exclusion rule was binding. The United States wished to separate the discussion of war debts from other issues, but not to prevent such discussion entirely. This was the same approach taken to tripartite exchange-rate stabilization talks, namely, to segregate them from the proceedings of the World Economic Conference on the grounds that they directly involved only a subset of countries. During the Washington Conversations, extensive discussion of war debts had ensued, covering reduction of capital, elimination of interest, and other options. Formal cancellation may have been impossible, but this did not necessarily exclude close substitutes. When the June 15 payment came due, in the midst of the conference, the U.S. agreed to accept token payment of 10 million dollars. The U.S. strategy prevented a war-debt settlement from being negotiated at the conference itself, but it did not prevent the negotiation of debt revision as part of a broader agreement.

The other explanation, emphasizing Roosevelt's refusal to stabilize, is not so much flawed but incomplete. That the President's bombshell halted negotiations is indisputable; the question is what led him to take that step. The literature tends to portray Roosevelt's action as idiosyncratic. In the remainder of this chapter we suggest that two more systematic factors were at work: the incompatibility of the conceptual frameworks that informed national negotiating positions, and domestic politics.

THE ROLE OF COMPETING CONCEPTUAL FRAMEWORKS

The Nature of the Frameworks

One reason that French, British, and U.S. representatives found it difficult to agree was that their negotiating positions were informed by different conceptual frameworks.[16] By 1933 the interpretation of the slump presented by Keynes to the Macmillan Committee three years earlier had been accepted by the British Treasury and, with reservations, by the Bank of England. In this view, Britain's Depression had resulted from a deflationary shock imported from abroad. World prices had collapsed starting in 1929. The decline of international prices had not reduced domestic prices commensurately; instead, rigidities in the domestic wage-price structure had produced the macroeconomic slump. Financial contracts were nominally denominated and ran many years to maturity. Hence the fall in prices had raised the real burden of debts, eroding the creditworthiness of borrowers and discouraging investment. The failure of money wages to fall proportionately had inflated real labor costs, discouraging production and employment. The growing market power of unions had reinforced labor's traditional desire for a wage structure that was stable across workers and over time; this had contributed to the failure of money wages to adjust. Trade Boards, established just prior to World War I, set minimum rates of pay for unskilled workers, effectively placing a floor below the entire structure of labor costs. The authorities' failure to reduce unemployment benefits along with wages further exacerbated the problem.[17]

This interpretation of the crisis pointed to an obvious policy response. Monetary policy should be used to stabilize prices and eventually to restore them to 1929 levels. Starting in 1932, the Bank of England had begun to take the necessary action. Bank rate had been reduced to 2 percent. Credit had been provided in quantities sufficient to halt the decline of prices.

Central to the British view was a preoccupation with the external constraint. If the exchange rate was fixed, it was impossible for any one central bank to pursue reflationary initiatives. Measures to raise the domestic price level would erode international competitiveness, undermining the balance of payments. If the central bank reduced domestic interest rates, capital would flow out, worsening the capital account of the balance of payments. If it stimulated domestic demand, imports would flow in, worsening the current account. In effect, a central bank committed to defending a fixed exchange rate lacked the capacity to run independent reflationary policies. Unless reflationary initiatives were coordinated internationally, currency depreciation was a necessary concomitant of cheap money.

French policy-makers attributed the crisis neither to deflation nor to the passivity of policy-makers, but to monetary instability. Unlike the British, who argued that under the gold standard monetary authorities possessed inadequate discretion, in the prevailing French view the opposite was true. Growing reliance on foreign-exchange reserves had relaxed the gold-standard constraints. Central banks had willingly accumulated sterling and dollar balances over the second half of the 1920s, allowing the Bank of England and the Federal Reserve System to indulge in excessively expansionary monetary policies. In this view, productive capacity worldwide had expanded more rapidly since 1913 than the supply of monetary gold. Since the demand for money rose with the level of activity, lower prices were necessary to provide a matching increase in the supply of real balances. Under the gold standard, a smooth deflation like that of 1873–93 was the normal response. But in the 1920s central banks had used their discretionary power to block the downward adjustment of prices. They recklessly pyramided domestic credit on foreign-exchange reserves. Liberal supplies of credit had fueled speculation, raising asset prices to unsustainable heights and setting the stage for the stock-market crash. Following this shock, central banks rushed to liquidate exchange reserves, and prices fell abruptly. One point on which French and British experts agreed was that this sudden deflation was far from smooth: it produced bankruptcies among debtors, discouraged investment, and disrupted activity. The insufficiency of investment that resulted was the proximate source of the slump.[18]

In France, then, the Depression was seen as an inevitable consequence of the unrealistic policies pursued by central banks in preceding years. To now prevent deflation from running its course threatened to inaugurate another era of speculative excess and, ultimately, another depression. It was better to allow excess liquidity to be purged and prices to fall to sustainable levels. Only then would the confidence of investors be restored. Only then could sustainable recovery commence.[19]

Nothing more dramatically symbolized this problem of financial instability than disarray in the international monetary sphere. Exchange-rate instability discouraged domestic investment and international trade. Restoring the international gold standard was the single most important step policy-makers might take to promote investor confidence.

In contrast to France and Britain, there existed no dominant economic model in the United States.[20] In part this reflected the ongoing transition from the Hoover to the Roosevelt administration. In part it reflected Hoover's eclecticism and Roosevelt's taste for experimentation. In part it was symptomatic of deep disagreement in academic and official circles. The American model, insofar as the label has content, incorporated elements of both its French and British counterparts, taking on a more British flavor with the passage of time. In addition, however, the American framework had distinctive elements of its own.

Hoover shared the French explanation for the slump that emphasized the abuse of credit.[21] He blamed excessively accommodating Federal Reserve policy between 1925 and 1927 for provoking the stock-market boom and the crash to whose effects the economy was still striving to adjust. But Hoover and his colleagues supplemented the French explanation with one akin to the British, holding that the unregulated economy was inherently unstable. Economic activity, they held, was given to periodic slumps that should be offset by measures to stimulate demand. Demand could be sustained during cyclical downturns by accelerating the rate of public-works spending, by reducing interest rates, and by preventing management from cutting wages. The appropriate policy response to the slump was to cut interest rates and stabilize prices in order to stimulate capital investment, to persuade employers to pay stable wages in order to stimulate consumer demand, and to increase government spending to stimulate employment directly.[22]

When the Hooverites contemplated the external constraint, the inconsistencies in their conceptual framework became apparent. Adopting the French explanation of the slump as a result of a massive abuse of credit, they attached priority to maintenance of investor confidence and to prevent renewed speculative excesses. During the 1932 electoral campaign, Hoover continued to tie his political fortunes to the gold standard. An absence of speculative excesses was not sufficient, however, to stabilize an unstable economy. Demand stimulus was also required. But each of the demand-side measures the Hooverites proposed threatened gold convertibility. Increased public spending promised to suck in imports. Low interest rates threatened to provoke a capital outflow. High wages eroded the competitiveness of U.S. exports. The two strands of thought proved incompatible.

Previous authors have noted that the Hoover Administration had in its portfolio all the policy instruments needed to counter the Depression, but was strangely hesitant to utilize them on the requisite scale.[23] Public works spending remained tentative. Aside from the spring of 1932, the Federal Reserve engaged in few expansionary open-market operations. The administration's high-wage policy was abandoned in 1931. The explanation is simple enough. Deficit spending, monetary expansion, and high wages threatened the gold standard. Absent a willingness to abandon gold, demand-side policies could be used only with moderation.

The relationship of Hoover's model to Roosevelt's is a contested issue among historians. Most writers have portrayed the Roosevelt Administration's model circa June 1933 as a revolutionary break with its predecessor. In fact, Roosevelt's model can be seen as essentially the same as Hoover's in its emphases on high wages (New Deal Labor codes), farm purchasing power (agricultural set asides), slowly rising prices (the gold-buying program and industrial price-maintenance schemes), public spending (the Tennessee Valley Authority and other New Deal programs), and the need for financial stability (to be obtained through banking reform). Roosevelt, like Hoover, apparently shared the diagnosis of the Depression as a reflection of insufficient demand.[24] Roosevelt simply reversed the priority Hoover had attached to exchange-rate stability over demand stimulus.

Origins of the Frameworks

It seems extraordinary that policy-makers in these three countries could have perceived the causes of the slump in such radically different ways. In fact, their divergent conceptual frameworks directly reflected their nations' different historical experiences. Britain had endured deflation throughout the 1920s. The Bank of England had first pursued restrictive policies in order to restore the pre-war sterling parity in 1925. Prices had continued to fall, albeit at a slower pace, over the second half of the 1920s. Recorded unemployment had hovered in double digits, suggesting an association between deflation and joblessness. Britain had experienced a series of exchange-rate crises, in 1927, in 1929, and most seriously in 1931, each of which had forced the Bank of England to tighten the monetary screws.

A decade of high unemployment and labor disputes had focused attention on nominal wage inertia as a central factor in the propagation of the deflationary impulse. The downward inflexibility of money wages, it was widely believed, reflected the spread of unionism and the growth of labor militancy. Union density declined in the 1920s from its immediate postwar peak, but labor organization continued to exceed the levels reached before the war.

Just as the 1920s had sensitized the British to the dangers of deflation and fixed exchange rates, the abandonment of gold in September 1931, and its aftermath, had impressed them with the advantages of the alternative. At last the Bank of England had been able to relax its monetary stance. Following a short period of adjustment, industrial production had begun to rise. The efficacy of monetary reflation and of a floating pound sterling was readily evident to British observers.

British insistence that an international commitment to reflationary measures precede the restoration of fixed parities similarly reflected the experience of preceding years. At the Genoa Conference in 1922, British Treasury experts had warned that restoration of the international gold standard might give rise to deflationary pressure. They had proposed a convention to supplement gold reserves with convertible foreign exchange. But the resolutions adopted at Genoa had not been systematically implemented, and consequently, the British believed, the disaster of which they had warned had come to pass. Starting in 1929, the British Treasury and the Bank of England had urged the U.S. Federal Reserve System and the Bank of France to expand, and thereby to relax the external constraint on British monetary policy. Neither foreign central bank had cooperated. This experience led British policy-makers to demand an explicit commitment to internationally coordinated reflationary initiatives before agreeing to return to gold.

Financial instability was the dominant characteristic of French experience in the postwar decade. During the period when gold convertibility was suspended, France had experienced persistent inflation accompanied by financial and political chaos. The Bank of France had used its discretion not to stabilize the economy but to finance government budget deficits through domestic credit creation. French observers consequently associated monetary discretion with financial instability. Only following the re-establishment of constraints on monetary policy, in the form of gold convertibility and statutes prohibiting the Bank of France from undertaking most open-market operations, had inflation been halted and a basis for sustainable growth bee laid. It is not surprising, then, that discretionary monetary policy was associated with financial instability in general, and exchange-rate instability in particular, and that the French sought an explanation for the slump in the breakdown of the international monetary system.

French observers did not share the worries of labor-market inflexibility characteristic of the British. Recorded unemployment had been low throughout the 1920s.[25] Mobility between the urban and rural sectors remained higher than in Britain. Nor did France possess an unemployment insurance system comparable to Britain's. Unemployment benefits were strictly limited, and public relief was provided locally. French experts such as Jacques Rueff ascribed British unemployment to the excessive generosity of its unemployment insurance system and attributed the smoother operation of the French labor market largely to the absence of such a system.[26]

The recent historical experience of the United States similarly helps to explain the Hoover Administration's failure to appreciate the conflict between the gold standard and demand stimulus. Ever since 1914, the U.S. gold standard had been secure. The U.S. was the one beligerent that had not been forced to suspend the gold standard during World War I. It had enjoyed persistent balance-of-payments surpluses throughout the 1920s. Gold reserves continued to flow toward the U.S. during the first two years of the slump. By 1931, there existed an entire generation of American policy-makers without firsthand experience with threats to gold convertibility. The situation changed following sterling's devaluation in September 1931, but policy-makers were slow to incorporate this new information.

Effects of the Frameworks

For competing conceptual frameworks to influence negotiations, they had to be embraced by government ministries. Officials from those ministries had to be vested with responsibility for negotiations.

The leading proponents of the French model were Charles Rist and Jacques Rueff. Rist was the preeminent French academic economist of his generation. He had been assistant governor of the Bank of France from 1926 through 1929 and advised a succession of governments. He had provided a fully articulated statement of the French model of the Depression as early as 1931.[27] The authority of Rist, combined with his connections to government, facilitated the acceptance of his views. Jacques Rueff, also a professional economist and long-time financial attaché to the French Embassy in London, played an important role in disseminating Rist's views within the French Treasury. Rueff authored a series of memoranda analyzing the international economic situation that circulated widely within the government.

Rist was appointed to the Committee of Experts and conferred with Ministry of France officials in the interval between successive meetings of the preparatory committee. At the critical stabilization negotiations, Rist's views were ably represented by Rueff.

Evolution of the British model was more complex. As mentioned above, Keynes had offered a statement of the model in private evidence to the Macmillan Committee. The Economic Advisory Committee, established by the second Labour Government in 1929, provided a vehicle through which Keynes and his followers within government were able to disseminate his views.[28] The Bank of England, and to a lesser extent the Treasury, resisted aspects of his analysis. The Bank continued to evince a strong preference for currency stabilization, but once establishment of the Exchange Equalisation Account transferred much responsibility for exchange-rate management from the Bank to the Treasury, its views carried less weight. The Treasury prepared the memoranda that informed the British negotiating position. Treasury officials represented Britain on the Committee of Experts and at the London Conference.

The absence of a dominant U.S. model was reflected in American representation at the London Conference. John H. Williams, though a leading academic authority, was not a member of Hoover or Roosevelt's inner circle or an intimate of the U.S. Treasury or the Federal Reserve Board. He was a strong proponent of fixed exchange rates, a fact indicative of his distance from Roosevelt. Oliver Sprague, a Harvard professor who previously advised the Bank of England on exchange-rat questions, had recently taken a similar position in the U.S. Treasury, but his influence over Roosevelt's opinions was not great. James P. Warburg, son of Paul Warburg and vice-president of the Bank of Manhattan, was the source of a series of creative proposals, but these were resisted by Roosevelt's other advisers and rejected by the President. Raymond Moley, Roosevelt's closest advisor, had been "a professor of Criminology at a girls' college" and was "almost completely lacking in detailed [financial] knowledge," as Leith-Ross disparagingly put it.[29] The composition of American representation seemed designed to maximize the distance between London and Washington.

The adherence of national representatives to these different models led to both general disagreements and specific misunderstandings. General disagreement made it impossible for the three national delegations to adjust exchange-rate and monetary policies in ways they all preferred. Had the representatives of the three governments all subscribed to the British model, it would have been straightforward to trade a French commitment to reflate for British and American commitments to stabilize their exchange rates. All three countries would have been able to expand supplies of money and credit, at the same time avoiding the disruptive effects of exchange-rate instability. All three, according to the British model, would have been better off.

Alternatively, had the representatives of all these governments subscribed to the French model, it would have been straightforward to agree to stabilize exchange rates and restore gold convertibility. Having eliminated the debilitating effects of exchange-rate instability, they all would have been better off. But lacking a common model, it was impossible for the three parties to agree on a package of exchange-rate cum monetary polices.

The predominance of different models also led to specific misunderstanding that disrupted communication and impeded negotiation. When, for instance, following Roosevelt's bombshell, the French attempted to negotiate a separate stabilization agreement with the British, French officials – Georges Bonnet in particular – assumed that their British counterparts shared their belief that exchange-rate variability handicapped recovery efforts. Bonnet had discussed financial issues with the British Chancellor, Neville Chamberlain, during a preconference visit to London. Chamberlain, in the British view, had agreed only on the desirability of limiting international financial instability. He had avoided the issue of what Britain would do in the event of dollar devaluation.[30]

In the French view, however, Chamberlain and the British shared the priority France attached to minimizing financial instability. Bonnet's impression was that he and the British Chancellor agreed completely on the need to restore exchange-rate stability. Bonnet came away convinced that the British would soon return to gold, presumably in the summer of 1933. The question was merely whether, before returning to gold, they would require an international convention on the operation of the monetary system, or whether British officials would settle for an informal understanding. The French misinterpreted British concern that dollar devaluation would transfer Britain's competitive advantage to the United States for an aversion to exchange-rate flexibility in general. Hence they were misled into believing that the British might agree to exchange-rate stabilization without U.S. participation.[31]

Similar factors appear to have influenced the perceptions of the American members of the Committee of Experts. Their cables to Washington did not provide a sense of British skepticism regarding stabilization or of the priority British negotiators attached to monetary reflation. They implied that their British counterparts shared their own desire for exchange-rate stabilization. Some of these cables mentioned in passing war-debt forgiveness and tariff concessions as the price that the British might demand for agreeing to stabilize sterling. When the American experts returned to Washington, even these caveats receded from view.[32]

Thus, the prevalence of different conceptual frameworks in different countries precluded the negotiation of a purely monetary deal. In principle, one can imagine that things could have turned out otherwise. One can imagine that representatives of the three nations could have agreed on a common set of actions for entirely different reasons. Frankel and Rockett show that there exist cases where policy-makers, despite subscribing to different models of the economy, can all be rendered better off by an agreement to cooperate.[33] But they also show that such cases are relatively rare, and the 1933 World Economic Conference does not appear to have been one of them. In 1933 the competing conceptual frameworks strongly pointed to the desirability of incompatible policies, causing negotiations to break down.

THE ROLE OF DOMESTIC POLITICS

Incompatible conceptual frameworks prevented the negotiation of a mutually acceptable package of exchange-rate and monetary reforms. In return for agreement to stabilize sterling, the British demanded structural reforms that guaranteed monetary reflation by France and dollar stabilization by the United States. The French viewed monetary reflation as counterproductive and therefore an unacceptable price to pay. The U.S. refused to stabilize the dollar because it did not see what it would get in return.

Yet exchange-rate and monetary policies were not the only variables that might have been bartered in London. In return for British and American agreement to stabilize their exchange rates, France might have agreed to relax its tariffs and quotas. Additional French imports from the United States and Britain would have permitted the Bank of England and the Federal Reserve System to expand domestic credit and stimulate demand without driving the British and American balances of payments into deficit and renewing the conflict between internal and external balance. France would have gained the exchange-rate stability she desired. The U.S. and Britain would have been able to engage in the monetary reflation to which they attached priority. French gold would have been redistributed to other countries without infringing on the autonomy of the Bank of France.

This chain of quid pro quos remained no less feasible after the United States abandoned gold. Before April 1933, a mutually acceptable package would have entailed British agreement to stabilize, French agreement to liberalize, and U.S. agreement to forgive war debts or reduce tariffs. After April 1933, it would have required Britain to stabilize, France to liberalize, and the U.S. to stabilize the dollar and perhaps grant war-debt or tariff concessions. Roosevelt's pre-emptive strike may have increased the tariff reductions that France (and perhaps also Britain) would have to offer, but it did not obviously alter the nature of the package.

The terms of this deal had been foreseen by Treasury Secretary Ogden Mills in the final months of the Hoover Administration.[34] The exchange of tariff concessions for exchange-rate stabilization had been implicit in the Draft Annotated Agenda of the Committee of Experts. Officials within the French Finance Ministry anticipated that the government would be asked to barter trade liberalization for monetary stabilization by countries that blamed French import quotas for the instability of currencies.[35] French officials envisaged the outlines of a trade in which Britain stabilized sterling, the United States forgave war debts, and France reduced its trade barriers and perhaps also adopted measures to redistribute its excess gold reserves.[36] Here, however, was where domestic politics entered the story. Domestic pressures made it impossible for France to offer tariff concessions. Pressures for reflation and silver monetization in the United States made Roosevelt hesitate to stabilize the dollar. Though there may have existed a policy trade acceptable to negotiators, it was not acceptable to those on whose support they relied.

French Politics

The Daladier government was in an extremely tenuous political position. It was one in a series of 11 ministries to hold power in the period of political instability from May 1932 to May 1936. Throughout the period, the Radical Party occupied the center of the political spectrum.[37] Though it gained 200,000 votes from the moderates and lost none to the Socialists in 1932, the party was still a minority in the Chamber of Deputies. To govern, a Radical premier had to satisfy the demands of his own constituency and at the same time retain the support of the Socialists and Rightists whose votes were needed to sustain the government.

The dominant characteristic of this polity was its fragmentation. The Right was split into two major parties, the Alliance Démocratique (representatives of big business who embraced the rhetoric of economic modernization) and the Fédération Républicaine (large land-owners and notables from predominantly Catholic regions). The Socialists were split between the more moderate Vie Socialiste, which favored cooperation with the Radicals, and the Bataille Socialiste, whose members advocated collective action and collaboration with the Communists.[38]

The Radical Party is itself best thought of as a loose coalition of moderate politicians representing rural, provincial regions. It was the party of the independent peasants and lower middle classes (independent proprietors, farmers, artisans, and civil servants).[39] Perhaps reflecting this diversity, the Radicals lacked a consistent economic program. The one economic goal that united them was the priority they attached to the maintenance of financial stability. A Radical government had presided over the inflation of the 1920s and had been brought down by the franc's collapse, opening the door to six years of conservative rule. At each party congress, the one issue on which there existed consensus was the need to prevent this from happening again.

The composition of the cabinet was critical to the formulation of economic policy. Until Leon Blum created a Ministry of National Economy in 1936, there was no office responsible for economics. The office of Undersecretary of State for Economic Affairs created by André Tardieu in 1930 possessed little influence. The economic policy of the Heriot and Daladier governments emerged from bargains between ministries representing different interest groups.[40]

From Poincaré's return to power in 1926 until the 1932 elections, France had been led by governments of the Right. The 1932 elections then returned a Left-wing majority. A coalition government of Radicals and Socialists would have possessed a comfortable majority. But the massive reduction of defense spending, tax increases, and national wheat and fertilizer boards demanded by the SFIO (Socialists) as their price for participation in a Cartel des Gauches were unacceptable to the executive committee of the Radical Party. Instead, Edouard Herriot formed a Radical government to pursue a more orthodox economic program in which the SFIO refused to participate, but to which it lent support. Herriot's government was continually harassed from the Left for its failure to raise taxes and reorganize the economy, and from the Right (including conservative Radicals) for its inability to cut public spending. Its downfall began in June 1932, when a bill to balance the budget which included a 5 percent reduction in the salaries of public servants was demolished by Left-wing Radicals and Socialists on the Finance Committee of the Chamber. Herriot fell in December 1932, ostensibly over his willingness to make another war-debt payment to the United States, in reality over his inability to break the budgetary deadlock.

Though Daladier was to the left of Herriot, the composition of his government was little different. Daladier was forced to make repeated concessions to both the Socialists and the moderate Right to retain their support.

For its survival, the Daladier government depended in particular on the support of deputies from predominantly agricultural *départements*, who returned Radical, Fédération Française, or Vie Socialiste deputies to the Chamber. This particular constituency was in dire straits. The crisis of French agriculture intensified as the London Conference approached. Since 1931, agricultural prices had been supported through the application of import quotas.[41] In 1932, an abundant harvest put further downward pressure on domestic prices. French wheat prices fell by 40 percent in the year ending in April 1933. A variety of measures had already been taken by previous governments to support the domestic wheat market. But in the spring of 1933 Daladier came under intense pressure from Socialists and Radicals in the Chamber of Deputies to introduce more comprehensive measures establishing a minimum wheat price. Though the bill was passed quickly, it was not clear that the government would in fact intervene to set a binding floor on domestic wheat prices, since it lacked financial resources. What was clear was that any attempt to support domestic wheat prices would be futile if import restrictions were relaxed.[42]

The French were perfectly aware that they would be asked at the London Conference to offer commercial concessions.[43] Georges Bonnet had in fact implied a willingness to consider relaxing French quotas in his preconference meeting with Chamberlain in London in March.[44] Agricultural interests were vigilant to this possibility, and made their objections known.[45] Each *département* had a Chamber of Agriculture which met regularly and lobbied elected representatives and ministerial officials. Following the example of the Confederations Générale de Planteurs de Betteraves (1921) and the Association Générale des Producteurs de Blé (1924), special associations were formed to represent the interests of producers of particular products. By the 1930s, half of the farmers belonged to such agricultural unions. These organizations have been called the "first really effective farm pressure groups France had ever known."[46]

Despite the inability of the farmers to unite behind a single political party, their interests were ably represented in the Chamber of Deputies. Though they made up only a third of the national electorate, rural voters accounted for the electoral majority in more than half of all districts. According to Gordon Wright, only one in four deputies could safely ignore rural interests if he hoped to be re-elected. The electorate for the Senate was if anything even more disproportionately rural.[47]

The effectiveness of the agricultural lobby is illustrated by an incident in early 1933. On February 27, Jacques Rueff had spoken to a conference at the Sorbonne presided over by Charles Rist. Rueff had emphasized the merits of trade liberalization. The speech provoked "acerbic" and "emotional" responses in the agricultural press, according to the Minister of Agriculture, Henri Queuille, who on March 11 sent a letter denouncing Rueff for his "total ignorance and lack of comprehension" of the question to various members of the government, and specifically to Rueff's superior, Georges Bonnet.[48]

Along with Queuille, the leading cabinet spokesman for the protectionists was Louis Serre, the Minister of Commerce. In early April, at an interministerial conference to determine the French position for the London Conference, Serrre noted that other countries would demand the suppression of quotas and the reduction of tariffs. He proposed raising tariffs immediately to provide scope for reducing them late without undercutting the protection afforded agriculture and industry. Those present unanimously agreed that the French government could not adopt an entirely negative attitude on trade liberalization which would isolate it at the conference. At the same time, it was regarded as unacceptable to renounce the policy of tariffs and quotas.[49]

The National Confederation of Agricultural Associations petitioned the government in April, protesting against the adoption of measures of trade liberalization proposed by the Preparatory Commission of Experts.[50] Departmental chambers of Agriculture and Commerce bombarded the Finance Commission of the Chamber of Deputies with letters denouncing commercial concessions. The Finance Commission forwarded these letters to the Ministry of Finance.[51] Most of the letters are dated late May and early June, as if the local chambers had the London Conference in mind. The text of each letter contained the resolution adopted (often unanimously) by members of the chamber. Many of these resolutions were virtually identical, suggesting a coordinated, concerted campaign.

These pressures clearly affected the negotiating position of the French delegation to the conference. In his opening statement, Daladier stressed the importance of currency stabilization, but made no mention of trade restrictions. He linked the plight of the farmers to the Depression in other sectors, asking, "How could the hundreds of millions of farmers, who had been suddenly deprived of their purchasing power and their ability to consume, continue as customers of industry, banking, and finance?"[52]

The tenuous political position of the Daladier government also reinforced its commitment to the gold standard. The year 1933 saw the first glimmerings of resistance on the Left to gold convertibility and monetary deflation.[53] Though it could not afford to antagonize the Socialists, the Daladier government did not budge. Its allegiance to the gold standard reflected the government's failure to contain the fiscal crisis and the price extracted by the Bank of France for continued assistance. Persistent budget deficits burdened the Herriot and Daladier ministries alike. The Right successfully resisted tax increases, while the Left rejected cuts in public services and veterans' pensions. There existed no viable parliamentary coalition to restore fiscal balance. Given the narrow French money market, it was difficult to finance deficits through sales of bonds to the public. Banks were willing to absorb treasury bills only if they were assured of Bank of France rediscounts in the event they needed additional cash. Successive governments were forced to rely on the central bank's willingness to discount treasury bills. Since the Bank of France could refuse to discount government paper, Daladier was forced to negotiate. The bank's governor, Clement Moret, attached the central banker's traditional priority to monetary orthodoxy, and specifically to maintenance of the gold standard. Moret and his colleagues demanded that Daladier reaffirm his commitment to gold convertibility. Unless it managed to construct a viable fiscal coalition, the government had no choice but to accept the bank's terms.[54]

U.S. Politics

Where Daladier's support was narrow, Roosevelt's was broad. Winning 472 electoral votes, he was supported by every region of the country. Urban workers, reacting against unemployment, voted for Roosevelt in large numbers. So did large numbers of midwestern farmers reacting against the slump in agricultural prices.

Nonetheless, two levels of politics impinged upon decision-making by the American chief executive: congressional politics and politics within the executive branch. Roosevelt's advisors had diverse views on international economic policy.[55] Cordell Hull, Roosevelt's Secretary of State, was the personification of internationalism; his Assistant Secretary, Raymond Moley, was a strong nationalist. Hull believed passionately in the need for tariff reductions; Moley worked to prevent them. The same tug-of-war occurred in other departments. Contemporaries viewed Roosevelt's appointments as indicative of indecisiveness or confusion; historians have come to view them as his systematic attempt to minimize dependence on particular ideological perspectives.[56] Whatever the case, the policy promoted rivalry and maneuvering within the administration, with leaders of each faction attempting unsuccessfully to control access to the President.

Turning to congressional politics, Roosevelt, like Daladier, was under pressure to do something for the farmers. Western and southern congressmen united in the campaign to secure agrarian relief. Even Republican progressives from rural districts joined what was traditionally a Democratic campaign. Demands for higher prices by this agrarian bloc complemented those of silver-mining interests urging reflation through silver monetization. A series of bills demanding silver coinage or reflationary open-market operations were introduced in 1932.

But it was only in 1933 that the agricultural bloc and the silverites formed an effective alliance.[57] In debate over Senator Burton Wheeler's amendment to the farm bill, senators from silver-mining states repeatedly invoked the plight of the farmers, prescribing monetary measures designed to raise prices. Senators from agricultural states stressed that their constituents' difficulties were shared by the residents of industrial regions as well. On April 17 the Senate, by 33 to 43, defeated the Wheeler Amendment, which would have permitted unlimited coinage of silver at a ratio to gold of 16 to 1. All 14 senators from the seven silver-mining states of the west voted for the amendment: they were joined by 19 others from the midwest and the south. The Administration was aware that at least 10 senators had withheld their support only because of the extremity of the measure.[58]

Roosevelt sought to channel these pressures by endorsing the more moderate Thomas Amendment. According to Raymond Moley, Roosevelt still had no specific economic program in mind and agreed to the Thomas Amendment only to contain the rebellion of the Senate inflationists. "The cold fact," wrote Moley, "is that the inflationary movement attained such formidable strength by April 18th that Roosevelt realized that he could not block it, that he could, at most, try to direct it."[59] The Thomas Amendment and the gold embargo were the most conservative steps that Roosevelt could take in response to inflationist pressure.[60]

The Thomas Amendment authorized but did not require the President to stimulate inflation in various ways. He could instruct the Federal Reserve System to purchase up to 3 billion dollars of government securities. If it refused, he could authorize the issue of 3 billion dollars of greenbacks. He could reduce the gold content of the dollar. He could authorize the coinage of silver. Roosevelt had been forced to accommodate mounting inflationist pressure in Congress, but he may have been happy to do so, both because the step was consistent with his own inflationist inclinations and because it permitted him to do so in a way that derailed more radical options.

If domestic politics mandated dollar devaluation, did they also preclude stabilization at a lower level? Three billion dollars of open-market purchases need not have depressed the dollar by more than 15 percent, a level at which the French and British were willing to contemplate stabilization. Had Roosevelt opted for additional silver monetization, however, he might have found himself unable to peg the dollar. Thus, silverites in Congress were certain to resist any stabilization plan, as Cordell Hull warned Ramsay MacDonald on June 19.[61]

It is not necessary to argue that domestic political pressures were wholly responsible for Roosevelt's decision. One must also consider the President's model of the economy and the failure of other countries to offer him something attractive in return. Roosevelt was gravitating toward the gold-buying program of the autumn, which was incompatible with a stabilization agreement. Such is the implication of his statement, on June 28, that it would not be a disaster if France was forced from the gold standard, since this would not interfere with his policy of raising domestic prices.[62] And France and Britain were unable to offer either commercial policy concessions or a credible commitment to reflate that might permit him to finesse this conflict.

Domestic political pressures also impeded efforts to extract commercial concessions from the United States. The Smoot-Hawley Tariff had been passed in 1930 by an alliance of agriculture (mainly representatives of the grain producers of the midwest) and light industry (such as New England textile, shoe, and glove manufacturers).[63] The traditionally protectionist Republicans had lost ground in Congress as a result of the 1932 elections, but pressure for protection emanating from agriculture and light industry had intensified as the slump deepened. The Americans on the Preparatory Committee of Experts, themselves sympathetic to tariff reduction, were instructed to veto statements to this effect because they were unacceptable to the U.S. Congress.[64] Tariff reduction was likely to antagonize the same agricultural interests pressing for silver inflation. Congressional leaders warned Roosevelt that significant changes in U.S. tariffs were impossible. On the eve of the conference, Roosevelt informed a disappointed Cordell Hull that the introduction of a bill that would have permitted the President to conclude trade agreements without Senate ratification was "highly inadvisable."[65]

British Politics

The National government that came to power in the summer of 1931 was a peculiar coalition led by a Labour Prime Minister, Ramsay MacDonald, but featuring Liberal and Conservative ministers. Following sterling's embarrassing devaluation in September, the Conservatives, campaigning on the need for sound finance and tariff protection, scored a resounding victory. In the new House of Commons, Conservatives occupied 473 of 615 seats. Thus, in contrast to the situation in France and the United States, the National Government did not have to worry about Parliamentary resistance to its policies so long as these remained consistent with the Conservative Party's election manifesto.

But Stanley Baldwin, the Conservative leader, could not force MacDonald's resignation, since the Conservative supporters of the National government had campaigned on the need for collaboration in time of crisis. Hence the Cabinet, not Parliament, was the principal battleground on which policy decisions were fought. On one side was MacDonald, an internationalist inclined toward collaboration with the United States and France. On the other was the new Chancellor of the Exchequer, Neville Chamberlain, heir to the fair-trade campaign initiated by his father, Joseph Chamberlain, and an advocate of tariffs and imperial preference. The Foreign Office and the Bank of England supported the Prime Minister. The Treasury and the Board of Trade fell in behind the Chancellor.

The nationalist position and its advocates were on the ascendant throughout 1932. Over Liberal opposition and Labour qualms, a general tariff was introduced in the early months of 1932.[66] The tariff bill passed its second reading by 454 votes to 78. Sterling was allowed to decline dramatically against the gold currencies. The locus of control over monetary policy shifted from the Bank of England to the Treasury, Chamberlain's bailiwick, following establishment of the Exchange Equalisation Account in the summer of 1932.[67]

The depth of support for tariff protection, which most Conservatives regarded as a matter of principle, would have made the extension of dramatic commercial concessions difficult. Neither Chamberlain nor his followers ruled out modest trade reforms, however. Chamberlain spoke of the need for tariff reductions and the abolition of quotas in his opening address to the conference.[68] No matter of principle stood in the way of agreement to stabilize currencies, which Chamberlain appears to have been willing to commit to in May and June of 1933. The problem was that the concessions offered by other governments were regarded as inadequate to justify this sacrifice.

IMPLICATIONS

The puzzle is that there existed one or more potential agreements that dominated the actual outcome in the sense that they would have enhanced the welfare of all three nations involved, and yet negotiations failed. We have argued that this failure can only be understood in terms of the importance of competing conceptual frameworks and domestic political constraints. In concluding, we explore the extent to which the factors highlighted by our account can be related to Putnam's concerns.[69]

The existence of competing conceptual frameworks can be thought of as limiting negotiators' "acceptability-set" (the set of policy trades that all negotiators regard as an improvement over the status quo). Trades that involved only exchange-rate stabilization by Britain and the U.S., and reductions in cover ratios and authorization to conduct open-market operations for the Bank of France, were unacceptable because of the different conceptual frameworks that informed national negotiating positions. An agreement that involved only exchange-rate and monetary policy would have been acceptable to all three countries had they embraced a common conceptual framework, whichever of the three frameworks they chose. But lacking a common framework, compromise on exchange-rate cum monetary disputes required at least one country to accept a position that was worse than the status quo. For such a compromise to lie in its "acceptability-set," that country required compensation, generally in the form of foreign commercial concessions.

The domestic political constraints confronting negotiators can be thought of as limiting their "win-set" (the subset of policy trades acceptable to negotiators that is also "ratifiable"). The opposition of the Bank of France, which exerted considerable leverage over government policy, in conjunction with the strong preferences of the government's own electoral constituency, prevented France from being the one to adopt an exchange-rate cum monetary position regarded as worse than the status quo. At the same time, the pivotal political position of farmers and other groups with protectionist inclinations prevented French negotiators, who would otherwise have been willing to do so, from offering the commercial concessions required if other countries were to adopt otherwise unacceptable exchange-rate and monetary policies. Domestic political constraints were also operative in the United States. Opposition of the silverites to exchange-rate stabilization, and of midwestern agriculture and light industry to trade liberalization, raised the costs to Roosevelt of stabilizing the dollar and of reducing U.S. tariffs, at least one of which would have been required by foreign countries.

Relative to other case studies collected in this volume, the role played by interest-group politics has two striking characteristics. First, transnational links among interest groups were relatively unimportant. Such alliances were not unknown, but in 1933 they had relatively little impact on negotiations. We conjecture that their relative significance reflects the fact that market structures likely to facilitate transnational alliances, such as multinational corporations and foreign branches of domestic banks, were not yet as pervasive as they became subsequently. In addition, in 1933 effective alliances would have had to cut across conventional lines. French free-traders would have had to ally not with American free-traders but with American advocates of debt forgiveness and the gold standard. These individuals were occasionally but not uniformly the same. Hence previous international contacts between special-interest groups did not provide a convenient basis for transnational alliances in 1933.

Domestic politics would not have posed an obstacle to agreement if side-payments could have been arranged for interest groups who would have been adversely affected. Why were additional agricultural subsidies not offered French farmers who resisted trade policy concessions, for example? Here the broader economic and political context in which negotiations took place was critically important. France was suffering through a series of severe budgetary crises that posed a threat to the stability of the franc. Deficit finance of additional agricultural subsidies threatened to drive her off the gold standard. Hence additional agricultural subsidies could be extended only if taxes could be raised. Once again, the fragility of parliamentary support for Daladier, and the ability of each member of the coalition to bring down the government through its defection, prevented the Chamber from raising the taxes of any interest group.

This study speaks to the question of how to conceptualize the role of chief executive. Is the head of government merely a cipher interested in staying in power? Does he simply mirror the preferences of the majority of interest groups? Or does the chief executive have independent capacity to shape opinion in ways that transform the scope for agreement? This case suggests that there exists no single answer to this question. In the United States the chief executive enjoyed considerable latitude. Possessing a comfortable Congressional majority, and with four years until the next presidential election, he could afford to adopt a policy that, in the short run, antagonized a portion of his constituency. In France the Prime Minister had little independence. A policy which alienated even a small fraction of his supporters promised to bring down the government.

This suggests that the latitude enjoyed by the chief executive in international negotiations depends on the structure of the institutions linking the head of government to his constituency.[70] Among the relevant institutional arrangements is the ratification process. In 1933, an agreement to reduce U.S. tariffs would have had to be ratified by a Congress in which protectionist interests possessed disproportionate influence.[71] This was regarded as infeasible, and tariff reductions were not seriously discussed at the London Conference. In 1934, with passage of the Reciprocal Trade Agreements Act, ratification was taken out of the hands of Congress, providing additional flexibility for a chief executive wishing to make trade liberalization part of a package deal. The institutions that structure the ratification process are bequeathed by history, but scope for altering them depends as well on domestic political constraints, as Roosevelt observed in 1933.

But to focus on institutional determinants of "ratifiability," narrowly defined, is to overlook other institutional arrangements that critically regulate the independence of the head of state. Chief among these is the structure of the electoral system. In France, a major part of the explanation for the government's fragility was the modified proportional representation system under which deputies were elected. This led to a proliferation of political parties and to the election of deputies who represented highly specialized interest groups. Assembling a viable coalition was difficult. Policies which alienated even a small number of deputies on the fringes of the governing coalition were infeasible. In the United States, in contrast, a majority-representation electoral system suppressed significant third parties even in the turbulent circumstances of the 1930s. Disaffected voters simply shifted parties, in this case from the Republicans to the Democrats, endowing Roosevelt with a comfortable majority and considerable latitude.

Ultimately, Roosevelt used the latitude he enjoyed not to engineer an agreement but to block one. The U.S. chief executive seems to have been personally uncertain about the comparative merits of dollar stabilization, expansionary open-market operations, and gold purchases. This uncertainty heightened his desire to keep all options open, which posed an obstacle to international agreement.

Rather than attributing the failure of the World Economic Conference to Roosevelt's personal characteristics, however, it is more useful to focus on systemic factors that impeded the successful conclusion of negotiations. In this chapter we have argued that competing conceptual frameworks and domestic politics were the most important such factors. The former precluded the negotiation of a purely monetary agreement, while the latter prevented the conclusion of a cross-issue deal involving monetary policy, tariffs, and war debts. Both factors are therefore necessary to explain the breakdown of the conference. The implication is that, even if the outcome of the 1932 elections in the United States had been different, the outcome in London might have been the same.

Much of the work on this paper was undertaken during visits by Eichengreen to the Ecole des Hautes Etudes en Sciences Sociales in Paris and by Uzan to the University of California at Berkeley. Eichengreen's research was supported in part by grants from the EHESS, the German Marshall Fund of the United States, and the National Science Foundation, Uzan's by the Caisse des Depots. We acknowledge the permission of the French Ministry of Finance, the Bank of France, and the British Public Record Office to cite documents in their possession. We thank Kenneth Mouré, Robert Putnam, Harold Jacobson, Peter Evans, and participants in the Stanford and Cape Cod meetings of the study group for comments on prior drafts.

NOTES

1 The first thesis is propounded by Sir Frederick Leith-Ross in *Money Talks: Fifty Years of International Finance* (London: Hutchinson, 1968), p. 125, for example; the second by Charles Kindelberger, *The World in Depression, 1929–1939* (Berkeley: University of California Press, 1973). We point to some limitations of these arguments below.

2 Ernst Haas, "Why Collaborate? Issue Linkage and International Regimes," *World Politics* 32 (1980): 357–405.

3 Robert Putnam, "Diplomacy and Domestic Politics: The Logic of Two-Level Games," *International Organization* 42 (1988): 287–316; James Alt and Barry Eichengreen, "Parallel and Overlapping Games: Theory and an Application to the European Natural Gas Trade," *Economics and Politics* 1 (1989): 119–144.

4 Peter Hall, *The Political Power of Economic Ideas* (Princeton, N.J.: Princeton University

Press, 1989); Judith Goldstein and Robert Keohane, "Ideas and Foreign Policy," unpub. ms., 1990.

5 Jeffrey Frankel, "Obstacles to International Economic Policy Coordination," *Essays in International Finance* no. 64 (Princeton, N.J.: Princeton University Press, 1988); Jeffrey Frankel and Katherine Rockett, "International Macroeconomic Policy Coordination When Policymakers Do Not Agree on the True Model," *American Economic Review* 78 (1988): 318–340.

6 Secondary sources upon which this account draws are H. V. Hodson, *Slump and Recovery, 1929–1937* (London: Oxford University Press, 1938); Abdul Hasib, *Monetary Negotiations in the World Economic Conference, 1933* (Allahabad, India: Muslim University, 1958); S. V. O. Clarke, "The Reconstruction of the International Monetary System: The Attempts of 1922 and 1933," *Essays in International Finance* no. 33 (Princeton, N.J.: Princeton University Press, 1973); Kindleberger, *World in Depression*; Ian Drummond, *The Floating Pound and the Sterling Area, 1931–1939* (Cambridge, Eng.: Cambridge University Press, 1981).

7 See League of Nations, *World Production and Prices, 1937/38* (Geneva: League of Nations, 1938).

8 A limitation of this discussion is its focus on the United States, France, and Britain. A comprehensive account would analyze also the role played by other countries. Our emphasis on exchange rate stabilization negotiations, in which these three were involved to the exclusion of other countries, provides some justification for the disproportionate attention they receive here.

9 A clear statement of French priorities is in French Ministry of Finance Archives (FMFA) B32319, "Position Française à la Conférence de Londres," June 8, 1933.

10 What follows is based largely on British Public Record Office (PRO) Cab 29/140, Committee on the Economic Conference, "Policy of United Kingdom on main questions raised on agenda," May 1933, and PRO T177/12, "Leith-Ross memorandum," Dec. 20, 1932.

11 U.S. Department of State, *Foreign Relations of the United State* (Washington, D.C.: GPO, 1933), 1:597–600.

12 Roosevelt had, however, publicly avowed his support for the principle of currency stabilization. A U.S. State Department press release, dated May 16, 1933, quoted him as stating that "The conference must establish order in place of the present chaos by a stabilization of currencies"; cited in Dean Traynor, *International Monetary and Financial Conferences in the Interwar Period* (Washington, D.C.: Catholic University Press, 1949), p. 114.

13 Details of Warburg's initial proposal are described in Daniel Bennett Smith, "Toward Internationalism: New Deal Foreign Economic Policy, 1933–39" (Ph.D. diss., Stanford University, 1983), p. 47.

14 These incarnations of the Warburg Plan are reviewed in Richard Sayers, *The Bank of England, 1891–1944* (Cambridge, Eng.: Cambridge University Press, 1976), app. 27. See also Susan Howson, "Sterling's Managed Float: The Operations of the Exchange Equalization Account, 1932–39," *Essays in International Finance* no. 46 (Princeton, N.J.: Princeton University Press, 1981). British and French objections are described in PRO T175/83, "Declarations by the Bank of England and the Bank of France," May 23, 1933.

15 France made one final attempt to secure separate British agreement, which the latter rebuffed. PRO Cab 29/142, part 2, "Note of a conversation in the Treasury Board Room on Sunday, 2nd July 1933, at 5.45 p.m." As Neville Chamberlain explained to Charles Rist, "Now that there had been a public refusal on the part of the United States, the government of the United Kingdom could not associate itself with a

European bloc, since this would be taken to mean that in the differences between the gold-standard countries and the United States, the United Kingdom joined with the former, whereas in credit policy we were more in sympathy with the United States."

16 Two previous studies of the period which make this same point are John S. O'Dell, "From London to Bretton Woods: Roots of Economic Diplomacy," *Journal of Public Policy* 8 (1989): 287–316; and Barry Eichengreen, *Golden Fetters: The Gold Standard and the Great Depression, 1919–1939* (New York: Oxford University Press, 1992).

17 Frederick Phillips provided an explicit statement of this view as early as September 1931: Susan Howson, *Domestic Monetary Management in Britain, 1919–38* (Cambridge, Eng.: Cambridge University Press, 1975), p. 83. In October 1932, he composed a memo emphasizing the relevance of the relationship between prices and costs and of impediments to cost adjustment to proposals that Britain return to gold: PRO Cab 58/183, "The foreign demand for the return of the United Kingdom to gold." Additional references to Treasury arguments along these lines are provided by Alan Booth, "Britain in the 1930s: A Managed Economy?" *Economic History Review* 40 (1987): 499–522.

18 See, for example, Charles Rist, "Caractère et origine de la crise de 1929," *Essais sur quelques problèmes économiques et monétaries* (Paris: Recueil Sirey, 1933), pp. 325–343. That the same model was prevalent in official circles is evident, for example, in the minutes of the proceedings of the Regents of the Bank of France: Bank of France Archives, "Procès verbaux," March 9, 1933.

19 Rist, "Caractère et origine," pp. 341–342, noted that monetary reflation was the alternative to further price declines. But, he observed, "qui, [après les expériences des quinze dernières années,] voudrait s'engager dans une voie aussi dangereuse?"

20 William J. Barber, *From New Era to New Deal* (Cambridge, Eng.: Cambridge University Press, 1985), and Daniel R. Fusfield, *The Economic Thought of Franklin D. Roosevelt and the Origins of the New Deal* (New York: Columbia University Press, 1955), are basic sources on the evolution of academic and official analyses of the macroeconomy in the United States.

21 See Herbert Hoover, *The Memoirs of Herbert Hoover: The Great Depression, 1929–1941* (New York: Macmillan, 1952), chaps 1–2, for what is admittedly a retrospective view.

22 The demand-oriented aspects of this model were not widely embraced within either the Treasury or the Federal Reserve System. For details, see Barber, *From New Era*.

23 Barber, *From New Era*, is a good example of the genre.

24 Fusfield, *Economic Thought*, pp. 254–255.

25 The low level of recorded unemployment reflected the limited data gathered on the subject as much as the state of the French economy, but this did not modify the outlook of officials. See Robert Salais, "Why Was Unemployment So Low in France During the 1930s?" in Barry Eichengreen and Timothy J. Hatton, eds., *Interwar Unemployment in International Perspective* (Dordrecht, Neth.: Kluwer, 1988), pp. 247–288.

26 His analysis of British unemployment may be found in Jacques Rueff, "L'assurance chômage cause du chômage permanent," *Revue d'economie politique* 45 (1931): 211–242.

27 Rist's "Caractère et origine" was prepared for and published by the League of Nations in June 1931.

28 Susan Howson and Donald Winch, *The Economic Advisory Council* (Cambridge, Eng.: Cambridge University Press, 1977), describe the activities of the Economic Advisory Council.

29 Leith-Ross, *Money Talks*, p. 165.

30 The British account of the Bonnet-Chamberlain talks to PRO 371/17304, "Notes of meetings held in the board room, Treasury, on Friday, 17 March 1933."
31 George Bonnet, *Vingt ans de la vie politique, 1918–1938* (Paris: Fayard, 1969), pp. 161–162. Secretary of State Cordell Hull's European contacts verified that Bonnet took away the impression that Britain was about to return to gold: *Foreign Relations* 1:471–472. The French record of the Bonnet-Chamberlain discussions, *Documents Diplomatiques Francais*, "Competes rendus: entertiens franco-britanniques du vendredi 17 mars 1933" (Paris: Imprimerie Nationale, 1st series, vol. 3, 1977), pp. 1–15, touches on this point on p. 10. Similarly, on the eve of the conference the French financial attaché in Britain erroneously reported that "British opinion has become almost unanimous in recognizing the necessity of returning to an international standard of values as soon as possible, and the Treasury as well as the Bank of England declares that this standard can only be the gold standard": FMFA B32321, "From the Financial Attaché to the French Embassy in London," May 31, 1933.
32 *Foreign Relations* 1:839–840 and 453–457, 463.
33 Frankel and Rockett, "International Macroeconomic Policy Coordination."
34 James Ray Moore, "A History of World Economic Conference, London 1933" (Ph.D. diss., State University of New York at Stony Brook, 1972), pp. 86–87.
35 Herbert Feis, *1933: Characters in Crisis* (Boston: Little, Brown, 1966), pp. 33, 116; Moore, "History," p. 74; FMFA B32317, "Note sur la 2nd réunion de la Commission préparatoire de la Conférence de Londres," Dec. 29, 1932; FMFA B32317, "Note au sujet de la Conference Mondiale, Nov. 15, 1932."
36 FMFA B32319, "Note sur la situation de la France à la Conférence Économique Mondiale," March 1, 1933.
37 Useful surveys of French politics in this period include Edward Mead Earle, *Modern France: Problems of the Third Republic and Fourth Republic* (Princeton, N.J.: Princeton University Press, 1951), and Edouard Dubief, *Le déclin de la Troisième République* (Paris: Seuil, 1984).
38 An explanation for this proliferation of parties is the modified form of proportional representation under which deputies were elected: see Peter Campbell, *French Electoral Systems and Elections, 1789–1957* (New York: Frederick A. Praeger, 1958). We return to this point in our concluding section.
39 Peter Larmour, *The French Radical Party in the 1930s* (Stanford, Calif: Sanford University Press, 1964), p. 31.
40 Julian Jackson, *The Politics of Depression in France, 1932–1936* (Cambridge, Eng.: Cambridge University Press, 1985), p. 20.
41 See Ethel B. Dietrich, "French Import Quotas," *American Economic Review* 23 (1933): 661–674; and Frank Arnold Haight, *A History of French Commercial Policies* (New York: Macmillan, 1941), pp. 163–165.
42 Jackson, *Politics of Depression*, pp. 63, 69.
43 FMFA B32319, untitled memorandum, Feb. 27, 1933.
44 Drummond, *The Floating Pound*, p. 142.
45 The 1920s had witnessed the emergence of a vocal, organized French peasantry. See Gordon Wright, "Peasant Politics in the Third French Republic," *Political Science Quarterly* 70 (1955): 75–86, and *Rural Revolution in France* (Stanford, Calif.: Stanford University Press, 1964).
46 Wright, "Peasant Politics," p. 79. Only in Brittany did agricultural unions fail to take root: see Annie Moulin, *Les paysans dans la société française* (Paris: Seuil, 1988), chap. 4.
47 Wright, *Rural Revolution*, p. 14.
48 The quotes are Rueff's characterization of the Queuille letter, which appears in Rueff's

autobiography, *Oeuvres complètes: I. De l'aube au crépuscule* (Paris: Plon, 1977), pp. 114–115; the conference presentation is given on pp. 321–332. Queuille was a long-time supporter of French import quotas, which he viewed as indispensable for the survival of French agriculture in the Depression: Frank Arnold Haight, *French Import Quotas* (London: P. S. King, 1935), p. 100.

49 FMFA B32317, "Compte-rendu de la 2ème séance de la commission interministérielle," April 8, 1933.

50 FMFA B32317, "Observations présentées au nom de l'agriculture française au gouvernement et à M. le Président Herriot," April 12, 1933.

51 The letters are collected in the French Ministry of Finance archives, FMFA B32321.

52 League of Nations, *Journal of the Monetary and Economic Conference* no. 4 (London, June 14, 1933), p. 12.

53 Kenneth Mouré, "As Good As Gold: French Monetary Management, 1928–1936" (Ph.D. diss., University of Toronto, 1988), pp. 274–277.

54 Moore, "History," pp. 117–119. Another option was to limit the bank's independence, as subsequent governments succeeded in doing. But in 1933, memories of inflation a decade earlier remained too vivid to allow Daladier to appoint a replacement for Moret or tamper with the composition of the Council of Regents.

55 A good source on internal politics in the Roosevelt Administration and their relationship to the World Economic Conference is Smith, "Toward Internationalism."

56 See, for example, Frank Freidel, *Franklin Roosevelt: Launching of the New Deal* (Boston: Little, Brown, 1973).

57 See Jeanette Nichols, "Silver Inflation and the Senate in 1933," *Social Studies* 25 (1934): 12–18; and John A. Brennen, "The Senate Silver Bloc and the First New Deal" (Ph.D. diss., University of Colorado, 1968).

58 Raymond Moley, *After Seven Years* (New York: Harper, 1939), p. 158.

59 Ibid., p. 157.

60 James Byrnes, *All in One Lifetime* (New York: Harper, 1958), p. 77. Some historians question whether Roosevelt was in fact forced by domestic political considerations to accept the Thomas Amendment. See Freidel, *Franklin Roosevelt*, pp. 331, 333. For present purposes it is necessary to observe that domestic politics influenced the decision.

61 See Nichols, "Silver Inflation." Cordell Hull alluded to such considerations in international discussions. "After some preliminary discussion Mr Hull raised the question of stabilisation. He had during the last 24 hours become very doubtful as to whether any measure of temporary stabilisation could be achieved. Speaking in great confidence, he said that the forces of inflation were at the moment rather powerful and had succeeded in preventing an agreement being approved. He thought that the best chance was for this conference to get some broad programme covering both the monetary and economic branches of the work which would be interdependent and coordinated." PRO Cab29/142, "Note of a conversation between the Prime Minister and Mr Hull on Monday, 19 June 1933, at 11.30 a.m."

62 *Foreign Relations* 1:660–661. The fact that U.S. prices had risen in the first month following the gold embargo should have worked to strengthen Roosevelt's belief in the efficacy of further depreciation.

63 The composition of support for Smoot-Hawley is analyzed in Barry Eichengreen, "The Political Economy of the Smoot-Hawley Tariff," *Research in Economic History* 12 (1989): 1–44. A different perspective, emphasizing the procedures by which tariff policy was made, is E. E. Schattschneider, *Politics, Pressures, and the Tariff* (New York: Prentice Hall, 1935).

64 Leith-Ross, *Money Talks*, p. 153.

65 Cordell Hull, *The Memoirs of Cordell Hull* (New York: Macmillan, 1948), vol. 1, p. 251; Moore, "History," p. 170. Thus, the Reciprocal Trade Agreements Act would have to wait until 1934: see Stephan Haggard, "The Institutional Foundations of Hegemony: Explaining the Reciprocal Trade Agreements Act of 1934," *International Organization* 42 (1988): 91–120.

66 The British debate over tariff protection in 1932 is analyzed in Barry Eichengreen, "Sterling and the Tariff, 1929–32," *Princeton Studies in International Finance* no. 48 (Princeton, N.J.: Princeton University Press, 1981).

67 French observers, noting "serious differences" between the Treasury and the Bank of England, concluded that it was "the position of the Treasury which is actually the one of the British Government": FMFA B32319, "Position du Gouvernement Britannique." According to the French, the Bank of England was skeptical that prices could be raised and prosperity restored simply through the application of a liberal credit policy. While cheap money was necessary for recovery, it was not sufficient. Also required were secure political conditions and a modicum of free international trade.

68 League of Nations, *Journal of the Monetary and Economic Conference*, 4 (June 14, 1933): 24–25.

69 From this point, all phrases in quotation marks are taken from Putnam's article.

70 Readers in international relations will recognize echoes of the strong state/weak state distinction – Peter Katzenstein, ed., *Between Power and Plenty* (Madison: University of Wisconsin Press, 1978) – although we qualify this view below.

71 This is the argument of Schattschneier, *Politics, Pressures*.

6. The GATT as an International Discipline over Trade Restrictions: A Public Choice Approach

J. M. Finger

Institutions do matter – over the long run perhaps far more than the adoption of this or that policy option or the election of that politician or party.

–James M. Buchanan

Reciprocal reductions of tariffs have been one of the success stories of post-World War II international cooperation. Through these reductions, negotiated since 1947 at a series of multilateral GATT "rounds," industrial country tariffs on manufactured goods, which ranged from 30 to 60 percent, have been reduced to an average of 4 to 8 percent. Parallel negotiations, in a different forum, restored the convertability of currencies and eliminated most of the quantitative restrictions in place in the industrial countries at the end of World War II. Together, these changes created a truly open international trading system among the major trading nations.

Yet there is increasing concern that the open international trading system is being seriously eroded. Even while the tariff cuts were being agreed on and implemented, voluntary export restraints, gray area measures, and other questionable trade practices began to appear and to close down the trading system. Free trade is advancing, it seems, at the same time as protection is becoming more frequent.

As demonstrated in this chapter, public choice theory provides the keys to understanding this apparent incongruity. The first key is that the institutions through which tariff decisions are made within the post-World War II GATT system are different from those through which decisions on other forms of trade restrictions are made. And, as James M. Buchanan reminds us in the quote at the beginning of this chapter, institutions do matter, so much so, this chapter will explain, that one institutional process can be moving the trading system toward free trade while another moves it toward protection.

But institutions are not immutable. Interests, over time, can reshape them. Post-World War II institutions for a while held at bay and even rolled back the dominance of concentrated producer interests over more dispersed consumer interests. But, as argued in this chapter, the shoe is on the other foot now. The processes that create trade restrictions are now dominant, and the forecast for the international trading system is pessimistic: continuing buildup of trade restrictions and continuing diminution of the breezes that disperse them.

1. THE LOGIC OF NEGOTIATED REDUCTIONS

Each country has the sovereign right to regulate its imports, and most tend to overdo it. This matter is well understood. When import restrictions are decided unilaterally, producer interests (the benefits of protection) are more effectively represented in the policy decision process than are consumer interests (the costs of protection), and the overall national economic interest is not well served. When import restrictions are determined through a process of negotiation with one's trading partners, an additional interest group is made effective. Determining trade restrictions on a reciprocal basis ties together (1) the access a country allows foreign suppliers to its domestic market, and (2) the access the country's exporters will have to foreign markets. This link brings exporters' interests to bear on the import restrictions, and the bias toward protection will be less.[1] As to the legal technicalities, each participating country agrees through the GATT to allow other participants access to its market at least as favorable as the tariff schedule it annexed to the agreement. When agreement involves reductions in tariffs, the new rates are "annexed" in such schedules. Each country's schedule, the parties agree, is subject to most-favored-nation (MFN) treatment within the group.

The U.S. reciprocal trade agreements program and the adaptation through the GATT of the same process on a multilateral basis are familiar examples of MFN treatment. An equally appropriate, though perhaps less familiar, example is provided by Jan Tumlir (1985). Before World War I, European states maintained among themselves a system of bilateral commercial treaties in which tariffs were contractually bound for long periods, usually ten years. The treaties were tied to each other by the inclusion of an unconditional MFN clause in each. As in the later "GATT system," national legislatures tended to delegate the power to negotiate tariffs to the executive. Within this institutional structure, the participating countries were able to maintain an open trading system. The system's legal structure was a series of bilateral treaties of friendship, commerce, and navigation, linked together by including the MFN clause in each – quite different from the multilateral agreement that is the legal structure of the GATT. However, the public choice structures of the two were similar, as were the successes of the two systems to generate an open trading system.

2. THE LOGIC OF TRADE REMEDIES

The first functional part of the GATT provides the mechanics through which countries exchange access to each other's markets; the second functional part defines the circumstances under which a country might go back on such an exchange. It specifies when a country may impose restrictions to safeguard the balance of payments, may introduce antidumping and countervailing duties, etc. The inclusion of such provisions for trade restrictions in an agreement intended to promote free trade can be explained in two ways. First, including them in the GATT was part of the price national governments paid their import competing interests not to block the country's participation in the negotiations to reduce tariffs. Second, specifying the circumstances under which a government can restrict imports may help the government to resist pressures to do so in other circumstances.

Within a property-rights conception, the GATT is a contract through which a nation exchanges access to its domestic market for access to the domestic markets of the other nations. This exchange of market access is subject to extensive and specific reservations as to the circumstances under which the procedures through which a country may reduce this access, i.e., impose import restrictions. However, which GATT provisions advance the agreement's objective and which provide for exceptions depends on where one's interests lie. The GATT, when read by an import-competing enterprise, becomes a statement of the circumstances in and procedures by which a nation may impose import restrictions, subject however to reservations the nation has placed upon the more protectionist candidates for his party's 1984 U.S. presidential nomination was summed up in the slogan, The GATT permits such actions – and it's time we took them. Taken a step further, into national laws and regulations that provide actual legal substance to a protectionist perspective on this contract, the circumstances under which a country may impose import restrictions become the rights of particular interests within the country to protection from import competition.

The mechanics of these provisions are easier to explain in concrete terms than in generalities, so I will use the United States as an example. Current U.S. law provides six tracks to which a domestic firm or industry may petition the U.S. government for relief from import competition, i.e., for protection. These are:

1. escape clause or safeguards ("201" cases),
2. antidumping,
3. antisubsidy or countervailing duty,
4. unfair trade practices actions ("301" cases),
5. unfair import practices ("337" cases),
6. market disruption ("406" cases).

The centerpiece of an escape clause or safeguards case is an investigation by the International Trade Commission of injury to a U.S. industry resulting from increased imports. An investigation begins when an industry "petitions" the ITC for "import relief." If the injury determination is affirmative, the ITC recommends a remedy to the president. This remedy might be imposition of tariffs, imposition of quantitative restrictions or other forms of import controls, or it might be adjustment assistance without the imposition of any broader measure to restrict imports. U.S. law does not, however, require the president to follow the ITC's recommendation, but if the president chooses not to implement import relief when the ITC has so recommended or to implement a form of import relief different from that recommended by the ITC, his decision is subject to congressional override.

The escape clause does not raise questions about the "fairness" of imports, but other trade remedy tracks do. Antidumping petitions are field simultaneously with the ITC and with the International Trade Administrations (ITA) of the Department of Commerce. An antidumping case entails two separate investigations: a material injury investigation (conducted by the ITC) and a sales at "less than fair value" investigation (conduced by the ITA). If both material injury and sales at less than fair value are found to exist, the Department of Commerce is required by law to issue an antidumping order. An antidumping order means that unless the exporter raises his price accordingly he must pay an antidumping duty. Most choose to raise their price. The antidumping law provides specific opportunities for an agreement to terminate the case to be reached between the petitioning domestic party and the foreign party. Grounds for such agreed termination are almost always an enforceable and monitorable commitment by the foreign seller to eliminate the dumping practice, usually by raising the price he charges in the U.S. market.

Countervailing duty cases, like dumping cases, are carried out under the authority of the Department of Commerce by the ITA. Cases involve an investigation of subsidy conducted by the ITA, and in most instances, an injury investigation conducted by the ITC. Injury investigations are carried out in all cases concerning duty-free goods and involving signatories to the GATT-subsidies code, against Taiwan, and against all countries to whom the U.S. has extended by treaty unconditional most-favored-nation status. As with the antidumping law, the countervailing duty law provides opportunities for a case to be terminated upon agreement between the petitioning party and exporter. Again, such agreement is conditioned upon an enforceable and monitorable commitment by the foreign party to eliminate the subsidy practice.

Section 301 follows a similar petition-investigation format but is an outlet mainly for complaints by U.S. *exporters* of unfair treatment in foreign markets. It will be discussed below. Section 406 provides an easier safeguards procedure that may be used only against imports from communist countries; "337" cases are mainly about patent infringement.

In recent years, these trade remedies have eclipsed the trade negotiations process and have come to dominate trade policy. Again, the U.S. case, the archetype example of GATT-consistent institutions, is the easiest to document. In the 1950s and 1960s, U.S. trade legislation was mostly about granting the president authority to negotiate tariff reductions. But over time, a larger and larger share of trade legislation has dealt with the expansion and strengthening of trade remedies, particularly those that appear to correct "unfair" foreign trade practices. For example, the widely circulated and frequently praised U.S. Chamber of Commerce explanation of the 1988 U.S. trade bill devotes sixteen pages to the import relief clauses and six pages to "301." "Negotiating authority" gets two pages, the same number as "Adjustment Assistance," for which the Congress has provided no funding.

"Unfair" foreign practices provide the screen behind which a government can enjoy being seduced by special interests and yet pretend to act nobly. U.S. Treasury Secretary James A. Baker III, in defending the Reagan administration's trade policy, pointed out in 1987, "We have not neglected our responsibilities to fair trade. . . . President Reagan, in fact, has granted more import relief to US industry than any of his predecessors in more than half a century."[2] Half a century covers every president since Herbert Hoover, the president who signed the Smoot-Hawley tariff.

Table 1 tabulates 1980–1986 trade remedies cases in countries that are the major users of such GATT-formal mechanisms. Of a total of 2,024 cases, only 45 were safeguards cases, i.e., only 45 did not accuse the foreign party of unfairness.[3]

From a public choice perspective, the intriguing matter is not that the special-interest-arming trade remedies have come to dominate the trade negotiations. The intriguing question is why it took so long. How did the liberalizing trade negotiations dominate trade policy from the end of World War II perhaps through most of the 1970s? An obvious possibility – that the trade processes did not exist until recently – turns out not to be true. Provisions for safeguards, anti-dumping, and countervailing duties are in the GATT because they existed in national legislation when the GATT was negotiated, and national governments would not give them up.

Table 1: Number of Administered Protection Cases, 1980--86

	1980	1981	1982	1983	1984	1985	1986	1980–1986
Safeguards								
United States	2	6	4	2	6	3	5	28
Australia	1	0	1	2	0	0	0	4
Canada	0	1	2	0	0	1	0	4
EC	3	1	1	1	1	0	2	9
Countervailing actions								
United States	8	10	123	21	51	39	30	282
Australia	0	0	2	7	6	3	3	21
Canada	3	0	1	3	2	3	4	16
EC	0	1	3	2	1	0	0	7
Antidumping actions								
United States	22	14	61	47	71	65	71	351
Australia	62	50	78	87	56	60	63	456
Canada	25	19	72	36	31	36	74	293
EC	25	47	55	36	49	42	40	294
Other unfair trade practices – US	28	19	73	39	33	39	28	259
All Categories								
United States	60	49	261	109	161	146	134	920
Australia	63	50	81	96	62	63	66	481
Canada	28	20	75	39	33	40	78	313
EC	28	49	59	39	51	42	42	310
Total	179	168	476	283	307	291	320	2024

Sources: United States data, US International Trade Commission, ALLAD-CASIS Database; Other Countries, Finger and Olechowski (1987) – Tables A8.1, A8.3, for numbers of antidumping and countervailing duty cases: GATT Secretariat, for numbers of safeguards cases.

Part of the reason the trade remedies did not generate many trade restrictions was that the people who made up the government did not want them to. To many of them, trade policy was less economics than international diplomacy and the idea was widely shared that freedom of commerce could be an important instrument for maintaining world peace. To Cordell Hull, secretary of state for President Franklin D. Roosevelt, the link was straightforward "[U]nhampered trade dovetailed with peace; high tariffs, trade barriers and unfair economic competition with war."[4] The cold war with Russia allowed a vulgar version of this idea to generate wide public support for the government's trade policy: If the United States did not provide markets for these countries they would be taken over by the Communist bloc.

And in I. M. Destler's informative phrase, the trade remedies provided "protection for Congress" against the wrath of special interests that would press a congressperson who was sympathetic to the general thrust of U.S. trade policy. The ideology of interdependence to preserve global stability was part of it, but not all of it. Economics did matter, but not in the way an economist would explain the "gains from trade." In this regard the old metaphor about prosperity is informative. A rising tide lifts all boats. The 1950s and 1960s were generally prosperous times in which the U.S. enjoyed substantial trade surpluses.[5] Directing a protection-seeking industry into a maze of administrative procedures bought time, and before the industry came to realize there was no prize at the end of the maze it realized that business was better and pressed the case no further. Besides, the system satisfied the U.S. sense of fairness. There was a place to complain; they listened, they investigated, they held hearings. One had one's day in court. To complain further would be un-American, maybe even pro-Communist, if the closing of the U.S. market tipped a country over to the Russian side of the cold war. In sum, the trade remedies procedures could be calibrated to produce trade restrictions at a much lower rate than the trade negotiations were removing them.

Import Politics

But things would not stay that way forever. Consider one of E.E. Schattschneider's observations about the pressure group politics of the 1930 tariff: "A policy that is so hospitable and catholic as the protective tariff disorganizes its opposition." (1935, p. 88) The same would turn out to be true for the trade remedies. Yearly, the political motives for the trade liberalization program waned, and the capacity of the rest of the world to export to the United States increased. It is hard to remember U.S. idealism to build a better world after World War II, also hard to remember that forty years ago everyone *knew* that the LDCs would never export manufactured goods. To reverse the thrust of U.S. trade policy it was not necessary to create a new mechanism, only to recalibrate the trade remedies process so that it provided more import relief. And year by year the trade remedies process expanded:

1. Technical changes expanded definitions of "injury," "dumping," etc., i.e., expanded the specification of when an industry had a right to "import relief."

2. Loopholes were closed, loopholes that the President had exploited to set aside determinations that an industry was eligible for import relief.

3. Judicial review was imposed to force administration of the trade remedy laws toward what Congress intended, away from the loopholes the president tried to find to allow him to meet his international obligations to keep the U.S. market open to import competition.[6]

The unfair trade laws in the judgment of two of Washington's top trade lawyers are now "the usual first choice for industries seeking protection from imports into the United States."[7] They have been made broad enough that they can now give expression to almost every pressure for protection.[8]

Is Export Politics Really Dead?

But the trade negotiations are still around, are they not? Do not the trade negotiations still provide the mechanics through which the politics of export expansion will dominate the politics of import restrictions?

The answer is no. U.S. exporters no longer need the trade negotiations to advance their interests. They have "301".

Section 301 was added to the list of trade remedies by the 1974 trade bill and has been modified and extended by the 1979, 1984, and 1989 trade bills. It authorizes the U.S. Trade Representative[9] to take action against foreign trade practices that violate international agreements or burden or otherwise restrict U.S. commerce in an unreasonable or discriminatory fashion. The instrument explicitly covers services, investment, and intellectual property.

Section 301 deals with two categories of practices: (1) violations of U.S. rights under a trade agreement, and (2) otherwise unjustifiable, unreasonable, or discriminatory actions or policies that burden or restrict U.S. commerce. When the GATT is the agreement that the petitioner alleges is violated, the U.S. trade representative is required to submit the matter to the GATT dispute settlement process simultaneous with his investigation under "301." If the U.S. trade representative (USTR) determines that a foreign violation of a trade agreement (category 1 above) does exist the trade representative must retaliate.[10] But the section also allows the USTR to waive retaliation if the GATT dispute settlement process decides against the United States, if the foreign government takes action to remove or offset the violation, or if retaliation would "backfire" or significantly harm U.S. commercial interests or U.S. national security. The law defines "unreasonable" as an act, policy, or practice that is unfair and inequitable, though not necessarily a violation of explicit U.S. legal rights. When the U.S. trade representative finds actions or policies of this sort, she has the authority to retaliate, but is not required to do so.

The intent and to a large extent the use of "301" has been to advance the interests of U.S. exporters. Of forty-seven cases that had come to conclusion by December 31, 1988, twenty-seven ended with some liberalization of a foreign restriction, one with a liberalization by the United States, eleven when USTR found that the foreign practice was legitimate or did not burden U.S. commerce, and eight with a trade restricting action by the United States.[11]

The menace of 301 is not that it serves U.S. export interests but that it unchains them from the necessity to oppose U.S. import competing interests. It arms the U.S. negotiator not with the authority to *remove* U.S. import restrictions, but with the threat to *impose* new ones. It provides the domestic political mechanics to press for export expansion without paying the price of removing U.S. import restrictions.

The basic public choice mechanics of the trade negotiations have been undone. Export interests no longer have to find the courage and the organization to overcome import-competing interests. The two interest groups can view the trade negotiations in the same manner. The multilateral negotiations, like the drafting of a U.S. trade bill, can be mostly a matter of searching for words to express a common standard of "fairness." What policies this standard in fact allows and disallows is left to be worked out in the bilateral disputes brought forward under 301 and other countries' equivalent instruments. The multilateral negotiations used to be a counter to the domestic politics of trade policy. Now they are an extension of it.

3. THE CODES APPROACH

By the middle 1960s, new trade restrictions were appearing in noticeable regularity. Most of the industrial countries had begun to limit textile imports and Japan, in acceding to the GATT, had been asked to restrain its exports of several products. Though many believed that the most effective way to retard the spread of new trade restrictions was to proceed with negotiations to reduce tariffs – the "bicycle theory," it was sometimes called – there was a growing feeling that the trend of nontariff barriers (NTBs) was shaking itself loose from the momentum of the negotiations to reduce tariffs, and some attempts at agreement to control NTBs were made at the 1960s Kennedy Round. Even though the Kennedy Round achieved broader and deeper tariff cuts than any other round, the NTB negotiations met with little success.

The international community then made NTBs the major concern of the 1974–1979 Tokyo Round. There, agreement was reached on six NTB "codes," the major of which were the subsidies, the countervailing-duties code, and the antidumping code. The codes are elaborations of the initial GATT specifications that were intended to limit when and how a country could impose an import restriction. The logic here, as in the original GATT, is that if the circumstances under which a country may impede trade are specified, the frequency with which it does so will be less. The formulators of this approach hoped that codification would make national procedures to impose trade restrictions the same in one country as in another and that as precedents built up each national government would have effective means for handling pressures for protection. Petitioners would be assured that their cases were decided on the same grounds as anyone else's (and that these grounds were the right grounds) and would thus be brought toward accepting a possibly negative decision.

As to effects, all reviewers agreed that the subsidies code had had little effect, either on the extent of the subsidization or on the prosperity of importing countries to take countervailing actions.[12] The antidumping code earns lowers marks. The number of cases by code signatories – 1,288 over the seven years 1980–1986, more than half of which led to antidumping duties or a restrictive consent arrangement – is alarming. Even more alarming is the considerable progress the code has made to promote the *acceptance* by one country of another's trade restricting actions – as if the objective were to bring order and agreement to the process of closing down the international trading system rather than to keep it open.

It is not hard to explain why the codes have not retarded the spread of trade restrictions. First, the codes provide a more elaborate specification of the circumstances under which a country could impose trade restrictions. But the specification of these circumstances, while legally complex, incorporates a very narrow economic perspective – the effects of imports on competing domestic producers. The institutional structure gives voice to no countervailing economic interests, and the more elaborate the institutional structure becomes the harder it is for counterveiling interests to make their voices heard.

A related matter: Although the intent of the codes' drafters may have been to *reduce* the degree of ambiguity over what "dumping" and other operative terms meant, it seems to have *submerged* an unchanged degree of ambiguity to a much more technical level. William B. Carmichael, drawing on twelve years' experience as head of the Australian Industries Assistance Commission, concluded that "the processes to be followed in antidumping investigations are not amenable to precise and consistent application. This means that the task of administering the legislation is not simply a task of following a set of unambiguous rules. To determine, for example, which good sold in the home market is like the good sold for export involves judgment and discretion about which technical rules to apply. That determination also demands expertise in the application of the technical procedures." (1986, p. 2)

It now requires more and more expensive legal, accounting, and economic skills to get to the level at which there is ambiguity, i.e., discretion, to be exploited. In short, more elaborate procedures make collective action even more expensive and thus tips the "concentrated vs. dispersed" dimension of the matter even further toward the more concentrated interests, the producer interests. Finally, the creation of more elaborate and more legalistic processes tends to legitimize the resulting restriction – in effect, to misuse the public's respect for due process.

4. VOLUNTARY EXPORT RESTRAINTS

When one recognizes which economic interests are given voice and what property rights are recognized and given exchange value in the GATT, it is easy to understand why the negotiated, or voluntary, export restraint (VER) has become a popular form of trade restriction. Although legally speaking, the GATT consistency of a VER is questionable, a VER is, from a public choice perspective, the ultimate or archetype GATT solution to a trade dispute.

First, a VER displays the involved parties' respect for the mercantilist sense of property rights the GATT negotiating procedure recognizes and reinforces.

The country wanting to withdraw access it has previously traded away negotiates to do so and pays for it through the higher price of imports generated by the restricted supply. Within this mercantilist sense of economic welfare, of each nation's property and of what has been exchanged, a VER is the least-cost solution for each government – certainly less costly than the compensation or retaliation that the letter of the GATT suggests. If say, the U.S. "paid for" new limits on imports of Japanese autos by liberalizing imports of Japanese electronics, the U.S. economy would bear the adjustment cost of a shift of resources from electronics to autos, and the U.S. government would have the political problem of explaining why the U.S. electronics industry has to pay for the protection given to autos. The Japanese economy is in the mirror-image situation – resources would have to move from the autos to the electronics industry. If the U.S. refused to provide compensation and the Japanese government retaliated against imports of U.S. beef, the situation would be similar. So long as the institutional structure "sells" a mercantilist conception of costs and benefits, a VER providing compensation through higher auto prices avoids the political and economic problems that would occur if the "injury" were borne by one sector and the "compensation" received by another.

GATT's "enforcement" provisions reinforce this mercantilist sense of national property rights. First of all, the power the GATT has been given to enforce its rules is quite different from the way one would think of enforcement in the context of a penal code and a police force. There is no police force. Rather, there is a "dispute settlement" process, whose power over national trade policies is limited to the power of persuasion, armed by appeal to an agreed international standard. Consistent with the absence of police powers, the thrust of the GATT's dispute settlement procedure is toward helping and encouraging the disputing parties to work things out. Robert Hudec, a leading expert on GATT dispute settlement, puts it this way, "The first principle of GATT dispute settlement theory is that a negotiated solution is the best solution."[13]

The procedures themselves are proof that Hudec's interpretation is correct. Under GATT's procedures, the government of a country that felt its "benefits" under the GATT were being "nullified or impaired" by, say, a U.S. action, must begin by asking for consultations with the United States, and the United States is obligated to enter into such consultations. The complaining country, the plaintiff, may refer the matter to the contracting parties, i.e., the entire GATT membership, after one round of consultation, but normal practice is for several rounds of consultation, sometimes with additional countries participating, and frequently with the informal assistance or good offices of the GATT staff.

If an acceptable solution does not result, the complaining party may notify the contracting parties that it wishes them to take up the matter. The GATT membership, called the GATT "Council" when they meet to conduct GATT affairs, then appoints a "panel" to look into the matter. A panel includes three to five individuals, but no nationals of countries party to the dispute.

The panel reviews written submissions from the disputant parties, listens to their oral arguments – generally speaking, does what is necessary to understand the case and to prepare its report. This report presents the facts of the matter as the panel has determined them, the panel's findings and conclusions on how

GATT rights and obligations have been affected, and its recommendations for appropriate actions by the parties to the dispute. But the panel's *process* is as important as its report, and the process is arranged to promote an agreed outcome. The panel is required to consult regularly with the disputants and to give them the opportunity to develop a mutually satisfactory solution. In this spirit, the panel's final report is delivered first to the parties to the dispute. One or two months later, if the dispute has not been withdrawn, the panel report is submitted to the contracting parties and placed on the GATT Council agenda for discussion. Consensus voting is the normal procedure, hence the report is not considered adopted if any country objects to its acceptance.

If the panel's report is adopted but its recommendations are not implemented within a reasonable period of time, the plaintiff may ask the contracting parties to help to find an appropriate solution. Under the GATT the contracting parties ultimately can authorize the plaintiff to retaliate against the defendant's action. But only once, in 1952, has the dispute settlement procedure gone to that point.[14] As GATT's drafters intended, a deal of some sort is almost always worked out.

5. CONCLUSIONS

The GATT was built on a mercantilist sense of economic welfare and a mercantilist sense that domestic producers had a higher claim than foreign producers to the domestic market. The trade negotiations process did not attack this claim – it gave producers in each country an opportunity to increase the claim's value through mutually beneficial exchanges with producers in other countries.

The process worked as long as institutions forced all producers in a country (import competing and exporting) to reach a collective decision on trade policy – as long as the trade remedies were subjugated by strategic and diplomatic concerns so that they did not provide import-competing interests an alternative.

Pressure from import-competing producers, whose interests are netted out in the trade negotiations process, eventually expanded the trade remedies into a policymaking institution and now eclipses the trade negotiations. Another mutation of GATT institutions has begun with the development in the United States of "301". Section 301 provides a way for exporting producers to advance their interests without bearing the burden of suppressing or buying off import-competing interests. It attacks foreign restrictions not with the possibility of *fewer* U.S. restrictions but with the threat of *more*. Trade remedies processes have been installed in many countries, "301s" should not be far behind.

The GATT system was devised to promote global security and free trade. It has been altered until, in the present system, export interests will generate trade conflicts, and import-competing interests will generate trade restrictions. Simply put, the institutions that shape the relevant public choices do not bring out the appropriate economic interests, and the resulting policy choices are not those that promote economic efficiency. To a reader familiar with economics history, this should not be a surprise. Institutions do not always get the underlying interests right – or as Douglas S. North might put it, not even often. "The fact that growth has been more exceptional than stagnation or decline suggests that 'efficient' property rights are unusual in history." (North 1981, p. 6)

NOTES

1 For lengthier expositions see Hauser (1986), Roesseler (1986), and Moser (1988).
2 Baker 1987, p. 4.
3 Unfairness provides the political rhetoric and the administrative process through which an interest group presents its case, but the unfair trade procedures do not always provide the *form* of the resulting trade restriction. Finger and Murray (1990) document that almost half of U.S. antidumping and countervailing duty cases end up with negotiated export restraints.
4 Quoted by Cooper (1987, p. 299) from Cordell Hull's *Memoirs*. Cooper provides similar quotes from Presidents Franklin D. Roosevelt and Harry S. Truman.
5 There has been a considerable amount of research on how aggregate economic conditions affect pressures for protection. Coughlin, et al. (1989); Feigenbaum, Ortiz, and Willett (1985); and Takacs (1981, 1985) are good examples that provide additional references.
6 Details of these changes are provided by Finger (1990).
7 Horlick and Oliver (1989, p. 5).
8 This brings to mind another lesson that E. E. Schattschneider drew from the politics of the Smoot-Hawley tariff: "One of the great defects of the protective system is that it provides no clear basis for discrimination, and that, since discrimination is politically difficult, Congress destroys the essential character of the policy in order to make it politically strong." (p. 85)
9 Until the 1988 amendments "301" authority was given to the president.
10 Since 1988, retaliation may not be on the case's subject product or service, e.g., if the subject practice affects U.S. exports of rice, retaliation cannot be a restriction on U.S. imports of rice.
11 The numbers in this paragraph are from the author's tabulation of information given in U.S. International Trade Commission, *Operation of the Trade Agreements Program*, 1975 through 1988 editions.
12 Stern and Hoekman (1987).
13 Hudec 1978, p. 6.
14 Plank 1987, p. 92.

REFERENCES

Baker, James A., III. "Remarks by Secretary of the Treasury James A. Baker III before a Conference Sponsored by the Institute for International Economics," *Treasury News*, Washington, D.C., September 14, 1987.

Blackhurst, Richard, "Strengthening GATT Surveillance of Trade Related Policies," in Hilf and Petersmann, *The New GATT Round of Multilateral Trade Negotiations: Legal and Economic Aspects*, Deventer, The Netherlands: Kluwer Law and Taxation Publishers, 1988.

Buchanan, James M. "Alternative Perspectives on Economics and Public Policy," *Policy Report*, Cato Institute, vol. 6, no. 1, pp. 1–5, January 1984.

——. "The Constitution of Political Economy," *American Economic Review*, vol. 77, no. 3, pp. 243–250, June 1987.

Carmichael, William B. "Review of the Customs Tariff (Antidumping Act)," Unpublished manuscript submitted to the Gruen Review, Canberra, 1986.

Chamber of Commerce of the United States. *The Omnibus Trade and Competitiveness Act of 1988*, Washington, D.C., 1988.

Contracting Parties to the General Agreement on Tariffs and Trade. *Basic Instruments and Selected Documents*, Twenty-sixth Supplement, *Protocols, Decisions, Reports 1978–79 and Thirty-fifth Session*, Geneva, March 1980.

Cooper, Richard N. "Trade Policy as Foreign Policy," in Robert M. Stern (ed) *U.S. Trade Policies in a Changing World Economy*, Cambridge, Mass.: MIT Press, 1987.

Coughlin, Cletus C., Joseph V. Terza, and Noor Aini Khalifah. "The Determinants of Escape Clause Petitions," *The Review of Economics and Statistics*, vol. 71, no. 2, pp. 341–347, May 1989.

Destler, I. M. *American Trade Politics: System Under Stress*, Washington, D.C.: Institute for International Economics, 1986.

Eichengreen, Barry. "The Political Economy of the Smoot-Hawley Tariff," National Bureau of Economic Research Working Paper #2001, Cambridge, Massachusetts: NBER, August 1986.

Feigenbaum, Susan, Henry Oritz, and Thomas D. Willett. "Protectionist Pressures and Aggregate Economic Conditions: Comments on Takacs, " *Economic Inquiry*, vol. 23, pp. 175–182, January 1985.

Finger, J. Michael. "Incorporating the Gains from Trade into Policy," *The World Economy*, vol. 5, no. 4, December 1982.

——. "Ideas Count, Words Inform," in R. H. Snape (ed) *Issues in World Trade Policy*, London: Macmillan, pp. 257–280, 1986.

——. "Protectionist Rules and Internationalist Discretion in the Making of National Trade Policy," in H. J. Vosgerau (ed) *New Institutional Arrangements for the World Economy*, New York: Springer-Verlag, 1988.

——. "Antidumping and Antisubsidy Measures," in Finger and Olechowski (eds) *The Uruguay Round: A Handbook for the Multilateral Trade Negotiations*, Washington, D.C.: The World Bank, pp. 153–161, 1987.

——. *Economists, Institutions and Trade Restrictions: A Review Article*, Washington, D.C.: The World Bank, PPR Working Paper #WPS78, September 1988.

Finger, J. M., and Andrzej Olechowski (eds). *The Uruguay Round: A Handbook for the Multilateral Trade Negotiations*, Washington, D.C.: The World Bank, 1987.

Finger, J. Michael, and Tracy Murray. "Policing Unfair Imports: The U.S. Example," *Journal of World Trade*, vol. 24, no. 4, pp. 39–53, August 1990.

Goldstein, Judith, and Stefanie Ann Lenway. "Interests or Institutions: An Inquiry to Congressional-ITC Relations," *International Studies Quarterly*, vol. 33, no. 3, pp. 303–328, September 1989.

Grinols, Earl. "Procedural Protectionism: The American Trade Bill and the New Interventionist Mode," paper presented at the NBER-CEPR International Seminar in International Trade, Oxford, England, August 24–25, 1988.

Hausser, Heinz. "Domestic Policy Foundation and Domestic Policy Function of International Trade Rules," *Aussenwirtschaft*, vol. 41, no. 2/3, pp. 171–184, 1986.

Hilf, Maynard, and Ernst-Ulrich Petersmann. *The New GATT Round of Multilateral Trade Negotiations: Legal and Economic Aspects*, Deventer, the Netherlands: Kluwer Law and Taxation Publishers, 1988.

Horlick, Gary N., and Geoffrey D. Oliver. "Antidumpting and Countervailing Duty Law Provisions of the Omnibus Trade and Competitiveness Act of 1988," *Journal of World Trade*, vol. 23, no. 3, pp. 5–49, 1989.

Hudec, Robert E. *Adjudication of International Trade Disputes*, London: Trade Policy Research Centre, Thames Essay No. 16, 1978.

——. "The Legal Status of GATT in the Domestic Law of the United States," in Meinhard Hilf, Francis G. Jacobs, and Ernst-Ulrich Petersmann (eds) *The European Community and the GATT*, Dordrecht, The Netherlands: Kluwer Law and Taxation Publishers, pp. 187–249, 1986.

——. *Developing Countries in the GATT Legal System*, London: Gower Press for the Trade Policy Research Centre, 1987.

——. "Reforming GATT Adjudication Procedures: The Lessons of the DISC case," *Minnesota Law Review*, vol. 72, no. 6, pp. 1443–1509, June 1988.

Hufbauer, Gray C. "Analyzing the Effects of US Trade Policy Instruments," Washington, D.C.: National Science Foundation, October 1981, mimeograph.

Jackson, John H., Jean-Victor Louis, and Mitsuo Matsushita. *Implementing the Tokyo Round, National Constitutions and International Rules*, Ann Arbor: University of Michigan Press, 1984.

——. "Comment on 'Protectionist Rules and Internationalist Discretion in the Making of National Trade Policy,'" in H. J. Vosgerau (ed), *New Institutional Arrangements for the World Economy*, New York: Springer-Verlag, 1988.

Moser, Peter, "Does GATT Matter: The Effect of the GATT on US Trade Policy," Fairfax, Virginia: Center for the Study of Public Choice, July 1988, unpublished manuscript.

North, Douglas C. *Structure and Change in Economic History*, New York: W. W. Norton, 1981.

Olson, Mancur. *The Logic of Collective Action: Public Goods and the Theory of Groups*, New York: Schocken Books, 1968.

Plank, Rosine. "An Unofficial Description of How a GATT Panel Works and Does Not," *Swiss Review of International Competition Law*, no. 29, March; reprinted in the *Journal of International Arbitration*, vol. 4, no. 4, pp. 53–102, 1987.

Roessler, Frieder. "The Constitutional Function of International Economic Law," *Aussenwirtschaft*, vol. 41, no. 2/3, pp. 303–328, 1986.

Salvatore, Dominick. "Import Penetration, Exchange Rates, and Protectionism in the Unites States," *Journal of Policy Modeling*, Vol. 9, pp. 125–141, Spring 1987.

Schattschneider, E. E. *Politics, Pressures and the Tariff*, New York: Prentice-Hall, 1935.

Stern, Robert and Bernard Hoekman. "The Codes Approach," in Finger and Olechowski (eds), *The Uruguay Round: A Handbook for the Multilateral Trade Negotiations*, Washington, D.C.: The World Bank, chapter 9, 1987.

Takacs, Wendy E. "More on Protectionist Pressure and Aggregate Economic Conditions: A Reply," *Economic Inquiry* vol. 23, 183–184, January 1985.

——. "Pressures for Protectionism: An Empirical Analysis," *Economic Inquiry*, vol. 19, 687–693, October 1981.

Tumlir, Jan. *Economic Policy as a Constitutional Problem*, Fifteenth Wincott Memorial Lecture delivered at the Royal Society for Arts, October 25, 1984, Institute of Economic Affairs, for the Wincott Foundation, London.

——. *Protectionism*, Washington, D.C.: American Enterprise Institute, 1985. United States International Trade Commission. *Operation of the Trade Arrangements Program*, Washington, D.C.: U.S. International Trade Commission, annual.

7. Creating the GATT Rules: Politics, Institutions, and American Policy

J. Goldstein

INTRODUCTION

The General Agreement on Tariffs and Trade (GATT) is among the most successful of the group of multilateral organizations built at the close of World War II. Created in 1947 as a temporary skeleton – its obsolescence was planned to coincide with the inauguration of the International Trade Organization (ITO) – the GATT subsequently orchestrated a radical reduction in international barriers to trade. In the past decade, the explanation for the success of this and other international organizations has focused on the role institutions can play in supporting cooperation. The virtues of reciprocity norms, of precise monitoring procedures, and of the dissemination of information have been cited as central elements in efficient international organization.[1]

This focus on organizational rules and norms reflects the current intellectual weight of "Prisoners' Dilemma" explanations for international cooperation. With this metaphor in hand, analysts have turned their attention to how nations with common interests – such as the potential welfare gains from trade liberalization – can overcome collective-action problems only if some mechanism is found to forestall cheating. According to such logic, GATT rules were appropriate because they assuaged the fears of potential regime participants that they would receive the "Sucker's Payoff" if they lowered tariff barriers. Interpreting the breakdown of the trading system in the interwar period as a market failure – mutual defection reflected the decline of rules, not of common interests, in international trade – the credit for the resurgence of trade under GATT is given to the institutionalization of efficient monitoring and enforcement procedures.

The problem is, however, that this analysis assumes far more common interest among the potential signatories of GATT than in fact existed. Although it may be true that the subsequent success of the GATT can be attributed to the inclusion of a clear set of procedures for punishing offenders, these were not the central issues of debate over regime rules. At the close of the war, significant differences existed in the trade preferences of the Western nations. While countries could agree on the general need to forestall a return to interwar trade competition, no common support was in place for a particular alternative. Rather, in GATT talks each nation defended the rules that they perceived as maximizing their particularistic economic interests.

Since distributional issues were in the forefront of debate, the game-theoretical metaphor that better captures GATT negotiations is a "Battle of the Sexes." Here, the issue is not getting to the "Pareto frontier," but rather where participants will settle along it.[2] Solutions to this problem have been many, ranging from focal points to the naked exercise of power.[3] In the case of the GATT, the asymmetry in capabilities suggests that the United States could have imposed the policy of its choosing.[4] Still, the observation derived from this metaphor – that the United States was powerful and could thus choose the rules of the game – merely begs the key question of why one set of rules for the new trade regime was preferred by American policymakers over others.

Seeking an explanation for America's preferences is especially important since with the benefits of hindsight, it is clear that GATT rules did not serve America's long-term economic interests. Most significantly, GATT rules facilitated the exclusion of agricultural trade from liberalization efforts. While this may have been consistent with American interests in the 1940s, the GATT's sanctioning of agricultural protectionism thereafter closed off foreign markets to America's most competitive products.[5]

How do we explain American trade policy preferences in the 1940s? Explanations that derive preferences from America's place in the international system have difficulty accounting for both the timing and the sectoral variation in American policies. For example, in the period between 1929 and 1947, America's commercial policy moved from nonnegotiable tariffs, to support for bilateral trade reductions, to advocacy for a multilateral trade regime. These considerable changes in economic policy in a relatively short time span dwarf changes in American power. Similarly, American reticence at the height of her power over support for a more open world economy suggests that theories that derive trading interests from the distribution of power do not explain this case.[6]

American indifference to higher levels of trade liberalization in the 1940s can be explained by the same variables that explain the inability of GATT to open up markets today. Policies, once adopted by governments and institutionalized in rules and procedures, spawn interests that make change difficult – even after the policy itself is recognized to be functionally deficient. In the United States, policies created in the 1930s subsidizing agricultural production created powerful domestic interests that foreclosed American support in the 1940s and 1950s for agreements that would reduce quantitative barriers to agricultural trade. Thereafter, GATT's agricultural exceptions legitimated antifree-trade constituencies in nations with uncompetitive agricultural sectors – in Europe and Asia – that subsequently made it hard for policymakers to trade off agricultural protections for other benefits from trade liberalization.

The explanation for American behavior suggested below relies on the conventional variables of international relations analysis, that is, power and interest. But as well, careful attention is paid to a third factor: the strategy chosen by political entrepreneurs to translate power resources into valued outcomes. Policies are chosen based on beliefs about their efficiency in a given environment. Objective "preferences" rarely translate into a singular method of reaching the desired goals. Political actors do not merely have preferences over "outcomes," they have preferences over "actions." Thus politics entails a fight not only over whose interests will be maximized *but also* over the method to be used to maximize those interests. Considerations of strategy are investigations into the beliefs – causal and normative – of political entrepreneurs who make decisions in an uncertain environment on how best to maximize their, their constituents, and the nation's interests.[7]

America entered GATT negotiations with specific preferences on the form and scope of the new trade regime. The most concise explanation for why the United States did not push for more "liberal" rules – as would have been predicted from America's relative economic position in world trade – was that domestic groups feared increased agricultural imports. These groups were efficacious not only because of their ability to organize effectively but also because institutional resources – the organization of Congress and existing legislation – biased policy in their direction.[8] The United States did not get what was in her objective best "interest," not because of a lack of power but because of domestic institutional, ideational, and social constraints.

To show how these domestic dynamics translated into GATT rules, this essay proceeds as follows. First, I examine the domestic determinants of America's trade preferences at the end of World War II. Second, I turn to the negotiations themselves and the translation of American preferences into international practice. Finally, I explore the deleterious consequences of this initial choice of rules – in light of changes in American preferences over time and in the legitimation of antifree-trade coalitions abroad.

AMERICAN TRADE POLICY PREFERENCES

When Roosevelt came into office – after years of Republican party hegemony – "New Deal" policies were still on the drawing boards. In the early days of his administration, Roosevelt's advisors – Cordell Hull, Rexford Tugwell, and George Peek – devised radically different trade strategies to combat growing economic malaise. On one hand, the administration unilaterally devalued the dollar (the equivalent of a 50 percent increase in tariffs), abstained from international attempts to stabilize currencies, and initiated programs that forestalled trade liberalization. Legislation indicative of this "nationalist" policy strategy included the Agriculture Adjustment Act and the National Industrial Recovery Act, both of which explicitly argued for higher, not lower, levels of import restrictions.[9] Simultaneously, however, the administration pursued programs that were potentially trade expansionist. Following on the President's first-year promise that a new trade program was imminent, for example, a trade reform act was passed in 1934.

Although not appreciated at the time, this 1934 legislation fundamentally altered American trade policy. Although members of the economic community had urged the liberalization of the U.S. export–import mix consistently after 1890, government officials knew little and cared less about their advice. And while America's status as a creditor nation after World War I further necessitated a change in import policy, Woodrow Wilson's attempt to lower tariffs had been short-lived. Once Congress confronted economic problems in the 1920s, they turned to their usual panacea: a high tariff policy. The 1934 act was critical because it generated a change in authority: once legislated, free traders were able to implement their particular vision of economic policy. Thus in mid-decade – after the National Recovery Administration (NRA) was ruled unconstitutional – Hull and others turned to the administrative structures legislated in 1934 to pursue trade liberalization.[10] Their efforts met with success for manufacturing products but were stymied in agricultural trade because preexisting legislation mandated explicit market controls.

Thus, a decade before the GATT was negotiated, agricultural and manufacturing trade policies had bifurcated in the United States. In the area of manufacturing trade, Congress repeatedly relegislated negotiating authority to the executive office, which facilitated, by the start of the war, the conclusion of trade agreements with twenty countries.[11] Agricultural subsidy programs forced trade polity in a second direction. Agricultural groups – well entrenched in Congress – made it impossible for American negotiators to gain congressional assent for any international agreement that undermined the ability of the United States to use import restraints to protect farm incomes. Farm incomes had risen substantially under price support programs. Between 1938 and 1948, wholesale prices for farm products increased 50 percent more than prices for nonagricultural goods did. Although this was due more to the war than to government programs, farm groups associated increased farm incomes with American subsidy programs.

Why did such different policies develop? Neither variations in interests nor the power of each sector explains these policy outcomes; neither bilateral tariff reductions nor agricultural protectionism was a functionally "optimal" economic policy. Policy preferences reflected different strategic choices by each sector on how to maximize economic growth. Whereas the policy on manufacturing trade was characterized by attention to the twin ideas of reciprocity and most-favored-nation (MFN) status, agricultural trade was guided foremost by the notion of parity, mandating overt government intervention to maintain high prices. The choice over strategy – the belief in one policy practice rather than another – became incorporated in legislation and split. America's foreign economic policy by sector.

Reciprocity and MFN Status

Until 1934, reciprocity was an idea closely associated with Republican high-tariff policy. Reciprocity legislation in the nineteenth century had given the executive authority to punish other nations that did not give American exporters "fair" access to their markets. As early as in 1883 President Arthur asked Congress whether it would be "advisable to provide some measure of equitable retaliation in our relations with governments which discriminate against our own."[12] Again in 1890, the idea appeared in section 3 of the trade act, which provided penalty duties on items imported from countries whose duties on American products were, in the opinion of the President, "unequal and unreasonable." Thus, reciprocity was seen as a way to penalize other countries – not a carrot to liberalize world trade, but a stick to be used if foreign nations discriminated against American products.[13]

Just as reciprocity could be used either to encourage or to discourage trade, the MFN principle was also potentially two-sided. By accepting an unconditional MFN principle, a country promised that it would give all importing nations the lowest tariff barrier it had negotiated with any one of them. Such a principle did not exist in the United States before the 1920s. Until that time, the United States negotiated agreements based on conditionality or on the provision that tariff concessions would be extended only to countries that gave the United States the same concessions. Such a proviso of conditionality led to discriminatory agreements among parties. If all nations could not benefit from a tariff reduction, then the agreement, by definition, would be discriminatory.

Thus, from February 1778 – when the United States concluded a trade treaty with France – until the 1920s, all American treaties retained this qualification:[14]

> The most Christian King and the United States engage mutually not to grant any particular favor to other nations, in respect of commerce and navigation, which shall not immediately become common to the other party, who shall enjoy the same favor *freely if the concession was freely made, or on allowing the same compensation if the concession was conditional.*

The *italicized* phrase guaranteed that third parties did not get the same treatment as the signor of the agreement unless a specific concession was made to the United States. Such disregard of the unconditional wording in MFN agreements was relatively unusual, even in the eighteenth century.[15]

The United States formally adopted the principle of unconditional MFN status in 1923. Acceptance of the principle was celebrated with little fanfare, and there was minimal understanding of the impact this small procedural change would have on future trade relations.[16] Perhaps because no mandate to lower tariffs existed in the 1920s, the issue of unconditionality was of little concern to those in Congress. Only when tariffs became negotiable in 1934 did this decision take on meaning. By then, however, the United States had a decade of these type of treaties.[17] Did Congress intend to liberalize trade in the 1920s when they adopted a change in MFN status? Some scholars have argued this was the case.[18] Such a position is, however, hard to defend since this same Republican Congress had previously endorsed high levels of trade protection! But whether knowingly or not, the United States had agreed to the policy that became the operational backbone of the postwar trading regime.[19]

Not only did a new form for trade treaties emerge in this period, but even more importantly, a fundamental change occurred in the interpretation and use of the term *reciprocity*. Before the 1930s, reciprocity was understood much as it had been in the 1840s when Congress first considered reciprocal treaties. Then, reciprocity referred to substantive bilateralism.[20] Agreements were exclusive. The United States negotiated to give and to gain equal concessions. At a time when the United States granted only conditional MFN status, such negotiations were discriminatory by definition and were difficult to expand multilaterally.

Such an approach was challenged by the supporters of liberalization, who spoke of reciprocity in terms of formal bilateralism, that is, bilateral action with multilateral implications.[21] Put more simply, negotiations, they suggested, should be conducted between countries whose import-export mix gave them an incentive to grant one another a trade concession (presumably with the low-cost producer). Once a concession was granted to the principal supplier, other nations were also to be granted that new tariff. In the United States, those who argued for formal bilateralism were, in effect, arguing for negotiations based on unconditional MFN principles. As long as the United States maintained a single-column tariff system (until 1934) a change in a tariff resulting from a bilateral agreement would benefit any importer of that product.

The change in thinking on reciprocity was gradual. In 1919, the Tariff Commission issued a report on the history of American reciprocity. The report concluded that the "policy of special arrangements, such as the United States has followed in recent decades, leads to troublesome complications."[22] But with the election of a Republican government came a return to isolation and little interest in using international bargains to maximize America's economic interests. Then, in 1931, in response to the failing economy, the Democrats promoted a bill at the start of the 72nd Congress that included, among other features, a call for reciprocal trade agreements "under a policy of mutual concessions." Although this bill was vetoed by Hoover, its reciprocity proposal appeared in the tariff plank of the Democratic platform and was endorsed by then governor Roosevelt, as well as by exporting interests and key academics.[23] Because of this change in sentiment, the 1934 act was unlike previous legislation supported by the Democrats. The Act gave the executive authority to negotiate with other nations reciprocally to lower tariffs – it was not a unilateral decree to lower tariffs.

Ambiguity remained, however, in both the Democratic party's position on trade negotiations and in the implications for trade of the 1934 endorsement of reciprocity and unconditional MFN treaties. Most members of the party still advocated the contradictory visions of reciprocity as retaliation *and* the idea of unconditional MFN agreements. Even the State Department's interpretation of the Trade Agreements Act of 1934 failed to absorb the new meaning of reciprocity, contending that the act "provides that the duties . . . shall be extended to all countries but provided that they may be confined to such countries as do not discriminate against American commerce.[24] The State Department's press release argued that such ability to punish was, in fact, "wholly in accord with the unconditional MFN principle."[25]

Different members of the administration voiced similar misunderstandings. Hull, who viewed the 1934 act as a doorway to liberalization, saw no contradiction between the 1922 and 1930 acts, which legislated retaliatory provisions through the maximum and minimum provision, and the 1923 decision to conclude only unconditional MFN agreements. He argued that if the United States signed with the principal low-cost producer, no industry would be hurt by secondary importers. This view was not universally shared. The more common view was represented by George Peek, the Special Advisor for Foreign Trade, who argued that the ideas of reciprocity and unconditional MFN principles were not compatible.[26] He continued to advocate barter and negotiations only on a country-by-country basis. In the short term, Peek's exit from government allowed Hull to orchestrate multilateral trade agreements. In the longer term, the successful culmination of trade agreements and the ensuing rapid recovery are what assured a multilateral meaning for reciprocity.

The 1934 Act

In all respects the 1934 trade act differed markedly from prior legislation. Politically, whereas the 1930 Smoot-Hawley Act had elicited 11,000 pages of testimony in forty-three days in the House, testimony on the proposed 1934 act was given by fourteen witnesses, six of whom were from the administration.[27] For the first time in years, the minority was permitted to help formulate the bill and to amend the act on the floor.[28] The week-long Senate committee hearings were brief, but considerably more discussion took place on the floor.[29] The chief controversy surrounded the delegation of authority to the executive.[30] In the end, the act passed as an amendment to the 1930 act in a nearly perfect partisan vote. The bill enabled the President to reduce rates up to 50 percent from Smoot-Hawley levels. Henceforth, he was also able to conclude trade agreements without further congressional action. Commenting on the loss of this traditional congressional power, the minority report stated that the bill "places in the hands of the President and those to whom he may delegate authority the absolute power of life and death over every industry dependent on tariff protection."[31]

Fundamentally, the 1934 law legislated into force new ideas on tariff adminstration and bargaining. No longer would the United States have a single-column tariff system. New trade agreements brought lower rates for all countries with MFN status while others would receive the higher Smoot-Hawley rates. Private parties, once so influential in setting their own rates, could still have their hearing, but now in an arena tangential to tariff setting. If interest groups were the big losers, the big winner was the President, who gained power over tariff classification and reclassification, control of valuation procedures, the statutory right to reduce rates, and the ability to prevent unfair competitive practices and discrimination against American exports.

As important as the creation of new organizational structures was the appointment of people whose professional and personal interests lay in tariff reductions. Within the Department of State, three committees focused exclusively on the foreign policy aspects of trade. These committees were America's first organizational advocates of multilateral trade. The Executive Commercial Policy Committee was created in November 1933 to coordinate American policy "with a view to centralizing in the hands of one agency supervision of all government action affecting our imports and export trade."[32] Members were high officials from various government departments. The Trade Agreements Committee, created after the 1934 act, included representatives from the Departments of State, Agriculture, Treasury, and Commerce. Finally, the Committee for Reciprocity Information was formed to ensure Roosevelt's promise that "no sound and important American interest (would) be injuriously disturbed" by the trade agreements program.[33] Its chief activity was to hold public hearings. Over the ensuing few years members of all three committees became convinced of the value of trade liberalization. Functionally, they diverted attention from Congress; professionally, they saw their jobs as assuring the continuation of the liberalization program.[34]

In sum, the 1934 trade act ushered in a new political era. In 1934, Congress abdicated direct tariff-making responsibility and adopted a new role for itself in the making of policy. Henceforth, Congress would act as a "balancer" and a broker; it would ensure the passage of "fair" trade bills and act as a watchdog for America's interests at home and abroad.[35] These changes allowed the United States to create a liberal trade regime a decade and a half later. But as will be shown below, a liberal trade policy was in no way guaranteed by America's ascendence to hegemony.

Agricultural Trade Policy and the Idea of Parity

The path to trade liberalization – from the 1923 decision on MFN agreements, to the 1934 act, and ultimately to the creation of a multilateral trade organization – was only one side of American trade policy. On the other side were events that occurred simultaneously in the area of agricultural trade.

If the 1934 trade act set the United States down a path of reducing barriers to manufacturing trade, the 1933 Agricultural Adjustment Act accomplished just the opposite. While liberalization in nonagricultural goods was guided by the twin assumptions of reciprocity and MFN agreements, agriculture policy was far more influenced by the idea of parity. Whereas the former concepts granted a place for international markets to regulate the demand and price of American products, the latter idea forced government to regulate just about all aspects of production.

The notion of a parity price developed in the 1920s. In essence, it implied that the agricultural sector should garner prices and profits akin to those found in industrial production, or at minimum, at a time when the agricultural sector was relatively prosperous. Legislative guarantees of a parity price were to be unrelated to economic factors, such as the world price for a particular commodity. Once established as the backbone of agricultural policy, competing notions that prices should be set by world supply-and-demand conditions were ignored.[36] The policy implication of guaranteed parity was problematic from the perspective of those who advocated open trade borders: the parity price maintained farm prices in the United States above those found on world markets, which created incentives for producers in other nations to export farm products to the United States. Without some controls, government-set prices would be undermined.

Farm Legislation

Legislators well understood that increased competition in the home market held the potential of undermining agricultural supports. The response was to enact trade restrictions. Thus Congress included in the original and subsequent authorizations on farm subsidies the right both to set import quotas and to give export subsidies, if necessary to maintain prices. The ideological underpinning of the trade liberalization – that is, that government should rely on markets to set price and quantity – was never accepted as a tenet of agricultural policy.

The 1933 act, which revolutionized American farm policy, was the last of a series of attempts to deal with an agricultural depression that began at the end of World War I.[37] Created by the 1933 act, the Agricultural Adjustment Administration (AAA) in the Department of Agriculture was given the authority to reduce production and to increase prices for seven basic crops – wheat, cotton, corn, hogs, rice, tobacco, and milk and its products. In subsequent acts, other commodities were added and other means were given to the administration to elevate farm prices. The focus of government activity was an attempt to reduce supply; ultimately, direct cash payments were used as an incentive for farmers to stop production. Between 1934 and the outbreak of the war, the government paid about $4.4 billion to producers in return for their not bringing crops to market.[38]

From the start, farm groups had little interest in and much apprehension about the reciprocal trade agreements program. In testimony, the Grange – one of the best organized of the farm groups – opposed all forms of trade liberalization, and the Farm Bureau argued that only industrial tariffs should be lowered. Their attempt to exclude agriculture from the program lost by a relatively small margin (54–33) in the Senate in 1934. Farm opposition did not, however, disappear with the passage of the 1934 act. As late as the 1945 extension of the Reciprocal Trade Agreements Act, wool, cattle, sugar, and dairy interests, among others, opposed the extension in testimony before the House.

In retrospect, these groups had little to fear. The Roosevelt administration showed itself willing to protect agricultural products if necessary to maintain farm incomes. On the heals of the 1934 trade act, Congress passed, and Roosevelt signed, the Jones-Costigan Act, explicitly mandating sugar import quotas. Further, under section 22 of the AAA, the administration authorized import quotas on wheat and wheat products, butter, milk products, cheese, oats, barley, rye, rye flour, peanuts, wheat, wheat flour, cotton, and cotton waste. The administration also limited import fees. Import licenses were deemed necessary for other products, including butter and applies. Wheat, wheat flour, cotton, and cotton waste imports were allocated by country, in direct conflict with the equal-treatment concept that was to become a central GATT norm.

But it was more than the use of import quotas that revealed fundamental conflict between free-trade ideas and American policy. Under section 32 of the AAA, the U.S. government was authorized to use export subsidies for agricultural exports. Under the 1935 version of the law, the Secretary of Agriculture was granted the right to use up to 30 percent of gross custom receipts to increase farm exports "by the payment of benefits . . . or of indemnities for losses incurred in connection with such exportation." In his January 1936 budget message to Congress, Roosevelt publicly acknowledged the contradictions in his legislative proposals. His public response was explicit support for liberalization. Roosevelt requested that export subsidy provisions be repealed. But indicative of sentiment at the time, he was ignored by Congress. Thus in 1944, just as Roosevelt's State Department declared America's intention to ensure a multilateral and liberal future for world trade, the Agricultural Department allocated $118 million to subsidize exports of wheat, cotton, corn, tobacco, fruits, tree nuts, and dairy and meat products.[39]

In general, the increased domestic and foreign demand for American farm products during World War II had made prewar agricultural programs inoperative. After the Lend-Lease Act passed Congress in 1941, agricultural products were shipped abroad in ever-increasing amounts. By the end of 1944, 5 billion dollars worth of agricultural products had been exported under the program's provisions. Cotton export subsidies were stopped in 1942; wheat export subsidies ended in 1943.[40] Although price supports were in effect for 166 different agricultural goods in 1945, the policy was cheap; the war kept market prices at about their price-support level. The result was that at the close of the war, the agricultural sector had expanded by 20 percent.[41] Prices paid to farmers were about 200 percent above their prewar levels.[42]

To encourage war production and assuage the fear of drastic price declines at the close of the war, the Steagall Amendment to the extension of commodity Credit Corporation in July 1941 increased government supports not only for the original group of protected products but also for expanded supports to other agricultural goods. Few forgot what increased output in WWI had done; government officials assumed and promised that at the end of the current war, price and production controls would be used to avert a second agricultural depression. Yet counter to these predictions, the war's end did not herald a slump in prices. The demand for American products actually rose, leading to even higher farm prices. Output reached unprecedented levels. By 1947, the average prices received by farmers were 25 percent above that received the year before! This meant that the provisions established by the Steagall Amendment remained dormant. Only in a few products – potatoes, eggs, butter, dried milk, wool, and turkey – did the government employ price support programs.

Even so, as American negotiators moved ahead on the trade regime, they found that agricultural supports and farm protections were difficult – if not impossible – to overturn. In the 1945 renewal of the trade act, Congressman Pace of Georgia had offered an amendment to safeguard further the farm program from trade treaties. Though not passed, it was clear that Congress, commitment to liberalization did not extend to the removal of protections to agriculture. When in 1948 the demand for agricultural goods finally fell, price support programs went immediately into force. The Steagall Amendment – which was set to expire – was replaced by similar and more permanent protections in the Agricultural Act of 1948.[43] And in 1951, the extension of the trade act formally stated that trade agreements could not be concluded in violation of existing agricultural programs.

In sum, as the United States embarked upon the creation of a new trade regime, its own domestic policy was mired with inconsistencies. Although the State Department was unequivocal on the benefits of multilateral trade liberalization for the American economy, the Department of Agriculture declared simultaneously that under no conditions could the United States delegate control over import protections for farm products. It was not that the intrinsic interests of the agricultural sector were orthogonal to trade liberalization. By the late 1940s, the prosperity of American agriculture was clearly associated with exports: the United States was supplying 39 percent of the world's wheat, 41 percent of the world's tobacco, and 49 percent of the world's cotton. Few could ignore the importance of agriculture to America's export economy (see table 7.1). Yet, both farm groups and elected officials were politically wedded – because of organized private interest, congressional committees and existing legislation – to government controls on price and supply. It would take twenty years for producers and political leaders to realize the costs of this strategy.

TABLE 7.1 *The Importance of Agricultural Trade 1945–58*

Year	% Total U.S. Exports	Index of Export Importance*
1945	34	41
1946	28	51
1947	25	51
1948	30	51
1949	30	40
1950	27	47
1951	26	54
1952	19	36
1953	19	37
1954	21	40
1955	21	43
1956	23	58
1957	21	50
1958	22	43

*Index is a measure of the changing importance of foreign trade to agriculture. Computed as total domestic exports of agricultural commodities divided by index of total farm output. 1967 = 100.

Sources: U.S. Bureau of the Census, *Historical Statistics of the United States* (1975), Series K 414–429; U.S. Department of Agriculture, *Agricultural Statistics* (1960), table 813.

CONSTRUCTING THE TRADE REGIME

During World War I, Cordell Hull proposed in a resolution to the House of Representatives that the United States establish a multilateral trade organization. Although dismissed at the time, the idea reappeared in State Department discussions as early as 1939. Post war planning, suggests Richard Gardner, was infused by a common interest in ensuring that unlike after the last great war, there would not be "inadequate handling of economic problems. Consequently, [planners] placed great emphasis on economics in drawing blue-prints for a better world."[44]

Early in the war State Department officials began formal and informal meetings with British and Canadian officials on postwar trade issues. In these talks and from ensuing policies, America's support for applying multilateral principles to commercial policy became increasingly apparent. In the Atlantic Charter in August 1941, in article VII of the Master Lend-Lease agreement in 1942, at Bretton Woods in 1944, and at the San Francisco conference to establish the United Nations, there were declarations of a causal relationship between commercial policies and peaceful relations among states. Then two documents – the *Proposals for Expansion of World Trade And Employment*, completed by State Department officials in December 1945 and the *Suggested Charter for an International Trade Organization of the United Nations* released in September of the following year – revealed specific plans for a trade regime that was both multilateral and nondiscriminatory. Both the GATT, which came into formal existence on January 1, 1948, and the ITO Charter, ratified in the fall of 1947 in Havana, have their intellectual origins in these American documents.

In moving from these blueprints, State Department officials confronted numerous problems. Perhaps most fundamental was that nations agreed only abstractly to a new multilateral trade regime. They disagreed, however, on just what the regime should do. The variation in greed, however, on just what the regime should do. The variation in national objectives was most visible in talks between the two key negotiating nations: Britain and the United States. The British argued that the goal of trade policy was full employment; trade liberalization was an acceptable strategy only to the extent that it met this goal. State Department negotiators, however, agreed only that changes in trade policy should not be at the cost of the economic vitality of particular sectors or producers. They – as opposed to America's own Department of Agriculture – never agreed that the trade regime should be created to meet domestic political goals. Indicatively, ITO negotiations were "a head-on collision between those who were wedded to the idea of a free multilateral trading system . . . and those who placed the whole emphasis on full employment policies on a national basis."[45]

In the original American *Proposal*, a general position was outlined:

> What is needed is a broad and yet detailed agreement among many nations, dealing at one time with many different sorts of government restrictions upon trade, reducing all of them at once on a balanced and equitable basis, and stating rules and principles within which the restrictions permitted to remain should be administered.[46]

Later in 1946, the American policy was further clarified by Clair Wilcox, the head of the American delegation in London negotiating with the British on the ITO:[47]

> Every nation stands to gain from the widest possible movement of goods and services . . . That international trade should be abundant, that it should be multilateral, that it should be non-discriminatory, that stabilization policies and trade policies should be consistent – these are propositions on which all nations, whatever their forms of economic organization, can agree.[48]

Whereas American negotiators argued that the primary principle of a trade organization was to reduce barriers to trade, Stafford Cripps, representing the

British, suggested that the prime object was to "achieve an agreement as to the manner in which the nations can co-operate for the promotion of the highest level of employment and the maintenance of demand and can bring some degree of regulation into world trade and commerce."[49] Such a position made little sense to American negotiators. The Americans doubted that nations could or should ask others to participate in domestic policies to maintain full employment. Employment, it was argued, could not be "as absolute as in the case of other matters which lie entirely within the volition and control of nations."[50] But it was not only the right of a multilateral organization to set domestic employment goals that sat poorly with the American delegation. As well, they differed on what should be the national employment objective. In 1945, the Full Employment Act had been rejected by Congress; its alternative in 1946 was far closer to the American conception of the responsibility of government, that is, ambiguity on both what constituted full employment and executive discretion over the use of economic tools to meet employment and executive discretion over the use of economic tools to meet employment goals. The Americans would only concede that nations should not use "measures likely to create unemployment in other countries."[51]

The British were, however, adamant on this point. Unlike the United States, their commitment to a Keynesian demand policy led to a fear that domestic expansion could be undermined by exports undercutting British production. Thus, the British proposed for the ITO Charter an unambiguous statement that full employment be "the main condition for the maintenance of satisfactory levels of living" and thus its maintenance on "a reasonably assured basis was essential . . . to the expansion of international trade."[52] And at minimum, the British wanted the ITO to allow them to resort to trade protection to defend employment goals.

The outcome on the ITO was a series of compromises. The heart of the settlement was the exceptions to rules under specific conditions relating to balance of payments adjustments. In London, the British got the assurance that

> in case of a fundamental disequilibrium in their balance of payments involving other countries in persistent balance of payments difficulties, which handicap them in maintaining employment, [nations] will make their full contribution to action designed to correct the maladjustment.[53]

Among actions to be taken, countries could, when necessary, resort to quantitative restrictions.

In any respects, quantitative restrictions were the fundamental issue of the times. When the Gold Standard collapsed in 1931, competitive devaluations made tariffs an insufficient mechanism for the protection of the economy. Nations then moved to explicit quantitative controls as a means of sheltering domestic industry. From the perspective of the State Department, quotas – unlike tariffs – not only were inherently discriminatory but also were associated with the economic nationalism of the interwar period. As early as 1933, the State Department pointed to quotas as the more onerous form of trade restriction, explaining that at least tariffs were potentially open to reciprocal bargaining.[54]

Although the trade regime ultimately allowed quotas, both British and American negotiators shared a general distaste for quantitative restrictions. Thus, they agreed that the trade regime should prohibit quantitative restrictions. But confronted with domestic political pressures, both agreed that special circumstances must occur when that principle could be ignored. To accommodate both parties, these exceptions grew to include a range of situations, from postwar transition, to balance of payment disequilibrium and domestic support programs.

This last category was introduced specifically by the American delegation. Before the war ended, American negotiators had informally indicated that they could sign no agreement that did not award special consideration to American agriculture. In response, American negotiators argued that quantitative restrictions to protect either an international commodity agreement or a domestic commodity program were legitimate extensions of previous principles. Then in line with its own needs, the United States proposed that restrictions be allowed only for domestic programs that controlled output. And when used, quotas and other restrictions would operate in such a way "as would reduce imports relatively to domestic production as compared with the proportion prevailing in a previous representative period."[55]

In the spring of 1947, the United States further clarified its position to the fifty-six participating nations at the Geneva United Nations Conference on Trade and Employment. Now, American acceptance of a trade regime was contingent upon four exceptions being written into both the ITO charter and the General Agreement. First, in 1946 the United States had included a new safeguard in its trade treaty with Mexico that allowed for portions of that agreement to be rescinded under specific conditions. Now the United States asked that such an escape clause – allowing suspension or withdrawal or tariff agreements if serious injury occurred to a domestic producer – be included in all its future agreements. Second, although GATT and the ITO were to forbid quantitative restrictions, such restrictions were to be allowed for the protection of agricultural commodities under specified conditions. Third, agricultural exports were to be an exception to any general pledge against export subsidization.[56] And fourth, if necessary to protect essential security interests, any obligation specified in the charter could be abrogated.[57] These exceptions were not negotiable. Thus, the United States vetoed a motion by China to extend the exceptions to include manufactured goods; likewise, they refused a motion by China, India, and the Netherlands to allow quantitative restrictions to apply to all domestic price stabilization measures.[58]

But the inclusion of these exceptions was still insufficient to garner domestic approval.[59] By the time Congress considered the final ITO Charter, almost every important group was lined up against ratification. Some groups argued with the National Foreign Trade Council that the employment provisions, "would operate inexorably to transform the free enterprise system of this country into a . . . planned economy . . . and threat[en] the free institutions and liberties of the American people."[60] Others suggested that the ITO would allow countries to pursue inflationary policies and still maintain quantitative restrictions against American exports. The sanctioning of restrictions for balance-of-payments reasons and rules on foreign direct investment, argued business groups, were inconsistent with their interpretation of the purpose of the multilateral trade regime.[61]

The administration made an additional mistake that made passage difficult. Throughout the negotiation process, the State Department had insinuated that the price of American involvement in a trade regime was the demise of British imperial preferences. When it became clear in 1950 that negotiators had not procured the elimination of British tariff preferences, many in Congress failed to see how the ITO Charter served American interests in any way. Commenting on the failure of the ITO, Richard Gardner argued that

> the two major sponsors . . . sought to incorporate in the Charter a detailed statement of their favorite economic doctrines. . . . The result was an elaborate set of rules and counter-rules that offered imperfect standards for national policy. These rule and counter-rules satisfied nobody and alienated nearly everybody.[62]

The demise of the ITO was not the end of the multilateral trade regime. The heart of what America wanted in a trade regime, that is, the commercial policy provisions of chapter V, were incorporated into part II of the GATT. This new document now codified America's preferences on trading relations as stated at the start of the negotiating process. Like the ITO, the GATT was multilateral. Fundamental control of the organization was shared by all members; all agreed to give others MFN status, and nondiscrimination was a central norm. But in operation, the GATT was a network of simultaneous bilateral reciprocal agreements. Unlike the ITO, the GATT did not aspire to be a multilateral mechanism for the formal control of all aspects of trade.[63] In this way, the United States finessed demands by other nations to specify policy guidelines for the new regime. But this limited purpose was an asset; even while the ITO Charter was being discussed in national capitals, the GATT initiated its first round of trade talks. These talks, called in 1947, were the first of eight major bargaining sessions that GATT would sponsor.[64]

GATT's success was not due to its being a better multilateral organization. As with the ITO, the document was riddled with exceptions. Article 11 contained the attempt to eliminate quantitative restrictions, except for restrictions on agricultural or fisheries products, and article 19 included the escape clause. The only item that may be construed as bowing to British demands was inclusion of article 12, providing the general safeguard for restrictions, if necessary, for balance of payments reasons. This general safeguard was, however, consistent with international monetary policies simultaneously being pursued in Washington.

THE GATT REGIME: MULTILATERALISM WITH EXCEPTIONS

By the late 1960s America's vision of the GATT had changed. Congress began to place pressure on GATT negotiators to get results on agricultural as well as manufacturing trade liberalization. But, as opposed to the 1950s when other countries were willing to entertain agreements in all trade arenas, American negotiators now found America's trading partners unable or unwilling to ignore farm constituencies that stood to lose from any liberalizing agreement. American policies of the 1940s and 1950s were coming "home to roost."

Finally, in 1948, on the eve of the first GATT talks, the demand for American farm products plummeted. As had been feared, the United States now had an oversupply of agricultural products, much as in the post-WWI years. But farm product price increases in the previous decade now exacerbated the problem. By 1948 the index of farm prices had reached 307, compared with an index of industrial prices that stood at 265. The parity price in 1948 – 116 – was the highest level reached since 1918. From an index of 76 in the period 1935–39, farm output advanced to 104 in 1948. Further, between 1938 and 1948, wholesale prices of farm products had increased 50 percent more than the prices of nonfarm products did.

To maintain incomes, policymakers eschewed trade liberalization as a policy option and turned instead to existing regulatory policies. But a program of substantial government intervention to control production, prices, and imports now meant that the United States would need a further waiver by the GATT.[65] Thus, in 1954, the United States went to GATT where it requested, and received, approval for a further change in GATT rules. To maintain prices the United States now needed GATT to allow it to halt imports even if there was no domestic program restricting output. This exception would become the legal basis for European claims that the Common Agricultural Policy (CAP) did not defy GATT rules.

Further, in this ninth GATT session, American negotiators made clear that the United States would condone no commodity agreement and would invoke the GATT principle if one was passed that any new activity by GATT would not automatically obligate existing members.[66] The formal American position as stated in these talks was that "the United States feels that the further venture into the commodity field . . . is unwise and unnecessary . . . because we believe that enough machinery already exists for dealing with commodity problems."[67]

Not only did the United States halt early talks on commodity trade, but also these actions encouraged others to increase barriers to American products. This is most clear in the case of European policy on agriculture

The CAP

At the time of the writing of the Treaty of Rome in 1957, the six signatories operated different types of agricultural support programs. Germany and Belgium, dependent on agricultural imports, used both trade restrictions and price supports to provide an income supplement to farmers. In contrast, France and Italy were self-sufficient in agricultural products, suffering instead from periodic surpluses. These countries not only restricted imports but also subsidized exports. The Netherlands and Luxembourg maintained relatively more liberal agricultural trade policy.

The Common Policy for Agriculture, adopted in January 1962, integrated these policies. Under the new rules, all national policies affecting prices, such as trading restrictions, local usage regulations, and subsidies were replaced by regulations for the Community as a whole. The marketing conditions for most agricultural products were fully controlled through direct market intervention. Target prices for individual products were set for the market as a whole. To ensure that these prices were not undermined by world market conditions, a system of variable import levies was created. These levies were calculated so as to offset any price advantage for imports, completely insulating producers from world price developments. To ensure that surpluses would not undermine target prices, the CAP provided for disposal of excess production through subsidized exports and subsidized consumption.

In practice, the target prices in the 1960s were not a weighted average of the previously ruling national prices but rather were a figure that exceeded that figure. In brussels, it was far easier to agree to higher prices than to lower individual price levels. Thus the Community maintained higher levels of protection for agricultural products after the CAP than had previously been in force by any individual states.[68]

The Europeans offered two legal defenses of the CAP to GATT members. First, they argued that the restrictions that had previously affected agricultural production and trade in each state were simply being substituted for a comprehensive program that was not ruled out by any provision of the GATT. Second, and more important, the Europeans relied on American precedent. The variable levy was compared with the American system of price supports. Both, it was suggested, maintained a domestic price unrelated to the world price; both called for us of import restrictions and export subsidies. Europeans suggested that article 11, which provided that imports be restricted only if domestic production or marketing was also curtailed, was no longer pertinent. The United States itself, in 1951, had legislated an amendment to the Defense Production Act requiring the Secretary of Agriculture to impose restrictions on imports of a number of products, including dairy, for which no domestic production controls existed. Further, in 1955, GATT had granted a general waiver for these quotas and others imposed under the 1951 extension of section 22 provisions. Given the U.S. example, GATT had no legal grounds to constrain the Community from enacting barriers to agricultural trade.[69]

In sum, the United States constrained GATT's efforts to deal with agricultural protectionism in two ways. First, in the 1950s, the United States refused to participate in any new agreements on commodity trade. The United States vetoed all proposals to have agricultural trade covered in separate commodity agreements, and in the GATT – as in the ITO charter – agriculture products were included in the general framework.[70] Thus, attempts by other GATT members to create separate agreements that would cover agricultural products were stymied by a lack of American participation.

Second, the United State undermined article 11 as a means of ending reliance on quantitative restrictions. While other primary commodity exporters waited for the time when countries would no longer rely on the exceptions to the use of quantitative restrictions for reasons of balance-of-payment disequilibrium, the United States itself actively used its waiver to impose such restrictions on agricultural products. The United States provided neither leadership nor support for the expansion of GATT into commodity trade. With agricultural trade restrictions off the agenda, nations recovering from the war were free to grant trade protection to inefficient agricultural producers for domestic political purposes. Before the late 1950s, no country on the continent made the argument that their participation in GATT was contingent on the exclusion of agricultural products. In the 1940s, Italy and France, the two countries with the least efficient farm sectors, were far more interested in an uninterrupted supply of agricultural supplies from the United States than in the needs of their nascent agricultural sectors. While dependent upon American food, there was no defiance to America's interests in reducing existing quantitative and nonquantitative restrictions. Agricultural protectionism returned to Europe and elsewhere with the tacit support of the United States.

CONCLUSIONS

Three general points may be drawn from this essay. First, GATT's creation stemmed from American power. It was the United States that envisioned a multilateral postwar world. That vision motivated individuals in the State Department to embark upon multilateral discussions that led to both the ITO Charter and the GATT. The specific rules written into both documents reflected American ideas on trade policy. Yet, American power did not ensure that the document constructed would adhere to the functional needs of the United States. Although negotiators might have thought that the agreement served the long-term interests of the American economy, neither the original GATT document nor the stickiness of these rules over time has proved optimal from the American perspective. In short, it may be true – but uninteresting – that regimes are created by the powerful. Power alone can explain neither the choice of rules nor the distributional implications of a particular regime.

How do we explain the choice of rules for a multilateral organization? Some suggest that GATT rules reflect an international "logroll." The United States agreed to exceptions in order to gain approval from other nations. There is little evidence to support this hypothesis. Only for the British – and only minimally – did the United States agree to deviate from the original American proposals. GATT rules and the structure of trade liberalization were absolutely consistent with America's original design for a trade regime. Whereas the ITO charter included compromise, especially to British interests, the GATT did not. In short, America had sufficient power and influence in 1947 to ensure that GATT rules reflected American demands.

Even so, the American delegation neither demanded nor obtained an unadulterated liberal trade order. Although the United States espoused multilateral principles, the American position on specific policy issues was a hybrid. In the 1940s, liberal trade ideas were relatively new; their worth was still an open question. Especially in the field of agricultural trade, no policymaker was willing to give up control to market forces when the alternative was a politically salient system of rules and procedures that had proved capable of ensuring agricultural growth. In short, no consensus existed in 1947 that liberalizing trade would be sufficient to ensure economic stability. Instead, a fear arose that the return to normalcy would bring on the agricultural depression akin to the one that followed World War I.

Thus, the United States limited its delegation of authority to the ITO and GATT through a series of escape clauses and exceptions.

By the 1960s, American opinion had changed.[71] But GATT rules had not. Thus, the problem for the United States thereafter was to attempt, through diplomacy, to establish new operating procedures by which to liberalize agricultural trade. As evidenced by the Uruguay Round, Americans have had only limited success. Where in the 1940s the United States could use either of two strategies to ensure compliance from her trading partners, that is, the United States could threaten to "exit" from negotiations or offer lucrative side payments, the decline of American power makes both of these strategies costly. In short, although America's commitment to liberal trade increased over the century, GATT's rules continued to allow other nations to pursue particularistic trade policies.

This suggests a second point. Policies once institutionalized are difficult to uproot. This is true in both domestic and international organizations, essentially for the same reason. Once in force, policies create interests who benefit from that particular constellation of rules and procedures. These interests – within and outside government – become a formidable political force, making change difficult. Thus, once agricultural subsidies became American policy, even groups who once scorned such government intervention found themselves aligned together defending the distributional aspects of the policy. This group made it impossible for American negotiators to delegate any authority to the GATT that would undermine the subsidy program. Similarly, once GATT allowed quantitative exceptions for agricultural products, it encouraged the creation of agricultural protections abroad. Europe could construct the CAP, which in principle deviated from the liberal trade regime, and still be in compliance with GATT. And once protected, European agricultural groups made it politically impossible for governments to withdraw aid.

On both the domestic and international level organizations codify a particular set of ideas. But although the organization may be the creation of the powerful and represent the strategy of the "winning coalition," the distributional aspects of the new regime may deviate markedly from that predicted by its creators. Not only may the strategy selected be suboptimal in the short term, but also in the long term, unintended consequences may follow from the creation of a set of rules and procedures that ultimately counter the interests of the organization's creators.

This is no more evident than in the case of agricultural trade. American negotiators wanted agricultural markets opened to American products. Thus they were adamant about not separating agricultural negotiations from talks on manufacturers. But simultaneously, the American Congress demanded the writing of an exception into the rules for agricultural subsidies. Once the rule existed, it created the incentive for both Europe and Japan to protect inefficient agricultural producers. The political coalitions that developed from such protections left the United States at a disadvantage, with little it could either offer or threaten in order to gain concessions from these governments.

This suggests a last point. From the American perspective, the GATT has serious flaws. Central among these problems is the continued inability of GATT to liberalize trade for America's key export items. Although true, such a perspective may be shortsighted. While these exceptions undermined the creation of a truly liberal trade regime, they may have been the regime's great strength. By allowing governments to pursue domestic interventionist policies – by supporting "embedded" and not orthodox liberalism – the regime retained the support of members and succeeded, with minimal resources, in fundamentally changing postwar commercial relations.[72] This compromise between free-trade ideas and domestic autonomy was never formally decided in multilateral negotiations. Rather, it was the unintended consequence of a series of compromises to ensure British and, more important, American involvement in the regime.

ACKNOWLEDGEMENT

I would like to thank Jeffry Frieden, Geoff Garrett, Robert Keohane, John Ruggie, Steven Weber, and the other participants in this project for excellent comments on previous drafts. Georgia Markou, Qurania Markou, and Scott Wilson provided valuable research assistance.

NOTES

1 See, for instance, Robert Keohane, *After Hegemony*, (Princeton: Princeton University Press, 1984); Kenneth Oye, *Cooperation Under Anarchy* (Princeton: Princeton University Press, 1986); Stephen Krasner *International Regime* (Ithaca: Cornell University Press, 1983).

2 Stephen Krasner, "Global Communications and National Power: Life on the Pareto Frontier" *World Politics*, (July 1991) vol. 43.

3 Focal points were first considered by Thomas Schelling *Strategy of Conflict* (Cambridge: Harvard University Press, 1960). For a more recent application see: Geoffrey Garret and Barry Weingast, "Ideas, Interests and Institutions: Constructing the EC's Internal Market," MS. 1991. On the ability of the powerful to get its desired outcome see: Stephen Krasner, "State Power and the Structure of International Trade," *World Politics*, (April 1976) vol 28, and Duncan Snidal, "The limits of hegemonic stability theory" *International Organization* (Autumn 1985) vol. 39(4).

4 On American power after the war and the creation of regimes see: Krasner, "State Power" *and International Regimes*; Robert Keohane, "The Theory of Hegemonic Stability and Changes in International Economic Regimes," in O. Holsti, R. Siverson, and A. George, eds. *Change in the International System* (Boulder: Westview, 1980); Snidal, "Limits of Hegemonic Stability Theory."

5 It is interesting to speculate about what would be the condition of America's trade deficit if farm products were traded as freely as are nonfarm products. One cannot ignore the radical shifts in American trade account in years in which some exogenous variable caused an increase in demand for American farm products, for example, famines or worldwide bad weather. By one estimate, access to European and Japanese markets would bring in more than 25 billion dollars to the trade account and balance the American budget.

6 On why hegemons would favor liberal trading regime see: Krasner, "State Power"; Keohane, "Hegemonic Stability."

7 See Judith Goldstein and Robert Keohane, "Introduction," *Ideas and Foreign Policy*, MS, 1991.

8 This does not suggest that a policy of price supports did not meet the needs of the agricultural producers. The more autarchic policies promoted by agricultural groups was "functional" in the 1940s. However, worldwide trade liberation was a superior policy choice since it would have met both the short-term and long-term interests of the farming sector.

9 Section 3(e) of the NIRA gave the president broad powers over imports so that the United States would not "render ineffective or seriously . . . endanger the maintenance of any code or agreement." In section 22 of the AAA it is stated that imports ought not to "render ineffective, tend to render ineffective or materially interfere with" AAA programs; Section 32 authorized the secretary of agriculture to set aside 30 percent of annual customs revenues to subsidize exports.

10 Although a counterfactual, we can imagine that if liberals had not been able to influence trade policy, the executive's enlarged power could well have been used for many other purposes. For example, if influenced by the existing German model, a much more mercantile or hierarchical system could have been inaugurated under American hegemony. What is apparent from congressional votes is that was not until the 1950s that the liberalization of trade policy had bipartisan support. On the 1930s and trade liberalization see: Judith Goldstein, *Ideas, Interests and American Trade Policy* (Ithaca: Cornell University Press, forthcoming).

11 By 1938 the U.S. was claiming concessions on more than half its exports and declared a 45 percent reduction in tariffs. Curzon notes, however, that half of the agreements concluded before World War II were with Latin America and on noncompetitive products. Only the agreements with Canada, Europe, and Great Britain covered products in which American producers lost their price advantage. In general, these agreements did little to increase world trade since American tariffs remained very high and most-favored nation status was extended to few countries. Gerard Curzon, *Multilateral Commercial Diplomacy* (London: Michael Joseph, 1965), p. 27.

12 Quoted in John Day Larkin, *The President's Control of the Tariff* (Cambridge: Harvard University Press) 1936, p. 48.

13 It was not until 1940 that both political parties agreed to any notion of reciprocity. Indicative of the slow change in preferences, the 1936 Republican platform still advocated repeal of the Reciprocal Trade Agreements legislation. The 1940 platform however, undertook to distinguish between "genuine reciprocity and so called reciprocal trade agreements." Thus, for the first time, both parties ran simultaneously on a platform of reciprocity. Thereafter, the Republican criticism moved to executive control of tariff treaties and multilateralism. In 1944 the party platform argued that, "We will always bear in mind that the domestic market is America's greatest market and that tariffs which protect it against foreign competition should be modified only by reciprocal bilateral trade agreements approved by Congress." Porter and Johnson, *National Party Platforms* (Urbana: University of Illinois Press, 1961).

14 Richard Carlton Snyder, *The Most-Favored-Nation Clause* (N.Y.: Kings Crown Press, 1948), p. 29.

15 In 1933, even as countries were increasing protections against their trade partners, the vast majority of agreements included an unconditional MFN statement. Out of the 625 most-favored-nation agreements in force, only 48 were conditional. Snyder, *Most-Favored-Nation Clause*, p. 211.

16 The move to unconditionality developed out of a controversy over differing interpretations of the powers granted in the flexible tariff provision of the Tariff Act of 1922. As understood at time of passage, flexibility was supposed to stop discrimination against U.S. exports in the tradition of earlier reciprocity clauses. Its inclusion was championed by Senator Reed Smoot (of Smoot-Hawley fame). Congress gave no hint

in its discussion that it interpreted this section to mean that, in the future, the United States should avoid discriminatory agreements. However, one member of the Tariff Commission, a proponent of unconditionality, understood the legal implications of the wording of the section. After passage, William Culbertson wrote to Secretary of State Hughes explaining that if the intent of Congress were to be followed, all discriminatory agreements had to be eliminated. According to Culbertson, Congress had mandated that the United States increase duties in all cases in which a nation did not give U.S. exports the same preferential treatment given to those of another country. This meant that the President must increase the tariff on the goods of all nations that were party to a tariff agreement without the United States. Culbertson went on to argue that Congress could not have intended Section 317 to be used in this fashion. So, to fulfil the will of Congress, the United States would need to render all treaties unconditional. Secretary Hughes communicated this to President Harding, who with little thought, approved this new policy. In August, it was announced that all future treaties would contain an unconditional MFN clause. See: William J. Culbertson, *Reciprocity* (New York: McGraw-Hill, 1937), pp. 244–58.

17 At the time of passage of the 1934 Act, the US had negotiated unconditional form treaties with 10 countries representing 12 percent of total American exports. In addition, there were executive agreements with 17 other countries representing 10 percent of total exports. Still in force were 13 conditional treaties and conditional executive agreements covering 34 percent of exports. Previous to the change in policy in 1923, the U.S. had signed only 3 unconditional treaties in 1850, 1871 and 1881, and these were recognized as exceptions to policy. Percy W. Bidwell, *Tariff Policy of the United States: A Study of Recent Experience: Report to the Second International Studies Conference on The State and Economic Life* (New York: Council on Foreign Relations, 1933), pp. 4, 5, 8.

18 Culbertson, *Reciprocity*, p. 69; and Henry J. Tasca, *The Reciprocal Trade Policy of the United States* (Philadelphia: University of Pennsylvania Press, 1938), pp. 116–21.

19 There were sound, functional reasons for a shift from conditional to unconditional MFN policies after World War I. In William B. Kelly, Jr., ed. *Studies in United States Commercial Policy* (Chapel Hill: University of North Carolina Press, 1963), pp. 44–98, Kelly argues that the United States enjoyed relative immunity from discrimination before the war because 1) few U.S. actions before 1890 might have inspired foreign retaliation; 2) the United States benefited from the unconditional treaties of other nations (particularly European treaties); and 3) noncompetitive agricultural goods dominated American exports. However, increasingly hostile trade, the necessity of new treaties, growing reliance on manufactured goods, and the shift from debtor to creditor made the United States vulnerable to discrimination after World War I.

20 Tasca, *Reciprocal Trade Policy* p. 6. On the history of reciprocity see: Robert O. Keohane, "Reciprocity in International Relations" *International Organization* (Winter 1986) 40:1–28.

21 Tasca, *Reciprocal Trade Policy* p. 6.

22 Bidwell, *Tariff Policy of the United States*, p. 52.

23 Ibid. pp. 57–59.

24 Cited in Larkin, *President's Control*, p. 54.

25 Ibid., 1936, p. 54.

26 Ibid., 1936, p. 55.

27 Lawrence Chamberlain, *President, Congress and Legislation* (New York: Columbia University Press, 1946), p. 133. All but two of the nonadministration witnesses opposed the bill, although all supported the general objective of increasing trade. For a more thorough study of the 1934 Act see: Stephen Haggard, "The Institutional Foundations

of Hegemony: Explaining the Reciprocal Trade Agreement Act of 1934," *International Organization* (Winter 1988), vol. 42.

28 The act came to the floor without a closed rule but with a large enough majority to ensure that all opposition amendments were rejected. One of the more telling points made by the minority was that the position now advocated by the Democrats on the issue of Presidential control was contradictory: in 1929, eight democratic members of the Senate Finance Committee had publicly declared themselves unalterably opposed to the principle of permitting the President to control tariff rates.

29 Hearings ran from April 26 through May 1. Sixty-five witnesses either appeared or filed briefs. Chamberlain, *President, Congress and Legislation*, p. 135.

30 One significant addition to the administration's act was a Finance Committee amendment to require "public notice of the intention to negotiate an agreement." Widespread sentiment in both houses had favored integrating public hearings into the process. In keeping with this provision, the interdepartmental Trade Agreements Committee and the Committee for Reciprocity Information were later formed. These became the progenitor of the interbranch committees that characterized the American trade program throughout the century.

31 Cited in E. E. Schattschneider, *Politics, Pressures and the Tariff: A Study of Free Enterprise in Pressure Politics* (New York: Prentice-Hall, 1935), p. 145.

32 Tasca, *Reciprocal Trade Policy*, p. 29.

33 John Day Larkin, *Trade Agreements: A Study in Democratic Methods* (New York: Columbia University Press, 1940), p. 69.

34 For a thorough explanation of the initial state groups charged with trade liberalization, see Tasca, *Reciprocal Trade Policy*, pp. 45–73. The Trade Agreements Committee continued to exist until 1962 when it was replaced by the Cabinet-level Trade Information Committee, chaired by the Special Trade Representative.

35 On the post-1934 role of congress see: Robert A. Pastor, *Congress and the Politics of U.S. Foreign Economic Policy, 1929–76* (Berkeley: University of California Press, 1980) and I. M. Destler, *American Trade Politics: System Under Stress* (Washington, D.C.: Institute for International Economics, 1986).

36 In the Agricultural Adjustment Act of 1933, prices were to be set so as "to reestablish prices to farmers at a level that will give agricultural commodities a purchasing power of agricultural commodities in the basic period (i.e., 1909–1914)." In the Soil Conservation and Domestic Allotment Act of 1936, the parity goal shifted from price equality of agricultural commodities and the prices of things farmers purchased to income equality between farm and nonfarm populations. In 1938, the Act moved back to an emphasis on agricultural incomes and the products farmers consume by providing for direct parity payments to producers of the basic crops equal to the difference between the market price and the fair exchange value. As one commentator noted in 1938, "The congressmen did not want to hear any more nonsense about equalizing incomes – what they wanted was a proper price for their cotton and corn. If they got that, income would take care of itself. John Black, *Parity, Parity, Parity* (Cambridge: The Harvard Committee on Research in the Social Sciences, 1942), p. 57.

37 See Judith Goldstein, "The Impact of Ideas on Trade Policy: The Origins of U.S. Agricultural and Manufacturing Policies" *International Organization* (Winter 1989), vol. 43, no. 1.

38 Allan Rau *Agricultural Policy and Trade Liberalization in the United States, 1934–1956* (Geneva: E. Droz 1957), p. 66.

39 Roosevelt's response to the lack of congressional action was to use his control of the Agricultural Department to limit use of supports. This led to some success in keeping export subsidies down. The 118 million dollar figure is relatively small considering

that in 1935 alone, congress allocated $90 million for export subsidization. Rau, *Agricultural Policy*, p. 80.

40 Under the Surplus Property Act of 1940, export subsidies for cotton were begun again in 1944.

41 Compared with WWI, the agricultural sector produced 50 percent more during WWII with only five percent more land and 10 percent fewer employees. Rau, *Agricultural Policy*, p. 88.

42 Rau, p. 88.

43 Even in the face of GATT rules, the 1948 Act endorsed export subsidies, budgeting $300 million for such supports. In addition, Section 22 authority was expanded to allow the imposition of import fees or quotas whenever unrestricted imports interfered with "any loan, purchase or other program or operation undertaken by the Department of Agriculture or any agency operation under its jurisdiction." Any product could now be protected under the provision.

44 Richard N. Gardner, *Sterling-Dollar Diplomacy*, (New York: McGraw-Hill 1969), p. 4.

45 Cited from an address by Eric Wyndham While, Executive Secretary of the GATT, at the Fletcher School, April, 1949. In Curzon, *Multilateral Commercial Diplomacy*, p. 31.

46 Cited in Edna Wilgress, *A New Attempt at Internationalism*, (Paris: Societe D'edition D'enseignmement Superieur, 1949) p. 12.

47 Cited in Gardner, *Sterling-Dollar Diplomacy*, p. 270.

48 In a speech during the London conference, Wilcox clarified what multilateral trade meant:
"International trade should be multilateral rather than bilateral. Particular transactions, of course, are always bilateral. One seller deals with one buyer. But under multilateralism, the pattern of trade is, in general, many-sided. Sellers are not compelled to confine their sales to buyers who will deliver them equivalent values in other goods. Buyers are not required to find sellers who will accept payment in goods that buyers have produced. Traders sell where they please, exchanging goods for money, and buy where they please, exchanging goods for money for goods. Bilateralism, by contrast, is akin to barter. Under this system, you may sell for money but you cannot use your money where you please. . . . Imports are directly tied to exports and each country must balance its accounts, not only with the world as a whole but separately with every other country with whom it deals." Wilgress, *New Attempts at Internationalism*, p. 37–38.

49 Gardner, *Sterling-Dollar Diplomacy*, p. 271.

50 Ibid.

51 Ibid., p. 272.

52 Ibid., p. 274.

53 Ibid., p. 276.

54 At the London Conference of 1933 a draft annotated agenda stressed the necessity of doing away with import quotas "whether they take the form of prohibitions or of quotas or licence, have in recent years become exceptionally widespread and are so numerous that they now constitute an almost insurmountable barrier to international exchanges." Curzon, *Multilateral Commercial Diplomacy*, p. 128.

55 Gardner, *Sterling-Dollar Diplomacy* p. 150.

56 The proposal specified that members who were paying export subsidies on agricultural commodities cooperate in negotiations of commodity agreements. But if no agreement was reached, export subsidies would be allowed provided they did not increase the products share of the world market relative to a past representative period.

57 The elasticity of this proposal was quickly recognized when the United States used

the security release to justify import restrictions on cheese and on wool.

58 Rau, *Agricultural Policy* pp. 111–12.

59 See Gardner, *Sterling-Dollar Diplomacy*, pp. 348–81.

60 Ibid., p. 376.

61 The condemnation of the International Chamber of Commerce was sweeping. "It [ITO charter] is a dangerous document because it accepts practically all of the policies of economic nationalism; because it jeopardizes the free enterprise system by giving priority to centralized national governmental planning of foreign trade; because it leaves a wide scope to discrimination, accepts the principle of economic insulation and in effect commits all members of the ITO to state planning for full employment." Ibid., p. 377.

62 Ibid., p. 379.

63 Because of its more minimalist task, the GATT was authorized through presidential decree under rights given by the trade agreements program instead of through congressional assent. In practice, this meant that its legal basis was somewhat unclear. It was not until 1968 that the President asked Congress for and received permanent authorization for contributions to the running of the organization. Previously, American contributions were buried in a State Department line item entitled "international conferences and contingencies". *Ibid.*, p. xxxiv.

64 The other talks were the Annecy in 1949, Torquay in 1951, Geneva in 1956, the Dillon Round in 1960–61, Kennedy Round in 1964–67, the Tokyo Round concluded in 1979, and the ongoing Uruguay round.

65 In the mid-1950s, policymakers began to see the costs associated with American actions. At the sixth session of GATT in 1951, Denmark, the Netherlands, Canada, Australia, New Zealand, Italy, Norway, and France lodged a formal protest against restriction under section 104 of the 1950 Defense Production Act, stating it was a violation of the agreement. The following year these countries demanded compensation, which they received.

66 The leader of the United States delegation stated that the "real reason for standing aside was that the extension of the scope of activities into the commodity field, beyond the trade aspects which were already within the scope of the General Agreement, would endanger the full and firm participation of the United States in the new organization, under explicit congressional approval, which the U.S. government hoped to see accomplished." Curzon, *Multilateral Commercial Diplomacy*, p. 169.

67 Ibid., p. 169.

68 For example, Hill gives figures for pre- and post-CAP levels of protection for the following items. Live animals, 14.4 to 48.5 percent; meat, 19.0 to 52.1 percent; dairy products, 18.6 to 137.3 percent; cereals, 13.5 to 72.4 percent. See: Brian Hill, *The Common Agricultural Policy: Past, Present and Future* (London: Methuen), 1984.

69 John Evans *The Kennedy Round in American Trade Policy: The Twilight of the GATT?* (Cambridge: Harvard University Press, 1971) pp. 70–86.

70 Here, the United States had sided with the other agricultural exporting nations, including some of the European nations – such as Denmark and Holland – whose interests in the trading organization were tied to agricultural trade liberalization.

71 If we look at section 22 petitions as a measure of interest in agricultural quotas, we see petition activity declining from seven a year in the 1950s to less than two a year in the early 1960s, a little more than one a year in the late 1960s and less than one a year by the mid-1970s. Similarly, acceptance rates go down 50 percent in this period. Goldstein, *Ideas, Interests*, p. 70.

72 On the idea of embedded liberalism see: John Ruggie, "International Regimes, Transactions, and Change: Embedded Liberalism in the Postwar Economic Order" in Stephen Krasner, *International Regimes* (Ithaca: Cornell University Press, 1983).

8. GATT: A Cooperative Equilibrium in a Noncooperative Trading Regime?

T. L. Hungerford

1. INTRODUCTION

MANY OBSERVERS OF THE international economy claim that the General Agreement on Tariffs and Trade (GATT) is not working – that many of the major international players are not abiding by the rules and are instead impeding trade through the use of nontariff restrictions [Stern (1987)]. Besides nontariff measures, many point to defects in the dispute settlement mechanism as a contributing factor to this breakdown [Jackson (1979)]. This paper will examine this 'breakdown' of GATT by specifically modeling the dispute settlement procedure with nontariff barriers (NTBs). It is found that the equilibrium outcome(s) involves each country imposing nontariff barriers to trade.

One well-known reason to impose trade barriers is to increase welfare, and one common policy is the import tariff. The theoretical possibility of improving the terms of trade has long been recognized: if a country is a large enough buyer in world markets, it can improve its terms of trade in a monopolistic manner by imposing tariffs on imports (i.e. the optimal tariff) and thus improve welfare [Meade (1952)]. This gives each large country an incentive to set the optimal tariff. However, improving the terms of trade in one country necessarily means a worsening of the terms of trade and declining welfare for the country's trading partners.

Since a country's trade policies have effects on other countries, we have an environment that gives rise to the possibility of strategic interaction. If one country's trade policy harms another country, then the harmed country has an incentive to retaliate. Several investigators [Dixit (1987), Johnson (1953–54) and McMillan (1986)] have formally analyzed this idea in a static 2 x 2 trade model with the result that both countries levy tariffs. On the other hand, other researchers [Dixit (1987) and Jensen and Thursby (1980)] have shown that cooperative behavior (free trade) is an equilibrium strategy in a dynamic noncooperative tariff game.

However, none of these studies explains why countries are resorting to NTBs. Deardorff (1987) reviews various reasons why NTBs are preferred to tariffs. The most compelling reason, he concludes, is the perception on the part of policy-makers and their constituents that tariffs will not reduce imports. As will be seen, simply substituting NTBs in place of tariffs into a dynamic game does not change the outcome: cooperative behavior is still an equilibrium strategy. NTB must somehow be different from tariffs in terms of how trade is restricted.

One important difference is that NTBs are not as transparent as tariffs. Some claim that NTBs are essentially invisible and can take virtually an unlimited number of forms [Economic Report of the President (1988)]. Since they are difficult to detect, their use will not invite retaliation. Some NTBs, such as the nonenforcement of certain intellectual property right laws, were initially invisible and were discovered only after an investigation. Some domestic measures, for example health and safety rules, while visible, have an ambiguous status. An investigation may be required to determine if a particular rule is a NTB or a legitimate health rule.[1] In either case, once a nontariff barrier is identified it is difficult to measure its effect on trade [Deardorff and Stern (1984)].

Some recent studies have incorporated NTBs into game-theoretic trade models. Riezman (1987), in an infinitely repeated game with uncertainty and asymmetric information (NTBs), shows that 'free trade will never occur'. But Riezman's result crucially depends on countries reverting to 'reversionary' (retaliation) times even when their terms of trade improve too much. A country's term of trade will improve for any of three reasons: (1) the country set its own optimal trade barrier: (2) there are random economic fluctuations; and (3) the other country lowers its trade barriers below the optimum. None of these reasons provides a country with an incentive to change its trade policy to 'reversionary' times.

On the other hand, Copeland (1986), using a two-stage game with a cooperative first stage (negotiations) and a noncooperative second stage to model trade policy, demonstrates that countries will use 'alternative types of barriers' (i.e. NTBs) in the second stage. But this set-up precludes the use of retaliation to enforce this spirit of the negotiated settlement from the first stage of the game. In a related paper, Copeland (1989) examined tariffs and quotas in a game with the possibility of retaliation. One case involves the negotiated setting of tariffs but not quotas. He shows that if tariffs are 'properly' set in the co-operative stage, then no quota war will start in the noncooperative stage. However, Rodriguez's (1974) trade eliminating quota war will break out if the tariff negotiations break down or some other mistake occurs in the tariff negotiations. The final outcome of this case is one of extremes: no quotas or no trade.

This paper examines the problems that NTBs created for the dispute-settlement mechanism of GATT in a two-country infinitely repeated game with uncertainty and asymmetric information. The next section sets up the model and examines the case where retaliation is certain when NTBs are suspected. The GATT investigation requirement of the dispute-settlement procedure is added and analyzed in section 3. Concluding remarks are offered in the final section of the paper.

2. THE GAME WITH A SIMPLE TRIGGER STRATEGY

For the purposes of this paper, the dispute settlement mechanism[2] will be stripped down to its barest essential features. It will be modeled as a trigger strategy. A trigger strategy is a strategy where a player will do action *a* if the state of the world is *A* and will do action *b* if the state is not *A*. Specifically, in the context of the GATT this means that a country will levy its GATT bound tariff as long as all others do so, but should a trading partner cheat by raising its tariff or imposing some other trade barrier, then the country will retaliate against its offending partner by increasing its tariff on imports.[3]

In this paper, the stylized dispute-settlement mechanism will be analyzed within the context of a two-country, two-good trade model. While each country has some power to affect world prices it is assumed that each industry is competitive. The use of export taxes as a way of exploiting monopoly power is ruled out.[4] Since trade relations are long-lived, it is assumed that the game is infinitely played. The whole game consisting of the infinite repetitions is called a supergame, and each play of the supergame is a subgame. The payoff (or welfare level) to the supergame is the sum of payoffs of each subgame appropriately discounted. In this supergame each country chooses a strategy that determines what action to take at each play of the game. These choices depend on the history of prior actions taken by each player. The present model draws on Green and Porter's (1984) analysis of cartels under price uncertainty.

Assume that each country has an indirect utility function representing consumer preferences. The indirect utility function, $U_i(p_i, I_i)$, is a nonincreasing function of domestic prices and a nondecreasing function of income in country $i \in \{1, 2\}$. Domestic prices and income are in turn functions of country i's terms of trade,[5] π_i, the domestic tariff on the imported good, τ_i, and nontariff barriers [see Copeland (1986) and Woodland (1982) for the derivation].

The set-up used here for the incorporation of NTBs has some elements in common with Copeland (1986). The first step is to determine the monetary equivalent of NTBs. Define ρ_i as the vector of country i's policy instruments. Some of the policy instruments could have as their main purpose the limitation of imports, while others may have purely domestic goals but have the effect of adversely interfering with trade. Next, let κ_i, the level of trade barrier resulting from ρ_i, be defined as the level of tariffs that would lead to the same reduction in imports, given world prices. In other words, it is assumed that there exists a function such that $\kappa_i = h(\rho_i)$.

Since κ_i is the level of the trade barriers in tariff units induced by ρ_i and τ_i is the tariff level that is included in ρ_i, the protective impact of the NTBs in the policy instrument vector (assumed to be everything but τ_i) is

$$\mu_i = \kappa_i - \tau_i.$$

In other words, the protective effects of NTBs are treated as residuals between tariff levels, which are negotiated at GATT sponsored multilateral trade negotiations (MTNs), and the total protective impact of ρ_i. It should be noted that the protective effect of NTBs can be redundant with other NTBs or the tariff.

Import demands also depend on economic conditions. There are various random supply and demand shocks that affect the economy. Let these various shocks in each country be summarized by a single random variable, δ_i, which neither country can directly observe, such that increases in δ_i decrease import demand in country i. Next, let $g(\delta_1, \delta_2)$ be the joint distribution function of the two random variables. Now each country's import demand function can be represented as $M_i(\pi_i, \tau_i, \mu_i, \delta_i)$. The balance of trade condition,

$$\pi_1 M_1(\pi_1, \tau_1, \mu_1, \delta_1) = M_2(\pi_2, \tau_2, \mu_2, \delta_2),$$

implicitly defines π_1 (and thus π_2) as

$$\pi_1 = \pi_1(\tau_1, \mu_1, \tau_2, \mu_2, \delta_1, \delta_2).$$

Assuming the Marshall-Lerner condition holds and that tariff revenues and quota rents are redistributed to consumers, then it is easily shown that the following set of four inequalities hold:

$$\frac{\partial \pi_i}{\partial \mu_i} < 0; \quad \frac{\partial \pi_i}{\partial \delta_i} < 0; \quad \frac{\partial \pi_i}{\partial \mu_j} > 0; \quad \frac{\partial \pi_i}{\partial \delta_j} > 0. \qquad (1)$$

Define national income as

$$I_i = G(p_i) + r(\pi_i, \tau_i, \mu_i),$$

where $r(\cdot)$ is government revenue from the trade barriers,[6] and $G(p_i)$ is the value of domestic output.[7] Domestic prices, q_i and p_i (consumer and producer prices, respectively) are functions of π_i, μ_i and τ_i. Substituting all this into the indirect utility function yields

$$U_i(q_i, G(p_i) + r(\pi_i, \tau_i, \mu_i)) = H_i(\tau_i, \mu_i, \tau_j, \mu_j, \delta_i, \delta_j),$$

which is assumed concave and twice continuously differentiable in τ_i and μ_i. Given the derivation of H_i the following inequalities hold at $\mu_i = \tau_i = 0$:

$$\frac{\partial H_i}{\partial \mu_i} > 0; \quad \frac{\partial H_i}{\partial \tau_i} > 0; \quad \frac{\partial H_i}{\partial \delta_i} > 0; \quad \frac{\partial H_i}{\partial \mu_j} < 0; \quad \frac{\partial H_i}{\tau_j} < 0; \quad \frac{\partial H_i}{\partial \delta_j} < 0. \qquad (2)$$

Since NTBs are assumed initially invisible, their effects cannot directly be observed. Therefore each country must use some observable variable as an instrument for the level of μ_i. The most handy variable in this set-up is the terms of trade. Consequently, it is maintained in this section that a country will retaliate if its terms of trade rises (and hence worsens) above some trigger level, $\bar{\pi}_i$, that is if $\pi_i(\tau_i, \mu_i, \tau_j, \mu_j, \delta_i, \delta_j) > \bar{\pi}_i$.[8] Condition (1) suggests that π_i could rise above the trigger for any of three reasons: (i) increases in foreign tariffs or NTBs; (ii) a rise in the foreign country's random shock term; and/or (iii) a fall in the domestic random shock term.

Define a contingent strategy for country i as the infinite sequence $s_i = \{s_{i0}, s_{i1}, s_{i2}, \ldots\}$, where s_{i0} is an initial action, and s_{it} determines i's action in period t given the history of previous actions of the other player in the game. Each country's action in any period is an ordered pair, $s_{it}=(\tau_i, \mu_i)$. The cooperative strategy is $s_i^*=(\bar{\tau}_i, 0)$, where $\bar{\tau}_i$ is country i's GATT tariff binding (it could be zero if there is free trade) and the retaliation action, s_i^i, is country i's response action to country j's retaliatory tariff, s_j^i, after country i has been suspected of imposing NTBs. It is assumed that a country retaliates by raising its tariff to its optimal tariff level.[9]

Now let $H_i(\mu_i) = E_\delta H_i(\bar{\tau}_i, \mu_i, \bar{\tau}_j, 0, \delta_i, \delta_\tau)$, be country i's single-period expected payoff from playing μ_i and let $H_i^i=E_\delta H_i(s_i^i, s_j^i, \delta_i, \delta_j)$ be the single-period expected payoff to country i after country j has retaliated by levying a compensatory tariff and country i plays its best response strategy (i.e. it adjusts its level of protective effect of NTBs, perhaps even to zero). Given this set-up it is safe to assume that

$$H_i(\mu_i) > E_\delta H_i(s_i^*, s_j^*, \cdot, \cdot) > H_i^i. \tag{3}$$

That is, the single-period payoff to defecting is greater than the payoff to cooperating, which is greater than the payoff when the other country is retaliating.[10] Time periods can be categorized into two groups: 'normal' periods and retaliatory periods. In retaliatory periods one country will retaliate for a past defection by the other country and the defecting country will play its best response. Normal periods are characterized by the absence of retaliation.

Let $V_i(\mu_i)$ be the expected discounted present value payoff to country i if it sets its NTB protective level to μ_i. Then $V_i(\mu_i)$ can be written as:

$$V_i(\mu_i)=H_i(\mu_i) + \Pr(\pi_j > \bar{\pi}_j)\left\{\sum_{t=1}^{t_i^*-1} \beta_i^t H_i^i+\beta_i^{t_i^*} V_i(\mu_i)\right\}$$

$$+ \beta_i \Pr(\pi_j \leqq \bar{\pi}_j)\, V_i(\mu_i), \tag{4}$$

where t_i^* is the number of retaliation periods and β_i is country i's discount factor. The payoff is the single-period gain from defecting (before the other country can react) plus the expected gains from continued defection. Country j will retaliate whenever $\pi_j > \bar{\pi}_j$.

Since $\pi_j(\ldots)$ is a function of two random variables (δ_1 and δ_2) it is therefore itself a random variable with distribution $F(\pi_j; \tau_i, \mu_i, \tau_j, \mu_j)(=F(\pi_j))$. Substituting this into eq. (4), solving $V_i(\cdot)$, and adding and subtracting $H_i^i/(1-\beta_i)(1-\beta_i^{t_i^*}-F(\bar{\pi}_j)(\beta_i-\beta_i^{t_i^*}))$ to the right-hand side, yields

$$V_i(\mu_i)=\frac{H_i(\mu_i) - H_i^i}{1-\beta_i^{t_i^*}-F(\bar{\pi}_j)(\beta_i-\beta_i^{t_i^*})} \quad \frac{H_i^i}{1-\beta_i} \tag{5}$$

This shows that the discounted present value payoff is what it would be in retaliation periods plus the single-period payoff gain to playing μ_i in 'normal' periods, appropriately discounted.

A Nash equilibrium[11] requires, in this case, that $V_i(\mu_i=0) \geqq V_i(\mu_i=0)$ for all i. In order to determine the optimal value of μ_i, we need to examine the first-order conditions of country i's optimization problem. The first-order necessary conditions for eq. (5) yield after some cancellation:

$$V_i'(\mu_i)=(1-\beta_i^{t_i^*}-F(\bar{\pi}_j)(\beta_i-\beta_i^{t_i^*}))\frac{\partial H_i(\mu_i)}{\partial \mu_i}$$

$$+(\beta_i-\beta_i^{t_i^*})(H_i(\mu_i)-H_i^{t})\frac{\partial F(\bar{\pi}_j)}{\partial \mu_i}$$

$$=0. \tag{6}$$

That is, country i will set μ_i at the level where the marginal gain to increasing its NTB protective level is just offset by the increase in the risk of triggering retaliation and suffering a loss.

The same condition holds for country j. When both of these conditions hold, it places two constraints on the equilibrium vector of NTB protective levels. This outcome demonstrates that the fact that NTBs are not observable does not necessarily lead to each country defecting. The intuitive idea is that country j punishes country i's defection by retaliating for a sufficient number of periods to wipe out the single-period gain country i receives from defecting. But this trigger mechanism has the undesirable property of having retaliatory periods when neither country has defected. Countries will have to retaliate when the random economic conditions push their terms of trade past their preset trigger in order to keep the threat of retaliation credible. Furthermore, this game ignores the institutional constraint that the GATT places on the trading environment.

3. THE GAME UNDER THE GATT TRADING ENVIRONMENT

The GATT dispute-settlement mechanism requires that an investigation be conducted before countries retaliate. In addition trade laws in many countries require that an investigation be launched when trading partners are suspected of engaging in unfair trade practices. The cost of any investigation must therefore be added to the model. Let the cost incurred by country i in its investigation of country j's trade practices be denoted as b_i. National income can now be rewritten as $G(p_i)+r(\pi_i,\tau_i,\mu_i,b_i)$. Substituting this expression into the indirect utility function yields country i's single-period payoff function, $H_i(\tau_i,\mu_i,\tau_j,\mu_j,b_i,\delta_i,\delta_j)$, where

$$\frac{\partial H_i}{\partial b_i}<0.$$

The full impact of NTBs is difficult to detect, let alone measure. Let the probability of country j detecting country i's NTB after an investigation be denoted as y^i_j. It is assumed to be an increasing and concave function of μ_i and b_j such that

$$0 \leqq y^i_j(b_j, \mu_i) \leqq 1; \quad y^i_j(0, \mu_i)=0; \quad y^i_j(\infty, \mu_i)=1; \quad y^i_j(b_j, 0) \quad 0. \tag{7}$$

It is assumed that the investigation is conducted instantaneously, that is, if country i's terms of trade rises above the trigger in period t, the results of the investigation are known by period $t + 1$, and so retaliation, if warranted, begins in period $t + 1$.

Now a country will launch an investigation if its terms of trade rise above some predetermined trigger, but it is quite possible that the other country's NTBs may not be detected, in which case 'normal' times prevail. If the other country's NTBs are detected,[12] then the aggrieved country will retaliate.

Country i's optimal policy is to play s^i_i (its best response action) in retaliation periods after being caught defecting, and μ_i in 'normal' times. Now $V_i(\mu_i)$ has the functional form:

$$V_i(\mu_i)=H_i(\mu_i) + \Pr(\pi_j > \bar{\pi}_j) \left\{ y^i_j(b_j, \mu_i) \left(\sum_{t=1}^{t^*_i - 1} \beta^t_i H^i_i + \beta_i^{t^*_i} V_i(\mu_i) \right) \right.$$

$$\left. + (1 - y^i_j(b_j, \mu_i))\beta_i V_i(\mu_i) \right\} + \beta_i \Pr(\pi_j \leqq \bar{\pi}_j) V_i(\mu_i). \tag{8}$$

Solving for $V_i(\cdot)$ yields

$$V_i(\mu_i)=\frac{H_i(\mu_i) - H^i_i}{1 - \beta_i + (1-F(\bar{\pi}_j))y^i_j(b_j, \mu_i)(\beta_i - \beta_i^{t^*_i})} + \frac{H^i_i}{1 - \beta_i}. \tag{9}$$

Again, this shows that the discounted present value payoff is what it would be in retaliation periods plus the single-period payoff gain to playing μ_i in 'normal' periods, appropriately discounted.

In order to determine the optimal value of μ_i, we need to examine the first-order conditions of country i's optimization problem. The first-order condition of eq. (9) yields the necessary condition:[13]

$$V'_i(\mu_i)=0. \tag{10}$$

Again country i will set μ_i at the level where the marginal gain to increasing its NTB protective level is just offset by the increase in the risk of getting caught and suffering a loss. Condition (10) places two rigid constraints on the equilibrium vector of NTB protective levels. Notice that the optimal μ_i depends on country j's effort at uncovering i's use of NTBs. It is clear that when $b_j=0$, country i's optimal $\mu_i(=\bar{\mu}_i)$ is greater than zero, since the first-order condition evaluated at $b_j=0$ and $\mu_i=0$ is positive. It is reasonable to suppose that there exists a $b_j(=\bar{b}_j)$ large enough such that μ_i will equal zero. Given this the locus of points satisfying

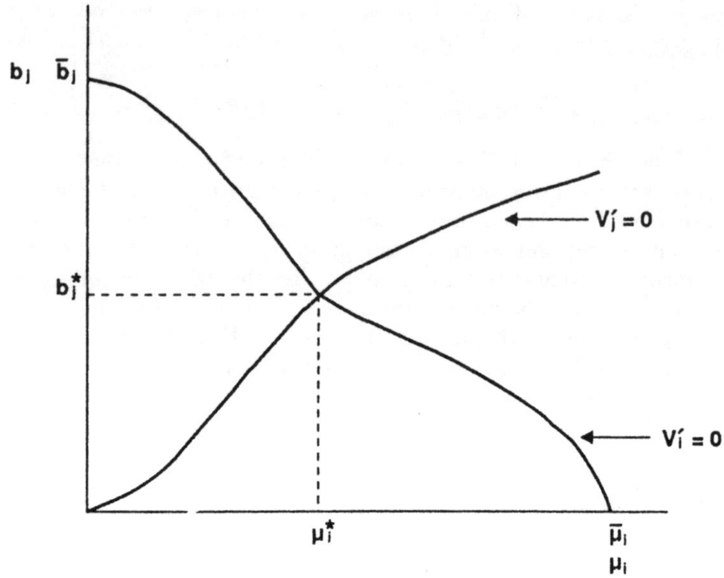

FIGURE 1 The NTB equilibrium.

condition (10) is shown in fig. 1. It is assumed that the second-order conditions for a maximum hold.

The next question to be answered is: Does country j have an incentive to launch an investigation when its terms of trade worsen (i.e. set $b_j > 0$)? In order to examine this question, let $V_j(b_j)$ be country j's discounted present value payoff from cooperating and spending b_j on trade investigations. In this case V_j has the functional form:

$$V_j(b_j) = H_j(\mu_i) + \Pr(\pi_j > \bar{\pi}_j)\, y_j^i(b_j, \mu_i)\left\{\beta_j H_j^i(b_j) + \sum_{t=2}^{t_i^*-1} \beta_j^t H_j^i + \beta_i^{t_i^*} V_j(b_j)\right\}$$

$$+ \Pr(\pi_j > \bar{\pi}_j)(1 - y_j^i(b_j, \mu_i))(\beta_j H_j(\mu_i, b_j) + \beta_j^2 V_j(b_j)).$$

$$+ \beta_j \Pr(\pi_j \leqq \bar{\pi}_j)\, V_j(b_j), \tag{11}$$

where

$$H_j(\mu_i) = E_\delta(H_j(\bar{\tau}_j, 0, \bar{\tau}_i, \mu_i, 0, \delta_i, \delta_j),$$

$$H_j^i = E_\delta H_j(s_j^i, s_i^i, 0, \delta_i, \delta_j),$$

$$H_j(\mu_i, b_j) = E_\delta H_j(\bar{\tau}_j, 0, \bar{\tau}_i, \mu_i, b_j, \delta_i, \delta_j),$$

and

$$H_j^i(b_j)=E_\delta H_j(s_j^i, s_i^i, b_j, \delta_i, \delta_j),$$

Some manipulation of eq. (11) gives

$$V_j(b_j)=\frac{H_j^i}{1-\beta_j}$$

$$-\frac{H_j^i - H_j(\mu_i) + \beta_j(1-F(\bar{\pi}_j))\{H_j^i - (y_j^i H_j^i(b_j)+(1-y_j^i)H_j(\mu_i, b_j))\}}{1-\beta_j(\beta_j + F(\bar{\pi}_j) - \beta_j F(\bar{\pi}_j)) + y_j^i(1-F(\bar{\pi}_j))(\beta_j^2 - \beta_i^{t*})}, \qquad (12)$$

of country *j*'s payoff if country *i* defects is what it would receive in retaliatory periods *minus* a weighted average of the difference between its single-period payoff from retaliation and the 'suckers' payoff ($H_j(\mu_i)$), and the difference between retaliation and the expected single-period payoff from launching an investigation.

The first-order condition for expression (12) yields the necessary condition for a maximum[14] with respect to b_j:

$$V'_j(b_j)=0. \qquad (13)$$

The expression gives two more constraints on the equilibrium vector. This expression is also a function of both b_j and μ_i. When μ_i equals zero the optimal value of b_j is zero since expression (13) is negative at μ_i=0. The locus of points satisfying condition (13) is shown in fig. 1.

The intersection of the two curves gives the equilibrium values of b_j and μ_i.[15] It should be noted that the equilibrium involves positive NTB levels. Furthermore, it is interesting that country *j* does not spend enough on its investigation to guarantee that country *i* will not spend enough on its investigation to guarantee that country *i* will not erect nontariff barriers to trade.

4. CONCLUDING REMARKS

This paper has examined the use of nontariff barriers to trade in a two-country infinitely repeated game. A country's incentive to impose trade barriers was to increase welfare (the optimal tariff argument). Therefore the results apply only to large countries. This paper differs from other investigations of NTBs in that GATT procedures on dispute settlement are incorporated into the analysis. The dispute-settlement procedure is modeled as a trigger strategy.

There are two results of the paper. The first, from section 2, is that the addition of uncertainty and asymmetric information (NTBs) into a tariff game do not necessarily lead to noncooperative behavior. However, the equilibrium strategy has the undesirable property of having retaliatory periods when neither country has defected. Countries have to retaliate when random economic conditions push their terms of trade past their preset trigger in order to keep the threat of retaliation credible. The full explanation for the prevalence of NTBs among large countries must lie elsewhere.

The second and major result shows that with the addition of the investigation technology the free trade outcome is not achieved. Both countries will impose NTBs even in the face of threatened retaliation. The main reason behind this is that the risk of getting caught and the associated losses are not great enough to outweigh the gains from impeding trade. While this result agrees with both Copeland's (1986) and Riezman's (1987) results, the present model incorporates the salient features of the trading environment (i.e. the GATT). This paper has shown that there is an equilibrium (possibly multiple equilibria) in an infinitely repeated game with the threat of punishment, but free trade (or some other negotiated *tariff* binding) is not the equilibrium outcome. The present results fit with reality: the record shows that today most industrialized countries impede trade with NTBs [Nogués, Olechowski and Winters (1986)].

APPENDIX: FIRST-ORDER CONDITIONS

The first-order necessary condition for a maximum of expression (9) is

$$V'_i(\mu_i) = (1 - \beta_i + (1 - F(\bar{\pi}_j))y^i_j(b_j, \mu_i)(\beta_i - \beta_i^{t^*_i}))\frac{\partial H_i(\mu_i)}{\partial \mu_i}$$

$$- (\beta_i - \beta_i^{t^*_i})(H_i(\mu_i) - H^i_i)\left(\frac{\partial y^i_j}{\partial \mu_i}(1 - \mathrm{F}(\bar{\pi}_j)) - y^i_j(b_j - \mu_i)\frac{\partial F(\bar{\pi}_j)}{\partial \mu_i}\right)$$

$$= 0. \qquad \text{(A.1)}$$

The first-order necessary condition for a maximum of expression (12) is

$$V'_j(b_j) = \beta_j\left\{\frac{\partial y^i_j}{\partial b_j}(H^i_j(b_j) - H_j(\mu_i, b_j)) + y^i_j\frac{\partial H^i_j(b_i)}{\partial b_j} + (1 - y^i_j)\frac{\partial H_j(\mu_i, b_j)}{\partial b_j}\right\}$$

$$+ Z(\beta^2_j - \beta_j^{t^*_i})\frac{\partial y^i_j}{\partial b_j}$$

$$= 0, \qquad \text{(B.1)}$$

where

$$Z = \frac{H_j^i - H_j(\mu_i) + \beta_j(1 - F(\bar{\pi}_j))\{H_j^i - (y_j^i H_j^i(b_j) + (1 - y_j^i)H_j(\mu_i, b_j))\}}{1 - \beta_j(\beta_j + F(\bar{\pi}_j) - \beta_j F(\bar{\pi}_j)) + y_j^i(1 - F(\bar{\pi}_j))(\beta_j^2 - \beta_i^{t*})}.$$

NOTES

I wish to thank John Chamberlain, Ted Bertstrom, Mark Bagnoli, Alan Deardorff, seminar participants at Michigan, Wayne State and the Midwest International Economics Conference, and two anonymous referees, for comments on earlier versions of this paper. Any remaining errors are, of course, my own.

1 The recent EEC ban on the importation of hormone-treated beef is an example. At one point the United States asked for a GATT panel to be set up to determine if the ban was a health regulation or a trade barrier.
2 The primary GATT article dealing with dispute settlement is Article XXIII.
3 In the language of the GATT this is referred to as a compensatory suspension of concessions [Dam (1970)].
4 Export taxes and duties are published in the United States by article 1, section 8, clause 5 of the Constitution.
5 A country's terms of trade is defined here as the relative world price of the imported good to the exported good.
6 It is possible that $r(\cdot)$ could be negative, implying that the NTBs entail some administrative costs and generate no revenue for the government.
7 Woodland defines the GNP function and includes factor endowments as an argument. I assume, in order to keep the analysis traceable, that factor endowments are constant and therefore suppress the argument.
8 Recently, Rep. Grephardt suggested that the United States focus on the bilateral trade deficit as an instrument for another country's use of NTBs. The assumption of balanced trade in this paper rules out the use of such an instrument. Another variable that countries could monitor is the level of exports. In this case a country will retaliate whenever their exports fall below some trigger. The results in this paper are independent of the choice of the trigger.
9 The GATT requires that countries retaliate by suspending tariff concessions (i.e. by increasing their tariffs).
10 This ranking is consistent with that obtained when analyzing the optimal tariff using offer curves.
11 See Green and Porter (1984) for the definition of a Nash equilibrium.
12 I am assuming here that a country will not mistakenly detect NTBs that are not present.
13 The full expression is shown in the appendix.
14 The full expression is found in the appendix.
15 The slope of the locus of points satisfying condition (10) has an ambiguous sign, but is continuous and connects points $\bar{b}_j$ and $\bar{\mu}_i$. This fact suggests that there may be more than one equilibrium pair. The important point, however, is that none of the equilibrium points includes $(\mu_i)=0$.

REFERENCES

Copeland, B., 1986, Strategic interaction among nations: Negotiable and non-negotiable trade barriers, Mimeo. (University of British Columbia).

Copeland, B., 1989, Tariffs and quotas: Retaliation and negotiation with two instruments of protection, Journal of International Economics 26, 179–188.
Dam, K. W., 1970. The GATT: Law and international economic organizations (University of Chicago Press, Chicago, IL.).
Deardorff, A. V., 1987, Why do governments prefer nontariff barriers?, Carnegie-Rochester Conference Series on Public Policy 26.
Deardorff, A. V. and R. M. Stern, 1984, Methods of measurement of nontariff barriers, UNCTAD/ST/MD/28 (United Nations, Geneva).
Dixit, A. K., 1987, Strategic aspects of trade policy, in: T. F. Bewley, ed., Advances in economic theory: Fifth World Congress (Cambridge University Press, Cambridge).
Economic Report of the President 1988 (GPO, Washington, DC).
Green, E. J. and R. H. Porter, 1984, Noncooperative collusion under imperfect price information, Econometrica 52, no. 1, 87–100.
Jackson, J. H., 1979, Governmental disputes in international trade relations: A proposal in the context of GATT, Journal of World Trade Law 13, no. 1, 1–21.
Jensen, R. and M. Thursby, 1980, Free trade: Two non-cooperative equilibrium approaches, Ohio State University Working paper no. 58.
Johnson, H. G., 1953–54, Optimum tariff and retaliation, Review of Economic Studies 21, 142–153.
McMillan, J., 1986, Game theory in international economics (Harwood Academic Publishers, Chur, Switzerland).
Meade, J. E., 1952. A geometry of international trade (Allen and Unwin, London).
Nogués, J. J., A. Olechowski and L. A. Winters, 1986, The extent of nontariff barriers to industrial countries' imports, The World Bank Economic Review 1, no. 1, 181–199.
Riezman, R., 1987, Dynamic tariffs with asymmetric information, Mimeo. (University of Iowa).
Rodriguez, C. A., 1974, The nonequivalence of tariffs and quotas under retaliation, Journal of International Economics 4, 295–298.
Stern, R. M., 1987, U.S. trade policies in a changing world economy (MIT Press, Cambridge, MA).
Woodland, A. D., 1982, International trade and resource allocation (North-Holland, Amsterdam).

9. Multilateral and Bilateral Trade Policies in the World Trading System: An Historical Perspective

D. A. Irwin

1 INTRODUCTION

Events of the past two decades have generated increasing concern about the direction of the world trading system. While the General Agreement on Tariffs and Trade (GATT) helped orchestrate the substantial reduction in tariffs after World War II, the multilateral approach to trade liberalisation has encountered difficulty in stemming the proliferation of non-tariff trade barriers and in extending international rules to new areas of trade. Meanwhile, the appearance of bilateral or regional trade arrangements in Europe, the Americas, and elsewhere provides an alternative track for expediting trade reform, but also risks deteriorating into exclusionary, trade-diverting blocs that possibly may bring harm to world welfare.

The loss of momentum in the multilateral system and the movement toward bilateral agreements have sparked renewed debate over the relative merits of the two approaches to trade liberalisation.[1] This chapter aims to provide some historical insight into this debate by examining whether multilateral or bilateral trade policies have been more effective in promoting trade reforms in the past. How has trade liberalisation been achieved in the past, and which types of policies have proved constructive or detrimental to multilateral cooperation on trade policy? Throughout the chapter the focus will be almost exclusively on trade policies in Europe, not only because Europe accounted for the bulk of international trade during these periods but because the trade policies set much of the agenda for the rest of the world.

Historical analysis is useful for a related reason. Because most economists and policy analysts agree that multilateral free trade should be the ultimate objective of international commercial diplomacy, concern is often expressed that bilateral agreements may divert attention away from this goal, and thus substitute for rather than complement efforts of multilateral reform. This deep-seated support for the multilateral framework and critical caution about the bilateral approach is derived in part from a common generalisation about two historical episodes in which international trade policies differed sharply. In the late 19th century, a network of treaties containing the most favoured nation (MFN) clause spurred major tariff reductions in Europe and around the world. These treaties ushered in a harmonious period of multilateral free trade that compares favourably with – and in certain respects was even superior to – the recent GATT era. In the interwar period, by contrast, discriminatory trade blocs and protectionist bilateral arrangements contributed to the severe contraction of world trade that accompanied the Great Depression. The disaster of the interwar period strengthened the resolve of policymakers during World War II to construct a sound multilateral trading system that would prevent any return to discriminatory bilateralism in trade policy.

These two periods have indelibly shaped our ideas about multilateral and bilateral trade policies. The architects of the postwar world trading system, who lived through both periods, concluded that the 19th century exemplified the virtues of non-discriminatory multilateralism and the interwar experience demonstrated the vices of preferential bilateralism. These conclusions continue to underlie the trade-policy debate about whether bilateral or regional agreements contribute to or detract from the ultimate objective of multilateral free trade. In probing these conclusions by focusing on these two key historical episodes, this chapter finds that these generalisations are somewhat inaccurate. The 19th-century liberalisation was attained entirely through bilateral agreements, with an utter absence of multilateral cooperation. In the interwar period, multilateral institutions and negotiations failed to reverse the spread of protectionism and promising bilateral attempts at trade reforms were actually discouraged by these multilateral gatherings.

This chapter first discusses the formation of customs unions (CUs) within a sovereign state as an important prelude to trade negotiations between nations, negotiations that had their European origins in the 1780s. Then the growth, maintenance, and decline of the 19th-century multilateral treaty network is described, along with a comparison of its strengths and weaknesses in relation to the current GATT system. Finally, the contribution of bilateralism to the unveiling of the world economy during the interwar period is anlaysed, with particular attention being paid to the forms of bilateralism that emerged and the obstacles they posed to multilateral cooperation in trade policy. A conclusion draws together the themes and lessons that emerge from this retrospective look at the world trading system.

2 THE ORIGINS OF EUROPEAN TRADE LIBERALISATION

Mercantilist trade policies of the 17th and 18th centuries aimed to achieve several objectives, such as an inflow of species via a balance of trade surplus or a large market share in world trade. The mutually advantageous expansion of trade through tariff reductions was not one of these objectives. The most prominent commercial treaty of the period was based explicitly on mercantilist grounds and gave bilateral trade agreements a poor reputation among economists that has continued to this day. The Methuen treaty between England and Portugal in 1703, granting Portuguese wines preferential access to the English market and English woollens to the Portuguese market, was sought by England to improve its trade balance with a country that had a direct source of bullion through its new world colonies. Adam Smith ridiculed the treaty for encapsulating what he thought was the mercantilist error of confounding specie with wealth. David

Hume heaped scorn on the treaty on grounds of trade diversion: 'But what have we gained by the bargain? We have lost the French market for our woollen manufacturers, and transferred the commerce of wine to Spain and Portugal, where we buy worse liquor at a higher price'. The English classical economists continued this tradition of hostility toward discriminatory or preferential trade arrangements, with J. R. McCulloch calling all treaties of commerce 'radically objectionable'.[2]

While commercial treaties between sovereignties on the treatment of each others' merchants and shipping can be traced back centuries, negotiations over tariffs became a significant feature of the world economy only when full CUs (i.e., internal free trade with a unified external tariff) had been established within the nation-state. Nearly all European states emerged from the medieval period riddled with internal tolls and customs areas that reflected remnants of local power. The centralisation of political control within a given region, however, provided no guarantee that a national CU could be easily or quickly formed. England and Scotland united under a single monarch in 1603, for example, but successive attempts to reach agreement on commercial union failed until the Act of Union in 1707. Although politically unified under the king for centuries, France remained divided – even after several reforms – by 1600 internal tolls and tariffs when the French Revolution enabled their abolition in 1790. At this same time over 1800 customs frontiers littered the various states in central Europe that later comprised Germany. Prussia made incremental moves toward economic union from 1808, culminating in the formation of the Zollverein in 1834 when most German states adopted Prussia's external tariff. Each canton in Switzerland retained tariff autonomy until 1848 and the Italian CU was not completed until the 1860s.[3]

Successful European tariff negotiations also had to wait for an opportune political environment. The Treaty of Utrecht in 1713, for example, governed Anglo-French trade for much of the 18th century, but the important Articles 8 (establishing MFN treatment) and 9 (abolishing prohibitions) were never passed by the British parliament for fear that they would undermine the Methuen treaty and harm the balance of payments. Furthermore, as long as the colonial trade of major European countries was flourishing, there was no pressing need to undertake efforts to expand intra-European trade, which was less complementary and hence more apt to increase import competition and offend domestic producers.

The first real impetus to negotiations on liberalising European trade came with the collapse of colonial trade routes in the 1770s, when Britain and France lost among others their North American colonies. This shock severely affected Britain's trade in particular – export volume fell nearly 20 percent between 1772–3 and 1780–1 – and the share of British exports destined for north-western Europe rose from 15 percent to 28 percent over the same interval (Mitchell, 1988, p. 496). These events naturally shifted British attention to the high tariff barriers impeding trade with the continent. Indeed, writing in 1783 to a government official named William Eden, Adam Smith saw opportunity in the colonial loss: 'By an equality of treatment to all nations, we might soon open a commerce with the neighbouring nations of Europe infinitely more advantageous than that of so distant a country as America' (Ehrman, 1962, p. 202).

Prime Minister William Pitt shared this recognition, and dispatched Eden to conclude treaties of commerce and major European countries. The resulting Anglo-French accord of 1783 involved the elimination of prohibitions and a modest reduction of duties on bilateral trade to eliminate smuggling and raise tariff revenues for both governments. While this agreement ranks among the first significant modern action on mutually advantageous trade liberalisation, Britain's unprecedented attempt at a trade negotiations was most notable for its utter failure. From 1785–93, interminable negotiations with Portugal, Spain, Poland, Prussia, and several other important trading partners in Europe (and even Ireland) failed to produce any agreements. European fears of import competition and a variety of political and diplomatic considerations account for this failure. Even the accord with France lasted less than six years as the French revolution led to cross-channel tensions. The subsequent Napoleonic wars severely disrupted European trade for nearly two decades and extinguished any immediate hopes for progress on tariff reform.

2.1 Britain's Lead to Free Trade

The end of European hostilities in 1815 brought a steep fall in agricultural prices as normal commerce resumed. Import protection for agricultural producers was established throughout Europe in response as landowners, not merchants, retained control of economic policy. Yet this only temporarily delayed continuation of the prewar liberalisation effort: despite the passage of the highly protectionist Corn Law of 1815, Britain still recognised the value of foreign markets for its manufactures. With the Reciprocity of Duties Act (1823), the Board of Trade strove to conclude reciprocal agreements with foreign governments for MFN treatment of goods and shipping. Although several such agreements were signed, they did not eliminate prohibitions or reduce tariffs, and were therefore of limited consequence. Tariffs were later the subject of what proved to be unsuccessful negotiation. Britain deliberately maintained high tariffs on sugar, coffee, wines, and spirits for bargaining purposes, but all to no avail. In 1836 Britain offered to abolish its timber duties for Prussia in exchange for lower tariffs on British textiles, but Prussia held out for a reduction of the Corn Laws and no agreement was reached.

Efforts at reciprocal tariff reductions thus failed in the 1830s and 1840s, just as they had in the 1780s and 1790s.[4] As Brown (1958, p. 132) put it, 'the drive to open markets in the countries of western Europe for British industry, and particularly in the years 1838–40 the British cotton industry, was uniformly unsuccessful'. Frustration and discouragement with reciprocity accumulated: trade negotiations were 'ever pending, never ending'. This lack of progress set the stage for unilateral tariff reforms in the early 1840s, which culminated in the repeal of the Corn Laws in 1846.[5] As Prime Minister Robert Peel explained that year, 'Wearied with our long and unavailing efforts to enter into satisfactory commercial treaties with other nations, we have resolved at length to consult our own interests, and not to punish those other countries for the wrong they do us in continuing their high duties upon the importation of our products and manufactures, by continuing high duties ourselves'.[6] By adopting unilateral free trade,

Britain resolved to forsake the bargaining motive for tariffs henceforth applying its tariff without discrimination, enacting tariff reforms on its own timetable, and leaving other countries free to determine their own tariff policies.

So complete was the conversion to unilateral free trade that treaties came to be viewed as dangerous, as tempting compromise with Britain's principles of non-discrimination and of bargaining abstinence. No longer desirable yet unobtainable, treaties of commerce became entirely disreputable and any effort toward them was dismissed as entirely counterproductive. W. E. Gladstone, the future Prime Minister who served at the Board of Trade during this period, later reflected about the legacy of the 1830s and 1840s, which was

> the period during which England was most actively engaged in the endeavour to negotiate, with the principal states of the civilized world, Treaties for the reciprocal reduction of duties on Imports. The task was supplied on our side with sufficient zeal; *but in every case we failed. I am sorry to add my opinion, that we did more than fail.* The whole operation seemed to place us in a false position. Its tendency was to lead countries to regard with jealousy and suspicion, as boons to foreigners, alterations in their laws, which, though doubtless of advantage to foreigners, would have been of far greater advantage to their own inhabitants (Tooke and Newmarch, 1857, p. 398, emphasis in original).

Foreign countries were unprepared to reduce trade barriers in part because of the suspicion that to do so would be mainly to Britain's advantage.

British policymakers were left to hope that other countries would see the benefits of unilateral free trade and follow Britain's example. In the decade following the repeal of the Corn Laws, Britain's unilateral policy was not an overwhelming success in establishing free trade abroad, although free-trade activism was widespread (see Kindleberger, 1975). Some trade liberalisation occurred in the United States, which passed its most liberal tariff of the *ante bellum* period (timed clearly in conjunction with the Corn Law repeal) in 1846, and in Holland, Switzerland, and Portugal, where tariffs were eased significantly in the early 1850s. But the movement toward free trade did not overtake the rest of Europe until the Anglo-French commercial treaty of 1860, a treaty that heralded the beginning of a liberal international trading order which lasted until the outbreak of World War I in 1914.

2.2 The Anglo-French Commercial Treaty (1860)

Diplomatic considerations weighed most for both France and Britain in deciding whether to pursue a trade agreement. Tensions were high in Europe – indeed, there was a real possibility of war – as result of France's opposition to Austria's influence in Italy. Domestic political and economic factors generally ran against such an agreement. Though the French emperor Napoleon III had initiated some tariff reforms in the 1850s, he worried about reducing tariffs too much and offending protectionist interests in the legislature. Britain was also somewhat reluctant to pursue an agreement as that would violate its policy of unilateral free trade. But both governments saw a commercial treaty as a way of defusing tensions and improving diplomatic relations, and an agreement was quickly reached.

There was one important political economy reason for pursuing an agreement as well. Though abandoning its policy against bargaining over tariffs, Britain had a rare opportunity to provide a mechanism that would enable the French emperor to circumvent domestic protectionist interests. Unlike the strong support for free trade in the British parliament, the French legislature overrepresented import-competing interests that wholly opposed lower tariffs. Although the legislature was responsible for all tariff legislation, Napoleon III had the authority under the constitution of 1851 to sign foreign treaties without legislative approval. Consequently he embedded the tariff changes in a diplomatic accord with Britain.[7]

According to the terms of the treaty, France abolished all prohibitions and imposed specific duties not exceeding 30 percent *ad valorem*, or 25 percent after 1865, although in practice most duties were set at 10–15 percent (Ashley, 1926, pp. 299–300). Britain cut the number of dutiable goods from 419 to 48 and reduced the wine tariff. The treaty was subject to renewal after 10 years, and either party could withdraw from the agreement after giving a year's notice. Perhaps the most important element of the treaty was Article V of the complementary convention, which stated: 'Each of the contracting powers engages to extend to the other any favor, any privilege or diminution of tariff which either of them may grant to a third power in regard to the importation of goods whether mentioned or not mentioned in the treaty of 23d of January, 1860' (US Tariff Commission, 1991, p. 395). Inclusion of the MFN clause eliminated the need for renegotiation in the event that either country lowered tariffs with a third country and automatically preserved non-discriminatory access of both countries in each other's markets. The unconditional MFN clause became the linchpin of the 19th-century commercial treaty network.

3 THE 19TH-CENTURY OPEN TRADING REGIME

The systemic effects of the Anglo-French treaty were of much greater significance than its importance to either country alone. The treaty sparked a spectacular movement toward the liberalisation of world trade, the initial impetus for which was the trade diversion that promised to accompany the integration of Europe's two largest economies. While Britain insisted on making its own tariff reductions applicable to all nations, France lowered his import duties on British goods only, adopting a two-tired tariff system of 'autonomous' tariff rates for MFN countries and higher 'conventional' rates for others. Only Britain benefited from the new lower rates and other countries were left at a substantial disadvantage in exporting to the large French market.

As other European states quickly sought agreements with France to secure equal treatment for their own goods, the Anglo-French treaty – which began as a purely bilateral agreement without abiding support in either country – rapidly cascaded into a series of bilateral trade agreements, all linked by the inclusion of an unconditional MFN clause. France extended the unconditional MFN trade network by concluding commercial treaties with Belgium in 1861, the Zollverein in 1862 (effective in 1865), Italy in 1863, Switzerland in 1864, Swede, Norway, Spain, and the Netherlands in 1865, and Austria in 1866. These agreements entailed significant new tariff reductions for those joining the arrangement, and the unconditional MFN clause proved to be a remarkably efficient instrument that encouraged other countries to join and also receive MFN treatment. The increase in treaty participants extended the coverage of low tariffs to virtually all of Europe.[8]

What triggered the swift acceptance of a new, low-tariff regime in Europe? Some bargaining models suggest that free-rider and other problems create difficulties in sustaining trade liberalisation under the MFN clause.[9] But in this period when MFN treatment was *sought* by most countries in Europe, the clause propelled trade liberalisation and acted as a strong inducement for others to join the treaty network, thereby building the number of treaty participants. Once Britain and France initiated the move to lower tariffs, the smaller countries of Europe clearly had an economic interest in obtaining equal treatment in the French market. The addition of the Zollverein, where a mix of political and economic motives were present, built particular momentum to the Europe-wide movement and added further incentives for other European states to join the chain of unconditional MFN treaties.[10] Britain, Belgium, Italy and others then signed agreements with the Zollverein in 1865 to receive MFN treatment.

Thus, through a variety of fortuitous circumstances, a single bilateral agreement to reduce tariffs blossomed into dozens of bilateral accords, resulting in an effectively multilateral arrangement under which international trade entered an unprecedentedly liberal era. Under the treaty arrangement, tariffs were generally set at about 8–15 percent with a maximum of 25 percent (Liepmann, 1938, p. 369). Bairoch (1989) suggests that the period of free trade in Europe peaked from 1866 to 1877, although not just this narrow window but much of the half-century to 1914 was marked by low government barriers to trade. At the start of 1908, Britain and MFN agreements with forty-six countries, Germany with thirty countries, and France with over twenty countries (Hornbeck, 1910, p. 57).

It is important to note that diplomatic objectives and tariff-bargaining were not the sole impetus behind European trade liberalisation. Additional unilateral reforms by Britain resulted in essentially four items taxed for revenue purposes (i.e., tariffs as the application of domestic excise duties to comparable imports) by the 1880s. Internal free-trade interests prompted Germany to enact substantial tariff reforms independently of treaty obligations when the Reichstag voted in 1873 to eliminate virtually all import tariffs by 1877 and to reduce those on textiles substantially. Consequently, tariffs on chemicals were eliminated at the beginning of the 1870s and all tariffs on grains and iron products (except fine iron goods) were to be phased out by the end of the decade (Ashley, 1926, p. 40). The same was true to varying degrees in other countries, even if protection was not entirely erased across Europe.

Even the colonies were brought into the liberal trading order. In the 19th century, the developing countries of today were, for the most part, colonies of the major European countries of today were, for the most part, colonies of the major European countries, each traditionally maintaining reciprocal preferences for each other's goods. In the mid-1840s and 1850s, Britain eliminated all tariff preferences for colonial supplies of timber, sugar, and other raw materials and also granted tariff autonomy to its self-governing colonies, allowing them to abolish preferences that favoured British manufacturers. In dependencies such as India, Britain maintained a non-discriminatory 'open-door' policy of applying the same low tariffs on foreign and British goods.[11]

In the trade treaties signed after 1860, the MFN clause was widely interpreted to include colonial trade and open-door policies were practised by other countries.[12] French colonies adopted the same tariff code as France, thus completing a full CU. German, Belgian, and Dutch colonies operated with low, non-discriminatory tariffs. At the Conference of Berlin in 1885, the European powers established that all colonies in central Africa would be open to trade with any country on the same terms, and this practice was maintained elsewhere to a remarkable degree. The European powers also took active steps to open up new regions to international trade on a non-discriminatory basis, often using military power to force autarkic countries to trade and fixing their tariffs at low levels. China lost its tariff autonomy with the Treaty of Nanking of 1842, which set its import duties at 5 percent *ad valorem* for over fifty years, and Japan faced similar externally-imposed constraints on its tariffs after 1858.[13]

3.1 The 19th-century Treaty System and the GATT

The 19th-century treaty system invites comparison with the post-World War II trade regime led by the GATT. The main features of the two regimes are compared in Table 4.1. A key similarity between the 19th-century order and the postwar GATT system is the principle of non-discrimination through the use of the MFN clause in its unexceptional and unconditional formulation. In the 19th century, MFN treatment would be granted to all countries with which the MFN agreement had been signed, and not just countries explicitly named in the treaties, as had been earlier practice. The MFN clause was also unconditional, meaning that the lowest available tariff would be applied automatically without requiring reciprocal concessions. The MFN clause ensured that all countries participating in the treaty network would continue to receive the best available tariff treatment, even if other countries engaged in further tariff reductions. Either an exceptional or a conditional interpretation would have slowed the initial advance of trade liberalisation by complication or extending the process of negotiation, although it is less clear that MFN was useful in sustaining lower tariffs. The unconditional form of the MFN clause became so well established that, despite the growth of protectionist pressures after the late 1870s, the conditional interpretation was not adopted. As with the treaty network, the GATT is based on the similar rule of granting unconditional MFN treatment to member states.

The treaty system also had significant weaknesses *vis-à-vis* the GATT. After the initial tariff cuts embodied in the agreements of the 1860s had formed the core of the 19th-century treaty arrangement, further progress on tariff reductions was not guaranteed. Most of the commercial treaties after this initial negotiating period ensured only non-discriminatory tariff treatment and did not place any limit on tariff rates, leaving each country free to set their tariffs without an

Table 4.1 *Features of two world trade regimes*

	The 19th-century regime (c. 1860–1914)	The GATT system (c. 1947–)
Underlying principle	Unconditional MFN treatment for treaty signatories	Unconditional MFN treatment for member states
Coverage	Effectively multilateral via bilateral treaties	Multilateral agreement
Terms of accord	Often subject to renewal after 10 years	Life of agreement
Permissible methods of protection	Tariffs only (*de facto*)	Tariffs only (*de jure*)
Restrictions on tariff level	Generally unrestricted	Bounded by agreement
Institutional basis	None	The GATT
Countervailing and anti-dumping duties	Virtually non-existent	Permissible under Article VI
Preferential arrangements	Presumption against as violation of MFN	Permissible under criteria in Article XXIV

effective external constraint on tariff behaviour. Nor was there any commitment to ensure progress toward even lower tariffs. In addition, the treaties were subject to periodic renewal and set to expire with regularity. The GATT, by contrast, established a contract in perpetuity that fixes and binds tariffs at a low level for the life of the agreement and provides for trade negotiating rounds. In principle the GATT also details a mechanism for compensation to penalise countries that nullify tariff obligations. At least in the 19th century, tariffs – with very few exceptions – were the only major government policy impeding international trade. While this has been legally true under the GATT, quantitative restrictions (QRs), orderly marketing arrangements (OMAs), and voluntary trade restraints (VTRs) continued to exist outside of the GATT's purview. It could have been that tariff flexibility in the 19th century enabled countries to avoid resorting to these more pernicious barriers.

Unlike the GATT which arose as an institution by design, the 19th-century trade regime arose spontaneously from an uncommon confluence of events. Indeed, the 19th-century order was more an informal arrangement than a system. There was no primary sponsor with the economic standing or diplomatic ability or willingness to cajole or manage the arrangement, to punish defectors or free-riders, or to consolidate the abundance of bilateral treaties into a more soundly-based multilateral system. The most obvious candidate to play such a central role, Britain, failed to nurture the treaty network, provided no systemic guidance, and clung to a unilateral, *laissez faire* policy regarding international trade. Soon many of these weaknesses came to the fore.

3.2 The Erosion of the Liberal Economic Order

The outbreak of World War I in 1914 ensured that the treaty network never had the chance to break down completely. But tariff rates began to rise and tariff disputes became more frequent after the late 1870s, even if adherence to unconditional MFN remained intact and there was no turn to regional or preferential arrangements.

The general turn to higher tariffs in Europe in the late 1870s can be traced to one key source: the decline in agricultural prices in the late 1860s and into the 1870s, which created difficulties for the liberal trading order just as the oil shocks of 1970s contributed to a revival of protectionist pressures in the postwar period. The extension of railway networks into Russia and the United States brought a flood of cheap grain to Europe: grain imports by Belgium, France and Germany averaged only 3 percent of domestic production a year in 1862–6, but had climbed to 20 percent by 1876–80 (Bairoch, 1989, p. 47). With Prussia having shifted from a net exporter to a net importer of grains, the 'iron and rye' coalition facilitated passage of the Bismark tariff of 1879 that increased protection to agriculture and, to a lesser extent, manufacturers. Other countries, such as France, Belgium, Switzerland, and Sweden, followed with tariff increases in 1880s.

The backsliding in trade policy that followed the decline in agricultural prices was later compounded by a concentration of expiry dates for the European trade treaties. According to Bairoch (1989, p. 54), of the fifty-three treaties with expiry dates in force in 1889, twenty-seven were due to lapse in 1892 and twenty-one by 1895. Renegotiation of these treaties was more contentious than earlier because protectionist pressures were greater. The result was increasing acrimony and even tariff wars after 1885. Tariff was often originated with a country repudiating a trade agreement to establish higher tariff rates. France and Italy (1888–9). Germany and Russia (1892–4), and France and Switzerland (1892–5) engaged in some of the more disputatious trade wars of the period. In a 'non-system' such as that in the 19th century, the threat of retaliation served as a constraint on domestic discretion in tariff matters and helped to maintain a low tariff equilibrium. But the realisation of retaliation, as during this period, suggests that the threat of retaliation was no longer a sufficient deterrent to ensure continuity of the low-tariff status quo.

Multilateral action was not taken to contain the rise in protectionist pressures. As early as 1875, several British officials sought to persuade their government that a European tariff conference should be convened to stem the growing threat of protectionism. But the government, specifically the first Gladstone Administration, remained firmly opposed to tariff-bargaining and still adhered to unilateral free trade as the basis for its policy (see Gaston, 1987). Britain also had precious few tariffs with which to bargain (the Treasury objected to reducing any revenue duties) and threats to exclude others from its market were not credible and were never made. While perhaps there was little it could do about higher European tariffs, Britain did not even attempt to seize the initiative and seek a multilateral agreement that would freeze tariff levels at existing levels.

The European trade policy environment did deteriorate after 1879, but the extent of the deterioration should not be exaggerated. Capie (1983), for example, suggests that effective rates of tariff protection remained relatively low through the final quarter of the 19th century to 1914. Germany returned to a more liberal policy in the 1890s and, under Chancellor Caprivi, signed several treaties that again reduced tariffs on agricultural goods and textiles. Yet tariffs were now being established for bargaining purposes; according to the US Tariff Commission (1919, p. 467), countries (particularly in central Europe) 'framed their general schedules not with a view to their being made operative but with reference to the advantages which they may offer as a basis for negotiations'. Furthermore, the increased specialisation of tariff categories meant effective tariff discrimination, with maximum advantage given to treaty partners and minimum advantage to other countries despite the MFN clause. The number of items in the German tariff code, for example, rose from 387 in 1879 to 946 in 1906.[14]

In several respects, however, the recent deterioration of the GATT system has been sharper than that of the 19th-century treaties. In the 19th century, unconditional MFN did not give way to regional or colonial preferences, as previously mentioned, and quantitative restrictions or prohibitions did not reemerge. Perhaps more significantly, unlike the present there was no recourse to anti-dumping (AD) actions or countervailing duties (CVDs) despite the appearance of a 'fair trade' movement in Europe in the 1890s (see Viner, 1923). Canada enacted a 'less-than-fair-value' law in 1904 and was soon followed by other self-governing colonies, but such laws were entirely absent in Europe despite increased concern about dumping. In 1892, Belgium was the first European country to institute a CVD law, but few countries followed this practice before 1914. Many commercial treaties of the period contained anti-bounty pledges, but they neither prevented export subsidies (which were uncommon) nor were they enforced. Even the first prominent 'managed trade' issue was resolved in a rare multilateral agreement that achieved a liberal outcome.[15]

The foremost achievement and great success of the 19th-century treaty network was the establishment – through the widespread use of the MFN clause – of non-discrimination as the fundamental principle of European trade policy. This achievement stood as a solid advance over the centuries of discrimination in European markets. In addition, for at least twenty years after 1860 European countries enacted unprecedented tariff reductions. However, the 19th century achieved only part of what might have been hoped for. The lack of binding constraints on tariff levels allowed countries to backslide toward greater protection after 1879. The interwar period would see not only the absence of movement toward this higher objective, but even the substantial loss of the principal 19th-century accomplishment.

4 THE INTERWAR TRADE POLICY EXPERIENCE

The bilateral treaty regime ended abruptly in August 1914 with the outbreak of World War I. Tariffs, quantitative restrictions, prohibitions, and exchange controls were rapidly instituted around Europe to protect industries associated with national security and to secure foreign exchange for state-determined allocation. At the Allied Economic Conference of 1916, Britain, France, and Italy gave the first indication that the postwar international economic order would not resemble the prewar one. They resolved to cooperate on commercial policy after the war, but hinted at creating trade preferences for Allied countries by ruling out the extension of MFN treatment to Germany and other wartime opponents. The United States – now taking a more prominent role in the world trade arena – opposed any such discrimination and the third of President Wilson's Fourteen Points called for 'the removal so far as possible of all economic barriers and the establishment of an equality of trade conditions among all the nations consenting to the Peace and associating themselves for its maintenance' (League of Nations, 1942, p. 15).

But European countries were ill-inclined, and interwar institutions were ill-equipped, to restore commercial policy to its prewar basis. The Covenant of the League of Nations in 1919 weakened Wilson's call for 'equality' of treatment, insisting in Article 23(e) only upon 'equitable treatment' in trade. And making no provision to ensure the reduction of trade barriers, the Covenant instead invited departures from this course by sanctioning trade controls owing to the 'special necessities' of economic recovery.

To be sure, the depression of economic activity and high rates of unemployment in the early 1920s were scarcely conducive to achieving progress on liberalising European trade policies. But efforts to coordinate the reduction of trade barriers after Word War I were slow to get on track: no formal, multilateral action was ever taken to abolish prohibitions, reduce tariffs, or restore the MFN treaty network, and a consensus in favour of serious cooperative action was never achieved. Although most wartime controls were gradually phased out on a unilateral basis, the far-reaching degree of wartime intervention ensured that the pace of liberalisation was slow and uneven and extended well into the 1920s. As late as 1927 the League of Nations was still calling for the eradication of prohibitions and other restrictions that had been instituted during the war.

In instances where strict wartime controls were abolished, other barriers – mainly tariffs – rose to take their place. The United Kingdom, for example, did not return to its prewar free trade policy, but enacted the Safeguarding of Industries Act (1921) to extend wartime tariff protection to scientific instruments and other goods. After President Wilson left office, the United States passed the Fordney-McCumber tariff in 1922 to raise import tariffs substantially. Throughout the 1920s, European countries also took the opportunity to raise tariffs as normal commerce resumed. As Table 4.2 indicates, even by 1927 when many wartime prohibitions and restrictions had been eliminated or scaled back, tariffs – particularly on manufactured goods – were higher than before the war.

The restoration of some degree of economic stability in Europe by around 1925 put efforts to reach a European trade accord on a firmer basis. The World Economic Conference of 1927 called for any action whatsoever – unilateral, bilateral, or collective – to stabilise and then reduce trade barriers and restore the effectiveness of the MFN clause. Though the conference was not an official diplomatic meeting, many governments endorsed its recommendations and it was hailed as a success when several countries abandoned plans to revise their tariff codes. Stabilisation of tariff levels was thought to have been achieved when the number of countries revising their tariffs fell from sixteen in 1926 to five in 1928 (League of Nations, 1942, p. 42). A committee of the League even began considering particular formulae – either specifying maximum tariffs or taking percentage reductions – to be used in multilateral negotiations for tariff reductions on semi-manufactured goods. In addition, the MFN treaty network showed faint signs of resurrection. The failure of the United States to join the League of Nations was compensated in part by its adoption of the unconditional interpretation of the MFN clause in 1922. France readopted the MFN clause when signing a trade agreement with Germany in 1927, and the number of countries linked by commercial treaties rose from thirty in 1927 to forty-two in 1928.

Although serious discussion of tariff reductions on either a multilateral or a bilateral basis had yet to be undertaken, the upward drift in tariffs appeared to have been broken and a path to freer trade was emerging. At this point scarcely a decade had passed since the end of the war and continued economic recovery in Europe promised an ever-improving environment for the reform of trade policy. But a year later any hope of progress on trade liberalisation was dashed with the onset of the Great Depression.

4.1 The Onset of the Depression

The temporary respite from higher tariffs ended in the summer of 1929 when a sharp fall in agricultural prices prompted tariff hikes in Germany, France, Italy, and elsewhere by the year's end. The initial outbreak of protection in response to lower agricultural prices had some similarities with the late 1870s, but the

TABLE 4.2 *Potential tariff[a] levels in selected European countries, % 1913–31*

	Foodstuffs			Manufactures		
	1913	1927	1931	1913	1927	1931
Germany	21.8	27.4	82.5	10.0	19.0	18.3
France	29.3	19.1	53.0	16.3	25.8	29.0
Italy	22.0	24.5	66.0	14.6	28.3	41.8
Belgium	25.5	11.8	23.7	9.5	11.6	13.0
Austria	29.1	16.5	59.5	19.3	21.0	27.7
Yugoslavia	31.6	43.7	75.0	18.0	28.0	32.8

Note: [a]The 'potential' tariff level refers to each country's tariff on 144 representative commodities using European-wide trade weights.

Source: Liepmann (1938) p. 413.

situation deteriorated much more rapidly in the early 1930s. The passage of the Smoot-Hawley tariff in the United States in June 1930 sparked another round of tariff increases, retaliatory and otherwise, throughout Europe. As the depression deepened, even the United Kingdom imposed emergency duties in late 1931, followed by the general tariff of February 1932. Table 4.2 illustrates how tariffs rose substantially in many other European countries between 1927 and 1931 and were heavily skewed toward protecting agriculture.

The unravelling of the world trade regime after 1929 made the mild erosion in the low-tariff era prior to World War I appear entirely trivial. Widespread deflation, increasing unemployment, and financial crises in the early 1930s landed devastating blows at what remained of the open trading system. Agricultural interests were behind the initial resort to higher tariffs and achieved some sectoral favouritism, but protection arose so rapidly and became so broadly based as the depression spread and deepened that its rise can perhaps be explained only as a desperate attempt to insulate all sectors from falling prices and to stimulate overall economic activity in response to a crisis of major proportions.

And further unlike the period after 1879 when there was no multilateral conferences held or actions taken to resist the tariff increases, the interwar period was replete with meetings and pronouncements reflecting international concern about maintaining open trade, but without any real political resolve to resist growing protectionism in the face of economic collapse. As Gordon (1941), p. 33) put it, 'the complete failure of every attempt to secure multilateral action in the sphere of commercial policy in 1930 and 1931 resulted in large part from the unwillingness of nations to commit themselves to international obligations which would limit their freedom to combat the depression through autonomous measures'. Conferences sponsored by the League of Nations aimed to declare a 'tariff truce' in 1930 and 1931, for example, but failed in part because agricultural states in central and eastern Europe insisted on further protection and demanded preferential treatment for their goods in industrial Europe. As the League of Nations (1942, p. 101) later observed, 'the international conferences unanimously recommended, and the great majority of Governments repeatedly proclaimed their intention to pursue, policies designed to bring about conditions of "freer and more equal trade"; yet never before in history were trade barriers raised so rapidly or discrimination so generally practiced'.

The policy instruments of the 'new proclamation' of the 1930s were blunt: quantitative restrictions, prohibitions, exchange controls, and clearing agreements. State bureaucracies were created to monitor or manage each international transaction, whether financial or merchandise. The market mechanism in international trade was subordinated to state planning and the priority of state requirements; the extent of government regulation of international trade across Europe had perhaps never been so pervasive and detailed. Protectionism consequently became much more entrenched than in the 19th century when only non-discriminatory tariff barriers had to be grappled with.

Yet countries varied distinctly in the degree to which they adopted protectionist measures. Just as Eichengreen (1992) describes how the magnitude of a country's macroeconomic difficulties during this period can be linked to its policy was also crucially related to its position in the international monetary system. In the early 1930s, deflationary pressures in many countries arose from a loss of foreign exchange or gold reserves. These countries faced a choice between import restrictions or devaluation as a means to stimulate the domestic economy while preserving external balance. The gold-bloc countries led by France clung to the gold standard and strove to maintain their currencies at par. In acceding to the accompanying deflationary pressures, these countries experienced a severe overvaluation of their currencies. This worsened the merchandise trade balance and forced resort to quantitative restrictions and import licensing to stem the further loss of reserves so that gold-standard parity could be maintained and devaluation avoided. By contrast, the sterling-bloc countries led by Britain took their currencies off the gold standard in September 1931. The depreciation of sterling against gold relieved the deflationary pressures arising from the balance of payments, alleviated macroeconomic distress, and consequently tempered the demand for severe import restrictions.

This relationship between direct controls on trade and commitment to the gold standard is illustrated in Figure 4.1. The proportion of total imports (by value) subject to licensing or quota restrictions in 1937 (for countries that maintained freedom in foreign exchange dealings) was highest for the gold-bloc countries – France, Switzerland, the Netherlands, and Belgium. Particularly surprising is the degree to which Switzerland and the Netherlands, traditionally free-trade countries, adopted direct trade controls. By contrast, the sterling-bloc countries – Sweden, the United Kingdom, Norway, and Ireland among them – faced less pressure to institute import restrictions because they opted for exchange rate depreciation. This cross-country pattern of import regulation appears more consistent with trade protection that had its origins in the macroeconomic depression rather than in the lobbying efforts of various interest groups.[16]

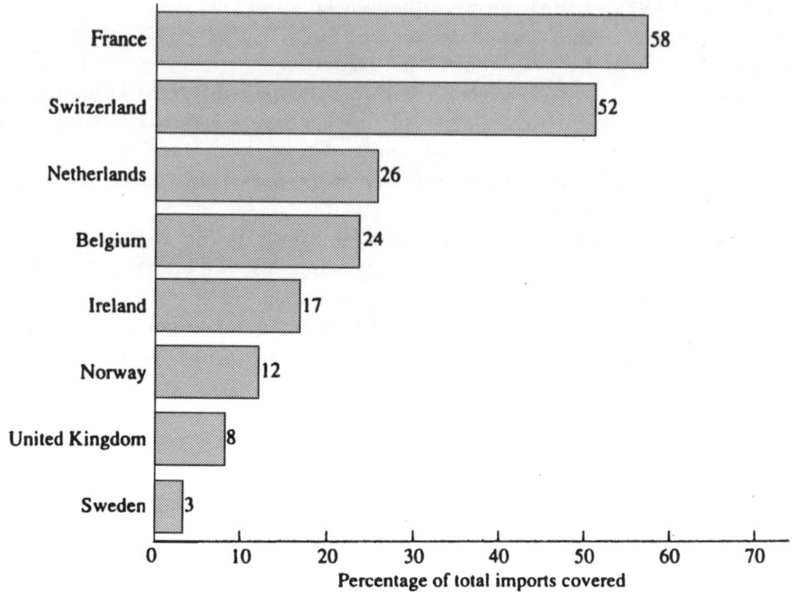

FIGURE 4.1 Licence or quota restrictions in 1937
Source: Haberler (1943, p. 19)

A third group of countries, mainly those in central and eastern Europe, curtailed trade directly through stringent controls on foreign exchange transactions. The collapse of international lending by western creditors to Germany and eastern Europe after 1929 resulted in severe balance of payments difficulties for these debtors. A financial panic in 1931 prompted Germany to lead these countries to restrict international payments by introducing controls on foreign exchange. Virtually every other east European country, from Poland and the Baltics in the north of Yugoslavia and Greece in the south, followed in rapid succession. Italy and Poland regulated nearly every foreign exchange transaction, while other countries such as Austria, Czechoslovakia, and Greece restricted substantial shares of such transactions (see Haberler, 1943).

While varying in their degree of stringency, these controls choked international trade and were followed by exchange-clearing arrangements aimed at eliminating bilateral trade imbalances and stemming the flight of capital. Clearing agreements were instituted to avoid the use of foreign exchange transactions in international trade to preserve liquidity and reserves. Through the Schacht agreements, Germany took deliberate steps to divert imports from those countries demanding payment in convertible currencies to those accepting German exports as payment, mainly countries in south-eastern Europe and Latin America. In many instances, trade in eastern and central Europe was reduced to barter. In South America, different exchange rates and multiple tariff rates were used to discriminate against countries with which a country had a trade deficit.

TABLE 4.3 *Share of gold value of world exports, excluding the United States, %, 1931 and 1937*

	1931	1937
Exchange control countries[a]	27.2	22.5
Gold-bloc countries[b]	15.9	12.1
Other countries[c]	56.8	65.4

Notes: [a]Austria, Bulgaria, Czechoslovakia, Denmark, Estonia, Germany, Greece, Hungary, Italy, Latvia, Lithuania, Poland, Portugal, Roumania, Turkey, Yugoslavia.
[b]France, Belgium, the Netherlands, and Switzerland.
[c]Principally sterling-bloc countries.

Source: League of Nations (1938), p. 30.

The consequences for world trade for this pattern of restrictions among the exchange control group and the gold- and sterling-bloc countries are not difficult to predict. Table 4.3 shows that the restrictions imposed by the exchange control group were so severe that even the depreciation of their currencies against gold could not stimulate their trade. Their share of world exports fell from 27 percent in 1931, when the controls were largely introduced, to 22 percent in 1937. Gold-bloc countries also saw their share of trade shrink in the face of quantitative restrictions and overvalued currencies. The trade of other countries, mainly the sterling group, accounted for a larger proportion of world trade as exchange rate depreciation boosted trade directly and avoided need for trade restrictions. The share of these countries rose despite 'exchange-dumping' measures, i.e., tariff surcharges to offset exchange rate changes, taken against them by other countries.

In seeking to eliminate all losses of foreign exchange reserves by ensuring balanced trade on a bilateral basis, the exchange control group gave rise to a 'pernicious' bilateralism in trade policy. This bilateralism stifled and diverted trade by bureaucratic fiat. Similarly, the harsh trade measures adopted by the gold-bloc countries were also inherently discriminatory, if not strictly 'bilateral' in nature. However, these polices were rooted in the difficulties of the international monetary system. Countries that opted for exchange rate depreciation did not resort to protectionist trade barriers to the same degree.

To be sure, explicit discrimination through tariff preferences was a feature of European trade policies during the 1930s, and this discrimination was heavily slanted toward diverting the source of imports rather than expanding trade overall. The open-door policies of the 19th century were abandoned and forgotten. Britain reinstated limited tariff preferences for the former colonies in 1919, but the Ottawa Agreement of 1932 raised general import duties to establish substantial tariff preferences for goods imported from Commonwealth countries. France and other European countries took similar steps to implement preferences with their colonies and dependencies. Germany and Japan roughly doubled the share of their trade with neighbouring countries that came under their political influence. As shown in Table 4.4, trade patterns shifted dramatically in the decade after 1929 as a result of these actions.

But preferential tariff treatment should hardly have been the major concern of the day. The shift in trade patterns described in Table 4.4 was probably accomplished more through exchange rate agreements, clearing and payments arrangements, bureaucratic allocation of import quotas and the like rather than through tariff preferences. The League of Nations (1942, p. 119) observed that 'effective discrimination by methods which did not violate the letter of the [MFN] clause continued to be widely practiced' throughout the 1930s. Non-tariff restrictions became so far reaching as to render tariffs – even discriminatory tariffs – the least important trade barrier to be surmounted. In an environment of quotas and exchange controls, attempts to reestablish non-discriminatory MFN tariff treatment among major countries were absolutely meaningless. As Nurkse (1944, p. 175) observed, 'Real equality of treatment, aimed at ensuring multilateral trade in accordance with market criteria, is . . . impossible when the control determines not only the purposes, commodities and firms but also the countries to which exchange is allotted.'

Yet the League and other international gatherings during this period constantly emphasised the need to restore MFN treatment in Europe. These efforts were misplaced and probably even counterproductive by harming the chances of trade liberalisation. The instability in the international financial system that bred the use of 'hard core' non-tariff barriers (such as licences, quotas, and exchange controls) was the root source of the protectionist trade policies in the 1930s. Removal of the underlying instability by improving international macroeconomic policy and the 'tariffication' of existing restrictions would have been a more useful allocation of multilateral effort. With an international economic environment so vastly different from that in the 19th century, stress on unconditional MFN in the 1930s stymied what little effective support there was for trade liberalisation. High-tariff countries refused to accept any exception to MFN treatment by others unless they were to be recipients of the lower tariffs. This intransigence over the interpretation of the MFN clause posed a barrier to regional liberalisation that at least would have allowed some countries to end and reverse the upward movements in tariffs. With the benefit of hindsight, even the League of Nations (1942, pp. 119–20) conceded that 'instead of facilitating, the clause tended to obstruct the reduction of tariffs', noting that

> when it became apparent that multilateral negotiations on an almost universal scale were not likely to succeed, certain groups, especially the Oslo group of countries, were anxious to achieve the general objects advocated in international conference within a more restricted area. Had general support of such endeavours been forthcoming, it is possible that the practice of reduction through group agreements might have spread and the groups gradually have extended their size. Such a procedure might have been less favourable to world trade as a whole than the rapid conclusion between a large number of countries of bilateral treaties embracing the MFN clause, but not less favourable than the failure to grant concessions owing to the quasi-universal implications of the MFN.

TABLE 4.4 *Shift in trade patterns, 1929–38*

(a) Share of intra-imperial trade, 1929 and 1938, %

		Imports		Exports	
Trade of	Share of	1929	1938	1929	1938
United Kingdom	British Commonwealth, colonies, protectorates	30.2	41.9	44.4	49.9
France	French colonies, protectorates, mandated territories	12.0	27.1	18.8	27.5
Belgium	Belgian Congo	3.9	8.3	2.6	1.9
Netherlands	Overseas territories	5.5	8.8	2.6	1.9
Portugal	Overseas territories	7.9	10.2	12.7	12.2
Italy	Colonies and Ethiopia	0.5	1.8	2.1	3.3

(b) Regional preferences in the trade of Japan and Germany, 1929 and 1938, %

		Imports		Exports	
Trade of	Share of	1929	1938	1929	1938
Japan	Korea, Formosa, Kwantung, Manchuria	20.2	40.6	24.1	54.7
Germany	Six south-eastern European countries and Latin America	16.7	27.6	12.8	24.7

Source: League of Nations (1939) pp. 34–5.

For example, the Second Conference with a View to Concerted Economic Action, in late 1930, recognised that the chances for a multilateral agreement did not exist and that bilateral agreement was the only feasible path to liberalisation. But the conference encouraged this path only if tariff reductions from those agreements were extended to others through unconditional MFN treatment. Later, in mid-1932, Belgium, Luxembourg, and the Netherlands signed the Ouchy Convention in which they and any other willing participants agreed to staged tariff reductions amounting to 50 percent of existing tariffs. This could have formed the nucleus of a movement toward freer trade, but Britain and others insisted that the convention would be a violation of the unconditional

MFN principle unless the tariff cuts were generalised. This undermined the agreement and the convention never entered into force.

This 'progressive' bilateralism, allowing a subset of countries to expand trade through tariff reductions and thereby giving an incentive for others to follow, was squelched while the 'pernicious' bilateralism of quantitative restrictions and bureaucracy-administered exchange controls was allowed to fester unchecked. The result was a sharp reduction in world trade: the volume of trade declined 40 percent from 1929 to 1932, while real world output fell only 20 percent. When economic recovery had gradually been restored by the mid-1930s, the volume of trade lagged severely behind the rebound in income.

4.2 Toward Another Postwar Order

The seeds of more effectual international cooperation were sown in the mid-1930s after the trough in economic activity had passed. Though not of sufficient strength to save the decade of the 1930s, international cooperation, particularly between Britain and the United States, helped set the groundwork for the next postwar international economic order.

The Tripartite Agreement of 1936 was a success in initiating cooperation on financial matters between the United States and western Europe. France, Switzerland, the Netherlands, and Italy finally devalued their currencies against gold, thus enabling the gold-bloc countries to dismantle some of their import quotas and licences. The recision of 1937, however, ended this liberalisation of import restrictions.

Of greater significance was the stirring international activism of the United States. Having contributed in no small degree to increased world protection by instituting the Smooth-Hawley tariff in 1930, the United States now played a key role in the Montevideo conference in December 1933 which promised negotiations among western hemisphere republics to reduce tariffs on trade in the Americas. By the Reciprocal Trade Agreements Act of 1934, subsequently renewed in 1937 and 1940, the Congress delegated limited tariff-negotiating powers to the president, enabling him to offer reciprocal concessions amounting to up to a 50 percent reduction in tariffs. The United States had mixed success with the purely bilateral approach to trade liberalisation, although some tangible progress on creating momentum toward lower tariffs was made. By 1938, a full third of American tariffs had been cut by at least 20 percent, and many by the full 40–50 percent, with countries signing agreements with the United States. By 1939, the United States had signed 20 MFN treaties with countries that accounted for 60 percent of its trade. Most notable was the agreement with Britain in 1938 that set the stage for the great Anglo-American cooperation during World War II that eventually led to the Bretton Woods conference in 1944 where the cornerstones for the postwar economic order were established.

While the economic environment for trade liberalisation was improving if still shaky, after 1934, the political situation in Europe began to deteriorate with the rise of fascism. After the mid-1930s, the League of Nations (1942, p. 149) observed, 'the political foundations for any liberalization of commercial policy had been shattered and the tendencies towards closed economies and rigid state regulation gained impetus from year to year under the exigencies of a near-war economy'.

5 TRADE LIBERALISATION IN HISTORICAL PERSPECTIVE

The lessons to be drawn from the trade policy experience of past decades for current concerns about the direction of the world trading system are, unfortunately, somewhat limited. The relative serenity and simplicity of the 19th-century order, with its absence of discrimination, quantitative restrictions, 'fair trade' laws, or industrial policies, cannot be replicated today. And the challenges for trade policy today are nowhere near as urgent as those experienced in the interwar period. Nonetheless, certain themes that have relevance for today's concerns do emerge from this retrospective look at trade policy.

One important lesson about facilitating multilateral free trade is that long periods of macroeconomic stability provide an environment conducive for the adoption of liberal trade policies. That is, based on the 19th-century and postwar experiences, a sound international monetary and financial system appears to be a prerequisite for (or at least an important complement to) an open trading system. Major supply disruptions such as large positive or negative price shocks had proved to be detrimental to an open trade regime. The agricultural and raw material price shocks of 1815, 1879, 1929, and 1973 are each associated with an important shift in the direction of world trade policies toward greater protection.[17]

But avoiding macroeconomic difficulties and large price shocks lie outside the realm of what trade policy can achieve. What lessons emerge about the types of policies that change the world trading system for the better? Here again, the trade policy experience of the past 150 years does not provide clear guidance. Multilateral cooperation on trade policy is not necessary either for the liberalisation of trade policy or for the prevention of illiberal trade policies. Multilateralism was not a feature of the 19th century, whereas multilateral talks were repeatedly held in the 1920s and 1930s to no avail. Similarly, bilateral trade policies cannot be uniquely praised or condemned. A progressive bilateralism flourished in the 19th century, with the prospect of trade diversion from the Anglo-French accord of 1860 leading other countries to join and reduce tariffs rather than to retaliate and raise them. In the interwar period, such progressive bilateralism – the sole hope for freer trade – was extinguished in the misplaced desire to restore unconditional MFN treatment first. At the same time, the pernicious bilateralism that emerged was rooted not so much in terms of international trade policy and tariff discrimination as in the malfunction of the international monetary system, which prompted the bureaucratic allocation of import quotas and foreign exchange to eliminate all bilateral payments' imbalances.

Although the complexity of international economic issues was greater in the interwar period than in the 19th century, the number and size distribution of European countries did not change considerably between these periods. Britain provided no leadership on international trade negotiations in the 19th century and it is not clear that the vacuum of leadership in the 1920s and 1930s (on the trade policy front, if not in the international monetary system) was the primary source of the period's failures.

Yet the fact that multilateral cooperation was absent in the 19th century and failed in the interwar period is no excuse to ignore its great success since 1947 and abandon this path to the reform of policy owing to current difficulties. The GATT eliminated the tariffs and the discrimination in international trade that was established in the interwar period, thereby restoring world trade to its pre-World War I basis. To top the 19th-century achievement, the GATT also imposed restrictions on the imposition of new trade barriers, however imperfect those restrictions may be, and set up a dispute settlements mechanism, however weak that mechanism may be, and ensured ongoing liberalisation, however time-consuming and complex these negotiations have become. While there remain major gaps in its effectiveness, notably dispute settlement and the control of fair trade laws, the GATT in principle represents a substantial improvement over the 19th-century treaty network.

As for bilateralism, it is extremely difficult to judge the trade policy environment and to determine whether the regional blocs of today constitute the progressive or the pernicious variety of bilateralism. Fortunately, the trade blocs of today are at least predicated on the notion of reducing barriers among participants and not raising barriers against non-participants. That the EFTA countries seek links with the European Community and that the several South American trading arrangements have as their ultimate aim to join the North American Free Trade Agreement (NAFTA) provides at least one signal that recent regional blocs exhibit the ability to expand membership rather than remain exclusive. If this expansion can be accomplished without harming efforts to strengthen the multilateral GATT approach, then the liberal postwar open trading system will be far from finished.

NOTES

1 Bhagwati (1991) makes a vigorous case for preferring multilateralism, and urges that regional trade agreements be harnessed toward improving the multilateral GATT system. Dornbusch (1990) expresses greater scepticism about the viability of the multilateral approach, and argues that bilateral agreements can restore progress on world trade liberalization.

2 See O'Brien (1976) for a discussion.

3 Although political union often precedes customs union, the converse is less frequent. According to Viner (1950, p. 96), 'aside from the German Zollverein case, there appear to have been only three instances where substantial tariff unification preceded political union, and in none of these cases can it be held that the tariff unification was in any way responsible for creating a sentiment favorable to political union, or that in any other significant way made a substantial contribution to the eventual realization of political unity'.

4 Britain encountered difficulty in tariff bargaining in part because it refused to grant preferential access to other countries in its own market. Export interests demanded that raw materials, which comprised much of Britain's imports, be obtained at the lowest possible cost, while Richard Cobden (a founder of the Anti-Corn Law League)

argued for non-discrimination in trade as fostering international peace. In addition, Britain found no need to strive for preferential access in foreign markets, remaining confident that its comparative advantage in manufactured goods would ensure the success of exporters, provided only that non-discriminatory treatment of its goods abroad was assured.

5 The crisis sparked by the harvest failure in Ireland paved the way for the repeal of the Corn Laws, leaving no time for them to be used as a bargaining tool.

6 Hansard's *Parliamentary Debates* (27 January 1846), p. 601.

7 Commercial agreements in the form of foreign treaties proved useful in circumventing protectionist interests in the legislature throughout Europe. The treaty mechanism allowed European countries to reduce legislative discretion over tariffs far in advance of the United States and thereby liberalise their policies sooner. In the United States, only with the Reciprocal Trade Agreements Act of 1934 were limited tariff-making powers formally delegated from the legislative to the executive branch. In the absence of a pro-trade executive, however, the lack of broadly-based domestic support for trade liberalisation meant the underlying commitment to such reforms was weak. In France, for example, the Anglo-French treaty was weakened and eventually abandoned after Napoleon was replaced in 1870.

8 The only major European state that resisted joining the spate of trade treaties in early 1860s was Russia, which finally acceded in 1874. Britain signed a similar number of agreements to secure the MFN treatment it had already granted to others, though it was unable to sign treaties with Spain and Portugal which demanded preferential treatment. The United States also stood outside of the treaty system and sought (by and large unsuccessfully) preferential trade agreements with Latin America. The United States also held to a conditional MFN policy, wherein reciprocal concessions were required before extending MFN treatment to third countries.

9 See Caplin and Krishna (1988). However, in a more general model Ludema (1991) finds that the MFN clause does not give rise to the free-rider problem because countries will opt to continue rather than conclude the process of negotiations.

10 A change in the Zollverein's tariff required unanimous agreement among members, and Prussian grain producers and western German merchants had long been prevented from enacting lower tariffs by the protectionist states in southern Germany. Prussia also sought to maintain its preeminent status in the Zollverein by excluding its rival Austria. Knowing that the current Zollverein agreements were soon up for renewal, Prussia approached France about a trade pact two days after their signing of the Anglo-French treaty and then committed itself to substantially freer trade by signing an agreement with France in 1861. Prussian leaders reasoned that Austria would have no interest in joining the Zollverein at such low tariff levels, and that the southern German states would have either to endorse the accord and align their tariff with Prussia's or leave the Zollverein. The tactic worked: after sharp resistance, the south German states agreed to stay in the Zollverein, Austria remained outside the agreement, and Prussia achieved greatly enhanced power in the Zollverein. See the discussion in Henderson (1957, 1959).

11 Sometimes it is asserted that there was a 'free-trade imperialism' in China, Argentina, and elsewhere such that the open-door policy was more posture than reality. But Platt (1968a, p. 297) found that 'the range of government action on behalf of overseas trade permitted by the *laissez faire* tradition of the time was extraordinarily narrow; official demands on behalf of British interests overseas never went beyond equal favour and open competition'. High trade volumes between the colonies and the European coloniser could persist not because of discriminatory government policy, but because of monetary integration, transactions costs (such as telegraph and shipping links), and trade-related foreign direct investment.

12 For a detailed study, see US Tariff Commission (1922).

13 According to Huber (1971), as a result of the forced opening by the West, Japan's terms of trade improved by a factor of three and its national income rose roughly 65 percent in the transition from autarky to free trade.

14 In the German tariff of 1902, according to Platt (1968a, p. 93), there was even a tariff category for 'large dappled mountain cattle or brown cattle, reared at a spot at least 300 meters above sea level, and which have at least one month's grazing each year at a spot at least 800 meters above sea level'.

15 A convention in 1864 among major European powers failed to end the subsidisation of domestic sugar beet producers in many European countries. After removing the sugar tariff in 1874, Britain's colonies complained about competing against subsidised sugar in the British market. Law officers of the Crown ruled in 1880 that CVDs could not be imposed because they would violate the MFN clause of various commercial treaties. The Brussels convention on sugar in 1902 abolished all direct and indirect support for sugar and called for CVDs against countries that continued to subsidise sugar and called for CVDs against countries that continued to subsidise sugar exports. The convention was generally a success, but Britain was so adamant about not violating the MFN clause that it withdrew from the convention in 1912 on the grounds that either quantitative restrictions or CVDs would violate it.

16 See Dornbusch and Frankel (1987). State bureaucracies as interest groups, however, would have a much greater stake in import regulation than in allowing the market to function anonymously through a change in relative prices brought about by a devaluation.

17 It is also instructive to note that the agricultural sector has long been a chronic stumbling block on the path toward free trade. Local 'policies of provision' ensured regional self-sufficiency in the mercantilist period, the Corn Laws hindered trade liberalisation in the aftermath of the Napoleonic Wars, the Russian and American grain shock triggered a move to protection and significantly weakened the 19th-century trading system, acute agricultural distress spared the return to protection in the 1930s, and, of course, agricultural trade has stubbornly resisted all attempts to be brought under the rules of the GATT.

REFERENCES

Ashley, P. (1926) *Modern Tariff History*, 3rd edn; New York: Dutton.

Bairoch, P. (1989) 'European Trade Policy, 1815–1914', in P. Mathias and S. Pollard (eds), *The Cambridge Economic History of Europe*, vol. viii, *The Industrial Economies: The Development of Economic and Social Policies*, New York: Cambridge University Press, pp. 1–160.

Bhagwati, J. (1991) *The World Trading System at Risk*, Princeton: Princeton University Press and Harvester Wheatsheaf.

Brown, L. (1958) *The Board of Trade and the Free-Trade Movement, 1830–42*, Oxford: Clarendon Press.

Capie, F. (1983) 'Tariff Protection and Economic Performance in the Nineteenth Century' in J. Black and L. A. Winters (eds), *Policy and Performance in International Trade*, New York: St Martin's Press.

Caplin, A. and K. Krishna (1988) 'Tariffs and the Most-Favored-Nation Clause: A Game Theoretic Approach', *Seoul Journal of Economics*, I (September) pp. 267–89.

Dornbusch, R. (1990) 'Policy Options for Freer Trade: The Case for Bilateralism', in R. A. Lawrence and C. L. Schultz (eds), *American Trade Strategy: Options for the 1990s*, Washington, DC: Brookings Institution.

Dornbusch, R. and J. Frankel (1987) 'Macroeconomics and Protection', in R. M. Stern (ed.), *U.S. Trade Politics in a Changing World Economy*, Cambridge, Mass: MIT Press.
Ehrman, J. (1962) *The British Government and Commercial Negotiations with Europe, 1783–93*, Cambridge: Cambridge University Press.
Eichengreen, B. (1992) *Golden Fetters: The Gold Standard and the Great Depression, 1919–1939*, New York: Oxford University Press.
Gaston, J. (1987) 'The Free Trade Diplomacy Debate and the Victorian European Common Market Initiative', *Canadian Journal of History*, **22** (April) pp. 59–82.
Gordon, M. S. (1941) *Barriers to World Trade*, New York: Macmillan.
Haberler, G. (1943) *Quantitative Trade Controls: Their Causes and Nature*, Geneva: League of Nations.
Henderson, W. O. (1957) 'A Nineteenth Century Approach to a West European Common Market', *Kyklos*, **10**, pp. 448–57.
(1959) *The Zollverein*, Chicago: Quadrangle Books.
Hornbeck, S. K. (1910) 'The Most-Favored-Nation Clause in Commercial Treaties', *Bulletin of the University of Wisconsin*, **343** (February).
Huber, J. R. (1971) 'Effects on Prices of Japan's Entry into World Commerce After 1858', *Journal of Political Economy*, **79** (May/June) pp. 614–28.
Kindelberger, C. P. (1975) 'The Rise of Free Trade in Western Europe', *Journal of Economic History*, **35** (March) pp. 20–55.
League of Nations (1938) *Report on Exchange Controls*, Geneva: League of Nations.
(1939) *Review of World Trade, 1938*, Geneva: League of Nations.
(1942) *Commercial Policy in the Interwar Period: International Proposals and National Policies*, Geneva: League of Nations.
Liepmann, H. (1938) *Tariff Levels and the Economic Unity of Europe*, New York: Macmillan
Ludema, R. D. (1991) 'International Bargaining and the Most-Favored-Nation Clause', *Economics and Politics*, **3** (March) pp. 1–20.
Mitchell, B. R. (1988) *British Historical Statistics*, New York: Cambridge University Press.
Nurkse, R. (1944) *The International Currency Experience: Lessons of the InterWar Period*, Geneva: League of Nations.
O'Brien, D. P. (1976) 'Customs Unions: Trade Creation and Trade Diversion in Historical Perspective', *History of Political Economy*, **8** (Winter) pp. 540–63.
Platt, D. M. C. (1968a) 'The Imperialism of Free Trade: Some Reservations', *Economic History Review*, 2nd ser. **21** (August) pp. 296–306.
(1968b) *Finance, Trade and Politics in British Foreign Policy*, Oxford: Clarendon Press.
Tooke, T. and W. Newmarch (1857) *A History of Prices*, 6 vols, London: Longman, Brown, Green, Longmans and Robert.
United States Tariff Commission (1919) *Reciprocity and Commercial Treaties,* Washington, DC: Government Printing Office.
(1992) *Colonial Tariff Policies,* Washington, DC: Government Printing Office.
Viner, J. (1923) *Dumping: A Problem in International Trade,* Chicago: University of Chicago Press.
(1950) *The Customs Union Issue,* New York: Carnegie Endowment for International Peace.

10. The GATT in Historical Perspective

D. A. Irwin

The transformation of the General Agreement on Tariffs and Trade (GATT) into the World Trade Organization (WTO) on January 1, 1995, provides an opportune moment to take stock of the GATT's achievements and shortcomings alongside those of its 50-year-old sister international institutions set up at Bretton Woods. It is temptingly easy to attribute the astounding postwar economic expansion, particularly when set against the turbulent interwar period when multilateral efforts to contain protectionist pressures failed miserably, to the economic policies embodied in the GATT and to the initial stability provided by the Bretton Woods institutions. Yet a closer look at precisely what the GATT accomplished in its first decade suggests that trade liberalization under its auspices alone is far from sufficient to explain the postwar economic boom.

I TRADE RELATIONS PRIOR TO THE GATT

Prior to World War I, the world economy enjoyed several decades of relative serenity in terms of both international trade and monetary relations. During 1860–1913, world trade relations centered around a network of bilateral trade treaties containing the most-favored-nation (MFN) clause. Each country was generally free to set and change its tariff code so long as it adhered to the MFN clause. These arrangements arose without multilateral cooperation. Yet despite the lack of any oversight mechanism or institutional basis, this regime (if it can be called that) brought about relatively low trade barriers – almost exclusively tariffs, with an absence of quantitative restrictions, voluntary restraint agreements, exchange controls, and the like – along with very little trade discrimination.[1]

International trade flourished during this period. Figure 1 plots the trade-weighted export volume and real output of 11 major countries during 1870–1913.[2] Although both enjoyed a smooth expansion for nearly half a century, export volume grew much faster than real output, expanding fourfold in the 43 years prior to World War I, compared to a near tripling in output.

World War I shattered the treaty network as countries imposed higher tariffs, import quotas, licensing requirements, and foreign-exchange controls. Economic reconstruction following the war lacked any institutional mechanism to facilitate the reduction of the extensive trade barriers that had arisen during the war and had become entrenched thereafter. The political weakness of European countries

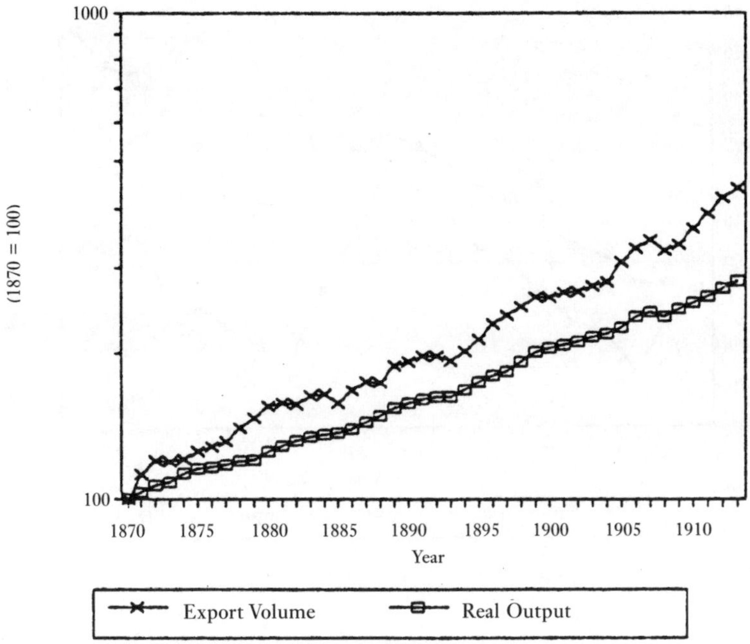

FIGURE 1 Pre-World War I Trade and Output

in trade policy was evident when a proposal for "equality of trade conditions" in a draft League of Nations charter was rejected in favor of a weaker provision for "equitable treatment." The World Economic Conference in 1927 found it necessary to call upon governments to remove the still pervasive controls on trade. A decade after its formation, the League of Nations had yet to sponsor any negotiations on liberalizing world trade from high tariffs.

The onset of the depression vanquished any serious prospect of trade reform in Europe and elsewhere, and the 1930's were a disaster in the field of commercial policy. An outbreak of even greater protectionism supplemented by discriminatory trade and currency blocs created innumerable impediments to international commerce and hampered economic recovery.[3] Multilateral and bilateral efforts to remove these barriers and to end this discrimination were feeble and amounted to virtually nothing.

Partly as a result, economic performance in the interwar period was dismal. As Figure 2 illustrates, exports grew more rapidly than output in the decade after World War I, although that growth was not robust. Between 1929 and 1932, exports plunged more than output, but the real debacle is illustrated by the failure of trade to follow the path of output after 1932. Trade failed to expand in the 1930's not because output growth was sluggish, but because the previous relationship between trade and growth no longer held. Although real output was roughly 15-percent higher in 1938 than in 1929, exports were roughly 15-percent

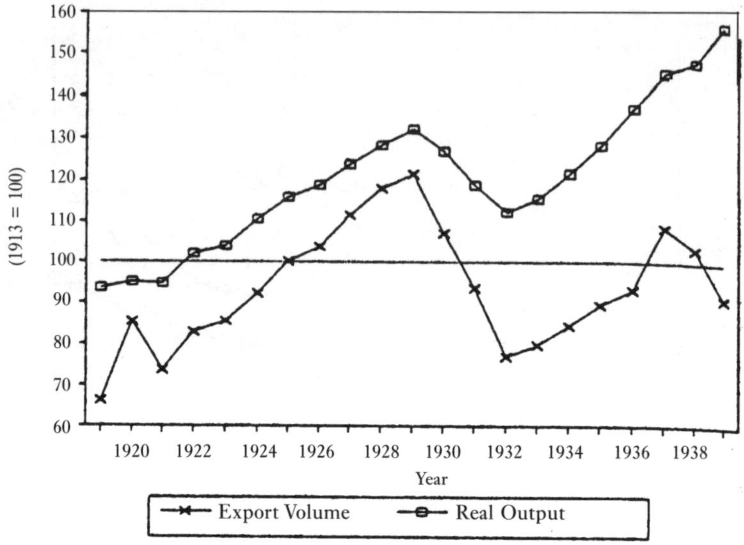

FIGURE 2 Interwar Trade and Output

below where they stood in 1929 and had scarcely returned to their prewar level. Greater protectionism and trade discrimination, as well as a breakdown in multilateral financing arrangements, were probably the major causes.

After the interwar catastrophe, the notion that a beneficent, decentralized, noncooperative equilibrium (like that prior to World War I) could possibly emerge after World War II seemed fanciful. Certain that the "nonsystem" of the late 19th century would not be automatically resurrected after World War II, the United States and the United Kingdom began preparing the ground during the early 1940's for a postwar international agreement on commercial policy to reduce trade barriers and limit discriminatory tariff preferences.

II. EARLY GATT EFFORTS ON TRADE LIBERALIZATION

The driving force behind the GATT was the same as that which motivated the Bretton Wood conference in 1944: the interwar disaster. The interwar period should not be viewed just as a series of domestic economic failures, but as an international economic failure as well. Just as the architects of the Bretton Woods system envisioned restoring the international monetary system to a sound footing, the purpose of the GATT was to roll back trade barriers and end discriminatory trade policies.

The architects of the postwar international economic framework believed that trade liberalization had an important supporting role in achieving the principal economic goals of monetary stability and full employment. But trade reform was not considered an urgent priority in itself, and negotiations over the creation of an International Trade Organization (ITO), designed to take a place alongside the World Bank and International Monetary Fund, were not successfully completed until 1948. In the end, the ITO never came to fruition.[4] This may have been a blessing in disguise: with a multifaceted agenda ranging from restrictive business practices to intergovernmental commodity agreements, the ITO risked devolving into a large bureaucracy that would have institutionalized and sanctioned state regulation of international commerce as much as it would have freed trade from such controls.

The GATT was formed by carving out and implementing the commercial-policy sections of the Havana Charter that was to have guided the ITO. The narrow focus of the GATT served the process of trade liberalization (and the institution itself) well because the GATT's mission was simple and straightforward. The purpose of the GATT, as stated in its preamble, was to contribute to rising standards of living and full employment by "entering into reciprocal and mutually advantageous arrangements directed to the substantial reduction of tariffs and other barriers to trade and to the elimination of discriminatory treatment in international commerce."

In contrast to the inaction after World War I, trade relations began the postwar period on an encouraging note. Just two years after Germany's surrender, 23 countries established a General Agreement on Tariffs and Trade that set rules to restrict national trade policies and even started to decrease tariffs in binding agreements. Just five years after the end of the war, all major Western European countries had participated in three separate negotiating rounds that had expanded GATT membership and further reduced import tariffs. The first GATT negotiating round, held in Geneva in 1947, was a tremendous success. The 23 participating countries (accounting for 80 percent of world trade) implemented tariff cuts (of a still undetermined magnitude) and implemented those cuts on an MFN basis. The United States took the lead by cutting its tariffs by 35 percent, on average.

But the postwar period did not see steady, consistent progress in the reduction of tariff barriers. Rather, such progress came in fits and starts. Indeed, the GATT achieved remarkably little in the 15 years after the Geneva Round. The Annecy (1949) and Torquay (1950–1951) rounds expanded GATT membership but made only minor progress in reducing tariffs. the GATT's momentum stalled very early into the post-war economic recovery, and there was widespread pessimism and frustration with the GATT process throughout the 1950's. It is doubtful that the ITO could have expedited this process; negotiations might have proceeded even more slowly under the ITO owing to the greater complexity of issues it was designed to address. Fortunately, as world trade reform paused, a European program of trade liberalization proceeded under the auspices of the Organization for European Economic Cooperation (OEEC) and the European Economic Community (EEC).[5]

A crucial achievement of the GATT during the 1950's came in preserving the sanctity of the early tariff reductions. Although tariff concessions embodied in Article II of the GATT were considered fixed indefinitely, countries retained the right under Article XXVIII to revoke them in negotiations with their principal supplier. To prevent an erosion in the 1947 tariff cuts, the GATT members agreed to forgo the right to invoke Article XXVIII for three years. This pledge was renewed throughout the 1950's to ensure the continuity and integrity of the tariff reductions and thereby helped prevent the GATT's early successes from unraveling.

This lock-in feature prevented backsliding toward higher tariffs and proved particularly important as other trade barriers, notably quantitative restrictions and exchange controls, were being phased out during the 1950's. As these other trade impediments were being removed, the tariff cuts negotiated in the early rounds took on increasing bite and thereby more directly affected domestic import-competing interests.

The success of the European program of trade liberalization, capped by the formation of the EEC in 1958, prompted the United States once again to initiate multilateral trade negotiations. Aiming to reduce the EEC's common external tariff, Congress gave the president authority to reduce tariffs up to 50 percent. The resulting Kennedy Round of trade negotiations during the 1960's concluded with the most substantial tariff reductions of the postwar period. The Tokyo Round of the 1970's made further progress in reducing tariff and nontariff trade barriers.

III. WAS THE GATT A SUCCESS?

The postwar economic expansion in trade and income surely exceeded all the expectations of those involved in designing the GATT. The main goal, avoiding a repetition of the interwar experience, was clearly averted. Figure 3 illustrates, once again, export volume and real output for the 10 countries for which data exist back to 1870. Because Figure 3 closely resembles Figure 1, the major goal of the GATT founders was achieved: once again, the world economy experienced expanding international commerce facilitated by lower trade barriers, a record that continued after the breakdown of the fixed-exchange-rate regime in the early 1970's.

To what extent can the GATT take credit for this happy happenstance? Here it should be noted that the successes and failures of the GATT need to be viewed somewhat differently from those of the World Bank and the International Monetary Fund. The Bank and the Fund are autonomous institutions that use lending power to affect the economic policies of member countries. The GATT had no autonomous power, independent leverage, or financial sanction. The GATT, in some sense, did not exist beyond the commitment of its members, particularly the United States and the European Community, to reach certain goals through a negotiated consensus. The GATT could have done no more than what these countries, in conjunction with others, were willing to achieve.

With this in mind, the GATT process with U.S. leadership did secure the very real accomplishment of eliminating the very real accomplishment of eliminating a host of impediments to international trade. Tariffs of the industrialized countries have fallen from roughly 40 percent after World War II, on average, to about 5 percent now, according to the GATT. On nondis-

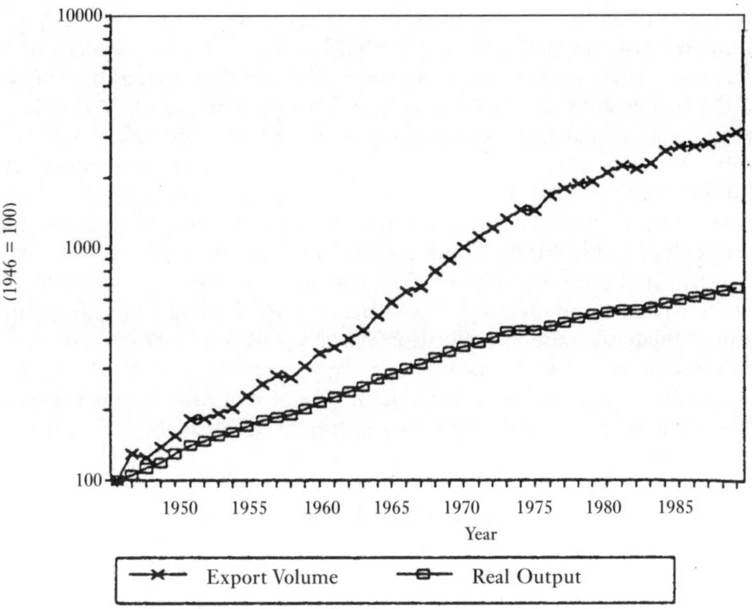

FIGURE 3 Post-World War II Trade and Output

crimination, the GATT period is perhaps less successful than the late 19th-century era, but certainly an improvement over the interwar period.

Of course, this broad record of success is marred by several gaping holes in the GATT's coverage. Whole areas of trade escaped GATT rules; agriculture and textiles come quickly to mind. New policy instruments arose to replace the reduced tariffs and quotas; voluntary restraint agreements and antidumping measures also come quickly to mind. The developing countries for much of the postwar period, stood largely outside the GATT system in that membership did not require them to reciprocate fully the actions of other participants.[6]

Several factors also moderate one's conclusions about the GATT's responsibility for the post-war boom. First there is the issue of timing. If the economic expansion of the 1950's and 1960's is to be attributed to the GATT, then the Geneva Round in 1947 appears pivotal. After all, the GATT was largely inactive during the 1950's, and the Kennedy Round was not concluded until 1967, and implemented thereafter. To say that this first negotiating round stimulated two decades of rapidly expanding international trade stretches the imagination and suggests that other sources of trade liberalization (such as by the OEEC and the EEC) or technological catch-up need to be examined. However, the GATT's role in preserving the early tariff cuts cannot be denied.

Yet the GATT may be as important for what it represents in terms of process as for what it has accomplished as an institution. The GATT set a standard for commercial policies and stood as a reminder that striving for the objective of freer multilateral trade was worthwhile. As a set of rules, the GATT provided some credible assurance that tariff levels could move in only one direction, unless specific escape-clause procedures were invoked. Providing a quantitative assessment of the importance of these factors, of course, is extremely difficult.

By some ideal standard, the GATT has been far from a complete success. But it is also necessary to consider the counterfactual: how would trade policies have evolved in the absence of the GATT? Given the interwar experience, the founders of the postwar system surely could not imagine a much better scenario unfolding than the one depicted in Figure 3 and could easily envision much worse outcomes occurring. But had there been no GATT, the postwar system would not necessarily have reverted to the interwar chaos. Because the United States had initiated a program of bilateral trade liberalization (largely with Latin American countries) after the passage of the Reciprocal Trade Agreements Act of 1934, the United States might have become the central node of a series of bilateral trade agreements, although not necessarily with unconditional MFN as the ruling principle.[7]

IV. CONCLUSION

One should neither overstate nor understate the impact of the GATT on the post-war world economy. The GATT deserves some contributory credit for the post-World War II economic boom. The GATT scraped along at times but had a distinct, downward rachet effect on world trade barriers. For this reason, in spite of its small size and uncertain place as an economic institution, the GATT's long-run impact on the world economy has (arguably) been more significant than either that of the World Bank or the International Monetary Fund.

The GATT's success was by no means uniform. In replacing the GATT, the WTO promises to fill in some gaps – liberalizing agricultural trade, eliminating voluntary restraint agreements, and strengthening dispute settlement procedures – without entailing a radical innovation in the GATT's primary purposes. Whether these promises will be fulfilled remains to be seen.

NOTES

I thank the discussants, Peter Kenen and Michael Mussa, for helpful comments on an earlier draft.

1 For further analysis of the strengths and weaknesses of international trade arrangements during 1860–1913, see Irwin (1993).

2 The countries are Australia, Belgium, Canada, France, Germany, Italy, Japan, Norway, Sweden, the United Kingdom, and the United States. The data are from Angus Maddison (1991).

3 Barry Eichengreen and Irwin (1995) examine the effects of these trade and monetary arrangements on trade flows.

4 With U.S. business support weakening and the international political situation changing, as described by William Diebold (1952), the Truman administration never submitted the ITO to Congress for its approval.

5 See the discussion in Irwin (1994).

6 As John Whalley (1989) and Dani Rodrik (1992) note, many developing countries are currently embarking upon trade reforms not in the context of the GATT, but at their own unilateral initiative.

7 This is similar to what we may see with an expanded membership of the North American Free Trade Agreement.

REFERENCES

Diebold, William, Jr. "The End of the ITO." Essays in International Finance No. 16, International Finance Section, Princeton University, October 1952.

Eichengreen, Barry and Irwin, Douglas A. "Trade Blocs, Currency Blocs, and the Reorientation of World Trade in the 1930's." *Journal of International Economics*, February 1995, *30*(1), pp. 1–24.

Irwin, Douglas A. "Multilateral and Bilateral Trade Liberalization in the World Trading System: An Historical Perspective," in Jaime de Melo and Arvind Panagariya, eds., *New dimensions in regional integration*. New York: Cambridge University Press, 1993, pp. 90–119.

——. "The GATT's Contribution to Economic Recovery in Post-War Western Europe." National Bureau of Economic Research (Cambridge, MA) Working Paper No. 4944, December 1994; In Barry Eichengreen, ed., *Europe's post-war recovery, revisited*. New York: Cambridge University Press, 1995 (forthcoming).

Maddison, Angus. *Dynamic forces in capitalist development*. New York: Oxford University Press, 1991.

Rodrik, Dani. "The Rush to Free Trade in the Developing World: Why So Late? Why Now? Will it Last? National Bureau of Economic Research (Cambridge, MA) Working Paper No. 3947, January 1992.

Whalley, John. "Recent Trade Liberalization in the Developing World: What Is Behind It and Where Is It Headed?" National Bureau of Economic Research (Cambridge, MA) Working Paper No. 3057, August 1989.

11. An Economic Theory of Protectionism, Tariff Bargaining, and the Formation of Customs Unions

H. G. Johnson

I. INTRODUCTION

The traditional approach to the theory of tariffs, which is embodied in the recently elaborated analysis of the effects of customs unions pioneered by Viner, Meade, Lipsey, and others, is concerned with such matters as the possibility of increasing real income by using the tariff to exploit monopoly or monopsony power in world markets, the 'welfare costs' of the tariff in terms of foregone real income, and the effects on real income of changes in particular tariffs or in tariff structures, such as are entailed by the formation of customs unions and free-trade areas. Implicit in this approach is the assumption that 'real income' is identifiable, on social welfare function lines, with the utility derived by individuals from their personal consumption of goods and services; and, except in the optimum tariff analysis, the further assumption that tariffs are arbitrary interferences with the freedom of international exchange, which may be changed equally arbitrarily by governments.

In two previous papers, written within the traditional approach, I have called attention to the special and restrictive nature of these assumptions and the implications of abandoning them. In my 'The Cost of Protection and the Scientific Tariff'[1] I assumed that the authorities of a country were attempting to achieve certain non-economical objectives by the use of the tariff, and worked out the implications for the structure of tariff rates of a 'scientific' effort to achieve these objectives at minimum cost in terms of foregone real income. In my 'Optimal Trade Intervention in the Presence of Domestic Distortions,'[2] I remarked that the relevance of the traditional theory to the problems of economic policy depends on a particular assumption about the nature of government, namely, that government seeks to maximize real income but is ill informed about how to do this. I also pointed out that under different assumptions about the nature of government the analysis would have to be interpreted differently: if government were assumed to be all wise, the traditional measures of marginal welfare loss would have to be reinterpreted as measures of the divergence of social from private costs or benefits of protection; if, on the other hand, government is regarded as an extra-market system for modifying the distribution of income and wealth, interest would focus on the tariff structure as measuring the political power of various claimants to the national income, and the traditional welfare costs would measure the inefficiency of the political process as a redistributor of income.

The traditional approach explicitly adopts the orthodox economist's judgment of what economic welfare consists in, which runs in terms of individual consumption of goods and services. This definition of welfare leads virtually automatically to the recommendation of what Meade has called the 'modified free-trade position,'[3] a position exemplified by my paper on 'Distortions', previously mentioned. This policy recommendation, in turn, puts the economist in opposition to dominant strands in the actual formulation of international economic policy, which have to be treated by definition as 'irrational' or 'non-economic,' or as arbitrarily constraining analysis to the realm of 'second-best theory.' At the same time, the economist is left without a theory capable of explaining a variety of important and observable phenomena, such as the nature of tariff bargaining, the commercial policies adopted by various countries, the conditions under which countries are willing to embark on customs unions, and the arguments and considerations that have weight in persuading countries to change their commercial policies.

This chapter attempts a sketch of such a theory.[4] The theory derives from the underlying analysis of my two previous papers, in that it accepts the relevance of 'non-economic' objectives and utilizes the suggested hypothesis that government action represents a rational attempt to offset divergences between private and social costs or benefits. But it departs from that analysis in abandoning the distinction between economic and non-economic objectives, which is ethically biased in favour of private consumption as the exclusive measure of welfare, in favour of a distinction between private and public consumption goods, and between 'real income' in the sense of utility enjoyed from both private and public consumption and 'real product' defined as total production of privately appropriable goods and services. The theory employs building blocks provided by a variety of recent contributions, notably Downs' economic theory of democracy, Becker's theory of discrimination, and Breton's economic theory of nationalism.[5] The theory presented does not claim to account for all aspects of commercial policy formation, only to provide a tool for dealing with some practically important aspects; in particular, it concentrates on industrial protection, to the exclusion of agricultural protection, though the latter may be dealt with by obvious extensions of the theory.[6]

II. THE THEORY OF PROTECTIONISM AND TARIFF BARGAINING: INDUSTRIAL PRODUCTION AS AN AGGREGATE

The theory assumes, following Downs, that political parties in democratic countries (and, to a sufficient extent, in dictatorial systems) seek to gain and hold power by promising and implementing policies desired by the electorate; and that competition for office will result in the adoption of policies that tend to maximize the satisfaction enjoyed by the electorate. That satisfaction flows from two sources; private consumption of privately provided goods and services, and collective consumption of goods and services provided through the government at the cost of sacrifices of private consumption. (Consumption is used here as shorthand for both investment and consumption proper.) Competition among parties will tend to carry the allocation of the economy's productive resources between private and collective consumption to the point where the marginal return of satisfaction per unit of resources expended is the same in the two uses.

It is further assumed that there exists a collective preference for industrial production, in the sense that the electorate is willing to spend real resources through government action in order to make the volume of industrial production and employment larger than it would be under free international competition. Industrial production, in other words, appears as a collective consumption good yielding a flow of satisfaction to the electorate independent of the satisfaction they derive directly from the consumption of industrial products. The origins of the preference for industrial production may lie in any one of a number of sources – nationalist aspirations and rivalry with other countries, the power of owners of and workers in industrial facilities to achieve a redistribution of income toward themselves by political means,[7] or the belief that industrial activity involves beneficial 'externalities' of various kinds. The precise source of the preference for industrial production will influence the form of expenditure of resources through government action, and especially the distribution of resources so spent among particular industries. In a detailed analysis of a particular nation's tariff policy, the nature of the preference for industrial production would be an important question, and could be inferred from the relative magnitudes of the premiums the public is willing to pay for different kinds of industrial production; for the present purpose, however, it is sufficient to work with a generalized preference for industrial production.

Resources for the support of industrial activity as a collective consumption good have to be provided by government action, since it is in no one's individual interest to provide them voluntarily. Such resources could be supplied in various ways: fundamentally, the choice lies between direct subsidy from tax revenue, indirect subsidy through tax concessions involving loss of tax revenue, and indirect subsidy through a tariff. The tariff involves the equivalent of an excise tax on the consumer the proceeds of which are paid to the producer to the extent that he produces the good and to the government to the extent that the producer is unable to compete with imports. Subsidy through tax concessions depends on the existence of sufficiently heavy taxes on productive activity, and hence has only become an important technique since World War II. Direct subsidy can be shown to be more efficient than the tariff as a means of promoting production, since it avoids the consumption cost of the tariff. But the tariff is invariably favoured, generally on the grounds that the revenue to finance a subsidy is difficult to collect. Other explanations are that the politicians and businessmen who exploit the preference for industrial production do not wish its alternative opportunity costs to be readily ascertainable, and that the preference for industrial production includes the specification that the country's industry must appear to be able to compete with imports without explicit governmental support. In other words, the collective utility derived from industrial production is conditional on the maintenance of the appearance of competitiveness.

On the assumption of the rationality of governmental processes, the government will tend to carry protection to the point where the value of the marginal collective utility derived from collective consumption of domestic industrial activity is just equal to the marginal excess private cost of protected industrial production. In so doing, the government will be maximizing the country's real income, properly defined. But it will not be maximizing the country's real product, since maximization of real income requires sacrificing real product in order to gratify the preference for collective consumption of industrial production.

The marginal private excess cost of protected industrial production consists of two components, the marginal production cost and the marginal private consumption cost. The marginal production cost, expressed as the proportion by which domestic cost exceeds world market cost, would be measured by the tariff rate, in the usual simple model of trade in which goods are assumed to be produced by production processes employing only original factors of production. In a more complex input-output model of production, the marginal production cost, similarly expressed as a proportional excess above world cost, would be measured by the tariff rate minus the proportion of world cost by which other tariffs on goods sued as inputs raised domestic costs above world costs, all divided by the proportion of the value of the final product considered to constitute collective consumption. (If, for example, the country derives collective satisfaction from the sales value of automobiles assembled in the country, the divisor is unity; if it derives satisfaction from the value added in assembly, the divisor will be substantially less than one, for the automobile assembly industry.)

The marginal private consumption cost of protected industrial production comprises the loss of consumers' surplus due to the restriction of consumption by the increase in the tariff rate necessary to induce the marginal unit of domestic production. The magnitude of this marginal cost depends on the tariff rate and on the price sensitivity of demand relative to supply, increasing with the relative price sensitivity of demand.[8]

If account were taken of the variety of industrial products available for protection, and the possibility that their contributions to satisfaction of the collective preference for industrial production might well vary were recognized, the foregoing principle that the government would equate marginal social utility of collective consumption of domestic industry to marginal excess private cost of protected production would have to be elaborated into the principle that the government would equate the values of the marginal utilities derived from the various lines of industrial production to their marginal excess private costs. This principle would not imply equalization of tariff rates, both because the marginal collective utility of a dollar's worth of industrial production might depend on what was produced, and because the relation of the proportional excess cost of marginal protected production to the tariff rate associated with it would vary, for two reasons. First, the relation of the tariff rate to the marginal excess production cost would vary due to the input-output complications just mentioned,[9] second, the relation of the consumption to the production cost component of the marginal excess private cost of protected production would, as already mentioned, vary with the price sensitivity of demand relative to supply. For all these reasons, the real-income-maximizing tariff structure would not entail equal tariff rates on all protected products. Thus variations in the tariff rates levied under existing national tariff structures cannot be adduced as evidence of

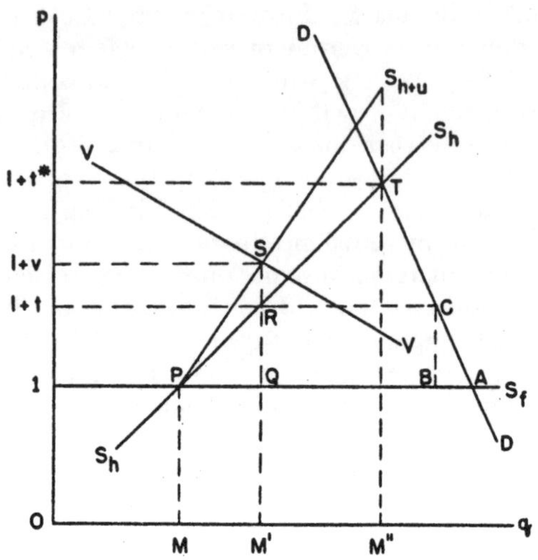

FIGURE 1

'irrationality' in tariff-making, contradicting the theory presented here. In what follows, these complications will be ignored, and industrial production treated as a single aggregate, produced entirely with domestic inputs.

In equilibrium, the proportional marginal excess private cost of protected production measures the marginal 'degree of preference' for industrial production. Its magnitude reflects the interaction of the demand for collective consumption of industrial production and the cost of supplying it. This interaction is depicted in Figure 1.

In Figure 1, $1S_f$ is the supply curve of industrial products (measured in unit values at world market prices) from the world market, assumed to be perfectly elastic (probably a reasonably realistic assumption for most countries), and *DD* is a compensated (constant-utility) demand curve for such products (at the free-trade private utility level). S_hS_h is the domestic supply curve, and PS_{h+u} is the marginal private cost curve of protected production, including excess private consumption cost, the vertical distance between PS_{h+u} and S_f representing the marginal excess private cost, of protected production, geometrically, PS_{h+u} must be so constructed in relation to S_hS_h that, for any tariff *t*, the area *PSR* is equal to the area *ABC*. The height of the curve *VV* above S_f represents the marginal value of industrial production in collective consumption, measured in units of world purchasing power. The maximization of real national income is achieved at the intersection *S* of *VV* with PS_{h+u}, requiring the use of the tariff rate *t* to induce an increase in industrial production from *OM* to *OM*$'$, and involving the marginal degree of preference for industrial production *v*.

The marginal 'degree of preference' for industrial production *v* will be higher, the higher is *VV* and the more elastic it is a the free-trade output, and the farther left and less elastic is PS_{h+u}. Given the slope of *DD* relative to that of S_hS_h, which determines the ratio of *SR* to *RQ* and hence of *v* to *t*, the higher also will be *t*, the tariff rate. It follows that, if the demand conditions and the preference for industrial production tend to be the same in all countries, the lower is a country's ability to compete in industrial production (as represented by the location of *P.* relative to *A*, the free-trade production and consumption points, respectively), the higher will be its marginal degree of preference for industrial production, and (except in certain circumstances detailed in the next footnote) the higher will be its tariff level (degree of protection). In other words, the degree of protection will tend to vary inversely with ability to compete with foreign industrial producers. This is a testable implication of the theory, which seems confirmed by reality. Similarly, if a country's competitive ability should change adversely (that is, S_hS_h shift leftward), continued maximization of real income would require an increase in the degree of protection; and vice versa. This is another testable implication of the theory, which again seems confirmed by reality.[10]

As Figure 1 is drawn, the preference for industrial production is satisfied with the country producing less industrial goods than it consumes. The limit to the gratification of the preference for industrial production that can be achieved by protection is the level of industrial production OM'' achievable by the self-sufficiency tariff rate t^*. Beyond that point, the country can gratify the preference for industrial production only by resorting to export subsidies. Since the domestic price is unsubsidized, and must rise with increased output if domestic sales are to be profitable to producers, the tariff must be increased along with the export subsidy to prevent imports (and reimports) from undercutting sales in the domestic market; thus this policy will continue to involve both excess production costs and excess consumption costs. The marginal private cost of such a policy would be represented in Figure 1 by an extension of PS_{h+u} beyond S_{h+u}.

Figure 1 assumes that the country depicted would be a net importer of industrial products under free trade. Countries that are net exporters of industrial products may also have a preference for industrial production. The preference of exporting countries for industrial production may be satiated by the level of industrial production their exports permit them (that is, *VV* may joint S_hS_h at a point below the world market price of industrial goods). If the preference is not satiated, the only policy open to the country is export subsidization coupled with a tariff at the same rate as the subsidy to prevent reimportation. This case is shown in Figure 2, which is the same as Figure 1 except that the locations of *P* and *A* are reversed, the world demand curve $1D_f$ replaces the world supply curve, and *s*, the subsidy and tariff rate, replaces *t*.

These last two implications of the theory – subsidization of industrial exports by both high-cost protectionist countries and countries competitive in the world market – are again testable and confirmed to some extent by practical experience. Examples are the practice of subsidizing exports of the products of 'new industries' in the less developed countries such as India, and the various arrangements for subsidizing exports through tax incentives, easy export credit, and so forth maintained by countries that have no balance-of-payments reason to transfer real product to foreigners by these means. Another implication, again in conformity with experience, is that industrial exporting countries faced with

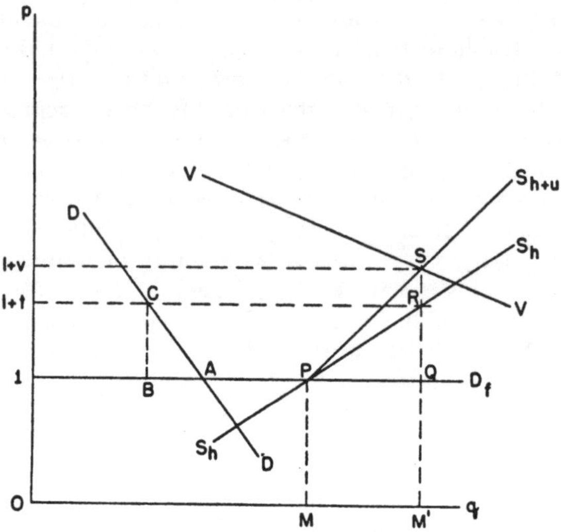

FIGURE 2

adverse changes in their international competitive position will introduce export subsidies or raise existing export subsidies. (For possible exceptions to this proposition, refer back to the discussion of the effects of the same change on the industrial importing countries, and especially n.10.).

The subsidization of exports just discussed is, however, not a widespread practice and is usually disguised in some subtle fashion. The reason is that there is an international convention against explicit export subsidization, incorporated in the principles of GATT and backed up by national antidumping legislation. This convention and the associated national legislation are themselves explainable by reference to the preference for industrial production and the free enterprise philosophy that underlies the preference for tariffs over production subsidies. Export subsidization by a foreign country appears as an attempt by the foreigner to increase his collective utility from industrial production at the expense of one's own by unfair means. What is more important, direct export subsidization is visible and can be counteracted by use of one's own tariff. Enforcement of a prohibition on export subsidization implies that only industrial importing countries are free to maximize their real incomes by gratifying the preference for industrial production: industrial exporting countries are (or may be) confined to a suboptimal level of real income by the inability to subsidize exports. This constraint has important consequences for tariff policy and bargaining, which will be developed subsequently.

The analysis thus far has implicitly assumed a typical country small enough for changes in the volume of its imports or exports of industrial products to make no difference in the price it pays for its imports (if it is a net industrial importer) or receives for its exports of the other products (if it is a net industrial exporter).[11] If this is not true, and the terms of trade are affected by the country's tariff policy, the conditions of optimum tariff theory exist; and by the initial assumption of governmental rationality they will be exploited. It is clear, however, that importers of industrial products will adopt a higher tariff level (against industrial products) than the optimum tariff of conventional analysis, and conversely that countries that are net exporters of industrial products will adopt a lower tariff level (against non-industrial products) then the conventional optimum tariff – always provided that the preference for industrial production does not become satiated.[12] In both cases real income is maximized, and thus is higher than it would be under the conventionally determined optimum tariff. But in the net industrial importing country real product must be lower than it would have been under the conventional optimum tariff, and may be lower than it would have been under free trade; whereas in the net industrial exporting country, real product, though less than it would have been under the conventional optimum tariff, must be higher than it would have been under free trade – provided that the preference for industrial production is not strong enough to lead to free trade (or to export subsidization, if that is possible) rather than a tax on imports.

The introduction of monopoly-monopsony power in the world market into a model in which industrial production is treated as a single aggregate provides a motive for industrial exporting countries as well as industrial importing countries to have tariffs, and therefore introduces the possibility of negotiation for the reciprocal reduction of tariffs. To investigate this possibility, I assume a world of two countries only, an industrial exporting ('advanced') country and an industrially importing ('less developed') country, each with a tariff on imports.[13] To allow scope for tariff bargaining, these tariffs must be seemed to have been arrived at by some process of independent tariff formation in the two countries, though this process may or may not be assumed to have involved recognition of the dependence of the welfare-maximizing tariff policy of each on the tariff policy of the other, without affecting the conclusions.[14]

Under what condition will a reciprocal reduction of tariffs by the two countries be mutually beneficial, in the sense that some combination of tariff reductions can be found that will raise the real income of both countries? In the traditional analysis, where the initial existence of tariffs is derived from the exercise of monopoly-monopsony power on the part of each country, reciprocal tariff reduction is always beneficial, and it can be shown that tariff bargaining would proceed to reduce tariffs until at least one country had eliminated its tariff entirely.[15] In the presence of a preference for industrial production, however, this proposition no longer holds, since this preference gives the less developed country a motive for imposing a tariff independent of the exploitation of monopoly-monopsony power, so that the existence of its tariff does not necessarily imply the presence of such power. In this case, mutually beneficial tariff reduction is possible only to the extent that the less-developed country's tariff involves the exploitation of monopoly-monopsomy power, and would never lead to that country's abandoning protection in favour of free trade.

The point may be illustrated, without loss of generality, by considering the attractiveness to the two countries of a proposed slight reciprocal reduction of tariffs, so designed as to expand trade without changing the terms of trade. In the traditional model the presence of tariffs means that in each country the marginal private value of an increment of imports exceeds its price (the tariff having been imposed because the marginal social cost of imports exceeds price), so that each country will proceed until one country reaches the free-trade point. In the present model, the marginal private value of an increment of imports also exceeds its price, owing to the tariff. But in the advanced country the marginal social value of an increment of imports is above the marginal private value, because an increment of imports carries with it an increment of exports and therefore of industrial production and utility of collective consumption associated with industry. In the less developed country, on the other hand, the marginal social value of an increment of imports is below the marginal private value, because an expansion of trade entails a contraction of industrial production and a loss of utility from the collective consumption of industry. Given rational maximization of real income, the country will have fixed its tariff so that the marginal social value of an increment of imports is initially just equal to its marginal social cost, and unless the presence of monopoly-monopsony power makes marginal social cost exceed price, the country will derive no gain in real income (as distinct from real product) from an expansion of trade at constant terms of trade. In fact, a non-infinitesimal expansion of trade would impose a loss on it. Thus while the advanced country will have an incentive to accept the proposed reciprocal tariff reduction, the less developed country will have no incentive to do so unless it possesses monopoly-monopsony power that its tariff has exploited. If it possesses no monopoly-monopsony power, it would only accept a reciprocal tariff reduction proposal that promised an improvement in its terms of trade; but the advanced country would have no incentive to offer such a proposal since to do so would entail an unrequited sacrifice of the exploitation of its own monopoly-monopsony power.[16] If it does possess monopoly-monopsony power, it would be willing to accept reciprocal tariff reduction of the type described, but only to the point at which its tariff rate equalized the marginal excess private cost of protected production with the marginal degree of preference for industrial production. Thus reciprocal tariff reduction could only lead to one country's following a free-trade policy if that country were the advanced country; and this would require that country's monopoly-monopsony power be relatively less, in some sense difficult to define except by its results, than that of the less developed country.

The case in which the less developed country has no monopoly-monopsony power is of special interest, since for the analysis of tariff bargaining (though not of the actual results of bargains) it can be taken to represent the more realistic situation in which there are a large number of less developed countries, each too small to exercise any independent monopoly-monopsony power, even though the aggregate of less developed countries may possess such power. To be acceptable, a tariff-reducing bargain in this case must promise to improve the terms of trade of the less developed country and turn them against the advanced country; in monetary terms, it must threaten to worsen the advanced country's balance of payments at the existing exchange and money wage rates. If, as a matter of rational exploitation of monopoly-monopsony power (as in the preceding analysis), or more generally of bargaining tactics, balance of payments considerations or other reasons, the advanced country's negotiators insist that equity of bargains necessitates reciprocal tariff reductions that would produce a balanced expansion of trade at unchanged terms of trade (that is, equal increases in export and import values at current prices) the less developed country will refuse any bargain proposed, as involving a loss of real income to it. This point explains one aspect of the dissatisfaction that the less developed countries have recently been manifesting with respect to the GATT mechanism of bargaining for tariff reduction. Given the preference for industrial production, bargaining on GATT rules appears to offer no attractions to countries that do not export industrial products and lack monopoly-monopsony power in world markets; instead, it appears to such countries as a mechanism designed to enable the advanced countries to win benefits at their expense.[17]

The aggregated two-good model of this section does not lend itself readily to extension to tariff-bargaining among a number of countries, which introduces the possibility of preferential arrangements. The analysis does, however, indicate the reasons why preferential arrangements between advanced and less developed countries may be attractive to both sides. The convention against export subsidies may prevent the advanced country from achieving a level of industrial production high enough to maximize its real income, and this may make it willing to pay a price, in terms of a preference-created increase in the cost of its imports of non-industrial goods, for a preference-created increase in its exports. To the less developed country, on the other hand, a preference toward a particular advanced country has the advantage that its price is an increase in the social cost of existing imports, rather than a decrease in the country's industrial production, which loss may be more than offset by the increased prices the country may obtain for its exports of non-industrial products.

III. THE THEORY OF PROTECTIONISM AND TARIFF BARGAINING: VARIETY OF INDUSTRIAL PRODUCTION

In this section, I abandon the assumption that industrial production is a single aggregate, with countries having varying comparative advantage in industry as opposed to non-industrial production. Instead, I assume that industrial production comprises a variety of products, in which countries have varying degrees of comparative advantage. Such differences in comparative advantage among industries may be assumed to result from differences in the local availability of natural resources, in the general level of labour or management skill, in the availability of capital, in technological level, or in the size of the domestic market combined with the existence of economies of scale in certain industries, I continue to assume that countries differ in their over-all comparative advantage in industry as compared with non-industrial production.

The variety of industrial production allows countries to be both importers and exporters of industrial products, and in combination with the preference for industrial production will motivate each country to practice some degree of protection. It is therefore not necessary to appeal to monopoly-monopsony power in world markets to provide an environment of universal protection within which reciprocal tariff reduction is possible; and for analytical simplicity it will be assumed that no country has such power. It will also be assumed that the convention against export subsidization is fully effective; this is an important assumption, in that it creates an opportunity for mutually profitable tariff reduction, and in certain circumstances a motive for protection itself.

In the circumstances posited, a country can gratify its preference for industrial production only by protecting the domestic producers of commodities it imports. Acting rationally, it will carry protection to the point where the marginal social value of collective consumption of industrial production is equal to the marginal excess cost of industrial production. The latter, however, will be constituted somewhat differently in this model than in the previous one. Protection of import-competing industries will tend to some extent to reduce industrial exports, as well as non-industrial production; hence, in order to increase total industrial production by one unit, it will be necessary to increase protected industrial production by more than one unit to compensate for the induced loss of industrial exports, so that the marginal excess private production cost and consumption cost must be reckoned accordingly.[18]

Protection of import-competing industries reduces industrial exports by raising their cost of production, either by raising the prices of factors of production common to the two sectors of industry, or by raising the cost of outputs of the protected sector used as inputs in the export sector. The stronger are these effects of protection, other things equal, the higher will be the marginal excess cost of industrial production. These effects are likely to be larger, the larger the size of the total industrial sector relative to the non-industrial sector and the larger the size of the protected industrial sector relative to the exporting industrial sector.

These relationships would imply that the same marginal degree of preference for industrial production would entail (a) lower tariff rates in a country with a relatively small non-industrial sector than in one with a relatively large non-industrial sector, and (b) higher tariff rates in countries a relatively small proportion of whose industrial production is protected than in countries a relatively large proportion of whose industrial production is protected. These would appear to be testable implications of the theory: and the former seems in conformity with reality, while the latter does not. The tests, however, are not valid ones, because the marginal degree of preference for industrial production is not independent of the characteristics of the economy to which the implication refer. A country with a small non-industrial sector is virtually certain to be a net industrial exporter, and vice versa, so that with identical preferences for industrial production among nations a country with a small non-industrial sector would necessarily have a more fully gratified preference and hence a lower marginal degree of preference for industrial production: hence its tariff rates would tend to be lower anyway. Similarly, a country that protects relatively much of its industrial production presumably does so because it has a comparative disadvantage in industrial production, so that its marginal degree of preference for industrial production and hence its tariff rates would tend to be higher than those of a country which protects relatively little of its industrial production. Higher tariff rates in the former than in the latter are therefore not inconsistent with the theory.

As in the previous model, the theory implies that the degree of protection practiced by the various countries will vary inversely with their net industrial export position; and that an improvement in a country's comparative advantage in industrial production as against non-industrial production will lead it to reduce its degree of protection, and vice versa. As already mentioned, these implications are consistent with experience – countries whose competitiveness in world markets is improving tend to move in the free trade direction, while countries whose competitiveness is deteriorating tend to move toward increased protectionism.[19]

The analysis just presented assumes that domestic and international trade is organized competitively, so that protection tends to divert resources away from production for export. If production is assumed to be carried on by monopolistic enterprises, so that discrimination by the producer between markets is possible, and these enterprises are assumed to be multiproduct firms operating under joint cost conditions, so that discrimination between the domestic and the foreign markets can be effected by loading different products with different prices for the same product in the two markets (thus circumventing the convention against dumping), the foregoing conclusions will be altered. A tariff will permit the protected producer to charge his overheads against the home-market consumer and, indirectly, to subsidize exports. By so doing, monopolistic market organization may permit the country, through its tariff policy, to achieve a given level of industrial production of a lower marginal excess cost than would rule under competition. Under these conditions, the tariff might increase rather than decrease industrial exports, thus yielding a double gain from protection. The implications of monopolistic market organization for the theory of tariff bargaining are obviously both complex and interesting; the former characteristic prevents them from being pursued further in this chapter.

The analysis thus far has provided a rationale for the existence of universal tariff protection of industrial production and examined some of the implications of differences or changes in countries' circumstances for their protectionist policies. I now introduce the possibility of bargaining for reciprocal tariff reduction. To begin with, I assume a world of only two countries, though this does some violence to the assumption that no country has monopoly-monopsony power in the world market. One of these countries must be a net exporter, and the other a net importer, of industrial products; but it is no longer true (as in the previous model) that the expansion of industrial production in one must entail a contraction of industrial production in the other, since industrial production in both can expand at the expense of production of non-industrial products.

At the outset, it should be emphasized that for each country the prospective gain from reciprocal tariff reduction must lie in the expansion of exports of industrial products. By assumption, each country has been willing to reduce its real product by protection of domestic industrial producers against foreign competition in order to maximize its real income (including utility from collective consumption of industrial production), and any reduction in industrial production due to an expansion of imports adds less to real product than it subtracts from collective utility. Thus reduction of one's own tariffs is a source of loss, which can only be compensated for by a reduction of the other country's tariff. On the other hand, a reduction of the other country's tariff is a source of gain, since it expands one's own industrial production and yields an increased flow of utility from collective consumption of industrial production. The theory therefore accounts for the form and logic of bargaining for reciprocal tariff reduction, phenomena which are incomprehensible to the classical approach to tariff theory, according to which the source of gain is the replacement of domestic production by lower-cost imports, whereas increased exports yield no gain (improved terms of trade apart) to the exporting country, but a gain to the foreigner through the same replacement of domestic production by lower-cost imports. Since these gains are attainable by unilateral action, the classical approach provides no explanation of the necessity and nature of the bargaining process.

The gains from reciprocal tariff reduction are nevertheless of the same basic nature in this model as in the classical analysis, though their outward character is different; they result from the substitution of lower-cost for higher-cost sources of want satisfaction. The difference is that in the classical analysis it is lower-cost satisfaction of private consumer wants that is involved, and this could be achieved without the co-operation of the other country through unilateral tariff reduction; whereas in the preference for industrial production model it is lower-cost satisfaction that is involved, and this can only be achieved through the co-operation (via bargaining) of the other country. Because of the convention preventing export subsidization, a country enters the bargaining situation in a 'second-best' equilibrium position, in which the marginal excess cost of industrial production achieved by additional exports is zero, whereas the marginal excess cost of additional industrial production achieved by protection is positive. Each country therefore stands to gain, in terms of real income, by exchanging a reduction of its industrial production through its own tariff reduction for an equal expansion of its industrial production through the other country's tariff reduction. Actually, however, reciprocal tariff reductions can be arranged that will increase each country's aggregate consumption of industrial goods at the expense of its consumption of non-industrial goods.[20] And an individual country could gain from negotiated reciprocal tariff reductions that reduced its aggregate industrial production, providing that the resulting increase in real product outweighed the loss of utility from collective consumption of industrial production; at the initiation of bargaining it could gain from any reciprocal tariff reduction that offered it any slight increase in exports.[21] It follows that reciprocal tariff-cutting would proceed so long as each country could offer the other a tariff reduction that would increase the other's exports. Consequently, just as in the classical model in which tariffs exist due to monopoly-monopsony power in world markets, bargaining for mutually beneficial tariff reductions would eliminate tariffs in one of the countries, and possibly in both.

This result depends, of course, on the assumptions of the model, and especially on the assumption that the preference for industrial production does not discriminate between industries. If countries attached separate collective consumption utility to different industries, a position could be reached in which a country could not be compensated for further reductions in the tariff on one of its (more highly valued) industries by a reduction in the other country's tariff or one of its (less highly valued) industries. Also, if a country's production is concentrated in the hands of monopolistic enterprises capable of effective price discrimination between the domestic and foreign market, reciprocal tariff reduction might involve a loss rather than a gain for that country.

The assumption of a two-country world and a general preference for industrial production leads to the conclusion that bargaining will result in the elimination of the tariffs of at least one of the countries. This result is due to the fact that in a two-country world it is always possible to arrange reciprocal tariff reductions that will increase industrial production in both countries while reducing the excess cost of industrial production. I now abandon the two-country assumption and assume the existence of many countries. In this case, as will be shown, there are limits to the extent of the reciprocal reduction of tariffs that can be negotiated on a most-favoured-nation basis; furthermore these limits introduce the possibility that reciprocal preferential tariff reduction, that is, tariff reductions discriminating among foreign countries, will be more attractive than non-discriminatory tariff reduction, a possibility that would not exist apart from the preference for industrial production.

Assume that all reciprocal tariff reductions must be arrived at on a most-favored-nation basis; that is, that each partner in the negotiation must extend the tariff reduction to all other nations, not merely to the negotiating partner. Reduction of a country's tariff on a particular item will then increase its total imports of that item by more than it increases imports from the partner country; it may or may not decrease the country's industrial production by more than it increases industrial production in the partner country, depending on the magnitudes of the parameters involved.[22] The same holds for a reduction of the partner country's tariff.

It follows, first, that countries negotiating for reciprocal tariff reductions will offer concessions on those items for which a reduction in their own tariff will yield the maximum increase in partner industrial production per unit reduction in domestic industrial production, and demand concessions on those items for which a reduction in the partner's tariff will yield the maximum increase in their own industrial production per unit reduction in the partner's industrial production. By so doing, they maximize their joint gains from the combination of substitution of lower-cost (exported) for higher-cost (protected import-competing) industrial production and expansion of aggregate industrial production. In other words, each country has an incentive to choose items for negotiation in a fashion that discriminates against expansion of trade with third parties in favour of expansion of trade with the partner country. In this way the most-favoured-nation principle, which proscribes tariff discrimination among countries, leads to indirect discrimination among countries through the choice of commodities for reciprocal tariff reduction.

Second, it follows that the process of reciprocal tariff reduction is likely to come to a halt well before either country approaches anything like complete elimination of tariffs. This is so because sooner or later the only reciprocal tariff reductions possible will be the ones that will reduce the aggregate industrial production of one or both countries. And while reciprocal reductions of this kind will be mutually advantageous over a certain range, in the sense that the loss of utility from collective consumption of industrial production in a country whose industrial production fell would initially be outweighed by the gain in real product resulting from tariff elimination, this must cease to be the case before the country's tariffs have been completely eliminated, because the loss of utility is constant or rising per unit of industrial production sacrificed while the gain of real product must fall as the tariff is reduced.[23]

The foregoing propositions relate to the nature and effects of bilateral negotiation for reciprocal tariff reduction, subject to the rule of non-discrimination, in a multicountry world; and they bear a reasonably close relationship to the nature and results of tariff negotiations under the GATT system. In a rational world, however, negotiations for reciprocal tariff reduction would not be confined to bilateral negotiations between pairs of nations; and this is not entirely the case under GATT. What would be the results of multilateral negotiations for reciprocal tariff reductions?

It seems likely, on the analogy of Marcus Fleming's treatment of the problem of making the best of balance-of-payments restrictions on imports,[24] that the outcome would be a situation in which countries could be arranged in an order of decreasing industrial strength (comparative advantage in industrial production) and increasing protectionism – though it is difficult to construct a rigorous formal argument leading to this conclusion, owing to the difficulty of defining 'industrial strength.' The basic logic behind the conclusion stems from the preceding analyses of two-country models, where it was shown (in the aggregate industrial production model) that a country with no industrial exports and no monopoly-monopsony power would have no incentive to negotiate tariff reductions; and (in the disaggregated industrial production model) that both countries would gain from negotiating reciprocal tariff reductions until at least one of them practiced free trade. Multilateral negotiation, it may be presumed, will permit one country to deal with the rest as if they constituted a single country.

In a multicountry world it should always be possible to find at least one country ('the strongest industrial country') so situated with respect to its initial trade position in industrial products and the elasticities of demand and supply governing them that universal adoption of free trade would increase its industrial exports more than its industrial imports. Such a country could always gain by offering to pursue a free-trade policy in exchange for tariff concessions by the others, providing that it received sufficient concessions for its aggregate industrial production to remain unchanged or increase; and the other countries – except for the non-exporters of industrial products, who would have no incentive to participate – should always be able to find some set of individual non-discriminatory tariff concessions that, in combination with the effects of free trade in the strongest industrial country, would leave unchanged or increase their individual aggregates of industrial production.[25] Thus one country at least would end up with a commercial policy of free trade. After this negotiation, the next strongest industrial country would have an incentive to negotiate reciprocal tariff reductions with the rest; but the free-trade country would now appear as the third party in the preceding analysis of bilateral negotiation, since it would gain automatically from the non-discriminatory reciprocal tariff reductions of the rest without being able to offer them export-increasing tariff concessions in return. Thus this negotiation might or might not bring the second-strongest industrial country to free trade. At the opposite extreme, countries with no comparative advantage in industrial production – countries all of whose industrial production has to be protected – would have nothing to gain from reciprocal tariff negotiation, but industrial production to lose, and would retain their original tariffs. Thus some arrangement of countries in order of increasing protectionism and decreasing industrial strength would emerge from multilateral negotiation of reciprocal tariff reduction. But this arrangement would be subject to some indeterminacy, since the outcome would depend in part on the order in which negotiations took place and the way in which the gains from negotiated tariff reductions were divided among the participating countries.

Now introduce, in place of the most-favoured-nation principle, the possibility of preferential (discriminatory) reciprocal tariff reduction, that is, of reciprocal reduction of tariffs on imports from the partner country, tariffs on imports of the same commodity from third countries remaining unchanged. Starting from an initial position of non-discrimination, discriminatory tariff reduction has the advantage over non-discriminatory tariff reduction that it permits a country to offer its partner an increase in exports and industrial production without suffering any loss of its own industrial production, through diverting imports from third countries to the partner. After all such possible trade diversion has occurred, further discriminatory tariff reduction has the advantage over non-discriminatory tariff reduction of yielding the partner the whole of any increase in the tariff-cutting country's imports (which now occur partly at the expense of its domestic industrial production), whereas under non-discriminatory tariff reduction the partner's exports would expand less than the tariff-reducing country's imports, so that the partner's industrial production expands more under the former than under the latter type of tariff-cutting. Thus discriminatory reciprocal tariff reduction costs each partner country less, in terms of the reduction in domestic industrial production (if any) incurred per unit increase in partner industrial production, than does non-discriminatory reciprocal tariff reduction. On the other hand, preferential tariff reduction imposes an additional cost on the tariff-reducing country, the excess of the cost of imports from the partner country over their cost in the world market.

For the initial slight preferential tariff reduction, this cost will be smaller, the smaller the amount of the partner country's exports to the world market. (Under the assumed conditions of perfect competition, the partner's exports may be sold anywhere under non-discrimination, but any slight preference will divert them to the market of the preference-granting country. It is obvious that the preference-receiving country will only benefit from the preference if its initial export sales are less than the import quantity that would be demanded by the preference-granting country under free trade, since only in this case can the preference increase its sales; this sets limits on the conditions under which preferential arrangements can be mutually beneficial.) For subsequent preferential tariff reductions, the marginal cost per unit of increased imports will rise, both because the excess cost of the marginal unit of imports increases and because this excess price is paid on a larger volume of intramarginal trade with the partner. Once the partner country's exports have replaced imports from other countries, further preferential tariff reductions entail an additional element of cost through

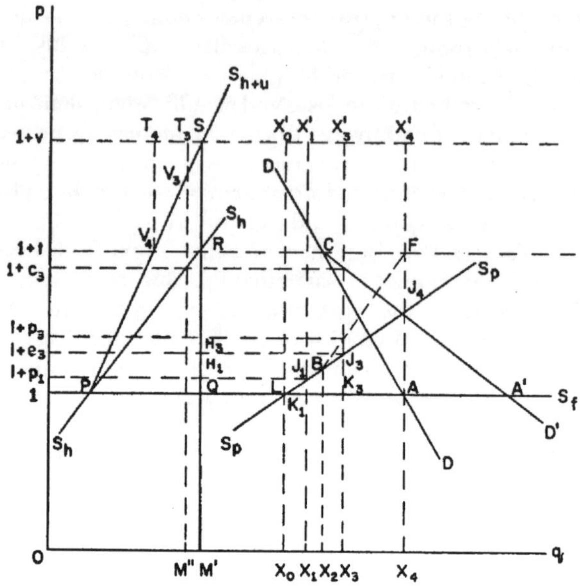

FIGURE 3

replacement of domestic by partner industrial production and a consequent loss of collective utility.

That part of the cost of the preference that corresponds to the higher price paid for intramarginal imports, however, is an income transfer to the partner, whose gains from the preference comprise this transfer and the collective utility derived from whatever expansion of its industrial exports results. Since the excess marginal cost of the increment of partner industrial exports resulting from an initial slight preferential tariff reduction is negligible, while there must be some increase in the partner's industrial production if the preference is to benefit it, it follows that an exchange of slight preferential tariff reductions between the partners must always be mutually beneficial. For further reciprocal tariff reductions, however, the increasing marginal cost of preferential tariff reduction will not proceed to the point of 100 per cent preferences (reciprocal free trade in the commodities under negotiation). This conclusion parallels a proposition in standard customs union theory, to the effect that a partial preferential arrangement is more likely to raise the real income (real product, in the present terminology) of the preference-granting countries than a 100 per cent preferential arrangement.

The cost of giving a preference is illustrated in Figure 3, which reproduces the relevant parts of Figure 1. For simplicity, it is assumed that the quantity of resources used in domestic production of the imported commodity has no influence on the quantity of resources used in the country's production of other industrial products, and that the marginal degree of preference for industrial production v is constant. The partner country's supply curve is represented by S_pS_p, quantity supplied being measured from the vertical SM'; the partner is assumed to be capable of supplying less than the total quantity of imports demanded when the country imposes a non-discriminatory tariff and the partner receives the world price, but more than that quantity of imports if it receives the domestic price. For simplicity, it is arbitrarily assumed that all of the exports of the partner in the initial non-discriminatory situation are directed to the preference-granting country.

So long as the preference is insufficient to enable the partner to supply the whole of the quantity of imports initially demanded, the granting of the preference simply enables the partner suppliers to charge a higher price than the world market price, and induces substitution of partner for foreign supplies (trade diversion). This case is represented in the figure by the preference p_1, which increases partner exports to the country from $M'X_0$ to $M'X_1$ (by X_0X_1); the cost of this preference to the country is $QH_1J_1K_1$, of which QH_1J_1L is an income transfer to the partner and J_1K_1L is the excess of the real production cost of the additional partner exports above the world market price.

Once the preference has become large enough for the partner country to supply the initial level of imports, the situation changes. For partner exports to increase, the domestic price must fall, to induce increased consumption and decreased domestic production (trade creation). In the figure, the effect on the quantity of imports demanded of the contraction of domestic production as the domestic price falls is represented by shifting the demand curve DD to the right below the point C by the amount of the corresponding contraction of domestic output, to give the demand curve for imports CA' continued (in the figure, $PQ=AA'$). The necessity for the domestic price to fall to induce increased imports means that part of any additional preference is absorbed in price reduction to domestic consumers, so that only a part of it accrues as an increase in the price received by partner suppliers. To represent this in the figure, the vertical distance between the horizontal line at $1+t$ and CA' is added to S_pS_p to give the line BF, which represents the locus of the preferences necessary to induce various quantities of partner exports. With the preference p_3, for example, imports from the partner would be $M'X_3$; the excess of the price received by the partner over the world market price would be e_3; the domestic price would be above the world market price by c_3 and below the price in the absence of the preference by $t-c_3$; and domestic production would be below its level under non-discriminatory protection by the amount $M''M'$. The cost of the preference p_3 would consist of two parts: $QH_3J_3K_3$, the excess of the cost of imports from the partner country above world market prices, of which QH_3J_3L is an income transfer to the partner and J_3K_3L is the excess of the real production cost of the additional partner exports above the world market price; and ST_3V_3, the excess of the loss of utility from domestic industrial production over the saving of excess private cost of protected production.

Figure 3 can also be used to depict the gains from preferential tariff reduction to the partner country, if it is assumed that the increase in partner exports represents the net increase in its industrial production resulting from the preference and that the partner country's marginal preference for industrial production is also v. Under the preference p_1, the partner gains an increment of producer's surplus (income transfer) equal to QH_1J_1L, and an increment of collective utility from industrial production $LX'_0X'_1K_1$; under the preference p_3, the corresponding gains are QH_3J_3L and $LX'_0X'_3K_3$.

Taking the two countries together, and cancelling out the income transfer, there is for preference p_1 a net benefit for the two together of $LX'_0X'_1J_1$; for preference p_3, there is a net benefit of $LX_0X'_3J_3 - ST_3V_3$. From the assumptions on which the figure is constructed it is obvious that the latter measure must be positive and must increase as the preference increases up to a 100 per cent preference (a change from a preference p_3 to a preference t involves an addition to net benefit of $J_3X'_3X'_4J_4 - T_3V_3V_4T_4$, and since T_4T_3 is less than $X'_3X'_4$, and T_3V_3 *and* T_4V_4 are less than X'_3J_3 and X'_4J_4, this must be positive). If these assumptions held in both countries, the partners would therefore negotiate 100 per cent preferences (reciprocal free trade) in the commodities concerned. The assumptions of the figure are highly restrictive, however: if the industrial production of the preference-receiving country increases by less than its exports, the gain of collective utility to the partner country will be less (say) than the area $LX'_0X'_3K_3$ and may fall short of the sum of the areas LJ_3K_3 (the excess real production cost of the increased exports) and ST_3V_3 (the net loss of real income to the home country from the reduction of its domestic production).

The potential benefit from discriminatory reciprocal tariff reduction, it should be noted, derives from two assumptions of the mode: the preference for industrial production, and the convention against export subsidization. The first involves a willingness to sacrifice real product for the sake of greater industrial production, the second prevents countries from implementing the preference for industrial production by direct subsidization of exports. Reciprocal preferential tariff reduction is in fact an arrangement by which each partner indirectly subsidizes its own industrial exports by subsidizing its industrial imports from the other, the subsidy being given in the disguised form of preferential relief from tariffs otherwise payable.

It should also be noted that the foregoing analysis involves both of the effects considered in the standard analysis of preferential tariff reduction – trade diversion and trade creation – and that contrary to the standard analysis trade diversion as well as trade creation yields a gain to the partners; in fact, trade diversion is preferable to trade creation, for the preference-granting country, because it entails no sacrifice of domestic industrial production. This reversal of the usual conclusions is due to the presence of the preference for industrial production, and its frustration by the convention against export subsidization. In these circumstances, the gain of real product from trade creation to the importing country is insufficient to compensate for the loss of real income due to the resulting sacrifice of utility from collective consumption of domestic industrial production; and trade diversion is preferable because, though it involves a real product loss, it does not involve a sacrifice of domestic industrial production.[26] In both cases, however, the gain in a country's real income comes, not from a preponderance of the real product gains from trade creation over the real product losses from trade diversion resulting from the effects of the country's own preferential tariff reduction on its own imports, but from the increase in the country's exports of industrial products resulting from the trade-diverting and trade-creating effects of the partner country's preferential tariff reduction in its favour. Consequently, preferential reciprocal tariff reductions may be negotiated even if they lead to a loss of real product for one or both parties.[27]

The foregoing analysis also indicates the conditions under which reciprocal preferential tariff reduction will be beneficial to the countries concerned, and will therefore be resorted to. Implicit in the analysis are the assumptions that the parties concerned have a strong preference for industrial production, and a weak comparative advantage in industrial production, so that they each export relatively small quantities of industrial products, and gratify their preference for industrial production largely through protection of domestic industry against imports. A country with strong comparative advantage in industrial production would both be able to seek expansion of its industrial production through multilateral tariff bargaining, and might be unable to benefit (in the competitive conditions of the model) from preferential entry to the other country's market, because such preferential entry might merely divert its exports from other countries' markets without significantly affecting their prices. The analysis also requires that the partners have differing comparative advantages (disadvantages) in the various lines of industrial production, so that each can benefit from preferences given by the other. In the preceding analysis, this was implicit in the assumption that each could export some quantity of a product that the other imported in spite of its protection of its domestic industry; that assumption is unnecessarily strong, all that is required being that tariff rates vary so that domestic costs of production of the various commodities exceed their world prices by different proportions in the two countries, the lower costs being found sometimes in one country and sometimes in the other.

Since in the model of protectionism presented above the marginal degree of preference for industrial production is equal in all industries, differences in tariff rates among industries must be due to differences in the behaviour of the consumption cost of protection among industries, or to differences in the extent to which resources employed in one branch of industry reduce production in others, and differences in tariff rate structures among countries must be due to differences in these factors among countries. For tariff rates to be sometimes higher and sometimes lower in one protectionist country than in the other, the latter differences must outweigh any differences in the marginal degree of preference for industrial production among countries. This last requirement implies that only countries with comparable degrees of preference for industrial production are likely to be in a position to benefit extensively from preferential reciprocal tariff-cutting schemes, a point relevant to the prediction of what countries or groups of countries are likely to engage in such schemes.[28]

Under these conditions, countries can obtain increases in their individual aggregates of industrial production through preferential reciprocal tariff reduction that they could not obtain otherwise, while at the same time increasing their real incomes, and possibly but not necessarily their real products. The benefits accrue primarily through balanced exchanges of lower-cost industrial production in one country for higher-cost industrial production in the other (trade creation) and through balanced substitutions for foreign production of domestic industrial production whose collective consumption value exceeds its excess cost (trade diversion). There is, however, a further possible source of gain not comprehended in the preceding analysis: if the reason for the excess cost of domestic industrial production is inefficiency promoted by the small scale of the domestic market and the monopolistic tendencies fostered by the tariff in each country, the trade-creating and especially the trade-diverting effects of reciprocal preferential tariff reduction may permit the harvesting of economies of scale. The preference for industrial production on which the analysis is posited will require that industries subject to the economies of scale be fairly divided up among the participants in the preferential arrangements. This consideration, however, is more relevant to the theory of customs union formation, the subject of the next section.[29]

IV. THE THEORY OF CUSTOMS UNION FORMATION

Preferential tariff arrangements of the type discussed at the end of the previous section are inconsistent with the most-favoured-nation principle, and are frowned on for the quite valid reason that they are likely to be used mainly for protectionist rather than trade-liberalizing purposes. The most-favoured-nation principle can in fact be interpreted as a convention designed to protect the third parties at the expense of whose industrial production the mutual benefits of preferential reciprocal tariff reduction are in part obtained. Under the rules of GATT, however, an exception to the most-favoured-nation principle is made for customs unions and free-trade areas, on the quite questionable assumption that, since these arrangements demand 100 per cent preferences across the board, they are likely to constitute movements in the free-trade rather than the protectionist direction. The standard theory of customs unions has shown that this is not necessarily so, if by 'the free-trade direction' is meant the direction of maximization of real product, while the emergence of the European Common Market has provided a practical demonstration of the protective potentialities of customs unions.

That customs unions will be formed with a protective intent is one of the implications of the analysis of protectionism in the preceding sections, and especially of the assumption of a preference for industrial production. The analysis of preferential tariff reduction is especially relevant, the customs union differing from preferential tariff reduction only in that preferences granted to participants in the arrangement have to be at the rate of 100 per cent, and to apply across the board, and that the tariff rates of members against imports from the rest of the world have to be unified. The purpose of the present section is to apply the theory developed in the preceding sections to various aspects of the formation of customs unions (free-trade areas can be analyzed by obvious extensions of the analysis).

The first problem to be considered is the nature of the gains that are generally alleged to follow from the formation of customs unions. The standard economic analysis of customs unions stresses the gains from trade diversion; and some weight is put on economies of scale and the promotion of efficiency through competition in a larger market area. These arguments, however, are equally arguments for unilateral tariff elimination, which would have the advantage of entailing no losses from trade diversion; and, apart from the economies of scale argument, which begs the question of why such economies are not exploitable through the world market but can be obtained by customs union, the only economic argument on classical lines for pursuing these gains through customs union rather than unilateral tariff elimination must rest on the possible terms-of-trade loss from unilateral tariff reduction and on the possible terms-of-trade gain for the union as a whole from discrimination against the outside world. The arguments usually advanced for customs unions in political discussion, however, generally ignore any possible gain from trade creation, in the sense of replacement of domestic production by cheaper imports, and instead regard this as a price to be paid for the benefits of expanded export markets, those benefits to result from both trade creation and trade diversion in favour of domestically produced products; and stress is laid on the gains to domestic industry from economies of scale and increased competition in a large market, as well as the 'growth potential' of a larger market area. In these arguments, trade diversion is valued for its effects in increasing production within the union, not for its effects in improving the terms of trade with the outside world; this is significant, because the conditions under which a customs union will divert the most trade are those under which its terms-of-trade effects will be least.

The difference between the two sets of arguments is clearly explainable by the hypothesis that standard economic analysis is concerned with maximization of real product, whereas political discussion derives from a preference for industrial production and is concerned with the maximization of real income conceived to include utility from the collective consumption of industrial production. The latter concern is bound to concentrate on the potentialities of a customs union for increasing the industrial output of the country and the efficiency of its industrial production, rather than on its potentialities for satisfying private consumption demand at lower cost by increased imports; and to regard such imports as a necessary cost of rather than a benefit from joining a customs union.

A second problem is the characteristics of countries likely to be successful in forming a customs union. As the preceding analysis of preferential reciprocal tariff reduction has shown, an arrangement of this kind will be attractive to countries with a strong preference for industrial production that are (or feel themselves to be) at a comparative disadvantage in industrial production in relation to the world market. A customs union enables them to gratify the preference for industrial production through trade creation and trade diversion, to an extent that would not be possible through negotiation of non-discriminatory tariff reduction.

In contrast to preferential tariff reduction, however, a customs union involves 100 per cent preferential treatment of partners on an across-the-board basis. Instead of being able to pick and choose among commodities on which to give and demand preferences, a country must choose whether or not to participate in the customs union; and it will only choose to participate if there is a reasonable probability of a net gain, by comparison with *either* the situation in the absence of a customs union, *or* the situation in the presence of a union to which it does not belong. In either case, broadly speaking, a country will be motivated to join the union only if it judges that its industrial competitiveness or comparative advantage in industrial production is strong enough for its industrial production to increase within the union (or for any loss in aggregate industrial production to be compensated by increased efficiency). Conversely, the other members will be willing to have it join only if its membership does not threaten to increase its industrial production unduly at the expense of their own. Consequently, customs unions are most likely to be negotiable among countries with a similar degree of preference for industrial production, and with a similar degree of comparative advantage in industrial production,[30] or, as it is sometimes put, countries at a similar stage of economic development. This implication of the theory of protectionism advanced here is confirmed by the formation of the European Common Market, and by the actual and prospective formation of customs unions among groups of less developed countries, in both of which connections much has been made of the 'similar stage of economic development' argument.

A third and final problem concerns the internal arrangements of the customs union. Standard trade theory would suggest that these arrangements would seek to maximize efficiency of production within the union, regardless of where production was located. The preference for industrial production hypothesis, however, would imply that any customs union agreement would include provisions to insure that each member obtains a 'fair share' of industrial production, and particularly that the growth of production in the union does not concentrate in one or a few countries at the expense of the rest. Such provisions are written into the Treaty of Rome, in the arrangements for a Development Fund, and incorporated more generally in the Common Market through the recognition of an obligation to contribute to the development of southern Italy. They are even more explicit in the provisions of the Latin American Free Trade Area Treaty, which envisage the Treaty as applying mostly to the establishment of new industries, and are concerned with a fair allocation of the new industries among the participating countries.

V. CONCLUDING COMMENTS

This chapter has departed from the conventional assumptions of international trade theory and welfare economics, that welfare depends on private consumption of goods and services, in an attempt to construct a theory of protectionism, tariff bargaining, and customs union formation. In order to do so, it has posited a 'preference for industrial production,' involving the treatment of industrial production as a collective consumption good the quantity of which is governed by commercial policy. The intention has been to provide a logically coherent explanation of why commercial policy is conducted the way it is.

Any such attempt runs the risk of being misinterpreted as a justification of whatever countries have chosen to choose to do, and a demonstration that economics has nothing to say about what public policy should be. These are misinterpretations, because they fail to distinguish between two separate levels of analysis. At one level an economic decision unit is treated, as in this chapter, as an objective actor in the economic process, with certain preferences whose satisfaction it seeks to maximize, the assumption being that the actor rationally connects means with ends. At a different level of analysis, the analytical problem is precisely what the actor should do to maximize its satisfaction, the assumption being that the actor does not, or does not fully, understand the connections between means and ends. Thus one branch of economics is concerned with the consequences of the assumption that firms act rationally to maximize profits, while another branch is concerned with devising decision rules and operations on data that will yield the profit-maximizing decisions. In this chapter, problems at the second level of analysis have been deliberately concealed in the concept of 'a preference for industrial production,' in order to explore and rationalize the behaviour of governments. That preference, it will be recalled, was so defined as to comprise the effects of electoral ignorance and the influence of power groups on government policy. There is nothing in the analysis of this chapter to prevent an economist from asking whether industrial production yields the economic benefits believed to flow from it, from calculating the real product cost of protection and asking whether the benefits repay this cost, or from insisting that the consumer's interest in low-cost consumption, as contrasted with the producer's interest in high-priced production, deserves more representation in government policy-making than it usually receives.

APPENDIX A: THE LIMITS OF NON-DISCRIMINATORY RECIPROCAL TARIFF REDUCTION

This appendix develops a simple and somewhat artificial model to demonstrate the proposition stated in the text, that bilaterally negotiated reciprocal tariff reduction on a non-discriminatory basis may cease to be profitable before free trade is reached.

Assume that each country produces exports at constant cost, and import substitutes at increasing cost. Let each country's import demand function (imports being measured in dollar's worth at workd market prices) be $M_i(1 - m_i t_i)$, where M_i is the free-trade level of imports, m_i is the slope of the demand curve for imports, and t_i is the tariff rate (expressed as a proportion). The slope of the import demand curve is the absolute sum of the consumption demand and domestic supply curves; let x_i be the proportion of $m_i (0 < x_i \leq 1)$ composed of the domestic supply slope. Assume further that each country j receives a fixed share s_{ij} in country i's imports

$$0 < s_{ij} \leq 1, \quad \sum_{j \neq i} s_{ij} = 1,$$

this share being determined by some economic mechanism not investigated here. (In fact, these shares can be defined less restrictively, as applying only to the imports excluded by country i's tariff.) Finally, assume that each country attaches a constant social value v_i to a unit increase in industrial production achieved through an increase in exports or in production for the domestic market (by protection). The cost of protection, is, of course, approximately equal to $^1/_2 m_i t_i^2 M_i$.

The difference between the real income of the country under general protection and under general free trade is

$$R_i = -\,v_i \sum_{j \neq i} s_{ji}\, M_j m_j t_j + v_i x_i m_i t_i M_i - {}^1/_2 m_i\, t_i^2 M_i. \tag{1}$$

If each country takes the tariffs of the others as given, it will maximize its real income by setting its tariff rate at the level required by

$$\frac{\partial Ri}{\partial t_i} = m_i M_i (v_i x_i - t_i) = 0, \tag{2}$$

that is, it will establish the tariff rate $t_i = v_i x_i$. This is the tariff rate from which bilaterally negotiated tariff reductions are assumed to commerce.

Now consider reciprocal tariff reduction by countries i and j. Assume that the negotiation comprises a series of exchanges of small tariff reductions, symbolized by $T_i = -dt_i$ and $T_i = dt_j$. The effects on the respective real incomes of the two countries at each step will be

$$dR_i = v_i\, s_{ji} m_j M_j T_j - (v_i x_i - t_i) m_i M_i T_i, \tag{3}$$

$$dR_j = v_j\, s_{ij} m_i M_i T_i - (v_j x_j - t_j) T_j, \tag{4}$$

where t_i and t_j represent the tariff rates established at the termination of the previous step. Note that there must be some gain from non-discriminatory tariff reduction at the first step, because in each question the first term on the right-hand side is positive, while at the beginning of negotiations the second term on the right-hand side is zero [by maximization condition of eq. (2)].

The limits to which non-discriminatory reciprocal tariff reduction may go can be investigated by using equations (3) and (4) to define two 'boundary' loci of possible reciprocal tariff reductions, representing successive pairs of marginal tariff reductions that would leave one of the two countries no better off in terms of real income than it was initially. These loci, obtained by setting dR_i and dR_j, respectively, equal to zero are

$$\frac{T_i}{T_j} = \frac{v_i\, s_{ji}}{v_i\, X_i - t_i} \quad \frac{m_j M_j}{m_i M_i}, \tag{5}$$

$$\frac{T_i}{T_j} = \frac{v_j x_j - t_j}{v_j\, s_{ij}} \quad \frac{m_j M_j}{m_i M_i}. \tag{6}$$

Reciprocal tariff reductions on a non-discriminatory basis that will benefit both countries will be possible only so long as the value of T_i / T_j given by equation (5) exceeds the value given by equation (6); that is, so long as

$$\frac{v_i\, s_{ji}}{v_i\, x_i - t_i} > \frac{v_j x_j - t_j}{v_j s_{ij}}. \tag{7}$$

This condition must hold for the first step of tariff reductions from the initial level, since initially the denominator of the left-hand side and the numerator of the right-hand side are zero. Thereafter, however, the left-hand fraction falls and the right-hand fraction rises, as the tariff rates are reduced.

Will it be possible to reach free trade in the two countries by non-discriminatory reciprocal tariff-cutting? Substitution of $t_i = t_j = 0$ into equation (7) yields the necessary condition

$$\frac{s_{ji}\, s_{ij}}{x_i x_j} > 1. \tag{8}$$

This condition can be given an economic interpretation in several ways; the simplest approach is to express it in terms of conditions on the (geometric) average values of the parameters. Alternative statement of the condition can then be made as follows. Free trade on both sides is attainable through non-discriminatory reciprocal tariff reduction if

(a) the average share of a country in the expansion of the other's imports exceeds the average proportion of the increase in a country's imports resulting from tariff reduction by which its domestic production of import substitutes is reduced ($s_{ji} s_{ij} > x_i x_j$), *or*

(b) on the average an increase in a country's imports reduces its domestic production by less than it increases the other country's exports [$(x_j/s_{ji})(x_i/s_{ij}) < 1$].

Version (b) amounts to the requirement that reciprocal tariff reduction must increase total industrial production in the negotiating countries, as stated in n. 23. Note that this condition is incapable of fulfilment unless an expansion of imports involves some increase in total consumption, and does not merely replace domestic production (in the latter case, the condition reduces to $s_{ji} s_{ij} > 1$, which is by assumption impossible). In general terms, the condition implies that the possibility of reciprocal non-discriminatory tariff reduction proceeding to free trade will be greater, the larger the shares of the negotiating countries in each other's markets, and the more responsive their domestic demand and the less responsive their domestic supply of import substitutes to reduction in the landed price if imports.

Finally, the condition of equation (8) can be used to illustrate the proposition, presented in the text, that preferential arrangements may be more attractive than tariffs. By preferential arrangements, s_{ji} and s_{ij} can be made equal to or greater than unity, so that a free-trade area between the two countries would always be mutually beneficial. This conclusion, however, is limited to this particular model:

since exports are assumed to be in perfectly elastic supply, a country incurs no loss from trade diversion effected by preferential tariff reduction.

NOTES

1 *Journal of Political Economy*, Vol. LXVIII (August 1960) pp. 327–45.
2 In R. E. Caves, H. G. Johnson, and P. B. Kenen (eds.), *Trade, Growth and the Balance of Payments: Essays in Honor of Gottfried Haberler* (Chicago: Rand McNally Co., 1965).
3 J. E. Meade, *The Theory of International Economic Policy*, Vol. I: *The Balance of Payments* (London: Macmillan & Co., 1951).
4 The stimulus to develop this theory comes partly from my former colleague J. A. Knapp, of Manchester University, who has persistently posed the question why, if reduction of tariffs is economically beneficial, tariff negotiators always regard a tariff reduction as a concession that must be compensated by reciprocal tariff reductions by the other party to the bargain.
5 See Anthony J. Downs, 'An Economic Theory of Political Action in a Democracy,' *Journal of Political Economy*, Vol. LXV (April 1957) pp. 135–50 and his *An Economic Theory of Democracy* (New York: Harper & Bros., 1957); Gary S. Becker, *The Economics of Discrimination* (Chicago: University of Chicago Press, 1957); and Albert Breton, 'The Economics of Nationalism,' *Journal of Political Economy*, Vol. LXXII (August 1961) pp. 376–87.
From Downs I take the notion of government policy in a democracy as a rational response to the demands of the electorate; Becker's work contributed the notion (already present in my analysis of the scientific tariff) of conceptualizing 'irrational' behavior as a preference and measuring it by the marginal premium (discount) individuals would pay (give) to gratify it; Breton's work contributed the notion of conceptualizing certain kinds of government policies as providing a collective consumption good. I have used these building blocks in an earlier and more general paper prepared for the University of Chicago Committee for the Comparative Study of New Nations Seminar on Nationalism and Economic Policy in Developing Nations ('A Theoretical Model of Economic Nationalism in New and Developing States,' *Political Science Quarterly*, Vol. LXXX, No. 2 (June 1965) pp. 169–85.
6 The theory presented below is derived from the assumption of a 'preference for industrial production'; by extension, agricultural protectionism can be explained by an assumed 'preference for agricultural production.' Since industrial protectionism is a major common policy of less developed countries (which are predominantly agricultural in economic structure) and agricultural protectionism is a major common policy of advanced countries (which are predominantly industrial in economic structure), the two preferences could be synthesized in the concept of a 'preference for economic balance.' This concept was indeed suggested by R. A. Mundell, in discussion of an early draft of this article. Such a concept has the appeal of formal elegance and symmetry in explaining the commercial policies of countries at all stages of development. I have not pursued it, however, for two reasons: (1) policies of agricultural protection are implemented by different means than policies of industrial protectionism, and, more important, agriculture commodities are treated differently than industrial commodities under GATT; (2) advanced countries protect their industry or parts of it as well as their agriculture, and do bargain over reductions of tariffs on industrial goods in a manner explained by the theory presented here.
7 Downs (*op. cit.*) explains the dominance of producer over consumer interests in a democracy by the costs of acquiring information and taking action, which generally

exceed the potential benefits for the consumer, whose economic interests are diffuse, but not for the producer, whose interests are concentrated; the dominance of producer interests in political decisions is therefore a consequence of economic rationality.

8 According to a well known formula, the welfare cost of a small increase in the tariff rate, for a simple model ignoring cross-effects in production and consumption and input-output complications, may be written

$$-\frac{dW}{dt} = t\frac{dP}{dp} - t\frac{dC}{dp},$$

where t is the tariff rate, p the domestic price, P domestic output of the protected good, and C domestic consumption of it (quantities being measured in unit values at free-trade prices, so that $dp = dt$); the two terms on the right-hand side are, respectively, the marginal production and marginal consumption costs of protection (dC/dp being negative). The present analysis, however, is concerned with the welfare cost, not of an increase in the tariff rate, but of an increase in protected output. Division of the foregoing expression by dP/dp yield this welfare costs as

$$-\frac{dW}{dP} = t - t\left(\frac{dC/dp}{dP/dp}\right),$$

the second expression on the right-hand side being the marginal private consumption cost of protected industrial production. The ratio $[(dC/dp)/(dP/dp)]$ is a ratio of the price slopes of the demand and supply curves, referred to in the text as 'the relative price sensitivity of demand.' The marginal excess private cost of protected industrial production may also be expressed in terms of elasticities of supply and demand as

$$-\frac{dW}{dP} = t\left(1 + \frac{P}{C}\cdot\frac{\eta}{\epsilon}\right),$$

where η and ϵ are, respectively, the elasticities of consumption demand and domestic supply.

9 An important implication of the theory is that inputs not counted as part of 'industrial production' will not be subject to protection. This implication is confirmed empirically by the escalation of tariff rates by stage of production typical of national tariff structures. On the protective effects of such escalation see my 'The Theory of Tariff Structure with Special Reference to World Trade and Development,' in Harry G. Johnson and Peter B. Kenen, *Trade and Development* (Geneva: Etudes et Travaux de l'Institut Universitaire de Hautes Etudes Internationales, 1965).

10 Using the mathematical expression of n. 8, and the equality of the marginal degree of preference for industrial production v with its marginal private excess cost,

$$\frac{v}{t} = 1 - \left(\frac{dC/dp}{dP/dp}\right) = 1 + \frac{P}{C}\cdot\frac{\eta}{\epsilon}$$

If $-[(dC/dp)/(dP/dp)]$ is constant, v/t will be constant, and t will vary with v. If, on the other hand, η/ϵ is constant, v/t will decrease with P/C (which may be taken as an index of ability to compete with foreign producers). In both cases, differences in v due to differences in P/C must necessarily be accompanied by differences in t in the same direction. A decrease in t could accompany an increase in v only if the slope (elasticity) of the demand curve increased relatively to the slope (elasticity) of the supply curve as t (and P/C) increased.

11 For simplicity, industrial products are here taken as *numéraire*, so that all terms of trade effects appear as changes in the prices of non-industrial goods.

12 The orthodox optimum tariff formula for the two-community case may be derived as follows. Maximization of social welfare requires $U_m/U_x = dX/dM$, where X and M, respectively, represent export and import quantities and U_x and U_m the marginal utilities of X and M in domestic consumption. Here dX/dM is the marginal cost of additional imports, derived from the balance of trade equality $X = pM$ or $M = \pi X$ (where $p = 1/\pi$ is the price of M in terms of X) and the foreign supply of imports or demand for exports,

$$\frac{dX}{dM} = p\left(1 + \frac{1}{\epsilon}\right) = \frac{1}{\pi} \cdot \frac{\eta}{\eta - 1}$$

where ϵ is the elasticity of foreign supply of imports and η the corresponding elasticity of foreign demand for exports as functions, respectively of p and π. Welfare maximization requires the imposition of an import tariff such that

$$\frac{U_m}{U_x} = (1 + t)\, p = \frac{dX}{dM}, \text{ that is,}$$

$$t = \frac{1}{\epsilon} \quad \text{or} \quad t = \frac{1}{\eta - 1}$$

With a preference for industrial production, however, the loss of social utility from an additional unit of exports for the industrial exporter is not U_x and $U_x - vaU_x$, where v is the proportional marginal preference for industrial production and a is the proportion of the increase in exports effected by increased domestic industrial production; similarly for the industrial importer, the gain in utility from an additional unit of imports is not U_m but $U_m - vbU_m$, where v is defined as before and b is the proportion of the increase in imports effected by decreased domestic industrial production. Substitution of these expressions yields the results $t = 1/\epsilon - av\,(1 + 1/\epsilon)$ for the industrial exporter, and $t = 1(\eta - 1) + bv$ for the industrial importer.

13 The problem of many countries, which involves the possibility of preferential tariff reductions, is most conveniently dealt with in conjunction with differentiation of industrial production. It is difficult to deal with in the present model, since industrial exporting countries will have tariffs only if they possess monopoly – monopoly power, and this creates analytical complexities in a multicountry system.
The terminology of 'advanced' and 'less developed' employed in the text is, of course, misleading, since neither real product nor real income is necessarily higher for net industrial exporting than for net industrial importing nations; but the terminology does reflect a judgement that follows naturally from the preference for industrial production.

14 The adjustment of the tariff of one country to changes in the other, based on the objective of maximizing national welfare, is to be distinguished from 'tariff retaliation' in the pure sense, which implies that a country derives utility by reducing the welfare of the other country through increasing its tariffs. The latter means that one country's welfare is a function of the other's, and introduces considerations that are excluded at this point, though they will be introduced briefly later in the argument.

15 One country may possess sufficiently superior monopoly power to be better off when both follow optimum tariff policies than it would be under free trade; negotiation for reciprocal tariff reduction cannot bring such a country to practice free trade.

16 Recall that the exercise of this monopoly-monopsony power is assumed to have already been tempered by the preference for industrial production.

17 Both the theoretical conclusion and its application to the contemporary situation are strengthened if the less developed country of the analysis is assumed to derive positive disutility from its 'collective consumption' of the industrial production of the advanced country.

18 Another way of making this point is to say that the marginal cost of protected industrial production in this case includes an additional element not encountered in the previous year, namely, the loss of utility from collective consumption of industrial production due to the decrease in industrial exports induced by protection.

19 Outstanding examples are the adoption of free trade by Britain in the nineteenth century and her retreat into protectionism in the period after World War I, the espousal of freer trade by the United States and Canada in the period after World War II, and the growth of protectionism in both countries when they encountered difficulties in international industrial competition after 1957.

20 The reduction in a country's industrial production will be less than the increase in its industrial imports to the extent that its consumption switches from non-industrial products to industrial imports, and that contraction of protected industrial production increases industrial production in the non-protected sector. Each country will therefore have an incentive to offer the other concessions on items that are close substitutes for non-industrial products in consumption and for non-protected industrial products in production, rather than on items that are close substitutes in consumption for its other industrial products and in production for its non-industrial products.

21 At the margin, the marginal excess cost of protected industrial production is just equal to its marginal social utility; a small contraction of protected production occasions negligible loss, while an expansion of industrial exports yields a surplus of utility from collective consumption of industrial production.

22 The relative magnitudes of the reduction in domestic production and the increase in imports will depend on the elasticities of demand and domestic supply of the good in question and the extent to which demand shifts from, and production shifts to, non-industrial production; the share of the increase in demand for imports that goes to the partner country depends on the magnitude of its elasticity of supply of exports relative to those of other countries, and the magnitude of the increase in the partner's industrial production relative to the increase in its exports depends on the relative magnitudes of the elasticities of domestic demand and supply of the commodity in the partner country. In all cases the elasticities have to be weighed appropriately by ratios of quantities initially produced, consumed, or traded.

23 Suppose the value of the marginal utility of collective consumption of industrial production is a constant v, initially equal to the marginal excess cost of protected production e; and that for every unit reduction in protected industrial production through reduction of its own tariff the country receives an increase in its industrial exports equal to $1 - a > 0$, from the reduction in the partner country's tariff. Its net

gain is initially $e - av > 0$; but it gains from further reciprocal tariff reduction only so long as e does not fall to av.

A simple mathematical model designed for analysis of the limits of non-discriminatory reciprocal tariff reduction is presented in the Appendix. It is there shown that such tariff reduction can only reach free trade if it would increase industrial production in the two countries combined.

24 J. M. Fleming, 'On Making the Best of Balance of Payments Restrictions on Imports,' *Economic Journal*, Vol. LXI (March 1951) pp. 48–71, esp. 48–54. Fleming's problem is analytically both more interesting and more clear cut than the present one, since it explicitly comprehends discrimination among countries, and can use the equivalent of a simple 'bargaining' rule, that the trade of all countries must always be exactly balanced.

25 Though the argument is couched in terms of increased industrial production, it will be recalled from the preceding analysis that within limits a country could gain from reciprocal tariff reduction that reduced its aggregate industrial production, if the resulting increase in its real product exceeded the value of the corresponding loss of utility from collective consumption of industrial production.

26 Trade diversion will be relatively still more attractive if the discriminating countries attach positive disutility to the industrial production of the countries discriminated against.

27 Whether a country's real product rises or falls depends on the net outcome of the trade-creating and trade-diverting effects of the reciprocal tariff reductions, as the standard theory has demonstrated.

28 In the real world, preferences have frequently been exchanged between industrially advanced countries and their less developed colonies or close political allies; these cases can be fitted into the argument by postulating that the advanced country includes the less developed territory in its concept of 'domestic.' Preferences given unilaterally to an industrially advanced country by its colonial dependencies of course fit perfectly into the theory presented here, which offers another way of looking at the phenomena of economic imperialism.

29 A number of the propositions stated in this and the preceding three paragraphs have been arrived at independently by C. A. Cooper and B. F. Massell, 'Toward a General Theory of Customs Unions for Developing Countries,' *Journal of Political Economy*, Vol. 73, No. 5 (October 1965) pp. 461–76.

30 These prerequisites are suggested by consideration of the determinants of the impact of customs union on trade – the initial individual country tariff levels and the industrial structures of the countries – and also by the necessity of the members agreeing on a common tariff level.

12. Group Behavior and International Trade

C. P. Kindleberger

I

The primary tool of analysis in economics is the market. But Walker has expressed the opinion that an economics adequate for prediction and policy must include a theory of extra-market behavior.[1] Polanyi, further, has attempted to demonstrate that the emphasis on the market is likely to be misleading and that a rounded theory of social behavior would include economic drives as only one stand in a broad web of social motivation.[2] The present article is designed to suggest that, in certain situations in international trade, a useful tool of analysis may be found in a theory of group behavior at the national level. Unhappily, no such theory adequate for the task appears to have been developed. A few suggestions will be offered as to the types of variables with which such a theory should deal.

The method followed is to take the world decline in the price of wheat after 1870 and to indicate the responses to it in Great Britain, Germany, France, Italy, and Denmark. If a theory of market behavior were sufficient for prediction, it might be expected that the reduction in the price of wheat in Europe would lead to increased imports. Foreign sources of supply would be substituted for domestic. Resources engaged in the production of wheat would shift to less remunerative occupations. Some increase in wheat consumption would take place at the expense of other grains, to the extent that wheat would fall more in price than rye, oats, and barley would. Some of these changes did, in fact, occur, but the results were not uniformly of this character.

After the differences in response have been established, attention will be turned to a series of explanations dependent on nonmarket factors. None of these is completely satisfactory. What appears to be needed is a comprehensive theory of group behavior to deal with groups as large as nations – in particular, a theory which systematically makes allowances for variation in the relation among the subgroups which make up the larger entity.

I am conscious of the amateurish character of the economic history and sociology in what follows, and I am not inclined to apologize for this inevitable shortcoming. Interdisciplinary co-operation must begin with the utilization, however crude, of the products of other social sciences by practitioners in separate fields. I have greatly benefited from the assistance of experts in other fields;[3] but I have been obliged to restrict my use of their techniques, lest my special focus of interest be lost among a host of fine points.

II

The main facts concerning the world decline in the price of wheat after the American Civil War and its causes are generally understood and accepted. The rapid spread of the American rail network in the 1870's and 1880's made it possible to transport wheat to tidewater more cheaply and in far greater quantities than the canal system had been able to handle. A parallel development occurred in railroad construction from the Ukrainian wheat fields to Crimean ports. The technological shift from wooden to iron ships – another indirect effect of the Civil War – reduced trans-Atlantic freight rates and those to western Europe from the Crimea. The availability of demobilized manpower, untilled land, and wartime accumulations of money capital, coupled with the development of farm machinery for extensive cultivation, resulted in an expansion of the American supply, which passed the economies of production and distribution on to the consumer in Europe as cheaper wheat. In addition, the weather was favorable during the 1880's, and yields were high. The European peasant and landowner met increased competition in grain production from overseas.[4]

The difficulties of European wheat-growers were not solely caused by overseas competition. A series of bad seasons reduced yields and brought about a deterioration in quality. A Royal Commission of Inquiry, sitting from 1879 to 1882, reached the conclusion that the loss of British farm income was due primarily to untoward weather and only secondarily to foreign competition. The effects of the two causes were not unconnected. In a closed economy a short crop is at least partially compensated for, so far as farm income is concerned, by an increase in price. In an international, bi-hemispheric economy, an increase in the local price produced by a series of short crops is likely to be forestalled by imports from overseas.[5]

The view exists, however, that what hurt European agriculture was not overseas competition or any other factor peculiar to agriculture but over-all depression, lasting from 1873 to 1896. It is recognized that the price of wheat fell somewhat more than prices in general, and this is ascribed to the growth of production in the United States. This relative decline, given by one writer as only 10 per cent, is regarded as much less significant for the agricultural depression than was the general fall in prices.[6] The reasoning, however, is not persuasive in the light of price developments on, say, the Copenhagen market, which was unaffected by tariffs. Between 1873 and 1896 wheat fell in price by 53 per cent and rye by 48 per cent, as compared with a decline of 36 per cent in the *Statist's* index of wholesale prices. And after 1873 American wheat appeared in European markets which had never before known it, including some cities, such as Trieste, which were known as export centers for European supplies.[7]

The combination of weather and overseas competition, then, produced potential economic distress for the farming community in the form of short crops and low prices. The remainder of this analysis, for convenience, treats this as a question solely of prices. In this connection, some importance attaches to the question of timing. The price of wheat fell from $1.70 to $0.66 a bushel in England from 1873 to 1894, and the sharpest decline was probably that from $1.31 in 1882 to $0.90 in 1886.[8] Action to meet the collapse in the price of wheat was taken, if at all, primarily in response to this pressure. But the nature of the response and the timing differed from country to country.

III

No action was taken in Britain. The issue had already been settled some years before, in 1846, with the repeal of the Corn Laws. The decline in the world price of wheat produced an improvement in the terms of trade for the rising industrial classes and a basis for lowering, or withholding increases in, the wages of the industrial labor force. The latter, in turn, received a new batch of recruits in the form of agricultural workers displaced from the farm by the unprofitability of wheat growing.

The repeal of the Corn Laws in 1846, fourteen years after the political settlement between the landed gentry and industry and commerce in the Reform Bill, produced no immediate economic effect. The period of high farming in Britain continued uninterrupted. British agriculture in general was efficient and profitable from 1837, when the long period of distress after the Napoleonic Wars came to an end, until 1873. The American Civil War and the Crimean War had helped to postpone the effects of cheap wheat imports, but even in the 1850's there had been no significant effects of the repeal. Land under the plow in Britain reached a peak in 1872 never again attained, even in World War II.[9]

The bad summers from 1875 to 1879, the rinderpest attack of 1877, and the widespread loss of sheep to liver rot in 1879 may have convinced the farmers that their difficulties were due to the vindictiveness of nature rather than to a change in their position in the community. Landowners remained the richest class in the country for several years after the disaster of 1879. By 1886 their relative position had begun to slip.[10] No action was taken to halt the decline in farm prices or to assist the farming community.[11] The dominant group in the society – the rising industrial class – was content to have cheaper food and cheaper labor. Rents fell, young men left the farm for the town, land planted to crops shrank rapidly. The response to the decline in the world price of wheat was to complete the liquidation of agriculture as the most powerful economic group in Britain.

IV

In Germany, France, and Italy the farmer was protected by the imposition of tariffs. In Germany the tariff on grain was enacted first in 1879, after fourteen years of free trade. Duties under this law were almost purely nominal, but rates were sharply raised in 1885 and again in 1887. The timing of tariff enactments in France and Italy was broadly similar, with the exception of the first step and with a significant difference in so far as Italy was concerned. Major increases in grain tariffs took place in Germany and France in 1885 and 1887. In Italy the first step was delayed until 1887, though the second followed more quickly in 1888.

The German situation is more properly analyzed in terms of the tariff on rye, which in the period to 1890 was identical with that on wheat. Gerschenkron makes clear that Bismarck's alliance ran not between industry and agriculture, as such, but between two powerful components of each, iron and rye.[12] Within industry the interests of the expanding steel industry were opposed to those of the fabricators of metal, who wanted cheap supplies. In this capital-intensive industry, moreover, the level of wages was relatively unimportant. In agriculture the large farms of the Junkers in eastern Germany produced rye as a cash crop for shipment to western Germany and for export. Their interest in high prices should have been opposed by the peasants of northern and western Germany, who bought grain for animal feed and had an interest in low prices. Despite this interest, however, the peasants of Germany politically followed the leadership of the landed nobility and supported tariffs on grain. Gerschenkron claims that they were deluged with propaganda and deluded by the concurrent imposition of tariffs on pigs and other animals, which, however, afforded a much lower level of protection.[13] Even within the ranks of labor there were groups which appeared not to oppose the tariffs.

The enactment of the tariff on wheat in France required the repeal of the Le Chapelier Law of 1791 which forbade associations based upon economic interest. A modification of this law in 1865 had made it possible to establish associations for the improvement of agricultural techniques. Its final repeal in 1884 paved the way for agricultural syndicates, which began by acting as producer cooperatives in the buying of fertilizer and agricultural machinery and in establishing credit unions. Very shortly these groups began to agitate for higher tariffs. The owners of large farms, marketing a larger proportion of their crop for cash than did the owners of small farms, had a greater interest in the price of wheat; but all farmers were affected by it. In only 10 of 87 departments of France did grain occupy less than half the tillable land in 1882, and only in one, Corsica, did the percentage fall below 40.[14] There is some evidence that the leadership in the political drive for protection was taken by the cattle interests of Normandy and Brittany. But all parts of the country, from the northern wheat districts to the southern wine areas (suffering from the depredations of *Phylloxera*), were united in their zeal to raise the relative level of French farm prices.

The success of efforts to obtain protection for agriculture was aided by a compromise with industrial interests. Agriculture and industry had not always readily adjusted their conflicts of interest. In the time of Napoleon, French commercial policy had favored industrial exports at the same time that it forbade the export of wheat or of agricultural products used by industry. Agricultural interests thereafter tried on several occasions to secure protection on such industrial supplies as hides, wool, oil seeds, and silk. In 1881 the farm interests hoped that commerce and industry would agree to a tariff of 10 per cent on foodstuffs in exchange for the concession of freedom to import agricultural raw materials. The compromise of 5 per cent, which did not apply to wheat, produced little satisfaction. After the final repeal of the Le Chapelier Law in 1884 and more effective organization, the markedly higher rates on grain and animals of 1885 and 1887 were won with the assistance of threats of retaliation against industry.

Italian tariff policy in the 1870's and 1880's favored industry over agriculture. In 1864 wheat had been subjected to a duty of $^1/_2$ lira per quintal to raise revenue. This was increased to $^3/_4$ lira in 1866 to meet the costs of the war. The tariff revision of 1878, undertaken primarily to regularize the duties of the newly formed kingdom, increased the rate on wheat to 1.40 lire per quintal. These rates were low. In other directions there was no protection for agriculture. Imports of rice and barley, for example, were free of duty. Yet industry enjoyed a considerable measure of protection.

The question of taxes on food was widely discussed. An excise tax of 2 lire per quintal of wheat had been imposed internally in 1869 to improve governmental finances; and although vigorously opposed by urban and industrial interests, it continued in effect for fourteen years. The experience with this tax appears to have given the Italian government pause when increasing imports of grain from overseas, encouraged by the appreciation of the lire, began in 1884. Three years later, in 1887, the tariff was raised to 3 lire, a full two years after similar action was taken in France and Germany. The rate was increased again to 5 lire in 1888, after the tariff war with France led to the loss of the French market for the wines of southern Italy, to compound the distress of the region.[15] But by this time it was too late. The Italian peasant had already begun to emigrate. Gross emigration across the Atlantic, primarily from agricultural regions of Italy, increased from an average age of 25,000 annually in the period 1876–80 to 73,000 in 1885, 83,00 in 1886, 130,000 in 1887, and 205,000 in 1888.[16] The 1888 figure, which is presumed to reflect the period of nominal tariff rates before April, 1887, with a time lag, was to remain the peak for thirteen years. Recovery of wheat prices under the impact of the tariffs and other factors slowed down the pace of emigration somewhat. The flow, once started, however, became cumulative and self-perpetuating. Early emigrants encouraged first their families and then their relatives and neighbors to follow.

The response of Germany, France, and Italy to the decline in the world price of wheat was to impose tariffs in an attempt to maintain the relative price of wheat and to protect grain producers. In Germany the movement was led by Bismarck as a step toward a new political alignment of Junkers and steelmakers, but it had the consent of many of those whose interests were adversely affected. In France agriculture, more or less as a whole, negotiated through the tariff in reaching a settlement with industry. The reluctance of Italian industry to agree to increased tariffs and the delay in imposing them meant that the Italian response to the decline in prices was to quit Europe.[17]

V

Like Britain, the Netherlands, and Belgium, Denmark did not impose a tariff on wheat. Instead, it gave up the attempt to compete in the world export market for wheat and became a wheat importer. This shift was incidental, however, to a revolution in Danish agriculture, which was converted from the growing of grain to animal husbandry. Denmark was assisted in responding thus by its proximity to the rapidly industrializing markets of England and Germany, with their expanding national incomes, and by the high income elasticity of demand for butter and bacon. Given the demand, however, there are certain remarkable features about the response of supply which merit investigation. Of particular importance are the middle-sized farm, which predominated in Danish agriculture, the agricultural school system, and the co-operative movement. The second of these, at least, and perhaps the whole response to the decline in wheat prices was deeply affected by the defeat of Denmark by Germany in 1864 and the loss of the province of Schleswig.

Of all the countries of Europe, only in Denmark has the size of the productive unit been stabilized at the medium-sized farm – around fifty acres.[18] In other countries, over considerable periods of time, farm size has been increasing or decreasing. Periodic reversals occur under the influence of such discontinuous events as land reform – primarily the distribution of church or noble lands and parcellation of peasant strips (or inclosures) when these became too many and too narrow to work (or extensive farming became more profitable than intensive). Aside from these turning points, however, farm size appears to have a tendency to increase, as in Hungary, East Prussia, and England up to World War I, or to decrease, as in France, Switzerland, and western Germany. In some countries, like Italy and Poland, the two processes take place side by side. Land purchases by the wealthy, primogeniture, high income taxes, poaching laws, veneration of blood sports in the culture, etc., tend to increase farm size. Equal inheritance and rapid population growth tend to reduce the size of the farm unit.[19]

In Denmark a variety of factors appears to have established and maintained the middle-sized farm. The principle of equal inheritance was offset by small family size, by a frontier of the sea to which extra sons could escape, and by easy credit, enabling farmer brothers to buy out their share of the patrimony. High land taxes made the maintenance of unproductive estates expensive. But the state intervened from an early date and continuously (1682, 1725, 1769, 1819) to prevent the landed aristocracy from adding peasant land to their holdings and to prevent undue subdivision as well. A policy of dividing large holdings into small, but not minuscule, units prevailed for several centuries and was reaffirmed in legislation providing for small holdings in 1899 and 1909. The institution of the middle-sized farm, which happens to be inefficient for grain production but is well suited to certain types of animal output, goes deep into Danish agricultural life.

The Folk School, or agricultural high school, was originated in 1844 by a remarkable man, Bishop N. F. S. Grundtvig, for the purpose of educating the rural population not in scientific agriculture but in "the Danish language and history and . . . its constitution and economic life." Classes are held in the five winter months for men and for three months in the summer for women, normally in some other part of the country than that in which the student lives. The schools attempt to provide the agricultural segment of the population with a unity of background and an awareness of the life of the urban population of the country.

The first Folk School was founded in Schleswig. After the loss of the province to Germany, this school was moved to Danish territory. Thereafter the movement spread rapidly.[20] By 1870, before the collapse of wheat prices, there were sixty or seventy in the country.

The co-operative movements in Sweden and Denmark have been widely studied. For present purposes, therefore, it is sufficient to make a limited series of points. To sell butter in international trade required bringing the "peasant" butter of uneven taste and texture up to "manor" quality. This meant a standardized product. After the invention of the cream separator, the manufacture of butter could take place on a large scale, even though the labor-intensive production of milk still required the medium-sized farm. Economies of scale in marketing were available not only in butter but in eggs and bacon as well. In this situation the spread of the producers' cooperative movement in Danish agriculture was rapid after the establishment of the first co-operative dairy in Jutland in 1882.[21]

Denmark's response to the decline in world wheat prices, then, was to revolutionize her agriculture and to change from an exporter of grains to an importer. It may be observed that the acreage devoted to cereal production in Denmark increased rather than declined after animal industry had developed.

VI

These differences in European responses to the decline in the world price of wheat in the 1870's and 1880's may be summarized as follows: In Britain agriculture was permitted to be liquidated. In Germany large-scale agriculture sought and obtained protection for itself. In France, where the demography, pattern of resources, and small scale of industrial enterprise favored farming, agriculture as a whole successfully defended its position with tariffs. In Italy the response was to emigrate. In Denmark grain production was converted to animal husbandry. What factors outside the market account for these national differences? A number of attempts have been made to explain at least some of these various responses. The present section undertakes to review and comment upon these efforts.

The most familiar contrast, perhaps, is between the free-trade ideas developed in Britain by Smith, Ricardo, and Mill and the theory of national economy propounded in Germany, especially by Friederich List. A variant of the List doctrine can be found in the "nationalist economics" of Paul-Louis Cauwès in France,[22] although it is difficult to make the case that Cauwès' ideas were more than an aberration in an intellectual atmosphere which was much more sympathetic to the doctrines of the Manchester School. The place of Smith and List in Denmark appears to have been taken by Bishop Grundtvig, whose métier was poetry and national mysticism rather than economics; and no particular figure rationalized the action taken in Italy. It might be fair to say that the economists of Britain and the national economists of Germany provided the rationale for the action taken rather than its impetus.[23] And the relative unimportance of this function may be indicated by the action of France and Italy, taken in the absence of any distinctive rationale.

In its vulgar version the foregoing explanation is reduced to the single word "nationalism". Britain adhered to the international system; Germany and France were nationalistic in their responses. But this reasoning has evident weaknesses.

Italy's solution was essentially international or one possible only in an international world, although the attempt was made to apply the "nationalist" solution of tariffs. It could be said that the Italian solution was more international than the British, where the displaced agricultural workers shifted into industry within their own country. The international solution, that is, may involve a shift in international trade or an international movement in factors. The explanation breaks down, further, on the side of nationalism. Leaving aside for the moment the subtle differences between the French and the German behavior, the Danish solution, like the French and the German, was a highly nationalistic one, taken without tariffs, to be sure, but in an atmosphere of nationalist emotion. Nationalism and internationalism in this context are compound variables of great complexity. They require, rather than furnish, explanation.

A more elaborate analysis, which fits the present case to a degree, though it makes no mention of it, is that developed by the Danish economist, Carl Major Wright, in his *Economic Adaptation to a Changing World Market*.[24] Wright observes that a country can respond to an adverse change in world market conditions by intervention to correct the world situation, by isolation from it, or by adaptation to it. His book contains a message for small countries like his own. These, he believes, are too weak to intervene in the world market and will not be allowed by the great powers to isolate themselves from it. In consequence, they have to adapt themselves to it. Toward this end he advocates increasing mobility of factors and competition among producers.

The contrast among intervention, isolation, and adaptation is suggestive as far as it goes, but it fails to canvass the alternatives fully or to explain the factors affecting choice among them. France and Germany isolated themselves from the world market, to the extent of the tariff. No country intervened to raise the world price of wheat, though this has been undertaken through international cooperation in the present century. England, Italy, and Denmark all adapted to the change, but in a variety of ways. Since a series of alternative adaptations was available and since adaptation was undertaken by large countries as well as by small, Wright's analysis fails to explain the differences in behavior which did occur. His emphasis on the necessity of small countries to adapt, however, suggests that larger countries are unable to adapt in the same way that is open to small countries. In Britain, for example, some substitution of cattle for sheep occurred, and over a longer period animal husbandry expanded to fill part of the gap left by a decline in croplands.[25] But, on the whole, Britain was content to import its wheat and its high-value protein foods as well. British agriculture lacked the energy, the resources, and the ability to devise the institutions which would have been necessary for large-scale conversion from arable cropping to animal husbandry.

Several Continental writers have provided an illuminating framework of analysis against which to contrast the behavior of Italy (and southeastern Europe from Hungary to the Volga) with that of the other countries. In *Les deux Europes*,[26] for example, F. Delaisi distinguishes between Europe A, lying within a circle drawn through Stockholm, Vienna, Barcelona, Bilbao, and Glasgow, and Europe B, outside the circle. Europe A includes northern Italy, upper Austria, and Bohemia and Moravia but leaves out Ireland, northern Scotland, and most of

Spain. In Europe A industrialization was possible because of the rise of the bourgeois and their insistence on the spread of education; even in agriculture there was established a basis for rural democracy as peasants acquired land. In Europe B, however, constitutions and parliaments had no roots, illiteracy prevailed, and bourgeois class was small and timid, working with the aristocracy against the peasant and urban laborer rather than challenging the power of the feudal nobility.

When technological advance made industrialization possible, Europe A adopted it; Europe B, consisting particularly of Italy, Austria-Hungary, Spain, Portugal, and Finland, as far as Delaisi's statistics went, but including also Russia, Yugoslavia, and Greece. For the countries covered by Delaisi, emigration overseas in the decade 1881–90 amounted to 180,000 annually. In successive decades the annual average climbed to 265,000, 629,000, and 907,000 by 1901–13.[27] In Europe A, on the other hand, emigration to overseas areas declined, after hitting new peaks in 1881–85. This was because of the opportunities afforded by the expansion in industry.

But this explanation by no means covers the situation in its entirety. Britain was much further along in the urbanization process than was Germany or France. This may help to a degree to explain why industry was ready to permit the liquidation of agriculture and why emigrants from agriculture found their way into cities rather than abroad. After industrialization has started, however, and has reached a point where the process is self-generating and cumulative, the rate of growth should be more important than the existing level of industry. And this pace after 1870 was faster in Germany than in Britain. Nor was industrialization meaningless in France: "While France accepted the new techniques and institutions of industry, and even played a significant role in developing them, she did not permit agriculture to be eclipsed, or to suffer revolutionary change."[28]

As between Italy and Denmark, the quality of agriculture was evidently more important than the proportions of population engaged in rural pursuits (which were of the same order of magnitude after adjustment for definitions of urban life). Delaisi's division of Europe into two and his discussion of the extent to which the collapsing feudal structure was replaced by modern industrial and national institutions are interesting. The fact of industrialization and the explanation of its concentration in northwestern Europe, however, fail to account for the differences among the responses of the several countries to the decline in the price of wheat.[28a]

VII

None of the foregoing explanations completely accounts for the differences in response to the market; and perhaps the differences should be approached from the standpoint of a theory of group behavior. To be adequate, such a theory must include not only criteria for differentiating the responses of national groups as a unit but also a system of analysis for interrelations among the subgroups within the larger unit. The theory of group behavior appears not to have coped adequately with this sort of question. In the main, social psychologists, sociologists, anthropologists, etc., have concentrated their attention on the relation of the individual to the group, to the relative neglect of the structure of the very large group (the nation) and of functional groups within it. [29] Where intergroup relations have attracted attention, it has been focused on the problems posed by cultural minorities and the relations between groups differentiated by age, sex, etc., rather than on large functional groups. Lacking a foundation in scientific literature, the following notions on group behavior are general and tentative.

A group must exist in space and time. To be effective, a group must have a system of communications and a set of common values. The existence of the national group in *space* hardly merits discussion. It is an elementary principle of the geography that mountain ridges make the best national boundaries – though they are disliked by the military interests charged with protecting the group – since they are the national barriers of language, culture, and commerce. Rivers provide a system of intercommunication rather than a barrier to it, and a country lying in a great plain, like Poland, has uncertain limits. Water in larger amounts is helpful in demarcating the national space. The existence of Britons as a homogeneous group has been assisted by their insular position, while subgroups are demarcated by highlands. Changes in the national space have an important reaction on national cohesion. The Danish "groupiness" or group consciousness was enhanced by the loss of Schleswig; the French by that of Alsace-Lorraine. Italy and Germany, at the same time, gained group solidarity from unification in space.

The existence of a group in *time* is connected with its set of *values*. This must be sufficiently attractive or forceful in the spiritual or emotional life of the group for its members to express their loyalty to the group by remaining a part of it through time and bringing their children up as members. The existence of the group in time suggests a difference between material things and social institutions. Matter can wear out evenly over time; when a functional group recognizes that it is doomed to extinction, however, it is difficult to let it decline slowly at the normal rate of depreciation by refusal to maintain it. When faith in the continuity of the organization or group is lost, the group is likely to disintegrate.

The importance of *communication* to the group is increasingly emphasized by social psychologists working with small functional groups, such as the personnel of factories, unions, etc. It is equally important in larger groups. Switzerland, where four languages are spoken, is cited as an illustration of its unimportance in certain situations. In this case space and a powerful set of values are sufficient to hold the group together. The subgroup of agriculture is typically weaker in cohesion than urban groups because of its dispersal in space and the resultant difficulty of communication among its members. The Folk Schools in Denmark and the formation of agricultural syndicates in France were requirements for the maintenance of the agricultural group in the face of the threat from reduced wheat prices.

An existence in space and a system of communication are not enough to constitute a functional group. The parts of the group must share a sense of identification and emotional involvement and a feeling of participation and purpose before the separate subgroups can be considered to make up a group. This sense of unity and purpose may be enhanced by the existence of an antithetical "out-group." If the sense is insufficiently developed to begin with, however, the development of an "out-group" may lead to the disintegration of the "in-group."

The major contrast lies between Denmark and Italy. In the former, national feeling was intense, as a result of territorial loss, and social cohesion was high. The rural population felt itself a unit and identified itself with the larger national unit. In Italy, despite the recent unification of 1871, the peasant's sense of belonging to the national group was feeble. A blow to his means of livelihood led to the disintegration of the national group, as far as he was concerned. He withdrew – the type of reaction which the classical economists thought was difficult because of cultural barriers and which, indeed, is today barred by the xenophobia of other national groups. Similar responses took place in the Balkans, the Iberian Peninsula, and through the rest of the feudalistic Europe.

The weakness of the national group in Europe B, to use Delaisi's designation, was due to the failure of national unity to replace the disintegrated feudal group structure. National groups lacked inter-communication and common values. Illiteracy, for example, ran from 10 per cent in the Po Valley in Italy to 30 per cent in Florence and Rome, 50 per cent in Naples, and 70 per cent in Calabria.[30] No new emotional attachment replaced the feudal ties which had bound the peasant to the latifundium. Group cohesion was too weak to meet the challenge, and the group, under pressure, collapsed.

The importance of the out-group to the cohesion and efficiency of the national group is illustrated effectively by the role played by German aggression and the loss of Schleswig in the Danish response to the decline in wheat prices. Other examples are not lacking in economic history. The French payment of the five-billion-mark indemnity in 1871 was an act of national dedication – and even immolation. To generalize from this experience as to the behavior of exports, imports, prices, and the banking system in similar situations where the group stimulus is absent is a familiar practice of economists,[31] but it is highly questionable.

VIII

The contrasting behavior of Britain, Germany, and France requires an understanding of more than the over-all degree of group cohesion at the national level. Attention must be given to the relations among the separate subgroups. This, to be sure, has a bearing on the over-all cohesiveness of the nation: a country in which the subgroups are not sharply differentiated and where a degree of social mobility between them exists is likely to have greater cohesion. For the moment, however, out attention is restricted to the relations among the economic subgroups.[32]

E. R. Walker asks, "When do men accept the verdict of the market, and when do they attempt to alter it?" A parallel question can be put for group behavior: When does an ascendant subgroup liquidate another subgroup within the large group, and when does it make adjustment with it? Under what circumstances do relationships among subgroups tend to stay in continuous equilibrium, and when do divergences of interest lead in cumulative fashion (as Marx predicted) to schism and clash? Why did industry allow the liquidation of agriculture in Britain, but not in Germany or France? The question appears not to be a simple one of relative strengths or even of more complex strategies of coalition, such as those suggested in *The Theory of Games*. There was no reason for the German steel manufacturer to accept coalition with an essentially backward[34] group of agriculturists or of French industry to make concessions to the pre-scientific peasant. The answer may be found in areas outside the normal province of the economic theorist or the economic historian. The decisive factors do not appear to lie in the field of economics at all but in that of sociology.

One clue to the intergroup behavior may be found in the notion that not all group relations are competitive. Bateson, the anthropologist, has listed a series of stable interdependent subgroup relationships, which, to be sure, primarily apply to subgroups based on age and sex. These include bipolar relations, such as spectator-exhibitionist, dominance-submission, succoring-dependence, aggression-passivity, and the like, but may extend to more complex arrangements. Among the latter, Bateson distinguishes what he calls the "ternary relationship," which contains serial elements but includes face-to-face contact between the first and third elements. The function of the middle member in his illustrations – parent-nurse-child and officer-n.c.o.-enlisted man – is to discipline the third member in the forms of behavior which he should adopt toward the first.[35] The relations of the middle class to the wealthy and to the working classes may partake of this character in some political and social respects.[36]

This clue, by no means unambiguous, may assist in explaining what took place in Germany. Gerschenkron expresses the view that the Junkers deceived the peasants of western Germany, whose interest lay in cheaper grain prices, by provision for a tariff on animals and by other means. The reaction, however, may contain elements of submission of the peasant groups before the will of the Junker with higher status. Residual traces of the feudal relationship existed; probably more important were the battles won for the glory of the national group in 1864, 1866, and 1870. Part of labor and even the steel barons were content to maintain the economic position of the Junkers, in the face of opportunity to liquidate them, because of the element of status which in the former case outweighed class interest. The leadership and dominance exhibited by the Junker class probably explain the major part of its success in maintaining its position through the Caprivi tariff, World War I, the inflation, and the Nazi regime.

Another clue may lie in that most complex conception, the basic personality type of a culture or subculture. This notion, developed by the social psychologist with the help of anthropological data, denies that human nature is a constant in time or space but holds that the basic personality type of a culture will condition responses to external stimuli and, in turn, be altered by them. Of particular importance, it is held, is the way in which the society rears its children.[37]

This matter is far too complex and elusive to pursue here beyond the rough generalization that the basic personality type differs among England, France, and Germany, in putting primary emphasis in the culture, below the level of the national group, on, respectively, the individual, the family, and the class. If this be accepted, it may assist in explaining why Britain was willing to liquidate agriculture, while France and Germany were not.

Economic and political liberalism, born in Britain, required social mobility to give importance to the individual at the level next below the national group. Mobility in space was provided for Britain, as for Scandinavia and the Netherlands, by the sea, which served as a frontier.[38] At home, despite the class structure, social mobility upward derived from the willingness of the aristocracy to admit successful commercial and industrial interests to the ownership of land and their sons to the public schools. Downward mobility was provided by primorgeniture, which drew off the increase in the aristocracy into the middle class. Whatever the facts, the concept of class as a functional subgroup was not recognized in the culture. A blow to a broad economic interest was regarded as affecting not a class but a loose aggregation of individuals.[39] This may account for the passivity of the nation in watching unmoved the liquidation of agriculture in the thirty years after 1879.[40]

The opposition of industry and agriculture in France was more apparent than real; both were concerned not with economic interest as such but with economic interest in a context of the dominant social institution of the family. This has been studied in industry, where the conclusion has been reached that the size of firm which could be kept in the family from generation to generation limited the growth of industry.[41] The unwillingness to the French to emigrate is further evidence. And the continuity of the French farm in the family group from generation to generation is a commonplace.

In Germany the major subgroup, at least at the extremes, was the class. To the extent that the nobility was a farming group in occupation, group solidarity and economic interest were unified in the Junker portion of agriculture, while they were opposed among the peasants. Such conflict of group and economic interest is not, however, unusual: Walker has expressed surprise that the farmers of Australia support a program of land settlement contrary to their economic interest.[42] But these farmers gained more through the growth in numbers of their group than they lost through the increase of supply. The question was one of class and, within the total class structure, of dominance.

IX

The Danish response to the decline in the world price of wheat was by far the most satisfactory, whether in social and economic terms or in economic terms alone. It raised the level of real income for the producer group at the same time that it preserved the gain of cheaper bread for the consumer. Social upheaval was avoided. Was the whole episode an accident? Was this sort of solution possible for the other countries? To what extent is it possible to capitalize disaster in this fashion on a general scale?

The mind of the economist is likely to try to find a parallel in certain situations which occur when wage increases lead to expansion rather than to contraction of output because they provide the incentive to a recombination of factors in a more efficient fashion. The classic example is the elimination of the sweatshop through the efforts of union leaders, which increased incomes for both laborers and enterprisers and also reduced the cost of clothing. This was brought about by requiring firms in the garment industry to employ their newly expensive labor efficiently. The market opportunity for combining capital and labor in more efficient fashion had existed before the success of the union drive. Until the system was pushed off dead center, however, the path of least resistance was resistance to the demands of the union.

The parallel is not exact. A beginning of dairying to replace grain cultivation had been made in the 1860's before the decline in the price of wheat, primarily, however, on large estates.[43] The motive was only partly economic. In part it was observed that the soil was being impoverished by grain crops. There was still another difference. Although a market opportunity offered by the relative prices of grain and butter already existed, it was considerably increased by the decline in the price of wheat in the 1870's and 1880's and the rise in the demand for butter in the growing urban centers of England. A real impetus to the conversion came from the price decline. Particularly remarkable was the capacity of Danish economy, or polity, to develop the institutions which were necessary to complete the conversion on a large scale to take maximum advantage of the economic opportunity.

It may be contended that there was a marked degree of accident in the existence of the middle-sized farm, which was inefficient for wheat, and in the development of the agricultural high school, in response to the loss of Schleswig. The explanation for the prevalence of the middle-sized farm would appear to lie deep in the Danish basic personality type, which emphasizes stability rather than growth.[44] The development of the Folk School was perhaps partly an accident, but the Danish peasant had always shown a communicating tendency,[45] and this fact may be more important than the particular form of institution devised at the particular time.

The development of the co-operative in response to a technological need raises more fundamental problems. What factors govern the capacity of a society to develop institutions required to enable it to take advantage of economic, political, and social opportunities? Are these adaptations always accidental? Under certain conditions, are they made automatically; or can they be contrived through direction after conscious decision?

Most commentators on the co-operative believe that this development was the product of the prevalence of the freehold in Danish land tenure, together with the high degree of education in Danish farmers. "Tenant farmers will not co-operate because, co-operative accounts being open to inspection, they fear their landlords might raise the rents if it were found that they were prospering."[46] But the emphasis given to the form of land tenure goes deeper than this. The point is that co-operation in Denmark flourished, because of the social cohesion which enabled the farmers to create the necessary institutions, when the occasion demanded economies of scale in marketing along with labor-intensive production. The prevalence of freeholds bespeaks equality of status, which makes communication freer in all directions. Education increases the quantity and quality of communication. Together with a high degree of communication, a closely held set of values, and internal social mobility – all of which are interrelated – Denmark had social cohesion. It was this factor which enabled her to create institutions needed to take advantage of an economic opportunity. In the absence of the economic opportunity, however, the institutions would not have been devised.

In general, then, the suggestion is offered that the flexibility in a society in devising institutions to accomplish its purposes under changing conditions is a function of its social cohesion which, in turn, depends upon its internal social mobility, system of communications, and set of values. If social cohesion is high, it may be possible to find a response to external change which will bring about a new identification of the interests of the subgroups with those of the total group at an improved level of satisfaction for all. If the system of communication is sufficiently effective, moreover, it may be impossible to isolate the decision-making process so that the response of the society appears to be automatic.

X

What I have said can be reduced to some fairly elementary propositions. The response that will be made to an economic stimulus in international trade cannot always be predicted from the nature and extent of the stimulus. It may require a knowledge of the group situation within the separate countries affected. The response may be the disintegration of the group, leading to emigration if that is possible, or, if no such outlet is available, to pathological political behavior. The effect, on the other hand, may range from the liquidation of a particular subgroup in the society, for the benefit of others, as in Britain; through the protection of the affected group at the general expense, as in France and Germany; to an inspired act of readjustment undertaken by the group as a whole. Which of these actions will be taken lies deep in the structure of the society. For accurate prediction and policy-formation, an adequate theory of the behavior of large groups and their components is needed as an adjunct to the analytical tools of the market.

NOTES

1 Ronald Walker, *From Economic Theory to Policy* (Chicago: University of Chicago Press, 1943), *passim.*

2 K. Polanyi, *The Great Transportation* (New York: Rinehart, 1944), *passim.*

3 Especially helpful have been Duncan Ballantine, John Blum, K. W. Deutsch, A. Gerschenkron, Bert F. Hoselitz, G. K. Krulee, E. E. Morison, W. W. Rostow, and J. E. Sawyer.

4 See E. G. Nourse, *American Agriculture and the European Market* (New York: McGraw-Hill Book Co., 1924), Appendix A. An earlier and entirely orthodox account is furnished by Thorstein B. Veblen in "The Price of Wheat since 1867," *Journal of Political Economy*, I (December, 1892), 70–103.

5 See Lord Ernle, *English Farming, Past and Present* (5th ed.; New York: Longmans, Green & Co., 1936), pp. 379–81; and R. C. K. Ensor, *England, 1870–1914* (Oxford: Oxford University Press, 1936), p. 116.

6 See Einar Jensen, *Danish Agriculture: Its Economic Development* (Copenhagen: Munksgaard, 1937), pp. 192 ff. and esp. 212.

7 *Ibid.*, statistical appendix. For a series of interesting contemporary European views see the *Report of the U.S. Commissioner of Agriculture* (1883), pp. 326–51 (quoted by Nourse, *op. cit.*, pp. 271 ff.).

8 Slight differences in range and timing existed in separate markets because of differing transfer costs and the accessibility of different sources of supply. In Sweden, for example, which is not covered below, the comparable decline was from $1.34 per bushel in 1881 to $0.78 in 1887. See Table II of the Appendix to the useful "Decline and Recovery of Wheat Prices," *Wheat Studies* (Food Research Institute), X, Nos. 8 and 9 (June and July, 1934), 347, which gives annual figures for a large number of countries.

9 Roy Lewis and Angus Maude, *The English Middle Classes* (London: Phoenix House, 1949), p. 171.

10 See Ensor, *op. cit.*, p. 117.

11 This statement should perhaps be qualified by reference to the fair-trade agitation of the 1880's and the rise of protectionist sentiment in the 1890's under Joseph Chamberlain. Both these movements, however, were industrial in origin and sought to enlist rural support as an afterthought.
Some weight should perhaps also be given to the roles of bad weather and pestilence which delayed recognition of the importance of overseas competition. It is not certain that the reaction would have been equally passive had the country as a whole clearly understood the deep-seated nature of agriculture's troubles.

12 See Alexander Gerschenkron, *Bread and Democracy in Germany* (Berkeley: University of California Press, 1943), p. 45.

13 *Ibid.*, pp. 26–29 and 57–58.

14 E. O. Golob, *The Mèline Tariff: French Agriculture and Nationalist Economic Policy* (New York: Columbia University Press, 1944), pp. 81–82. I rely heavily on Golob's treatment.

15 International Institute of Agriculture, *World Trade in Agricultural Products* (Rome, 1940), pp. 794–98.

16 I. A. Hourwich (*Immigration and Labor* [New York: Huebsch, 1922], p. 201) notes for a somewhat later period that more than 70 per cent of Italian immigrants to the United States came from agricultural regions. Gross emigration rates differ from net, it may be observed, by rather sizable amounts because of the practice of trans-Atlantic migration on a seasonal basis for harvesting, particularly to Argentina, by so-called *golondrinos* ("swallows").

17 For lack of readily available secondary material, I have not investigated the course of events in Austria-Hungary, Sweden, Spain, and Portugal, which took action against new wheat imports, or in the Netherlands, Belgium, or Switzerland, which did not. A cursory examination of the tariff schedules (see "Decline and Recovery of Wheat Prices in the 'Nineties," Table VII, p. 350) and of annual figures for gross emigration overseas (*Annuaire statistique de France* (1914–15), Part III, p. 164) suggests that Austria-Hungary and Sweden were equally tardy in protecting agriculture and equally affected by emigration. Gerschenkron (*op. cit.*, pp. 40–41) gives an interpretation of the Swiss experience.

18 See Jensen, *op. cit.*, p. 133.

19 A more complete statement might attach importance to types of soil.

20 Jensen, *op. cit.*, p. 101: "After the defeat in the war of 1864, the work which was already begun was taken up by able and enthusiastic men." See also Harald Westergaard, *Economic Developments in Denmark* (Oxford: Oxford University Press, 1992), p. 13: "For the economic life of Denmark, [the War of 1864] was of still greater importance in that it gave industry a strong impetus for attacking and solving the many problems which pressed upon it within the country's narrowed boundaries."

21 For an account of forerunners see Harald Faber, *Co-operation in Danish Agriculture* (2d ed.; London: Longmans, Green & Co., 1931), pp. 25–30.

22 See Golob, *op. cit.*, pp. 145 ff.

23 I have discussed elsewhere the antithesis between the views of Keynes, who asserted that the world is ruled by little else than the theories of economists and political philosophers, and those of Arnold, who classes the economist with the lawyer and the scholar as performing a purely ceremonial role (see Lord Keynes, *The General Theory of Employment, Interest, and Money* [New Uork: Harcourt, Brace & Co., 1936), p. 383; and Thurman W. Arnold, *The Folklore of Capitalism* [New Haven: Yale University Press, 1937), esp. chap. iv).

24 Copenhagen: Munksgaard, 1939.

25 Ensor, *op. cit.*, p. 117. It may be observed that some protection was afforded to the cattle interests by the sanitary regulations, passed in the 1890's, forbidding the import of live animals from the Continent and overseas. The principal competition for home-grown meat, even at this time, however, was in meat imported from the Southern Hemisphere, a trade which developed with the innovation of refrigerated ships in the 1880's. Beef grazing, however, is far less labor-intensive than dairying and would have been, from the point of view of employment, a much less satisfactory adaptation.

26 Paris: Payot, 1929.

27 *Ibid.*, p. 207. These sources are called "new," in contrast with Germany, Ireland, Britain, etc., in H. Jerome, *Migration and Business Cycles* (New York: National Bureau of Economic Research, 1926). It may be noted that emigration from Ireland fluctuated parallel to that of Europe A, though it lies in Europe B in Delaisi's scheme.

28 Golob, *op. cit.*, p. 8.

28a W. Röpke (*The Social Crisis of Our Times*, [Chicago: University of Chicago Press, 1950] finds the clue to the development of agriculture in the various countries of Europe in the existence or absence of a sturdy peasant body. Its absence accounts for the injury to British agriculture; its presence for the Danish success (pp. 245–46). The peasantry of Italy and "SE Europe lacked soundness" (p. 204). Wheat protection favors large estates and is detrimental to peasant agriculture (p. 247). But this analysis fails to cover the French case, where peasants gained from protection; and Röpke himself fatally damages the consistency of his position in the statement (p. 205): "Admittedly, agriculture is that part of the national economic system to which the principles of a free market economy could only be applied with broad reservations. . . ."

29 This statement is perhaps unfair to Talcott Parsons and Robert K. Merton and their structural-functional approach to sociology, with which I am inadequately acquainted. For an attempt to apply this to the French economy see the forthcoming essay by John E. Sawyer, "Strains in the Social Structure of Modern France," to be published in a volume on France by the Princeton University Press.

30 Delaisi, *op. cit.*, pp. 46–47.

31 See, e.g., F. Machlup, "Three Concepts, the Balance of Payments," *Economic Journal*, March, 1950, p. 59 n.

32 An individual in the society, of course, will belong to a variety of subgroups based on his occupation, class religion, avocations, age, sex, race, etc.

33 *Op. cit.*, p. 109.

34 This characterization is objected to as unfair to the Junkers, who, whatever their disagreeable attributes, were men of responsibility who energetically farmed their own land in the face of natural difficulties rather than live off the unearned increment *in absentia*. Yet they were backward in the sense that they clung to traditional crops farmed with traditional techniques. Perhaps a more appropriate adjective is "static."

35 Gregory Bateson, "Morale and National Character," in G. Watson (ed.), *Civilian Morale* (Cambridge: At the University Press, 1942), pp. 71–81.

36 See, e.g., Maude and Lewis, *op. cit.*, *passim*.

37 See A. Kardiner, *The Psychological Frontiers of Society* (New York: Columbia University

Press, 1945); Ruth Benedict, *Patterns of Culture* (Cambridge, Mass.: Houghton Mifflin Co., 1934); Clyde Kluckhohn, *Mirror for Man* (New York: Whittlesey House, 1949), etc. Given the emphasis on anthropological data, primary attention has been devoted to the personality types of cultures rather than subcultures, and Kardiner, for example, regards Western man as a homogeneous type. This notion is in process of correction at the hands of Meade, Bateson, Gorer, and others.

38 See H. A. Innis, "Economic Significance of Cultural Factors," in his *Political Science in the Modern State* (Toronto: Toronto University Press, 1946), p. 87.

39 A number of writers have referred to the alleged inability of the British farmer to co-operate because of his individualism. See, e.g., E. J. Russell, who states in the Foreword to Faber, *op. cit.*, pp. vi–viii: "The British method, in short, proved less capable of adaptation to new and adverse conditions than the Danish. Critics may argue . . . that the British farmer is so confirmed an individualist and so imbued with the idea of running his own farm in his own way that he cannot co-operate with his neighbor. It may or may not be so." See also H. Rider Haggard, *Rural Denmark and Its Lessons* (London: Longmans Green & Co., 1911), p. 273: "The Danes look upon their land as a principal means of livelihood . . . – in short, as a business proposition in which the Nation is most vitally concerned. In the main, although we [Britain] may not acknowledge it, we look upon our land, or much of it, as a pleasure proposition in which the individual only is concerned." Haggard also cites (pp. 192–93) the sad case of a Norfolk honorable secretary of a rat and sparrow club who was unable to enlist any co-operation from potential benefactees.

40 See n. 11, above.

41 David S. Landes, "French Entrepreneurship and Industrial Growth in the Nineteenth Century," *Journal of Economic History*, IX (1949), 45–61.

42 Walker, *op. cit.*, pp. 123 and 222–23. Another case is probably that of the American Medical Association, which is unified in opposing expenditures on health by governmental bodies which would increase the incomes of the vast majority of its members.

43 Faber, *op. cit.*, pp. 31–32.

44 See Benedict, *op. cit.*, pp. 53–56 and chap. iv for a discussion of the Spenglerian contrast between Apollonian and Faustian cultures and the description of a self-balancing society. Bateson has described another such primitive society in *Naven* (Cambridge: At the University Press, 1936). Franz Oppenheimer mentions other instances of the prevalence of small and medium-sized landholdings in Utah, Iowa, and New Zealand in "The Tendency of the Development of the State," in V. F. Calverton, *The Making of Society* (New York: Random House, 1937), pp. 40–42. Cf. H. Rider Haggard's literary description of the Danes as "tolerant-minded" (*op. cit.*, p. 212).

45 See Faber, *op. cit.*, p. 7.

46 Haggard, *op. cit.*, p. 190.

13. Commercial Policy between the Wars

C. P. Kindleberger

I. WAR AND POST-WAR RECONSTRUCTION

The First World War marked the end of an era in the history of commercial relations among countries. New boundaries set in the peace treaties, especially with Austria and Hungary, converted pre-1914 internal trade to international trade. Trade relations interrupted by war could not always be restored. Extended fighting and disruption of peacetime economic intercourse produced substantial changes in the economic capacities and interests of major trading nations. Monetary disturbance evoked responses in trade policy, especially increases in tariffs, to offset effects of exchange depreciation abroad. A loosely concerted attempt was made after the war to patch up the fabric of trade relationships, but with nothing like the fervour exhibited after the Second World War. There was virtually no planning to post-war trade policies, despite President Wilson's third of the fourteen points that called for 'removal, as far as possible, of all economic barriers and the establishment of an equality of trade conditions among all nations consenting to the peace and associating themselves with its maintenance'.

Exigencies of war led to changes in commercial policy. The McKenna budget in Britain in 1915 imposed duties of 33 $^{1}/_{3}$ per cent on motor cars and parts, musical instruments, clocks, watches, and cinematographic film in an effort to reduce imports of luxuries and to save shipping space – although the point has been made that the shipping space taken by watches is minimal (Kreider, 1943, p. 13). Unlike previous luxury taxes in Britain, these duties on imports were not matched by domestic excises to eliminate the protective effect. The tariffs, moreover, made it possible for the United Kingdom to discriminate in trade in favour of the British Empire, something it could not do under the regime of free trade which had prevailed since the 1850s. Canada had granted preferential tariff treatment to Britain on a unilateral and non-reciprocal basis since 1898 – Britain assenting to the extent that it denounced the trade treaties with Germany and Belgium going back to the 1860s under which those countries had the right to claim concessions made by one of the Empire to another on a most-favoured-nation basis. The Finance Act of 1919 further reduced excise taxes on Empire tea, cocoa, coffee, chicory, currants, and certain dried fruits by one-sixth, and on Empire wines by one-third. The Key Industries Act of 1919 designed to strengthen defence industries equally contained preferences for the Empire, as did the Safeguarding of Industries Act of 1921. If the McKenna duties were designed to economize shipping and foreign exchange, the Finance Act of 1919 to raise revenue, and the Key Industries Act of 1919 to serve national defence, the Safeguarding of Industries Act levying tariffs on imports of gloves, domestic, glassware, gas mantles – a list extended in 1925 to include leather, lace, cutlery, pottery, packing paper, and enamelled hollow ware – represented straightforward protection of industries hurt by foreign competition.

A number of countries increased tariff coverage and raised rates to gain revenue. French minimum tariff rates had been raised by 1918 from 5 to 20 per cent, and maximum rates from 10 to 40 per cent. The use of import quotas in France dates from 1919, rather than the depression in 1930, although export and import prohibitions were a widespread feature of Colbert's mercantilism two and a half centuries earlier. In countries where the principal fiscal instrument was the tariff, such as Canada, tariff duties were increased early after the outbreak of war.

Fitful attention was given to commodity problems by Britain. Long concerned about the prospect of interruption of cotton supplies from the Southern United States as a result either of boll weevil or black rebellion, she had contemplated an Empire scheme for producing cotton. The planting of Gezira in the Sudan was started in 1914 with the decision to irrigate 300,000 acres, but the Empire Cotton Growing Corporation was not chartered until November 1921, sometime after the acute shortage of cotton fibre during the war and early post-war period. An Empire Resources Development Committee proposed in 1915 a scheme for producing palm kernel in West Africa and processing it in the United Kingdom, foreshadowing the East African groundnut scheme after the Second World War. The technique envisaged was an export tax of £2 per ton to be continued for five years after the war, but that was to be rebated in favour of British processors. The scheme was started in October 1919 but met sharp Gold Coast resistance. When the price of palm kernel fell, the project became untenable and the duty was withdrawn in July 1922 (Hancock, 1940, pp. 113–18).

Limited as it was, post-war planning took place along lines of military alliance. France took the lead in an Allied economic conference in June 1916 that produced a resolution committing the Allies to take first temporary and then permanent steps to make themselves independent of enemy countries in matters of raw-material supply, essential manufactures, and the organization of trade, finance and shipping (Drummond, 1972, p. 56). Neutral reaction, including that of the United States neutral at that time, was hostile. When the United States entered the war, the notion was dropped despite French efforts to revive it at Versailles (Viner, 1950, pp. 24–5). On the other side, Germany and Austria concluded a treaty before the Armistice in 1918, providing for customs union after the war; the arrangement was not for complete free trade within the union, but permitted Austria-Hungary to retain protection at a preferential level in certain weak industries (*ibid.*, pp. 105–6). In defeat it proved academic, except perhaps as a precedent to the 1931 proposal for *Zollunion* (customs union) between Austria and Germany, and the 1937 *Anschluss*.

Commercial-policy features of the treaties ending the First World War were minimal. Germany was required to agree to apply the tariff nomenclature worked out at The Hague in 1913 (as well as to accept the international conventions of 1904 and 1910 suppressing the white slave trade, the conventions of 16 and 19

November 1885 regarding the establishment of a concert pitch (the wavelength of the musical note of A) and a host of others). The principal effect of these measures seems to have been to stiffen German resistance to subscribing to the agreements. More significantly, Germany was required by the treaty of Versailles to grant the Allies unilateral and unconditional most-favoured-nation treatment for five years. On 10 January 1925 when the five years elapsed and Germany was free to negotiate trade agreements on her own, the post-war period of reconstruction may be said to have come to an end – at least in the area of trade. The lapse of these provisions helped Germany but posed a problem for France which now had to negotiate to obtain outlets for Alsatian textiles and Lorraine minette iron ore which earlier had been marketed in Germany without payment of duties (Schuker, 1976, pp. 219–27).

These five years, however, constituted a period of considerable disorder in fluctuations of business and of exchange rates, and, in consequence, in policies relating to international trade. Anti-dumping legislation was enacted in Japan in 1920, in Australia, Britain, New Zealand and the United States in 1921, when also earlier legislation dating from 1904 in Canada was amended; the anti-dumping provisions of the Fordney-McCumber tariff took effect in 1922 (Viner, 1923, repr. 1966, pp. 192, 219, 227, 231, 246, 258). The United Kingdom further authorized 33 1/3 per cent duties against countries devaluing their currencies, although these were never imposed and were allowed to lapse in 1930. With the franc free to fluctuate, France initiated a system of tariff coefficients which could be adjusted to compensate for inflation at home or revaluations of the exchange rate. The Fordney-McCumber Act of 1922 in the United States not only extended anti-dumping provisions but raised tariffs on a variety of materials which had fallen in price in the sharp recession of 1920–1. Insult was added to injury from this and from the wartime enactment of Prohibition in the United States that cut off imports of wine, beer, and spirits, when the United States took sanitary measures against Spanish grapes and oranges to limit the danger of entry of fruit flies, without giving consideration to the possibility of refrigeration which kills the fruit fly (Jones, 1934, p. 35).

In Eastern Europe, new countries struggled with inflation, depreciation and inadequate sources of revenue, and were forced to levy heavy taxes on trade in a vain effort to restore financial balance. Export taxes were imposed along with import duties, despite a variety of international resolutions urging strongly against prohibitions of exports, and taxation, on the basis of equal access to materials (Bergsten, 1974, pp. 23–4). The finances of Austria and Hungary were supervized by experts under programmes of the Finance Committee of the League of Nations – Austria in 1922, Hungary in 1924 – which experts exerted strenuous efforts to liberalize trade.

As the world economy slowly settled down, the pre-war system of trade treaties was resumed, with extension of the principle of high legislative tariffs – so-called 'bargaining' or 'fighting' tariffs – which would be reduced through the most-favoured-nation clause. To a degree, the initial increases in tariff rates succeeded better than the subsequent reduction through negotiation, especially as not all countries were prepared to subscribe to the unconditional version of the most-favoured-nation clause (League of Nations (W. T. Page), 1927). The

United States especially, with its high Fordney-McCumber tariff, stood aloof from the system. Except in the period from 1890 to 1909 the United States Administration was not empowered to enter into tariff treaties; under the Dingley tariff from 1897 to 1919, no tariff treaties came into force since Senate approval was required but not forthcoming. The Fordney-McCumber tariff of 1922, however, changed United States policy from conditional most-favoured-nation to unconditional treatment. Under the conditional version, concessions offered to one country were made available to others only in exchange for a reciprocal concession. The Tariff Act of 1922's provision for retaliation by the United States against countries which discriminated against American exports was judged to require the more general form of the non-discrimination clause (US Department of State, *Foreign Relations of the United States*, 1923, 1, pp. 131–3). Exceptions to the unconditional most-favoured-nation clause were recognized for specific countries, such as Cuba and the Philippines insofar as the United States was concerned, and regional arrangements, in which 'propinquity' was a usual characteristic (Viner, 1950, p. 19). The British position, opposed by the United States, was that a further exception could be based on 'historical associations, such as were generally recognized'. This referred to Empire preference.

As a policy, Empire preference meant more the relations of the United Kingdom with the Dominions than those with the colonies, including India. 'Tariff reformers' at the turn of the century would have welcomed an imperial *Zollverein*, eliminating all tariffs between the mother country and the rest of the Empire. This was opposed not only by British free traders, who viewed free-trade and preferences both as disguises for protectionism, but also by the Dominions that regarded tariffs as a symbol of sovereignty and were unwilling to remove all vestiges of protection for their manufactures against British products. Preferences in the Dominions meant largely tariffs to be levied in Britain against non-Empire foodstuffs, and higher domestic tariffs on foreign manufacturers, rather than reductions in existing duties on British goods. Resistance to Empire preference in Britain came not only from the free traders, but from those who wanted to hold down the price of food on the one hand, and on the other, those who sought protection against Empire as well as against foreign food producers.

The slogan of Empire visionaries in Britain and the Dominions after the war was 'men, money, and markets'. 'Men' meant assisted settlement of British workers in the Dominions; 'money' help for Empire borrowers in various ways, ranging from preferences in the queue to guaranteed interest; 'Markets' referred to Empire preference, to a considerable degree in new products that especially Australia wished to have produced for export by immigrants settled on new farms – particularly dried fruit and frozen beef – rather than the traditional wheat, butter, wool, apples, bacon, cheese.

The Imperial Economic Conference of 1923 made little progress toward tariff preferences; the election called by Stanley Baldwin in 1924 to provide tariffs that could be used for the purpose ended in a Labour victory and even repeal of the McKenna duties and the preferences granted under them. The return of Baldwin to power eleven months later restored the McKenna duties, with lorries added to motor cars, but the Conservatives stopped short of extending tariff discrimination. Feeble efforts were made to undertake non-tariff discrimination through an Empire Marketing Board which was to perform research and promotion. Empire settlement fizzled gently. Empire preference was postponed.

The reconstruction period to 1925 or so was characterized by instability. Rapidly changing exchange rates required rapidly changing tariffs through countervailing charges, or the application of coefficients. Trade agreements were frequently contracted for only three months. Where changes in tariff rates did not occur, administrative regulation was applied. The League of Nations Economic Committee worked to improve the position through such actions as the International Convention Relating to the Simplification of Custom Formalities of 1923, although this soon proved inadequate as far as worst practices were concerned (Winslow, 1936, p. 182).

II. NORMALIZATION OF WORLD TRADE

The end of the reconstruction period about the middle of the decade was marked by the opening up of capital markets, following the success of the Dawes Loan in 1924 that primed the resumption of German reparations after the hyperinflation of 1923, by the restoration of the pound sterling to par on the gold standard in 1925, or perhaps by the expiration of the Versailles restriction on Germany's right to conclude commercial treaties, and with it the rapid extension of trade agreements in Europe. Whatever the event, it marked the initiation of increased efforts for trade normalization. A minor effort was represented by the International Convention for the Protection of Industrial Property of 1925 (Brown, 1950, p. 34). Of greater weight were the convention for the Abolition of Import and Export Prohibitions and Restrictions, with which was associated a special agreement on hides, skins and bones, and a World Economic Conference on trade expansion, all in 1927. In 1929 a special conference produced a convention calling for national treatment for foreign nationals and enterprises. A modernized tariff nomenclature to replace the 1913 Hague list was started in the 1920s, produced a first draft in 1931, and a final one in 1937 (League of Nations, 1942, p. 45).

A number of these conventions failed to be ratified. That on the treatment of foreign nationals fell through because some states were unwilling to liberalize, and the liberal states were unwilling to sign an agreement which would have weakened the force of the principle of national treatment (League of Nations, 1942, p. 27). The Convention on Imports and Exports prohibitions finally lapsed when the Poles refused to sign, because of an exception made for Germany, which reduced the value of the treaty in their eyes. Agreement on a tariff truce and subsequent reductions in rates was reached at the 1927 World Economic Conference, but this meeting was attended by delegations in their individual capacities and did not bind governments. Governments agreed on the necessity of reducing tariffs but did nothing about it. The League of Nations review of commercial policies in the inter-war period called it a striking paradox that conferences unanimously adopted recommendations, and governments proclaimed their intentions to lower tariffs, but did nothing (League of Nations, 1942, p. 101), asking why governments made such recommendations if they did not propose to carry them out (*ibid.*, p. 109). The answer furnished by one economist who had served on the economic secretariat of the League was that 'the pseudo-internationalism of the Nineteenth century was clearly an outgrowth of British financial leadership and trading enterprise, backed by the economic supremacy of London and by the British Navy (Condliffe, 1940, p. 118). With British hegemony lost and nothing to take its place, international relations lapsed into anarchy. Britain lost the will and lacked the power to enforce international cooperation as she had done in the nineteenth century (*ibid.*, p. 145).

Discouragement over the failure of tariffs to come down despite agreement to lower them led to an attempt at a commodity-by-commodity approach, foreshadowing the free trade for iron and steel undertaken in the European Coal and Steel Community on Robert Schuman's initiative in May 1950. The Economic Committee of the League of Nations reported in March 1928 that there was no prospect of a general tariff reduction by means of standard cuts or the setting of a maximum scale of duties. Cement and aluminium were chosen for a case-by-case approach. A year of negotiation, however, produced no result. The League's account of the attempt cites as reasons (1) that reductions in duties in single products would upset national industrial structures; (2) that it would increase the protection of finished goods – implying the so-called effective-rate-of-protection argument which was more fully developed in the 1960s; and (3) that among the limited groups of commodities and countries concerned, compensatory reductions were hard to find (League of Nations, 1942, pp. 128–9).

While governments were agreeing to the necessity to lower tariffs but doing nothing about it, action was taken directly on a number of commodity fronts. Most conspicuous was the Stevenson rubber plan of 1923–4 which raised the price of rubber by 1926 to almost four times its 1923 level. To American protests, the British replied that it was 'impossible to argue that the present high price is attributable solely or even mainly to the operation of the rubber restriction scheme. It is due to the great expansion of the demand for rubber. Only one half of the supply comes from the restricted area' (*Foreign Relations of the United States*, 1926, vol. II, p. 359). The fact that the other half – the Netherlands East Indies – had been left out of the scheme contributed to its early breakdown (Knorr, 1946).

More cartels were formed in a variety of commodities, that Mason divides into three groups (1) industrial raw materials and foodstuffs, like tin, oil, wheat, sugar, etc.; (2) standardized processed and semi-fabricated goods such as steel rails, cement, tinplate, plate glass, dyes, etc.; and (3) highly fabricated, specialized, and frequently patented items such as electrical equipment, pharmaceuticals, glass etc. (Mason, 1946, p. 16). Mason notes that the Soviet Union was a party to at least three international control schemes and eight cartel arrangements, despite its hostility to capitalism (*ibid.*, p. 14n.). Most of the commodity agreements begun in the 1920s broke down in the depression of the 1930s. The rubber scheme collapsed in 1928. Prices of agricultural commodities levelled off in 1925 and declined thereafter, faster after 1928, as European reconstruction crowded the extra-European supplies expanded to fill the gap left by war and post-war shortages, and demand shrank with such changes as the replacement of oats for horses by gasoline for motor cars.

Two of the most durable agreements were in oil: the As-Is Agreement concluded at Achnacarry, Scotland in 1928 between Sir Henry Detering of the Shell Oil Company and Walter Teagle of the Standard Oil Company of New Jersey, that provided that no oil company would seek to penetrate into markets where it was not already distributing, so that everything would stay 'as is'; and in the same year the Red-Line Agreement, among members of the Turkish Petroleum Company, that drew a line across the Middle East (through what is now Kuwait) and limited exploration by partners below that line, thereby ultimately making it possible for the Standard Oil Company of California, which was not a partner, to discover oil in Saudi Arabia (Federal Trade Commission, 1952, pp. 199f., 63).

National programmes further affected world markets in wheat and sugar. The Italian 'battle for grain' begun by Mussolini in 1925 was of limited economic significance, since Italy could not escape dependence on foreign supplies, but provided a disturbing symptom of the troubles of the 1930s. Great Britain expanded production of beet sugar through a bounty; Japan undertook sugar production in Formosa (Taiwan) and ceased to buy from Java. As the price of wheat declined, Germany raised tariffs in 1928 to slow down the movement of labour off the farm. From 1927 to 1931, German tariffs on foodstuffs were broadly doubled. France raised tariffs in 1928 and 1929 before resorting to quotas. Mixing provisions, under which foreign grain had to be mixed with domestic, were undertaken from 1929 on, patterned after the practice in motion pictures which allowed exhibitors to show foreign films only in fixed proportions to those domestically produced. In the United States, help for agriculture took the form of proposals for export subsidies, but President Coolidge's veto of the McNary-Haugen bill in 1928 led presidential candidate Herbert Hoover to seek other means of agricultural relief, and to promote help for farmers in his campaign speeches in the summer and autumn of that year. The League of Nations commented in 1942 that 'before the end of 1928 it was evident that the United States tariff was going to be raised above the formidable level of 1922' (League of Nations, 1942, p. 126).

Grain exporters of Eastern Europe were especially affected by the world decline in price and sought solutions in meetings at Warsaw in August 1930. Bucharest in October 1930, Belgrade in November 1930, and Warsaw again in the same month. They tried on the one hand to limit exports of grain to improve the terms of trade, and on the other to obtain preferences in import markets of Western Europe. The first proposal was never adopted. After the 1932 Stresa meeting, some reciprocal preferences were worked out between Austria and Hungary on one side and Italy on the other, but with poor results.

A strenuous effort was made to halt tariff increases. The World Economic Conference of 1927 recognized that general demobilization of tariffs would be slow, and the Economic Committee of the League of Nations in March 1928 saw no prospect of general reduction. The September 1929 General Assembly of the League moved from attempts at reduction to an effort to halt increases. It called for a conference to stabilize rates for two or three years and then to lower them. The Preliminary Conference with a View to Concerned Action met in February 1930, but too late. It proposed extending existing agreements to 1 April 1931 and to provide opportunities for negotiation before tariffs were raised. By this time, however, retaliation against the forthcoming Hawley-Smoot tariff bill was far along. A second Conference with a View to Concerted Economic Action in November 1930 failed equally. The Netherlands, which, along with Britain, had pressed for the tariff truce, turned to a smaller group and organized the Oslo group. On 22 December, Norway, Sweden, Holland, and Belgium signed an agreement undertaking not to raise tariffs without giving notice to other members. It was a brave example without much impact.

Quite unrelated to the fortunes of world incomes, prices, or trade, a highly original argument for tariffs emerged in Australia at the end of the prosperity of the 1920s. It bore resemblance to an earlier argument put forward by Alvin S. Johnson in 1908 that tariffs could add to capital formation by reallocating income from spenders to savers – an argument which went unnoticed until Harvey Leibenstein introduced similar notions into the discussion of economic growth in the 1960s. J. B. Brigden published an article in the *Economic Record* of November 1925 on 'The Australian Tariff and the Standard of Living'. He concluded that whereas the tariff on wheat in Britain favoured the landed classes, that on manufactured goods in Australia would redound to the standard of living of wage-earners, and increase the population of the country. Subsequently the Australian government appointed a committee of experts, including Brigden, D. B. Copland, E. O. Dayson, L. F. Giblin, and Wickens, which in 1929 produced *The Australian Tariff: An Economic Enquiry* that supported Brigden's conclusion. The analysis remained to be worked out by W. F. Stolper and P. A. Samuelson in their classic article of 1941, 'Protection and Real Wages', and was to be rediscovered for Canada in the post-war period by C. L. Barber. It was heatedly debated during the 1930s both in Australia and in Anglo-Saxon economic literature. What was clear, however, was that Australia chose not to be guided by the neo-classical static maximizing calculus of foreign-trade theory, but rather to introduce into the discussion dynamic considerations of economic growth, migration, as well as income redistribution.

III. THE DISINTEGRATION OF WORLD TRADE

A. The Hawley-Smoot Tariff

The origins of the Hawley-Smoot tariff, as already noted, reach back to the autumn of 1928 when Herbert Hoover, campaigning for the presidency, promised to do something to help farmers suffering under the weight of declining agricultural prices. A special session of the Congress was called in January 1929, long in advance of the stock-market crash of October of that year, and began to prepare a tariff bill. Its scope was widened from agriculture to include industry; Democrats joined Republicans in their support for tariffs for all who sought them; and both Republicans and Democrats were ultimately pushed from the committee room as lobbyists took over the task of setting the rates (Schattschneider, 1935). A groundswell of resentment spread around the world and quickly led to retaliation. Italy objected to duties on hats and bonnets of straw, wool-felt hats, and olive oil; Spain reacted sharply to increases on cork and onions; Canada took umbrage at increases on maple sugar and syrup, potatoes, cream, butter, buttermilk, and skimmed milk. Switzerland was moved to boycott American typewriters, fountain pens, motor cars, and films because of increased duties on watches, clocks, embroidery, cheese, and shoes (Jones, 1934). Retaliation was begun long before the bill was enacted into law in June 1930. As it passed the House of Representatives in May 1929, boycotts broke out and foreign governments moved to raise rates against United States products, even though rates could be moved up or down in the Senate or by the conference committee. In all, 34 formal protests were lodged with the Department of State from foreign countries. One thousand and twenty-eight economists in the United States, organized by Paul Douglas, Irving Fisher, Frank Graham, Ernest Patterson, Henry Seager, Frank Taussig, and Clair Wilcox, and representing the 'Who's Who' of the profession, asked President Hoover to veto the legislation (*New York Times*, 5 May 1930). A weak defence was offered contemporaneously by President Hoover as he signed the bill, saying 'No tariff act is perfect' (Hoover, 1952, p. 291), and another 45 years later by Joseph S. Davis, who claimed that the Senate got out of hand, but that Hoover had won two key points: inclusion of the flexible provisions permitting the Tariff Commission to consider complaints and recommend to the president higher or lower rates, and exclusion of an export-debenture plan along the lines of the McNary-Haugen bill (Davis, 1975, p. 239). Both views were in the minority.

The high tariffs of 1921, 1922, and *a fortiori* 1930 were generally attacked on the grounds that the United States was a creditor nation, and that creditor nations were required to maintain low tariffs or free trade in order that their debtors might earn the foreign exchange to pay their debt service. This view is now regarded as fallacious since the macro-economic impacts effects of tariffs on the balance of payments are typically reversed, wholly or in large part, by the income changes which they generate. Under the post-Second World War General Agreement on Tariffs and Trade, balance of payments considerations are ignored in settling on tariff reductions in bilateral or multilateral bargaining. In addition, a careful study for the Department of Commerce by Hal. B. Lary states that the effect of the tariff increases of 1922 and 1930, and those of the reductions after 1930, cannot be detected in the import statistics. This was partly perhaps because tariffs were already close to prohibitive and early reductions were minimal, but mainly for the reason that wide fluctuations in world economic activity and prices overwhelmed any lasting impact of tariffs on trade (Lary, 1943, pp. 53–4).

The significance of the Hawley-Smoot tariff goes far beyond its effect on American imports and the balance of payments to the core of the question of the stability of the world economy. President Hoover let Congress get out of hand and failed to govern (Schattschneider, 1935, p. 293); by taking national action and continuing on its own course through the early stages of the depression, the United States served notice on the world that it was unwilling to take responsibility for world economic stability. Sir Arthur Salter's view (1932, pp. 172–3) that Hawley-Smoot marked a turning point in world history is excessive if it was meant in causal terms, apposite if taken symbolically.

Retaliation and business decline wound down the volume and value of world trade. The earliest retaliations were taken by France and Italy in 1929. In Canada the Liberal government kept parliament in session during the final days when the conference committee was completing the bill, and then put through increases in tariff rates affecting one-quarter of Canadian imports from the United States. Despite this resistance to its neighbour, the government lost the August 1930 election to the Conservatives, who then raised tariffs in September 1930, June 1931, and again in connection with the 1932 Ottawa agreements (McDiarmid, 1946, p. 273). The action in May under the Liberal, W. L. Mackenzie King involved both increases and decreases in duties, with Empire preference extended through raising and lowering about one-half each of general and intermediate rates, but lowering the bulk of those applicable to Empire goods. Subsequent measures typically raised Empire rates, but general and intermediate rates more. In September 1930, anti-dumping rates were increased from 15 to 50 per cent.

B. Deepening Depression

The Hawley-Smoot tariff began as a response to the decline in agricultural prices and was signed into law as the decline in business picked up speed. For a time during the second quarter of 1930, it looked as though the world economy might recover from the deflationary shock of the New York stock-market crash in October 1929, which had come on the heels of the failure in London of the Clarence Hatry conglomerate after the discovery of fraudulent collateral used to support bank loans in September and the failure of the Frankfurt Insurance Company in Germany in August. This is not the place to set forth the cause of the depression in agricultural overproduction, the halt to foreign lending by the United States in 1928, the end of the housing boom, the stock-market crash, frightened short-term capital movements, United States monetary policy and the like. It is sufficient to observe that the dance of recovery was seen to fade at the end of June 1930 with the signing of the Hawley-Smoot tariff, the outbreak of retaliatory cuts in international trade, and the near-failure of the Young loan (to reprime German reparations) in international capital markets. Events thereafter were uniformly depressing from Nazi gains in German elections in September 1930, the collapse of the Creditanstalt in Vienna in May 1931, the run on German banks in June and July, until the Standstill Agreement that blocked repayment of all German bank credits shifted the attack to sterling, which went off the gold standard in September 1931, followed by the yen in December.

One item of commercial policy contributed to the spreading deflation. In the autumn of 1930, Austria and Germany announced an intention to form a customs union. The proposal had its proximate origin in a working paper prepared by the German Foreign Ministry for the World Economic Conference in 1927. It was discussed on the side by Austrian and German Foreign Ministers at the August 1929 meeting on the Young Plan at The Hague. Germany took it up seriously, however, only after the September 1930 elections which recorded alarming gains for the National Socialists, and Brüning, the Chancellor, felt a strong need for a foreign-policy success. The French immediately objected on the grounds that customs union between Austria and Germany violated the provision of the treaty of Trianon which required Austria to uphold her political independence. France took the case to the International Court of Justice at The

Hague for an interpretation of the treaty. Other French and British and Czechoslovak objections on the grounds of violation of the most-favoured-nation clause were laid before the League of Nations Council (Viner, 1950, p. 10). The International Court ultimately ruled in favour of the French position in the summer of 1932. By this time, however, the Austrian Creditanstalt had collapsed – barely possible because of French action in pulling credits out of Austria, though the evidence is scanty – the Austrian government responsible for the proposal of customs union had long since fallen, and the run against banks and currencies had moved on from Austria to Germany and Britain.

In the autumn of 1931, appreciation of the mark, the dollar and the gold-bloc currencies as a consequence of the depreciation of sterling and the currencies associated with it, applied strenuous deflation to Germany, the United States and to Western Europe from September 1931 to June 1932. Depreciation of the yen in December 1931 marked the start of a drive of Japanese exports into British and Dutch colonies in Asia and Africa, and of colonial and metropolitan steps to hold them down. June 1932 was the bottom of the depression for most of the world. The United States economy registered a double bottom, in June 1932 and again in March 1933, when spreading collapse of the system of many small separate banks climaxed in the closing of all banks for a time, and recovery thereafter. German recovery started in 1932 after the resignation of Brüning, who had hoped to throw off reparations by deflation to demonstrate the impossibility of paying them, the succession of von Papen as Chancellor, and finally the takeover of the chancellorship by Hitler in February 1933. The gold-bloc countries remained depressed until they abandoned the gold parties of the 1920s, first Belgium in 1935, and the remaining countries in September 1936.

In these circumstances, there was little if any room for expansive commercial policy. Virtually every step taken was restrictive.

C. Ottawa

The Hawley-Smoot Tariff Act occupied most of the time of the Congress for a year and a half (Smith, 1936, p. 177). Empire preference was the major issue in Canadian policies for more than half a century (Drummond, 1975, p. 378). The Imperial Economic Policy Cabinet worried more about tariffs than about any other issue (*ibid.*, p. 426), though much of it dealt with objectively insignificant goods (Drummond, 1972, p. 25). Drummond several times expresses the opinion that the Ottawa discussions in the summer of 1932 should have abandoned the question of tariff preferences and focused on monetary policy, and especially exchange rate policy. In fact Prime Minister Bennett of Canada sought to raise the issue of the sterling exchange rate prior to Ottawa only to be rebuffed by Neville Chamberlain with the statement that the Treasury could not admit the Dominions to the management of sterling. Canada did succeed in getting exchange rates put on the Ottawa agenda, but the Treasury insisted that the question was minor and nothing came of it (Drummond, 1975, pp. 214–16).

Monetary policy and tariff policy were occasionally complements, occasionally substitutes. The Macmillan Committee report contained an addendum, no. 1, by Ernest Bevin, J. M. Keynes, R. McKenna and three others recommending import duties, and, insofar as existing treaties permitted, a bounty on exports, the combination being put forward as a substitute for devaluation of sterling (Committee on Finance and Industry, 1931). In the event, Britain undertook both depreciation of sterling and the imposition of import duties.

Sterling left the gold standard on 21 September 1931 and depreciated rapidly from $4.86 to a low of $3.24 in December, a depreciation of 30 per cent. Canada and South Africa adopted anti-dumping duties against British goods. On its side, Britain enacted an Abnormal Importations Act on 20 November 1931 that gave the Board of Trade the right to impose duties up to 100 per cent as a means of stopping a short-run scramble to ship goods to Britain before the exchange rate depreciated further. While 100 per cent tariffs were authorized, only 50 per cent were imposed. This act was followed in a few weeks by a similar Horticultural Products Act. Both the Abnormal Importations Act and the Horticultural Products Act exempted the Empire from their provisions (Kreider, 1943, p. 20).

In the Christmas recess of parliament, Lord Runciman, President of the Board of Trade, persuaded Chamberlain to take up protection as a long-run policy, as had been recommended by Keynes and the Macmillan Committee, prior to the September depreciation, and opposed by Beveridge (1931), since without tariffs, Britain had nothing to exchange with the Dominions for preferences in their markets. The resultant Import Duties Act of February 1932 established a 10 per cent duty on a wide number of imported products – but not copper, wheat, or meat – and created an Import Duties Advisory board, charged with recommending increases in particular duties above the flat 10 per cent level. At the last minute a concession was made to the Dominions and colonies. The latter were entirely exempted from the increase, and the former were granted exemption until November 1932, by which time it was expected that mutually satisfactory arrangements for preferences would have been reached. Eighteen countries responded to the Import Duties Act by asking Britain to undertake negotiations for mutual reductions. The reply was universally negative on the grounds that it was first necessary to arrive at understandings with the Empire (Condliffe, 1940, pp. 300–8). In the spring of 1932, the Import Duties Advisory Board was hard at work raising duties above the 10 per cent level, with the notable increase in iron and steel duties were increased to 50 per cent in order to assist the British industry in negotiating a satisfactory basis with the European iron and steel cartel (Hexner, 1946, p. 118).

Imperial economic conferences held in 1923, 1926, and 1930 had all broken down on the failure of Britain to raise tariffs which would have put her in a position to extend preferences to the Empire. Substitute assistance in the form of arrangements for Empire settlement or Empire marketing boards failed to produce significant effects on either migration or trade. British bulk-purchase schemes sought especially by Australia had been halted as early as 1922 and had not been resumed. Hopes were high for the Imperial Economic Conference of 1932 in Ottawa which now had British tariffs to work with.

Canada cared about wheat, butter, cheese, cheese, bacon, lamb, and apples; Australia about wheat, chilled meat, butter, cheese, currants, dried fruits, canned fruits; South Africa about wine and dried and canned fruits; New Zealand, butter and mutton. The position differed in those commodities that the Dominions produced in greater amounts than Britain could absorb, like wheat, in which diversion of Dominion supplies to Britain from third markets would produce an offsetting increase in non-Dominion sales in non-British markets, and leave Dominion export prices overall unchanged, from those in which Britain depended upon both Dominion and foreign sources of supply, among the latter notably Argentina in meat, Denmark in butter, Greece in dried currants and raisins, and it would like to think, the United States in apples. Trade diversion from foreign to Dominion sources was possible in this latter group, but only at some cost in British goodwill in the indicated import markets. On this score, the United Kingdom was obliged to negotiate at Ottawa with an uneasy glance over its shoulder.

A significant Dominion manufacture, as opposed to agricultural product, which had earlier received preference in the British market, in 1919 under the McKenna duties, was motor cars. This preference had led to the establishment of tariff factories in Canada, owned and operated by United States manufacturers. Its extension in the Ottawa agreement led to the unhappy necessity of defining more precisely what a Canadian manufactured motor car consisted of, and whether United States-made motor parts merely assembled in Canada qualified as Canadian motor cars.

In exchange for concession in primary products in the British market, the United Kingdom expected to get reductions in Dominion duties on her manufacturers. But it proved impossible at Ottawa to fix levels of Dominion tariffs on British goods. Instead, the Dominions undertook to instruct their respective tariff boards to adjust the British preference tariff to that level which would make British producers competitive with domestic industry. Resting on the notion of horizontal supply curves, rather than the more usually hypothesized and far more realistic upward-sloping curves, the concept was clearly unworkable and gave rise to unending contention. It was abandoned in 1936.

Argentina, Denmark, Greece, Norway, and Sweden were not content to yield their positions in the British market without a struggle. Even before the Import Duties Act had taken effect, Denmark in January 1932 legislated preferences favouring Britain, and on raw materials used in manufactured exports. By June 1932, total imports had been reduced 30 to 40 per cent, but import permits issued for British goods allowed for a 15 per cent increase (Gordon, 1941, p. 80). In similar fashion Uruguay undertook to discriminate in the allocation of import licences in favour of countries that bought from her. The threat to discriminate against Britain was clear. Quickly after Ottawa British customers pressed to take up negotiations postponed from early 1932 and to settle the extent to which Ottawa would be allowed to squeeze them out of the British market.

In the Roca-Runciman Agreement of 1 May 1933, Britain agreed not to cut back imports of chilled beef from Argentina by more than 10 per cent of the volume imported in the year ended 30 June 1932, unless at the same time it reduced imports from the Dominions below 90 per cent of the same base year. This was disagreeable to Australia which was seeking through the Ottawa agreements to break into the chilled-beef market in Britain in which it had previously not been strong (Drummond, 1975, p. 310). Three-year agreements with Denmark, Norway, and Sweden, running from various dates of ratification about mid-1933, provided minimum butter quotas to Denmark and (much smaller) to Sweden, a minimum bacon quota to Denmark amounting to 62 per cent of the market, and agreement not to regulate the small and irregular shipments of bacon, ham, butter, and cheese by Norway. But guarantees to these producers left it necessary, of domestic British producers of, say, butter were to be protected, to go back on the Ottawa agreements which guaranteed unlimited free entry into the British market. The position was complicated by New Zealand's backward-bending supply curve which increased butter production and shipments as the price declined, and Australian policy, which evoked the most profound distrust from New Zealand, of subsidizing the export of butter to solve a domestic disposal problem (Drummond, 1975, pp. 320ff., 475). The problems of the Dominions and of the major foreign suppliers of the British markets of foodstuffs compounded the difficulties of British agriculture. In defence of the lost interest, the British agricultural authorities developed a levy-subsidy scheme under which tariffs imposed on imports were segregated to create a fund to be used to provide subsidies to domestic producers. The levy-subsidy scheme was first applied in Britain on wheat in 1932; strong voices inside the British cabinet urged its application to beef, dairy products, and bacon and ham. Wrangling over these proposals went on between British and Commonwealth negotiators for the next several years as Britain tried to modify the Ottawa agreements, with Dominion and foreign-supplier consent, in order to limit imports. In the background, dispute deepened within the British cabinet between the Agricultural Minister, Walter Elliott, who wanted subsidies, and the Chancellor of the Exchequer, Neville Chamberlain, who feared their effect on the budget and consistently favoured raising prices and farm incomes, in Britain and abroad, by cutting production and limiting imports.

In its agreements in Scandinavia, Britain sought to bind its trading partners to give preferences to British exports, and especially to guarantee a percentage share of the market to British suppliers in that sorely affected export industry, coal. In eight trade agreements, British coal exporters were guaranteed generally the major share of import volume, with quotas as follows: Denmark, 90 per cent; Estonia, 85 per cent; Lithuania, 80 per cent; Iceland, 77 per cent; Finland, 75 per cent; Norway, 70 per cent; Sweden, 47 per cent. In addition, Denmark agreed that all bacon and ham exported to the United Kingdom should be wrapped in jute cloth woven in the United Kingdom from jute yarn spun in the United Kingdom (Kreider, 1943, pp. 61–2). The Danish government gave British firms to 10 per cent preference for government purchases, and undertook to urge private Danish firms to buy their iron and steel in the United Kingdom wherever possible. Kreider notes that these agreements constrained British trade into a bilateral mode: British agreements with Finland lifted the unfavourable import balance from 1 to 5 against Britain in 1931 to 1 to 2 in 1935. The agreement with Russia called for the import/export ratio to go from 1 to 1.7 against Britain in 1934 to 1 to 1.5 in 1935, 1 to 1.4 in 1936 and 1 to 1.2 in 1937 and thereafter. Argentina agreed to allocate the sterling earned by exports to Britain to purchases from Britain.

The Ottawa agreement dominated British commercial policy from 1932 to the Anglo-American Commercial Agreement of 1938, and to a lesser extent thereafter. It was continuously under attack from foreign suppliers other than the United States that entered into trade and financial agreements with the United Kingdom, and from the United States which undertook to attack it as early as the World Economic Conference of 1933. But at no time could the agreement have been regarded as a great success for the Empire. It produced endless discussion, frequently bitter in character, and dissatisfaction on both sides that each felt they had given too much and gained too little. By 1936 and 1937, there was a general disposition to give up the attempt, or at least to downgrade its priority.

D. The Netherlands

The United Kingdom embraced free trade, broadly speaking, with the repeal of the Corn Laws in 1846, and gave it up with the McKenna duties in 1916. The Netherlands' support goes back at least to the sixteenth century, and lasted until 1931. A faithful supporter of attempts to spread freer trade throughout the world from the World Economic Conference in 1927 until the Convention on Import and Export Prohibitions and the Conference with a View to Concreted Economic Action. The Netherlands ultimately turned to the smaller arena of the Oslo agreement of Scandinavia and the Low Countries. The pressure from declining wheat prices, however, proved too severe. In 1931 The Netherlands undertook to regulate farm prices and marketing. The Wheat Act of 1931 set the domestic price at 12 florins per 100 kg at a time when the world price had fallen to 5 florins, necessitating the first major break with the policy of free trade in nearly three centuries. There followed in 1932 as a response to the depreciation of sterling, first an emergency fiscal measure establishing 25 per cent duties generally, and then in agriculture the Dairy Crisis Act and the Hog Crisis Act, which were generalized in the following year as the Agricultural Crisis Act of 1933 (Gordon, 1941, p. 307). The freer-trade tradition of the Oslo group continued, however. At the depth of the depression in June 1932, the Oslo group concluded an agreement to reduce tariffs among themselves on a mutual basis by 10 per cent per annum for five years. Though it was already blocking out the discrimination to be achieved at Ottawa two months later, the United Kingdom objected on the grounds that the arrangement would violate the most-favoured-nation clause. After dissolution of the gold bloc in 1936, the Oslo group resumed its example-setting work in reducing trade barriers, agreeing first to impose no new tariffs and then to eliminate quotas applied to one another's trade on a mutual basis. Since the most-favoured-nation clause applied only to tariffs and not to quotas, there was no basis for an objection or to claim extension of the concession.

During the period of restricted trade, The Netherlands licensed not only imports, but in some cases exports. The latter practice was followed where quotas in foreign import markets left open the question whether the difference between the domestic price and the world price would go to importers or exporters. A law of 24 December 1931 established a system of licensing exports in instances of foreign import quotas, with permits distributed among exporters in accordance with the volumes of some historical base period. Licence fees were then imposed, in the amount of 70–100 per cent of the difference between the world price and the domestic price in the import market, with the collected proceeds distributed to Dutch producers. The purpose of the fees was to divert the scarcity rents available from import restriction, first to the exporting country as a whole, and then, within the exporting country, from exporting firms to agricultural producers (Gordon, 1941, p. 356).

E. France

The French are often given the credit in commercial policy between the wars for the invention of the quota, a protective device which was to flourish until well into the 1950s, and even then to experience revival in various forms in the 1970s. While its origins go well back in time, the proximate causes of the quota in 1930 were the limitation on France's freedom of action imposed by the network of trade treaties it had fashioned, beginning with that with Germany in 1927, and the difficulty of ensuring a restriction of imports sufficient to raise domestic prices – the object of the exercise – in the face of inelastic excess supplies abroad. Like the Hawley-Smoot tariff increases in committee, quotas spread from agricultural produce to goods in general.

Under an old law of December 1897 – the so-called *loi de cadenas* – the French government had authority in emergency to change the rate of duty on any one of 46 agricultural items. The emergency of falling agricultural prices after 1928 caused the laws of 1929 and 1931 which extended the list. With especially wheat in excess supply overseas in regions of recent settlement like Australia and Canada, the French decided that raising the tariff under their authority would not only pose questions about their obligations under trade treaties, but might well not limit imports, serving only to reduce world prices and improve the terms of trade. Australia, in particular, lacked adequate storage capacity for its wheat and had no choice but to sell, no matter how high the price obstacles erected abroad. The decision was accordingly taken to restrict quantity rather than to levy a customs duty (Haight, 1941, p. 145). The device was effective. As the depression deepened, and as imports grew with the overvaluation of the franc, it was extended to industrial goods. Other countries follows suit, especially Germany with its foreign exchange control. In 1931, Brüning and Pierre Laval, the then French premier reached an agreement establishing industrial understandings to coordinate production and trade between German and French industries. One such understanding in electrical materials developed into a cartel. The rest were concerned primarily with restricting German exports to France. When they failed to do so, they were replaced by French quotas (Hexner, 1946, pp. 119, 136). After a time, the French undertook bilateral bargaining over quotas, which led in time to reducing quotas below desired limits in order to have room to make concessions during negotiations.

F. Germany

Less by design than by a series of evolutionary steps, Germany developed the most elaborate and thorough-going system of control of foreign trade and payments. Foreign claims on Germany were blocked on 15 July 1931, when Germany could no longer pay out gold and foreign exchange to meet the demands of foreign lenders withdrawing funds. This default was followed by a negotiated Standstill Agreement between creditors and Germany, involving a six-month moratorium on withdrawals, subsequently renewed. The decision not to adjust the value of the Reichsmark after the depreciation of sterling in September 1931 made it necessary to establish foreign exchange control, and to prevent the free purchase and sale of foreign currencies in the private market. The proceeds of exports were collected and allocated to claimants of foreign exchange seeking to purchase imports. Clearing agreements developed under which German importers paid Reichsmarks into special accounts at the Reichsbank in favour of foreign central banks, which then allocated them to their national importers of German goods. The foreign central bank faced a particular problem whether or not to pay out local currency to the exporter in advance of its receipts of local currency from national importers of German goods. Some central banks did pay off local exporters against claims on the German clearing, following what was later called the 'payments principle', and experienced inflation through the resultant credit expansion. Other central banks made their exporters wait for payment which both avoided monetary expansion and held down the incentive to export to Germany (Andersen, 1946).

A number of countries with large financial claims on Germany, such as Switzerland, insisted that the proceeds of German exports be used in part to pay off creditors abroad, thus converting 'clearing' into 'payments' agreements. These payments agreements were also used in a few cases to require Germany to continue spending on non-essential imports of importance to the exporter, such as tourism in Austria.

Germany set limits on the use of foreign-owned marks within Germany as well as against their convention into foreign exchange. They were not permitted to be used for many classes of exports, capable of earning new foreign exchange, but only for incremental exports which could be sold only at implicit depreciated exchange rates, for travel within Germany – the so-called Reisemark – and under certain limitations for investment in Germany. Foreshadowing some post-war limitations on foreign direct investment, permission was granted for investment by foreigners in Germany with outstanding mark balances only when the investment was considered generally beneficial to the German economy, was made for at least five years, did not involve a foreign controlling interest in a German enterprise, and did not exceed a stipulated rate of interest (Gordon, 1941, pp. 92–3).

In August 1934, the New Plan was adopted under the leadership of the German Minister for Economics, Hjalmar Schacht. In the words of Emil Puhl, an associate of Dr Schacht's at the Reichsbank, it provided totalitarian control over commodities and foreign exchange, with stringent controls on imports and on foreign travel, administered through supervisory boards for a long list of commodities and foreign exchange boards in the Reichsbank (Office of the Chief Council for Prosecution of Nazi Criminality, *Nazi Conspiracy and Aggression*, vol. VII, 1946, p. 496). Along with trade and clearing agreements, designed especially to ensure German access to food and raw materials, and to promote exports, the Reichsbank developed a series of special marks for particular purposes. In addition to the Reisemarks for travel, there were special-account (*Auslands-Sonder-Konto*, or 'Aski') marks which came into existence through imports of raw materials, especially from Latin America, and which were sold by the recipients at a discount and used by the buyers on a bilateral basis for purchases of incremental German goods. The incremental aspect of the exports was of course difficult to police. Because Aski-marks would be sold only at a discount, the raw-material supplies against them tended to raise their prices in the bilateral trade (Gordon, 1941, p. 180). On the German side, Schacht established a price-control agency in 1935 in each export group – amounting to 25 in all – to prevent German exporters from competing with one another for export orders and to assure that all exporters sold at the highest possible price (*Nazi Conspiracy*, vol. VII, 1946, p. 383).

Beginning in 1934. German foreign-trade plans were intended particularly to ensure access to imported food and raw materials. The New Plan, and especially the Four Year Plan which succeeded it in the fall of 1936, were designed to produce synthetic materials, especially Buna-S (synthetic rubber) and gasoline from coal, where foreign supplies for wartime needs should not be assured. Particular problems were encountered in non-ferrous metals, in iron ore, for which the low-grade Salzgitter project was developed in the Four Year Plan, and in synthetic fertilizer required for self-sufficiency in food. Schacht at the Reichsbank, Goering as Schacht's successor in the Economics Ministry and as the head of the Four Year Plan, the War and Food Ministries wrangled among themselves over policies, including especially whether to export wheat against foreign exchange following the bumper crops of 1933 and 1934 or conserve it as a war reserve; whether to hoard Germany's meagre free foreign exchange reserves or to spend them for crucially short raw materials; the mobilization of privately owned foreign securities and their conversion to cash for buying materials; the pricing of exports; the purchase of unnecessary imports like frozen meats from Argentina, for lack of which Schacht was unable to conclude a favourable trade treaty, etc. (*Nazi Conspiracy*, vol. VII, 1946). The documents published by the prosecution at the Nuremberg post-war trials reveal considerable internal dissention, especially in the exchanges between Schacht and Goering that lasted through 1937 and ended in Schacht's defeat and resignation.

German sentiment had continuously decried the loss of the country's African colonies in the Versailles treaty. Schacht continuously referred to the loss in Young Plan discussions of the late 1920s and was still harping on the issue in an article in *Foreign Affairs* in 1937. In a conversation with the American ambassador, Bullitt, in the autumn of 1937, Goering noted that Germany's demand for a return of the German colonies which had been taken away by the Versailles treaty was just, adding immediately that Germany had no right to demand anything but these colonies. Particularly sought were the Cameroons which could be developed by German energy (*Nazi Conspiracy,* vol. VII, 1946, pp. 890, 898). Three weeks earlier, however, in a private conference, Hitler had stated that it made more sense for Germany to seek material-producing territory adjoining the Reich and not overseas (*ibid.*, vol. I, 1946, p. 380). And at a final war-preparatory briefing in May 1939, he went further to explain the need for living space in the East to secure Germany's food supplies. It was necessary to beware of gifts of colonial territory which did not solve the food problem: 'Remember blockade' (*ibid.*, vol. I, 1946, p. 392). The directive to the Economic Staff Group on 23 May 1941 just before the attack on the Soviet Union stated that the offensive was designed to produce food in the East on a permanent basis.

It was widely claimed that Germany squeezed the countries of Southeast Europe through charging high prices for non-essential exports, while not permitting them to purchase the goods they needed, at the same time delaying payments for imports through piling up large debit balances in clearing arrangements. In a speech at Köningsberg in August 1935, Schacht expressed regret that Germany had defaulted on debts to numerous pro-German peoples abroad, indicated confidence that Germany could obtain the raw materials it needed, acknowledged that the trade relations of Germany with different countries had changed a great deal, but insisted that these new possibilities of exporting to Germany which had helped relieve them from the rigours of the world depression (*Nazi Conspiracy*, vol. VII, 1946, p. 486). In a polemical exchange in 1941, Einzig insisted that Benham was in error in holding that South-east European countries had improved their terms of trade in dealing with Germany, which paid higher prices than Western Europe was able to pay, and sold German goods competitively in the area. A post-war analysis of the matter tended to show that Benham and Schacht had been right (Kindleberger, 1956, pp. 120ff.).

An intellectual defence of the Benham-Schacht position had been offered in a somewhat different context as early as 1931 by Manoilesco who expressed the view that the theory of comparative advantage had to be qualified if the alternative to tariff protection for an industry were either unemployment, or employment at a wage below the going rate. His statement of this position in *The Theory of Protection and International Trade* (1931) was strongly attacked on analytical grounds by the leading international-trade theorists of the day – Habeler, Ohlin, and Viner, each in extended treatment – but was resurrected after the war by Hagen, and then generalized into a second-best argument for interference with free trade, e.g .by tariffs. When the conditions for a first-best solution under free trade do not exist, protection may be superior in welfare for a country to free trade. By the same token, export sales at less than optimal terms of trade may be superior to the exports and unemployment.

G. The Union of Soviet Socialist Republics

During the 1920s, commercial policy in the Soviet Union had been the subject of a great debate under the New Economic Plan, between the Right that advocated expansion of agriculture, and of other traditional exports, plus domestic production of manufactured consumer goods to provide incentives for farmers, and the Left that favoured development of domestic heavy industry and the relative neglect of agriculture. Under the proposals of the Right, exports of agricultural products would be expanded to obtain imports of machinery, metals, raw materials, and exotic foodstuffs such as coffee and tea. This was the trade-dependent strategy. The Left, on the other hand, sought to increase trade in order to achieve autarky as rapidly as possible, as it feared dependence on a hostile capitalist world. With Stalin's achievement of power, the Left strategy was adopted in the First and subsequent Five Year Plans. Strong efforts were made to reduce dependence on imports to a minimum. Territorial losses during the First World War, land reform which divided large estates, and the inherent bias of planning which favoured domestic users over foreign markets helped reduce the ratio of exports to national income, which fell from a figure variously estimated within the region of 7–12 per cent in 1913 to 3.5 at the inter-war peak in 1931. Estimates of the volume of Soviet exports vary, depending upon the weights chosen, but on the basis of 1927/8 weights, exports fell from 242 in 1913 to 53 in 1924/5 before recovering to 100 in 1929. Thereafter they rose sharply to 150 in 1930 and 164 in 1931 with disastrous consequences for the Russian peoples (Dohan and Hewett, 1973, p. 24).

In 1930 and 1931, Soviet exports conformed to the model of the backward-bending supply curve in which volume increases, rather than decreases, as price falls. Declines in the prices of grain, timber and oil, starting as early as 1925, had threatened the Soviet Union's capacity to pay for the machinery and materials necessary to complete its Five Year Plans, and threatened as well its capacity to service a small amount of foreign debt contracted in the 1920s. To counter this threat, the Soviet authorities diverted supplies of foodgrains from domestic consumption to export markets, shipping it from grain-surplus areas to export ports and leaving internal grain-deficit areas unsupplied. The result was starvation and death for an unknown number of the Russian people numbering in millions. The world price of wheat fell by half between June 1929 and December 1930, and more than half again by December 1932. So hard did the Soviet Union push exports that supplies of pulp wood, woodpulp, timber, lumber, and even coal, asbestos, and furs threatened to enter the Canadian Market, a notable exporter of these products in ordinary times, and led the Canadian government in February 1932 to prohibit the import of these commodities from the Soviet Union (Drummond, 1975, p. 205). Similar discriminatory restrictions were taken in many other markets. The dysfunctional character of forcing exports on the world market became clear and the volume of Soviet exports levelled off and started downward in 1932. As primary-product prices rose after 1936, moreover, the export volume declined sharply below the 1929 level.

H. Japan

Japan had not participated fully in the boom of the 1920s, but the fact that it had restored the yen to par after the First World War as late as January 1930 made it highly vulnerable to the liquidity crisis of 1930 and 1931. It was vulnerable, too, because of heavy dependence on silk, a luxury product, about to experience both a sharp decline in its income-elastic demand and severe competition from rayon and later from nylon. In 1929 silk was responsible for 36 per cent of Japanese exports by value, and produced 20 per cent of Japanese farm income. The price of silk fell by about half from September 1929 to December 1930. With the help of the depreciation of the yen after December 1931, it reached a level of $1.25 a pound in March 1933, compared with $5.20 in September 1929.

The combination of sharp exchange depreciation and the collapse of the American market in silk produced a drastic reorientation in Japanese export trade, away from North America and Europe and toward Asia, Africa, and Latin America. Export drives were especially intense in British and Dutch colonies, and in the so-called 'yen bloc' of Korea, Formosa, Kwantung, and Manchurai. The Japanese share of the Netherlands East Indies market, for example, rose from 10 per cent in the 1920s to 32 per cent in the 1934 before restrictive measures were applied under the Crisis Act of 1933 (Furnival, 1939, p. 431: Van Gelderen, 1939, p. 24). Japanese exports to the yen bloc rose from 24 per cent in 1929 to 55 per cent in 1938, with imports rising from 20 to 41 per cent over the same period (Gordon, 1941, p. 473). Within Asia, Japan developed sugar production in Formosa and stopped buying it in Java in the Netherlands East Indies. The British and Dutch Empires imposed quantitative restrictions on Japanese imports, especially in textiles. Foreshadowing a technique extensively used by the United States after the war, at one stage the British asked the Japanese to impose controls on shipments to India or face abrogation of the Indo-Japanese Commercial Convention of 1904 (Drummond, 1973, p. 133). By 1938 Netherlands East Indies imports from Japan were down to 14 per cent of the total from a high of 30 per cent in 1935 (Van Gelderen, 1935, p. 17). Japanese fear of reprisals led them to amend the Export Association Act of 1925, which had been enacted to promote exports, so as to control exports in accordance with restrictions imposed by importing countries (Gordon, 1941, p. 360).

I. The World Economic Conference of 1933

Sir Arthur Salter termed the Hawley-Smoot tariff a turning-point in world history. Lewis Douglas thought the Thomas amendment under which the dollar was devalued in March 1933 marked 'the end of Western civilization as we know it' (Kindleberger, 1973, p. 202). W. Arthur Lewis regarded the failure of the World Economic Conference of 1933 as 'the end of an era' (Lewis, 1950, p. 68). Each characterization contained an element of hyperbole. The World Economic Conference offered only the slightest of chances to reverse the avalanche of restrictions on world trade and to stabilize exchange rates. The reversal in tariffs came the next year with the June 1934 Reciprocal Trade Agreements Act in the United States. More stability in exchange rates took root with the Tripartite Monetary Agreement of September 1936 among, initially, the United Kingdom, France, and the United States.

The inspiration for a new world economic conference after 1927 went back to the early years of deflation and to a suggestion of Chancellor Brüning of Germany to treat disarmament, reparations, war debts and loans as a single package to be settled on a political basis, rather than separately in each case by economic experts. A preparatory commission of economic experts under the auspices of the League of Nations fashioned a package of somewhat different ingredients, in which the United States would lower the Hawley-Smoot tariff, France would reduce quota restrictions, Germany relax foreign exchange control and the United Kingdom would stabilize the pound. War debts were excluded from the agenda by the United States, and consequently reparations by France and Britain. Pending the convening of the conference, delayed first by the November 1932 elections in the United States and then by domestic preoccupations of the newly elected President Roosevelt, Secretary of State Cordell Hull tried to work out a new tariff truce, but ran into blocks. The United States desired new tariffs on farm products subject to processing taxes under the new Agricultural Adjustment Act; Britain had some pending obligations under the Ottawa agreements; France reserved her position until she could see what would happen to United States' prices as a response to the depreciation of the dollar initiated in April 1933. Only eight countries in all finally agreed to a truce on 12 May 1933, many with explicit reservations. In the final preparations for the conference, commercial-policy measures seemed secondary to all but Cordell Hull, as contrasted with the problem of raising international commodity prices and international public-works schemes, for neither of which could general solutions be found. In the end the United States broke up the conference by refusing to stabilize the exchange rate of the dollar (only to reverse its position seven months later in February 1934), the British felt moderately comfortable with their Empire solution in trade with the vast volume of wrangles still to come, and the gold bloc battened down to ride out the storm. The only positive results were an agreement on silver negotiated by Senator Key Pitman of the US delegation, and bases laid for subsequent international agreements in sugar and wheat. Perhaps a negative result was the *de facto* constitution of the steering bloc with most of the Commonwealth, save Canada and the subsequent withdrawal of the Union of South Africa, plus foreign adherents such as Sweden, Argentina, and a number of countries in the Middle East.

J. Commodity Agreements

From the decline in commodity prices in the mid-1920s, one after another attempt had been made to devise schemes for raising prices. Some were private, like aluminium, copper, mercury, diamonds, nickel, iron and steel; some were governmental. Of the governmental, some were under the control of a single government – Brazil in coffee, Chile in nitrates, the United States in cotton, the Netherlands East Indies in cinchona bark; others, especially in sugar and wheat, were world-wide. Some of the private/government agreements in iron and steel, petroleum, and aluminium were regional, especially European (Gordon, 1941, pp. 430ff.).

The Chadbourne Plan in sugar was reached in May 1931 among leading export countries – Belgium, Cuba, Czechoslovakia, Germany, Hungary, Java, Peru, and Poland – later joined by Yugoslavia. But British India, France, and United Kingdom, and the United States – important consumers that also maintained substantial production – remained outside the agreement. The United States formulated its own legislation, the Jones-Costigan Act of 1934, which assigned rigid quotas to imports from abroad and discriminated in favour of Cuba. Under the Chadbourne Plan, production declined among the signatories but rose almost as much outside. Particularly hard hit was Java which lost both the Japanese and the Indian markets, the former to Formosan production, the latter to domestic production. Unsold stocks in Java reached 2 1/2 million tons in 1932, and the government took over in January 1933 as the single seller. The failure of the Chadbourne scheme led the World Economic Conference to push for a new agreement, which was finally reached under League of Nations auspices only in May 1937 at the height of the recovery of primary-produce prices.

The World Economic Conference was the twentieth international meeting on the subject of wheat after 1928 when the price of wheat started to plummet – two on imperial preference, seven limited to Eastern Europe as already mentioned, and eleven general. The agreement that emerged after the World Economic Conference achieved a system of export quotas for major producers, but no agreement on acreage controls to limit production (Malenbaum, 1953).

Tea was regulated in this period by an international committee which met in London. In March 1931 the four leading producers of tin – Malaya, Boliva, Nigeria, and the Netherlands East Indies – cooperated in the Joint Tin Committee. In May 1934 nine countries in South-east Asia producing 95 per cent of the world's rubber supply undertook to impose export quotas to reconstitute the Stevenson rubber plan which had broken down in 1928 (Van Gelderen, 1939, pp. 51ff.). Their problem was complicated by sharply differing supply elasticities in the plantation and the native sectors, the latter characterized in many countries by backward-bending responses. As rubber prices rose in the 1936/7 inventory boom, a number of governments sought to tax away the price increase from the producers, but until the price collapse of September 1937 succeeded mainly in raising the price to buyers in a sellar's market. With the eventual decline in prices, the incidence of the export taxes shifted back from the foreign consumer to the domestic producer and in most instances they were quickly removed.

K. Sanctions

In December 1934 a border incident occurred between Italian Somalia and Ethiopia. Italy demanded an apology; Ethiopia refused. With tension rising, the League of Nations sought to arbitrate but received no help from Italy. After further border clashes, Italian troops invaded Ethiopia on 3 October 1935 without a declaration of war. Later in the month, the League of Nations declared Italy the aggressor and voted sanctions to be applied to her in arms supply, finance, and export-import restrictions. The League did not, however, decree sanction in the critical item, oil, Germany refused to comply with the League vote, the United States though not a member of the League of Nations was strongly sympathetic. Oil sanctions were discussed again in March 1936. At this time an attempt was made to apply them informally through major world oil companies. These companies stopped selling to Italy, but the increase in oil prices thereby brought about encouraged a vast number of small shippers to enter the business for the first time and to deliver oil to Italian troops at Red Sea ports in the full quantities required. With the fall of Addis Ababa, the Italians proclaimed empire over Ethiopia and withdrew from the League. League members continued to apply sanctions with increasing resolution until 15 July 1936 when sanctions were abandoned (Feis, 1946, vol. III).

IV. THE DISINTEGRATION OF THE WORLD ECONOMY

In a few countries – notably France and the United States – foreign trade fell by the same proportion as national income from 1929 to 1938. In others trade fell more than output. Thus the ratio of imports to industrial production declined by 10 per cent in the United Kingdom, nearly 20 per cent in Canada, 30 per cent in Germany, and 40 per cent in Italy. Crop failures in the United States in 1934 and 1936, and in Germany in 1937 and 1938, prevented the decline in the proportion of imports from being wider (League of Nations (Meade), 1939, pp. 107–8). Buy-British and Buy-American campaigns, involving government discrimination against foreign as against domestic suppliers with margins of initially 10 per cent, increased to 25 per cent, in the United States, and 100 per cent for items under $100, were often supported by programmers affecting state governments, and campaigns to persuade the general public to discriminate as well (Bidwell, 1939, pp. 70–1 and Appendix A). The major influences to be sure were higher tariffs, quotas, clearing and payments agreements, and preferential trade agreements.

What trade remained was distorted, as compared with the freer market system of the 1920s, both in commodity and in country terms. The index of German imports for 1937 with a base of 100 in 1929 strongly reflected *Wehrwirschaft*, and especially rearmament: 'other ores' 153, manganese ore 142, iron ore 122, iron and steel 121, copper 100, cotton 73, wool 62, coal 59, oil seeds 57, timber 28 (League of Nations (Meade), 1938, p. 128). The share of Germany in Turkish, Greek, and Italians imports rose between 1928 and 1939 respectively from 13 to 43 per cent, 27 to 39 per cent and 13 to 17 per cent for the same countries in the same order (Thorbecke, 1960, p. 100). By 1937, bilateral clearings amounted to 12 per cent of total world trade and 50 per cent of the trade of Bulgaria, Germany, Greece, Hungary, Romania, Turkey, and Yugoslavia (League of Nations, 1942, p. 70). Pioneering estimates of the shrinkage of multilaterally as opposed to bilaterally balanced trade were made for the League of Nations Economic and Financial Department by Folke Hilgerdt. In 1928, bilateral balancing of export and import values between pairs of countries on the average covered 70 per cent of merchandise trade, with about 5 per cent more covered by exports or imports of services or capital movements, and 25 per cent balanced multilaterally (League of Nations (Hilgerdt), 1941). Hilgerdt's two studies emphasized the shrinkage of the proportion of the trade balanced multilaterally during the depression years, without furnishing a precise estimate for the end of the 1930s (League of Nations (Hilgerdt), 1941 and League of Nations (Hilgerdt), 1942). A post-war study on a somewhat different basis furnished a comparison for 1938 with 1928, shown in Table 18.

Major changes occurred both world-wide and within Europe. On a world basis, the largest change shown in the Hilgerdt analysis derived from the fact that the developing countries or the tropics no longer earned large surpluses in merchandise trade with the United States to pay their interest on debts owed to Europe, and especially to the United Kingdom. Regionally, within Europe, the most important change was the failure of Germany to earn an export surplus in Europe, largely Britain, to enable her to pay for her net imports of raw materials

TABLE 18 *Proportions of world trade balanced bilaterally and multilaterally (in percentage of total)*

	By non-merchandise	Multilaterally	Bilaterally
1928	11.1	21.2	67.7
1918	14.3	16.9	68.8

Source: Thorbecke (1960) p. 82

from overseas. Another striking feature was the shift by Britain of procurement from Europe to the sterling area. France, The Netherlands, and especially Britain diverted trade from the rest of Europe to their colonial empires, a trend which would be reversed after the Second World War, and especially after the formation of the European Economic Community in 1957 and Britain's accession to it in 1973. In 1913 22 per cent of British exports went to the Empire. By 1938 the figure had more than doubled to 47 per cent. In imports, the proportion rose over the same period from 22.3 to close to 40 per cent. As noted earlier, the figures might have risen further had it not been for what has been called 'Imperial Insufficiency' (Hancock, 1940, p. 232; see also Drummond, 1972).

V. WORLD TRADING SYSTEMS

Recovery of raw-material prices from 1933 to 1937 was followed by some considerable reduction in tariffs, and relaxation of quota restrictions. The renewed, though less far-reaching, decline of these prices in September 1937, outside the fields dominated by European rearmament, set back the movement towards freer trade. The last five years of the inter-war period were most clearly characterized by what have been called disparate 'world trading system' (Tasca, 1939). At the limits were the system of German trade, locked into a network of bilateral clearing and payments agreements, and practising autarky for the sake of war economy (Petzina, 1968), and at the other extreme, the United States, which stood aloof from all payments and clearing agreements, with few quota restrictions, largely in agriculture, some subsidies to export in agricultural commodities, plus government credit through the Export-Import Bank for export promotion. Within Europe, the Balkan countries were nearer to the German model, the Oslo group to the American. Midway between was the Empire preference scheme of Britain, the Dominions, India, and the dependent colonies. Latin America had been hard hit by declines in raw-material prices and the decline in foreign lending, but was hopeful to trade expansion under the Roosevelt 'Good Neighbor' policy. The Soviet Union went its own way. Anxious to join a system, but largely orphaned outside them were the Middle East and Japan, the latter of which carved out its own Greater East Asia Co-Prosperity Sphere.

There were limited attempts at achieving a single unified world trading system. The League of Nations Committee for the Study of the Problem of Raw Materials reported in September 1937 at a time when payments difficulties had eased but the position was on the point of reversal (League of Nations (Meade), 1938, p. 162). It found few problems of supply or access to materials, and argued in favour of valorization schemes to raise prices provided that consumers' interests were safeguarded. The report went to the League of Nations Assembly where it was pigeonholed as a consequence of the sharp check to commodity prices and deterioration in payment balances.

Before that time, the British and French governments had asked Paul Van Zeeland, a former Belgian Prime Minister, to prepare a programme for world action in the commercial-policy field. In January 1938, the Van Zeeland report was presented to the public, equally an inopportune time. It called for reciprocal reductions of tariffs, generalized by the most-favoured-nation clause, replacement of industrial quotas by tariffs or by tariff quotas, removal of foreign exchange control, clearing agreements, and the ban on new lending in London; and, as a final step when all else was in operation, six-months agreements on foreign-exchange rates leading ultimately to the establishment of fixed rates under the gold standard (League of Nations (Meade), 1938, p. 159). The report was received with universal agreement that the restoration of trade was needed, but equally universal agreement that the restoration of trade was needed, but equally universal reluctance on the part of all governments to take any decisive initiative in the matter (Condliffe, 1940, p. 47).

The 1937–9 recession in fact led to increases in tariffs in Belgium, France, Greece, Italy, the Netherlands East Indies, Norway, Sweden, Switzerland, and Yugoslavia in 1938, and in that stronghold of free-trade sentiment, The Netherlands, in March 1939. Rubber and copper quotas which had been freed in 1937 under their commodity schemes were tightened down again. Brazil, Colombia, and Japan extended their foreign exchange restrictions. Germany and Italy introduced the death penalty for violations of foreign exchange regulations in December 1936 and June 1939, respectively. Italy also constituted a Supreme Autarky Commission in October 1937 (League of Nations (Meade), 1939, p. 197). In all, the number of clearing and payments agreements rose from 131 on 1 June 1936 to 171 by 1 January 1939 (Gordon, 1941, p. 131).

Meanwhile some considerable relaxation of commercial policy was underway in the United States, led by Cordell Hull, whom Herbert Freis, his economic adviser in the Department of State, called a monomaniac on the subject of tariff reductions (Freis, 1966, p. 262). Hull had long been a Congressman from eastern Tennessee, which specialized in tobacco for export, before becoming Secretary of State, and had been in opposition to the Fordney-McCumber and Hawley-Smoot tariff increases in 1922 and 1930 as a member of the House of Representatives Committee on Ways and Means. As early as the World Economic Conference of 1927, as a Congressman, he had been thought to believe that the tariff of the United States was the key to the entire world situation (US Department of State, *Foreign Relations of the United States* delegation to the World Economic Conference of 1933, he had been frustrated in his attempts to get world tariffs reduced by the repudiation of President

Roosevelt which prevented him from encountering the profound disinterest of the other countries. The tariff truce of May 1933 lapsed when the conference failed, but Secretary Hull persevered. At the Seventh Conference of American States at Montevideo in November 1933 – the first having been held in 1889 – he had tariffs put on the agenda for the first time and induced President Roosevelt to offer the Latin American republics tariff reductions (Gordon, 1941, p. 464). The main business accomplished at Montevideo was the strengthening of the most-favoured-nation clause, as Hull had tried to do at London, by government agreement not to invoke the clause in order to prevent the consummation of multilateral tariff reductions in agreements to which a government was not a party. The full agreement provided for no tariff reduction, and was signed by eight countries, though ratified only by the United States and Cuba (Viner, 1950, p. 37).

Upon his return from Montevideo, Secretary Hull found that the President had established an Executive Committee on Commercial Policy under the chairmanship of George Peck, agricultural expert and opponent of trade liberalization, and that the committee had already drafted a bill providing for trade treaties to be subject to Senate ratification. This was unsatisfactory to Hull. The Department of State had already been negotiating with Argentina, Brazil, Colombia, Portugal, and Sweden in the summer of 1933, had signed an agreement only with Colombia, but had not submitted it to the Senate for ratification. In early 1934 new legislation was drawn up that delegated authority from the Congress to the Executive branch of government to conclude reciprocal trade agreements on its own authority. The draft legislation was completed on 24 February, approved by President Roosevelt on 28 February, passed the House of Representatives on 20 March, the Senate on 4 June, and was signed into law on 13 June 1934 as the Reciprocal Trade Agreements Act. The initial delegation of authority was for a period of three years. The legislation was renewed in 1937 and 1940. It provided for mutual bilateral reductions in tariff duties, generalized by the most-favoured-nation clause, limited to 50 per cent of the existing (largely Hawley-Smoot) tariff levels.

Even before the legislation had been drafted, further talks were going forward to reduce tariffs, with Belgium and Denmark in January 1934, and with Canada. Canada and the United States each made official public statements on the subject in February 1934, emphasizing the importance of their mutual trade relations. A request for negotiations was made by the Canadian government in November 1934 and an agreement was achieved a year later to the effect on 1 January 1936. Canada received concessions on 88 items, largely primary products, including along with Hawley-Smoot items, the lumber and copper affected by the US Revenue Act of 1932. United States concessions obtained from Canada were largely in manufactured goods.

The first agreement under the Reciprocal Trade Agreements Act, however, was that concluded with Cuba in August 1934. By November 1939, agreements had been reached with twenty countries, eleven of them in Latin America. A second agreement was concluded with Canada in November 1938, but the most important was the British agreement concluded simultaneously with the revision of the Canadian agreement.

In the British and Canadian agreements, the United States hoped to break down Empire preference. This was beginning to happen of its own accord. In a British–Canadian trade agreement of 1937, five years following the Ottawa agreements of 1932, the British persuaded the Canadians to abolish the doctrine of equalizing competition and to substitute fixed tariff rates and fixed preferential margins in the agreements (McDiarmid, 1946, p. 295). New Zealand was ready to abandon the Ottawa agreements, and started to conclude agreements outside them with Sweden (1935), Greece (1936), Germany (1937), and was negotiating a dozen others (Hancock, 1940, p. 278). Britain meanwhile was highly critical of Australian performance under Ottawa, on the ground that Australia had persistently violated its commitments. Australian Tariff Board studies were limited, and even when the Tariff Board recommended reductions on British goods, the government often failed to introduce them in parliament (Drummond, 1975, pp. 392ff.) British and Australian interests were only partly complementary. Accordingly the United Kingdom, Canada, and the other Dominions as well were ready in their agreements with the United States to sacrifice advantages in each other's markets in return for significant compensation in the market in the United States (Hancock, 1940, p. 265).

To an extent, the Anglo-American trade agreement was more symbolic than effective. Two years of hard bargaining went into it, and it lasted only eight months, from 1 January 1939 until British wartime controls were imposed on the outbreak of war with Germany in September 1939. Reductions were agreed on nine items in which trade amounted to no more than $350 per annum. Important concessions, as in cotton textiles, were prevented from being generalized to Japan and other competitors through reclassification. Full 50 per cent reductions in the United States were made on 96 items but the total trade involved was only $14 million. Under all twenty agreements, the unweighted (equal weights) United States *ad valorem* duties were reduced from 57 per cent on products subject to the tariff to 35 per cent, a reduction of 39 per cent, whereas the reduction under the British agreement, from 42 to 30 per cent on the same basis, amounted only to a reduction of 28 per cent. The 35 per cent level achieved on 1 January 1939 was somewhat lower than the Fordney-McCumber average of 38.5 per cent and the Payne-Aldrich tariff (1909) of 40.8 per cent, and well below the Hawley-Smoot average of 51.5 per cent. It was nevertheless still well above the 1913 Underwood level of 27 per cent (Kreider, 1943, pp. 170ff.).

Moreover, the trade agreements applied largely to industrial products and materials. United States opposition to Empire preference had export concerns in view, especially in competition with Canada in pork and apples. The reductions in tariffs under the agreements, however, went side by side with continued US protection against agricultural imports and subsidies on agricultural exports. Protection was required under those domestic programmes which raised prices in the United States and would, without new restrictions, have attracted further supplies from abroad; and subsidies were deemed necessary to offset the price disadvantage this imposed on American producers in their traditional markets. The trade agreements reduced tariffs on a few items, such as maple sugar from Canada, which had been a particular irritant under the Hawley-Smoot Act, and altered the arbitrary valuations on fresh fruits and vegetables early in the season that had hitherto been kept out of Canada by this device. A sanitary agreement between the United States and Argentine on the regulation of foot-and-mouth disease was not ratified by the Congress (Bidwell, 1939, pp. 217–18); and independence for the Philippines was accelerated to push its sugar production outside the tariff borders of the United States. On the whole, the trade agreements marked the beginning of regarding liberal commercial policies as appropriate only for manufacturers, and their inputs, and leaving agricultural trade largely to special arrangements.

A small beginning was made by the United States on what was to be a major post-war issue. East-West trade. The United States was unwilling to recognize the government of the Soviet Union all through the 1920s. With President Roosevelt's New Deal, this was changed and recognition was accorded in 1933. In the mid-thirties, the United States and the Soviet Union undertook a series of trade agreements. In 1935, the Soviet Union contracted to purchase at least $30 million worth of US goods in the following year; in return, the United States accorded the Soviet Union most-favoured-nation treatment. In August 1937 under a new part, the Soviet Union agreed to step up its purchases from the United States to $40 million (Gordon, 1941, p. 407).

British adherence to the more liberal trade policies pursued by Cordell Hull was highly ambiguous. Kreider claims that the British concessions were not spectacular but represented a reversal of policy (1943, p. 240). At the same time, the British government was unwilling to repudiate the principle of Ottawa, despite its effects, as Mackenzie King claimed, in destroying the principle of imperial harmony (Drummond, 1975, p. 316).

Moreover, British ministers were experimenting with a new technique quite at variance with the American professed principle of increased reliance on the international market. Mention was made above of the special tariff assistance given to the iron and steel industry to assist in its negotiations with the International Steel Cartel. At the depth of the depression, in October 1933, the British had encouraged negotiations between Lancashire and Indian cotton-textile mill owners. The resultant Lees-Mody pact of October 1933 provided that India would lower her tariffs on British textiles to 20 per cent while holding those against other (i.e. Japanese) goods at 75, to which they had been raised from 31 ½ per cent in August 1932 in several steps. As part of the negotiation, involving governments and business groups on both sides, the British agreed to take one and a half million bales of cotton that had piled up as a result of a Japanese retaliatory boycott. At the time Lord Runciman stated, 'The work of the Delegation has gone some way in justifying the Government in their belief that best approach to the problem of international industrial cooperation is by the method of discussion between industrialists' (Drummond, 1972, p. 316).

In early 1939, immediately after signing the Anglo-American Reciprocal Trade Agreement in November 1938, and as part of an export drive, the British Board of Trade encouraged the visit to Düsseldorf of a delegation of the Federation of British Industry to meet with the Reichsgruppe Industrie, its institutional counterpart, and to fix quantitative relationships between the exports of the two countries in each commodity and market. In prospect, *The Economist* after some qualifications expressed itself as approving (cxxiv, no. 4585 (February 1939),

p. 383). The agreement was concluded on 16 March 1939, one day after the German invasion of Czechoslovakia (text in Hexner, 1946, Appendix III, pp. 402–4). The British government repudiated the agreement on political grounds, but not before *The Economist* had denounced it on the grounds that it involved cartelization of domestic industry as well as of trade, but it would extend Anglo-German subsidies to exports, and that it might involve joint action against competition who refused to join the arrangement, including possible American firms (March 1939, p. 607).

In Eastern Europe the German bloc was strengthened in ways to guarantee German access to raw materials and foodstuffs in short supply. An agrement with Hungary in 1934 provided for a shift of Hungarian agriculture from wheat to oilseeds with an assured outlet in Germany. German treaties with Romania in March 1935 and again four years later fostered the expansion of Romanian agriculture in oil seeds, feedgrains, vegetable fibres, as well as industrial and financial cooperation, including the development of Romanian transport and petroleum under German–Romanian companies supervized by joint government commissions (Gordon, 1941, pp. 425–6). In 1937, the proportion of German exports sold through clearing agreements amounted to 57 per cent, while 53 per cent of her imports came through clearings. The comparable figures for Turkey were 74 and 72 per cent respectively, for Romania 67 and 75 per cent, for Switzerland 28 and 36 per cent, for Sweden 17 and 24 per cent, and for the United Kingdom 2 and 2 per cent (Gordon, 1941, Table 7, p. 133).

The disintegration of world trade thus proceeded, despite the attempts of the United States, the Oslo group, Premier Van Zeeland under Anglo-French auspices and the economists of the Economic and Financial Department of the League of Nations. With some prescience Condliffe concluded his book written at the outbreak of the Second World War (1940, p. 394), 'If an international system is to be restored, it must be an American-dominated system, based on *Pax Americana*.'

NOTE

I am grateful for the comments on the original draft of Barry Eichengreen, Jonathan Hughes and Donald Moggridge

REFERENCES

For a useful, immediately post-war bibliography on international economics generally, with approximately seventeen pages on commercial policy, see American Economic Association (H. S. Ellis and L. Metzler), *Readings in the Theory of International Trade,* Homewood, III., 1950, pp. 555ff. and especially pp. 608–25.

Andersen, F. Nyboe, *Bilateral Exchange Clearing Policy.* Copenhagen, 1946.
Arndt, H. W. *The Economic Lessons of the Nineteen-Thirties.* London, 1944.
Australia: Committee on Economics (Brigden, J. B.) *The Australian Tariff, An Economic Enquiry.* Melbourne, Melbourne University Press, 1929.

Benham, Frederic C. *Great Britain under Protection.* New York, 1941.
Bergsten, C. Fred. *Completing the GATT: Toward New International Rules to Govern Export Controls.* No place stated, British–North-American Committee, 1974.
Beveridge, William H. *Tarrifs, The Case Examined by a Committee of Economists under the Chairmanship of Sir William Beveridge.* New York, 1931.
Bidwell, Percy W. *The Invisible Tariff. A Study of Control of Imports into the United States.* New York, 1939.
—— *Raw Materials: A Study of American Policy.* New York, 1958.
Brigden, J. L. 'The Australian Tariff and the Standard of Living', *Economic Record,* vol. 1, no. 1 (November 1925), pp. 29–46.
Brown, William Adams, Jr. *The United States and the Restoration of World Trade,* Washington, DC, 1950.
Childs, Frank C. *The Theory and Practice of Exchange Control in Germany.* The Hague, 1958.
Committee on Finance and Industry (United Kingdom, Macmillan Report, Cmd 1897), London, 1931.
Condliffe, J. B. *The Reconstruction of World Trade: A Survey of International Economic Relations.* New York, 1940.
Copland, Douglas B. and James, C. V. *Australian Tariff Policy: A Book of Documents, 1932–1937.* Melbourne. 1937.
Davis, Joseph S. *The World Between the Wars, 1919–1939: An Economist's View.* Baltimore, Md., 1975.
Dohan, Michael and Hewett, Edward. *Two Studies in Soviet Terms of Trade, 1918 1970.* Bloomington, Ind., 1973.
Drummond, Ian M. *British Economic Policy and the Empire, 1919–1939.* London, 1972.
—— *Imperial Economic Policy, 1917–1939: Studies in Expansion and Protection,* Toronto, 1975.
—— *Economist, The.*
Einzing, Paul J. *Bloodless Invasion: German Penetration into the Danube States and the Balkans.* London, 1938.
Elliott, William Y., May, Elizabeth S., Rowe, J. F. W., Skelton, Alex and Wallace, Donald H. *International Control in Non-ferrous Metals.* New York, 1937.
Federal Trade Commission. *The International Petroleum Cartel,* US Senate Select Committee on Small Business, 82nd Congress, Committee Print no. 6. Washington, DC, August 1952.
Feis, Herbert, *Three International Episodes seen from E.A.* New York, 1946.
—— *1933, Characters in Crisis.* Boston, 1966.
Friedman, Philip. *The Impact of Trade Destruction on National Income: A Study of Europe, 1924–38.* Gainesville, Fla., 1974.
Furnivall, J. S. *Netherlands India: A Study of Plural Economy.* Cambridge, 1939.
Gordon, Margaret S. *Barriers to World Trade: A Study of Recent Commercial Policy.* New York, 1941.
Haight, Frank Arnold. *A History of French Commercial Policies.* New York, 1941.
Hancock, W. Keith, *Survey of British Commonwealth Affairs,* vol. II: *Problems of Economic Policy,* London, 1940.
Hexner, Erwin. *International Cartels* Durham, NC, 1946.
Hoover, Herbert, *The Memoirs of Herbert Hoover,* vol. III, *The Great Depression, 1929–1941.* New York, 1952.
Hull, Cordell. *The Memoirs of Cordell Hull,* New York, 1948.
Johnson, Alvin S. 'Protection and the Formation of Capital', *Political Science Quarterly,* vol. XXIII (June 1908), pp. 220–41.
Johnson, D. Gale. *Trade and Agriculture; A Study of Inconsistent Policies.* New York, 1950.

Jones, Joseph M., Jr. *Tariff Retaliation, Repercussions of the Hawley-Smoot Bill.* Philadelphia, 1934.

Kindleberger, Charles P. *The Terms of Trade: A European Case Study.* New York, 1956.

—— *The World in Depression, 1929–1939.* Berkeley, 1973: revised edn. 1986.

Knorr, Klaus E. *World Rubber and its Regulation.* Stanford, 1946.

Kreider, Carl. *The Anglo-American Trade Agreement: A Study of British and American Commercial Policies, 1934–39.* Princeton, 1943.

Lary, Hal B. (US Department of Commerce, Bureau of Foreign and Domestic Commerce). *The United States in the World Economy,* Economic Series, no. 23. Washington, DC, 1943.

League of Nations. *Enquiry into Clearing Agreements.* Geneva, 1935.

—— *Commercial Policy in the Interwar Period: International Proposals and National Policies,* Geneva, 1942.

—— Economic Committee. *Considerations on the Present Evolution of Agricultural Tariffs,* Geneva. 1935.

—— (Folke Hilgerdt). *Europe's Trade, A Study of the Trade of European Countries with Each Other and with the Rest of the World.* Geneva, 1941.

—— (Folke Hilgerdt). *The Network of World Trade, A Companion Volume to 'Europe's Trade'.* Geneva, 1942.

—— (James E. Meade), *World Economic Survey, 1937/38.* Geneva, 1938.

—— (James E. Meade), *World Economic Survey, 1938/39.* Geneva, 1939.

—— (W. T. Page). *Memorandum on European Bargaining Tariffs.* Geneva, 1927.

—— (Jacob Viner). *Trade Relations between Free-market and Controlled Economics,* Geneva, 1943.

Lewis, Cleona, *Nazi Europe and World Trade.* Washington, DC, 1941.

Lewis, W. Arthur. *Economic Survey, 1919–1939.* Philadelphia, 1950.

Liepmann, H. *Tariff Levels and the Economic Unity of Europe.* London, 1938.

McDiarmid, Orville J. *Commercial Policy in the Canadian Economy.* Cambridge, Mass., 1946.

Malenbaum, Wilfrid. *The World Wheat Economy, 1895–1939.* Cambridge, Mass., 1953.

Manoilesco, Mihail. *The Theory of Protection and International Trade.* London, 1931.

Mason, Edward S. *Controlling World Trade, Cartels and Commodity Agreements,* New York, 1946.

Office of the Chief Counsel for Prosecution of Nazi Criminality. *Nazi Conspiracy and Aggression,* vols. I and VII. Washington, DC, 1946.

Petzina, Dieter. *Autarkiepolitik im dritten Reich, Der national-sozialistiche Vierjahresplan.* Stuttgart, 1968.

Reitsama, A. J. 'Trade and Redistribution of Income: Is There Still an Australian Case?'. *Economic Record,* vol. XXIV, no. 68 (August 1958). pp. 172–88.

Richardson, J. H. *British Economic Foreign Policy.* London, 1936.

Roepke, Wilhelm. *German Commercial Policy.* London, 1934.

—— *International Economic Disintegration.* London, 1942.

Rowe, J. W. F. *Markets and Men: A Study of Artificial Control Schemes.* New York 1936.

Salter, Sir Arthur. *Recovery, the Second Effort.* London and New York, 1932.

Schacht, Hjalmar 'Germany's Colonial Demand', *Foreign Affairs,* vol. XIV (January 1937), pp. 223–34.

Schattschneider, E. E. *Politics, Pressures and Tariffs: A Study of Free Private Enterprise in Pressure Politics as Shown by the 1929–30 Revision of the Tariff,* New York, 1935.

Schuker, Stephen A. *The End of French Predominance in Europe: The Financial Crisis of 1924 and the Adoption of the Dawes Plan,* Chapel Hill, NC, 1976.

Smith, Mark A. 'The United States Flexible Tariff', in *Explorations in Economics, Notes and Essays Contributed in Honor of F. W. Taussig.* New York, 1936.

Stolper, W. F. and Samuelson, P. A. 'Protection and Real Wages', *Review of Economic Studies*, vol. IX (November 1941), pp. 58–73.
Suctens, M. *Histoire de la politique commerciale de la Belgique jusqu'a nos jours.* Brussels, 1955.
Tasca, Henry J. *The Reciprocal Trade Agreement Policy of the United States: A Study in Trade Philosophy.* Philadelphia, 1938.
Thorbecke, Erik. *The Tendency toward Regionalization in International Trade, 1928–1956.* The Hague, 1960.
United Nations, Department of Economic Affairs. *Customs Union: A League of Nations Contribution to the Study of Custom Union Problems.* Lake Success, NY, 1947.
United States Department of State. *Foreign Relations of the United States.* Washington, DC, various years.
——Tariff Commission. *Foreign Trade and Exchange Controls,* Report no. 150. Washington, DC, 1942.
Van Gelderen, J. *The Recent Development of Economic Foreign Policy in the Netherlands East Indies,* London, 1939.
Viner, Jacob. *The Customs Union Issue.* New York, 1950.
—— *Dumping: A Problem in International Trade.* 1923, rep. New York, 1966.
Winslow, E. M. 'Administrative Protection: A Problem in Commercial Policy', in *Explorations in Economics: Notes and Essays in Honor of F. W. Taussig.* New York, 1936.
World Trading Systems. Paris, 1939.

14. A Proposal for an International Commercial Union

J. Meade

Note: This is the text of a proposal by James Meade on 25 July 1942 when he was in the Economic Section of the War Cabinet Secretariat in the British Government. The document was not published until 1987 when The World Economy *reproduced it (vol. 10, pp. 399–407).*

The acronyms in the document which appear in parentheses refer to committees in the Cabinet Office: E.C. = Post-war Employment; R. P. = Reconstruction Problems; and U.S.E. = Post-war Economic Problems of Anglo-American Co-operation.

1 OUR POST-WAR COMMERCIAL PROBLEMS

1. The United Kingdom will be in a difficult commercial position after the war. As a community we depend upon imports of essential foodstuffs and raw materials, which we must purchase by the export of manufactured goods. Developments during the war, such as the loss of income from foreign investments, will have increased our need for an expanded export trade, while at the same time the industrialisation which has taken or is likely to take place in certain overseas territories may well have restricted some of our export opportunities. We import essentials; we export goods with which our customers can more easily dispense. If ever there was a community which had an interest in the general removal of restrictions to international commerce, it is the United Kingdom.

2. Our trade in the past has been very largely of a multilateral character. We have brought goods from the United States with income obtained from the sale of our produce in other less well developed territories. If many of our most readily available sources of supply of essential imports are not to be closed to us, it is important that the opportunities for beneficial multilateral trade should be preserved to their fullest extent.

3. Our export possibilities would thus be directly and indirectly greatly improved if we could obtain the agreement, for example, of the United States to modify its pre-war excessive tariff barriers and of Germany to give up its pre-war policy of bilateralism and trade discrimination. These considerations suggest that we, above all other countries, stand to gain (i) from a policy of general world economic and financial expansion which will maintain a high level of buying power in export markets, (ii) from a general reduction of barriers and restrictions

in international markets and (iii) from a removal of those discriminations and rigidly bilateral bargains which remove the opportunities for multilateral trading.

4. Multilateral trading and the removal of trade restrictions do not, however, imply laissez-faire, and are in no way incompatible with a system of state trading. We shall wish to co-operate with the United States, on the basis of Article VII of the Mutual Aid Agreement of 23rd February, 1942, on 'action by the United States of America and the United Kingdom, open to participation by all other countries of like mind, directed to . . . the elimination of all forms of discriminatory treatment in international commerce, and to the reduction of tariffs and other trade barriers. . .' At the same time, we must aim at the formulation of such action by means which do not automatically preclude countries such as the USSR, which may be assumed to desire to continue a system of state trading, nor prevent us, if we so desire, from continuing a system of state importation for certain products.

5. After the war we shall not be in a position in which we can afford *unconditionally* to abandon all protective devices. We cannot readily indulge in a unilateral policy of removing our protective armour and shall thus desire to retain the right to restrict purchases from, and to discriminate against, those countries which themselves retain highly protective commercial policies or which discriminate against ours. We shall, moreover, need to retain the right to impose more general restrictions on purchases of unessential goods or on unnecessary payments abroad so long as we are faced with an acute problem of restoring equilibrium to our international balance of payments.

6. The essential features of our post-war commercial problems may, therefore, be summarised as follows:

(i) We shall need a large expansion of our export trade and shall stand to gain very greatly from a general world system in which there is a general expansion of world purchasing power and in which restrictions and discriminations on foreign trade are reduced or removed.

(ii) Apart from our interests we are committed under Article VII of the Mutual Aid Agreement to such a policy, and the future of our relations with the United States requires that we should implement this undertaking.

(iii) We need, however, to implement these undertakings in a way which leaves room for state trading and which does not preclude us (a) from imposing restrictions or discriminations against those countries which impose severe restrictions or discriminations against us or (b) from restricting our payments to other countries if and when balance-of-payments difficulties make such action inevitable.

II THE CONTRIBUTION OF OTHER PROPOSED INSTITUTIONS TO THE SOLUTION OF THE COMMERCIAL PROBLEM

7. The proposals which have already been made (R.P.[42] 2 paragraphs) for the institution of an International Clearing Union, if they are adopted, should much simplify our task in formulating far-reaching and imaginative proposals for the reduction of restrictions to international commerce.

8. In the first place, these and similar proposals would greatly help – indeed this is the essence of the proposals – to adjust the balance of payments without

undue strain on the debtor countries. Since a large number of protective devices are in origin essentially weapons of defence of countries which are faced with an undue pressure on their balances of international payments, an affective mechanism which makes the creditor nations responsible for a due part, if necessary, of adjustments of international payments should clear the way for attempts to mitigate protectionism.

9. But, in the second place, the machinery of the Clearing Union, through the debit and credit balances of its members, provides an effective and automatic measurement of existing maladjustments in balances of payments. A country which claims that it must be permitted to impose certain protective restrictions as a result of a serious maladjustment in its balance of payments can appeal to (or be referred to) a reasonably unambiguous index – its debit balance with the Clearing Union. It should, for example, be possible for a country to commit itself in commercial agreements to remove various protective devices, but, at the same time, to reserve the right to reimpose some of these devices when and for as long as its debit with the Clearing Union was in excess of a certain figure.

10. Thirdly, the Clearing Union may be expected to aid in promoting that general expansion of demand in world markets which, in Article VII of the Mutual Aid Agreement itself, comes before the removal of trade restrictions and discriminations as an objective of international co-operative action. Indeed, it is only in a general milieu of economic expansion that the pressure on the balance of payments of debtor countries is likely to be sufficiently relieved to make possible a really effective lowering of protective devices. There are other proposals under consideration which will help towards the same purpose of economic expansion. In particular the proposals for the development of international investment (R.P. [42] 2 paragraphs) and the proposals for a systematisation of buffer stock arrangements for primary products (U.S.E. [42]) should provide effective support to an expansive international policy.

III OUTLINE OF A POSSIBLE COMMERCIAL UNION

11. It is suggested, therefore, that the United Kingdom should propose the formation of an International Commercial Union for the purpose of achieving a general reduction of restrictions on international commerce. The Commercial Union would be founded on the following principles:

(i) Membership of the Union would be open to all states which applied for membership and which were willing to carry out the obligations of membership. Membership of the Commercial Union would not be confined to members of the Clearing Union (just as membership of the Clearing Union would in no way be confined to members of the Commercial Union) but, as is indicated in (iv) below, members of the Commercial Union who were also members of the Clearing Union would obtain certain privileges in the Commercial Union.

(ii) Members of the Commercial Union would undertake not to grant preferences or other price advantages to any other member of the Union without extending it to all members, except that certain moderate and defined degrees of preference might be given as between members of a recognised political or geographical group of nations. A clause of this kind would permit discrimination of any degree desired against countries which were not members of the Commercial Union and which had not, therefore, pledged themselves in turn not to discriminate. It would also permit discrimination of a defined and moderate degree in favour of a recognised political or geographical grouping of states and would thus permit the continuation of a moderate degree of Imperial Preference.

(iii) Members of the Commercial Union would undertake to remove altogether certain protective devices against the commerce of other members of the Union and to reduce to a defined maximum the degree of protection which they would afford to their own home producers against the produce of other members of the Union. A clause of this type would pledge members to eliminate or to limit their protective devices against other members of the Union who had undertaken a similar pledge, but would leave them free to introduce what protective measures they desired against non-members. Such an arrangement would be safeguarded by the right of any non-member state to join the Commercial Union.

(iv) Members of the Commercial Union, who were also members of the Clearing Union and whose accounts with the Clearing Union were in deficit by a certain defined amount, would be permitted to impose certain protective devices so long as their debt remained in excess of the prescribed amount.

(v) The Charter of the Commercial Union would expressly state that state trading by members of the Union was not precluded. An indication should be given of the way in which the provisions of the Charter of the Commercial Union should be applied both in the case of competitive trading and in the case of state trading.

(vi) The Charter of the Commercial Union would provide for the institution of an International Commerce Commission of a semi-arbitral semi-judicial nature. Members could refer complaints to this body in order to obtain an opinion whether the Charter or the Union was being broken by any particular action of a particular member of the Union.

(vii) Membership of the Commercial Union would in no way preclude any member from concluding any type of commercial treaty or agreement with any other state – whether a member of the Union or not – provided only that the terms of the treaty or agreement were not incompatible with its obligations as a member of the Union.

12. If an attempt were made to a Charter for a Commercial Union of this type, one of the most important questions would be how precisely worded should be the definition of the discriminations and degrees of protection that would be disallowed to members of the Union and of the actions which would be permitted or disallowed to state trading organisations. It is in this connection that the major dilemma is to be faced. If an attempt is made to define very rigidly and precisely exactly what any member may or may not do in all possible circumstances, it is probable that as circumstances change and as states introduce new methods of trading certain state measures may be precluded which it is not in the general intention of the Charter to disallow and certain other measures may be allowed which it is in the intention of the Charter to forbid. On the other hand, if the Charter is drawn up in much less precise terms and expresses only in the most

general terms the types of protective device which it is intended to allow, then very great responsibility will rest upon the International Commerce Commission or similar body whose duty it was to interpret the Charter. The success of the Union will depend upon the formulation of the Charter in terms, which, on the one hand, do not attempt to put international trade into an impossible strait jacket and, on the other hand, do not impose upon the International Commerce Commission such a burden of semi-legislative duties that it could not bear.

13. The following clauses are intended merely as an illustration of one possible set of conditions which might be included in that section of the Charter of the Commercial Union in which the limitations on members' discriminatory or protective policy are defined:

(i) Members would be forbidden to discriminate (whether by means of taxes, subsidies, preferential prices offered by state organisations, or other means) in the prices offered for the produce of other members of the Union.

(ii) Members would be bound to give other members of the Union as favourable prices for their produce as they gave for the similar produce from any non-member state.

(iii) As exceptions to Clauses (i) and (ii) above members could give price preferences up to a maximum of, say, 10 per cent to the produce of another state with which it formed a special recognised geographical or political union.

(iv) Members would be forbidden to give a preference (whether by tax, subsidy, price offered by state trading body or other means) in price to their home producers which was more than, say, 25 per cent greater than the price offered to similar goods produced by other members of the Union.

(v) Members would be forbidden to impose quantitative restrictions or prohibitions, other than for reasons of public health or public safety, on the import of goods from other members of the Commercial Union.

(vi) Members would undertake not to impose restrictions on payments for current (as opposed to capital) transactions to other members of the Union, except that a country which was also a member of the Clearing Union and was a 'deficiency' country with the Clearing Union would be permitted to impose restrictions on current payments for as long as it remained a 'deficiency' country.

(vii) Members would undertake not to impose quantitative restrictions or prohibitions on exports except as part of a recognised international regulation scheme for primary products (as arranged for in the scheme outlined in U.S.E. [42]).

(viii) Members would undertake not to impose open or hidden taxes or subsidies of more than, say, 10 per cent, on exports to any country whether a member of the Commercial Union or not.

14. The purpose of these various provisions is clear. Clauses (i) to (iii) in the preceding paragraph would limit price discrimination for imports. Clause (iv) would limit the degree of price protection which could be given to home production; Clauses (v) and (vi) would prevent quantitative or value restrictions on imports, except in the case of countries in a 'deficiency' position with the Clearing Union; and Clauses (vii) and (viii) would cover export policy, preventing both undue restriction of exports and export dumping – the latter of which may

be equally obnoxious whether it be to other member states or to non-member states.

IV THE PROBLEM OF STATE TRADING

15. The general principles of the application of these clauses to countries adopting a competitive trade organisation are clear, although there would, no doubt, be many difficult technical problems to be determined in border-line cases by the International Commerce Commission as to what exactly did or did not constitute a price preference or a restriction on payments. The problem of applying these clauses to cases of state trading would probably in practice present more difficulties since it is as yet a less familiar problem; but in principle it should no less be capable of satisfactory solution.

16. It resolves itself into a two-fold problem:

(i) That of determining the degree of price preference of protection which is being offered by the state trading organisation and
(ii) That of deciding whether a quantitative restriction on imports (or on exports) is being imposed.

In the case of a state which, while its trading system is mainly competitive, monopolises for itself the trade of a limited number of commodities, the problem of judging the degree of price discrimination or of price preference given as between one source of supply and another or as between one market and another does not present any additional difficulties of principle. This problem may become somewhat more complicated in practice, but it still remains in essence the same, even in the case of a country which has socialised trade in all or the majority of products; such extreme cases are, however, in the post-war world likely to be relatively few in number; and they will be still less important from the point of view of their share in the total of international trade.

17. The regulation of price preferences is not, however, sufficient to prevent discrimination or protection. A state trading organisation might, for example, discriminate in favour of one source of supply as opposed to another by buying much in the first and little in the second, even though it paid a non-discriminatory price. It is necessary to determine what corresponds in the case of state trading to the obligations (suggested in clauses [v]–[vii] of paragraph 14 above) not to impose quantitative restrictions on imports or exports except in certain clearly defined cases. This limitation corresponds in the case of state trading to an obligation (i) to take from each foreign market as much imports as each such market would wish to supply at the price which the importing state organisation is offering and (ii) to sell in all foreign markets as much foreign exports as each such market would wish to purchase at the price at which the goods are offered by the state exporting organisation.

18. These considerations suggest that the principles of membership of the Commercial Union should be applied in such a way as (i) to impose the same obligations both to competitive and to state trading in all matters of price

discrimination and price preference, (ii) to forbid in the case of competitive trading quantitative restrictions on imports and exports and on current payments and (iii) to impose in the case of state trading obligations to purchase from, or to sell to, each foreign market as much as that foreign market wishes to sell, or to purchase, at the prices offered by the state trading organisation. It would, however, be a matter for detailed consideration to determine the extent to which, and the conditions on which, long forward contracts could be entered into by state trading organisation within the framework of these principles. Such contracts should not be excluded; but they should be undertaken in such a way as to maintain a reasonable approximation to the principle outlined above.

V THE INTERNATIONAL COMMERCE COMMISSION

18. The existence of some international body which had the competence to interpret the Charter of the Commercial Union, and to arbitrate or to give decisions in case of disputes among its members, would be an essential part of the mechanism of such a union. It would, however, be premature at this stage to make detailed suggestions about the constitution of such a body. Its members should, no doubt, be appointed by the governments of the states making up the Commercial Union. It should, no doubt, have the power of expressing an opinion upon any complaint brought to its notice by one member of the Union against another member and of requiring members of the Union to provide it with the statistical and other information necessary to form a judgement in such cases. It might well be ruled that, in such cases, its findings – both its majority and minority findings – should be published. But it is a matter for further consideration how such findings should be binding on members of the Union. It might, for example, be provided, as a sanction against breaches of the Charter of the Union, that any member of the Union which refused to accept a majority finding of the Commission could be treated by other members as if it were no longer a member of the Union, in so far as the clauses prohibiting discriminatory practices were concerned. This, however, is a question which is probably best answered at a much later stage.

VI THE PROBLEM OF THE TRANSITION

19. Membership of the Commercial Union (at any rate on anything like the terms suggested above for illustrative purposes) would require an extensive re-adjustment of commercial policy in the case of a number of countries. If such major re-adjustment are desirable, there is much to be said for undertaking them after the cataclysm of a major war; for serious re-adjustments will be inevitable in such a period in any case and it is surely better to re-adjust then to the conditions which are most desired than to rebuild to an ancient plan which it is intended in any case to reconstruct sooner or later. Nevertheless, it would be out of the question to suggest this or any other country should commit itself to an immediate acceptance of all the principles of the Commercial Union immediately after the

war. What is required is some transitional arrangement whereby countries can become members of the Commercial Union during the period of, say, five years after the close of hostilities on condition:

(i) That they undertake to fulfil some of its obligations, such as the removal of quantitative import restrictions and prohibitions, within a short period of a year or two and
(ii) That they undertake to fulfil some of its obligations within a period of not less than, say, five years. Such an arrangement might serve to secure that certain protective devices were quickly eliminated, that a more gradual movement was initiated for the removal or reduction of others, and – most important of all – that each member could plan its economic development on the assumption that within a specified number of years other members would have contracted their protective and discriminatory devices within reasonably precise and clearly defined limits.

15. Do GATT Rules Help Governments Make Domestic Commitments?

R. W. Staiger and G. Tabellini

1. INTRODUCTION

Building on the seminal work of Kydland and Prescott (1977) on rules versus discretion, a number of theoretical papers have pointed out that international rules for trade policy, such as those embodied in the General Agreement on Tariffs and Trade (GATT) and its successor, the World Trade Organization (WTO), can help governments make commitments to superior trade policies that would not be credible to domestic agents in the absence of such rules. For example, Staiger and Tableini (1987) state the following:

> Finally, these theoretical results contain a clear normative implication for improving on the time-consistent but suboptimal equilibrium: the government should be enabled to undertake binding commitments concerning its future behavior. From an operational point of view, this is suggestive of the important role that could be performed by an international organization like the GATT: namely, to enforce the domestic commitments to a policy of free trade. The GATT was originally conceived to facilitate international cooperation among individual countries; the results of the paper suggest that this institution can – and presumably to some extent already does – perform an equally crucial role in enforcing the cooperative outcome in a setting in which the strategic interaction is between each country and its own domestic residents (p. 825).

Similar statements concerning the possible role of trade agreements in helping governments make commitments to their private sectors can be found in Matsuyama (1990), Brainard (1994), Mayer (1994), and most recently Maggi and Rodriguez-Clare (1998). Yet there is no empirical evidence as to whether international agreements such as GATT or the WTO do in fact offer member-governments a commitment technology with respect to their private sectors. The goal of this paper is to provide an initial empirical assessment of this issue.[1]

As an environment for the study of rules versus discretion in government policy-making, trade policy decisions may be uniquely suited among the many kinds of economic decisions that governments make. This is because governments confront similar trade policy decisions in a variety of institutional settings distinguished by the degree to which international rules apply. We exploit this by comparing US responses to injured import-competing sectors in two different institutional settings, one in which GATT rules explicitly apply and one in which they do not.

The first setting we consider is where the United States was faced with determination and implementation of tariff reductions as part of the Tokyo Round of GATT negotiations (1974–1979). The centerpiece of GATT is the tariff *binding*, the commitment made by each GATT contracting party not to raise tariffs above specified levels. These bindings, in turn, have been reduced over time through a series of multilateral negotiating rounds.

In the Tokyo Round, the *negotiated tariff reductions* were determined in two steps. First, a general formula for lowering each country's tariff bindings across all product categories was adopted; and second, faced with the implication of applying formula cuts across the board, each government then chose to *exclude* certain product categories from the general formula cuts and to substitute alternative tariff changes for these products.[2] The outcome of these two steps determined the tariff reductions that were to be implemented at the conclusion of the Tokyo Round. By excluding a product category from the tariff-cutting rule, a government could therefore choose to offer relief to an import-competing sector that would otherwise face injury associated with the formula tariff cut.

A similar two-step procedure determined the *speed of implementation* of the negotiated tariff reductions at the conclusion of the round. First, a general staging rule was adopted under which the negotiated tariff reductions would be phased in over eight years in eight equal parts; and second, faced with the implication of applying the general staging rule across the board, each government chose to *exclude* certain product categories from the general staging rule.[3] The outcome of these two steps determined the speed with which the tariff reductions negotiated in the Tokyo Round were to be implemented. By excluding a product category from the general staging rule and substituting a slower phase-in, a government could provide temporary relief from the negotiated tariff reductions.

Our empirical investigation beings by considering the determinants of the US exclusion decisions in the Tokyo Round. In facing these decisions, the government was confronted sector-by-sector with a tradeoff between distributive gains and efficiency losses. The distributive gain from exclusion comes from the prevention of injury that would otherwise occur in each import-competing sector if the formula cuts were applied. The efficiency loss is associated with the sectoral production and consumption distortions that are maintained as a result of the sectoral exclusion from tariff reduction. The issue of government *commitment* relative to the private sector when making the exclusion decision arises because the government's assessment of this distribution/efficiency tradeoff, and hence its sectoral exclusion decision, depends in part on the degree to which it can commit to a course of action before private sector decisions are made. In particular, a government that is unable to credibly commit to a trade policy before the relevant production decisions are made will take those production decisions as bygones when selecting the exclusions and will as a consequence neglect the production distortions associated with this trade policy choices. We therefore draw inferences about the ability of governments to commit to trade policy decisions under GATT rules by examining the degree to which trade-policy-induced production distortions were reflected in the US exclusion decisions of the Tokyo Round.

In the context of the Tokyo Round, GATT rules may have helped governments commit to the tariffs implied by their exclusion decisions by making explicit the threat of costly dispute settlement procedures and possible retaliation from trading partners if these decisions were not adhered to. In particular, each member-government was obligated in general under GATT rules to refrain in the future from unilaterally raising its tariffs above the bindings it negotiated in the round. The temporary unilateral suspension of specific bindings and the associated temporary tariff increases would be permitted in certain circumstances, but only under the rules governing *escape clause* actions, which required that substantial injury to the relevant import-competing industry first be established. Thus, following the Tokyo Round's completion, the exclusion decisions of member-governments could be reversed unilaterally and without threat of penalty only under the relatively stringent injury conditions that would activate the escape clause. By providing a degree of government commitment in this way, GATT rules should have induced Tokyo Round exclusion decisions to reflect the production distortions that the departures from the formula tariff cuts would cause, i.e., all else equal, departures from the formula tariff cuts should have been smaller in sectors where the production distortions induced by these departures were larger. In our empirical work, we will interpret evidence of such a pattern as indicating that trade policy decisions made under GATT rules are relatively unconstrained by domestic credibility issues.[4]

When international rules such as those provided by GATT are absent, this does not necessarily mean that government credibility will be lost and therefore that the production distortions introduced by protection will be ignored when setting tariff levels. Governments could in principle find other means of establishing and maintaining trade policy credibility with their private sectors, for instance through some domestic reputation mechanism. If governments can successfully do this, then GATT may not provide any additional credibility benefit of the sort discussed above. Thus, to address the question we set out to explore, it would not be enough to find evidence that decisions made under GATT rules appear unconstrained by domestic credibility issues: we must also ask whether decisions made in the absence of GATT rules share this characteristic.

To accomplish this second task, we look at trade policy decisions made under the escape clause. In particular, we examine government choices over whether or not to offer additional protection to industries that have passed the escape clause injury standard. In this setting, the government is faced with a decision very similar to the exclusion decisions of the Tokyo Round: whether or not to offer increased protection to an industry that faces the prospect of substantial injury. However, unlike the exclusion decisions of the Tokyo Round, when making escape clause decisions the government cannot rely on explicit GATT rules to limit its ability to reconsider those decisions. This is because GATT commitments are temporarily "unbound" under the conditions of the escape clause, so that once the injury determination has been established a government would be free to readjust unilaterally its tariff response at any time during the period of injury without fear of triggering dispute proceedings and possible retaliation from its trading partners (see, for example, Jackson, 1989, pp. 149–187).

Absent an alternative commitment mechanism, the lack of applicable GATT rules in these circumstances will undermine the credibility of escape clause decisions that attempt to take into account the costs of associated production distortions. Therefore, unless domestic reputation mechanisms are working to provide a substitute for explicit international rules in this case, the decision to offer increased protection under the escape clause should not be tempered by the magnitude of the production distortions induced by the added intervention. On the contrary, if, as theory would suggest, the commitment provided by GATT's rules enabled governments to sustain deeper negotiated tariff cuts in those industries where exclusions would have induced especially high production distortions, then in light of these prior decisions the escape clause's temporary suspension of GATT's rules (and the implied loss of government commitment) should lead governments to *undo* what the rules had accomplished. This suggests the perverse result that, if GATT rules are indeed contributing to the ability of governments to make trade policy commitments to their private sectors, then the *greatest* additional protection will be granted under the escape clause precisely where the associated production distortions would be *highest*, i.e., all else equal, additional protection under the escape clause should be more forthcoming where the magnitude of the production distortions induced by protection is highest.

Hence, if GATT rules are actually providing member governments with a commitment device relative to their private sectors that they would otherwise lack, we would expect to find that, ceteris paribus, the Tokyo Round exclusion decisions were *negatively* related to the production distortions they caused while escape clause decisions showed a *positive* sensitivity. This is in essence what we seek to determine in our empirical work.

To preview our findings, our empirical results are mixed, but overall they provide some support for the view that GATT rules help member-governments make trade policy commitments to their private sectors. We find some evidence that the United States granted exclusions from the Tokyo Round general tariff-cutting rule less readily in sectors where higher tariffs were more likely to significantly distort production decisions. When we consider US exclusions from the Tokyo Round general staging rules, stronger support for this inverse relationship between exclusions and associated production distortions is evident. These findings are consistent with the view that, at least when GATT rules apply, governments are able to make trade policy commitments to their private sectors. By contrast, we find no evidence of an inverse relationship between US escape clause protection and the implied production distortions, and in fact find some evidence of a positive association, as would be implied if GATT rules are providing member-governments with a commitment device relative to their private sectors which the member-governments do not otherwise possess (and which is therefore lost when GATT rules are temporarily suspended under the escape clause). While our empirical results are subject to a number of important caveats and must therefore be viewed as only a first step in providing an answer to this question, we interpret these findings overall as suggestive that GATT rules may indeed help governments make domestic commitments.

The next section presents a model of tariff determination which is meant to capture the main elements of trade policy decisions in these two settings. While stylized, this theoretical framework serves to motivate our empirical methodology, which we present in section 3. Our empirical results for the Tokyo Round are presented in section 4. In section 5 we present empirical results for escape clause decisions, and compare the impact of the different institutional settings and the relative degrees of policy discretion they permit on actual tariff choices. Finally, section 6 concludes. Our data sources are described in the Appendix.

2. THEORY

Our goal in this section is to present a simple theoretical framework within which to evaluate the impact that GATT rules may have on the strategic interaction between a government and its own domestic residents. In particular, we wish to contrast the choices a government would make to protect specific industries from injury in the context of a GATT-sponsored round of tariff negotiations with the choices it would make in responding to injury under the escape clause, with the key distinction across the two environments being the degree to which the government can commit to a tariff policy in advance of the resource allocation decisions of the private sector. To this end, we first describe the economic environment and then proceed to discuss the institutional setting within which trade policy decisions will be made.

2.1 Economic Environment

We consider a simple partial equilibrium model of two economies trading two non-numeraire goods as well as a numeraire good that enters linearly into utility and is consumed in positive amounts by both countries. Let x denote the home-country import good and let y be the corresponding import good for the foreign country. Each government has a specific import tariff at its disposal, which we denote by t_x (t_y^* for the home (foreign) government, with an "*" generally denoting a foreign-country variable. Arbitrage across the home and foreign market then ensures that home and foreign prices differ only by the relevant tariff, or $p_x = p_x^* + t_x$ and $p_y^* = p_y + t_y^*$, where $p_i(p_i^*)$ denotes the price of good $i \in \{x, y\}$ in the home (foreign) market. Initially these tariffs are set exogenously at the levels $\bar{t}_x$ and $\bar{t}_y^*$, possibly as the result of prior rounds of GATT negotiations.

Demands for x and y are presented in each country by decreasing functions of the relevant local price, with $D_i(p_i)$ [$D_i^*(p_i^*)$] denoting demand for good $i \in \{x, y\}$ in the home (foreign) country. The determination of supply in each country is more involved. First, each country is endowed with an inelastic supply of its export good, $\bar{E}_y$ for the home country and $\bar{E}_x^*$ for the foreign country, and its import good $\bar{E}_x$ for the home country and $\bar{E}_y^*$ for the foreign country. These endowments may be thought of as supplies of each good produced with factors that are not mobile during the time horizon relevant for the decisions to which our analysis applies. However, we wish to consider the implications of trade liberalization for resource allocation out of the import-competing sector, and so we must also introduce some factors that are mobile over this time horizon.

To accomplish this we assume that each country is also endowed with a supply of *skilled* labor, and a supply of *unskilled* labor. Unskilled labor comes in assorted types indexed by $\lambda \in [0, 1]$, and the distribution of types of unskilled labor in the home (foreign) country is described by the distribution function $F(\lambda)$ $[F^*(\lambda)]$ with associated density function $f(\lambda)$ $[f^*(\lambda)]$. Countries produce the numeraire good with a common *skill-sensitive* technology that can convert a unit of skilled labor into one unit of the numeraire good and a unit of unskilled labor of type λ into $\alpha \times \lambda$ units of the numeraire good where $\alpha \in (0, 1)$. By contrast, the common import-competing technology in each country is not skill-sensitive, and it converts a unit of either skilled or unskilled labor into one unit of the import-competing good. Hence, with $1 > \alpha \times \lambda$ for each λ all unskilled workers have a comparative advantage over skilled workers in import-competing production, and low-λ unskilled workers have a comparative advantage over high-λ unskilled workers in import-competing production as well. With all workers in an economy being paid the value of their marginal product, all workers employed in the domestic (foreign) import-competing sector will receive a wage equal to $p_x(p_y^*)$, while in the domestic (foreign) numeraire sector skilled workers receive a unitary wage and unskilled workers of type λ receive a wage of $\alpha \times \lambda$ $(\alpha^* \times \lambda)$. It therefore follows that the import-competing sector in each economy will employ all available unskilled workers before employing any skilled workers, and it will employ low-λ unskilled workers before employing high-λ unskilled workers.

A central feature of the model is the reallocation of workers from the import-competing to the numeraire sector in each economy in response to tariff liberalization. We assume that there are $\bar{N}_x$ $(\bar{N}_y^*)$ unskilled workers in the home (foreign) country, and that the initial tariff levels $\bar{t}_x$ and $\bar{t}_y^*$ are such that some skilled workers (and therefore all unskilled workers) are initially located in the import-competing sector of their respective country. This will be assured provided that the initial tariffs are sufficiently high, and we denote the critical levels above which $\bar{t}_x$ and $\bar{t}_y^*$ must reside as $\underline{I}$ and $\underline{I}^*$, respectively. Calculations yield the explicit expressions $\underline{I} \equiv [1 - D_x^{*-1}(\bar{N}_x+\bar{E}_x+\bar{E}_x^*-D(1))]$ and $I^* \equiv [1 - D_y^{-1}(\bar{N}_y^*+\bar{E}_y^*+\bar{E}_y-D_y^*(1))]$. With $\bar{t}_x > I$ and $\bar{t}_y^* > I^*$, each economy is initially in an equilibrium in which (i) all unskilled workers are employed in the import-competing sector and (ii) all workers in the economy receive the same (unitary) wage.

We now suppose that the opportunity arises for a new round of tariff negotiations.[5] As these negotiations will lead naturally to the possibility of mutual reductions in each country's tariff, we need to determine the equilibrium prices and labor allocations for tariffs below the critical domestic and foreign levels I and I^*, respectively, and we need to specify government preferences, including how governments feel about the wage inequality between skilled and unskilled workers that tariff liberalization may induce.

When the domestic tariff is set below the critical level I, the wages paid to unskilled workers in the domestic economy and the domestic price of the import-competing good will fall below unity, and unskilled workers may begin to leave the domestic import-competing sector for jobs in the numeraire sector. More specifically, define $M \equiv [\alpha - D_x^{*-1}(\bar{N}_x+\bar{E}_x+\bar{E}_x^*-D_x(\alpha))]$. Then for $t_x \in [M, I]$, no unskilled workers will be induced to leave the domestic import-competing sector, but the equilibrium wage paid to domestic unskilled workers will decline from one to α as t_x falls from I to M. This follows from the x-market equilibrium condition, which for $t_x \in [M, I]$ can be written as

$$\bar{N}_x+\bar{E}_x+\bar{E}_x^*=D_x(p_x^*+t_x)+D_x^*(p_x^*). \tag{1}$$

Condition (1) defines the equilibrium foreign price of x for $t_x \in [M, I]$ $\hat{p}_x^*(t_x)$, and therefore the equilibrium domestic price of x will be given by $\hat{p}_x(t_x) \equiv \hat{p}_x^*(t_x) + t_x$ and the equilibrium domestic wage paid to unskilled workers will be given by $\hat{w}_x(t_x) \equiv \hat{p}_x(t_x)$ for $t_x \in [M, I]$. As can be seen from (1)$\hat{p}_x^*$ is decreasing in t_x over this range while $\hat{p}_x$ and $\hat{w}_x$ are increasing in t_x. Moreover, it can be checked from (1) and the definitions of M and I that $\hat{w}_x(I) = 1$ and $\hat{w}_x(M) = \alpha$.

For any $t_x < M$, some domestic unskilled workers will choose to leave the import-competing sector. In particular, for domestic tariffs in this range, domestic unskilled workers can be partitioned into low-λ types, who choose to stay in the import-competing sector, and high-λ types, who choose to leave for employment in the numeraire sector, with the marginal type $\tilde{\lambda}$ defined by the condition that the wage earned in the import-competing sector (p_x) is the same as the wage that would be earned by this type of unskilled worker in the numeraire sector ($\alpha \times \tilde{\lambda}$), or $p_x = \alpha \times \tilde{\lambda}$. Recalling the goods-market arbitrage condition $p_x = p_x^* + t_x$, we now record the x-market equilibrium condition for $t_x \leq M$, which defines as a function of t_x the market-clearing foreign price of good x, $\hat{p}_x^*(t_x)$:

$$\bar{N}_x F\left(\frac{p_x^*+t_x}{\alpha}\right)+\bar{E}_x+\bar{E}_x^*=D_x(p_x^*+t_x)+D_x^*(p_x^*). \tag{2}$$

From (2) it follows that $\hat{p}_x^*$ is a decreasing function of t_x over this range. We then have the equilibrium domestic price of x defined by $\hat{p}_x(t_x) \equiv \hat{p}_x^*(t_x) + t_x$, and it again follows form (2) that $\hat{p}_x$ will be an increasing function of t_x over this range. The equilibrium allocation of unskilled workers in the domestic economy is determined by the equilibrium marginal type $\hat{\lambda}(t_x) \equiv \hat{p}_x(t_x)/\alpha$, with the number of workers remaining in the domestic import-competing sector given by $\bar{N}_x F(\hat{\lambda}(t_x))$ and thus increasing in t_x. Domestic wages of skilled workers are still unity, but the wages of unskilled workers in the domestic economy are now given by $\hat{w}_x(t_x) \equiv \hat{p}_x(t_x)$ for domestic unskilled workers of type $\lambda \in [0, \hat{\lambda}(t_x)]$, who choose to remain in the import-competing sector, and by $\alpha \times \lambda$ for domestic unskilled workers of type $\lambda \in [\hat{\lambda}(t_x), 1]$, who choose to leave the import-competing sector and produce the numerate good. Hence, as t_x is increased, the number of unskilled workers staying in the domestic import-competing sector rises and the wage earned by all unskilled workers remaining in the domestic import-competing sector increases toward the skilled-labor wage of unity.

For any $t_y^* < I^*$, an analogous set of y-market equilibrium conditions (i.e., one for $t_y^* \in [M^*, I^*]$, and one for $t_y^* \leq M^*$, with M^* defined analogously to M) will determine the market-clearing domestic price of y, $\hat{p}_y(t_y^*)$, from which the equilibrium foreign price of y may then be defined by $\hat{p}_y^*(t_y^*) \equiv \hat{p}_y(t_y^*) + t_y^*$. The equilibrium allocation of unskilled workers in the foreign economy is then determined by the equilibrium marginal type $\hat{\lambda}(t_y^*) \equiv \hat{p}_y^*(t_y^*)/\alpha^*$. As with the domestic economy, foreign wages of skilled workers are still unity, but the wages of unskilled workers in the foreign country are now given by $\hat{w}^*_y(t^*_y) \equiv \hat{p}^*_y(t^*_y)$ for foreign unskilled workers of type $\lambda \in [0, \hat{\lambda}^*(t^*_y)]$, and by $\alpha^* \times \lambda$ for foreign unskilled workers of type $\lambda \in [\hat{\lambda}^*(t^*_y), 1]$.

We now define the trade-policy objectives of each government. We wish to capture in a simple way the notion that a government may pursue the competing goals of enhancing efficiency and preventing serious adjustment costs/injury to specific groups (e.g. unskilled workers) as it enters into tariff negotiations with its trading partners. We also wish to allow for the fact that political motives may be important in shaping the government's trade-policy goals.

We therefore define the domestic government's trade-policy objectives by

$$W(t_x, t^*_y) = CS_x(\hat{p}_x(t_x)) + \gamma_x \times PS_x(\hat{p}_x(t_x)) + TR_x(t_x, \hat{p}^*_x(t_x))$$
$$+ \bar{N}_x \left\{ F(\hat{\lambda}(t_x)) \times g_x(\hat{w}_x(t_x)) + \int_{\hat{\lambda}(t_x)}^{1} f(\lambda) \times g_x(\alpha \times \lambda) d\lambda \right\}$$
$$+ CS_y(\hat{p}_y(t^*_y)) + PS_y(\hat{p}_y(t^*_y)), \tag{3}$$

where CS_i, PS_i and TR_i, denote domestic consumer surplus, producer surplus and tariff revenue associated with industry $i \in \{x, y\}$, where $\gamma_x \geq 1$ denotes a domestic government weighting factor on import-competing producer surplus, and where $g_x(\cdot)$ is a function which is increasing and concave in its argument with $g_x(1) = 0$. The parameter γ_x is meant to capture political economy motives of the domestic government in a simple way (see Baldwin, 1987), with $\gamma_x > 1$ reflecting a politically-motivated preference for channeling surplus toward producers in the domestic import-competing sector x. The function $g_x(\cdot)$ is meant to capture the domestic government's dislike for reducing the wage of domestic unskilled workers (who are located in its import-competing sector x at the time it initiates trade negotiations) below that of skilled workers as a result of its negotiated tariff reductions. In particular note that, for $t_x > I$ we have $\hat{\lambda}(t_x) = 1$ and $\hat{w}_x(t_x) = 1$ so that the term in curly brackets in (3) is zero, but that this term grows increasingly negative as t_x drops below I and the domestic wage of unskilled workers begins to fall below the domestic skilled-worker wage. We assume that the trade-policy objectives of the foreign government are similarly defined:

$$W^*(t^*_y, t_x) = CS^*_y(\hat{p}^*_y(t^*_y)) + \gamma^*_y \times PS^*_y(\hat{p}^*_y(t^*_y)) + TR^*_y(t^*_y, \hat{p}_y(t^*_y))$$
$$+ \bar{N}^*_y \left\{ F^*(\hat{\lambda}^*(t^*_y)) \times g^*_y(\hat{w}^*_y(t^*_y)) + \int_{\hat{\lambda}(t^*_y)}^{1} f^*(\lambda) \times g^*_y(\alpha^* \times \lambda) d\lambda \right\}$$
$$+ CS^*_x(\hat{p}^*_x(t_x)) + PS^*_x(\hat{p}^*_x(t_x)), \tag{4}$$

where CS^*_i, PS^*_i and TR^*_i denote foreign consumer surplus, producer surplus and tariff revenue associated with industry $i \in \{x, y\}$, where $\gamma^*_y \geq 1$ denotes a foreign government weighting factor on import-competing producer surplus, and where $g_y^*(\cdot)$ is a function which is increasing and concave in its argument with $g_y^*(1) = 0$.

Finally, in an effort to motivate the inclusion of an "escape clause" from negotiated tariff commitments, we wish to capture the notion that, at the time of initial negotiations, there is some uncertainty as to the degree of injury that a given amount of tariff liberalization will actually cause. We represent this in the home country by the assumption that the parameter α can take on either of two magnitudes, α_H or α_L with $\alpha_H > \alpha_L$. At the time of negotiations it is known only that, with probability $p \in (0, 1)$, the magnitude of α will be α_H, while with probability $(1 - p)$ the magnitude of α and α_L. The actual magnitude of α will be revealed only after the negotiations are completed. We make an analogous assumption with regard to the foreign country. Note that, for a given $t_x < M$, condition (2) implies that $\hat{p}_x$ is increasing in α but less than proportionately so, and so $\hat{\lambda}$ is declining in α. Hence, for a given domestic tariff, the realization of a lower value of α brings with it diminished adjustment out of the domestic import-competing sector [$\bar{N}_x F(\hat{\lambda}(t_x))$ will be larger] and lower domestic unskilled wages ($\hat{w}_x = \hat{p}_x$ will be lower, as will $\alpha \times \lambda$ the alternative wage for a type-λ domestic unskilled worker if it locates in the numeraire sector) than would be implied under a high value of α. We thus interpret the state of the world in which α turns out to be low as reflecting the realization of relatively high adjustment costs associated with the transfer of resources out of the domestic import-competing sector. The possibility of such a "shock" will motivate the inclusion of an "escape clause" which allowed governments to suspend their negotiated tariff commitments under certain circumstances.[6]

2.2 Institutional Setting: Credibility from GATT Rules

We are now ready to describe the timing of the tariff negotiations and private sector decisions, which we characterize as corresponding to three stages. Our description attempts to capture the stylized features of GATT's rules as they would apply in this setting.

We suppose that there is a first stage in which a round of tariff negotiations occurs. In this stage, the two governments jointly select tariffs and agree on payments of lump-sum transfers.[7] Upon completion of these negotiations, the first stage ends and the values of α and α^* are revealed. If the low value of $\alpha(\alpha^*)$ is realized, then adjustment costs turn out to be high in the domestic (foreign) country, and in the domestic (foreign) country the escape clause in invoked. In the second stage the government of this country is then permitted to select unilaterally a tariff increment for its import-competing sector at the same time that labor allocation decisions are made by the private sector. In conformity with GATT rules, we assume that "compensation" (in the form of a lump-sum transfer) must be paid to its trading partner for the export price effects of its escape clause action.[8] If instead the high value of $\alpha(\alpha^*)$ is realized at the end of the first stage, then adjustment costs turn out to be low in domestic (foreign) country, and in the domestic (foreign) country the escape clause is not triggered. Under these circumstances, the country will be held to the tariff commitment it negotiated in the first stage, and so in the second stage only the labor allocation decisions of the private sector remain to be made. Finally, all consumption decisions are made by the private sector in the third and final stage.

There are two important features of this setup that distinguish the tariff choices made in the stage-1 negotiations from the stage-2 escape clause tariffs, and both features follow from the fact that a country will have the opportunity to modify its stage-1 negotiated tariff commitment in stage 2 (via the escape clause) if and only if its adjustment costs turn out to be high. A first feature is that, while the escape clause tariff choice will reflect the knowledge that adjustment costs are high, the stage-1 negotiated tariff commitment will be designed to deliver its preferred outcome when adjustment costs are low, since only in this state of the world can a government's stage-1 commitment not later be modified by an escape clause action. Hence, one difference between the tariff choices made in the negotiating round and those made under the escape clause is that the latter are designed to respond to additional injury in the import-competing sector not anticipated in the calculations which lead to the former. A second feature is that, while the escape clause tariff choice is made simultaneously with the resource allocation decisions of the private sector and therefore treats these private sector decisions as given, the calculations which lead to the tariff choices made in the negotiating round are carried out in advance of the decisions of the private sector, and can therefore take into account the impact that negotiated tariff commitments will have on the allocation of resources across the economy. Hence, a second difference between the tariff choices made in the negotiating round and those made under the escape clause is that the former will account for production distortions induced by the tariff choices while the latter will not.

These two features account for the difference between the tariff choices made in the negotiating round and those made under the escape clause in our formal setting, and they capture in a stylized way the essential differences across the two decision-making environments upon which we wish to focus. We now characterize these tariff choices, and then compare them to derive the basic predictions that will guide our empirical work. We begin with the stage-1 negotiated tariffs.

Negotiated Tariff Commitments In light of the observations made above, the negotiated tariffs to be selected in stage 1 will reflect an underlying assumption that adjustment costs will turn out to be low ($\alpha = \alpha_H$, $\alpha^* = \alpha^*_H$) and will account fully for the production effects of the resulting tariff choices. As international lump-sum transfers can be used to divide the total surplus across the two countries, the negotiated tariff choices will maximize the sum of the government welfare functions, and hence negotiations will choose tariffs that solve

$$\max_{t_x, t^*_y} W(t_x, t^*_y, \alpha_H) + W^*(t^*_y, t_x, \alpha^*_H), \qquad (5)$$

where $W(t_x, t^*_y, \alpha_H)$ is defined as in (3) with $\alpha = \alpha_H$ and similarly $W^*(t^*_y, t_x, \alpha^*_H)$ is defined as in (4) with $\alpha^* = \alpha^*_H$. It is direct to show that the domestic ad valorem tariff (τ^1_x) that solves (5) is given by

$$\frac{\tau_x^1}{1+\tau_x^1} = \frac{(\gamma_x - 1) \times Q_x}{D_x \times \eta_{px}^{Dx} + Q_x \times \eta_{px}^{Qx}} + \frac{N_x \times g_x'(\hat{w}_x)}{D_x \times \eta_{px}^{Dx} + Q_x \times \eta_{px}^{Qx}}, \quad (6)$$

where τ_x^1 denotes the domestic tariff expressed in ad valorem terms, Q_x and N_x denote domestic output and employment, respectively, in sector x, η_{px}^{Dx} and η_{px}^{Qx} denote, respectively, the price elasticity of domestic demand (taken positively) and supply (reflecting the elasticity of domestic demand (taken positively) and supply (reflecting the elasticity of inter-sector labor movements) in sector x, and $g_x'(\cdot)$ denotes the derivative of g_x with respect to its argument. Implicit in (6) is the assumption that domestic political economy and labor income inequality concerns [i.e. γ_x and $g_x(\cdot)$, respectively] are not so strong as to prevent the domestic government from accepting a negotiated tariff commitment that implies resource movements out of the domestic import-competing sector. An analogous expression describes the foreign tariff that solves (5).

The right-hand side of (6) establishes that the negotiated domestic tariff may be written as the sum of two components. The first component will be zero if the government simply seeks to maximize domestic surplus with its tariff policy (i.e., $\gamma_x = 1$). But this component will be positive if the domestic government has a political desire to channel surplus toward import-competing producers (i.e., $\gamma_x > 1$). In this case, political motives will contribute toward a strictly positive negotiated domestic tariff, though these motives will be tempered on the margin by the additional domestic consumption and production distortions that a slightly higher tariff would introduce (i.e., the term $D_x \times \eta_{px}^{Dx} + Q_x \times \eta_{px}^{Qx}$). The second component embodies the response to the adjustment costs/injury that the negotiated trade liberalization may cause. This component reflects the domestic government's desire to prevent its negotiated tariff reduction from creating large discrepancies between skilled and unskilled wages in the domestic economy [i.e., the term $g_x'(\cdot) > 0$], a desire that is also tempered on the margin by the additional domestic consumption and production distortions that a slightly higher tariff would introduce. Notably absent from the expression for the negotiated domestic tariff is the inverse of the foreign export supply elasticity, which would reflect the domestic country's power over foreign export prices (the terms of trade) and which would contribute to its unilateral motives for raising import tariffs. Negotiations will eliminate this inefficient terms-of-trade incentive, leaving two remaining reasons for a positive tariff as reflected in (6).

Escape Clause Tariffs Now consider the escape clause tariff to be chosen in stage 2. We first consider the implications of the "compensation" requirement outlined above, and argue that this requirement helps to induce efficient escape clause choices by preventing a government from using the escape clauses as an excuse to reassert its power over export prices. To see this, observe that, from (3) and (4), each country's tariff alters the welfare of its trading partner only through the impact on its trading partner's export price (i.e., its terms of trade). It therefore follows that, when exercising the escape clause, a requirement of lump-sum compensation offered to one's trading partner in an amount that offsets the value to the country of the terms-of-trade improvement induced by its escape clause action will ensure that each country is confronted with the "right" (i.e., efficient) incentives relative to its trading partner when choosing its escape clause tariff.[9]

Under such a compensation requirement, each government will be induced to choose its escape clause tariff to maximize the same function as in (5), with two differences: first, the "shock" of high adjustment costs in the relevant country will have been realized, so that α_L replaces α_H (or α_L^* replaces α_H^*); and second, as the government will select an escape clause tariff simultaneously with the resource allocation decisions of the private sector, it will behave as if the allocation of resources – and hence output – is fixed, and so output elasticity will be treated as if it were zero. Of course, in equilibrium the resource allocation decisions of the private sector will fully reflect the escape clause tariff decisions, but it is just that the government is unable to take account of this sensitivity when selecting its escape clause actions. Solving (5) with these differences yields an expression for the domestic ad valorem tariff chosen under the escape clause, τ_x^2:

$$\frac{\tau_x^2}{1+\tau_x^2} = \frac{(\gamma_x - 1) \times Q_x}{D_x \times \eta_{px}^{Dx}} + \frac{N_x \times g_x'(\hat{w}_x)}{D_x \times \eta_{px}^{Dx}}. \tag{7}$$

Note that we have defined the escape clause tariff τ_x^2 as the desired tariff level at the time of the escape clause decision, so that the escape clause *response* would be $\tau_x^2 - \tau_x^1$. An analogous expression describes the foreign tariff chosen under the escape clause.

Negotiated and Escape Clause Tariffs Compared A comparison of (6) and (7) reveals that there are two distinct reasons for a positive escape clause response (i.e., $\tau_x^2 - \tau_x^1 > 0$). First, the larger shock associated with the escape clause decision (α_L as opposed to α_H) increases the marginal benefit to the home government of a higher tariff $[(\gamma_x - 1)Q_x + N_x \times g_x'(\cdot)]$ beyond its level at the time of the original (stage-1) tariff negotiations. And second, at the time of the escape clause decision the marginal cost of additional protection $D_x \times \eta_{px}^{Dx}$ appears lower, as the government now ignores the production distortions ($Q_x \times \eta_{px}^{Qx}$) that its tariff choices induce.

This decision suggests a basic empirical distinction between negotiated and escape clause tariffs that should arise if GATT's rules are providing governments with a way to make commitments to their private sectors which they could not make in the absence of these rules. That is, while negotiated tariff levels should be *negatively* related, ceteris paribus, to the production distortions they cause [as captured by the term $Q_x \times \eta_{px}^{Qx}$ which enters negatively in the expression for τ_x^1 in (6)], the escape clause tariff response (i.e., $\tau_x^2 - \tau_x^1$) should be *positively* related, ceteris paribus, to the size of the associated production distortion [as indicated by the absence of the term $Q_x \times \eta_{px}^{Qx}$ in the expression for τ_x^2 in (7)]. This observation reflects the basic point that, by permitting a country to temporarily suspend its GATT obligations when adjustment costs are sufficiently high, GATT's escape clause provides each member-government with the flexibility to respond to an unexpected shock but also with the opportunity in this circumstance to reverse any impacts that GATT obligations may have had on the ability to make commitments to the private sector. Our empirical investigation will focus on this simple observation.

2.3 The Failure of GATT Rules to Enhance Credibility

How might GATT rules *fail* to enhance the credibility of trade policy decisions? And what would constitute empirical evidence to this effect? There re two possibilities which we now briefly discuss. A first possibility is that GATT rules are simply not needed for this purpose, as governments have found other means to secure the credibility of their trade policy programs. A second possibility is that, while governments could gain from additional means to enhance their credibility, GATT rules are ineffective for this purpose. We consider each in turn.

The first possibility may be captured in the framework outlined above by supposing that the government makes any stage-2 trade policy decisions *before* the resource allocation decisions of the private sector. Such a timing assumption would reflect the view that, even with GATT rules suspended under the escape clause, governments have the ability to commit through other means to trade policy decisions in advance of the resource allocation decisions of the private sector. Under this timing assumption, the domestic ad valorem stage-1 negotiated tariff will still be given by (6), but now the stage-2 escape clause tariff will be characterized by an expression analogous to (6) as well, with the only difference between the two tariff choices being that the former embodies the smaller shock (α_H) while the latter embodies the larger shock (α_L). Hence, if governments find trade policy commitments feasible independent of the application of GATT rules, then both negotiated tariffs and escape clause responses should be negatively related to the production distortions they induce.[10]

It is also possible that GATT rules are simply ineffective in enhancing the credibility of government trade policy decisions. This would be the case if the threat of costly dispute settlement procedures and possible retaliation from trading partners in response to violation of GATT rules were largely empty. Here, GATT rules might not stop governments from reconsidering in stage 2 their stage-1 tariff choices even when the escape clause cannot be legitimately invoked. In the limit, as all such threats become empty, the ability of a government to reconsider its trade policy decisions would be effectively unconstrained by GATT rules, and an expression analogous to (7) would characterize both stage-1 and stage-2 tariff choices. In this case, neither the negotiated tariffs nor escape clause responses will show any sensitivity to the production distortions they induce.

2.4 Summary

Gathering these theoretical results together, it is now apparent that observations on negotiated and escape clause tariffs can be used to draw inferences about the extent to which GATT rules help governments make domestic commitments. In particular, evidence that both negotiated tariffs and escape clause responses are *unrelated* to the magnitudes of the production distortions they induce would be consistent with the view that GATT's rules are weak and ineffective and that governments are unable to make domestic commitments (with or without these rules). Alternatively, evidence that both negotiated tariffs and escape clause responses are *negatively* related to the magnitudes of the production distortions they induce would be consistent with the view that GATT's rules are irrelevant from the point of view of domestic commitments with regard to their private sectors. And finally, evidence that the negotiated tariffs are *negatively* related and that escape clause responses are *positively* related to the magnitudes of the production distortions they induce would be consistent with the view that GATT's rules do indeed provide governments with an ability to commit that they would otherwise not possess.

3. EMPIRICAL METHODOLOGY

We now use the theoretical results of the previous section to motivate the basic empirical relationships which we will investigate. We consider first the exclusion decisions of the Tokyo Round (we focus here on exclusions from the tariff-cutting rule, though analogous statements apply to exclusions from the staging rule).

As noted in the Introduction, the negotiated tariff reductions of the Tokyo Round were determined in two steps. First, a general formula for lowering each country's tariff bindings across all product categories was adopted; and second, faced with the implication of applying formula cuts across the board, each government then chose to exclude certain product categories from the general formula cuts and to substitute alternative tariff changes for these products. When added to the tariffs implied by the formula cuts, the Tokyo Round exclusions determined the final outcomes of the negotiations. According to our theory, if GATT's rules were helping governments commit to trade policy decisions then these final negotiating outcomes should correspond to τ_x^1 as defined in (6).

However, rather than trying to explain the final negotiating outcomes of the Tokyo Round, we wish to focus instead on the exclusion decisions themselves, as these decisions confronted governments with choices very similar to those they would face under the escape clause, i.e, whether or not to offer protection to an industry that faces the prospect of substantial adjustment costs/injury. If the Tokyo Round exclusion decisions can be interpreted as a response to the anticipated adjustment costs/injury implied by the formula cuts, then we can use (6) to disentangle the final negotiating outcome into two component parts, one [corresponding to the first term on the right-hand side of (6)] which represents the tariff implied by a hypothetical "formula cut," and other [corresponding to the second term on the right-hand side of (6)] then representing the Tokyo Round exclusion. According to this interpretation, the formula cut delivers a tariff, $(\gamma_x - 1) \times Q_x/[D_x \times \eta_{px}^{Dx} + Q_x \times \eta_{px}^{Qx}]$, which by (6) would be optimal in the absence of concerns about adjustment costs [i.e., when $g_x'(\cdot) \equiv 0$].[11]

Denoting by τ_x^R the home-country's Tokyo Round ad valorem exclusion, we may then use (6) to express this exclusion as

$$\frac{\tau_x^R}{1+\tau_x^R} = \frac{N_x \times g_x'(\hat{w}_x)}{D_x \times \eta_{px}^{Dx} + Q_x \times \eta_{px}^{Qx}}, \tag{8}$$

where it is understood that the right-hand-side magnitudes are evaluated at τ_x^1 and α_H. If we use expression (8) to compare exclusion decisions across hypothetical import-competing industries, we can infer that the industries receiving the most substantial exclusions from the formula tariff cuts will be those industries in which (i) the government cares most strongly about preventing adjustment costs/injury, (ii) the largest numbers of workers suffer the greatest wage reductions as a result of the round, and (iii) product demands and supplies are the least responsive to price movements.

Recalling now that the commitment which is hypothetically made possible by GATT rules simply allows the government, when selecting a negotiated tariff, to take account not only of the consumption distortions induced by its tariff choice but of the production distortions induced by its tariff choice as well, it is evident from (i) that the government's ability to commit when making its Tokyo Round exclusion decisions will be signaled by an inverse relationship, ceteris paribus, between its elected exclusions across industries and $Q_x \times \eta_{px}^{Qx}$, the price-responsiveness of industrial supply (which would be treated as zero absent the ability to commit). This observation can be given a very simple empirical representation under the further assumptions that demands take a constant-elasticity (η) form, and that the labor adjustment-cost parameter λ is distributed uniformly. Under this last assumption, the inter-sectoral labor supply elasticity becomes unity, allowing (8) to be written in the form

$$\frac{\tau_x^R}{1+\tau_x^R} = \frac{N_x \times g_x'(\hat{w}_x)}{D_x \times [\eta + \theta_x]}, \tag{8}$$

where $\theta_x \equiv [\hat{w}_x N_x]/[\hat{p}_x D_x]$ or, equivalently, θ_x is the elasticity of industry-x output with respect to employment weighted by the ratio in industry-x of output to consumption. The implication of the assumed ability to commit embedded in the derivation of (9) is embodied in the presence of the term θ_x, which would be absent were the government unable to commit to its exclusion decisions in advance of the resource allocation decisions of the private sector. Accordingly, ceteris paribus, an inverse relationship between the magnitude of the Tokyo Round exclusions and θ_x can be interpreted as evidence of government commitment, as this signals that the government is least likely to offer exclusions from the Tokyo Round formula cuts in industries where the induced production distortions are, relative to the associated consumption distortions, the most prominent.

With (9) serving as motivation, we evaluate the US government's ability to commit to its Tokyo Round exclusion decisions by estimating the parameters of the simple linear relationship

$$\tau_x = \beta_0 + \beta_1 n_x + \beta_2 c_x + \beta_3 \theta_x + \beta_4 \Gamma_x + \epsilon_x, \tag{10}$$

where τ_x is the US ad valorem Tokyo Round exclusion for industry x, n_x is production worker employment in industry x as a fraction of production worker employment in total manufacturing, c_x is "consumption" (domestic absorption) of industry x as a fraction of GNP, θ_x is the industry-x production worker wage bill divided by the value of industry-x consumption, Γ_x, is a vector of variables that depict the strength of the government's concern for preventing adjustment costs/injury in industry x, the β's denote parameters to be estimated, and ϵ_x is assumed to be a classical disturbance term. On the basis of our earlier theoretical discussion, we expect β_1 to be positive whether or not the US government was able to commit to its exclusion decisions, as in either case the prospect of injury to a greater fraction of US production workers should have evoked, all else equal, a greater tariff response. Similarly, we expect β_2 to be negative independent of the ability of the government to commit, as products that loom large in consumption should in any event receive, all else equal, less protection. However, we expect β_3 to be negative if and only if the US government was able to commit to its exclusion decisions in the Tokyo Round (and we expect it to be zero otherwise), as only under commitment will a government be less willing to provide exclusions where the production distortions associated with doing so would be highest.

Turning now to the US escape clause decisions, we noted earlier from (7) that GATT's escape clause provides each member-government with the flexibility to respond to any impacts that GATT obligations may have had on the ability to make commitments to the private sector. Hence, if we view (10) as continuing to provide the basis for an explanation of government tariff choices in response to a shock, the central difference when (10) is estimated with observations on US escape clause decisions rather than Tokyo Round exclusion decisions should be with regard to β_3.

In particular, on the basis of our theoretical discussion there are three inferences that can be drawn depending on the estimated sign of β_3 under the escape clause in light of the estimated sign of β_3 under the Tokyo Round exclusions. If β_3 is estimated to be negative under the Tokyo Round exclusions, then a negative value for β_3 under the escape clause would be consistent with the view that the US government found commitments possible even absent GATT rules, and consequently that GATT rules provided no additional commitment ability in our sample. By contrast, if β_3 is estimated to be negative under the Tokyo Round exclusions but is found to be positive under the escape clause, then this would be consistent with the view that GATT rules can help governments make commitments, as it would imply that the lifting of these rules under the escape clause led the US government to reverse the relationship between tariffs and production distortions that the rules had facilitated. Finally, if β_3 is estimated to be zero under both Tokyo Round exclusion and escape clause decisions, then this would be consistent with the view that GATT's rules are weak and ineffective and that governments have difficulty making trade policy commitments with or without GATT. We now turn to our estimation results, beginning with the US Tokyo Round exclusions.

4. ESTIMATION RESULTS FROM THE TOKYO ROUND

In this section we estimate (10) with data on US exclusion decisions in the Tokyo Round. A complete list of data sources is provided in the Appendix. We first consider the extent to which US industries were granted exclusions from the general formula Tokyo Round tariff cuts. We then turn to an analysis of the US decisions to grant exclusions from the general staging rules of the Tokyo Round.

With regard to US exclusions from the general formula Tokyo Round tariff cuts, we have constructed ad valorem exclusion measures for 199 four-digit SIC sectors. To see how the exclusions are calculated, consider a product whose pre-Tokyo Round ad valorem tariff was 14 percent. According to the general tariff-cutting formula adopted in the Tokyo Round (the "Swiss rule"), this product would receive a 7 percentage point reduction in its ad valorem tariff. If, say, the actual tariff change emerging from the Tokyo Round for that product was a 3 percentage point reduction in the pre-Tokyo-Round ad valorem tariff, then the ad valorem exclusion from the general formula cut for that product would be 4 percentage points. With the exclusions calculated in this way, US trade weights for 1980 were then used to aggregate the product-level exclusions to the four-digit SIC level. A common practice in the Tokyo Round was for a country to offer negative exclusions on low-tariff products as a way of maintaining deep average cuts in the face of exclusions in other sectors. In light of this, it might be argued that a separate model would be appropriate to explain the exclusion decisions on low-tariff products. We thus restrict our sample to four-digit sectors with ad valorem pre-Tokyo Round tariffs greater than 5 percent, leaving a total sample size of 199 sectors. This sample selection also provides a "minimum injury" standard associated with the general formula cuts: all sectors in the sample faced formula tariff cuts of no less than 1.3 percentage points.[12]

The estimating (10) for the four-digit SIC Tokyo Round exclusions, 1978 values at the four-digit SIC level were used for all explanatory variables, on the grounds that this was the most recent year of data that could enter into decisions that were completed in 1979. As noted in the previous section and embodied in (10), the explanatory variables by sector suggested by our theory include the ratio of production worker employment to total manufacturing production worker employment ($n_x \equiv PREMP$), the ratio of consumption to national income ($c_x \equiv CONS$), the ratio of the production worker wage bill to consumption ($\theta_x \equiv COMMIT$), and a set of variables that depict the strength of the government's concern for preventing adjustment costs/injury in each sector (Γ_x).

We experiment in our representation of Γ_x with a number of political variables discussed by Baldwin (1985), in an effort to account for variation across industries in the degree to which the US government may have been motivated to prevent injury associated with trade liberalization. These include a measure by industry of establishment size (ESTSIZE), four-firm concentration ratio (CONCEN), value-added share of output (VALOUT), and import penetration ratio (IMPEN). Baldwin (1985) argues that industries with low import penetration ratios are unlikely to be viewed by government officials as attractive candidates for protection, implying that the expected sign of the coefficient on the political variable IMPEN is positive. However, Grossman and Helpman (1994) have observed that this relationship may in fact be negative, as high import penetration in an industry can imply that the cost to domestic consumers from protection will be relatively large as compared to the political payoff from helping domestic producers. Inclusion of the variable VALOUT is motivated by the "pressure group" model of tariff determination (Olson, 1965), on the basis of the observation that the smaller an industry's value-added share of output, the larger is the percentage change in factor rewards associated with a given tariff change (assuming fixed prices of intermediate inputs), and thus the greater the industry's incentive to fight for protection. Thus, the expected sign of the coefficient on the political variable VALOUT is negative. Also, according to the pressure group model, variables such as ESTSIZE and CONCEN, which are related to the ability of an industry to internalize free-rider problems, should be important determinants of industry protection According to this argument, the coefficient on ESTSIZE and CONCEN are expected to be positive. However, under the "adding machine" model as put forth by Caves (1976), governments are more concerned with protecting industries composed of a larger number of small firms than industries which are highly concentrated, suggesting that the coefficients on ESTSIE and CONCEN should be negative. As each of the foregoing observations is subject to various qualifications, we have no strong prior beliefs on the signs of the associated coefficients for these variables, and we will report estimates of the central parameters of interest (β_1, β_2 and β_3) both with these political variables included and in their absence.

Table 1 presents the results of estimation for the US exclusions from the general formula Tokyo Round tariff cuts. Column 1 presents ordinary least squares (OLS) estimates of the parameters of (10) with all variables expressed in levels, column 2 presents estimates of (10) when all variables are expressed in logs, and column 3 provides parameter estimates when COMMIT is entered in level form and PREMP and CONS are entered as logs, as would be suggested by (9) expressed in log form provided that the elasticity of demand η is close to one (for the estimates presented in column 3, the remaining variables are entered as levels). A first observation is that the parameter estimates vary substantially across specifications. When (10) is estimated on levels (column 1), none of the parameter estimates are statistically different from zero at standard confidence levels, suggesting that the theory motivating (10) misses the central features of what went in to the Tokyo Round exclusion decisions. However, when estimated in logs (column 2), most parameters are estimated to be statistically different from zero, and the parameters of primary interest are each significant and of the theoretically expected sign in light of (9). Moreover, many of the coefficients on the political variables shown in column 2 are also significant, and take signs that are typically found by earlier researchers in this area (see Baldwin, 1985).

Of particular interest across the three specifications is the parameter estimate on COMMIT. This coefficient is found to be negative and significant when the other economic variables PREMP and CONS are also significant and of the theoretically expected sign (column 2). This result lends some support to the view that Tokyo Round exclusion decisions were made with commitment. In particular, when the economic model guiding our empirical exercise finds *any* support in the data, it does so in a way that is consistent with the conclusion

TABLE 1 *Tokyo Round Exclusions from General Formula Cuts**

Variable**	Eq. 1	Eq. 2	Eq. 3	Eq. 4	Eq. 5
CONSTANT	0.012	–0.027	0.012	–0.056	–0.043
	(1.49)	(–1.13)	(0.83)	(–2.77)	(–1.41)
COMMIT	0.007	–0.021	–0.057	–0.025	–0.021
	(0.16)	(–2.34)	(–0.96)	(–3.13)	(–2.42)
PREMP	0.604	0.016	0.009	0.017	0.017
	(0.51)	(2.39)	(1.55)	(2.56)	(2.37)
CONS	–1.258	–0.018	–0.009	–0.017	–0.019
	(–0.77)	(–2.86)	(–1.70)	(–2.73)	(–2.89)
VALOUT	–0.032	–0.013	–0.030	—	–0.009
	(–1.63)	(–1.53)	(–1.52)		(–0.99)
IMPEN	0.025	0.002	0.019	—	0.002
	(1.85)	(2.08)	(1.37)		(1.73)
ESTSIZE	0.016	0.008	0.016	—	0.007
	(1.44)	(3.26)	(1.48)		(1.99)
CONCEN	0.001	–0.005	0.001	—	–0.005
	(0.37)	(–1.17)	(0.58)		(–0.92)
R^2	0.05	0.15	0.06	0.05	—
Obs.	199	199	199	199	345

* Dependent variable: ad valorem exclusion from Tokyo Round general formula cuts.
** See text for variable descriptions and differences among equations; *t*-statistics in parentheses.

that the US government exhibited an ability to commit with regard to the private sector when it selected its exclusions from the Tokyo Round general formula cuts. To check that this conclusion is not sensitive to the inclusion of political variables for which our theory gives little guidance, we also estimated (10) in logs but excluding all political variables. The estimation results, contained in column 4 of Table 1, confirm that the presence or absence of political variables has virtually no impact on this conclusion. Despite the sensitivity across specifications, we therefore interpret the finding of a negative and significant coefficient on COMMIT in the (logs) exclusion equation as providing some support for the notion that the US government showed an ability to commit in its determination of exclusions from the Tokyo Round general tariff-cutting rules.[13]

The OLS results presented in the first four columns of Table 1 ignore the possible effect that our sample selection procedure may have on the properties of the error term. We now re-estimate (10) in a censored regression framework to account explicitly for our selection of sectors with pre-Tokyo Round tariff rates in excess of 5 percent.

In particular, we use maximum likelihood techniques to jointly estimate the parameters of a selection equation and a regression equation, with the selection equation governing when the dependent variable of the regression equation is observed. The dependent variable of the selection equation is the pre-Tokyo Round ad valorem tariff, for which we have 345 four-digit SIC observations. While we experimented with various forms for this equation, our reported results specify this equation in the form of (10), with all variables measured in logs at their 1968 values (this year conforms to the year following the conclusion of the Kennedy Round, the set of multilateral tariff negotiations which shaped the structure of pre-Tokyo Round tariffs). The list of explanatory variables for this equation is the same as that used throughout our analysis of Tokyo Round decisions, with the exception of CONCEN which was not available for that year. The regression equation is simply the Tokyo Round exclusion equation as specified by (10), with the dependent variable observed only if the pre-Tokyo Round ad valorem tariff exceeds 5 percent. The error terms of the two equations are assumed to have a bivariate normal distribution.

The last column (column 5) of Table 1 reports the results of estimation of (10) for the Tokyo Round exclusion equation when all variables are measured in logs. For conformity with the rest of the table, we report only the parameters of the regression equation. Comparing these results with the analogous OLS estimates (column 2 of Table 1), it is apparent that accounting for the sample selection process has little effect on the parameter estimates of interest. In particular, the coefficient on COMMIT continues to be negative and significant even after accounting for the sample selection process.

As a second piece of evidence regarding the ability of the US government to commit to its Tokyo Round decisions, we now present estimates of (10) as applied to US decisions to grant exclusions from the general staging rules of the Tokyo Round. As noted previously, while a general staging rule was agreed upon (cuts were to be implemented in eight equal stages), the actual staging rule for many products was in fact quite different. In this way, the government in effect provided temporary relief from the negotiationed tariff reduction in those sectors where the staging rule was substantially slowed from the general rule, e.g. textiles and steel. Hence, these decisions provide an additional set of observations upon which the ability of the US government to make commitments within the context of the Tokyo Round may be checked.

We measure these staging rule exclusions with reference to the percentage of negotiated Tokyo Round tariff cuts that were in place as of 1984, the midpoint of the eight-year general staging process. Table 2 presents the results of estimating (10) over the entire sample for which Tokyo Round tariff reductions were implemented. Because the dependent variable is truncated below at zero and above at one, we assume (10) as a two-limit Tobit. We note, however, that OLS estimates are virtually the same as the two-limit Tobit estimates which we present. As before, we present the specification in levels (column 1), in logs (column 2), and in the form suggested by (9) expressed in log form (column 3). As with the earlier results on exclusions from the Tokyo Round general tariff-cutting rules, there is evidence that the pattern of exclusions from the general staging rule reflects the government's ability to commit: the parameter estimate on COMMIT is negative and significant whenever the coefficients on each of the other economic variables PREMP and CONS are also significant and of the theoretically expected sign (columns 2 and 3). The signs of the estimated coefficients on the political

TABLE 2 *Tokyo Round Exclusions from General Staging Rules**

Variable**	Eq. 1	Eq. 2	Eq. 3	Eq. 4
CONSTANT	0.310	0.073	0.262	0.319
	(9.18)	(0.49)	(3.15)	(4.26)
COMMIT	–0.147	–0.104	–0.900	–0.549
	(–0.66)	(–2.20)	(–2.68)	(–1.93)
PREMP	9.626	0.102	0.105	0.095
	(1.31)	(2.16)	(3.60)	(3.92)
CONS	–18.114	–0.117	–0.117	–0.107
	(–2.31)	(–2.98)	(–4.70)	(–5.07)
VALOUT	0.197	0.103	0.179	—
	(2.39)	(3.43)	(2.25)	
IMPEN	–0.058	–0.008	–0.110	—
	(–1.24)	(–1.45)	(–2.28)	
ESTSIZE	–0.011	0.013	0.012	—
	(–0.27)	(1.06)	(0.28)	
CONCEN	0.000	0.002	0.000	—
	(0.43)	(0.07)	(0.79)	
log(*L*)	153.22	162.40	164.24	159.69
Obs.	316	316	316	316

* Dependent variable: one minus percentage of negotiated Tokyo Round tariff reduction in place as of 1984.
** See text for variable descriptions and differences among equations; *t*-statistics in parentheses.

variables are in some cases reversed from their signs in the estimates presented in Table 1, reinforcing further the concern that the parameter estimates are quite sensitive to specification issues. Nevertheless, as a check that our basic conclusion regarding the parameters of primary interest is not sensitive to the inclusion of political variables for which our theory gives little guidance, we again estimated (10) in logs but excluding all political variables. The estimation results, contained in column 4 of Table 2, confirm once again that the presence or absence of political variables has little impact on this conclusion.[14]

Despite the sensitivity across specifications, we therefore interpret the results of Tables 1 and 2 as providing some support for the notion that the US government showed an ability to commit in its Tokyo Round exclusions decisions. We turn next to an examination of US escape clause decisions to see whether there is evidence that the US government was able to commit as effectively when GATT's rules were not in force.

5. EMPIRICAL RESULTS FROM ESCAPE CLAUSE ACTIONS

In this section we present the results of estimating (10) for escape clause decisions over the period 1975–1986. An immediate problem we face is that protective responses under the escape clause often take the form of quantitative restrictions. Rather than employing various elasticity measures to convert these to tariff equivalents, we simply treat the decision to offer protection under the escape clause as a 0/1 variable. We thus estimate (10) as a Probit model under the assumption that the likelihood of import relief is increasing in the size of the equilibrium tariff response as characterized by (10). Of the 40 escape clause decisions in our sample, 15 cases ended in some form of protection being granted, with protection being denied in the remaining 25 cases.

A second problem we face is that our sample of escape clause cases spans a dozen years, and therefore escape clause decisions may be influenced by additional dynamic considerations, such as changes in political preferences over time or business cycle conditions, which we did not need to consider in our estimation of the Tokyo Round exclusion equation. This suggests that the inclusion of a number of additional controls on the right-hand side of (10) might be warranted, such as the political party of the President at the time of an escape clause decision, the proximity of the escape clause decision to an election date, the value of the aggregate trade balance relative to GNP, and so on. We experimented with these and other measures, and found empirical support for the inclusion of only one additional right-hand-side variable when estimating (10) on escape clause data – a dummy (*REP201*) indicating whether the industry had filed a previous escape clause petition.

It should also be borne in mind that the escape clause is designed to allow governments to respond with temporary protective measures to greater-than-anticipated injury in import-competing sectors. This has two implications for our empirical analysis of escape clause protection. First, we need to include a measure of the sectoral shock as a right-hand-side variable when estimating (10), to control for shocks of different magnitudes hitting different sectors. We experiment with several different measures of SHOCK, employing both the change in industry import penetration ratio and the change in industry wage. And second, as a matter of interpretation, the explicitly temporary nature of escape clause protection might by itself keep to a minimum the resource allocation decisions that would actually hinge on this protection, thereby relieving governments of the need to consider the possibility of serious production distortions associated with their escape clause decisions at all. Such an interpretation cannot be ruled out, and it should be kept in mind as a potential caveat throughout this section. But it is made less compelling by the Tokyo Round staging rule exclusion results reported in the previous section. After all, the staging rule exclusion decisions amounted to protective measures of an explicitly temporary nature as well, and yet we found evidence there that the government was indeed sensitive to the potential production distortions associated with its trade policy decisions. As a consequence, a natural (but by no means the only) interpretation of a failure to find such evidence here is that the production distortions are still present but that the government's ability to account for them in its tariff decisions is lost in the absence of GATT's rules.

Measures of the explanatory variables were taken from the relevant four-digit SIC sector in which the petitioning industry belonged for the year prior to that in which the determination of escape clause protection was made. Unfortunately, these data are not tailored to the particular industries represented by each escape clause petition. While in principle such data could be collected from the published case reports, in practice the data published in these reports are irregular and incomplete. Moreover, it is not uncommon for the reports to provide four-digit SIC data when more detailed data are unavailable. Nevertheless, to check the robustness of our results with respect to this measurement problem, we have also constructed as complete a data set as possible from the individual reports and supplemented this with four-digit SIC data where necessary, and we will discuss our results with this alternative data set as well.

Finally, there is an important issue of sample selection. The 40 observations on escape clause decisions in our sample were not generated randomly, but were instead determined by the joint requirement that (i) the industry chose to file an escape clause petition under US law and (ii) the US International Trade Commission (ITC) found the industry to be facing serious injury or a threat thereof. If the random factors influencing the decisions at either of the first two stages are correlated with the error term in the tariff equation (10), as they would be for example if an unobserved industry characteristic influenced decisions at all three stages, then simple Probit estimators of the coefficients of (10) will be biased and inconsistent. We will attempt to go part way to address the issue of sample selection later in this section, but must in the end acknowledge this as an important caveat in interpreting our results.

Table 3 presents Probit estimates of (10) under the same three specifications as presented earlier in Tables 1 and 2 in the context of the Tokyo Round exclusions: in levels (column 1), in logs (column 2), and in the form (column 3) which is suggested by (9) – *COMMIT* in levels and *PREMP* and *CONS* in logs (with political variables in levels). The variable *SHOCK* is measured as the change in import penetration ratio. Its coefficient is always of the expected sign, but never significant at the 5 per cent level, though it is occasionally significant at the 10 percent level (this is also true when *SHOCK* is measured as the change in wage). The coefficient on the dummy variable *REP201* is always positive and typically significant, implying that industries which have previously filed an escape clause petition have a better chance of receiving protection. The coefficients in other political variables are typically significant, and again take signs that are typically found by earlier researchers in this area (see Baldwin, 1985). The coefficients on *PREMP* and *CONS* are often of the wrong sign but never significant. Most importantly, however, and in contrast to our Tokyo Round findings, the coefficient on *COMMIT* across escape clause equations is always positive and sometimes (column 1) significant. To see whether the estimated coefficient on *COMMIT* – and in particular the failure to find a negative coefficient – might be sensitive to the inclusion of political variables, in column 4 we estimate (10) in logs but excluding all political variables. The significance levels on all remaining variables drop, but the signs of the estimated coefficients remain as before and, in particular, there is no evidence that our failure to find a negative and significant coefficient on COMMIT in the escape clause equation is sensitive to the inclusion or exclusion of political economy variables..

While the lack of significance across specifications of the coefficients on *PREMP* and *CONS* is discouraging and a cause for some concern, the absence

TABLE 3 *Determination of Escape Clause Protection**

Variable**	Eq. 1	Eq. 2	Eq. 3	Eq. 4	Eq. 5
CONSTANT	–8.78	4.74	6.91	1.77	2.37
	(–1.74)	(0.73)	(0.76)	(0.56)	(0.98)
COMMIT	191.64	6.32	24.57	0.29	—
	(2.39)	(1.74)	(1.47)	(0.34)	
PREMP	703.13	–0.39	0.77	0.28	1,178.96
	(0.60)	(–0.26)	(0.71)	(0.39)	(2.23)
CONS	2.49	2.80	0.42	0.17	–0.70
	(1.37)	(1.51)	(0.45)	(0.26)	(–1.55)
SHOCK	29.93	10.37	10.37	0.58	15.44
	(1.73)	(1.22)	(1.22)	(0.10)	(1.58)
REP201	9.56	3.13	1.31	0.90	2.21
	(2.32)	(2.11)	(1.97)	(1.84)	(2.18)
VALOUT	–65.88	–8.32	–13.67	—	–12.95
	(–2.40)	(–2.03)	(–2.09)		(–2.12)
IMPEN	28.00	2.32	4.71	—	2.37
	(2.47)	(1.98)	(1.84)		(1.25)
ESTSIZE	–28.40	–1.81	–1.44	—	–8.46
	(–2.06)	(–2.07)	(–0.62)		(–1.44)
CONCEN	0.04	–0.69	–0.02	—	0.01
	(1.03)	(–0.76)	(–0.80)		(0.25)
Obs.	40	40	40	40	40

* Dependent variable: 1 if escape clause protection imposed, 0 otherwise.
** See text for variable descriptions and differences among equations; *t*-statistics in parentheses.

of a negative and significant coefficient on *COMMIT* in any of our escape clause equations in Table 3 does offer some support for the view that the government lacks commitment ability under the escape clause procedure. Moreover, the presence of a positive and significant coefficient on *COMMIT* in one of the escape clause equations of Table 3 (column 1) indicates a lack of commitment in the escape clause decisions at the same time that it reinforces our earlier finding that the US government *was* able to make commitments to the private sector in the context of its exclusion decisions in the Tokyo Round. According to our theoretical results of section 2 and their interpretation in section 3, the results in column 1 of Table 3 would, in combination with the Tokyo Round exclusion results of Tables 1 and 2, provide strong evidence that GATT's rules help governments make domestic commitments.

Of course, in light of the poor performance of the variables *PREMP* and *CONS* and the mixed evidence in favor of a positive coefficient on *COMMIT* in Table 3, an alternative interpretation of our escape clause results is that *none* of the variables specifically identified by our model performs particularly well in the escape clause equation, and that therefore the model simply fails to capture what governments care about in determining escape clause protection. However, it is also possible that our small number of escape clause observations is incapable of revealing in a strong and consistent way the relatively subtle effects that we are looking for, but that more central features of the model would find support. One way to explore this possibility is to consider what additional structure might be imposed on the escape clause estimating equation under the basic hypothesis that the government cannot commit in the escape clause decision-making environment, and to ask whether there is more support for the economic model when this additional structure is imposed. A natural candidate in this regard would be to abstract from the more subtle interactions between escape clause decisions and previous Tokyo Round commitments that give rise to the prediction of a positive coefficient on *COMMIT* under the escape clause, and to simply impose on the escape clause estimating equation a restriction that the coefficient on *COMMIT* is zero, as would be the case in the absence of any interaction between escape clause and Tokyo Round tariffs if the government could not commit to its escape clause decisions.

The fifth column of Table 3 presents the results of estimating (10) on escape clause data (in levels) when *COMMIT* is dropped from the equation. Now, all coefficients take their theoretically expected signs. In particular, the coefficients on each of the economic variables *PREMP*, *CONS*, and *SHOCK* take their expected signs, though only the coefficient on *PREMP* is significant. The insignificant coefficient on *CONS* is consistent with the empirical findings of other studies and reflects perhaps a greater concern with producer as opposed to consumer interests in setting escape clause tariffs. The uniformly poor performance of our *SHOCK* measures in the escape clause equations is not entirely surprising either; it may reflect the sample selection issues discussed above, that protection decisions under the escape clause are only made in cases where the ITC has determined that the industry is facing serious injury or an established threat thereof. In any event, we view the results in column 5 of Table 3 as providing some evidence in support of the economic model as applied to escape clause decisions under the assumption that the government cannot commit to these decisions. Together with the other results contained in Table 3, they suggest that the absence of a negative coefficient on *COMMIT* in the escape clause equation is not simply a reflection of a general failure of the theory to account for systematic features of the escape clause decision.

Nevertheless, our failure to find any evidence that escape clause decisions take account of the production distortions may reflect problems of measurement and sample selection. In the remainder of this section we attempt to address both problems.

The most serious potential measurement problem is that, as discussed in the previous subsection, measures of all explanatory variables have been taken from the relevant four-digit SIC sectors rather than from the ITC reports themselves. In Table 4 we re-estimate columns 1 and 5 of Table 3 using a data set constructed as completely as possible from data provided in the ITC reports. This alternative data set combines the four-digit SIC data with more disaggregated data found in the ITC reports. The Appendix contains a detailed description of how these data have been constructed.

TABLE 4 *Determination of Escape Clause Protection: Sensitivity**

Variable**	Eq. 1	Eq. 2	Eq. 3
CONSTANT	–1.45	0.48	–8.81
	(–0.53)	(0.22)	(–0.42)
COMMIT	27.87	—	194.27
	(1.59)		(1.44)
PREMP	768.02	711.10	731.45
	(1.54)	(1.78)	(0.14)
CONS	–0.20	–0.50	2.50
	(–0.25)	(–0.94)	(0.34)
SHOCK	–0.40	0.38	30.74
	(–0.06)	(0.07)	(0.57)
REP201	1.78	1.42	9.73
	(2.29)	(2.22)	(1.48)
VALOUT	–14.97	–7.34	–67.01
	(–2.33)	(–1.84)	(–1.54)
IMPEN	6.60	2.52	28.38
	(1.82)	(1.20)	(1.57)
ESTSIZE	1.31	0.56	–29.00
	(0.80)	(0.40)	(–0.62)
CONCEN	–0.01	–0.01	0.04
	(–0.22)	(–0.46)	(0.20)
CONSTANT	—	—	–0.09
			(–0.35)
LRSHOCK	—	—	5.00
			(2.35)
ρ	—	—	0.00
			(0.00)
Obs.	40	40	63

* Dependent variable: 1 if escape clause protection imposed, 0 otherwise.
** See text for variable descriptions and differences among equations; *t*-statistics in parentheses.

Columns 1 and 2 of Table 4 present our results of estimating the escape clause equations with report-based measures of the explanatory variables. All equations are estimated in levels. Column 1 presents the results of estimating (10) with report-based data with *COMMIT* included, while column 2 drops *COMMIT* from the equation. The results in columns 1 and 2 of Table 3 are broadly similar to the escape clause results presented in columns 1 and 5 of Table 3. The estimated coefficients on the variables *REP201*, *VALOUT*, and *IMPEN* are of the same sign as before and are significant with roughly the same frequency. The estimated coefficients on *CONS*, *SHOCK*, and *CONCEN* continue to be insignificant as before. The main difference is that the estimated coefficient on *PREMP* when *COMMIT* is excluded from the regression is no longer significant at the 5 percent level, though it maintains significance at the 10 percent level (column 2 of Table 4). Most importantly, however, the estimated coefficient on *COMMIT* in column 1 of Table 4 is still positive, though its significance level has dropped. In short, our estimates with this more disaggregated data continue to provide no evidence that escape clause decisions are made with commitment while at the same time they continue to reinforce (albeit weakly) our earlier finding that the US government *was* able to make commitments to the private sector in the context of its exclusion decisions in the Tokyo Round.

Finally, in an attempt to partially address the sample selection problem discussed above, we estimate a bivariate Probit model by full information maximum likelihood methods.[15] The model consists of two equations, one corresponding to the ITC injury determinations and the other corresponding to the (President's) decision of whether or not to grant protection. The dependent variable for the first equation takes a value of one in the event of a positive injury determination by the ITC, and zero otherwise. The dependent variable for the second equation relates to the protection decision, and is defined as before; it is observed only if the ITC decision is positive. Our total sample consists of 63 escape clause decisions made by the ITC during the period 1975–1986, of which 40 were affirmative.

According to US law, the ITC must determine whether or not there has been serious injury as a result of imports, or the threat thereof. It is therefore natural to specify the ITC regression by including as right-hand-side variables alternative measures of the extent of injury and the change in imports. We measure the change in imports as the average percentage change in import penetration over the five years prior to the ITC decision (*LRSHOCK*). The regressions that we report below include only this explanatory variable (plus the intercept) in the ITC equations. We tried other measures of injury and a richer set of explanatory variables, but their estimated coefficients generally turned out to be insignificant or of the wrong sign; moreover, the results of interest (the coefficient on the variable *COMMIT* in the protection regression) were never affected by the specification of the ITC regression.

Column 3 of Table 4 reports the results of the joint estimation of the two Probit regressions. The first 11 coefficients refer to the protection equation and are based on the selected sample of 40 observations. The next two coefficients refer to the ITC equation, and are based on the full sample of 63 observations. The last estimated coefficient, p, is the correlation coefficient between the error terms. All variables are measured in levels. Column 3 in Table 4 is the analogue of column 1 in Table 3, with the variable *COMMIT* included in the protection equation. The estimated correlation coefficient is zero. As a result, the estimated coefficients of column 3 in Table 4 are nearly identical to those of column 1 in Table 3. The only difference is that the standard errors are much larger in the latter. As a consequence, almost all estimated coefficients turn out to be insignificant when the system is jointly estimated. Despite this fact, the results are robust to alternative initial conditions for the parameters and for the correlation coefficient.

While our robustness checks are limited by available data, we infer from the results of Table 4 that the broad findings reported in Table 3 regarding the escape clause are likely to be robust to measurement issues and to the sample selection problem. The strength of the evidence that the estimated coefficient on *COMMIT* in the escape clause equation is non-negative (and possibly strictly positive) does not appear to be particularly sensitive to the level of aggregation of the explanatory variables, or to whether the protection regression is estimated in isolation or jointly with the ITC decision. When viewed in light of the evidence presented in the previous section supporting a negative coefficient on *COMMIT* in the Tokyo Round exclusion equations, we interpret our escape clause findings as suggesting that the commitment which governments evidently achieve under the rule of GATT is not easily achieved in its absence.

6. CONCLUSION

The debate on rules versus discretion has received a great deal of attention in the theory of economic policy, in macroeconomics, public finance and trade policy. A central question is whether the institutional environment really matters, or whether instead the policy-maker's reputation can substitute for commitment. While there is a large theoretical literature addressing this question, to date there has been little empirical study of how relevant the distinction between rules and discretion is, and no study within the context of trade policy.

Trade policy lends itself particularly well to an empirical investigation of these issues, for two reasons. First, as shown in section 2, the theory yields very sharp predictions of how trade policy chosen under discretion differs from that chosen under rules. Second, and perhaps more important, trade policy in the US is implemented under a variety of institutional arrangements. A major difference between some of these arrangements is the commitment technologies that they provide. Hence, by comparing the policies implemented within these different environments, one can examine whether or not the capacity to undertake binding policy commitments matters.

We have attempted to do just that by comparing trade policy actions taken in the highly discretionary environment of escape clause decisions with those taken under less discretion within the context of the Tokyo Round. Our empirical results are mixed, but overall they provide some support for the view that GATT rules help member-governments make trade policy commitments to their private sectors. We find some evidence that the United States granted exclusions from the Tokyo Round general tariff-cutting rule less readily in sectors where higher tariffs were more likely to significantly distort production decisions. When we consider US exclusions from the Tokyo Round general staging rules, stronger support for this inverse relationship between exclusions and associated production distortions is evident. These findings are consistent with the view that, at least when GATT rules apply, governments are able to make trade policy commitments to their private sectors. By contrast, we find no evidence of an inverse relationships between US escape clause protection and the implied production distortions, and in fact find some evidence of a positive association, as would be implied if GATT rules are providing member-governments with a commitment device relative to their private sectors which the member-governments do not otherwise possess (and which is therefore lost when GATT rules are temporarily suspended under the escape clause). While our empirical results cannot be viewed as conclusive, they are nevertheless suggestive that GATT's rules do indeed help governments make domestic commitments.

7. APPENDIX

This appendix defines the variables and describes the data sources underlying our reported empirical results. We do not include sources for those variables, e.g., certain political variables, which we experimented with but did not report. With the exception of the ITC report-based data to be discussed below, all of the independent variables used in this study were constructed from data contained in the National Bureau of Economic Research (NBER) Immigration, Trade, and Labor Markets Data Files. This is an annual data set covering four-digit SIC manufacturing industries from 1958 through 1986, and more recently updated through 1994. A detailed description of the data is contained in Abowd (1990).

All independent variables in the Tokyo Round regressions were constructed using 1978 values (1968 values for the selection equation in the censored regression model), except for the four-firm concentration ratio which was available only for 1976. All independent variables for the escape clause regressions were taken from the four-digit industry (or industries) associated with the petition, with the year being that associated with the month 15 months prior to the ITC ruling date. Where a single petition spanned several four-digit SIC industries, we treated each four-digit industry as a separate Presidential decision on the grounds that the President did often distinguish among industries or products that the President did often distinguish among industries or products of a given petition in the final escape clause determination [e.g., Color TV (TA-201-19), and Non-Electric Cookware (TA-201-39)]. The rule for choosing the year associated with each escape clause petition reflects our attempt to generate pre-shock variables, and leads to independent variables which are measured generally one to two years prior to the year of the ITC ruling. We experimented with other rules, with no change in the results. The one exception to this rule was the four-firm concentration ratio which, as noted, was available only for 1976.

We also constructed an alternative data set for the escape clause regressions by combining four-digit SIC data with more disaggregated data found in the ITC reports. For 22 of our 40 observations, we collected measures of (apparent) consumption, sales, import penetration, change in import penetration, and establishment size directly from the relevant reports. We then supplemented the missing values with their four-digit counterparts. While data on production worker employment were also generally available from the ITC reports, the figure reported was total employment of production workers by firms involved in the petition, regardless of whether these workers were employed in the production of the products named in the petition. Thus, as an alternative to the four-digit production worker employment figures, we also constructed an employment series as the product of the ITC reported sales and ratio of production worker employment to less for the relevant four-digit industry, under the assumption that all production within a four-digit industry shares a common labor-to-sales ratio. As it turns out, our results were largely the same regardless of which employment figure we used. We thus present results only with the four-digit employment figure. No consistent data on wages or concentration were available as an alternative to the four-digit data. The absence of wage (or payroll) data from the ITC reports also means that our variable *COMMIT* could not be constructed entirely from report data. However, in addition to the four-digit measure, we constructed a measure of this variable using four-digit wage data but with our report-based employment and consumption series. Again, our results were unaffected by the use of this alternative measure of *COMMIT*, and we report results using the four-digit measure of *COMMIT*. Finally, for each report-based data series we experimented with the last year of data available in each report and alternatively with the second to last year of data available, and found that it made no difference in our results. Thus, we present our findings with all variables corresponding to the last year of available data in the ITC report.

The dependent variables for the Tokyo Round regressions were constructed from World Bank data supplied to us by Kishore Gawande and Daniel Trefler. The exclusions from both the Swiss rule cuts and the general staging rule were constructed by beginning with line-item changes and aggregating up to the four-digit SIC level using 1980 US trade weights. The dependent variable for the escape clause regressions was constructed by assigning a zero to Presidential decisions which ended in no action or expedited adjustment assistance procedures, and a one otherwise. Our escape clause sample is limited to Presidential decisions involving manufacturing products during the period 1975 through 1986.

The variable definitions follow:

COMMIT	Ratio of production worker payroll to consumption.
WAGE	Average production worker wage, deflated by CPI.
PREMP	Ration of production worker employment to total production worker employment in US manufacturing sector.
CONS	Ratio of shipments minus net exports to GNP.
VALOUT	Ratio of value-added to shipments.
IMPEN	Ratio of imports to consumption.
ESTSIZE	Average employment per establishment.
CONCEN	Four-firm concentration ratio for 1976.
SHOCK	Annual percentage change in *IMPEN* or *WAGE*.
REP201	Dummy variable that takes a value of one if a President has considered an escape clause petition from the industry before or during the sample period, and zero otherwise.

ACKNOWLEDGMENTS

We are greatly indebted to John Alfaro, Robert Baldwin, Drusilla Brown, Kishore Gawande, Howard Gruenspecht, William Hart, Edward Leamer, Terry Obrien, Kerry Pannell, and Daniel Trefler for help with various aspects of the data. Phil Levy and Tom Harris provided outstanding research assistance on early portions of this work. This research was funded by the National Science Foundation under grant SES89-1118. Some preliminary results from this research were presented at the NBER Conference on Empirical Studies of Commercial Policy, March 1990, and are contained in Staiger and Tabellini (1991). An earlier version of this paper was circulated under the title "Does Commitment Matter in Trade Policy?"

NOTES

Corresponding author, Robert W. Staiger, Department of Economics, The University of Wisconsin, 1180 Observatory Drive, Madison, WI 53706, USA.

1 The theoretical literature has also identified a second, logically distinct but possibly complementary role for trade agreements: in a setting where the important strategic interaction occurs across individual countries, a trade agreement can provide member governments with an escape from a terms-of-trade-driven prisoners' dilemma. See Johnson (1953/54), for the classic formalization of this more traditional view of what trade agreements do. More recent interpretations and extensions of this view are contained in Dixit (1987), Staiger (1995a), and Bagwell and Staiger (1990, 1999). To our knowledge, there are as yet no empirical studies that explore the extent to which trade agreements serve this purpose either.

2 This two-step procedure also characterized the Kennedy Round, but was not followed in the recently completed Uruguay Round.

3 The list of items for which the actual staging rule differed from the general staging rule is contained in Annex I of GATT (1979).

4 GATT rules also afford member-governments the opportunity to reverse their exclusion decisions by entering into *renegotiations* over tariff bindings with their trading partners subsequent to the conclusion of a round. Where the strategic interaction across governments presents the main problem to be solved by a trade agreement (see also note 1), GATT's provision for renegotiation can have important implications for the outcome of the original tariff negotiations (see Bagwell and Staiger, 1999). However, when considering the impact that GATT rules may have on the strategic interaction between a government and its own domestic residents, the important feature of this provision is simply the requirement that the procedures for renegotiation with one's trading partners must be carried out before any tariff changes can be made, which by itself serves to limit the flexibility with which a government could lawfully reverse exclusion decisions through this channel, much as the injury condition limits a government's flexibility in using escape clause actions for this purpose. Hence, despite the opportunities for reconsideration granted in these provisions, GATT's rules at least in principle place limits on the flexibility with which member-governments may lawfully exceed the tariff bindings negotiated in a round, and hence these rules could in principle help governments make domestic commitments. The empirical question is then whether this effect is evident in practice.

5 We do not attempt to explain why the opportunity to negotiate a round of table liberalization arises at a particular time, nor why any further liberalization would be desired in light of previous rounds. These are important questions, but they lie well outside the scope of this paper. For attempts to answer these questions from the perspective of enforcement difficulties at the international level, see Staiger (1995b), Devereux (1997). Bond and Park (1998) and Furusawa and Lai (forthcoming).

6 Note that we do not make a distinction here between temporary and permanent suspension, as there is essentially only a single period after the tariffs are implemented.

In a multi-period model, such a distinction could be added without upsetting the basic flavor of our results, but at the cost of substantial additional complexity. We also note that GATT's escape clause can be given alternative interpretations to the one that we consider here (see, for example, Bagwell and Staiger, 1990).

7 The ability to make international lump-sum transfers simplifies our characterization of the outcome of tariff negotiations between the two governments, but is otherwise not crucial to our argument.

8 By stabilizing the export price effects of a government's decision to raise tariffs, GATT's compensation requirement effectively induces "large" countries, i.e. those with the power to influence the prices received by foreign exporters, to act as if they had no ability to affect export prices when making their tariff determinations. In the present setting, this requirement ensures that a government will not use the escape clause as an excuse to reassert its power over export prices. Bagwell and Staiger (1999) consider the efficiency properties of this kind of rule more broadly.

9 It can further be shown (see Bagwell and Staiger, 1999) that such a requirement can be given an interpretation along the lines of GATT's norm of *reciprocity*, which neutralizes terms-of-trade movements associated with trade policy choices by calling the tariff adjustments that lead to equal changes in import and export volumes.

10 Inspection of (6) confirms this negative relationship for negotiated tariffs. For the escape clause response, which is an increment to the negotiated tariff in light of higher-than-anticipated adjustment costs, this negative relationship can be confirmed under mild regularity conditions.

11 This interpretation would imply an additional empirical relationship once the determinants of γ_x are specified. For example, if the domestic government sought to maximize national surplus with its tariff policy, then we would have $\gamma_x = 1$, and this would imply that the formula cut should be designed to reduce $\bar{t}_x$ to zero, from which the domestic government could then contemplate an exclusion on the grounds of adjustment costs. Alternatively, if the domestic government valued channeling national surplus toward producers in sector x, then we would have $\gamma_x > 1$, and so the formula cut would be designed to preserve a positive level of protection in sector x, from which the domestic government would again contemplate an adjustment-cost-based exclusion. Similar statements might be derived with respect to the general staging rules and their exclusions. However, while the determinants of γ_x and an explanation of the general formula cuts and staging rules are interesting topics in their own right, they are not the focus of this paper.

12 While we do not present results on the full sample, they are roughly equivalent. Below we do present results that account for the sample selection process.

13 When the estimated coefficient on COMMIT is statistically significant in the Tokyo Round exclusions, it is also quite large from a quantitative point of view: the standardized beta coefficients on COMMIT in column 2 of Table 1 is –0.38. Finally, the White (1980) test rejects the hypothesis of no heteroscedasticity; when the standard errors are re-estimated using White's (1980) procedure that insures consistency under heteroscedasticity, the t-statistic for COMMIT drops slightly and becomes just insignificant at the 5 percent confidence level. However, if the model is re-estimated dropping four outlier observations, the results remain essentially unchanged, and the t-statistics conform to the results of Table 1, even when the standard errors are estimated using White's (1980) procedure.

14 Again, there is evidence of heteroscedasticity, but the results do not change when the standard errors are re-estimated using White's (1980) procedure. Also the results do not change when a big outlier is removed from the sample.

15 This estimator is based on Wynand and Bernard (1981). The estimation employs the software "Limdep," by W. Greene. The details of the estimation procedure are

illustrated in Greene (1989, chapters 12 and 20). For computational simplicity, we are forced to neglect the self-selection problem in the sample of observations on which the ITC decides. Thus, our procedure yields unbiased and consistent estimates only if the error term in the ITC Probit equation is uncorrelated with the variables that determine the filing decisions of firms.

REFERENCES

Abowd, J. M., 1990, The NBER immigration, trade, and labor markets data files. NBER Working Paper No. 3351, May.

Bagwell, K. and R. W. Staiger, 1990, A theory of managed trade. *American Economic Review* 80, 779–795.

—— and ——, 1999, An economic theory of GATT. *American Economic Review* 89, 215–248.

Baldwin, R. E., 1985, *The political economy of US import policy* (MIT Press, Cambridge, MA).

——, 1987, Politically realistic objective functions and trade policy. *Economic Letters* 24.

Bond, Eric W. and Jee-Hyeong Park, 1998, Gradualism in trade agreements with asymmetric countries. Mimeo, Pennsylvania State University, October.

Brainard, S. L., 1994, Last one out wins: trade policy in an international exit game. *International Economic Review* 35, 151–172.

Caves, R. E., 1976, Economic models of political choice: Canada's tariff structure. *Canadian Journal of Economics* 9, 278–300.

Devereux, M. B., 1977, Growth, specialization, and trade liberalization. *International Economic Review* 38(3), 565–585.

Director-General of General Agreement on Tariffs and Trade (GATT), 1979, *The Tokyo Round of multilateral trade negotiations* (Geneva).

Dixit, A., 1987, Strategic aspects of trade policy, in: T. F. Bewley, ed., *Advances in economic theory: fifth world congress* (Cambridge University Press, New York).

Furusawa, T. and E. Lai, forthcoming, Adjustment costs and gradual trade liberalization. *Journal of International Economics.*

Greene, William, 1989, *Econometric analysis* (Macmillan, New York).

Grossman, G. M. and E. Helpman, 1994, Protection for sale. *American Economic Review* 84, September, 833–850.

Jackson, John H., 1989, *The world trading system: law and policy of international economic relations* (MIT Press, Cambridge, MA).

Johnson, H. G., 1953/54, Optimal tariffs and retaliation. *Review of Economic Studies* 21(2), 142–153.

Kydland, F. and E. Prescott, 1977, Rules rather than discretion: the inconsistency of optimal plans. *Journal of Political Economy* 85, 473–491.

Maggi, Giovanni and Andres Rodriguez-Clare, 1998. The value of trade agreements in the presence of political pressures. *Journal of Political Economy* 106, June, 574–601.

Matsuyama, K., 1990. Perfect equilibria in a trade liberalization game. *American Economic Review* 80, 480–492.

Mayer, W., 1994, Optimal pursuit of safeguard actions over time, in: A. V. Deardorff and R. M. Sterm, eds., *Analytical and negotiating issues in the global trading system* (University of Michigan Press, Ann Arbor, MI).

Olson, Mancur, 1965, *The logic of collective action: public goods and the theory of groups* (Harvard University Press, Cambridge, MA).

Staiger, R. W., 1995a, International rules and institutions for trade policy, in: G. M.

Grossman and K. Rogoff, eds., *Handbook of international economics: Vol. 3* (North-Holland/Elsevier, Amsterdam).
——, 1995b, A theory of gradual trade liberalization, in: A. V. Deardorff, J. Levinsohn, and R. M. Stern, eds., *New directions in trade theory* (University of Michigan Press, Ann Arbor, MI).
—— and G. Tabellini, 1987, Discretionary trade policy and excessive protection. *American Economic Review* 77, 823–837.
—— and ——, 1991, Rules versus discretion in trade policy: an empirical analysis, in: R. E. Baldwin, ed., *Empirical Studies of Commercial Policy* (University of Chicago Press, Chicago and London).
White, H., 1980, A heteroskedasticity-consistent covariance matrix estimator and a direct test for heteroskedasticity. *Econometrica* 48, 817–838.
Wynand, P. and M. Bernard, 1981, The demand for deductibles in private health insurance. *Journal of Econometrics* 17(2), 229–252.

16. Reciprocity and Commercial Treaties

United States Tariff Commission

Subject and scope of this report.—The present report is concerned primarily with the reciprocity experiences of the United States, and, in connection with and in relation thereto, the American theory and practice of most-favored-nation treatment. It gives also somewhat extensive attention to the tariff systems and commercial treaty practices of other, and especially of European, countries.

Commercial treaties.—Modern commercial treaties cover a wide variety of subjects. They relate to the treatment to be accorded to persons, to vehicles of communication and transportation, and to commerce in all its phases. Within them there appear provisions as to admission of diplomatic and consular officials, and their rights and activities; immigration and emigration; police protection and civil rights; conditions of travel, residence, and trade; exemptions from extraordinary levies, forced loans, and military service; navigation, quarantine, and harbor regulations and dues; conditions for importation, exportation, transit, transfer, warehousing; tariffs and customs laws; protection to patents, copyrights, and trade-marks. In a tariff study those provisions are of chief concern which have to do with trade and with customs laws and regulations.

Reciprocity agreements.—In the adoption of a commercial policy and in the making of arrangements connected therewith, every State has a twofold object—it seeks to gain and to preserve for itself advantages, and to escape, avoid, and guard against disadvantages. This being the case, the making of a commercial treaty becomes a form of concluding a bargain.

Where each of the parties to a treaty makes special concessions to the other with the intention that the transaction shall be looked upon as a particular bargain and with the understanding that its benefits are not to be extended automatically, generally, and freely to other states, the agreement is called a "reciprocity" agreement.

The most-favored-nation clause.—In the making of commercial treaties a State may or may not seek a special and privileged position, but it has been a matter of especial concern to each State to be assured that it shall receive treatment at the hands of other States at least as favorable as that which the latter accord to any others. Each State desires that such concessions and guarantees as have been made to other States shall be extended to it; also that all which may in the future be granted to other States shall equally be granted to it.

In order to safeguard against oversight at the moment of making a treaty, and to reduce the necessity for repetitions, an instrument was devised which should automatically assure or offer to newly contracting States the benefit of concessions made, previously or afterwards, to third States. That instrument was the "most-favored-nation clause." It is neither the purpose nor the effect of the most-favored-nation clause to establish a "most-favored-nation;" on the contrary, its use implies the intention that the maximum of advantages which either of the parties to a treaty has extended or shall extend to any third State—for the moment the "most-favored" – shall be given or be made accessible to the other party; thus in practice to prevent the establishing of distinctions or discrimination in the extending of concessions and guarantees.

Conditional and unconditional forms of the most-favored-nation clause.—Up to the time of the American Revolution the most-favored-nation provision appeared in but one form: the pledge was not qualified; no limitations were laid down as to the circumstances under which concessions granted to other States should be extended as between the contracting parties. But in the first American treaty, that made by the American Confederation with France on February 6, 1778, the clause was given a new phraseology. In this treaty there appeared the usual pledge that advantages which either of the contracting parties had granted or might grant to a third State should be granted to the other, but there was attached a qualifying conditional provision, "... freely, if the concession (to the third State) was freely made, or on allowing the same compensation, if the concession was conditional." From that time forward the most-favored-nation clause has been used sometimes with the qualifying stipulation and sometimes without it. Where no such stipulation is attached, it is customary to speak of the clause as being "unconditional;" when it is specified that there shall bc compensation, the clause is described as "conditional."

European and American practice.—From the time when its representatives first subscribed to the conditional form of the clause, the United States, when pledging itself to favored-nation treatment, has employed that form almost without exception. The States of Europe, which had previously used the unconditional form only, have since employed sometimes the one and sometimes the other of the two forms—up to 1850 very frequently the conditional, after 1860 almost exclusively the unconditional. At the same time, in the negotiation of their earlier treaties the European States had been governed strictly by the principle of making concessions only in return for concessions sought: they had been in the habit of making treaty bargains with those States only from which they wished at a particular time to secure particular concessions. The American Government adopted a policy of offering favorable treatment to all who would reciprocate; it was frankly seeking to secure equality of opportunity in foreign markets, and it offered equality of opportunity to all countries seeking American markets on the basis of mutual concessions.

The willingness to treat with all nations equally and to offer the same concessions to all in return for compensatory concessions by each was essentially a step forward. It was no part, however, of the American policy to give to some

States "freely" such concessions as were given to others in consideration of reciprocal concessions. The earliest American statesmen adopted the "special bargain," principle, and the American Government has acted ever since in conformity with the conception that commercial concessions are to be given for specific compensation, and that most-favored-nation treatment implies and requires nothing more than the granting of opportunity to purchase, on the basis of reciprocal give and take, treatment identical with, or similar to, that accorded other States.

Changes in European practice—Tariff schedules by negotiations.—European States have long since altered their commercial policies: they have experimented with various tariff systems; or they have adopted new theories and practices in regard to commercial treaties and treaty bargaining. The commercial liberalism which met with favor in the leading States of Europe after the middle of the nineteenth century emphasized the theory and practice of generalizing concessions—that is, of extending, without condition, to all nations entitled to most-favored-nation treatment, the benefit of concessions made to any. Thus the use of the unconditional form of the most-favored-nation clause, together with the application of the unconditional interpretation, became the common European practice. Notwithstanding later changes in their commercial policies and tariff systems, European States have found it still convenient to generalize the concessions which they make, and such being the case, their most-favored-nation practice has remained, and is, "unconditional."

Many of these States now devise the rates in their statutory tariff schedules with distinct and particular reference to bargaining possibilities; they expect to make reductions, on the basis of concession for concession, by negotiation with other States individually, and then to extend the benefit of all their reductions, generalizing them, to all the States with which they have most-favored-nation agreements.

Practice of the United States—Single-tariff system.—These practices the United States has not adopted. Throughout the tariff history of the United States there has been an unbroken line of tariff laws on which it has been the uniform practice, except for the slight deviation in 1909, to employ a single list of fixed duties intended for general application to imports from all countries alike. It has not been the policy of the United States to modify its schedule of duties by granting concessions to various nations with the intention that all the concessions shall be grouped into a supplementary tariff schedule and be extended to all.

As a result of the continuity of its tariff policy in this respect, the commercial treaty pledges to which the United States has subscribed exhibit less variation in intent and wording than appears in European treaties. There has been a continuity in the American conception and construction of these pledges, particularly of the most-favored-nation clause, which has not been paralleled in the course of the European conception and interpretation.

While the United States has not practiced the type of commercial treaty bargaining now prevalent in Europe, it has, however, had no little experience with tariff treaties in the pursuance of "reciprocity." The American conception of a commercial treaty as an agreement based on the principle of bargaining has made it possible for the United States to enter in good faith into "reciprocity" agreements with individual countries, giving and receiving special concessions. By means of reciprocity treaties, the United States has granted various concessions to certain countries, for compensation, and has accepted concessions from them. This has involved in each case particular reductions from the rates established in the general tariff. In most cases the determination to enter into such agreement has come as a result of unusual circumstances, such as a peculiar geographical factor or peculiar particular relations. Having made concessions under special circumstances or for special compensation, the United States has not considered it obligatory or even just to extend the same favors to third states "freely."

Differences in principles and practices.—The principle which has consistently guided the practice of the United States in respect to treaty bargaining is thus different from that which has prevailed in Europe in recent decades. The American and the European conceptions of reciprocity and of the proper function of the most-favored-nation clause have differed. Proper appraisement of either requires an understanding of the commercial theories and policies and of the tariff systems and practices with which it is associated and of which it is made an instrument. To make possible such an appraisement, the Tariff Commission has made the studies which constitute the basis of this report.

I. RECIPROCITY AND TARIFF AGREEMENTS OF THE UNITED STATES

The reciprocity experiences of the United States.—Reciprocity treaties, in the specialized sense indicated above, have been an increasingly important factor in the commercial policies of the United States. Before 1890 seven such treaties had been negotiated; but of these only two, those made with Canada in 1854 and with Hawaii in 1875, became effective. A commercial agreement of minor importance was concluded with Spain—for Cuba and Porto Rico—in 1883, which agreement remained in effect until 1892.

In accordance with section 3 of the tariff act of 1890, reciprocity agreements of a more generalized type were made with six American countries, and with Austria-Hungary, Germany, Great Britain (for the West Indies) and Spain (for Cuba and Port Rico). These were terminated when the tariff act of 1894 went into effect.

Under the provision of section 4 of the tariff act of 1897, treaties, also of a more generalized type, were negotiated with Great Britain (for certain colonies), Denmark (for the Danish West Indies), Nicaragua, Ecuador, the Argentine, and France. These were, however, never ratified. Agreements more restricted in scope were concluded under section 3 of this act with France, Portugal, Germany, Italy, Switzerland, Spain, Bulgaria, Great Britain, and the Netherlands. These were terminated by the act of 1909.

Since 1904 special treatment for United States imports into Brazil has been established by a special arrangement. In 1903 a treaty, independent of general tariff legislation, was made with Cuba. This treaty is still in effect. In 1909–1911 President Taft arranged with representatives of the Canadian Government for a reciprocity agreement between Canada and the United States, but this failed of ratification by Canada.

1. The Canadian Reciprocity Treaty of 1854

The arrangement which the Canadian people rejected in 1911 was but the least of a long series of attempts which have been made to bring Canada and the United States, by the removal of commercial restrictions, into closer commercial relations. Only once has such an attempt been successful. A reciprocity treaty negotiated in 1854 was ratified, was put into force in 1855, and remained in force for eleven years. The great revolution in colonial and commercial policy which was carried through by the British Government in and after 1846 had thrown the British North American Provinces very much upon their own resources economically. Among policies possible at the moment, the most promising was that of close commercial relations with the United States, and to this the Canadian Government committed itself.

Tentative negotiations looking to reciprocity were begun in 1846. It was agreed in 1848 that reciprocity should be secured by concurrent legislation. The necessary legislation was passed by the Canadian Parliament and by the House of Representatives in the United States, but it never came to a vote in the Senate. The British Government Tyler objected to this on constitutional grounds. In 1852 the fisheries question assumed very serious aspects, and the British Government refused to discuss the diplomatic points therein involved if the discussion of reciprocity were excluded. Concerned over the political consequences much more than over the trade relations of the Canadian Provinces, the British Government finally pushed negotiations to a successful conclusion in Washington in 1854. A treaty was signed and ratified which provided that the United States and Canada should enjoy mutually the Atlantic coast fisheries and the canal systems of both countries and which provided also for the use by Americans of the St Lawrence River and by British subjects of Lake Michigan. With respect to commerce, it virtually established free trade in natural products between the United States and the British North American Provinces. The legislation necessary to make the treaty effective was passed on both sides, and the treaty was put into effect by proclamation of President Pierce on March 16, 1855. It was to run for ten years, and thereafter subject to two years' notice for termination.

The operation of the treaty.—The treaty achieved the main purpose for which it was negotiated—relief of the tension over the fisheries controversy; but it did not have the effect of stimulating the American fishing industry. The opening of the St Lawrence River and the Canadian canals to American shipping did not result in an increase in American traffic on those highways, but it did afford a choice of routes, which relieved congestion and insured reasonable railway rates to the Atlantic seaboard.

In any attempt to estimate the effect of the tariff changes on the trade between Canada and the United States, cognizance must be taken of a number of factors which complicated the situation and of facts which make calculations difficult. The investment in Canada of great sums of English capital, the Crimean War, the opening of new settlement areas in the West, increase in population, improvement of transportation facilities, speculation, a commercial crisis in both countries in 1857, financial difficulties leading to a fundamental change in Canadian fiscal policy, and, finally, the Civil War—all these influenced the course of developments both within each country and between the two, making it impossible to determine conclusively with regard to various increases and decreases whether they were or were not consequences of the treaty. The trade statistics of the period, also, both Canadian and American, are by no means satisfactory for the purpose of making accurate calculations.

There resulted from the treaty increased trade with Canada, which was more marked in regard to imports from Canada than in regard to exports to Canada. During the treaty period, the relative share of the United States in Canada's import trade increased; after the termination of the treaty, it decreased. While the treaty actually benefited some American producers and injured none save fishing, lumber, and possibly coal interests—and these in small degree—it was, on the whole, of greater benefit to the export-trade of Canada than to that of the United States. It was anticipated when the treaty was concluded that such would be the case, but it was expected that the United States would be compensated for this by the opening of the Canadian coast fisheries and waterways and by the benefits to American railways and commission houses. These expectations were fulfilled in a considerable measure until the revision of fiscal policy in Canada and the conditions of the Civil War in the United States altered the situation. During the eleven years of the reciprocity period, the total trade between the two countries increased approximately threefold, and, for the United States, the trade with Canada became second in importance only to that with Great Britain. How much of this was due to the improvement in general relations between the two countries and how much to the reciprocity provisions of the treaty can not be determined. But it may safely be asserted that, in its several features the reciprocity arrangement contributed largely to the very considerable growth of trade and that both countries were benefited by it.

Abrogation of the treaty.—The main causes which brought about the abrogation of the treaty were the adoption of protectionist principles and practices in Canada, the resentment aroused in the United States by the attitude of Canada during the Civil War, and the need of increased revenue in both countries. To these may be added the dissatisfaction of the fish, lumber, and coal interests in the United States.

The denunciation of the treaty came from the side of the United States. In the winter of 1863–64, a bill calling for abrogation was passed in Congress, and on March 17 the President gave the required year's notice for termination.

Effects of the abrogation.—The termination of the treaty involved the termination of the arrangements which had relieved the political tension in Canadian-American relations. It offered the possibility of serious political consequences. The action of the United States and the hostile attitude of the American people, of which it was an evidence, were prominent among the factors which brought about, in 1867, the uniting of the Canadian Provinces into the Dominion of Canada.

The commercial effects of the abrogation were less than had been expected. In so far as trade was affected at all, it was the United States rather than Canada that suffered. The chief direct effects of the United States seem to have been to lay the burden of certain duties on the American consumer and to divert from American railways and merchants a part of the business of transporting, handling, and reexporting Canadian produce. The chief indirect result was to establish among the Canadian people a sense of grievance which affected trade to some extent and which undoubtedly contributed in a small measure later to Canada's rejection of reciprocity when the United States finally proposed it.

Efforts to restore reciprocity.—For thirty years after the termination of the treaty, Canadians continued to express a desire for reciprocity, and they made overtures several times to that end.

The treaty of Washington of 1871, disposing, among other things of the fisheries and the waterways controversies, was a bitter disappointment to the people of Canada. They felt that the British Government had thrown away the most effective lever for opening the American market. When the Liberals entered office in 1874, they sent Mr George Brown to the United States to negotiate for reciprocity. Mr Brown offered reciprocity, not only in reference to natural products, but also on a long list of manufactures. A treaty was drafted but with the provision that everything made free by Canada to the United States should also be made free to Great Britain, and the Senate rejected the draft. The Conservative party in Canada thereafter urged a policy of consistent retaliation against the United States, and they secured an overwhelming victory at the polls in 1878. In the ensuing tariff act of 1879 the Canadian free list was materially abbreviated. In 1887 Canadian commissioners offered to negotiate a treaty combining a settlement of the fisheries question with reciprocity, but this proposal was rejected by Secretary of State Bayard. The hostility which had characterized the relations of the two countries for twenty years was by this time rapidly decreasing and official attitudes became more conciliatory. In the spring of 1888 the House Committee on Foreign Affairs recommended that a commission be appointed to meet with Canadian commissioners and prepare a plan for commercial union, and at the next session a bill to that end was passed in the House, but was not acted upon in the Senate.

In 1890 a reciprocity treaty with Newfoundland was drafted at Washington, but this was withheld by the British foreign office at the insistance of Canada.

Between 1890 and 1892 the Conservative Government in Canada made another effort to secure reciprocity, but the terms which it proposed were not acceptable to Mr Blaine, nor were his proposals acceptable to the British and Canadian representatives. This was the last effort of the Conservatives on behalf of reciprocity. Thereafter Canadian public sentiment even among the Liberals swung strongly toward the "National," self-sufficiency policy, and from 1891 to 1910 the reciprocity question ceased to be a live issue.

2. The Hawaiian Reciprocity Treaty of 1875

The reciprocity treaty concluded between Hawaii and the United States in 1875, which was in operation for twenty-five years, was a product of political rather than of economic considerations.

The location, resources, and political weakness of Hawaii made the islands, from the early part of the nineteenth century, attractive to several strong powers. Their strategic position made it inevitable that the United States should view the uneasiness and dissatisfaction their being brought under the control of any other power.

Several times before the middle of the nineteenth century, European States had made attempts upon the political integrity of Hawaii. In 1851 the King of Hawaii actually prepared to place his Kingdom under the protection of the United States in order to escape the aggression of a European power. In the years which followed, it became evident that protection by the United States was necessary, and the choice of methods lay between reciprocity and annexation. An annexation treaty was negotiated in 1854, but was not concluded. In the next year a reciprocity treaty was negotiated, but this failed ratification. In 1867, for the second time, a reciprocity treaty was negotiated, but the attention of Congress was very much taken up with other matters, problems of reconstruction were imperative, and the treaty did not secure ratification. In 1874 the question was brought up under peculiarly favorable circumstances, and in the next year a reciprocity treaty was negotiated and ratified. Congress thereafter passed the legislation necessary for putting it into effect, and it went into force on September 9, 1876.

In the treaty there were no political concessions other than the pledge that while the treaty remained in force Hawaii would not lease territory or grant special privileges to any other power, or make any treaty by which any other powers should obtain the same privileges which were assured by the treaty to the United States. The commercial provisions involved the admission by each country of a considerable number of products of the other, free of duty. Claims of right to the benefit of the commercial concessions were soon advanced by certain nations, on the basis of the most-favored-nation clause. The United States combatted these claims, on the score both of the conditional interpretation of the most-favored-nation clause and of the special and peculiar circumstances governing the relations between Hawaii and the United States, and the American contention was ultimately accepted.

The question of the renewal of the treaty came up in 1882. A convention to extend its term was negotiated in 1884. It was recognized that the operation of the treaty was more advantageous commercially to Hawaii than to the United States, but, even more than in 1875, political considerations weighed in the minds of American statesmen. There was incorporated in the convention which was to extend the treaty, a provision for the cession of Pearl River Harbor to the United States as a naval base. This became an item in the bargain. The convention was finally ratified, after its adoption had been strongly urged by President Cleveland, in 1887. It extended the duration of the original treaty, without any alteration in the commercial reciprocity provision, for a period of seven years from the moment of ratification, and thereafter subject to one year's notice.

Effects of the treaty.—The most important articles of Hawaiian export in the reciprocity group were brown sugar, molasses, fruits and nuts, and rice. These comprised at all times more than three-fourths of the aggregate exports of the islands. Sugar was first in importance, in a class by itself. The chief consideration which Hawaii received was the admission into the United States, duty free, of the specified products originating in the islands, while similar commodities, when coming from other sources were subjected to substantial rates of duty. The special preference, not the free admission, was the significant feature so far as the effect on Hawaiian exports was concerned.

Even before the establishment of reciprocity, the bulk of the Hawaiian exports had gone to the United States. Under reciprocity the percentage increased, and after annexation the Unites States absorbed practically the whole of the Hawaiian exports.

Reciprocity was more conspicuously effective in increasing the absolute amount of Hawaiian exports to the United States than in increasing the share which these formed of the total Hawaiian exports. The exports multiplied to many times the maximum figures which they had reached previously. The one commodity signally affected was sugar, the Hawaiian production and export of which increased enormously, beyond all expectation and imagination. The remission of duty on this sugar was not followed by a reduction in price to the American consumer; the gain went to the sugar producers. Under this stimulus the cultivation of sugar in the islands became highly intensified.

The effects of the United States tariff act of 1890 emphasized among Hawaiian commercial interests the insecurity of a position dependent on reciprocity alone, and the question of annexation came again strongly to the fore. Dissatisfaction with the government of the islands together with actual political disturbances, strengthened the desire, as well as the case, of those who favored putting the islands under the control of the United States. The political disturbances ended in a revolution in 1893, and the temporary government which came into control asked immediately for annexation, but this the United States refused. A permanent government of republican form was thereupon organized in Hawaii. With the passage in the United States of the tariff act of 1894, which once more put Hawaiian sugar in a favored position, economic conditions in the Islands improved. But the failure of reciprocity to assure constantly favorable conditions was remembered, and in 1897 the agitation for annexation was renewed. In the course of the next year, in view of the fact that the United States was at war, annexation appeared highly desirable, and the administration resorted to the procedure of a joint resolution of both Houses. Such a resolution was passed in the summer of 1898, and the President of Hawaii surrendered the sovereignty of the islands on August 12, 1898. The tariff arrangements of the treaty continued in effect until June 15, 1900, when the Organic Act providing for the political reorganization of the islands became operative.

The prosperity and greatly increased purchasing power which reciprocity had brought Hawaii under the influence of the tariff preference to Hawaiian producers had resulted in an increase of imports into Hawaii from the United States. This was not, however, comparable in volume to the increase of imports from Hawaii into the United States. The commercial development of Hawaii had led also to increased demand for the services of American shipping, banking, insurance, and the like. But when all the various factors have been taken into account, the conclusion is inevitable that the reciprocity relationship with Hawaii was economically unprofitable to the United States. However, in a comprehensive estimate, the fact must not be overlooked that in entering into the reciprocity arrangement Congress had not been actuated primarily by economic considerations.

3. Negotiations, 1882–1890

In the decade following 1880, repeated efforts were made to develop closer trade relations with Latin America, and several treaties were negotiated, but these did not secure the ratification of the United States Senate.

4. Treaties and Agreements under the Tariff Act of 1890

The legislative record.—The provision in the tariff act of 1890 for the imposition of penalty duties upon imports from countries which discriminated in their tariff treatment against goods from the United States may be considered the first authorization ever given by Congress for a comprehensive program of tariff bargaining.

Early in 1890, with the Republican party in power, the McKinley tariff bill was introduced. It provided for several changes in the tariff schedules, important among them being the free admission of sugar and molasses; but it contained no reciprocity provision, in spite of the strong recommendation of Mr Blaine, Secretary of State, that such a provision be incorporated in the bill. The bill passed the House on May 21.

In the Senate an amendment was offered which would have practically established, through negotiation, free trade between the United States and the Latin-American countries. This never came to a vote. The Finance Committee finally recommended an amendment which would leave coffee, tea, hides, sugar, and molasses on the free list, but at the same time would provide that the President might suspend, by proclamation, their free admission from countries imposing unequal or unreasonable duties on products of the United States, and instead might impose thereon a stated list of penalty duties. The bill, so amended, was passed by the Senate, and, after going to conference without receiving any modification of its bargaining features, became law on October 1, 1890. Congress aimed by this act to secure more favorable trade relations with other countries by penalizing such countries as did not treat American products favorably, rather than by following the method which had been favored by the administration—that of remitting or lowering duties on the products of countries which in return would make similar tariff concessions. The act gave the President, within prescribed limits, a free hand in negotiations. The articles upon which penalty duties could be imposed, especially sugar, were particularly adapted in bargaining with South and Central American countries and also with the great beet-sugar producing States of Europe.

Under the terms of this act, Secretary Blaine began the negotiation of a series of agreements. Between January 31, 1891, and May 26, 1892, ten reciprocity arrangements were concluded, all but two of them being with countries of the Western Hemisphere. In each of these agreements the United States undertook to admit free of duty, when coming from the other country, the five articles—coffee, tea, hides, sugar, and molasses—enumerated in the penalizing provision in the act. In most cases the other contracting party agreed to admit free or at substantially reduced tariff rates the bulk of its imports from the United States.

The penalty duties were imposed only on Colombia, Venezuela, and Haiti, after these States had been asked to negotiate and had failed satisfactorily to respond. Several other countries, producers of the specified articles, conspicuously the Argentine and Mexico, failed to conclude agreements, but the penalty duties were not imposed on them; and this led to protests by Colombia and Venezuela against what they considered to be unfair discrimination.

Effect of the treaties on the trade of the United States.—An analysis of imports and exports during the period covered by these reciprocity treaties indicates that the penalty duties were moderately effective both as a measure of retaliation and as a means of securing tariff favors. There was a marked decrease in the imports from the penalized countries. The conditions of the sugar industry made it possible to secure liberal tariff concessions in return for a free market for sugar in the United States, while at the same time the imposition of the penalty duties did not prevent the consumer from profiting through the fall in the price of sugar in the American market.

Exports from the United States to the reciprocity States, favored by special reductions of duty, showed a substantial increase, in spite of the handicap of severe industrial depression and revolutionary disturbances existing in many of these States, while at the same time there were decreases in the aggregate exports to all other countries.

The termination of the reciprocity agreements.—In 1894, under a Democratic administration, a new tariff act was passed which did away with the reciprocity provision. It imposed a duty on raw sugar, raised that on refined sugar, and repealed the bounty on the domestic product. It further provided that treaties not inconsistent with this new provision might remain in force; but the reimposition of the duty on raw sugar acted almost automatically to annul the agreements made under the act of 1890, and was so interpreted by the State Department. Protests were made against the reimposition of the duty on sugar and against the abrupt termination of the agreements of the act of 1890 by several of the countries concerned. Considerable resentment was shown, and measures of retaliation followed in certain cases.

The termination of these agreements left only the treaty with Hawaii in operation.

5. Treaties and Agreements under the Tariff Act of 1897

In the congressional elections of 1896 the Republican Party once more came into power. Reciprocity, as a means of securing fairness of treatment for the expanding export trade of the United States in Europe, had been made a plank in the platform upon which the election was carried.

The passing of the tariff act of 1897.—At a special session of Congress, called on March 18, 1897, the Dingley tariff bill was introduced. This provided, in section 3, for tariff bargaining by two methods. The first part of the section contained a provision empowering the President to reduce duties on a specified list of articles (including argols, wines, and sugar) when coming from countries making equivalent concessions to the products of the United States. The second part consisted of a penalizing provision, also to be used at the discretion of the President, imposing an additional duty on coffee, tea, and hides when coming from countries deemed to be subjecting products of the United States to unequal or unreasonable treatment.

Less than two weeks after its introduction, and with very little attention to the reciprocity provisions, the bill was passed in the House. In the Senate the question of reciprocity was given careful consideration. An amendment was inserted, as a substitute for section 3 of the House bill, giving the President the right to negotiate commercial treaties, and, in return for concessions to the United States, to grant reciprocal reductions on the products of the treaty countries. The opposition to this amendment contended emphatically that the conferring of this power on the President and the Senate would take from the House its constitutional right to levy revenue taxes, but both the amendment and the bill were passed by the Senate.

The conference committee restored the original House measure as section 3, but from the list of articles upon which penalty duties could be imposed they removed sugar, hides, skins, and certain other items of less importance and substituted in their place tonka and vanilla beans, articles of little commercial importance. The committee retained the Senate amendment as section 4, but with a provision requiring that treaties negotiated under it must be submitted for approval to Congress, instead of merely for ratification to the Senate. Thus altered, the bill was accepted and passed by both Houses, and it became law on July 24, 1897.

Provision for negotiation of agreements.—President McKinley appointed John A. Kasson, of Iowa, as special commissioner, to be assisted by a "reciprocity commission," for the negotiation of agreements under the new tariff act.

The "argol agreements," negotiated under section 3 of the act of 1897.—In conformity with the provisions of the first part of section 3, two series of agreements, known from the first article specified on the list as "argol agreements," were concluded. The first series, agreements with France, Portugal, Germany, and Italy, was negotiated by Mr Kasson during the McKinley administration. The concessions obtained by the United States, in return for a few and small reductions of duty, were of some importance. In general this series of agreements was received with satisfaction by the American public.

An indirect result of the conclusion of these agreements was that Switzerland, through the unconditional most-favored-nation clause of her treaty of 1850 with the United States, claimed and was given, without compensation, the benefit of the concessions extended by treaty to France. The most-favored-nation treaty provision upon which Switzerland based her claim was promptly denounced by the United States Government with due notice, and in March, 1900, ceased to be operative.

During President Roosevelt's administration, the United States negotiated a second series of "argol agreements." In this, new agreements similar to those of the first series were made with Spain and Bulgaria, and, of a more limited character, with Great Britain and the Netherlands; the treaties with France, Portugal, Germany, and Italy were supplemented or extended; sparkling wines were added to the list of articles upon which concessions were granted by the United States; and Switzerland and the United States once more resumed reciprocal commercial relations, although without the negotiation of a formal agreement.

Commercial treaties concluded (but not ratified) under section 4 of the tariff act of 1897.–Section 4 of the tariff act of 1897 authorized the President to negotiate treaties providing for the reduction by not more than 20 per cent of the duties on any articles imported into the United States in return for equivalent concessions by the other party. Accordingly, Mr Kasson negotiated a series of treaties, all of which made provision for tariff reductions of considerable importance.

Of these treaties the first to be agreed upon, and the one which aroused the most interest, was that with France, in 1899. After lengthy negotiations, the French conceded the rates of their minimum schedule on all but a few articles. In return the United States was to admit a long list of French products at reductions of from 5 to 20 per cent from the rates of the tariff of 1897.

Other treaties negotiated under this section of the act promised also to prove of considerable importance. They were all with or on behalf of American countries—the Argentine, Ecuador, Nicaragua, the Dominican Republic, Denmark (for St Croix), and Great Britain (for various American colonies). The concessions made to the United States by these countries were numerous and varied; coal was one thing in particular for which favorable terms were secured. Important items upon which the United States agreed to make concessions were sugar, molasses, hides, and wool.

An attempt was made to conclude an agreement with Russia, but the imposition of a countervailing duty on Russian sugar in 1901 caused the breaking off of negotiations and was followed by retaliatory measures on Russia's part. Not until 1905, when Russia withdrew her retaliatory duties, were satisfactory commercial relations between the two countries reestablished.

The treaties submitted for ratification.—In December, 1899, the Kasson treaties were presented to the Senate for ratification, and early in 1900 the Committee on Foreign Relations took up their study. Popular interest was keen and much attention was given to the discussion, especially to that of the treaty with France. Two groups of interests finally stood in opposition—on the one side the representatives of American industries which were on an export basis, such as the iron and steel and the agricultural implement trades; on the other, both domestic producers who feared foreign competition and those persons who saw in the treaties an undesirable infringement of the principle of protection. Mr Kasson strongly urged ratification of the treaties; President McKinley was in favor of them. No action was taken in 1900 and 1901, however, other than to extend the time during which ratifications might be secured.

Disheartened by his failure to secure ratification, Mr Kasson resigned in March 1901. The administration still supported the ratification of the treaties, and, in his last speech, at Buffalo, President McKinley expressed himself more strongly than ever in favor of the policy of reciprocity.

On November 19, 1901, the Manufacturers' Reciprocity Convention met in Washington and declared itself for protection and favorable to reciprocity only when the latter could be secured without injury to any of the domestic interests of manufacturing, commerce, or farming. Although President Roosevelt adhered to the views of his predecessor with regard to reciprocity, he likewise found it impossible to secure for the treaties the necessary approval of the Senate.

Finally, in 1903, action on the treaties was considered to have been abandoned; no mention of reciprocity was made in the President's message of 1904; and the treaties remained pigeonholed, without further action, in the Senate Committee on Foreign Relations.

Termination of the argol agreements by the act of 1909.—Six years after, the tariff act of 1909 provided for giving to all countries other than Cuba notice of termination of their reciprocity agreements with the United States.

Effect of the argol agreements upon trade.—The articles upon which the United States had made reductions of duty in the argol agreements were few, and although some of these articles were imported in quantities and to values not inconsiderable, the reductions of duty were often small, and they were not exclusive, but were shared by most of the important countries. As regards imports, the influence of reciprocity was to be seen most clearly in increased imports of – and sparkling wines from the reciprocity countries. As regards exports, the result appeared in a number of instances in increased shipments of articles upon which reductions of duty had been made. In most cases, however, the terms secured for the United States were merely a continuance of the most-favored-nation treatment, to which the United States had already been entitled under treaties in existence previous to the conclusion of the agreements. The only general conclusion derivable is negative. When reductions obtained by agreement are few and small, and are shared by all or most of the competing countries, the agreements will have very limited influence on the amount or the direction of trade.

6. Two-Schedule Provision of the Tariff Act of 1909

The movement of reciprocity gradually lost vigor. When, in 1909, the Republican Party began the revision of the tariff, provision was made in the bill introduced in the House for a two-schedule system, the minimum to be the general rates and the maximum the penalizing rates, the latter to be applied, at the discretion of the Treasury Department, to products from countries discriminating against the United States. All existing reciprocity treaties other than the one with Cuba were, after due notice, to be terminated.

The bill was amended in the Senate to provide that the free list of the rates in the general schedule of the House bill should constitute the minimum rates, while the maximum schedule should be made up by adding to the minimum 25 per cent of the values of the articles; the maximum schedule should be the general tariff, applicable to all countries, but the President should be authorized to extend the benefit of the minimum schedule to all countries found not discriminating against the United States.

The act, as passed August 5, 1909, followed the plan of the Senate amendment for making the maximum the general schedule. It marked a distinct departure from the policy of seeking special favors in granting reciprocal concessions. Though in form the policy was that of the concession of a minimum tariff, virtually it amounted to a provision to impose maximum rates by way of penalty against mutual treatment of American products.

France was the only country that protested, the protest being on the score that, on account of the wording of her 1908 agreement, the notice given her was shorter than that to the other reciprocity countries.

Before the maximum tariff was applied to any country, the Tariff Board, which had been created for the purpose under authority of the act (sec. 2), made an investigation of the existing tariff treatment of products of the United States by other countries. Discrimination was discovered in the case of a number of countries, and negotiations with such countries were entered into. In consequence of the negotiations, there were issued prior to April 1, 1910, proclamations applying the minimum rates to the countries comprising the entire commercial world; in no case was the maximum rate applied. In certain important instances, however, notably those of Germany and France, full equality of treatment was not extended to imports from the United States, and it would appear therefore that the act of 1909 did not provide a penalty method effective for the total elimination of all discrimination against American products in European markets.

7. Reciprocity Section of the Tariff Act of 1913

In 1913 the Democratic Party gained control of both the executive and the legislative branches of the Government. They at once prepared to revise the tariff. The Underwood bill as first drafted contained no provision for maximum and minimum schedules, but included a section authorizing the President to negotiate reciprocity agreements with foreign countries, such agreements, however, to be submitted to Congress for ratification or rejection. In the House a proposed amendment that there should be added a provision for maximum and minimum duties were rejected. In the Senate the bill was amended to include a provision for penalty duties to be imposed by the President at his discretion upon imports from countries whose treatment of American products was not "reciprocal and equivalent." In conference the Senate amendment was withdrawn and the bill was passed on October 3 1913, with the reciprocity provision left as it had stood in the original bill.

8. Brazilian Preferential Arrangement

Brazil had been among the countries with which, as has already been mentioned, the United States made reciprocity agreements under the provisions of the tariff act of 1890. The Brazilian agreement was terminated with the others by the tariff act of 1894.

The chief items in the Brazilian export trade to the United States were coffee and rubber, and these had both been duty-free in the United States without a reciprocity agreement. The articles of the export trade from the United States to Brazil were, however, in the absence of a special arrangement, subject to very heavy import duties on entering Brazil.

Such were the conditions governing the trade between the two countries from 1894 to 1897. The United States tariff act of 1897 authorized the President to impose a penalty duty of 3 cents a pound on coffee from countries according unequal or unreasonable treatment to American products. For various reasons it was not attempted to make an arrangement with Brazil by treaty. In 1904, moved by the possibility that this duty might be imposed on its coffee, and by representations of the United States minister, the Brazilian Government was induced to plan considerable reductions in a number of its rates in favor of United States products, the most important of the articles thus provided for being wheat flour.

Much opposition to this measure, especially from the wheat and flour interests, developed in the Brazilian Congress and the reduction was effected only by an order of the President, under the authority of an old law which empowered him to reduce certain duties by as much as 20 per cent. The Brazilian Congress in the next year repealed the legislation which gave this authority, and from January 1, 1905, to July 1, 1906, the preference was not in effect. But on July 1, 1906, legislation restoring this authority to the President and adding a number of items to the original list became effective.

Upon the passage in the United States of the tariff act of 1909, the State Department negotiated with Brazil for tariff reductions in return for which Brazil might be entitled to the minimum rates. This, it may be noted, was an attempt to use the bargaining provisions of the act of 1909 as a means of securing special treatment for American products in a foreign market. As a result, numerous articles were added to the Brazilian list of 1906, and later the President of Brazil was given authority to extend this list at his discretion. In 1911 the preference on American flour was raised to 30 per cent. In 1916 the stipulation was made that the imports given this preferential treatment must be the product of the United States, and not merely imported via that country. In 1917 and 1918 the preferential list was renewed without change.

Effect of the Brazilian preferential treatment on American exports.—The important article on the Brazilian preferential list was wheat flour, and an analysis of the figures indicates that the United States exports to Brazil of this product did not increase, though the preference undoubtedly tended to check a decrease which other factors were bringing about. Other preferred articles were less important, forming only a small fraction of the total American exports to Brazil; but the preference had more effect on them, producing an appreciable increase, both absolutely and in relation to the total of Brazilian imports from all sources. Certain lines of trade, as, for instance, pianos and cement, were practically established by the preference.

In addition to a growth in the trade in the preferred articles, there was an increase in the general trade, due in part to the aroused interest in the new field. It would appear that although preference did not secure the desired results with respect to the chief item, wheat flour, it was moderately successful in stimulating an expansion of American trade in general with Brazil.

9. The Cuban Reciprocity Treaty of 1902

The close political relations of the United States with Cuba after the conclusion of the Spanish-American War turned the attention of the Cubans to the United States as a possible friend, who might rescue them from the depressed economic condition into which the years of revolution and war had thrown the island. The American administration in Cuba and President Roosevelt in Washington were in favor of giving Cuban products special tariff privileges in the American market, but the attitude of Congress was at first adverse. Many members looked upon any reductions of duty as a possible starting point for others less desirable. They, together with the domestic beet-sugar and cane-sugar producers, were opposed to any action which would involve a lowering of the tariff.

Public opinion, however, developed favorably toward closer economic relations between the two countries, and when the Fifty-seventh Congress convened for the second time, in January, 1902, the question became the subject of extended hearings, followed by the introduction of a bill in the House on March 19, 1902. The bill provided for reciprocal reductions of duties of 20 per cent, upon condition that Cuba should first adopt immigration laws as fully restrictive as were the laws of the United States. The arguments in support of reciprocal relations with Cuba emphasized particularly the alleged moral obligations of the United States toward Cuba and made no great claims for the economic desirability of the arrangement. After long debate, the bill passed the House by a large majority, but Congress adjourned before it came to a vote in the Senate.

President Roosevelt next sought to attain the same end by the negotiation of a treaty. His efforts resulted in the signing, on December 11, 1902, of a convention providing for a reduction of 20 per cent from the American duties on Cuban imports and reductions of from 20 to 40 per cent from the Cuban rates on American products. The Senate advised ratification, and the Cuban Government signified its approval of the treaty. The treaty required, however, the approval of Congress. Early in November, 1903, it was submitted to the Fifty-eighth Congress for approval. In the debates the arguments were similar to those in the earlier discussions. The measure was finally passed by both Houses, and on December 17, 1903, it was formally proclaimed.

This treaty was independent of the reciprocal provisions of the act of 1897, and was in no way connected with the treaties negotiated under the act. It contained in Article VIII some unusual provisions, namely, that the reductions in duty specified should not be extended to any other country, that during the continuance of the treaty no Cuban sugar should be admitted to the United States at a rate of duty less by more than 20 per cent than the rate imposed by the tariff act of 1897, and that no sugar from countries other than Cuba should be admitted by treaty or convention into the United States at a rate of duty lower than that provided by the act of 1897. The agreement has been in force continuously since 1903, with the exception that a portion of Article VIII was abrogated by a provision in the United States tariff act of 1913.

Second treaty with Cuba.—In addition to this commercial arrangement, another treaty had been negotiated, signed May 22, 1903, which prescribed the conditions under which American military authority would be withdrawn from and those under which it might be reinstated in the island. The guaranty of public order which this second treaty insured to labor and capital contributed much to the great commercial development which has subsequently occurred in the island, and any estimate of the effects of the first treaty must take into consideration the influence of the second.

Effect of the treaty on trade.—The supporters of the treaty had placed but little emphasis upon its possible commercial results. The major portion of the Cuban exports already found their market in the United States, and it did not appear likely that great benefits would accrue from an increase in the share of the Cuban imports which was or would be contributed by the United States. The years immediately preceding the treaty had formed a period of gradual and halting recovery of Cuban industry. The first years under the treaty showed a decided increase for both American exports to and imports from Cuba. Following the depression of 1907, the growth showed a relative decrease, but after 1908 there was again a tendency toward increase in value in both the imports and the exports.

The imports into the United States from Cuba have reflected the influence of reciprocity in a less significant degree than have the exports from the United States to Cuba. The principal gains made by the imports have been due to the fact that several important staple articles of Cuban production, especially sugar and tobacco, have found a steady and growing market in the United States, a market which would probably have expanded in some measure without the extension of tariff preferences.

A comparison of the United States exports to China with similar exports to a group of Caribbean countries, which in a general way resemble Cuba as regards location, climatic conditions, and economic development, shows that the exports to Cuba increased immediately after the conclusion of the treaty, whereas those to the other countries did not. But since 1907 the rates of growth of the two trades have not been substantially different.

When the articles of export are examined in groups according to the amount of tariff preference received, it appears that the increases of the American exports to Cuba for the several groups have varied directly with the amount of the preference. From another classification of Cuban imports—grouping selected articles in which the United States encountered competition from other countries—it again appears that the increases in the American exports have varied directly with the amount of the preference. The fact must not be overlooked, however, that these increases in trade with Cuba have been due not only to the treaty of 1902, but also in considerable part to the favorable influence upon Cuba of the reconstruction program carried out under the assurance of law and order guaranteed by the treaty of 1903. The close political relations between the United States and Cuba, the investment of American capital, the development in the United States of a large-scale export trade in manufactures, and the settlement in Cuba of Americans—these and other factors have operated along with the tariff preference to increase the trade between the two countries.

10. Commercial Relations of the United States with Newfoundland

Newfoundland was included with the Canadian Provinces in the ratification of the reciprocity treaty of 1854. The treaty of Washington, of 1871, contained provisions for reciprocal free admission of products of the fisheries of the United States on the one hand and British North American colonies on the other, but these ceased to operate in 1885. A treaty relating to Canadian and Newfoundland fisheries products was negotiated in 1888, which failed of ratification by the Senate of the United States. A convention for reciprocity between the United States and Newfoundland was negotiated in 1890, but in view of the objections of the Canadian Government, the British Government was not prepared to ratify this. A similar treaty was negotiated in 1902, but this was later so amended by the Senate Committee on Foreign Affairs that it became unacceptable to Newfoundland. Finally, in 1910, the fisheries question was settled by arbitration proceedings between the United States and Great Britain.

11. The Attempt to Establish a Reciprocity Arrangement with Canada, 1910–1911

Ever since the precipitate termination of the reciprocity treaty in 1865, there have been a number of obstacles operating to check the flow of trade between the United States and Canada, but not sufficient to discourage or to divert it. The United States tariff had always been something of a barrier. In Canada the Conservative Party framed a tariff (1879) intended especially to curtail the volume of importations from the United States, and when the Liberals came into power (1896) under Sir Wilfrid Laurier and adopted the "National Policy" of their opponents, they framed a tariff little less exclusive than that of the Conservatives.

The United States tariff act of 1897 contained a provision for increasing the import duties upon lumber by an amount equal to the export duties imposed by Canada upon logs. This threat was sufficient to cause Canada to remove her export duty, but several of the Canadian Provinces subsequently placed restrictions upon the exporting of timber, with the result that American capital went into the forests of those Provinces. The rates of the tariff of 1897 were almost prohibitive for certain Canadian products. The influence of that fact was shown in the failure of the imports of these articles to increase in proportion to the growing ability of Canada to compete in the American market. On their side the Canadians had adopted the preferential tariff system and were turning their attention to developing better markets in the mother country and the other British colonies. Nevertheless, in spite of commercial policies, a number of factors—geographic, social, and industrial—tended to offset or nullify artificial restrictions upon the trade between the two countries.

The years at the end of the nineteenth century and the beginning of the twentieth were the most prosperous that Canada had ever experienced. This prosperity and the visions which it aroused of future development account, along with the influence of the tariff legislation of the United States, for the almost universal approval in Canada of the protective and preferential tariff policy. Yet the growth of Canadian manufactures and the establishing of protective duties, aimed principally at the wares of the United States, had remarkably little effect in reducing the imports from the latter country.

In operation, the preferential system, however it may have encouraged British-Canadian commerce, did not prevent American–Canadian commerce from growing rapidly. The United States had advantages in competition for the Canadian market which the measures actually adopted could not overcome.

When the Canadian Government revised the tariff in 1907, the most important feature of the revision was the adoption of an intermediate schedule of duties framed and intended for bargaining purposes. When in the United States the Republican Congress revised the tariff in 1909, it was no part of its purpose to weaken the principle of protection. Such reductions of duty as were made were chiefly in reference to foodstuffs and raw materials. The distinctive feature of the tariff act of 1909 was the approach to the two-schedule tariff system in the adoption of a general schedule and a maximum schedule, making it possible, without special negotiation, to invite favorable treatment of United States products and to penalize unfavorable treatment.

When the tariff act of 1909 went into effect, Canada was threatened with the maximum duties. Their imposition would probably have provoked a tariff war. To avert this, President Taft made advances to the Canadian Government which resulted finally in formal negotiations at Washington. An arrangement was agreed upon whereby Canada should give to certain specified imports from the United States the benefit of her intermediate instead of her general rates, and should in return be given the general, or minimum, rates of the American tariff. Slight though the Canadian concessions were, the arrangement was attacked by the Conservative Party in the Canadian Parliament.

The concluding conferences between the representatives of the two Governments were held in Washington in January, 1911. It was decided that a reciprocity arrangement should be framed, after which its provisions should be brought into effect by means of concurrent legislation rather than by treaty. The Canadians refused to grant the use of the inshore fisheries in return for the free admission of fish to the United States, but they consented to annul the license charges which had been required under the *modus vivendi* of 1887. It was found impossible to arrive at an agreement concerning pulp and paper duties, but it was agreed that the United States should admit free of duty Canadian wood pulp and paper upon which no export duty had been charged in Canada. This provision was later a part of the legislation passed by Congress and it became effective in spite of the defeat of the reciprocity measure in Canada. The proposed changes in the general tariff rates affected a considerable number of articles listed in four schedules. The arrangement was such that Canada was to obtain practically all the advantages that she had sought formerly in reciprocity proposals, while she was to concede little more than what she was already extending to most countries, but not to the United States, through the operation of her concessional tariff schedule.

Legislation to carry the arrangement into effect was introduced concurrently in the Congress of the United States and the Parliament of Canada on January 26, 1911. This legislation was passed by Congress. In Canada it became the subject of extended parliamentary debate and widespread and vigorous public discussion. The Conservative Party made the issue the basis of a concerted effort to drive the Liberals from power. Reasons of great variety were urged why the arrangement should not be approved. The past unconciliatory attitude of the United States and the allegation of sinister political designs—nothing less than a policy of annexation—were made use of as powerful arguments. The possibility of an injurious effect upon commerce within the Empire, with the consequent disadvantageous effect upon imperial relations, was strongly and effectively urged. Economic arguments of various types were presented. After several months' debate in the House of Commons, the Government appealed to the country. In the elections which followed, the Liberals were defeated and the Conservatives returned to power. The most potent among the causes which brought about the defeat of the Liberals appears to have been the argument that the adoption of the reciprocity policy would have as a consequence annexation. Other considerations, however, in no way connected with the reciprocity issue, contributed to the defeat.

The result of the Canadian election put an end to further consideration of the reciprocity measure. In 1913 a resolution was introduced in the House of Representatives in the United States, calling for the repeal of the reciprocity legislation of 1911, but this was rejected. The act providing for reciprocity with Canada still stands upon the statute books of the United States. The passage of a like act by the Canadian Parliament would put the arrangement, as negotiated in 1911, into effect.

II. THE MOST-FAVORED-NATION CLAUSE AND RECIPROCITY ARRANGEMENTS

The most-favored-nation clause and the practice of reciprocity—No single feature of modern commercial treaties has occasioned more or greater difficulty of interpretation than the presence therein of the most-favored-nation clause. Occurring almost universally, under widely differing conditions, in both the unconditional and the conditional forms, and in a veritable network of treaties, this clause has contributed at once to the solution of some and to the creation of other serious problems in commercial relations. Many such problems are bound to arise where and when some States do and some do not make reciprocity treaties.

As has already been mentioned, it has been the practice of the United States almost without exception to employ the conditional form of the most-favored-nation clause and to maintain the conditional construction. It is the practice of the European States to-day, though it has not always been, to employ the unconditional form and to maintain the unconditional construction.

The present European attitude is essentially a development of the past fifty years. The American position began with the making of the very first treaty of the United States, and from then until the present time the guiding principle in the commercial treaty-making policy of the United States has been that of bargaining between individual nations on the basis of reciprocal and progressive giving of favor for favor and concession for concession.

American statesmen have contended for equality of opportunity to bargain, but not for identity of treatment; for the removal and prevention of discrimination, but not for the same terms to all States at all times and in relation to all trade. A survey of the treaties to which the Unites States has been a party shows that this principle has been written expressly into nearly all of the most-favored-nation clauses. It further shows that since 1890 the United States has employed the favored-nation clause by no means as regularly as it did before that date; and that it has employed it in a less number of agreements, proportionately, than have some other States. In late years the United States has made various commercial agreements wherein most-favored-nation clauses have not been included; also, other types of commercial treaties and conventions wherein, because of previous difficulty over the interpretation of the most-favored-nation clause, it has apparently seemed advisable to both parties not to include the most-favored-nation provision specifically.

Theories and practices.—A survey of the United States practice in treaty construction shows that both the executive and the judicial departments of the American Government have consistently interpreted the favored-nation pledge as conditional and contingent upon the offering and acceptance of compensation. The leading commercial countries of Europe have moved first from the unconditional toward the conditional, and later back to the unconditional interpretation. British practice exhibits with greater regularity, with greater consistency, and with greater simplicity than does that of any other State the possibilities of unconditional most-favored-nation treatment. The British attitude may be explained in part by reference to the fact of the free-trade policy and the peculiar commercial position of the United Kingdom, but it by no means follows that such circumstances are essential to the acceptance and maintenance of the unconditional favored-nation practice. The States of continental Europe, a few of them free trade, most of them protectionist, all practice unconditional favored-nation treatment. However, the views and practices of the European States have been subject to change and there are evidences that they may not hereafter continue what they have been in recent years.

Relation to the negotiations and application of reciprocity agreements.—In the controversy with Great Britain over the construction of the United States-Hawaiian treaty, both the Hawaiian and by the United States Governments, the latter pointed out that "special privileges had been given in return for special, valuable considerations," and took the position that this was, because of geographical and political circumstances, a special and extraordinary case. Ultimately the logic of this position was accepted.

The application of the unconditional interpretation would have rendered of little effect the provisions of the United States tariff acts of 1890 and 1897, which authorized the negotiation of reciprocity agreements. To render the policy of special reciprocity effective, it is essential that the "American" interpretation of favored-nation obligations be applied. But the penalty-duties clause in the act of 1890 presented an issue which even the conditional interpretation would not properly meet. The principle of applying penalties on the basis of comparison of the relative heights of the tariff rates of the United States and those of the countries whose treatment of American goods laid them open to penalty is altogether different from that of bargaining with a view to securing and giving equality of treatment. It would leave it possible for some States, charging relatively low duties, to discriminate against the United States and yet escape the imposition of penalty duties. Penalty duties were actually thus applied to Columbia and Haiti, although those countries did not discriminate against the United States, while at the same time the benefit of the ordinary rates was extended to several countries which made no special concession to the United States.

In the course of a discussion which arose during the negotiation of reciprocity treaties under the tariff act of 1897, Mr Sherman, Secretary of State, made a lengthy statement, thoroughly in conformity with views expressed by the long line of his predecessors, which succinctly sets forth the American conception of most-favored-nation obligations. Among other things, he said:

> [The most-favored-nation clause] does not control the right of he nation adopting it to make exclusive compensatory agreements in just reciprocity with other nations …; the allowance of the same privileges and the same sacrifice of revenue duties, to a nation which makes no compensation, that has been conceded to another nation for an adequate compensation … destroys that equality of market privileges which … the clause was intended to secure. … The right of other nations to enjoy the same special concessions depends on their ability to offer an equivalent compensation. … Such is the construction of the treaty clauses in question which the Government of the United States adopts in carrying out the late provisions of law for reciprocal conventions with other States.

The experience of the United States in meeting the claim of Switzerland in 1898 affords an excellent example of the impossibility of reconciling the practice of entering into reciprocity agreements with the giving of unconditional most-favored-nation pledges. It had to be admitted that, in the negotiation of the treaty of 1850 with Switzerland, the American plenipotentiary had pledged the United States to unconditional most-favored-nation treatment. The Government stood by the pledge. Switzerland was therefore given, without compensation, the benefit of concessions made to France in the special reciprocity treaty which had been concluded under the provisions of the act of 1897. Other States at once claimed the right to the same treatment, and it became necessary to denounce the favored nation provision in the Swiss treaty.

Relations and discussions with Germany.—Not until the enactment of the bargaining provisions of the act of 1890 was the United States Government in a position to bargain effectively with Germany. Then, possessed of the necessity instruments, it did not undertake to enforce the claim of being entitled, without compensation, to the concessions which Germany made in her new treaties to European countries. Instead, in 1891, it entered into a bargain, which took form in the Saratoga convention, giving concessions for concessions.

In the course of the diplomatic controversies which arose and continued intermittently, and in which various claims were made by Germany on the basis of the treaty of 1828 between the United States and Prussia, the status of the treaty itself was finally brought into question. Although neither Government has ever officially declared the treaty not in force, it is possible to show that neither in theory nor in practice were its terms applied to German-American commercial relations after about 1890. The Saratoga convention of 1891 amounted to an admission on the part of each Government that it was not entitled automatically to concessions which the other had made to third nations. In 1900 the two countries negotiated a reciprocity convention whose terms were in conformity with the requirements of conditional most-favored-nation practice, but in 1903 Count Posadowsky declared, "The United States no longer enjoys most-favored-nation treatment in Germany." Nevertheless, when the reciprocity treaty was concluded between the United States and Cuba, the German Government contended that it should be given the opportunity to offer a concession through which to secure the benefit of the concessions made to Cuba. The circumstances being in several respects similar to those which had earlier attended Hawaiian-United States reciprocity relations, the United States did not in any way concede the German claim.

After the new German tariff law went into effect in 1906 a *modus vivendi* was arranged by which the United States secured the reduced rates made in the German treaties with European States, but this was not interpreted by Germany to include reductions subsequently made to other States.

Difficulty of reconciling reciprocity and most-favored-nation pledges.—The evidences show that the conclusion of reciprocity treaties is likely to lead to claims from States outside the agreement which, if granted, will defeat the purposes of the treaties, and which, if not granted, occasion the preferring of a charge of disloyalty to treaty obligations. The practice of making reciprocity treaties requires the conditional construction of the most-favored-nation clause. But the use by the United States of the conditional interpretation of the most-favored-nation clause has for half a century occasioned, and, if it is persisted in, will continue to occasion frequent controversies between the United States and European countries.

Possible developments.—So many have been the inconveniences and difficulties of most-favored-nation practice, it has frequently been suggested that the pledge be done away with. Any proposal entirely to eliminate it would call for very careful scrutiny of the arguments by which such proposal may be accompanied. The clause has performed, undoubtedly, very useful functions. The fact that it has had its inconveniences is not sufficient reason for abandoning it. Such a proposal, to merit consideration should offer a substitute affording promise of more satisfactory performance.

On the other hand, if the clause is to be retained, it should be possible for the nations either to agree by common stipulation upon the meanings to be attached to each of the various forms and types of the clause or to adopt one standard form whose phraseology shall be unequivocal and whose function shall be clearly defined.

The effect, whether the conditional or the unconditional practice is followed, depends most of all upon the honesty, consistency, and rigidity or liberality with which the application is made to conform to the principle.

Whatever the relative advantages and whatever the difference in net results, the practice of "preference," "reciprocity," and conditional most-favored-nation treatment necessitate frequent and repeated special negotiations, constant bargaining, inevitable delays actual inequality of treatment. There are without question circumstances in which special treatment is warranted; this is recognized in relation to certain circumstances in the favored-nation practice of all nations. But in the absence of special circumstances or special relations, special treatment inevitably creates unwarranted distinctions and tends to perpetuate discriminations.

When the peace settlement is being decided, it should be found possible to frame a model pledge or pledges intended to secure equality of treatment; also to devise machinery for the construction and enforcement of such, along with other international pledges.

III. BARGAINING TARIFFS AND COMMERCIAL TREATIES OF EUROPEAN STATES

Tariff systems.—Practically every nation frames its tariff policy with the primary aim of promoting domestic industries. Most nations add to this primary object that of encouraging their export trade. To carry out its policy, each country chooses that system which appears to it best adapted to its circumstances and purposes. Various tariff systems may be distinguished according to the methods by which the lists of duties are made and by the numbers of lists employed. Thus there are statutory tariffs and conventional tariffs, single-schedule systems and multiple-schedule systems. Among multiple-schedule systems are the preferential, the maximum-and-minimum, and the general-and-conventional, and there are combinations of these. Of European States, five have single-schedule systems; the others have all adopted one or another of the multiple-schedule systems, most of them the general-and-conventional.

History of recent tariff and tariff treaty policies.—The most conspicuous single event in the commercial history of the nineteenth century was the conclusion of the Cobden treaty of 1860 between England and France, which marked the full acceptance by Great Britain of the principle of free trade. The contracting parties agreed to unconditional most-favored-nation treatment. Almost at once England generalized the concessions which she had made. There followed among European States a rapid succession of treaties, involving tariff reductions and including the unconditional most-favored-nation clause. The tendency of the period was toward free trade.

After 1875 protectionist sentiment began again to prevail, Germany taking the lead in a movement for the restoration and raising of rates of duty. New tariffs and new treaties superseded those which had been made after 1860.

In 1891 France adopted the maximum-and-minimum tariff system, and at about the same time Germany adopted the general and conventional system.

Thenceforth and until the beginning of the present war there might be distinguished in Europe three groups of States, representing three types of commercial policy and practice—a free trade, single-schedule tariff group; a protectionist, maximum and minimum tariff group; and a protectionist, general-and-conventional group. In the realm of treaty-making, all have retained the principle of most-favored-nation treatment, but the practical effect of the favored-nation pledge has been limited very decidedly by increased specialization of tariff schedules. The importance of the bargaining or bartering process has been constantly and considerably increased.

The commercial policy and tariff system of Germany.—Among the Central European States, commercial policy has been in no small measure made a means to political ends. First, Prussian policy was directed with a view to the unification of Germany; then, German policy was directed with a view to consolidating the interests of the Central European States. In 1871 Bismarck concluded with France the treaty of Frankfort, in which article XI provided for permanent, unconditional most-favored-nation treatment between Germany and France. This agreement has had, in operation, some advantages and some disadvantages for each of the contracting parties; it has operated, however, probably more than any other single treaty provision or other law, as a stabilizer of European commercial policy.

In 1879 Germany adopted a new tariff law whereby many protective duties were revived, duties on manufactured articles were increased, and the country was definitely committed to the policy of protection. In 1891 the Government presented to the Reichstag a new series of treaties, the Caprivi Treaties, which it had negotiated with neighboring countries, and these were soon confirmed almost without opposition. The characteristic feature of these treaties was that of tariff bargaining. The concessions made to each State were in the long run extended, by the operation of the most-favored-nation clause, to all the others of the treaty group and to some not in the group. The chief advantage which the treaties brought both to Germany and to the countries with which they were concluded lay in the fact that the duties in the conventional schedules could be counted on as fixed for a considerable and definite period. The effect upon German trade was far from decisive, but the treaties doubtless prevented certain undesirable developments which were imminent at the time when they were made.

Russia, following a tariff policy decidedly hostile to Germany, had raised the rates of her tariff, already high. Germany was provoked to retaliation, and there ensued a brief but bitter tariff war. In 1893 Russia adopted a maximum-and-minimum tariff, and subsequently each of the two countries raised its duties on the products which it imported from the other. So injurious were the effects on both that an agreement was effected and a new commercial treaty concluded between them in 1894, in which each made concessions to the other and most-favored-nation treatment was mutually pledged. There ensued a rapid revival of the trade which had suffered.

In 1892 Spain, the originator of the maximum-and-minimum system, though not the most conspicuous user, raised the rates of her schedules. This led to a tariff war between that country and Germany, which continued until, in 1906, each agreed to grant the other its lowest normal rates.

The adoption of the preferential system by Canada in 1897 led to strong representations by the German Government to the British Government, but to no actual disturbance of the commercial relations between Germany and the United Kingdom. Against Canada, Germany put into force the rates of her general tariff, and a tariff war ensued which lasted until a working arrangement was effected in 1910.

As between the United States and Germany, the trade was such that Germany was in no position to follow an aggressive tariff policy. An agreement was affected by the Saragota convention of 1891, already mentioned, but it appears that during the years which followed nothing but the circumspection of the two Governments averted the tariff war. A convention was made in 1900 whereby Germany granted the United States the benefits of her conventional tariff and was given in return the rates which the United States had already extended on certain articles to France, Italy, and Portugal.

In 1897 the German Government appointed a commission which made extensive investigations by way of preparation for revision of the tariff and the making of new treaties. In 1901, in the face of bitter opposition from the agrarians, the Government introduced its proposals, involving the retention of the general-and-conventional system; a new tariff law was passed in 1902; new treaties were forthwith negotiated; and the new tariff and the new treaties went into effect in 1906.

The rates of the German tariff of 1906 evinced an inclination toward stricter application of the policy of protection. In the arrangement of schedules, though the general-and-conventional principle was retained, there was a partial adoption of features of the maximum-and-minimum system. The rates of the general schedule were specialized to an extent previously unknown. They were prepared with a view to negotiation, adjusted to the balancing of concession against concession with all the nicety of the most minute distinctions. The Government was authorized to employ penalty duties to enforce satisfactory treatment from States inclined to discriminate.

Treaties were concluded with eleven States, and from the concessions there was made up the conventional schedule, which was to be in force for twelve years from 1906. Though it may not be susceptible of conclusive proof, Germany appears on the whole to have bargained more successfully than the other parties to the treaties. She had had the advantage of superior organization and of patient and painstaking preparation for the negotiations.

In 1907 an agreement was made between the German and the American Governments whereby the United States was given the benefit of the German conventional rates. In 1909 the United States granted to Germany the minimum rates of the new tariff. After the passage of the United States tariff act of 1913, Germany attempted to negotiate a special agreement, but the response to her proposals was not favorable.

The commercial policy and tariff systems of France.—Although the Emperor, Napoleon III, had accepted the lead of England in making the Cobden treaty and others which followed, there remained in France strong opposition to the policy represented by these treaties. In 1875–76 the Government made an extensive investigation, from the returns of which it was evident that there was a preponderance of opinion favoring the multiple rather than the single-schedule tariff system.

In 1881 a new tariff law was passed, in which the rates on manufactured wares were increased, while raw materials and foodstuffs remained, as a rule, on the free list or were made subject to low rates. The general schedule was to be modified in operation by agreements with other powers. On the basis of this law, the Government negotiated treaties with seven European powers in which rates were fixed, thereby establishing a new conventional schedule. With Great Britain, Germany, and Austria-Hungary there were framed simple conventions granting most-favored-nation treatment.

In 1887 Italy promulgated a new tariff with sharp increases of rates, terminated her treaty with France, and demanded new and greater concessions. This led in 1888 to a tariff war, from which both countries suffered—Italy the more—and the two countries did not come to an agreement until 1898.

In 1892 France adopted a new tariff law which altered the whole basis of her commercial relations. She abandoned the general-and-conventional system in favor of an autonomous "maximum-and-minimum" system. The difference between the minimum and the maximum rates was approximately 25 per cent, and the law provided that the minimum rates should be applied to goods the produce of countries where French goods enjoyed equivalent concessions and were admitted at the lowest rates of duty. The Government was empowered to prolong the expiring commercial treaties, except in so far as they involved fixed rates of duty, and to apply the minimum rates to the wares of countries which would promise most-favored-nation treatment to France.

Several States were unwilling to make treaties on the basis of the concessions which France offered, and against such countries France put into effect the general tariff. Switzerland insisted upon modifications which the French Government refused to concede, and there resulted a tariff war which led to a considerable shrinkage in the trade between the two countries. Finally, in 1905, a convention was signed on the basis of a compromise on both sides. During the tariff war there had been a diversion of trade of both countries to other States, by which several of the latter, especially Germany and Belgium, profited.

A threatened tariff war with Spain was averted by an exchange of notes which did not involve changes of rates of duty. A short tariff war with Roumania was brought to an end by an agreement on the basis of most-favored-nation treatment.

Although France succeeded eventually in making agreements with all countries of commercial importance and in securing most-favored-nation pledges from most of these, she reached this end only after serious complications, which caused losses and left a permanent and somewhat adverse effect on her commercial relations. She did establish and maintain her autonomy in rate-making. The maximum tariff schedule stood essentially as a standardized warning. For the measure of autonomy which she gained, France paid by conceding a like measure to other countries, and she sacrificed guaranties of stability which the treaties of a former period had established.

When the time came for revision, the principles of autonomy and of the double schedule were accepted as established. The revision was confined to the rates. In the new law of 1910 the rates of both schedules were in general increased, though some were reduced. The disparity between the two was made almost systematically 50 per cent. The proposal of an intermediate tariff was rejected, but it was provided that the Government might under exceptional circumstances, and temporarily, apply the rates of the general tariff to products originating in countries where French products were not discriminated against, measures to carry out this provision to be submitted for ratification to the Parliament.

France had not, since 1892, extended her minimum rates in their entirety to the United States. A convention, signed in 1899, which would have given the United States most of the rates of the minimum tariff was not ratified by the American Government. Special provision for American trade was made in the French law of February 24, 1900, but all arrangements between the two countries were rendered void by the passage of the American tariff act of 1909, which terminated all reciprocity agreements.

On the day on which it enacted the tariff law of 1910, the French Parliament passed a law regulating commercial relations with the United States. This authorized the admission of certain products from the United States at the minimum rates and of certain other products at the rates of the old general tariff. More than two-thirds of the American imports into France were already entitled to enter free of duty. It was estimated that 29.3 per cent of the total imports would be admitted at the minimum rates, 0.4 per cent would be admitted at the old general rates, and 3.2 per cent of the total imports would be subjected to the new general rates.

The commercial policy and tariff system of Russia.—In Russia, as in the neighboring countries, the last quarter of the nineteenth century was marked by a movement toward higher rates of duty. The Russian Government was influenced, in addition to the usual motives, by a desire to make use of the tariff to control the balance of trade and to protect the national currency from an outflow of specie. Russia employed at that time the autonomous, single-schedule tariff system. In her treaties, she had in some cases the unconditional and in some the conditional most-favored-nation clause, but in her relations with Austria and Germany she had no claim for favored-nation treatment. In 1893 the Russian Government adopted the machinery both of the maximum-and-minimum and of the general-and-conventional tariff systems. The application of the maximum schedule to imports from Germany led to a tariff war, which was brought to an end by a commercial treaty whose conclusion marked the definite acceptance by Russia of the general-and-conventional tariff system. This was the product of political as well as economic considerations. Other treaties, on the model of the German treaty, followed with several countries.

Between 1901 and 1905 Russia applied penalty duties to various imports from the United States, in retaliation for the levying of countervailing duties on Russian sugar and petroleum. These punitive rates were withdrawn in 1905.

In 1903 Russia adopted a new general tariff designed for bargaining purposes, in which the rates were raised on many items, particularly manufactured wares, and the schedule was more sharply specialized than before. Commercial treaties followed with Germany, France, and several other States, and the new tariff went into effect in 1906. The system thus established was not materially altered until after the beginning of the European war.

Classification and characteristics of tariff systems.—Germany, Russia, Austria-Hungary, Bulgaria, Greece, Italy, Portugal, Roumania, Sweden, and Switzerland have adopted the general-and-conventional system and have made with their neighbors treaties involving reciprocal tariff concessions. Spain originated the maximum-and-minimum system and is still classed as a maximum-and-minimum country, but her practice has become essentially that of the general-and-conventional system.

France and Norway employ the maximum-and-minimum system. The theory of this system is that there shall be two schedules of rates, made autonomously, below the lower of which the treaty making authorities may not make concessions. In practice, however, it has been found necessary to make concessions.

The preferential system requires at least two schedules and is autonomous, but its minimum schedule is intended, not for the most favored nation, but for specially "preferred" nations. There is in Europe no State which employs a tariff which may properly be designated as "preferential"; but preferential practices in some form and degree are in force between several European countries and their colonies.

The countries of Europe which still adhere to the single schedule system are either "free-trade" countries with peculiar advantages or countries of minor commercial importance. There has been a marked tendency toward the abandonment of a single-schedule system, especially among countries whose tariff policy has a "protective" feature.

As matters stood until 1914, it was the universal practice of European States to extend unconditional favored-nation treatment to each other. But the tendency in framing tariff schedules was toward detailed specifications, with the intent frequently and with the result that numerous concessions apparently generalized, were in application particular and exclusive. As a consequence, it is by no means the case that the generalizing of concessions under the European construction of the most-favored-nation clause effects or maintains complete equality of treatment in a given market. One thing, however, tariff treaties do accomplish positively and effectively: they fix, or "bind," rates of duty for a specified term of years, thus creating an assurance that during that term these rates will not be increased.

As with constitutions, so with commercial policies and tariff systems—the advantages or disadvantages of a particular type or feature must be estimated from the point of view of the situation and circumstances, the needs and the possibilities of each individual country at a particular time.

IV. CONCLUSIONS AND RECOMMENDATIONS

The Commission begs to submit to the Congress the following conclusions and recommendations:

Absence of a continuous policy in the past.—The survey of the reciprocity experiences and commercial arrangements of the United States which is made in this report shows that the country has not in the past followed a consistent and continuous policy. It is true that there has been a steady current of opinion in favor of the principle of securing for ourselves and of extending to others equality of treatment. Early American statesmen believed that the offer of equality of opportunity of access to American markets, in return for the removal of the discriminatory barriers which then prevailed in other countries, together with denial of equal treatment to those countries which persisted in discrimination against the trade of the United States, would bring about a general regime of liberal and equal treatment. The method to be employed, however, was that of individual negotiation. Hence arose the special form and interpretation given by the United States to the clause in commercial agreements by which nations engage to extend to each other the most-favored-nation treatment, a clause to whose history and significance detailed consideration is given in Part II of the report.[1] The practice of individual bargaining, which followed inevitably in view of the national circumstances and international situation of the United States through the larger part of its history, has led to special arrangements and has stood in the way of the adoption of a general policy.

To the early liberal attitude of the United States, the States of Europe did not on the whole respond. In the course of these, therefore, as separate and independent commercial arrangements were entered into, the treatment accorded by the United States to different countries became not infrequently unequal. Special agreements and provisions were made in separate cases as they arose. Having begun with the intention to offer equality of treatment, and with the hope of securing such equality in return, the United States has nevertheless been led into commercial relations with individual nations of which the effect was inequality.

During the period before 1890 two isolated agreements were made, those with Canada and with the Hawaiian Islands. Others were negotiated during this period, but were not consummated. Both those projected and those carried out were determined by the particular circumstances of time and conditions. The reciprocity agreements made, subsequently, under the acts of 1890 and 1897, were intended, it is true, to conform to the principles of a fixed general policy.

But in operation even these acquired the character of special agreements. Both the policy and the agreements have since been given up.

An opportunist attitude was natural so long as the United States kept aloof from foreign complications and was intent on avoiding them. Now, however, the situation is completely altered. The United States has become committed to far-reaching participation in world politics. The American Government can no longer shape its commercial negotiations solely with reference to the results of each particular arrangement. It must consider the world at large and must shape its commercial policy in conformity with the political and humanitarian principles which govern its general attitude in the international sphere.

So far as commercial policy and commercial negotiations are concerned, the evidence presented in the present report indicates that a policy of special arrangements, such as the United States has followed in recent decades, leads to troublesome complications. Whether as regards our reciprocity treaties or as regards our interpretation of the most-favored-nation clause, the separate and individual treatment of each case tends to create misunderstanding and friction with countries which, though supposed to be not concerned, yet are in reality much concerned. When each country with which we negotiate is treated by itself, and separate arrangements are made with the expectation that they shall be applicable individually, claims are none the less made by other States with whom such arrangements have not been made. Concessions are asked; they are sometimes refused; counter concessions are proposed; reprisal and retaliation are suggested; unpleasant controversies and sometimes international friction result.

A clear and simple policy needed for the future—Equality of treatment.—A great gain would be secured, now that the United States is committed to wide participation in world politics, if a clear and simple policy could be adopted and follows. The guiding principle might well be that of equality of treatment—a principle in accord with American ideals of the past and of the present. Equality of treatment should mean that the United States treat all countries on the same terms, and in turn require equal treatment from every other country. So far as concerns general industrial policy and general tariff legislation, each country—the United States as well as others—should be left free to enact such measures as it deems expedient for its own welfare. But the measures adopted, whatever they be, should be carried out with the same terms and the same treatment for all nations.

Possible exceptions to the principle of equal treatment.—In the application of any general principle of this kind, there may be occasion for qualifications or exceptions. Some allowance for exceptional treatment, not inconsistent, under certain circumstances, with the principle of equality of treatment, has been made by almost all countries in connection with discussions and negotiations with reference to the most-favored-nation clause. Special treatment, or the concession of special rates of duty, has been regarded as admissible, particularly in two sets of cases. First, it has been on occasions recognised that where one country has a long frontier line in common with another country, the unique ties of geographical connection give ground for exceptional arrangements. Considerations and exceptions of this kind are exemplified in the relations between Spain and Portugal, and those between Canada and the United States. Second, special political ties and political responsibilities have led to commercial relations also of a special character. Such were the relations that existed for a considerable time between the United States and Cuba. But these cases of exception, whether they are universally admitted to rest upon valid grounds or are debatable, do not make it impossible to carry out, with reference to the great mass of international relations and negotiations, the principle of equality of treatment.

It must be further admitted that, just as special political ties may lead to exceptional treatment, so also the severance of normal international relations may be followed by exceptional treatment. It remains to be seen what conditions of peace will be established and what commercial relations will ensue on the termination of the war. The nature of the settlement must affect the commercial arrangements also. Political and perhaps military considerations may compel modification of a policy which nevertheless should aim in general at reciprocal equality of commercial treatment.

So far as concerns existing commercial treaties and arrangements, the international relations of the United States, as they have been gradually shaped since the opening of the present century, are in conformity with the principle of equality of treatment, when interpreted and qualified with regard to special political affiliations and special geographical ties. The treaty between the United States and Cuba, providing for special remissions of duty on both sides, is to be judged in the light of the special political relations between the two countries. The act which stands upon our statute book, making possible a reciprocity arrangement with Canada, also rests upon grounds of its own, being influenced by the exceptional geographical relations. Only one commercial arrangement of the United States now in effect can be said to be inconsistent with the general principle, namely, that with Brazil. And this rests, not upon a treaty to which the Unites States is formally a party, but upon legislative and administrative measures of Brazil.

Methods of enforcing equality of treatment.—If, however, the principle of equality of treatment is to be adopted, something more than a bare declaration of policy is needed. In view of the divergent attitudes and demands of different countries, and of the undeniable possibility that other countries may not follow, in their own dealings with the United States, the principle of equality of treatment, some method of enforcement is indispensable.

As matters now stand, the United States has know way of bringing pressure to bear, or rather, none that is immediately available. If not accorded equality of treatment by other countries, this country is almost helpless. There has been provided no authorization for action on the part of the Executive. If the United States wishes to exercise pressure upon another country for the purpose of bringing that country's measures into conformity with demands of the United States for equality of treatment, the slow-moving process of legislative enactment alone is now available.

Measures for the purpose of securing just treatment by other countries may take one of two forms. The first of these is that of concessions, or of concessional arrangements, by which reductions of duty may be conceded to countries which grant the United States equality of treatment. The second is that of additional studies, in tries which fail to give the United States satisfactory treatment. Each of these methods has its advantages and its disadvantages.

The method of concessions.—The main advantage of the concessional method—that of reductions of duty—is that it appears more conciliatory. To offer a concession is less irritating than to impose a penalty. But it must be borne in mind that if the granting of a concession be carried out with full effect and in full accord with the principle of equality of treatment, the concession must be extended alike to all countries which conform to the principle. Only a few countries are then left unaffected, and, as regards its effect upon these, a concessional method becomes the equivalent of a penalizing method.

A disadvantage of the concessional method, when the concessional schedule includes a considerable number of items, is that it causes the effective tariff schedules of the country in respect to those items for which concessional rates are provided to consist largely of those items for which concessional rates are provided to consist largely or mainly of the concessional or reduced rates of duty. It involves, if carried out fully and with the desired effect, a lowering of what is declared to be the general tariff. This brings it about that the general tariff becomes nominal; it contains rates higher than those which are expected actually to go into effect. This leads in turn to some uncertainty, at the time when the general rates are fixed, as to the extent to which they will be modified by the concessional arrangements. The outcome is likely to be virtually a maximum-and-minimum tariff, with possible uncertainty as to the extent to which the minimum rates shall be applied.

As regards economic effect, reductions of duty under the concessional method have different consequences under varying conditions of supply as regards the article affected. Where a reduction of duty affects only a fraction of the imports of a particular article, and the major portion of the imports of that article is still left subject to the main, or non-concessional duty, the result is not only a loss of revenue to the Treasury, because of the lower rates of duty, but absence of any gain to consumers. The reduction of duty redounds only to the advantage of the foreign producer. This situation was exemplified by our experience with Hawaii, as detailed in this report, under the reciprocity treaty of 1875.[2] That experience was not indeed part of a general concessional policy; but it, nevertheless, supplies an example of the working of a limited concession. If, on the other hand, virtually the entire imported supply of a given article is admitted at the lowered concessional rates, the effect is that of a general reduction of duty. Such a result ensued, at least in the more recent years of the operation of the reciprocity treaty with Cuba, as a consequence of our concession of a reduced duty upon Cuban sugar. As shown in the discussion of Cuban relations,[3] this concession resulted in a gain to the Cuban sugar producer during the first years after the reciprocity arrangement went into effect, but had come to redound, during the years immediately preceding the European war, mainly to the advantage of the domestic consumer.

The method of additional duties.—The other method—that of the imposition of additional duties on articles coming from countries which discriminate against the United States—has also its advantages and disadvantages. The main disadvantage is that, employing something in the nature of a threat, it seems combative in principle, unfriendly in appearance, and therefore irritating. In this respect it is in its outward aspect the reverse of the concessional method. But it should be borne in mind that when the additional duties are put into effect solely for the purpose of securing equality of treatment, and are therefore subject to termination as soon as such treatment has been attained, they can hardly give reasonable ground for complaint.

A distinct advantage of this method is that it does not affect the general tariff rates of the country which uses it. It is directed against those countries only which do not themselves apply the principle of equality of treatment. The probabilities are great—so great as almost to amount to a certainty—that it will not be applied to any considerable number of countries or articles. Administered with discretion, and with due regard to the character of the trade with different sources of supply, it leads to no substantial change in the general tariff system, and therefore leaves this to be determined solely with regard to the country's domestic needs and wishes.

As regards economic effect, additional duties, like the concessional, have different consequences according to their range of application. If a country to which such duties are applied sends to the United States only a fraction of the imports of a given article, the effect is simply that this fraction is excluded from the domestic market and is displaced by additional imports of the same commodity from elsewhere. Only in very rare cases would the domestic consumer be affected by the imposition of an additional duty on such fractional imports. If, indeed, a very large portion of the supply of a given article comes from the penalized country, the situation is different; still more is it different if the entire supply comes from that one country. In such cases additional duties are likely to entail a burden on the domestic consumer.

It follows that there is special need of care in the application of additional duties. They are most effective if there be competing countries, each desirous of sending to the United States the same or like goods, as is usually the case when applied to countries which send us manufactured products. For such, the conditions of production and the control of products are not determined by physical or climatic causes, and there is not likely to be found anything in the nature of exclusive control of a particular article by any single country. Additional duties then establish a preference of one foreign producer over another, but the pressure on the offending foreign country does not affect injuriously the domestic consumer.

Under the existing tariff system of the United States—that embodied in the tariff act of 1913—the method of additional duties would seem the only one that could be put at once into operation. For the time being it may be presumed that no concessions below the rates of the act of 1913 are likely to be proposed by the Executive or considered by Congress. Congress could provide for additional duties, the design being, not to bring about any substantial changes in the general tariff rates, and certainly not to entail increased prices to consumers, but to secure fair reciprocal treatment from foreign countries.

Possible problems of the future.—Looking to the more distant future, the choice between the additional and the concessional methods must be influenced by the international relations which may develop as a result of the war. The latter method may then seem as effective a method as the former for securing equality of treatment from other countries. More particularly may this be the case if the concessions—in the form of lowered rates, within limits set by Congress—be arranged with the intent and with the effect of their being applicable to almost all countries, the higher non-concessional rates being designed for application, if at all, to a few recalcitrant countries only. Thus applied, the concessional method, as has already been said, is virtually a more conciliatory form of the additional method. It still has the disadvantage that it does not clearly and unequivocally leave the country free in the independent determination of its own tariff policy. It is less satisfactorily adapted to the single-tariff system, which the Unites States has generally used in the settlement of its own internal problems.

Conclusion as to methods.—To conclude, the method of additional duties is that which can be put into effect by the United States at once, without disturbance of its general tariff policy, and without committing the country definitively as regards the permanent commercial arrangements which may be evolved as part of the coming international settlement. The necessary flexibility can be secured by leaving the actual imposition of additional duties to the discretion of the President, who shall act always in conformity with a stated general principle and subject to general limitations defined by statute. Indeed, either system, the concessional or the additional, can be safely applied only when there is a provision for elasticity in its application and administration. It would seem indispensable that a considerable degree of freedom be left to the executive department. The restrictions within which that freedom shall be exercised must be prescribed according to the judgment of Congress. They may take the form of limiting the additions or penalties to stated ad valorem supplements to the existing duties, or to stated ad valorem duties (or equivalent specific duties) on articles appearing upon the general free list. The early enactment of legislation authorizing the imposition of additional duties at the discretion of the President is accordingly recommended by the Tariff Commission.

Concerning the position which the United States should take with regard to the most-favored-nation clause the Commission now makes no recommendation. There has been shown in the body of the report sharp diversity between the usage of the United States and that of most other countries in the interpretation of that clause; and there is also diversity of opinion as to its present and future value. An attentive, even exhaustive, consideration of its form and interpretation, and of its substantive effect, will be necessary in the course of the coming international readjustments. The extent to which the clause may be embodied henceforth in commercial and tariff agreements will depend largely on the general character of those adjustments. The other policies which the Commission recommends for immediate consideration may be adopted consistently with the use of either of the two main forms of the most-favored-nation clause. It seems to the Commission premature for the United States to commit itself at this moment either to the maintenance without justification of the country's traditional most-favored-nation policy or to the advocacy or adoption of a different policy.

Finally, it can not be too much emphasized that any policy adopted by the United States should have for its object, on the one hand, the prevention of discrimination and the securing of equality of treatment for American commerce and for American citizens, and, on the other hand, the frank offer of the same equality of treatment to all countries that reciprocate in the same spirit and to the same effect. The United States should ask no special favors and should grant no special favors. It should exercise its powers and should impose its penalties, not for the purpose of securing discrimination in its favor, but to prevent discrimination to its disadvantage. Respectfully submitted.

F. W. Taussig, *Chairman*
Thomas Walker Page, *Vice Chairman*
David J. Lewis
William Kent
William S. Culbertson
Edward P. Costigan

NOTES

1 See also in the Summary, *infra*, p. 39.
2 See page 129, *infra*.
3 See page 330, *infra*.

17. The Most-Favored-Nation Clause in American Commercial Treaties

J. Viner

THE TWO INTERPRETATIONS

It has been a common practice of most nations since the beginning of the seventeenth century to insert in their commercial treaties a provision known as the most-favored-nation clause. In its multiform variations of phrasing this clause provided in effect that each of the contracting parties shall grant to the other any privilege or favor of commerce, navigation, or other specified matters, which it grants or may thereafter grant to third countries. The object of such a provision is to assure each of the contracting parties that its economic interests in the other country will not be discriminated against in comparison with the treatment given to the economic interests of other foreign countries.

Ignoring minor variations, the clause is to be found in two principal forms, known as the unconditional and the conditional. Before the American Revolution the clause had appeared only in the unconditional form, wherein there appears no limitation on the obligation of each of the contracting parties to extend to the other concessions granted to a third country. The conditional form made its initial appearance in the first commercial treaty signed by the United States, the treaty with France of February 6, 1778. Article II of this treaty contained what had hitherto been the usual most-favored-nation pledge: "The Most Christian King and the United States engage mutually not to grant any particular favor to other nations, in respect of commerce and navigation, which shall not immediately become common to the other party"; but it was followed by the qualification: "who shall enjoy the same favor, freely, if the concession was freely made, or on allowing the same compensation, if the concession was conditional." The most-favored-nation clause in American treaties has ever since as a general rule been phrased in conditional terms. It has even more uniformly been given the conditional interpretation by American authorities, whatever the particular phrasing may have been.

During the period from 1820 to 1860 the conditional form appeared frequently in treaties between European states and it has been used extensively by Latin-American countries and by Japan. In practice, however, there have been very few instances where countries other than the United States have used the conditional form as a basis for withholding from treaty countries privileges to which they would have been entitled if the clause had appeared in the unconditional form. The most important of such instances have been connected with special privileges granted to the United States. There has been no instance, I believe, where countries, other than the United States, and Hawaii under pressure from the United States, have attempted to interpret a clause appearing in the unqualified form as if it implied the conditional limitation.

The conditional interpretation, in consequence of this almost complete divergence of commercial treaty practice between the United States and the rest of the world, has commonly come to be known as the "American" interpretation. In an almost continuous series of diplomatic controversies beginning in 1787 and persisting up to the present time the United States has steadfastly defended against the protests of many countries both its use of the conditional form and its enforcement of the conditional interpretation regardless of the particular form in which the clause may have appeared. It is therefore a matter of some consequence that the State Department has suddenly abandoned the traditional American policy, that in treaties recently negotiated by the State Department the most-favored-nation provision has been phrased in what are specifically and unequivocally unconditional terms,[1] and that the State Department has announced that future treaties will likewise contain the most-favored-nation clause in the unconditional form, and that existing treaties will be revised, wherever other parties thereto consent, so as to conform to the unconditional principle.[2]

American economists have given but scant attention to the most-favored-nation clause. What academic discussion there has been in the country has been confined very largely to the writers in international law. These latter have been astonishingly uncritical in their treatment of the substantive effects of the two interpretations, and have limited themselves in large measure to approving statements of the arguments presented in support of the merits of the American interpretation by American officials. Their writings as a rule contain little which offers even a hint that the conditional form may not have been altogether superior, in its economic and in its political consequences, to the unconditional form.[3] The time is opportune, therefore, to compare the theoretical merits of the two forms, to survive the manner of operation of the conditional form, and to forecast the consequences which the abandonment of this form will have on American commercial relations, and thus to provide a basis for an appraisal of the action of the State Department.

ADVANTAGES CLAIMED FOR THE AMERICAN INTERPRETATION

The advantage most commonly claimed for the conditional as against the unconditional form of the clause is that it is manifestly unfair that a concession which has been granted for full compensation to one country should be extended without charge to other countries. This is probably the consideration which led to the adoption of the conditional form. John Jay in 1787, in a report to Congress, as Secretary for the Department of Foreign Affairs, concerning the proper interpretation of a most-favored-nation provision in the Treaty of 1782 with the Netherlands, wrote as follows:[4]

> It is observable that this article takes no notice of cases where compensation is granted for privileges. Reason and equity, however, in the opinion of your Secretary,

> will supply this deficiency. . . . Where a privilege is gratuitously granted, the nation to whom it is granted becomes in respect to that privilege a favored nation . . . but where the privilege is not gratuitous, but rests on compact, in such case the favor, if any there be, does not consist in the privilege yielded, but in the consent to make the contract by which it is yielded. . . . The favor, therefore, of being admitted to make a similar bargain, is all that in such cases can reasonably be demanded under the article. Besides, it would certainly be inconsistent with the most obvious principles of justice and fair construction, that because France purchases, at a great price, a privilege of the United States, that therefore the Dutch shall immediately insist, not on having the like privileges at the like price, but without any price at all.

This argument, however, fails to look beyond the particular transactions between states to their commercial intercourse as a whole. There is at least as complete and reciprocal an exchange of considerations between countries bound by an unconditional most-favored-nation contract as between countries in conditional and most-favored-nation relations with each other. Under the unconditional form of the pledge there is in a sense an exchange of concessions at the moment of the coming into effect of the treaty, but this exchange receives its execution gradually throughout the life of the treaty through the immediate extension by each country to the other of all privileges, favors, or concessions which it may grant to third countries. Country A has no ground for complaint if concessions to it from country B, for which it has given compensation, are extended gratuitously to countries C and D, for during the life of A's treaty with B country A will in like manner receive gratuitously concessions which were granted by B to C and D for compensation. Nor should country B feel aggrieved because under the unconditional most-favored-nation clause it is obligated to extend freely to A concessions for which C and D have given it full compensation, for A will in like manner be obligated to extend freely to B concessions which it had originally granted to other countries for compensation.

It is possible, of course, that a country which followed the unconditional practice may deliberately refrain from making concessions to any country in order that it may avoid the obligation of extending such concessions to other countries. If country A, which has been making a series of concessions, for compensation in each case, to countries D, E, and F, is obligated under an unconditional most-favored-nation pledge to extend such concessions to country B, and if country B deliberately refrains from making concessions to any country in order to be free from the obligation of extending them to other countries, country A may feel that it has not received and will not receive from B anything in return for the concessions which it has given to B. Even under such circumstances, however, which are for country A the least favourable imaginable under the unconditional practice, A has received from B the important and valuable pledge that no country will under any circumstances enjoy any privileges in B which will not be available in like measure to A. The guaranty to A of equality of treatment in B is a valuable consideration, in fact more valuable than any guaranty which it could receive under the conditional practice, even though in its execution it means merely that no worse treatment will be given to A's economic interests in B than to the interests of any third country and does not result in positive concessions to A of privileges not enjoyed by the latter prior to the signature of the treaty.

From the economic point of view, moreover, it is not a source of loss to A if its unconditional most-favored-nation treaties force it to generalize the tariff concessions which it had by special arrangement granted to particular countries. A remission of import duties on a specific commodity, if confined to imports from one country not capable of supplying the entire import needs, will reduce the customs revenue and will impair the protection to domestic industries without substantially lowering the price to the domestic consumer. It will operate virtually as a subsidy from the treasury of the importing country to the producers in the favored exporting country. The price in the importing country will continue to be the world-market price plus the full duty. The producer in the favored country will get for his product the world price plus the full duty, if the remission is of the entire duty, or the world price plus the difference between the full duty and the preferential duty, if the remission is of only part of the duty. If, on the other hand, the favored country can fully supply the import needs of the country granting the favor, and does so after the remission of duties on its product by the latter, there would be little or no difference in the situation if the concession were extended to the entire world. Whether the remission of duty were special or general, the imports would be supplied in whole, or almost so, by the country to which the remission was originally granted. The price in the importing country would be the same as the world price (assuming that the entire duty was remitted). The consumer would gain by substantially the full amount of reduction in duty on each unit of the product he consumed, whether it were of domestic or of foreign origin. There would be no subsidy from the treasury of the importing country to foreign producers. Finally, if the country originally receiving the concession cannot supply the full import needs and if the concession is generalized, the consumer in the importing country will likewise gain on each unit consumed by the amount of reduction in the duty and there will be no subsidy to foreign producers at the cost of the treasury of the importing country. The protection to domestic producers will be lessened only slightly more under a generalized concession than under an exclusive concession to an important producing country capable of supplying a large fraction of the import needs.[5]

An objection often raised against the unconditional pledge, that it is an obstacle to the negotiation of reciprocity agreements providing for the mutual exchange of special favors, is in large measure sound. The systematic grant of special concessions, i.e., concessions which are not to be automatically extended to other countries, is impossible without violation of unconditional most-favored-nation obligation. In general, however, this is an argument in favor of, instead of against, the unconditional practice. Most tariff discriminations are not wanton, but arise out of reciprocity agreements. It was precisely to bring about equality of treatment and to eliminate the economic disadvantages, the ill-feeling, and the diplomatic bickering resulting from such discriminations that the use of the most-favored-nation clause became common.[6]

It has already been argued that to the granting country the grant of special concessions is under ordinary circumstances less advantageous than the extension to the entire world of such concessions as it desires to make. To the world as a whole, also, reciprocity treaties, even on free-trade grounds, are ordinarily not an amelioration, but on the contrary are an intensification of the evils of customs tariffs. They not only do not counteract the tendency of protective import duties to divert international trade from the channels which it would follow under free trade, but they may cause an even wider departure of trade from its "natural" channels than would result from a régime of uniform protective tariffs at the levels prevalent prior to the grant of partial reductions of duties through reciprocity arrangements. Imports which come in over a uniform tariff barrier are still being produced where the conditions are economically most advantageous for their production. If the tariff is not uniform, however, the production of the commodities affected may be diverted from the foreign country best fitted to produce them to another foreign country not so well situated for their production, but able to compete on a price basis because of the tariff differential which has been given to it.

There are supposed to be circumstances under which propinquity, economic interdependence, geographical or political bonds, racial or linguistic kinship, etc., make reciprocity arrangements peculiarly profitable to both countries and peculiarly tolerable to the rest of the world.[7] In so far as the advantages derivable from such arrangements are economic, however, they are obtainable in at least equal degree through the outright reduction of their tariffs by both countries. Moreover, if the countries are really so related to each other economically that a mutual reduction in the tariffs on each other's products would result in a closer, instead of in a less close, conformity of trade to the channels which it would follow under universal free trade, a reciprocity treaty will not operate very differently from the outright extension to the entire world by both countries of the concessions granted to each other. Under the conditions described, no third countries will be in as good position to profit from the concessions as the parties to the original arrangement.

It may be objected against this reasoning that it is too "theoretical," and has no practical applicability, since it does not conform to the way in which statesmen approach these problems. Governments, it may be said, on the one hand cannot be induced to make concessions from their tariffs except in return for special concessions, and on the other hand will often refuse to make general concessions where they could be induced to make special ones. If the economic advantages of reciprocity arrangements, where there are such advantages, are to be secured, the defender of the conditional practice may argue, it must be through the reciprocal exchange of special concessions. Reciprocity treaties, moreover, may bring political and sentimental gains, such as the strengthening of political ties, or the smoothing of the path to eventual political union, which are not obtainable in equal measure through outright and general reductions in duties.

It must be conceded that this reasoning is not wholly without force. It is easy, however, to exaggerate its importance. European countries following the unconditional practice have shown little hesitation in entering into arrangements with each other whereby mutual reductions in duties were to be granted, even though they were fully aware of their obligation immediately to extend the benefit of such reductions to all countries entitled to most-favored-nation treatment. Each country would naturally seek in such arrangements those concessions which would be of greatest value to itself, and in many cases such concessions would be of little significance to other countries. By the process of "specialization," or the fine classification of commodities and rates in tariff schedules, it is possible to avoid applying a concession on, for example, one type of cotton cloth in which a negotiating country was alone or especially interested to all types of cotton cloths imported from all countries entitled to most-favored-nation treatment. If carried to extreme lengths, it is true, the practice of specialization may enable a country to grant what are in effect if not in form exclusive concessions, and thus to violate the spirit while adhering to the letter of its unconditional most-favoured-nation obligations. Much has been made by some writers of the alleged breakdown of the unconditional system through the abuse of the possibilities of tariff specialization. There is ground for belief, however, that there has been considerable exaggeration, both of the extent to which the practice has been carried in order to avoid the execution of treaty obligations, and of the degree to which it can successfully be carried without revealing an indisputable intent to escape such obligations and thus giving rise to the danger of the termination of amicable tariff relations with the countries suffering from such evasion.[8] It is in any case wholly beyond question that in the last sixty years European countries following the unconditional practice have made more frequent and more substantial mutual reductions of their statutory duties through diplomatic arrangements than has the United States with its conditional practice.[9]

Where there are strong motives, whether economic or political, for the entrance into special arrangements wherein two countries will stipulate the reciprocal exchange of *exclusive* favors, the unconditional most-favored-nation clause will not prove to be an absolute and inflexible barrier to the conclusion of such arrangements. The conditional pledge, it should be noted, permits only "special" concessions, not "exclusive" ones. In theory at least, any country, A, having a right to conditional most-favored-nation treatment in country B, has a right to claim from B, upon the offer of equivalent compensation, any privileges which B has given for compensation to a third country, C. The only way in which a country can grant specifically exclusive concessions under the conditional practice is on the plea of special relations with the country receiving such concessions, and this plea may equally be raised in support of exclusive concessions under the unconditional practice.[10] To maintain as an advantage of the conditional practice, as has sometimes been done, that it alone permits of exclusive concessions,[11] is, therefore, to misinterpret the intent of the conditional pledge and to minimize the possibilities under the unconditional pledge.

The most-favored-nation clause in American commercial treaties, as conditionally interpreted and applied by the United States, has probably been the cause in the last century of more diplomatic controversy, more variations in construction, more international ill-feeling, more conflict between international obligations and municipal law and between judicial interpretation and executive practice, more confusion and uncertainty of operation, than have developed under all the unconditional most-favored-nation pledges of all other countries combined. To claim for the conditional pledge, therefore, that "It also avoids the uncertainty on the part of legislators and the courts which must be of necessity be present when, due to the interlocking of the provisions of various treaties, it is not clear to what body of facts any law or treaty may apply"[12] is absolutely to ignore the history of the operation of the two forms of the clause. With almost the sole exception of the question of the compatibility of bounty-countervailing duties with most-favored-nation obligations, uncertainty as to rights under most-favored-nation pledges has been a peculiar characteristic of treaty practice under the conditional interpretation.

There is some evidence in the utterances of American official spokesmen and of American writers on international law that there exists an unreflecting prejudice against the unconditional practice resulting from the assumption that that practice is in some manner or other inimical to or inconsistent with high tariff protection.[13] The unconditional most-favored-nation pledge is not a free-trade device and is in no way hostile to the pursuit of an as unregenerate and extreme a policy of high tariffs as the most ardent protectionist would desire. Let tariffs be as high as they can be, they in no way violate unconditional obligations, provided only that they are uniform to all countries. It is true that the conditional practice is inconceivable on the part of genuinely free-trade countries, for the conditional practice involves the giving, the withholding, and the seeking of special tariff concessions, and a free-trade country has no special concessions to give and therefore cannot expect to receive any. It is true, also, that the mercantilist who thinks that in international trade one country must lose what another country gains and that the gains go in largest measure to the sharp-trading and keen-bargaining country is justified in thinking that the conditional practice offers more scope to the haggling proclivities of his country's statesmen. But that the unconditional practice in no way enforces any limitation on the height of the import duties which may be imposed by a country following that practice is demonstrated by the fact that Russia and France with their high protective tariffs, Switzerland and Belgium with their moderately protective tariffs, Great Britain with its strictly free-trade tariff, have all followed for many years the unconditional practice.

SOME PHASES OF AMERICAN MOST-FAVORED-NATION PRACTICE

The Conditional Interpretation of Pledges Unconditional in Form

The United States has, with one exception, uniformly maintained that the most-favored-nation pledges in its treaties, regardless of their phrasing, must in the light of traditional American policy be interpreted as conditional pledges, in so far as claims upon the United States are concerned. In a number of instances, the pledge appeared in American treaties in unqualified form. But it is questionable that the traditional American policy demanded the conditional practice for its execution. The instances of failure to express this policy by specific inclusion of a conditional pledge in most-favored-nation treaties must have been due either to inadvertence, ignorance, or carelessness on the part of American negotiators, or to their assumption that the American or conditional interpretation was the universal and the only acceptable one.[14] But where a pledge appears in the unconditional form in a treaty with a country whose traditional policy it is to maintain the unconditional practice, there would appear to be at least a moral obligation on the part of the United States to bear the consequences of the carelessness or incapacity of its diplomatic officers and to fulfil its obligations to the letter. Such, unfortunately, has not been the practice of the United States.

In many of the American most-favored-nation treaties there is both a specific pledge that "no higher or other duties shall be imposed" by either treaty country on the products of the other than are imposed on the products of any third country and a general or "covering" pledge of reciprocal most-favored-nation treatment. The relationship of the specific to the general pledge has been the subject of considerable diplomatic discussion.

The Treaty of August 27, 1829, with Austria-Hungary contained a general most-favored-nation pledge in the conditional form, accompanied by a specific pledge such as that described above. Under the United States–France Treaty of July 4, 1831, French wines, in return for French concessions to the United States, were admitted to the United States at lower duties than other wines. Austria-Hungary immediately requested the extension of the same low duties to her wines. Secretary of State Livingston refused to comply with this request, on the ground that the specific pledge did not cancel the conditional provision in the general pledge of most-favored-nation treatment.[15] The United States–Denmark Treaty of April 26, 1826, also contained a general most-favored-nation pledge in the conditional form accompanied by a specific pledge not to impose higher or other duties. After the conclusion of the reciprocity treaty between the United States and Hawaii, an importer of sugar from the Danish West Indies claimed that this sugar should share in the privilege of free admission enjoyed by Hawaiian sugar. The United States Supreme Court denied that there was anything in the treaty with Denmark which would entitle her to receive without compensation privileges granted to Hawaii for compensation.[16] In the following year the meaning of the specific "no higher or other duty" pledge was brought before the Supreme Court for determination under circumstances which isolated the issue from the question of the relationship to each other of two pledges stated in different and possibly inconsistent terms. An importer of sugar from the Dominican Republic sought admission for such sugar on the same terms as Hawaiian sugar, on the ground that the United States–Dominican Republic Treaty of February 8, 1867, contained only the specific pledge that neither country should impose on the products of the other higher or other duties than it imposed on the products of any third country, unaccompanied by a general pledge of most-favored-nation treatment. The Supreme Court again denied that the specific pledge imposed any obligations on the United States which would not have been equally imposed by a pledge formulated in general conditional most-favored-nation terms.[17]

It is not necessary for our present purposes to examine the soundness of these decisions. The Supreme Court, it was evident, was interpreting the traditional American commercial policy rather than the particular terms of the particular treaties involved in the cases at issue. Note, however, the effect of the decisions: foreign countries have no valid claim, on the strength of "no higher or other duties" pledges in their treaties, to receive freely from the United States tariff concessions given to other countries for compensation. Not many years after these decisions were rendered, the State Department, in negotiations with Russia (in 1895) and with Haiti (in 1901), blandly insisted that American exporters were entitled under the specific "no higher or other duties" pledges in the treaties with these countries to privileges which they admittedly could not claim under the conditional most-favored-nation pledges appearing in the same treaties.[18] In the negotiations with Russia, the American claim to share gratuitously, by virtue of the "no higher or other duty" pledge, in concessions granted by Russia to other countries for compensation was followed within a few months by an American denial that Russia could under the same pledge lay claim to share gratuitously in the American concessions to Hawaii, on the ground that Hawaii had given compensation for them![19]

What is Equivalent Compensation?

Country A negotiates a treaty with country B whereby, in return for the remission by A of its import duty on woolens from B, country B agrees to admit steel rails from A free of duty. Country C, which has a conditional most-favored-nation treaty with B, is an exporter of steel rails and admits woolens from any source free of duty. Must country B admit steel rails from C free of duty, on the ground that C is giving the same compensation as A for this privilege, namely, the free admission of B's woolens?

In general it would seem that reductions of duty established by legislative enactment to execute purposes of domestic policy, made general to the entire world, and not contingent upon the receipt of return concessions nor having such reciprocation in view, are free gifts and not "compensation." There would seem to be in such action no element of the "bargain" principle upon which the conditional practice is supposed to rest. As an eminent authority says:[20]

> If the privileges claimed have been specifically extended by treaty stipulations, they are presumed to have been based upon a consideration and not to have been gratuitous, for the usual purpose of a treaty is to secure benefits for concessions, not to record the exchange of free gifts. This presumption does not arise if the privileges have been extended unconditionally by acts of legislation, not in execution of treaty stipulation, for such acts are not presumably the result of negotiation with foreign nations.

American practice, however, has varied on this point. The above quotations, as far as I am aware, exhaust the literature on the problem, and American officials have shown such inconsistency in their actions with respect thereto as to indicate that they have never thought the problem through. As a general rule, the United States has not extended special concessions, originally granted to one country for compensation, to other countries entitled to conditional most-favored-nation treatment, even though these other countries were at the time giving to the United States as favourable treatment as that given in return for the American concessions by the country originally receiving them. To cite only one example, the United States, under authority of Section 3 of the Tariff Act of 1897, gave special reductions in duty to several European countries in return for minor concessions from their high tariffs – which in some cases continued to be discriminatory against the United States even after these concessions – but withheld them from Great

Britain, which had no concessions to make because it already admitted most American products free of duty.[21] It is obvious that such a policy operates unfairly toward the free-trade country, which is in no position to grant concessions because it has already given freely all that it has to give.

There are a number of instances, however, of the reverse practice by the United States. The United States–Belgium Treaty of July 17, 1858, provided for the freedom from tonnage dues of the shipping of each country in the ports of the other. The same freedom from tonnage tolls was extended by the United States to Bremen by virtue of the conditional most-favored-nation pledge of the united States–Hanseatic Republics Treaty of December 20, 1827, on the ground that there being no tonnage tolls on any vessels in the Port of Bremen, equivalent compensation had been received by the United States. The same concession was extended to Norway and Sweden, on the ground that there being no line of American vessels to these countries, it could not be presumed beforehand that if American vessels did call at ports of these countries, tonnage tolls would be imposed![22] Under Section 3 of the Tariff Act of 1890, the United States imposed special penalty duties on the imports from three small Caribbean republics, two of which had most-favored-nation treaties with the United States, on the ground that these countries levied duties on American products higher than the American duties on their products. Unless these penalty duties are to be regarded as having been in outright violation of American treaty obligations – which position it is not difficult to maintain[23] – it may be held that the free admission of the specified products, i.e., the withholding of the penalty duties, was a special concession granted to the non-penalized countries in return for low duties on American products. This free admission, not having been granted gratuitously, could not be claimed, therefore, by the penalized countries merely on the strength of their right to most-favored-nation treatment.[24] On this interpretation, it would follow that low duties on American products established by legislation already long in effect and originally enacted in execution of domestic policy were acceptable as compensation equivalent to new and special reductions of duty granted to the United States by other countries with the express purpose of receiving American concessions in return.

A more important instance of the acceptance by the United States of general low rates of duty in foreign tariff laws of some years standing as equivalent compensation for special American concessions is to be found in connection with the operation of the "contingent duties" which have been a feature of American tariff legislation since 1890. These duties are levied on specified commodities, but only if these commodities are imported from countries which levy import duties on similar commodities imported from the United States.[25] They would unquestionably be in violation of unconditional most-favored-nation obligations. They can be defended as compatible with conditional most-favored-nation obligations only on the ground that the withholding of the contingent duty on imports into the United States is a special concession granted in return for compensation, the compensation consisting of the admission of the American product free, or at rates of duty not higher than the American rates. Here again the sole defense available to the United States of its practice under these duties is the assertion of the principle that privileges freely given to the United States many years before the enactment of the American contingent duties are acceptable as "equivalent compensation."

Such in fact was the American defense in the one reported case in which the levy of the contingent duties gave rise to diplomatic protest by a foreign country. Paragraph 608 of the Tariff Act of 1894 placed salt on the free list, provided, however, that the rate of duty levied under the preceding tariff act should be collected on salt imported from any country which imposed a duty on American salt. Germany collected a duty on salt imported from the United States, but she presented a claim, nevertheless, for the free entry of her salt into the United States by virtue of the most-favored-nation clause in the United States-Prussia Treaty of May 1, 1828. The United States, following the opinion of Attorney-General Olney, denied the German claim:[26]

> The United States concedes "free salt" to any nation which concedes "free salt" to the United States. Germany, of course, is entitled to that concession upon returning the same equivalent. But otherwise she is not entitled, and there is nothing in the "most-favored-nation clause" which compels the United States to discriminate against other nations and favor of Germany by granting gratuitously to the latter privileges which it grants to the former only upon the payment of a stipulated price.

Incompatibility of Conditional and Unconditional Pledges in the same Treaty System

If a country enters into unconditional most-favored-nation relations with one or more countries and into conditional relations with other countries, it must in practice extend unconditional most-favored-nation treatment to all treaty contries. If country A, having an unconditional most-favored-nation treaty with country B and a conditional most-favored-nation treaty with country C, granted to country D concessions for compensation, it must extend them gratuitously to country B. Country C thereupon has a valid claim to the extension to itself without compensation of like concessions, on the ground that country B was receiving them gratuitously. A country which uniformly follows the conditional practice is therefore in the advantageous position, in its relations with countries following uniformly or in part the unconditional practice, of being entitled to receive gratuitously all concessions which such other countries grant for compensation without being under corresponding obligations itself.

The United States, as the only country which has uniformly followed the conditional practice, has alone been in this enviable position of having a valid right to receive unaccompanied by an obligation to give! In general, foreign countries conceded this right without awaiting demands from the United States. In some cases the United States appears to have made no complaint when this right was withheld. On at least one occasion, however, the Unites States has insisted upon receiving gratuitously, by virtue of a conditional pledge, concessions originally granted by a foreign country to another foreign country for compensation but extended gratuitously to third countries in compliance with unconditional pledges.[27]

> While we do not deny the right of Germany to adopt the same construction which controls the action of this Government, it should be remembered that whatever construction is adopted it must be applied uniformly to all governments whose interests are protected by the like treaty clauses. . . . If the compensatory privileges should be extended to any third nation, which has given no special compensation for them, it is evident that as to that nation the grant would be gratuitous, and, by the express provision of Article XXVI [of the United States-Prussia Treaty of May 1, 1828], "Shall immediately become common to the other party, freely." . . . It is evident that Germany can not apply one construction in her relations with this Government and another in her relations with an European government.

The treaty list of the United States, however, has not been completely free from treaties containing the unconditional pledge in such unequivocal and unmistakable terms that not even the subtlest of legalistic quibbling could make them appear other than what they were. The United States–Switzerland Treaty of November 25, 1850, contained provisions for *immediate* most-favored-nation treatment, and none of its provisions were such as to give any opening for a conditional construction of the treaty. The records of the original negotiations showed that Switzerland had refused to consent to the insertion of a conditional provision and that the treaty had been signed with the mutual recognition that it was an unconditional treaty. Upon the coming into force of the reciprocity agreement of May 28, 1898, between France and the United States, Switzerland demanded the extension to Swiss goods of the concessions made to France in this agreement. After an examination of the records of the original negotiations with Switzerland, the United States acknowledged the validity of the Swiss claim, but it soon thereafter gave notice of denunciation of the most-favored-nation provisions in the Treaty with Switzerland. Upon the extension to Switzerland gratuitously of the concessions granted to France for compensation, several European countries claimed the same privilege. The United States refused these claims, on the ground that "the gratuitous grant of the concessions to Switzerland was to be considered an exception to the regular practice of the United States, and would be no longer effective after the early termination of the treaty clauses upon which the obligation to Switzerland rested."[28]

Treaties of the United States with the Orange Free State (December 22, 1871), and Serbia (October 14, 1881), and an agreement with Spain (August 1, 1906) also provided in clear terms for unconditional most-favored-nation treatment. No claims ever appear to have been made by the Orange Free State or Serbia on the strength of their treaties, Spain, in 1909, requested that the reduction of duty on sparkling wines, which had been specially granted to France for compensation in 1908, be extended to her wines. The United States extended this reduction to Spain, in reality gratuitously. But in order to save appearances, Secretary of State Bacon notified Spain in substance that the extension was granted because the concessions made by Spain in 1906 in return for American concessions not including the low duty on sparkling wines were now found to be reciprocal and equivalent of the concessions granted to Spain by the United States in 1906 plus this additional concession.[29]

Concessions made by the United States because of Conditional Obligations

The advantages which a country can derive from its possession of a pledge of conditional most-favored-nation treatment from another country fall into two classes: (1) the right, upon offering equivalent compensation, to receive privileges extended by the treaty country for compensation to a third country; and (2), the right to receive gratuitously privileges extended gratuitously by the treaty country to a third country.

The right to receive upon the offer of equivalent compensation, concessions granted to a third country for compensation is of little practical value. The grantor of concessions to one country for compensation is itself the judge of the equivalence of the compensation offered for the same concessions by other countries. If it does not wish to extend its concessions to third countries, it need only deny the equivalence of the compensation offered. Or it may sometimes do as the United States has done in connection with special concessions to and from Cuba and from Hawaii – plead "special circumstances" as a justification for the denial to third countries of even the opportunity to make similar bargains. Moreover, any country which has valuable compensation to offer for concessions does not need – and is not substantially aided by – the possession of a pledge of conditional most-favored-nation treatment, in order to strike a bargain for a mutual exchange of concessions.

If the possession of a right to conditional most-favored-nation treatment is of value to the possessing country, the value, therefore, must reside largely in the right with which it is thereby endowed of receiving gratuitously any privileges which the pledged country may grant gratuitously to third countries. There are two phases to this right: security against wanton discrimination, and participation in gratuitous concessions. Wanton discriminations against specified countries, however, involve gratuitous concessions to all other countries. In practice, therefore, it is not necessary to attempt to discover whether differential treatment of countries, when not the result of reciprocal exchanges of concessions with some of these countries, has as its intent the penalization of the countries unfavorably treated or the extension of special privileges to the countries favorably treated. In any case, wanton discriminations are rare in modern times, and where they occur they are likely to be directed only against countries with which most-favored-nation treaty relations have been terminated in consequence of some tariff or other dispute.

There have been only a few cases in which the United States has given to a foreign country gratuitously, by virtue of its right to conditional most-favored-nation treatment, privileges which it did not extend by statute to all countries irrespective of their treaty claims. If the cases where the United States has accepted what were in fact free gifts as equivalent compensation for special American concessions are not deemed to fall in this class, the only instances have been due to inadvertences of American legislation. The Tariff Act of 1842 raised the duties on cotton goods, but provided that this increase in duties was not to apply to goods shipped in vessels which had left the last port of lading eastward of the Cape of Good Hope or beyond Cape Horn prior to September 1, 1842. Importers of goods shipped from Great Britain prior to this date paid the higher duties under protest. A commission to arbitrate claims between the two countries, appointed under the Convention of February 8, 1853, between the United States and Great Britain, decided in favor of the claims of these importers, on the ground that the most-favored-nation treaty of July 3, 1815, between the two countries entitled British imports to as favourable treatment as was granted gratuitously to imports from any other country.[30] A similar ruling was made by the Commission with reference to a provision in the Tariff Act of 1824, which increased the duties on cotton goods unless they were imported from ports or places eastward of the Cape of Good Hope or beyond Cape Horn prior to January 1, 1825.[31] In both of these instances the intent of the legislation was to exempt from the increased duties shipments which had left the place of exportation prior to, or within a short time of, the enactment of the new rates. The British claims would not have been conceded by the United States if the dispute had been left to administrative determination.

In the reciprocity arrangement of 1910 with Canada, the United States agreed, among other things, that Canadian wood pulp and paper should be admitted free of duty if manufactured from wood cut on lands not subject to the Canadian provincial export restrictions. The arrangement was to be made effective in the two countries by concurrent legislation to take effect simultaneously. Congress, on July 2, 1911, passed an act ratifying the reciprocity arrangement, but the act was not to become operative until Canada had passed like legislation. Important support for the reciprocity arrangement had come from American consumers of Canadian pulp wood and newsprint, who desired cheap raw materials for their industries. Under pressure from these interests, who were not willing to assume the risk that Canada would fail to ratify the reciprocity arrangement, the section of the Reciprocity Act admitting Canadian pulp and paper free of duty was, by exception, made immediately operative, irrespective of Canadian action with respect to the reciprocity arrangement. Canada failed to ratify the reciprocity pact, but under the provisions of the American act Canadian pulp and paper continued to enter the United States free of duty. Importers of similar products from a number of European countries claimed the benefit of the same privilege, by virtue of the rights of these countries to most-favored-nation treatment. The Court of Customs Appeals ceded the validity of these claims, on the ground, mainly, that the privilege extended to Canada had been granted freely and without receipt of compensation.[32]

The few instances, therefore, in which countries holding conditional most-favored-nation pledges from the United States obtained by virtue thereof any concession from the United States without giving in return compensation, or what was held by the United States to be compensation, were unintentional on the part of the United States and were the consequences of inadvertence in American legislation. Even in these cases the concessions were not ceded as a matter of course, but were yielded only after resort to arbitration or to the American courts.[33]

CAUSES AND PROBABLE CONSEQUENCES OF THE CHANGE IN AMERICAN POLICY

The preceding study of the manner of operation of the conditional practice has shown that in the main it served to gain for the United States concessions from other countries without involving it in the obligation of giving concessions in return. From the nationalistic point of view it would appear, therefore, that there was nothing less to be desired than the abandonment of a traditional policy operating so beneficently for a new and untried policy which would enforce upon the United States more generous treatment of foreign countries. An examination of some phases of American commercial relations with other countries will show, however, that conditions were not altogether satisfactory from the American point of view and that they promised to become less, instead of more, favourable in the near future.

The concessions secured by the United States in the various reciprocity arrangements into which it entered were on the whole of minor importance; they were often trivial in character. Many of these concessions were not special to the United States, but at the time of extension to this country were already being enjoyed by almost all other countries and would have been enjoyed by the United States as a matter of course if it followed the unconditional practice. While the United States succeeded in a few instances in getting special concessions and in a few other instances in securing gratuitously concessions for which some other country had originally given compensation, it failed, after 1890, with its conditional most-favored-nation practice and with its elaborate reciprocity negotiations, to obtain as favourable tariff treatment from Continental Europe as a whole as was enjoyed by Great Britain with its unconditional practice and with no concessions to make in return. France, Germany, Russia, Spain, Portugal, Austria-Hungary, Switzerland, Canada, have all at times or continuously since 1892 discriminated in tariff matters against the United States. France, Spain, and Canada are discriminating today. The United States during this period has been the one important commercial nation, with the exception since 1918 of vanquished Germany, which has not been reasonably certain of being given equality of treatment in tariff matters by the rest of the Western world. In most cases the reciprocity negotiations with European countries secured to the United States no special privileges, but merely effected a partial removal of the adverse discriminations to which American trade was subjected. The conditional practice, instead of operating, as its supporters contended, to gain specially advantageous conditions for American commerce, failed to secure for it mere equality of treatment with the commerce of other nations.

In earlier years the exports of the United States consisted predominantly of agricultural products and raw materials. Foreign countries were dependent on the United States for their supplies of many of these commodities. They were, therefore, little likely to apply discriminatory tariff duties to them. In any case, American commercial policy concerned itself but slightly with the interests of the producers of agricultural products and raw materials, and was directed mainly to the securing of a monopoly of the domestic market for American manufactures. The United States, moreover, as an important purchaser of the manufactured products of Europe, had it within its power vigorously and effectively to retaliate against hostile European legislation.

In the last decades of the nineteenth century, the situation began to change to the disadvantage of the United States. Manufactured and partly manufactured products acquired increasing importance in the exports; foodstuffs and raw materials became an increased and steadily growing proportion of the imports. European countries, irritated by the repeated refusals of the United States to acknowledge obligations under its most-favored-nation pledges and by the extraordinary heights to which American protectionism was carrying import duties on European products, began to denounce their most-favored-nation treaties with the United States, to consent to new tariff arrangements only on a temporary basis, and openly and otherwise to discriminate in their customs legislation against American products. The attempt of the United States to meet the situation by the insertion of elaborate bargaining provisions in its tariff laws failed to bring about a substantial amelioration of the situation.

This state of affairs was for the first time brought forcibly to the attention of American statesmen and the American public by the Tariff Commission in its Report on Reciprocity and Commercial Treaties. President Wilson, guided, it appears, by the advice of the Tariff Commission, formally committed the United States to the policy of equality of treatment and embodied the principle in the third of his famous Fourteen Points. At the time a one-sided Brazilian tariff preference to American products, established in response to American diplomatic pressure, was, with the exception of the reciprocity relations with Cuba and some minor preferences, of obscure origin, to American products in Haiti and San Salvador, the only instance in which the United States was either receiving or giving special favors. President Wilson made known that the United States would not object to the discontinuance by Brazil of its preference to American products. Thus the American slate was cleaned, and the United States put itself in position, in so far as existing circumstances were concerned, to demand consistently from all nations equality of treatment for American trade.

Secretary of State Hughes has recommitted the United States to the policy of equality of treatment to all, and from all, countries. He has taken the further logical step of abandoning the conditional most-favored-nation policy which stood in the way of the full execution of the equality of treatment policy. The makers of policy for the United States have apparently become convinced that this country has more to gain from giving and insisting upon receiving equality of treatment than it has to lose from the surrender of the right to strike special bargains with particular countries. Recent American history strongly supports the soundness of this belief, and condemns only the tardiness with which it has been reached. Those who can look beyond narrow nationalistic considerations will welcome the change in American commercial policy most of all because it will mark an important step toward the establishment of more friendly and more generous relations between the United States and other countries.

The practical consequences of the change in policy will not be such as to bring about very important changes in the tariff relations which have existed between the United States and foreign countries in the last few years. The reciprocity treaty with Cuba is the only diplomatic arrangement at present in effect which impairs the uniformity of the American tariff, and in the unconditional most-favored-nation treaties which the United States has so far negotiated the relations of the United States with Cuba are expressly exempted from the most-favored-nation obligations, on the plea of special circumstances.

The contingent duties in the Tariff Act of 1922, whose compatibility even with conditional most-favored-nation obligations is open to serious doubt, are unquestionably inconsistent with the unconditional practice. Whether the unconditional most-favored-nation treaties, assuming that the Senate duly ratifies them, automatically terminate these duties, i.e., whether most-favored-nation treaties are self-executing, is a matter of dispute upon which the Supreme Court has never expressed itself.[34] Administrative officers,[35] and lower courts,[36] have, however, conceded the self-executing character of most-favored-nation treaties. Congress, on the other hand, has always insisted upon the necessity of express legislative action before such treaties could come into actual operation, and "this practice has generally been acquiesced in by the other organs of government."[37] The United States, in consequence of its change of most-favored-nation treaty practice, must give up all hope of negotiating reciprocity agreements whereby special concessions are to be exchanged, except in cases which permit of the plea that special circumstances take them out of the sphere of most-favored-nation obligations. Since European countries have objected both to the conditional practice of the United States and to the height of its import duties, it is by no means certain that the abandonment of the conditional practice will of itself serve to secure equality of treatment for American trade in other countries. But with a clear slate itself, the United States can with easy conscience test the effectiveness of the penalizing device in Section 317 of the Tariff Act of 1922 as a means of securing equality of treatment by threat of retaliation where it is not given without such threat.

NOTES

1 Exchange of Notes with Brazil, October 18, 1923 (Press Notice issued by State Department, October 17, 1923); Draft of Treaty with Germany (*New York Times*, November 27, 1923); and apparently also the Treaty with Turkey.

2 Speech of Secretary of State Hughes at Philadelphia, November 30, 1923: "It should also be observed that in our commercial relations the United States is seeking unconditional most-favored-nation treatment in customs matters" (*New York Times*, December 1, 1923). Cf. also letter of Assistant Secretary of State Harrison to the New York correspondent of a South American newspaper (*ibid.*, November 24, 1923).

3 S. K. Hornbeck (*The Most-Favored-Nation Clause in Commercial Treaties*, 1910) is a notable exception. He supports the conditional form, but only after a careful and able discussion of the pros and cons.

4 S. B. Crandall, *Treaties, Their Making and Enforcement* (2d ed., 1916), pp. 404, 405.

5 For an inductive verification of this reasoning, in connection with the special American concessions on Hawaiian and on Cuban sugar, see U.S. Tariff Commission, *Report on Reciprocity and Commercial Treaties* (1919), pp. 127–36, 328–36.

6 It is difficult to understand, therefore, the statement by the U.S. Tariff Commission that "In the European view the function of the clause is automatically to distribute or generalize advantages. In the American view its proper function is to safeguard against the denial of opportunities; that is, to prevent discrimination." (*Report on Reciprocity and Commercial Treaties*, pp. 393, 394). It is difficult to reconcile this statement with the general mass of evidence presented in this report to the effect that the unconditional

practice is more effective than the conditional in securing equality of treatment, or with the statement that "Efforts to insure and to secure equality of treatment by the method of making and taking special concessions, with conditional favored-nation treatment, have not been successful" (*ibid.*, p. 439).

7 "The neighborhood of nations, their border interests, their differences of climate, soil, and production, their respective capacity for manufacture, their widely different demands for consumption, the magnitude of the reciprocal markets, are so many conditions which require special treatment. No general tariff can satisfy such demands. It would require a certainty of language which excludes the possibility of doubt to justify the opinion that the government of any commercial nation had annulled its natural right to meet these special conditions by compensatory concessions, or held the right only on condition of extending the same to a nation which had no compensation to offer. The fact that such concessions if made would inevitably inure to the equal benefit of a third competitor would often destroy the motive for, as well as the value of, such reciprocal concessions" (Secretary of State Sherman to Minister to Argentine Republic, 1898, cited in J. B. Moore, *Digest of International Law*, V, 278, 279).

8 Cf. T. E. G. Gregory, *Tariffs: a Study in Method* (1921), pp. 475, 476.

9 If it be objected that this has been due to the more extensive use in Europe of multiple-schedule tariffs and to the greater consideration which European countries have of necessity given to the safeguarding of their export trade, it at least remains true that the use of the unconditional form of most-favored-nation pledge has not been in practice an important obstacle to the making of mutually acceptable arrangements whereby reductions in duty were reciprocally extended.

10 For a list of most-favored-nation treaties, many of them unconditional, containing provisions exempting specified arrangements, or potential arrangements with specified countries, on the plea of special relations, from the obligations of the most-favored-nation pledge, see Memorandum presented to the House of Representatives by Mr McCall, on January 18, 1912 (*Congressional Record*, XLVIII, 1096 ff.). Whether or not exclusive concessions can be defended on the plea of special relations, where no express stipulation exempting them from the operation of the most-favored-nation clause is contained in the treaties containing the clause, is an open question. (Cf. S. K. Hornbeck, *The Most-Favored Nation Clause in Commercial Treaties* [1910], pp. 35, 95.)

11 E.g., in C. L. Jones, "The American Interpretation of the "Most Favored Nation' Clause," *Annals*, XXXLI (1908), 392.

12 *Ibid.*, p. 393.

13 Cf. S. K. Hornbeck, *op. cit.*, p. 102: "Logically, the universal acceptance of that form and interpretation of the clause which would satisfy the 'unconditional' school would eventually lead, whether that be its object or not, to absolute free trade."

14 As an instance of the assumption that the conditional interpretation was the only one acceptable in international law, cf. Secretary of State Bayard to Minister to Japan, 1886, cited in Moore's *Digest*, V. 273: "This [i.e., the conditional] proviso, when it occurs, is merely explanatory, inserted out of abundant caution. Its absence does not impair the rule of international law that such concessions are only gratuitous (and so transferable) as to third parties when not based on reciprocity or mutually reserved interests as between the contracting parties. This ground has been long and consistently maintained by the United States."

15 Moore's *Digest*, V, 261.

16 *Bartram v. Robertson* (1887), 122 U.S. 116.

17 *Whitney v. Robertson* (1888), 124 U.S. 190.

18 Secretary of State Gresham to the Russian Minister, *Foreign Relations*, 1895, II, 1119; Secretary of State Hay to the Minister to Haiti, *ibid.*, 1901, pp. 276 ff.

19 Acting Secretary of State Adee to the Russian Chargé d'Affaires ad interim, *Foreign Relations*, 1895, p. 1121.

20 S. B. Crandall, *Treaties, Their Making and Enforcement*, pp. 407, 408. Cf., also, Secretary of State Frelinghuysen to the Minister to Japan, June 11, 1884, cited in Moore's *Digest*, V, 267; "For example, the United States have just concluded a commercial treaty with Mexico by which each country especially favors the other by putting on its free list certain dutiable products. Under the favored-nation clause of our treaties with other nations we are not bound to give their products the benefit of our free list, even though such country may not impose any duty on the articles which Mexico has free-listed in our favor; but we would be willing to stipulate to give a third power the favor we give Mexico in exchange for some equivalent favor not general as towards the rest of the world."

21 Cf. *Report on Reciprocity and Commercial Treaties*, p. 214.

22 14 *Opinions of the Attorney General*, 468, 530; 16 *Op.* 276, 626.

23 Cf. *Report on Reciprocity and Commercial Treaties*, pp. 155 ff., 421 ff.; and Jacob Viner, *Dumping: a Problem in International Trade* (1923), pp. 311 ff.

24 The fact that the United States withheld the free admission of the specified commodities, not from all countries levying high duties on American products, but only from a few such countries which were not in a position, by their heavy purchases of American products, vigorously to retaliate, weakens the force of this reasoning.

25 See Paragraphs 369, 371, 1536, 1541, 1543, 1548, 1585, in the Tariff Act of 1922.

26 21 *Opinions of the Attorney-General*, 80. Cf. also *Foreign Relations*, 1896, pp. 205–9.

27 Secretary of State Hay to Ambassador to Germany, 1899, *Foreign Relations*, 1899, p. 301.

28 *Report on Reciprocity and Commercial Treaties*, pp. 428 ff.

29 *Ibid.*, pp. 435 f.

30 J. B. Moore, *International Arbitrations*, IV, 3361, 3362.

31 *Ibid.*, p. 3363.

32 *American Express Co. et al. v. United States*, and *Bertuch & Co. et al. v. United States*, Court of Customs Appeals, May 12, 1913, *Treasury Decisions*, XXIV, 724 ff.

33 In 1787, or prior to the ratification of the American Constitution, a gratuitous concession by the state of Virginia to France to the free admission of French brandies imported in French or American vessels was, upon the recommendation of John Jay, Secretary for the Department of Foreign Affairs, extended gratuitously to the Netherlands, on the strength of its most-favored-nation treaty of 1782 with the United States (S. B. Crandall, *Treaties, Their Making and Enforcement*, pp. 404, 405).

34 But compare, Quincy Wright (*The Control of American Foreign Relations*, 1922, p. 228) who interprets what on the surface appear to be merely hypothetical statements in *Bartram v. Robertson*, 122 U.S. 116, and *Whitney v Robertson*, 124 U.S. 190, as dicta in support of the self-executing character of most-favored-nation obligations. Cf., however, *American Express Co., et al. v. United States, Bertuch & Co. et al. v. United States*, Court of Customs Appeals May 12, 1913, *Treasury Decisions*, XXIV, 750, where Justice De Vries, in a minority opinion, interprets these same statements as explicitly declaring most-favored-nation treaties *not* to be self-executing.

35 The only instance I can find is the extension by the Treasury Department gratuitously to Switzerland in 1898, in compliance with the unconditional treaty with that country of November 25, 1850, of the concessions granted for compensation to France earlier in the same year (Moore's *Digest*, V, 283 ff.).

36 *Taylor v. Morton*, 23 Fed. Cases, 784 (1855) most-favored-nation treaty is *not* self-executing; *American Express Co., et al. v. United States, Bertuch & Co., et al. v. United States*, Court of Customs Appeals, May 12, 1913, *Treasury Decisions*, XXIV, 724 ff., most-favored-nation treaty *is* self-executing.

37 Quincy Wright, *op. cit.*, p. 299.